W9-CTH-702

CANADA
DEPARTMENT OF MINES
HON. CHARLES STEWART, MINISTER; CHARLES CAMSELL, DEPUTY MINISTER

NATIONAL MUSEUM OF CANADA
W. H. COLLINS, ACTING DIRECTOR

BULLETIN No. 60

ANTHROPOLOGICAL SERIES, No. 11

Sacred Stories of the Sweet Grass Cree

BY
L. Bloomfield

OTTAWA
F. A. ACLAND
PRINTER TO THE KING'S MOST EXCELLENT MAJESTY
1930

CONTENTS

83186—1½

SACRED STORIES OF THE SWEET GRASS CREE

INTRODUCTION

These texts are part of a series written from dictation during a five weeks' stay on Sweet Grass Reserve (Battleford Agency, Saskatchewan), in the summer of 1925.

The principal informants here represented are as follows:

Coming-Day (*kā-kīsikāw-pīhtukāw*), a blind old man; the Sweet Grass Cree say that he knows more traditional stories than any other member of the band. He was easily trained to dictate, but, to the end, could not be rid of certain faults. Especially when fatigued, he would simplify his stories or omit portions of them. Occasionally he would interrupt the dictation to tell me rapidly—by way of a footnote, as it were —the matter which he had omitted; or he would append it after finishing the dictation; he could not be persuaded to dictate these portions. Another of his faults is not uncommon among Indian informants: he will suddenly avoid using some perfectly common and harmless word. He explained by saying that he feared I might not understand the word. This is obviously a rationalization; Coming-Day knew that I had only a small vocabulary, that it did not matter whether I understood everything at the time of dictation, and, above all, he was extremely kind and patient in explaining (in Cree; he speaks no English) the meaning of expressions that I did not understand. I cannot explain the sporadic avoidance of words, but suspect it to be in some way an outgrowth (extension in the presence of a foreigner?) of the word-taboo that exists in every language. Similarly, Coming-Day will now and then, as though perversely, use the less appropriate of two synonyms, perhaps afterwards adding the right one. Thus, at the end of a story, he will characterize it as *ātsimōwin*, when it is *ātayōhkāwin* (*See* below), or vice versa, or he will use both terms. In spite of these faults, he is a splendid informant: a good dictator, a patient instructor, and a narrator generous of his immense lore.

Adam Sakewew (*sākāwāw*), his close companion, is stylistically more gifted, uses a greater vocabulary, but, especially in his earlier texts, did not dictate as well. He knows far less tradition than his friend, but when he tells a story, it is better told.

Mrs. Maggie Achenam (*kā-wīhkaskusahk*), a middle-aged woman, dictates poorly; in all her stories there were sentences which I did not get a chance to take down. Further, she insists that she is no story-teller, and, indeed, she omits parts of her stories, or gets them mixed up. Nevertheless, I took as much dictation from her as I could get, for she is full of interesting things (being, in fact, something of a sorceress); more than one archaic trait will be found in her texts.

Louis Moosomin (*nāh-nāmiskwākāpaw*), blind from childhood, a man of middle age, uses many archaic expressions, and dictates well, except that in the process of slow speech he often gets muddled in his construction.

I hazard the conjecture that the speech-mechanism of the Sweet Grass Cree represents an archaic type: speech about any exciting topic is usually accompanied by a higher degree of excitement (gesture and non-social symptoms) than is the case with us or with woodland Indians. This, however, is not true of all informants, notably not of Coming-Day, nor of Louis Moosomin, nor have I observed it in women.

None of the preceding speaks English. Two English-speaking Cree, Harry Watney and Norman Standinghorn (*māyiskinīkiw*), both young men, gave me my foundation in Cree. The former speaks Cree poorly; neither of them can translate. Baptiste Pooyak, a man of middle age, is the only person I found who can with any consistency tell in English the meaning of a Cree expression. Unfortunately his help was available only for short periods. Many a word or phrase in the texts has remained unintelligible to me.

In order to help the reader evaluate the texts I have dwelt too much, perhaps, on the shortcomings of the Sweet Grass informants. In reality, the Sweet Grass people were, without exception, kind, helpful, and hospitable. I owe thanks also to the untiring farm-instructor, Mr. Matthew Layton, and to Mrs. Layton; also to the Agency staff at Battleford, Mr. L. S. Macdonald, Dr. Norquay, and Mr. Smith; and to Father Lacombe (nephew of the author of "Grammaire et dictionnaire de la langue des Cris," Montreal, 1874).

The work was throughout made possible only by the kindness of officials of the National Museum of Canada, Mr. E. Sapir and Mr. L. L. Bolton, and by the courtesy of the Indian Department.

Distinctive Sounds of Plains Cree

(1) Consonants:

Bilabial:	*p*, *m*
Dental:	*t*, *ts*, *s*, *n*
Velar:	*k*
Glottal:	*h*

(2) Semivowels:

Labiovelar:	*w*
Palatal:	*y*

(3) Vowels:

Short, high:	*i*, *u*
Short, low:	*a*
Long, high:	*ī*, *ō*
Long, low:	*ä*, *ā*

The consonant combinations consist of *h* or *s* before *p*, *t*, *ts*, *k*.

For the general character and historical relations of these sounds, *see* the discussion of the Central Algonquian sound system in "Language," I, 130. A list of the symbols used in these texts with rough description of their sound values is given at the end of this introduction (page 6).

A non-significant stress accent falls on the third syllable from the end of words or close-knit phrases: *nä'hiyaw:* a Cree; *nähi'yawak:* Crees; *iskwä'w ana:* that woman.

Initial vowels have an on-glide of *h* under stress, especially in interjections; *hay hay !* splendid!

Final vowels have nearly always an off-glide of *h* ; *maskwa, maskwah :* bear. In the word *äha' :* yes, the off-glide always takes the form of a glottal stop; this I have indicated by the symbol '.

When final and initial vowels come together in the sentence, the *h*-glide may remain; this is the slow and full form of speech; *awa'h iskwäw :* this woman. In faster and more natural speech, the *h*-glide may disappear, or may be replaced by *w* (if one of the vowels is *u* or *ō*) or by *y* (if one of the vowels is *i*, *ī*, or *ä*); *awa' iskwäw, awa'y iskwäw :* this woman; *kīh-u'tinam, kī-u'tinam, kīw-u'tinam :* he has taken it.

If, however, the first of the two vowels is short, a different type of combination is more common: both the glide sound and the short final vowel are lost, and the initial vowel, if short, is lengthened; *aw ī'skwäw :* this woman. The stress, it will be noticed, of an elided short vowel, stays on the vowel with which it has merged. Final *u* deviates; before an unlike vowel it is replaced by *w*, and the following vowel, if short, is lengthened; *piku :* only, and *isi :* thus, give *pikw ī'si :* in every way; *piku* and *awiyak :* someone, give *pikw ā'wiyak :* anyone at all, everyone.

In certain combinations a final long vowel merges with an initial vowel. Thus *ā* and *i* give *ä ; kā'h-itwät, k-ä'twät :* what he said. Similarly, *ā* and *u* give *ō ; kāh-u'tinahk, k-ō'tinahk :* what he took. In some common combinations final *ā* merges with other vowels; *äkāh a'wiyak, äk ā'wiyak :* lest anyone.

Various modifications of these habits of vowel combination occur, but my knowledge of the dialect does not suffice to formulate them.

The unaccustomed ear has difficulty in distinguishing the vowel quantities, especially in certain positions, as: before *h* plus consonant; before *w ;* after consonant groups. Thus, *a'htsānis :* ring (I take this to be the actual, or, at any rate, the normal form of the word), sounded to me like *a'htsanis, ā'htsanis, ā'htsānis : ayahtsi'yiniw :* a Blackfoot, appears in my earlier texts as *ayāhtsi'yiniw*. To the end, I had no certainty on this point. Before *y* the distinction of *i* and *ī* seems entirely lacking; I have written *iy* uniformly, never *īy*.

Between like consonants, especially between labials and between dentals, a short vowel is often lost; *wāsaskutä'nikan :* lamp, *wās(s)kutä'nikan; nā'nitaw :* anywhere, *nā'ntaw*. When in such cases the group *nt* is formed after a short vowel, the *n* is long and probably always syllabic; *ku'nitah :* at random, variously, *ku'ntah* (with long, syllabic *n*). Similarly, when *tn, pm* so arise, the *n, m* is syllabic; *u'tinam :* he takes it, *u'tnam* (syllabic *n*); *a'stutin :* hat, *a'stutn* (syllabic *n*, as in English *button*); *pi'muhtäw :* he walks, *pm'uhtäw* (syllabic *m*). Occasionally two short vowels are thus lost; *pimi'pahtāw :* he runs, *pm'pahtāw* (syllabic *m*).

The sounds *h, w, y* alternate in rapid speech according to the surrounding vowels; *äh-nika'muyit :* when the other sings, *äh-nika'muwit ; ōmisi'h itwäw :* he says so, *ōmisi'y itwäw*, beside the more common *ōmis ī'twäw ;* cf. above.

The sound-group *hy* appears between *a*-vowels, e.g. *wāhyaw :* far, *ahyapiy :* net; but where it is historically to be expected before or after *i, ī, ä,* we have *h ; ahäw :* he places him (Menomini *a'new*, Fox *asäwa*), *pimihāw :* he flies (Menomini *pemē'new*, Fox *pemisäwa*). In these cases I seem to have heard occasional pronunciations with *hy*, but this may be an error of mine. I seem to have heard *hy* also occasionally in *pihäw (pihyäw) :* partridge, a word whose history I do not know.

Sequences of vowels and semivowels are subject to great variation. I have not succeeded in fully analysing this; the following are the clearest cases.

Short *a* before and after *y* may be replaced by *i*, and intermediate sounds (short *e*-vowels) occur; thus the second person singular conjunct ends in *-yan* or *-yin ; ayahtsiyiniw :* a Blackfoot, *iyahtsiyiniw*.

Short *a* before *w* is rounded; the usual pronunciation of a word like *mayaw :* straight might be symbolized by *mayow*. More complex is the phrase *nama' wiya :* not, *nama' wya, namō'ya*. In other positions the rounding or backing of short *a* is less marked than in other Central Algonquian; final *-ak* after *w*, as in *nāpäwak :* men, comes nearest to this.

The combination *-iw* at the end of a word is spoken with now one, now the other, element syllabic, or perhaps with balanced syllable stress; *apiw :* he sits there, *apyuw, apyw*.

Final *-äw* has the second element rather open, and probably often balanced stress; *nāpäw :* man, *nāpēō*.

Initial *uy-* similarly appears often as *wiy- ; uyākan :* bowl, *wiyākan*.

The combination *wä* after consonant is probably often *uy ; mwästas :* afterwards, *muystas*.

The combination *iyi* seems often to be merged to *ī ; kōhtā'wiyinaw :* our father, *kōhtā'wīnaw ;* in this instance and in some others the place of the stress presupposes *ī* rather than *iyi*.

The sound here represented by *ä* is a long mid front vowel (as in German *Tee*); the symbol *ä* is used for the sake of uniformity with other Algonquian texts; *ē* would be better. Indeed, the vowel is, to my ear, quite close to *ī*, and I have no doubt sometimes confused the two. In some words the variation of *ä* and *ī* is probably real and not merely my mishearing, as *käkway :* something, beside *kīkway ; kätahtawäh :* at a point in time, beside *kītahtawäh*.

The sound *s* varies freely between normal and abnormal sibilant. It is often spoken long, especially after stressed vowels (i.e., after the antepenultimate vowel), e.g. in *asiniy :* stone, *asamäw :* he gives him to eat, *misiwäh :* all over. It is tempting to view this long *s* as the reflex of old consonant groups that still appear in Menomini and are represented in Ojibwa by unvoiced *s* (as opposed to voiced *z*): Menomini *a'sen :* stone, *ahsāmäw:* he gives him to eat. This hypothesis, however, was not verified: the difference between shorter and longer *s* seems to be non-distinctive, for, firstly, all gradations between the shortest and longest forms seem to occur; secondly, both short and long forms are used in the same word; and, thirdly, the longer form is not confined to words that once had the consonant group, but seems to occur in any and all, as *misiwäh :* all over (Menomini *mesēwä*, but here Cree *ss* might be analogically due to *misi- :* big, Menomini *me'si-*), *isih :* thus (Menomini *is, isēh*). I soon found it impracticable to try to record the apparent quantitative fluctuations of *s*.

Medially *k* is often voiced, as, *uspwākan :* pipe; this has not been indicated, as it is not distinctive.

There seems to be some fluctuation between final *-h* (whether historically old *h* or a glide, is indifferent in Cree) and *-hk ;* thus the conjunct ending for *he . . . it*, as *äh-utinahk :* when he takes it, *äh-utinah*. Similarly between final *-s* and *-sk ; piyis :* at last, *piyisk*. In some words there seems to be no such fluctuation, as, *askihk :* kettle, *mänisk :* earthwork. If this observation be correct, the phenomenon is due to sandhi variants analogically turned loose; words with obvious inflectional parallels (*askihkwak :* kettles) would be protected.

In these texts I have used one, and only one, symbol for each Cree phoneme (a digraph for *ts*), and have not adopted extra symbols for variations within any Cree phoneme, such as fronted and backed *a*, or voiced *k;* such distinctions, however precious to a foreign ear, are irrelevant to the language we are considering.

But where variation involves different Cree phonemes, I have tried to record it; as, when *a* is fronted all the way to (Cree) *i* or backed all the way to (Cree) *u; äh-apiyan, ah-apiyin :* when thou sittest there; *āsawaham* he crosses it (water), *āsiwaham, āsuwaham, āsōwaham.*

In these texts I have kept the forms as they were actually taken from dictation. The only exceptions are, first, that my notes are here reduced to the distinctive sounds of Cree, irrelevant variations (such as attempts to note the fluctuating quantities of *s*) being eliminated; second, I have corrected forms which repeated experience showed to be, beyond reasonable doubt, errors of mine, the correct form being, again beyond reasonable doubt, available. In this I have been extremely conservative; the reader will be able to correct many a form that I have left in the text either because I am not absolutely sure that the deviation is due to my error, or because, having erred, I was not sure of the proper correction. Where the eccentric form seems to interfere with the sense, a note is appended; it is just in those cases that alteration is dangerous: the form may be rare or archaic; if not, even an informant's "slip of the tongue" may be of interest, and lies beyond our right of correction. Or again, in some of the texts a word will appear consistently in divergent form; I have left it so, for it may have been the speaker and not my ear that deviated.

I have tried to adapt punctuation and word division to the structure of Cree, making the former as intelligible and the latter as complete as possible.

The hyphen is used between members of compounds. In noun compounds the first member usually adds *-i ; paskwāwi-mustus :* buffalo (*paskwāw :* prairie). This merges with preceding postconsonantal *w* to *u; masku-pimiy :* bear's fat (*maskwah* bear, stem *maskw-*). In the remaining compound words the first member is a particle, e.g. *pōni-kimiwan :* it stops raining. The hyphen distinguishes these compounds from unit words, such as *pōnäyimäw :* he stops thinking of him (*-äyimäw* does not occur as an independent word).

This distinction has been partly troubled in Cree. For instance, historically, *atim :* dog, horse, is an independent word, whereas *-astim* in the same meaning, is a medial stem, as in *wāpastim :* white dog or horse. But actually we find, on the one hand, *misatim :* horse, where historically we should have either a compound word, **misih-atim, *mis-ātim* (*misih :* big), or a unit word **mistastim.* On the other hand, we have *matsastim :* evil dog, where historically we should have either the compound **matsih-atim, *mats-ātim,* or the unit word **matastim.* Similarly, we find forms like *kihtsäyimōw :* he is conceited, where the initial stem *kiht- :* big, has taken on the form of the independent particle *kihtsih :* big, beside the historically justified *kihtäyimōw.*

Consequently my use of hyphen will not always be found consistent. A form like *nahapiw :* he sits down, might well be taken as *nah-apiw,* since there is a particle *nahih :* well adjusted, and a verb *apiw :* he sits there. Yet we write *nahapiw* because the ordinary type of sandhi for a compound would give **nahih-apiw* or **nah-āpiw* (*See* page 5); hence *nahapiw* is parallel with the unmistakable unit word *itapiw* : he sits thus. Historically, we may compare Menomini *nanāhapiw* (reduplicated), which is in the phonetic system of Menomini characterized as an unmistakable unit word. But the historical criterion is irrelevant; the chief real criterion is negative (absence of certain sandhi forms); hence I could not always get it right. I have not used the hyphen in particle compounds with *ayihk* as second member, e.g. *pīhts-ayihk* : inside, although *ayihk* is plainly the local form of *ayih* : such and such a thing, and the first members are plainly derivatives with suffix *-i* forming particles: to use the hyphen here would demand setting up too many particles that occurred only in composition with *ayihk*.

An interesting case is that of the initial element *nisiwanāt-*: destroy, as in *nisiwanātsihäw* : he destroys him. This is an old form, cf. Menomini *ne'swanāt-* : mess, confusion. Here some speakers have an analogic reformation, as in *misi-wanātsihäw* : he destroys him, where the form is interpreted as having an initial element *wanāt-*, extended form of *wan-* : disappear (e.g. *wanihäw* : he loses him), with prefixed particle *misih* : big.

Reduplication which leaves the stem unchanged has been separated by a hyphen, as, *pa-pimuhtäw* : he walks and walks, but the (archaic) types where the stem is changed have been written as unit words; *papāmuhtäw* : he walks about.

General Nature of the Texts

The texts here given are stories of the kind called *ātayōhkäwin*. An *ātayōhkäwin* or sacred story is a traditional story concerning the time when the world was not yet in its present, definitive state. The actors are often the totem ancestors (I am not sure that this term is appropriate for the Plains Cree) before they took the shape of present-day animals. Or the stories are in the time when *wīsahkätsāhk* was on this earth. He, however, is not the high spirit that he is among the more easterly Algonquian-speaking tribes, and much about him is inexplicable. People wonder why he calls everybody "younger brother." The Sun-Dance is crowding out the Mitewin; at Sweet Grass the latter is viewed as black magic.

List of Symbols Used

The equivalents from European languages are in part rough approximations.

a short, low vowel, usually like the vowel of German *nass*, but varying occasionally forward, through the vowel of French *patte*, all the way to that of English *pet;* or backward, all the way to the vowel of American English *son*.

ā long, low vowel, as in English *father*, but tending in the direction of the vowel in English *saw*.

ä long, mid front vowel, as in German *Tee, geht*.

h as in English *hand;* it occurs, however, also finally and before *p, t, ts, k*.

i short, high front vowel, as in English *pin*, varying all the way to the type of French *fini*.

ī long, high front vowel, as in German *ihn*, French *rive*.

k unvoiced velar stop, as in English *kill, cow,* but usually unaspirated, as in English *skill,* French *coup*. Within the word after a vowel it is often voiced, hence like the initial of English *go*.

m voiced bilabial nasal, as in English *man*.

n voiced postdental nasal, as in French *nid*.

ō long, mid back vowel, rounded, as in German *so*, French *chose;* it varies all the way to a high vowel, as in German *tut*, French *rouge*.

p unvoiced bilabial stop, as in English *spin*, French *patte*.

s unvoiced sibilant, varying all the way from the normal sibilant as in English *see*, to the abnormal, as in English *she*.

t unvoiced postdental stop, as in French *tout*.

ts affricate of unvoiced postdental stop plus sibilant, varying all the way from the final of English *oats* to the sound in English *church*.

u short, high back vowel, rounded, varying all the way from that in English *put* to that in French *coupe*.

w unsyllabic *u*, as in English *well*.

y unsyllabic *i*, as in English *yes*.

' (superior comma) glottal stop, only in the word *äha'* : yes.

TEXTS AND TRANSLATIONS

(1) The Birth of Wisahketchahk and the Origin of Mankind

Louis Moosomin

nāh-namiskwäkāpaw.

kayās kītahtawä — äkwah nitātayōhkān — kītahtawä yāhkih päyak nāpäw päyakukamikisiw, wīwa äkwah nīs ōtawāsimisah. kītahtawä māna säpwähtätsi, uwīkimākana wawäsiyiwa. namuya kiskäyihtam tanähk ōhtsi äh-wawäsiyit uwīkimākana. kītahtawä kuntah sipwähtähkāsōw, äh-mätsīt; äkwah kāsōw, " mahtih kä-tōtahk, " äh-itäyimät. pōti äkwah kā-wāpamāt mistikwah äh-pah-pakamahwāyit, äkwah ka-pä-wayawiyit kinäpikwa, kā-wāpamāt uwīkimākana äh-uwītsimusiyit. sämāk mistahi kisiwāsiw. mistikwah äh-pakamahwāyit wīwa, " ninäpäm, äkwah nitakuhtān ! " itwäyiwa. kisiwāsiw mistahi. uhtäyihtam ; ayisk usām nawats sākihimāwa kinäpikwa. äyakunih ōhi kā-wi-ātayōhkātimak wīsähkätsähk ukāwiyah mīn ōhtāwiyah. äkwah awa nāpäw mistahi kisiwāsiw ; nama kīh-nipäw.

ōmis ītäw wīwa : " wāhyaw niwīh-isi-mätsīn, " itäw wīwa.

tāpwä mituni wāhyaw isi mätsīw. payakutipiskwäw.

" tānähki k-ōh-katikuniyan ? " itik uwīkimākana.

" wāhyaw nik-isi-mätsīn, " itäw ; " māka kiya kika-nātän wiyāsah, " itäw wīwa.

" äha' , " itwäw āw īskwäw.

mayaw ä-sipwähtäyit wīwa, uskutākayiw utinam, äh-pustiskahk. ituhtäw ōhi kinäpikwah itah k-āsiwasuyit mistikuhk.

" ninäpäm, nitakuhtān ! " itäw kinäpikwah.

tāpwäh pä-wayawiyiwa. mōhkumān uhtsih kīskikwäsäwätäw ; kīwähtahäw ōhih kinäpikwah ; mītsimāpuy usīhtäw. äkwah kätäw utawāsimisah.

tsikämā maywäs askiy ihtakuhk, nanātuhk isi kīsi-kaskihtāwak. kāhkutāwinäw utawāsimisah askīhk. äkwah awah iskwäw mistahi kahkiyaw käkway kaskihtäw, ahpōh kahkiyaw käkway äsah äh-pīkiskwātahk, äkusi äsa ä-naskuwasimikut. äkwah kahkiyaw käkway mīna nāpäw pīhtsāyihk ōtah k-āhtakuniyik kitahamawäw äkā käkway kita-wīhtamākuyit.

takuhtäyiwa äkwah wīwa. asamäw kinäpikwa kā-kīh-mītsimāpōhkākät.

" hwah, käkway ōma, " itwäw aw īskwäw, " mistahih kā-wīhkasik ? "

" kināpäm kinäpik umihkuh, äkutōwahk uhtsih k-ōsīhtamātān, " itäw. kisiwāsiw aw īskwäw.

" nama tsī tāpwä ahpōh äkus äh-tōtaman ? " itäw äsah.

ituhtäw itäh māna kinäpikwah kā-ntawāpamāt aw īskwäw. äkwah pakamahwäw mistikwah. namwāts kinäpikwah pä-wayawiyiwa. mistahi kisiwāsiw, kunt äh-pä-mawihkätät. äh-pä-pīhtukät, unāpäma kīskikwätahuk. äkus īs ōhpiskāw awa nāpäw, äh-tapasīt.

" ntawāts ōtah kīsikuhk nika-ntawih-utaskīn. nikah-atsahkusiwin ! " itwäw, äh-at-īsi-uhpiskät.

äkwah awa iskwäw, kītahtawä tōhkāpīmakan ōmah pisisik mistikwānis. äkwah kītahtawä kā-pīkiskwät um ōstikwān.

" ā, nitōyākan, tāniwähkāk ? "

sōskwāts kahkiyaw kakwätsimäw utāpatsihtsikanah. kahkiyaw mitunih kāh-kitōtam, äh-kakwätsihtahk. pōtih asiniya kā-wīhtamākut askīhk äh-kīh-kutāwināyit unāpäma. näu käkway kīh-miyäw utawāsimisah awa nāpäw, ispīhk ä-sipwätisahwāt, sīpiy kit-ōsīhtāyit, äkwah iskutäw, äkwah asinīwatsiy, äkwah sakäw, ukāminakasīwi-sakäw.

äkwah täpwäw awa ustikwānis awa. "ntawāsimisitik, pähik! kikitimahināwāw kā-nakasiyäk!" itwäw.

tahkih täpwäw awa iskwäw. äkwah awa nāpäsis itāmaskamik kāy-isihtapasīt, wāhyaw uhtsih wāpahtam ōma pisisik mistikwān äh-pīkiskwämakaniyik, äh-nayōmikut ustäsäh.

ōmis ītaw: "nistäsä, nama käkway kikāwiyinaw. ustikwān pikuh kā-pīkiskwämakahk," itwäw.

utinäw ōhtāwiyah kā-kīh-miyikut, iskutäw nähiyawak k-ōh-ōsīhtātsik[1]*; wäpinäw nāway isi.*

"ōtah iskutäw ta-wīh-ayāw!" itwäw.

tāpwäh mistahi nakānikōw awa, wāhyaw uhtsih iskutäw äy-isih-kwähkutäyik. ayis pisisik ustikwān pimuhtämakaniyiw. äwaku pikuh nähiyaw kāh-isiyīhkāsut äsah mats-āyisah ä-kīh-wītsihikut, pisisik ustikwān k-ō-tihtipipayiyik. piyisk miyāskam iskutäw. äkwah nawaswātäw sāsay mīna utawāsimisah. kahkiyaw saskitäyiwah wästakayah.

äkwah minah kītahtawä äh-ay-itāpit ana kā-nayōmiht awāsis, "namuya kikāwīnaw, nistäsä! kiyām sōhkih tapasītān!" itäw.

āsay mīna kīhtwām utinam ōhtāwiyah kā-kīh-miyikut ōkaminakasiyiwatsiy kit-ōsīhtāt. nāway isiwäpinäw. tāpwäh ātsisin aw ustikwān kā-tihtipipayiyit. äkwah atutäw misi-kinäpikwah, kita-kāh-kīskamāyit ukāminakasiya, kita-tawinamākut, sōskwāts kita-pimuhtät. tāpwä kaskihōw sōskwāts äh-pimuhtät.

äkwah āsay mīna wāhyaw äh-itāmutsik, āsay mīna pätisāpamäw ustikwān äh-pä-tihtipipayiyit awa awāsis kā-nayōmiht. āsay mina kā-kīh-miyikut ōhtāwiyah asinīwatsiy kitā-ōsihtāt āsay mīna nāway isiwäpinam. mistahi mis-īspayiw asinīwatsiy. nama kīh-kaskihōw awa ustikwānis ta-pāsituhtät. kwayask atutäw amiskwah ta-pīkwamāyit ōhi asiniya, äh-pīwāpiskōwiyikih wīpitiyiwa. äkwah kaskihōw sāsay mīna. āsay mīna nawaswātäw utawāsimisah.

āsay mina pätisāpamäw aw āwāsis kā-nayōmikut ustäsah. äkwah mīna sīpiy kit-ōh-ōsihtāt kā-kīh-miyikut ōhtāwiya ōtäh nīkān pistsih isiwäpinam. at-ītwäw aw āwāsis. mātōwak äkwah, äh-kustahkik ta-nipahikutsik ōma mistikwān ka-tihtipipayiyik, ukāwīwāwa ustikwāniyiw.

äkwah äh-mātutsik, "äkāya mātuk! kika-pihkuhitināwāw!" itikwak misi-kinäpikwah.

äkwah āsiwawihikuk.[2] *äkwah akāmihk ä-kih-takuhtahikutsik, kāwih āsiwaham awa kā-kiy-āsiwawahāt ōhi awāsisah.*

äh-wāpamāt äkutä awa mistikwān kā-tihtipipayit, ōmis ītwäw: "āsiwawahin niya mīna!" itäw.

"äkāya māka papāsäyihtah," itik.

tāpwä asiwahuhik. pōsiw uspiskwaniyihk.

mwähtsih tāwayihk nipīhk äh-ayātsik, "misi-kinäpik, wäsā kipäsiskān!" itwäw aw īskwäw.

äkwah pakastawähuk.

"'namäw' kik-äsiyīhkāsun!" itik awa ustikwān awa kā-tihtipipayit.

äkwah ōki nāpäsisak papāmātsihuwak, mistah ä-kwātakihtātsik. äwakw āwa utawāsisiwihtay wīsahkätsāhk.

äkuspīhk äkwah sipwähtäwak, usīmisah äh-wītsäwāt. pākahatōwānisah usīhtamawäw, ta-mätawākäyit.

---

[1] Word avoided, probably *pusākan*: "birch-fungus, used as tinder."

[2] Probably for *āsiwahuyikuk.*

kītahtawä tsīkih sīpīhk äh-pa-pimuhtätsik, äwaku ustäsimās, " āstam ! " k-ätikut kisäyiniwa utōsiyihk äh-pōsiyit. äh-pōsit, äkus īsi isi-kwāsihik. äkwah awa k-āpisīsisit awa nakatik.

äh-āt-īsi-mātut, " nistäsä, ntawāts niya nka-mahīhkaniwin ! " itwäw awa nāpäsis usīmimās.

äkusi äwaku pikuh kīh-utināw wīsahkätsāhk, äkwah äkutä wīkiyihk äh-takuhtahikut ōhi kisäyiniwa. kwatapinik utōsiyihk ; namuya ahpōh wīh-kīwähtayik. takuhtäw wīkiwāhk awa kisäyiniw, nīsu utānisa.

" ntawāsimisitik, nipäsiwāw kit-siw-unāpämiyäk , " itwäw äsa ; " ntawāpamihk , " itwäw.

wayawīw äh-umisimāwit, äh-ntawāpamāt. mistah ätsik āwa äh-māyātisiyit.

" namuya ta-kīh-unāpämiyān awāsis ! " itäw.

" āh, käyiwähk miyusiw. māskōts ahpōh usām mistah äh-mātut , " itwäw äsah.

äkwah ituhtäw usīmimāw. awa uskinīkiskwäw kīwähtahäw anihih awāsisah, ä-kīh-kāsīhkwänāt. pamihäw ; tāpwä unāpämiw äwaku. äkwah pakwātäw awa umisimāw, wāwāts māna uhtsitaw äh-tōtahk awa awāsis, äh-mīsīt utanāskāniyihk.

ä-kīh-näwu-tipiskāyik māka ōmis ītäw : " mahtih matōtisānihkäh ; nik-ōsīhtān niyaw , " itwäw.

tāpwä matōtisānihkäwān, äw-usīhtāt wiyaw. äkwa mistahi miyusiw äh-āhtsiyisut. akāwātäw äkwah awah kā-kī-pakwātāt. ātah kätutātsih, namwāts ahpōh nōhtä-kitōtik. äkwah awa käsäyiniwit sīhkimik utānisah ōh ōmisimāwa si-kakwäh-nipahāt.

äkwah tāpwäh, " aha' , nka-kakwä-nipahāw , " itwäw awa kisäyiniw.

" tāntäh ätukä nikah-kīh-uhtinän mistsikusah äh-miywāsikih ? " itwäw awa uskinīkiw.[1]

äkwah, " nk-ätuhtahāw ninahāhkisīm , " itwäw awa kisäyiniw.

äkwah tāpwä ituhtahäw äh-ministikōwiyik.

ōmis ītwäw awa kisäyiniw : " nipawākan, äwakw āna kitasamitin ! " itwäw.

mayaw utati-säskisihtay aw ōskinīkiw, ka-pä-mōskīstākut wākayōsah, itōwahk kā-wāpiskisitsik.

" ' nika-nipahāw , ' tsīw ōmah äh-itäyihtaman ? " itäw awa ; " nama ka-kih-nipahin , " itwäw ; " ayisk nīsta kōpawākanimitin , " itwäw.

tāpwäh nipahäw awa uskinīkiw. ustikwāniyiw utinamwäw. kīwähtatäw. āsiskawäw ōhi kisäyiniwa ; waskits nipīhk ati-pimuhtäw. äh-kīwāt awa kisäyiniw, kā-wāpahtahk wākayōs ustikwān äh-akutäyik utiskwähtämihk ; māka wiya kisäyiniw mawīhkātäw upōwākanah, äh-nipahimiht.

āsay mina kītahtawäh äh-ay-āyātsik, ōmis ītwäw aw ōskinīkiw : " tāntäh ätukä nkaw-uhtināwak mīkwanak äh-miyusitsik, nīpisisah kit-ōhts-ōsīhtāyān ? "

" ōtäh ōmah k-āsinīwatsīwik, äkutä mistahi miyusiwak mīkwanak. äkutä nik-ätuhtahaw , " itwäw awa kisäyiniw.

tāpwä sipwähtahäw äkutä isi. äkusi äkutä äh-takuhtahāt, piyäsiwa äh-uwatsistwaniyit.

" hāw, nipawākanitik, äwakw āna kitasamitināwāw ! " itäw.

äkusi isi-kīwäw. āsay mīna kahkiyaw nipahäw ōhih piyäsiwah.

---

[1] In the ensuing episodes he is spoken of not by name, but as "that youth."

āsay mina, " tāntäh ätukä nkah-kih-uhtinän nīpisiy äh-miywāsik, kitōsihak ?"

äkusi sāsay mīnah kisäyiniw, " nk-ätuhtahāw itäh äh-miywāsiniyik nīpisiyah."

tāpwä ituhtahäw.

āsay mina, " ā, nipawākan, häwakuh kitasamitin !" itäw misi-kinäpikwah.

āsay mina awa uskinīkiw k-āsamimiht misi-kinäpikwah nipahäw. ustikwāniyiw kīwähtatāw. āsay mina kisäyiniw nāway takuhtäw. mawīhkātäw mīna upawākanah.

" misi-kinäpik, nipawākan !" itwäw.

äkwah namuya kīh-kiskäyihtam tānis äkwah kita-kīh-isi-kawatimāt ta-k-īsi-nipahāt, ahpōh ta-kawatimāt.

äkwah ōmis ītwäw : " mātsītān, ntähkwāh[1] *!" itäw.*

tāpwä mātsīwak. äh-tipiskāyik iyikuhk, nipahäwak mōswah.

" wah ! piku ta-nipāyahk ! kimisi-kawātāpāwānānaw !" kisupwāmispuniyiw.

" pāsätān kitayōwinisinawa !" itäw.

tāpwä pāsamuk, mituni mistahi äh-pōnahkik minahikuskāhk. mayaw äh-kiskäyimāt unahāhksīmah äh-nipāyit, utinamwäw utayōwinisiyiwa kā-kīh-akutāyit. kahkiyaw mästihkasamwäw.

" käkway kā-saskitäk ? kitayōwinisah mästihkahtäwah !"

" hāh, ayisk kiwī-kakwä-nipahin ! — itāp nika-mōsōwin !" itwäw awa uskinīkiw.

ntumäw, äh-ati-sipwähtät awa kisäyiniw kisinwah. tāpwä mistahi kisināw. ayisk ntōmäw. äkwah awah uskinīkiw kīwäw. āsiskawäw usisah ; mōsōwiw, äh-kīwät.

äkwah, " tānähki ?" itik wiwa.

" kōhtāwiy äh-wīh-kakwä-nipahit, kahkiyaw ntayōwinisah kīh-mästihkasam."

täkuhtät awa kisäyiniw, apīwah unahāhkisīma. kīhkāmik utānisa.

" tānähki mīna k-ō-mästihkasamwat kitihkwatim utayōwinisah ?" itik utānisa.

" hā, äh-kīskwähkwasiyān," itwäw awa kisäyiniw.

" mahti päyakwāw āsay mīna !" itäyihtam awa kisäyiniw. " ninahāhkisīm, mahti mātsītān !" itäw.

tāpwä mātsīwak.

" namuya ta-kīh-kīwäyahk !" itäw sāsay mina.

iyikuhk äh-tipiskāyik, nipahäwak mōswah.

" kiyām ka-kapāsinānaw," itwäw awa kisäyiniw ; " kika-pāsänānaw kitayōwinisinawa," — " kīhkīhk äkusi nka-kakwä-isi-nipahāw," äh-itäyihtahk awa kisäyiniw.

äkwah akutāwak ä-kīh-pōnahkik utayōwinisiwāwa. mayaw äh-nipāyit, awa uskinīkiw nīhtinam kahkiyaw utayōwinisah. itah kā-nipāt astāw.

---

[1] Literally, "my sister's son (man speaking); my brother's son, my husband's sister's son (woman speaking)," often, as here, for *nahāhkis :* "son-in-law." Similarly, *nisis :* "my mother's brother" for "my father-in-law" (*See* below), and *nisikus :* "my father's sister; my mother's brother's wife" for "my mother-in-law," both of these being more specifically *manātsimākan :* "person one dare not address, parent-in-law." And *nahāhkaniskwäw :* "daughter-in-law" is little used beside *nistim :* "my sister's daughter (man speaking); my brother's daughter, my husband's sister's daughter (woman speaking)."

äkwah kisäyiniw waniskäw. pasakwāpiw, kuntah ä-kīskwähkwasīhkāsut. wiya käsäyiniwit kähtsiwāk utayōwinisah kahkiyaw mästihkasam.

" käkway kā-kīsitäk ? " itäw.

" ōhi niya k-āstäkih ntayōwinisah , " itwäw awa ōskinīkiw ; " kiy ätukä kähtsiwāk kitayōwinisah kā-pōnaman , " itäw ōhi kisäyiniwa ; " ayisk äkusi kikīh-tōtawin ; nīsta māka äkus īsi kik-äsi-nakatitin. "

" äha' ! itāp ätukä nka-mōsōwin ! " itwäw awa kisäyiniw.

nama kaskihtäw kita-mōsōwit. ntumäw kisinwa awa wīsahkätsāhk. nipahäw ōhi kisäyiniwa.

mātsikā äkwah nōtukäsiw näpahimiht unāpäma mistahi kisiwāsiw.

" kika-nōtinitunānaw ! " itäw unahākisīma ; " ahkāmasiniy äkutōwahk näwāw ka-nimahutin ; äkutah kä-pakamahutān ! " itwäw awa nōtukäsiw.

näwāw äh-nimahwāt nāpiwa,[1] *utinamiyiwa ; ustikwān uhtsih pīkwatahamiyiwa. mīna äwaku nipahik.*

äkusi äkwah awa kutak uskinīkiskwäw, mīna äwakuh nipahik. äkusi kahkiyaw äh-nipahikutsik. matsikah ayāwak äkutah wīsahkätsāhk.

äkwah sipwähtaw, äh-pähtahk usīma kā-kīh-mahīhkaniwiyit äh-nipahikuyit itāmi-nipīhk k-ōtaskiyit nanātuhk misi-pisiwah [2] *mina misi-kinäpikwah. äkwah mistahi kisiwāsiw.*

" tānis ätukä nikah-tōtän itāmi-nipīhk kit-ātuhtäyān ? "

kā-wāpamāt usīma, itah ä-kīh-nipahtsikāsuyit, nipīhk māna äh-ayitāpit, äh-ukimāwiyit kinusäwah utiskwāhtämiyihk äh-akutsiniyit, mistahi pakwātam. kītahtawäh ituhtäw ; natawi-pimwäw ōhi k-ōkimāwiyit kinusäwah. papāmuhtäw äkus īsi. kītahtawä kā-wāpamāt ayīkisah.

" tānähki ? " itäw.

" hā, nnatawi-nipiskäyān , " itwäw awa ayīkis.

" tānisi kä-tōtaman, wīh-nipiskäyani ? " itwäw awa wīsahkätsāhk.

ä-kīh-wīhtamākut, nipahäw ōhi. naspitamōhisōw ; usīhisōw t-āyikisiwit. ituhtäw äkwah ka-kanawäyihtsikāsuyit kā-mihkusiyit mahīhkaniwayānah.

mayaw äh-pīhtukät, " tawīstāhk ! äwakw äkwa kā-wīh-pä-pimātsihāt ōhi wīsahkätsāhkwah kākīh-pimwāyit , " itäw.

tāpwä tawīstawāw. äy-isi-tōtawāt ōhi kā-ntawi-nānapātsihāt, äkwah tāpwä sōhkih kihtsitānam ōma atsusis.

" käkway itahk ayīkis kä-nipiskät ! mistah ōma kikisiwāhinäwāw, nisīm äh-kīh-nipahāyäk ! " itwäw wīsahkätsāhk.

tapasīw äkus īsi.

" kikisiwāhāwak matsi-pisiskiwak ! " itik manitōwa ; " wīh-iskipäw askiy. kahkiyäw pāh-päyak pisiskiwak ōtinah, nanātuhk kā-papāmihātsik. äh-misāk ōsi usīhtāh , " itik.

äkuspihk äsa maywäs iskipäk ōma askiy, kahkiyaw käkway äsah ukīhmōtuhtāwāw pisiskiwak. ahpōh paskwāwi-mustuswak kī-mōwäwak ayīsiyiniwah, iyātah-ayāyitsih. äkusi kiy-ispayiw äsah. kahkiyaw pāh-päyak utinäw wīsahkätsāhk nāh-nīs ōhtsih, päyak nāpäw-āyisah, kiskisisah. kahkiyaw kā-papāmihāyit, mīna ōtah askīhk misiwä kā-ppāmuhtäyit, kahkiyaw nāh-nīsu uhtsi utinäw. äkusi usihtäw äh-misāyik ōsi. äkusi kīh-wanitipiskāyiw äsa. äkusi kahkiyaw atahkwak namuya uhts īhtakōwak. misiwä kīh-iskipäyiw askiy, ä-kīh-kīsihtāt äh-misāyik ōsi. äkwah misiwä äy-iskipäyik, kahkiyaw asinīwatsiyah äh-āyiwākipäyikih, äkwah papāmahukōwak.

---

[1] The Blackfoot name.

[2] Special mention of lynxes is perhaps to be discounted, as a compliment to me, who am called *misi-pisiw* : "Great Lynx."

piyisk wī-nipahāhkatusōw. wīwa nipahāhkatusōyiwa. äkwah ōmisi kahkiyaw käkwayah nipīhk k-ōtaskiyit mats-āyisah ä-wīh-kakwä-nipahikut, iyātah-päy-ituhtäyitsi äh-nipahāt, piyisk kahkiyaw käkwayah kustik. äkwah kītahtawä ksä-manitōwah kā-pakitsītutākut.

ōmis ītik : " kīspin äkā kīh-kāhtsitinamanä asiskiy, äkusi namuya wīhkāts kit-ähkipayiw ōma nipiy ," itik.

nämitanaw äskutōskwanähk itah äh-pāhkwāsik ; misiwä äsah kiy-iskipäpan.

" äkwah tānisi kä-tōtamān ? " itäyihtam āta wiya.

ayisk kahkiyaw kīh-pōsihäw pisiskiwah. kītahtawāh atutäw mākwa, ta-kakwäh-utinamiyit asiskiy. pōtih namwāts kīh-kaskihtāyiwa. kītahtawä mīna atutäw nikikwah. namwāts kaskihtāyiwa. kahkiyaw tahtuh kā-nihtā-kōkiyit āta äh-atutāt, namwāts kīh-kāhtsitinamiyiwa asiskiy. kītahtawä watsaskwah atutäw. nama mayaw mtunih takuhtäyiwa. äwakuni apisīs kīh-kikamuyiw asiskiy. āsay mīna kīhtwām sīhkimäw. āsay mīna pätāyiwa. näwāw sipwähtisahwäw kita-nātamiyit asiskiy.

" äkuyikuhk ! " itik manitōwa.

äkutah uhtsi kī-miyikōwisiwak ayīsiyiniwak nähiyawak, uskats askiy ōtah äh-ayātsik. äkusi kahkiyaw nipiy nama takun äkwa kahkiyaw.

äkusi sipwähtäw äkutah uhtsi wīsahkätsāhk. äkwah wiyasōwātäw ayīsiyiniwah kit-ōwītsäwākaniyit, ä-wīh-usihāt manitōw. asiskiy uhtsih usihäw nīsu ayīsiyiniwah. äkwah maywäs āpāhkawihāt nāpäwa, uspikä-kaniyiwa iskwäyānihk pāh-päyak uhtsih utinamwäw, äkwah k-āpāhkawihāt.

nistam äh-pīkiskwät ayīsiyiniw, ä-kīh-usihiht, " nipiy ! " kīh-itwäw äsah.

kīhtwām äh-pīkiskwät, " nimītsiwin ! " kīh-itwäw äsah.

kahkiyaw käkway nama käkway uhtsi kustikuk. nāpäw kī-wihāw äsah. " umihtikōs [1] " k-īsi-wihāw nistam nāpäw. äkwah iskwäw. näwu kiy-āhāwak, pāh-pītus äh-isi-wāhkōhtutsik.

äkutah äkwah kī-sipwähtisahwāw nistam kāhkākiw, kahkiyaw askiy ä-wāsakamät. pōtih ntsawāts kīh-asänāw.[2] äkwah kihiw kī-sipwähtisahwāw.

äkutah uhtsih nama wīhkāts äsah kīh-nipiwak ayīsiyiniwak. päyāhtik kīh-kāmwātsih-pimātisiwak, piyisk äh-atih-mihtsätitsik. kī-miskamwak tānisi äh-isi-pimātsihutsik. äkutah uhtsi ka-päw-uhpikihitut nähiyaw, ayīsiyiniw.

nanātuhk ayīsiyiniw kahkiyaw ninisituhtän ōma kā-ntawäyihtākwahk ātsimōwin. nähiyaw tānisi äy-isi-pimātisit, ä-kīh-päy-isih-uhpikihitutsik nähiyawak, kahkiyaw nikiskäyihtän. mīna wāpiski-wiyās ōtah kā-päh-takuhtatāt ayamihāwin, kahkiyaw min äōkō nikiskäyihtän, tānisi äh-päh-isih-wīhtsikātäyik. ōhtsitaw nitātayōhkātän nistam ayīsiyiniw, tānisi ä-kīh-isih-usīhtsikāsut nähiyaw. māskōts äkutōwahk kā-ntawäyihtsikātäk, māskōts äh-nuhtä-kiskäyihtamihk nähiyaw upimātisiwin, äy-itäyihtamān, k-ōh-isih-ātayōhkäyān.

nīswāw mitātahtumitanaw askiy ä-kīh-ispayik, äkuspihk äsa ukī-nipahikwah wākayōsah äwakuh nistam ayīsiyiniw, äsah äh-kīh-nipit. äwakuh niyanān kā-nähiyawiyāhk ōnipiwah utsāhtsāhkuyiwah ta-kanawäy-imāt kīh-itasōwātik äsa manitōwa. matwān tsī käyāpits äkusi ispayiw ;

---

[1] The word is in Ojibwa form.

[2] Or read *kīh-asähāw* : "he flew back."

namuya nika-kīh-itwān. ayisk usām ninisiwanātsihisunān. kih-kita-hamōwāw ayīsiyiniw äkā kit-ayamihāt ; äwakuh uhtsi kāh-itwäyān.

" nähiyaw kāy-isiyīhkāsut pikuh kāy-itak : äkāyah ayamihāhkan ! namuya kiya kā-miyitān. ntawāsimisah uhtsitaw nimiyāw wāpiski-wiyās, kita-kakwātakihut, wiya ä-kīh-nipahāt ntawāsimisah ," kīh-itwäw äsah manitōw.

äkuykikuhk äyakōw päyak pīkiskwäwin.

Once upon a time, long ago—I am now telling a sacred story—once upon a time, of old, a certain man dwelt in a lone lodge with his wife and his two children. Then presently, whenever he went away, his wife put on her finery. He did not know why his wife put on her finery. So then at one time he merely pretended to go away to hunt; he hid himself, thinking of her, "Let me see what she will do." And then he saw her beating a tree, and a serpent came out, and he saw that his wife had it for a lover, at once he was very angry. When his wife struck the tree, she said, "My husband, now I have come!" He was very angry. He was jealous; for the serpent was loved more than he. Those of whom I mean to tell the sacred story were Wisahketchahk's mother and father. So now that man was very angry; he could not sleep.

He said to his wife: "I am going far away to hunt."

He really went very far away to hunt. He stayed over one night.

"Why did you stay out over night?" his wife asked him.

"I have been far off to hunt," he told her; "But you, you are to fetch the meat," he told his wife.

"Very well," said she.

As soon as his wife had gone, he took her skirt and put it on. He went to where that serpent was inside the tree.

"My husband, I have come!" he said to the serpent.

Really, it came out. He cut through its neck with a knife; he took the serpent home; he made broth. Then he hid his children.

One must keep in mind that before the earth existed they had many kinds of power. He plunged his two children into the ground. And that woman, too, had great power for all things, and could talk even to every kind of thing and accordingly receive answer from it. And then the man forbade every object that was in their dwelling to tell her anything.

Then his wife arrived. He gave her the serpent to eat which he had cooked into broth.

"Oh, what is this," asked the woman, "which tastes so good?"

"The blood of your husband, the serpent; from it I have made this for you," he told her.

The woman was angry.

"It is not true, is it, that you have done even this?" she asked him.

She went to where she was in the habit of visiting the serpent. Then she struck the tree. The serpent did not come out. She was very angry, as she came back, loudly bewailing it. When she entered the dwelling, her husband cut off her head. Then he rose into the air, to flee.

"I shall needs go dwell there in the sky. Let me be a star!" he said, as he rose higher and higher.

And that woman, that severed head presently opened its eyes. Then presently that head spoke.

"Come, my dish, where are they?"

Without delay, she asked all her utensils. She spoke to every single one in turn, questioning it. At last a stone told her that her husband had sunk them into the earth. Four things that man had given his children, at the time when he started them off; that they might make a river, fire, a mountain of stone, and a forest; a forest of thorn-trees.

Then that head began to call. "My children, wait for me! You are making me wretched by leaving me!" it cried.

That woman called all the time. And that little boy who was fleeing under ground, from afar he saw that severed speaking head, as he was being carried on his elder brother's back.

He said to him, "Big brother, our mother is not there. It is only a talking head," he said.

He took that which his father had given him, that from which the Cree make fire; he threw it behind him.

"Let there be fire here!" he said.

And really that being was entirely brought to a stop, when far and wide the fire blazed. For it was but a severed head which went along. Because he, at any rate, who is called Indian was helped by evil beings, was why that severed head could roll along. Finally it passed the fire. Then it again pursued its children. All its hair was aflame.

Then presently when again that child looked about, who was being borne by the other, "It is not our mother, big brother! Let us flee with all our might!" he told him.

Again he took that which his father had given him that he might make a hill of thornberry-trees. He threw it behind him. That Rolling Skull was really blocked. Then it bade a Great Serpent to bite through the thorn-trees and make a passage through for it, that it might go unchecked. And so it managed to go on, unchecked.

Then, when again they had fled a long ways, again that child who was being carried saw the Skull come rolling. And again, he threw behind them that which he had been given by his father that he might make a mountain of rock. Vastly that rocky crag extended. That Skull-Being could not manage to go across it. At once it employed a beaver with iron teeth to bite that rock to pieces. Then it was able again to go on. Again it pursued its children.

Again that child who was being borne by his elder brother saw it coming. Then that which his father had given him that he might make a river, he threw it, by mistake, on ahead. The child kept crying its cry. Then they wept in terror that the Rolling Skull would kill them, their mother's skull.

Then, as they wept, "Do not weep! I will take you to safety!" a Great Serpent said to them.

Then he carried them across the water. When he had brought them to the far shore, he crossed back, who had taken those children across.

83186—2½

When the Rolling Skull saw him, it said, "Take me across, too!" it said to him.

"But do not be impatient" he told it.

So he carried it across. It rode on his back.

Just when they were in the middle of the stream, "Great Serpent, you are going altogether too slowly!" said that woman.

Then he threw her into the water.

" 'Sturgeon' will be your name!" he told that Rolling Head.

Then those boys wandered about, suffering many hardships. That boy was Wisahketchahk in his childhood.

Then they departed from there, he with his little brother. He made a ball for him to play with.

Then at one time, as they were walking by the river, the elder boy was told, "Come here!" by an old man in a canoe. When he stepped into the canoe, this person carried him off. They left the smaller boy behind.

Then as he began to weep, "Big brother, now I shall have to turn into a wolf!" cried that little boy, the younger one.

Thus only Wisahketchahk was taken, and the old man brought him over yonder to his dwelling. He put him under his canoe as he tipped it on the beach; he did not even care to take him home. The old man went to his abode, to his two daughters.

"My children, I have brought someone for you to marry," he said; "Go look at him," he said.

The older girl went out of the tent and looked at him. Why, he was very ugly!

"I cannot marry a child!" she said of him.

"Oh, he is handsome enough. Perhaps it is only because he has been weeping too much," he said.

Then the younger sister went there. This young woman brought the lad home, after washing his face. She took care of him; she really took him for her husband. The elder sister disliked him, and all the more so as the child wantonly played tricks, ...

On the fourth night, however, he said to them, "Do you build a lodge for the steam-bath; I shall make my body," he said.

Accordingly a sweat-lodge was built for him, and he made his body. Then he was very handsome, when he had made himself over. Then she who had disliked him conceived a passion for him. But even though she plied him with speech, he did not care to have her so much as speak to him. Then the old man was urged by that elder daughter of his to try and kill him.

And really, "Yes, I shall try to kill him," said the old man.

"I wonder where I can get good little arrow-sticks?" said the youth.

Then, "I shall take my son-in-law to such a place," said the old man.

And so he took him to an island.

Thus spoke the old man: "My dream guardian, I feed you this man!" he said.

Hardly had the youth gone into the brush, when out came a bear at him, one of those who are white.

" 'I shall kill him,' is that what you are thinking?" said he; "You cannot kill me," he said; "For I, too, have you as my dream spirit," he said.

The youth really slew it. He took its head. He took it home with him. He outdistanced the old man; he walked along on the surface of the water. When the old man went home, there he saw the bear's head hanging over the doorway; the old man bewailed his dream guardian who had been slain.

Presently, as they dwelt there, the youth spoke thus: "I wonder where I can get pretty feathers to make my arrows?"

"Over yonder amid the rocky cliffs, there the feathers are very fine. I shall take him there," said the old man.

Really, he led him off, to go there. And so he brought him there where the Thunderers had their nests.

"Come, my dream guardians, I feed you this man!" he said to them.

With that he turned to go home. Again, he killed all those Thunderers.

Once more, "I wonder where I can get a good osier to make my bow?"

Then again, the old man: "I shall take him where the willows are good."

Really, he took him there.

Again, "Come, my dream guardian, this one I feed to you!" he said to a Great Serpent.

And again, the youth slew the Great Serpent to whom he was being fed. He took home its head. Again the old man was the second to arrive. He grieved over this dream spirit, too.

"Great Serpent, my dream guardian!" he cried.

Then he did not know how he could freeze him to death, to kill him, but by freezing him.

So he said, "Let us hunt, my nephew!" he said to him.

Accordingly, they went hunting. At nightfall, no sooner, they killed a moose.

"Pshaw! We shall have to sleep out! We are soaked through to the bone!"

It was a warm-weather snowstorm.

"Let us dry our clothes," he said to him.

So they dried them, feeding up a huge fire in a cedar-grove. As soon as he knew that his son-in-law slept, he took the latter's clothes from where he had hung them. He burned them all.

"What is that burning? Your clothes have burned up!"

"Hah, of course, for you are trying to kill me!—So then I shall turn into a moose!" said the youth.

As the old man went away, he called the Cold. And really, it grew very cold. For he had called it. Then that youth went home. He outdistanced his uncle; he was in the form of a moose, as he went home.

Then, "Why thus?" his wife asked him.

"Because your father is trying to kill me, he burned up all my clothes."

When the old man arrived, his son-in-law sat there. His daughter upbraided him.

"Why now did you burn up your nephew's clothes?" his daughter asked him.

"Oh dear, because I was walking in my sleep," said the old man.

"Let me try once more!" thought the old man. "My son-in-law, let us hunt!" he said to him.

Accordingly, they went hunting.

"We shall not be able to go home!" he said to him, again.

Not before nightfall they killed a moose.

"Let us camp," said the old man; "We shall dry our clothes," for, "In spite of all, I shall try to kill him this way," thought the old man.

Then, after feeding up a fire, they hung up their clothes. As soon as the other slept, the youth took down all of his own garments. He put them down where he slept. Then the old man got up. He squinted from under his eyelids, pretending to walk in his sleep. The old man himself burned up all his own clothes.

"What is that burning?" he asked him.

"Here are my clothes, lying here," said the youth; "I daresay it is your own clothes you have put in the fire," he said to the old man; "But seeing that you did it to me, I too shall now leave you, as you left me."

"Very well! I suppose I shall then turn into a moose!" said the old man.

But he did not succeed in turning into a moose. Wisahketchahk called the Cold. He killed the old man.

Of course the old woman now was very angry, when her husband had been killed.

"We shall fight!" she said to her son-in-law; "With this pounding-stone four times I shall threaten you; then I shall strike you!" said the old woman.

When for the fourth time she held it over Napiw as if to strike, he took it; he smashed her head with it. He killed her too.

Thereupon that other young woman, her, too, he killed. So he killed them all. Of course Wisahketchahk and the other stayed there.

Then he set out, for he heard that his little brother who had turned into a wolf had been slain by the various Great Panthers and Great Serpents that dwell under water. He was very angry.

"I wonder what I shall do to go under the water!"

When he saw, as he always looked into the waters, his little brother, where he had been slain by them all, hanging over the doorway of the Chief Fish, he was filled with grief and hate. Presently he went there; he went and shot with an arrow that Chief Fish. Then he wandered about. Presently he saw a frog.

"What is your errand?" he asked it.

"Why, I am going to doctor by breathing," said the frog.

"What do you do, when you are breath-doctoring?" asked Wisahketchahk.

When it told him, he killed it. He turned himself into its form; he made himself to be a frog. He went to where they kept the Red Wolfskin.

As soon as he entered, "Make way for this person! This is the one who has come to cure him whom Wisahketchahk has shot with an arrow," was said of him.

Accordingly, they made way for him. When he was treating him whom he had come to tend, then, truly, with a vim he thrust in that arrow.

"What is that about a frog would be breathing on wounds! Rather, you have angered me much by killing my little brother!" cried Wisahketchahk.

Then he fled.

"You have enraged the evil beasts!" the Lord told him; "The earth will be flooded. Take one each of every beast, and of all those who fly. Build a great canoe," He told him.

At that time, we are told, before this earth was flooded, all kinds of animals ate each other. Even the buffalo ate men, no matter where they were. That is the way things were. Wisahketchahk took one of every kind, in pairs, one male and one female. Of all who fly and of all who walk about this earth, of each he took two. Then he built a great canoe. Then deep darkness came. All the stars ceased to be. Everywhere the earth was flooded, when he had finished the great canoe. Then, when the flood was everywhere, and all the mountains of rock were submerged, then they drifted about. At last he nearly starved to death. His wife starved to death. Then, when all the creatures that dwell in the water, the evil beings, tried to kill him, when in vain they came there, and he slew them, then at last all creatures feared him. Presently God descended to him.

Thus He spoke to him: "If you cannot scrape up some earth, then never will these waters recede," He told him.

It was forty cubits to the bottom; the flood had covered all.

"Now how am I to do?" he thought, none the less.

But he had all the beasts on his ship. Presently he bade the loon try to take up some soil. It turned out quite unable. Then presently he employed the otter. It was entirely unable to do it. Although he employed all, as many as are good divers, they could not at all scrape up any earth. Then in time he sent the muskrat. It was a long time coming back. A little earth was sticking to it. Again he bade it go. Again it brought some. Four times he sent it off to fetch earth.

"It is enough!" the Spirit told him.

Thus it was that the Indians were given this by the spirit powers, that first they had an earth here. For then all the water ceased to be.

Then Wisahketchahk went away from here. Then the Spirit decreed that he was to have man as a companion, and decided to create man. He made two human beings of earth. Then before He brought the men to life, from each of them He took the lowest rib, and then He brought them to life.

When man first spoke, after being created, we are told that he said, "Water!"

When he spoke again, we are told that he said "My food!"

They were feared by all creatures, for no cause. Then the man was named. "Dug-out-Canoe" the first man was named. Then the woman. Four of them dwelt there, being in different wise related, so as to make a family.

Then from there the raven was first sent out to make the circuit of the earth. In the outcome he was needs rejected. Then the eagle was sent out.

In the time that began then, people never died. They lived quietly and undisturbed, until at last they came to be many. They found how to keep themselves alive. From that time to this in successive generations has come the Cree, the Indian.

Of all the different peoples I understand this story which is desired. Of how the Cree lived, as the Cree have come down through the generations to this time, all of this I know. And of the Christian worship which the white man has brought here with him, of this, too, I know all, of how it has been announced to this time. I have chosen to tell the sacred story of how the first man was created, the Indian. Because I have thought that doubtless this is what is desired, that doubtless people wish to know of the life of the Indian, that is why I tell this sacred story.

When twice a hundred years had gone by, at that time, this first man was killed by a bear, and so he died. Then, we are told, he was assigned by the Spirit to care for the souls of the dead of us who are Indians. I question if it is still so; I cannot say. For too greatly are we destroying ourselves. The Indian was forbidden to practise the Christian religion; that is what I mean.

"I say this only to him who is called Indian: thou shalt not worship in Christian wise! Not to thee do I give this. I give my Son to the white man, that he may suffer for having slain my Son," said the Lord.

So much for this discourse.

(2) Wisahketchahk, the Partridges, and the Stone

Adam Sakewew

sākäwäw.

kītahtawä sipwähtäw wīsahkätsāhk. kītahtawä wāpamäw usk-āyīsisah watsistwanihk pihäsisah.

" nisīmitik, pihätik, tānisi äsiyīhkāsuyäk ? "

" ātah kiwīhinān, ' pihäwak ' k-ätwäyin ; äkusi pikuh äy-isiyīhkāsuyāhk. "

" namuya ! " itwäw wīsahkätsāhk ; " kahkiyaw käkway nīswayak isiyīhkātäw. "

" namuya , " itik ; " äkusi pikuh, ' pihäwak, ' äy-isiyīhkāsuyāhk. "

" namuya, nisīmitik ! mā-mitunäyihtamuk ; kutak minah wīhōwin kitayānāwāw. "

äkusi awah ustäsimās umis ītäw : " āta wiya māna nikāwiy nōhtāwiy, ' ukuskuhiwäsīsak ' kitisiyīhkāsunānaw, äkwah ' pihäwak ; ' kinīsuyīhkāsunānaw, ' ntikunān māna. "

" isay ! nitakis ōki kuskuhiwätsik ! " itäw, äh-mīsīt ustikwāniyihk, äh-pīwäyimāt ; " nama ta-kī-kuskuhiwäyäk ! " itäw ; " nam āwiyak ka-kī-säkihäwäw ! " itäw.

äkusi nakatäw. äkwah ōki pihäwak äh-kīwätsik, awän ōhi utawāsimisiwāwa ! kīh-mäyiwiyiwah ustikwāniyihk.

" tānihk um, nitawāsimisitik, k-ōh-isinākusiyäk, äh-wīhtsäkisiyäk ? " itikwak ōkāwiyiwāwah ōhtāwiyiwāwah mīna.

" wiy āna wīsahkätsāhk ä-kakwätsimikuyāhk, ' tānisi äsiyīhkāsuyäk, nisīmitik, pihätik ? ' äh-itikuyāhk, äkā ä-wīhtamōwāyāhk, ' āta kusā kiwīhinān, ' äh-itāyāhk, ' namuya ; kahkiyaw käkway nīsuyīhkātäw, ' nitikunān. piyisk niwīhtamawāw, ' ukuskuhiwäsīsak nitisiyīhkāsunān, ' äh-itak, ' ntakis ōki kuskuhiwätsik, ' k-ätikuyāhk, äh-mīsīt nistikwāninähk. äkusi āspin kā-sipwähtät, äh-pāhpit. "

" hāw, niwīkimākan, sipwähtä. māka mina sīpīsis utihtahkih, äkutah ka-wawiyasihānaw, ' ntakis ōki säkihiwätsik, ' k-ätāt kitawāsimisinawa ; kanōhkawātān. "

tāpwä pihäwah māwihkātäwak, äh-māwatsihitutsik. äkwah kītahtawä kā-wāpahtahk sīpīsis ä-sakāyik. äkwah āyītaw āyītawakām pihäwak apiwak äkutah, äh-kāsōtsik.

äkwah wīsahkätsāhk utihtam sīpīsis. wāsäkamiyiw. äkusi ä-wāpahtahk, mustuswayānah akwanahōw ; äkwah pahkäkin uskutākay ; äkwah pahkäkin utāsah.

äkwah umis ītwäw : " mahtih " — sōhki pīkiskwäw — " iskäkānih usk-āyih astutin astwātuhk, usk-āyah ayōwinisah, 'awiyak āsiwakāmä-uhpītsih, kit-āyāw ōhih,' itwähk. nistwāw nika-nōmiskän ; äkutah näwāw mwähtsi nik-uhpīn, " itwäw.

nituhtāk ōhi pihäwah ; māka namuya wāpamäw. äfwah kuspuhtäw.

" atsiyaw nika-wäpikātān, " itwäw ; ātsimustawäw tānisi äh-wīhtōtahk.

äkwah wāhyaw nīpawiw ; utakuhpah ōtah ahäw ; tāpiskawäw. äkwah pä-wayatsāwiw ; sisunä sīpīsisihk naki-kwāskuhtiw.

" yōhah, nahpihtsis nika-sāpupahāw, nōhtäpayiyānih, " itwäw ; " akāmihk ntäsiwäpināw. "

utinäw wahpihtsisah ; namuya kanawāpamäw, ōmisi äh-isiwäpināt ; akāmihk pahkisiniyiwa. äh-wäpināt, päyak pihäwa k-uhpahuyit.

" yōhu, māna tāpwä nka-kuskuwihikuh ! " itwäw.

" äkwah piku nistwāw ! "

min āsay nōhtsimihk ituhtäw. namuya kiskäyihtam itäh wahpihtsisah k-äsiwäpināt. äkwah pä-wayatsāwiw ; nakīw.

" nīsu ! äkwah piku nīswāw, " itwäw.

äkwah nīs uhpihāyiwah.

" yōhuh, mānah nika-säkihikuhtayik ōkih pihäwak ukuskuhiwäsīsak ! "

āsay mina sipwähtäw. āsay mina pä-mōskīstam uma sīpīsis.

" nistu ! äkwah anuhts äkwah nik-uhpīn. iskäkāniyah usk-āyah astwātuhk astutin ayōwinisah, 'awiyak āsiwākāmä-uhpītsih nika-miyāw,' itwähk. äkwah māka niwīh-uhpīn, " itwäw.

äkwah sipwähtäw ; äkwah äkutä sākuwäw : " äkwah niwīh-uhpīn ; niwīh-utinän usk-āyah ; niya nik-āyān ; niwīh-uhpīn ! namuya äkwah niwīh-nakīn ! " itwäw ; ātsimustawäw ōhih kā-kāsōhtākut.

äkwah pä-wäyatsāwiw, ä-pä-sākuwät. mituni kisiwāsiw pisisik. timīw uma sīpīsis. um äh-uhpīt āyītawakām pihäwah kā-uhpiyit, äh-pitihkuyit. säkisiw ; tāwakām pahkisin. ōhi kā-manātsihtāt umaskisinah, utāsah kātāpiskahk, kahkiyaw sāpupatāw, utakuhpah. " tsä ! matsastimwak kākuskuwihitsik, kā-sāpupatāwak ntayōwinisah ! " itwäw.

äkwah pāsam.

" hah, nika-pīhtwān ! kīh-pīhtwāyānih, äkuyikuhk ta-pāstäwah ōhi nitayōwinisah, " itwäw.

äkwah ä-ntunawāt wahpīhtsisah, nama miskawäw.

" tānitäh uma, nahpihtsis äsi-wanihak ? "

ntunawäw nipīhk, äkwah äkā ä-miskawāt. kītahtawä kā-wāpamāt äh-akutsiniyit.

" tsäyä ! mats-ahpihtsis awa kā-kāsōhtawit ! nikaskäyihtäh ä-wīhpīhtwāyān ! "

akuhtsiniyiwah ; utinäw ; nama käkway. piyisk umayikuhk ; nama käkway.

" äh, äh-tapasīt awa nahpihtsis ! " itäyihtam ; " nitsawāts kinwäs kīmīw. "

äkwah umis äh-tōtahk, piyisk nahapiw. nätä muhtsihk kāskatāwahkinikäw ; nama käkway.

itāpiw ; " äwakw āwa nahpihtsis ! " itwäw, " mahtih äkwah nikōtināw, " äh-itäyihtahk.

kisiwāsiw āsay.

äkwah umis äh-tōtahk, ōtah äh-akuhtsihk ōtah, " nk-āti-umis-ītiskwäyin, " äy-itäyihtahk, pōt ōhi ispimihk ōtah mistikuhk kīh-akutsiniyiwah.

" tsäh ! mats-ahpihtsis awa kā-wäh-wanihak, kā-kaskäyihtamihit ! niwīh-pīhtwāwā ! ätsik āwah itah äy-akutsihk ! " irwäw ; " ntsawāts namuy āwiyak, " itwäw, äh-utināt, " ntsawāts kika-nahihun, äkā kit-āpatisiyan. "

wäpināw. nama käkwayah ōh utōspwākana wahpīhtsisah minah. wäpināw.

kīsupwäyiw. nam äskwah pāstäyiwah utayōwinisah. nitsawāts sipwähtäw. kītahtawä sāpupäyiwa utakuhpah ; kusikwatäyiwah. usām ä-kīsupwäyik, äh-pimuhtät, pōtih usām äh-pwāwihāt ōh ōtakuhpah, ä-kisāstäyik, pōtih kā-wāpamāt asiniyah ä-misikitiyit. tuhtäw.

äw-utihtāt, " hāw, nisīm, " itäw ōh āsiniyah, " kimiyitin awa nitakuhp, " itäw.

akwanahäw. kāh-akwanahāt, ati-sipwähtäw ; musäskatäw. äkwah namuya wāhyaw äh-ihtāt, kā-pä-nōkwaniyik ä-wīh-kimiwaniyik, äh-pä-kāhkitōyit piyäsiwah.

" yōhō, nika-sāpupān ! nitsawāts kāwih nka-nātāw kā-kīh-mäkiyān, " itäyihtam, " nitakuhp. "

kīwäpahtäw ; takuhtäw ; utinäw.

" npä-nātāw awa nitakuhp, " itwäw.

" yahah, māka mīna nika-wiy-pimitisahuk awa kā-kīh-miyak nitakuhpah ! " itwäw, äh-itāt ōhih asiniyah.

ay-āpasāpiw. äkusi kītahtawä kā-waskawiyit ōh āsiniyah, piyätihtipiyit. mōskīstāk, tāpiskōts ōma äh-tihtipipayiyit.

" yahah, umīhkawikīh awa ! " itäw ; " isi tsikāhtaw ! "

piyisk kisiwāk ; wäyatsāwiw. kīsupwäyiw ; kīpah nayawapiw. āmatsiwäw ispatināhk.

" mahtih äk ä-kīh-päy-āmatsiwät awa kā-watakamisit, nitakuhpah ä-kīh-awihak ! "

äkwah tāpwä mīhkawikiyiwa. nitsawāts tapasīw.

ätāy ä-sakāyik itāmōw, " mahtih kit-ātisin awa kā-watakamisit ! " äh-itwät.

äkwah sakāw äw-utihtahk aw āsiniy, kāh-kawiskawäw ōhi mistikwah. āsay wīsahkätsāhk säkisiw ; äkwah wayatsāwiw.

" usām äk āwiyak ta-kīh-itāmuyān, kayās nōhtāwiy ä-kī-nipit, " itwäw ; " ta-kīh-nātamawit nam āwiyak, " itwäw.

paskwāhk itāmōw. mitunih nayawapiw.

" ntsawāts kiyām nka-nipahik, " äh-itäyihtahk, kawipayihōw.

usitihk māhtakuskāk ōhih asiniyah.

" āstam-itah nawats, nisīm ! " itäw.

päy-āhtapiyiwah uskātihk ; äkwah māhtakuskāk.

" āstam-itah nawats, nisīm ! "

" namuya ! " itik ; " kīspin itahk äpiyānih, nama wīhkāts nitāhtapin, " itik.

äkusi äkwah nama kih-pihkuhōw, kahkiyaw käkway pämuhtäyits äkutah, manitsōsah, " kakwä-pihkuhin, nisīm ! " äh-itāt, " namuya ! nikustāw ! " äy-itikut.

" nisīm, kiyām kitimākäyimin ! "

" namuya ! nikustäw usām !" kīh-itāw ; " päyakwanuhk kit-āpit, itah äpitsih," itik nanātuhk ōhih käkwah.

kītahtawä pīskwah kinwäs kā-kituyit ; äh-kituyit, kā-tsīpipayiyit.

" yōhōn, pakāhkam aw āsiniy kustäw äwakunih," itäyihtam ; " nisīm, āstam !"

" hāh, nistäsä, äyāh, māka minah wā-tōtawiyan !"

" namā wiya, nisīm ! kakwä-pihkuhin ; nitiskiskāk aw äsiniy. kik-äsi-miyusiyan kik-äsīhitin, kīspin pahkwatinatsi awa asiniy."

" häha', äkāya māka kiyāski ; nitaka nnōhtä-miyusin, nistäsä," itik pīskwah.

äkwah spāhkäpayihōw awa pīskwah ; äkutäw uhtsi pä-mōskīstawäw ōh āsiniyah ; pwäkitsitäw. pāstsipayiw aw āsiniy. käyāpits nama kīh-pihkuhōw awa wīsahkätsāhk.

" nisīm, āhkamäyimuh ! kakwä-pihkuhin ! kit-äsih-miyusiyin kik-äsihitin ; ka-wawäsihitin."

" äha', nistäsä, mitunih ninōhtä-miyusin ; usām niwiyīpisin," itik.

āsay minah ispāhkäpayihuyiwa ; āsay minah pä-mōskīstawäw asiniyah ; mituni kisiwāk pwäkitsitäw ōhī asiniyah. mitunih pīkupayiyiwa ; nanānis apiyiwa. pihkuhōw awa wīsahkätsāhk.

äkwah, " āstam, nisīm ; mistahi kitatamihin !"

äkwah wāpatuniskah, asiskiy äh-wāpiskāyik utinam wīsahkätsāhk ; äkwah awah pīskwah wā-wāpamisōw, pāh-pahkih äh-wāpiskisit.

äkwah umis ītäyihtam : "tāpwä nimiyusin !" itäyihtam.

" āstam, nisīm. mahtih kihkwākanihk mīn äkutah kik-ōsīhitin ; usām kinwāw kiskiwan. āstam ! iyikuhk kit-äspīhtsäw."

" äha'," itik.

äkwah umisi tōtawäw ; asānaskatinamwäw. äkwah sīsikuts utihtinäw, ōm ōtōniyiw umis äy-ispitamwāt. äkwah pakwātam awa pīskwah ä-misāyik utun.

äkuyikuhk kahkiyaw.

Once upon a time Wisahketchahk set out. Presently he saw some young partridges in a nest.

"My little brothers, partridges, what is your name?"

"But you just did name us, when you said, 'partridges'; that is the only name we have."

"No!" said Wisahketchahk; "Everything has two names."

"No," they told him; "For we have only this name, 'partridges'."

"No, little brother! Take thought upon it; you have some other name besides."

Thereupon the oldest of them said to him, "To be sure, my mother and father do say to us, 'Little Startlers,' we are called; and 'Partridges'; we have two names."

"Bosh! Fine ones these are to startle anyone!" he said to them,.... .... to show his contempt; "You couldn't startle anybody!" he told them; "You will never scare anybody!" he told them.

With that he left them. Then, when those partridges came home, what had happened to their children! ....

"Why is this, children, that you look like this ....?" their mother and their father asked them.

"Why, when that person Wisahketchahk asked us, 'What is your name, little brothers, partridges?' and we did not tell him, but said to him, 'But you have just spoken our name,' then he said to us, 'No; everything has two names.' At last I told him, saying to him, 'Little Startlers we are called,' whereupon he said of us, 'Fine ones these are to startle anyone,' .... With that he was off and away, laughing."

"Well, wife, come away. When he comes to the creek again, we shall make him a laughing-stock for saying to our children, 'Fine ones these, to startle anyone.' Let us attack him."

Accordingly they appealed to the other partridges, and all assembled. Then presently he came to the creek in the woods. And there on both sides, on both banks sat the partridges in concealment.

Then Wisahketchahk reached the creek. The water was bright and clear. When he came to it there, he had on a buffalo-robe; and leather was his coat; of leather were his breeches.

Then he spoke as follows: "Come"—and loudly he spoke—"I have a feeling that a new hat has been put up as a prize, and new clothes, and it has been announced, 'If anyone jumps to the far shore, he shall have these.' Three times I shall stop short; then, the fourth time, I shall jump," he said.

The partridges listened to him; but he did not see them. Then he walked back up the bank.

"For a short while I shall exercise my legs," he said; he simply told them what he meant to do.

Then he stood a ways off; he put his blanket-robe here, like this; he put it round his neck. Then he came on a running start; at the bank of the creek he stopped with a jump.

"Tut tut, I shall get my tobacco-pouch all wet, if I don't make it," he said; "I'll throw it across."

He took his tobacco-pouch; he did not keep his eye on it as he flung it; like this it fell somewhere on the other bank. When he threw it, one of the partridges flew up.

"Tut tut, really, he came very near startling me!" he said.

"Now only three times more!"

Again he went away from the water. He did not know the exact spot to which he had tossed his tobacco-pouch. Then he came with a running start; he stopped.

"Two! Now only twice more!" he said.

Then two of them flew up.

"Tut tut, they came mighty near scaring me, these partridges, these little startlers!"

Again he went off. Again he came running at that creek.

"Three! Now this time I shall jump. Without doubt a new hat has been put up as a prize, and new clothes, with the statement, 'If anyone jumps across the water, I shall give him these.' But now I shall jump," he said.

Then he was off; and then he shouted: "Now I am going to jump; I am going to take the new clothes; I, I shall have them; I am going to jump! This time I shan't stop!" he cried; he gave it all away to them who were hiding from him.

Then he came with a running start; he came a-shouting. He kept himself in a high state of excitement. When he jumped, up went the partridges from both banks with a whirr. He was scared; he fell into the middle of the water. Those moccasins of his, which he treated with such care, his breeches, which he had round his neck, he got them all drenched, and his blanket-robe. "Bah! Those dirty dogs startled me and made me get my clothes all wet!" he cried.

Then he dried them.

"Ha, I shall have a smoke! When I have smoked, these clothes of mine will be dry," he said.

Then, when he looked for his tobacco-pouch, he could not find it.

"Where can it be that I lost my tobacco-pouch?"

He looked for it in the water, but he did not find it. Then all at once he saw it lying in the water.

"Bah! This nasty tobacco-pouch has been hiding from me! I was getting sad for want of a smoke!"

It lay there in the water; he reached to take it; there was nothing. At last as far as this; nothing.

"Oho, and so this tobacco-pouch of mine is running away!" he thought; "It has been away a long time, for all I could do."

Then, when he reached like this, at last he was in a sitting position. Way out he was scratching up gravel from the bed of the stream; nothing.

He looked there; "There is my tobacco-pouch!" he cried; "Now do let me take it," he thought.

He was angry by this time.

Then, when he did like this, there where, by this time, he lay in the water, thinking, "I will turn my head like this when I reach," why, there, up aloft in a tree there, hung that thing.

"Bah! There is that nasty tobacco-pouch I kept losing till it made me miserable! As if I hadn't been longing for a smoke! And so there it hangs!" he cried; "Since you won't have it otherwise, be absent," he said, taking it; "Since you won't have it otherwise, I'll teach you how to be of no use."

He gave it a fling. Gone was his tobacco-pouch, and his pipe as well. He threw them away.

It was hot weather. His garments were not yet dry. So he needs went off without. Now his blanket was drenched through; it was heavy. And as the weather was very hot, as he walked along, he could hardly carry that blanket-robe of his, in the hot sun, when there he saw a big stone. He walked over there.

When he came up to it, "Now, brother," he said to that stone, "I give you this blanket of mine," he said to it.

He put the robe on the stone. When he had covered it, he went away; he went naked. Then, when he had not gone far, there came signs of rain, as the Thunderers sounded their approach.

"Tut tut, I shall be drenched! I shall have to get back the thing I gave away," he thought, "my blanket."

He ran back; he came to the place; he took it.

"I have come to get my blanket here," he said.

"Dear me, but now this fellow to whom I had given my blanket will come and chase me!" he said, speaking of that stone.

He kept looking behind him. And soon, there, that stone began to move and roll toward him. It went for him, rolling along, like this.

"Dear me, he runs fast, this fellow!" he said of it; "It's a close shave, this!"

At last it was near; he ran hard. It was hot weather; soon he was tired. He ran up a hill.

"Let's hope that he won't be able to come up the hill, this dangerous person to whom I lent my blanket!"

Truly, it went fast. There was nothing to do but flee.

He fled to a wooded place, "Let's hope that dangerous character will be blocked!" he said.

But when that stone reached the wooded place, it knocked over one tree after another. By this time Wisahketchahk was thoroughly frightened; he ran with all his might.

"And there is no one I can flee to, for my father died long ago," he said; "There isn't anyone could help me," he said.

He fled into the open country. He was very tired.

"There is no escape; he will kill me, that's all," he thought, and flung himself down.

The stone came down on his foot and held him fast.

"Farther up this way, brother!" he said to it.

It moved farther up, onto his leg; it held him fast with its weight.

"Farther up this way, brother!"

"No!" it answered him; "If I sit down anywhere, I never change my seat," it answered him.

So now he could not get himself free, and whenever any creature, even a worm or a beetle, went by, "Try and get me free, little brother!" he would say to it, but "No! I am afraid of him!" it would answer him.

"Little brother, please take pity on me!"

"No! I fear him too much!" he was told; "Let him stay where he is, when he takes his seat anywhere," those different creatures said to him.

Then at one time the mosquito-hawk gave a long, repeated cry; when it cried, the stone moved with a jerk.

"Hoho, plainly this stone fears this one creature," he thought; "Little brother, come here!"

"Hah, big brother, I wonder what you will be doing to me this time!"

"No, truly, little brother! Try to get me free; this stone is killing me with its weight. I will make you beautiful, if you move this stone away."

"Very well; but do not lie; I surely much want to be beautiful, big brother," the mosquito-hawk answered him.

Then the mosquito-hawk soared up into the air; from there it came attacking that stone; .... The stone split. Even yet Wisahketchahk could not get himself free.

"Little brother, keep at it! Do try to get me free! I will make you handsome; I will deck you out."

"Very well, big brother; I am very eager to be beautiful; I am too drab of colour," it answered him.

Again it rose soaring into the air; again it came and attacked the stone; .... The stone burst into many pieces; it lay here and there. Wisahketchahk was free.

Then, "Come here, little brother; you have greatly obliged me!"

Then Wisahketchahk took up some white clay, white earth; then that mosquito-hawk looked at itself, and saw that it was streaked with white.

Then thus it thought: "Surely I am beautiful!" it thought.

"Come here, little brother. Let me arrange your face as well; too long is your beak. Come here! It ought to be only as long as this."

"Very well," it answered him.

Then he did like this to it; he bent the thing crooked for it. And then suddenly he grabbed it and stretched out its mouth for it, like this. The mosquito-hawk hated having a big mouth.

That is all.

(3) Wisahketchahk Visits the Partridges

Mrs. Adam Sakewew

kiyākäskamikapiw.[1]

kisäyiniw sipwähtäw, äkwah äh-pipuniyik. äh-utākusiniyik, kītahtawā pähtawäw awāsisah. mihtsätukamikisiyiwa, mihtsät mīkiwahpah.

äh-ati-takuhtät ispatināhk, awāsisah, " ukiyutäw ! " itik.

" āh, ōtah ta-päy-ituhtäw ; ōtah ta-pämītssōw ! "

ha, ituhtäw äkutä, pīhtäyis äh-tsimatäyik. ā, pīhtukäw.

" ā, asam nistäs ; ta-mītsisōw. "

asamäw.

" pahkwäsikanāpuy, " itäyihtam.

" ōtah ta-pä-mītsisōw, " itäw, äh-nitumiht.

nam äskwa mītsisōw.

äkwah mwähtsi ä-wīh-mītsisut, āsay mina kutakihk kutakah äh-ntumikut.

äkwah äh-pīhtukät, ä-wīh-mītsisut, ōmisi äkwah : " nistäs ta-pä-kīwäw. "

kīwäw.

äh-pīhtukät, " hāw, nstäsä, kawisimuh ! kīpah māna pitsināniwiw, kīksäpā ä-wīh-pitsihk. kawisimuh ! "

käh-kätsīw.

" ā, nstäsä, kīpah māna pitsiwak ōki ayīsiyiniwak kīksäpā ! "

" pisinäw nītim kutawätsih, äkutah nika-päkupayin, " itäyihtam. kätayōwinisäw, " wätinahk nika-nipān, " äh-itäyihtahk.

äkwah kīksäpā pisinäw äh-wāsänākwaniyik, uhpiyiwah ōhi piyäsīsa, " ayīsiyiniwak " k-ätäyihtahk. sākākunäkāpawiw.

" tsä, wīnikunäwi-mahkayak ! "

äkwah pustayōwinisäw.

" nama kīhtwām nka-wayäsihikuk ! "

äkwah sipwähtäw.

" mahtih utäh kā-wīkihk ! "

---

[1] The narratress has since died.

One way—and no doubt an ancient one—of telling Culture-Hero stories (which are known to every listener) is in a series of laconic sentences, largely quotations of speeches.

In this anecdote Wisahketchahk visits the partridges in their camp. In each tent food is set before him, but before he can eat, he is dragged off by some other host. In the morning the partridges fly off before he wakes up, leaving him alone in the snow.

äkutä ituhtäw. mikunta sipwähtäw. mītusiskāhk, itah ä-sīpäyyāik, awāsisah äh-tatwäwitamiyit, ä-sōskwatsiwäyit, mistahi tahtakusiw kōnah, awāsisah itah äh-mätawätsik, äh-kīskwätsik.

āsay minah nitumāw. āsay tipiskāyiw. pimihkān asamāw.

mwähtsi äh-utinahk, " hāw, nipä-ntumāw kstäsinaw ; ta-pä-mītsisōw nīkihk, " itāw.

" hāw, nītim, pä-kīwäyāni, nika-mītsin ōma, " itäw ōhi iskwäwah.

āsay minah ntumāw : " pitah niya nistäs nīkihk kita-pä-mītsisōw ; usām kayās kā-wāpamak kistäsinaw. "

" hāw, nītim, itah kā-wīkihkämuyān, äkutah ituhtātān ōmah k-āsamiyin pimihkān, " itwäw.

āsay minah kīwäw.

" ā, nsīm, mistahi ninästuhtān ; äh-timikunik usätināhk niwī-nipān. "

" nstäsä, wīpats wīh-pitsiw awa ukimāw ! "

āsay miskākaniyiw itäh ä-wīh-ayuwäpihk.[1]

" pitah äkutah ä-wīh-mītsisuhk, maywäs mītsisuh ä-wīh-pitsihk. "

" ā, nisīm, kutawätsi nītim, āsay nka-waniskān, " itäw usīma.

äkusi kätsikunam umaskisina utāsa mīnah uskutākay, ä-aspiskwäsimut. nipāw. mituni kīksäpāw, wāhyaw äh-pä-wāpaniyik, mäkwäts äh-nipāt awa wīsahkätsāhk, kätahtawä sisikuts k-ōhpahuyit pihäwah. äkutōwihk kā-pīhtukät, itāmihk kōnihk äh-sīpāyākunakihiht.

" tsä ! wīnikunäyu-mahkayak kā-wayäsihitsik ! niya kahkiyaw awiyak kā-wayäsimak, kīhkīhk ka-wayäsimitināwāw ! " itäw.

äkusi äkuyikuhk.

The Old Man set out, and it was in winter. Presently, towards evening, he heard some children. Those people had many tents, many were the lodges.

When he arrived at the hill, the children said of him, "A visitor!"

"Ho, let him come here; let him come here and eat!"

So he went to the tent that stood in the centre. He entered.

"Hey, give my big brother something to eat; let him have a meal."

He was given food.

"Porridge," he thought.

"Let him come and eat over here," someone said to him, inviting him.

He had not yet begun to eat.

Then, just as he was about to begin eating, again he was invited by others to another tent.

Then, as he went in and was about to eat, then, "Let my big brother come back here."

He went back.

As he entered, "Well now, brother, go to bed! We always move camp early, when we move in the morning. Go to bed!"

He undressed.

"Ho, big brother, these folks always break camp very early of a morning!"

"As soon as my sister-in-law kindles the fire, I shall wake up," thought he. He took off his clothes, thinking "I do want to sleep in comfort."

---

[1] This sentence and the following speech are unintelligible to me.

Then in the morning, promptly with the first gleam of dawn, up flew those birds which he had taken for people. He stood there, deep in a snow-drift.

"Bah, the filthy brutes!"

Then he put on his clothes.

"They shan't fool me again!"

Then he went away.

"I'd better go to some inhabited place!"

He went over yonder. He set out at random. He went to a poplar-grove, to where there was an open place among the trees, where some children were playing noisily, sliding down a hill. Very hard and smooth was the snow where the children were playing and raising a rumpus.

This time, too, he was invited. It was already dark. He was given some pemmican.

Just as he took it, "Hullo, I've come to invite our big brother; he is to come eat at our house," he was told.

"Well, sister-in-law, when I come back here, I shall eat this," he told the woman there.

Again he was invited: "First let my big brother come eat at my house; it is really too long since I have seen our big brother."

"Well, sister-in-law, let us take the pemmican over to where I am visiting for the night," he said.

Again he went back.

"Now, little brother, I am tired from my long tramp; I want to sleep on the deep snow, on the hillside."

"Big brother, the chief here means to move camp promptly!"

They had already found the place to stop to rest.

"Wait and eat at the place where we are planning to eat, before we move on."

"Oh, little brother, when my sister-in-law kindles the fire, I shall get up all right," he told his younger brother.

Accordingly he took off his moccasins, his breeches, and his jacket; using them all for a pillow. He slept. Very early, at the first far-off sign of dawn, while that Wisahketchahk was yet asleep, suddenly up flew the partridges. For such they were whose tents he had entered, and he had been led to go deep under the snow.

"Bah, the filthy brutes have tricked me! I, who trick everyone, I shall trick you none the less!" he said of them.

That is all.

(4) Wisahketchahk Preaches to the Wolves

Coming-Day

kā-kīsikāw-pīhtukäw.

wīsahkätsāhk mistahi kitimākisiw; nama wya käkway utayōwinis ä-wīkitsik, äh-ayātsik. kītahtawä takusinwak wämistikōsiwak, äh-papā-atāwätsik ahtayah, mahīhkanah äkwah mustuswayānah. äkwah wīsahkätsāhk nama käkway ayāw atāwākan. kutakak ayīsiyiniwak mistahih ayāwak; atāwäwak äkunik mistahi ayōwinisah ; äkwah wīsahkätsāhk nama käkway.

äkwah ōmis ītäw wämistikōsiwah : " nama tsī nika-kī-masinahikān ? nama käkway atāwākan nitayān. māka kiyipah mihtsät nik-āyān ka-tipahikäyān. " äkus ōmis ītwäw ; wämistikōsiwah itäw wīsahkätsāhk awah : " nama käkway ka-kīh-tipahikākān. kīspin miyiyinih, kiyipah nik-āyān. "

" ahā' ! "—wämistikōsiwak—" käkway kintawäyihtän, wīsahkätsāhk ? "

" wāpuwiyānah nīsu, mīnah mitās nīsu, miskutākay mīna nīsu, pāsk-isikan. "

äkutah mistahi ayōwinis utinam. äkusi äkwah kīwäw wīsahkätsāhk. uwīkimākanah miyäw kahkiyaw.

umisiy itik uwīkimākanah : " muhtsu-kisäyiniw, tāntah ki-ōtinaman tah-tipahikākäyin ? "

äkusi itwäw, " nōtukäsiw, päyakwäw nna-ntawāpamäw[1] *wämistikōsiw . "*

äkusi äkwah sipwähtäw.

äh-pīhtukät, wämistikōsiw awah umis ītäw : " āh, wīsahkätsāhk, kipä-tipahikān ? "

" namuya, " itwäw wīsahkätsāhk ; " miyin pistsipōwin. "

" tānisi kitōtan ? "

" āh, mahīhkanak nika-nipahāwak. "

äkwah miyik maskihkiy, pistsipōwin. äkwah kīwäw wīsahkätsāhk.

äh-pīhtukät wīkiwāhk, " nōtukäsiw, miyin pimiy. "

miyik pimiy. äkwah äkutah pistsipōwin astäw pimīhk ; äkwa apisāsin uyākanis, sīkinam äkutah pimiy. mihtsät äkutah usihtäw apisāsikih pimīsah āhkwatinah.[2] *äkwah kahkiyaw utinam ; äkwah sipwähtäw ä-ntunawāt mahīhkanah.*

kītahtawä wāpamäw mahīhkanah päyak.

" āh, nisīm, āstam ! "—ōhi mahīhkanah.

" ā, namōya ! " itwäw mahīhkan, " ā, kiwīh-nipahin usām ! "

" namōya, nisīm. ä-wīh-masinahikähitan. "

" tānisi ä-wīh-isi-masinahikähiyin ? "

" ä-wīh-atuskahitān ka-papā-ntumatsik mahīhkanak mīna mahkäsīsak, kahkiyaw kā-miyusitsik mahkäsīsak. ōtah nik-āpin ispatināhk, ä-wīh-kakäskimitakuk, ä-miywāsihk ātsimōwin ka-wīhtamātakuk. "

äkwah tāpwä awa mahīhkan sipwähtäw, ä-nitumāt mahīhkanah mīna mahkäsīsah. tāpwä pätuhtäwak mihtsät mahīhkanak. mituni misiwä wāsakām apiyiwah, ä-wīh-ntuhtākut, tāpiskōts ayimihāwiyiniw wīsahkät-sāhk.

ōmisīh itäw : " nisīmitik, ayamihāwin kā-ntuhtamäk t-ōtinamäk ; äkusi äkwah namuy āwiyak ka-nipahikuwāwak, ayamihāyäkuh. māka äkāh tāpwähtamäkuh, ka-nipahikuwāwak. īh-ōhi wāpahtamuk, äh-ōhi ! " mahīhkanak mahkäsīsak ä-wāpahtahkik ōhi pimiyah, " hāw, umah awiyak umah mītsitsi kā-wīh-saskamuhak, kinwäs ka-pimātisiw, " äkusi itwäw wīsahkätsāhk.

äkwah kahkiyaw, " niya, niya ! " itwäwak mahīhkanak, äh-miywäy-ihtahkik kinwäs ka-pimātisitsik.

" äkwah umah, " äkwah miyäw pimiy.

---

[1] The combination *nt* does not exist in the full form of Cree words, but is due to the loss of an intermediate short vowel; *See* Introduction. Occasional forms like *na-ntawāpa-mäw :* "he goes to see him," are allegro variants for such as *na-nitawāpamäw ;* the first syllable here is reduplicative. This differs from Ojibwa, where *nand-* is probably the normal representation of older *nat-*.

[2] Probably an error.

mītsiw awa mahīhkan ; äkusi äkwah sipwähtäw.

pāh-päyak äh-saskamuhāt wāsakām, mīna mahkäsīsah, kahkiyaw mästinam ōmah pimiy.

" äkusi kinwäs ka-pimātisināwāw, nisīmitik, uma k-ōtinamäk ayamihāwin."

tāpiskōts ayamihäwiyiniw wīsahkätsāhk, äh-miyāt mahīhkanah ayamihāwin. kītahtawāh äh-apit mäkwāts wīsahkätsāhk, kahkiyaw kwāskwäpayihuyiwa mahīhkanah, äh-pahkisiniyit, äh-pistsipuyit, kahkiyaw äh-nipiyit.

" matsi-kakäpātisak ōki ! nik-ōh-ta-tipahikākäwā ! " itäw äs ōhi mahīhkanah wīsahkätsāhk.

äkwah wiyinihäw, äh-kīwähtahāt, äkwah mahkäsīsah mīnah kahkiyaw. mahīhkanah ayamihāwin kā-kiskinōhamawāt, kahkiyaw nipahäw. äkusi kahkiyaw tipaham umasinahikäwinah, äh-wayäsimāt mahīhkanah.

äkusi äkuyikuhk.

Wisahketchahk was very poor; he had not even clothing in his house, where he dwelt with his family. Then at one time arrived some Frenchmen who were going about buying furs, wolf-pelts and buffalo-robes. But Wisahketchahk had no furs to sell. The other people had many; they bought many clothes, but Wisahketchahk none at all.

Then he spoke to the Frenchmen as follows: "Won't you let me have credit? I haven't any furs. But in a short time I shall have a good many with which to pay my debt." Thus Wisahketchahk spoke to the Frenchman: "You will not need to pay anything. If you give me credit, in a short time I shall have them."

"Very well,"—the Frenchmen—"What do you want, Wisahketchahk?"

"Two blankets, two pairs of breeches, and two coats, and a gun."

Then he took a great deal of clothing. Then Wisahketchahk went home. He gave all of it to his wife.

This is what his wife said to him: "Crazy old man, where can you get anything with which to pay?"

He answered, "Old woman, once more I shall go see the Frenchmen."

So he set out.

When he entered, the Frenchmen said, "Well, Wisahketchahk, have you come to pay?"

"No," said Wisahketchahk; "Give me some poison."

"What do you want that for?"

"Oh, I am going to kill wolves."

So the other gave him some medicine, poison. Then Wisahketchahk went home.

When he came into the tent, "Old woman, give me some fat."

She gave him fat. Then he put the poison into the fat; and into a small dish he poured the fat. He shaped a great many little lumps of fat and cooled them until they were hard. He took them all, and went out to look for wolves.

Presently he saw a wolf.

"Hey, brother, come here!"—to that wolf.

"Oh dear, no!" said the wolf; "Why, you want to kill me!"

"No, little brother. I want to employ you."

"How do you want to employ me?"

"I want to give you the work of going round and summoning the wolves and foxes, all the good-looking foxes. I shall be sitting here on this knoll, ready to preach to you, to tell you good tidings."

So that wolf went off to call the wolves and foxes. Indeed, many wolves came. In great numbers they sat round in a circle, to listen to Wisahketchahk, exactly as if he were a missionary.

This is what he said: "My brothers, the tidings which you hear you should accept, and then no one will ever kill you, if you take on religion. But if you do not believe, someone will kill you. Look upon these things, these here!" As the wolves and foxes looked at those pieces of fat, "Now, then, if anyone eats this which I shall place between his teeth, long will he live," spoke Wisahketchahk.

Then all the wolves cried, "I, I!" glad that they were to live long.

"Here you are!" and he gave them the fat.

A wolf would eat it; then he would go.

He placed it in their mouths one by one, round the circle, the foxes' too, using up all the fat.

"So now long shall you live, brothers, now you have accepted this faith."

Just like a priest was Wisahketchahk, as he gave religious instruction to the wolves. Presently, as Wisahketchahk sat there, all the wolves leaped up in the air and fell down, poisoned, and they all died.

"These stupid fools! I surely did need something to pay my debts with!" Wisahketchahk must have said to those wolves.

Then he skinned them and took their skins home, and all the foxes' too. Having taught the wolves religion, he killed them all. In this way he paid all his debts, by deceiving the wolves with talk.

That is all.

(5) Wisahketchahk Stabs a Buffalo and Both His Arms

Coming-Day

kā-kīsikāw-pīhtukāw.

kätahtawä pimuhtäw wīsahkätsāhk ; māka mīnah nōhtähkatäw. kītahtawä wāpamäw mustuswah nīsu, takwahnawah päyak, päyak iyāpäsisah.

ōmisi itäyihtam : " tānisih nika-nipahāwak ? " itäyihtam.

nama käkway pāskisikan ayāw. äkwah sipwähtäw. äh-wāpamikut, wīh-tapasiyiwah.

" tsäskwah, nisīmitik ! miywāsin ātsimuwin k-ātsimustātināwāw. "

tsäskwah nīpawiwak mustuswak ; namuwya tapasīwak. äkwah takuhtäw wīsahkätsāhk.

ōmisī itäw : " ayisiyiniwak äh-itwätsik, ' takwahnaw wīhkimākusiw ; miyusiw,' äh-itwätsik, kutakak ayisiyiniwak ōmisih itwäwak : 'iyāpäsis miyusiw ; wīhkimākusiw,' äh-itwätsik, äh-kīh-kīhkihtutsik. äk ōhtsi wīh-kisiwāsiwak. 'mahti tsäskwah niyah nika-wāpamāwak ; awīnah wīhkimākusiw,' nititwān, kā-pä-nitawāpamitakuk, " ä-wīh-wayäsimāt ōhih mustuswah.

tāpwäh tāpwähtam awa mustus. äkwah tāhkinäw ; umis īsi miyāhtam utsihtsiy ; kutakah mīnah ōh ōtä. umōhkumān utinam.

umisīh itäw : " kiya kiwīhkimākusin ; kiyah kimiyusin, " itäw iyāpäsisah.

miywäyihtam iyāpäsis äh-miyusit, äh-itäyihtahk. umōhkumān tahkamäw watayihk. tapasiyiwa.

" matsih-kakäpātis ! tānitah kä-wīhkimākusit ! ninōhtähkatäwāh ! "

nipahäw ; nipiw awah iyāpäsis. äkusi äh-pahkisiniyit, äh-nipiyit, ituhtäw wīsahkätsāhk.

" hay hay hay ! äkwah nika-mītsisun, " itwäw.

äkwah wiyinihäw, äh-pahkwäkiswāt.

äkwah umis ītwäw wīsahkätsāhk : " wiyin nikah-ayān, " itwäw.

uma ōspitun, wīsahkätsāhk uspitun " namōya ! " itwäw, " niya nikah-ayān wiyin, " itwäw.

kutak uspitun : " namōya ! niyah nik-āyān. "

äkusi pīkiskwäwak, tāpiskōts nistu ayīsiyiniwak, äh-päyakut wīsahkätsāhk. kisiwāsiw āsay awa ; awa mīna kisiwāsiw.

" namuya kik-āyān wiyin ; niyah niwīh-ayān. "

wīsahkätsāhk ōmisi pīkiskwäw : " äkā wiyah, nisīmitik ! kuntah kiwīkisiwāsināwāw wiyās uhtsi. "

" ā, namuwya ! uhtsitaw äh-āspunisit."

" ā, äkāya nāntaw itwä ! kika-tahkamitin. "

" āh, nīsta ka-tahkamitn. "

" ā, tsäskwa nisīm ! namuya ta-miywāsin ta-nipahituyäk wiyās uhtsi. "

kunta māka kisiwāsiw.

" ā, äkā nāntaw twä ! "

mōhkumān ōmisi tahkamäw ; ōma uspitun tahkahtam. kwäski miyisōw umisi mōhkumān. kutak mīnah uspitun tahkahtam. äkusi äkwah pahkihtin mōhkumān ; nipahäw uspitunah. nipahitōwak.

äkwah wīsahkätsāhk nīpawiw, uspitunah ōmisi. äkwah wīsahkätsāhk namōya mītsisōw ; sipwähtäw ; nakatam wiyās. ayis uspitunah āhkusiw ; nipiyiwah uspitunah ; namuya kīh-mitsiminam mōhkumān.

äkusi äyakōw ātiyōhkäwin.

Once upon a time Wisahketchahk was walking along; as usual, he was hungry. Presently he saw two buffalos, a bull and a young steer.

This was what he thought: "How shall I kill them?" he thought.

He had no gun. Then he went from there. When they saw him, they wanted to run away.

"Wait a bit, my little brothers. I shall tell you a good story!"

Soon the buffalos stood still; they did not run away. Then Wisahketchahk walked up to them.

This is what he said to them: "Some men said, 'The bull smells good; he is beautiful,' but then some others said, 'The young steer is beautiful; he smells good,' and so they quarrelled. On this account they were getting quite angry. 'Just wait a bit, while I go look at them to find out which smells better,' said I, and so I have come to see you," he spoke to deceive those buffalos.

The buffalos really believed him. So he touched one; he smelled his hand like this; and then the other one. He took his knife.

He said to him, "You, you smell good; you, you are handsome," he said to the young steer.

The steer was glad to think himself beautiful. He stabbed him in the belly with his knife. The other one ran away.

'Stupid fool! How should he smell good? It is hungry I was!"

He killed it; the young steer died. So when it fell down dead, Wisahketchahk walked up to it.

"Splendid! Now I shall eat," he said.

Then he cut it up, stripping off the hide with his knife.

Then thus spoke Wisahketchahk: "I shall have the fat meat," he said.

His arm, Wisahketchahk's one arm, said, "No! It is I shall have the fat meat," it said.

His other arm said, "No! It is I shall have it."

So they spoke, as if they were three persons, though there was only Wisahketchahk. The one had already grown angry; now the other, too, got into a rage.

"You shan't have the fat meat! I, I shall have it!"

Wisahketchahk spoke thus: "Don't, little brothers! Needlessly you are growing angry over this meat."

"Oh, no! He simply insists on being selfish."

"Oh, keep still! I'll stab you."

"Oho, it's I who will stab you."

"Now, wait, little brother! It wouldn't do for you two to kill each other for the sake of this meat."

But he got into a foolish rage.

"Ho, keep still!"

With his knife he stabbed him like this; he stabbed that arm of his. Across to the other side he handed himself the knife, like this. He stabbed his other arm, too. And so then the knife fell down; he had killed his arms. They had killed each other.

There stood Wisahketchahk, with his arms like this. And Wisahketchahk did not eat; he went away; he left the meat. For he was sick in his arms; in fact, his arms had died; he was not able to hold a knife.

Thus goes this sacred story.

(6) The Shut-Eye Dancers

Coming-Day

kā-kīsikāw-pīhtukāw.

kītahtawä äh-pimuhtät wīsahkätsāhk,—nuhtähkatäw māka mīna,—äh-pimuhtät, kā-wāpamāt sīsīpah, äkwah niskah mihtsät, sīsīpah.

äkusi ōmisi itäyihtam : " tānisi k-äsi-nipahakik ? " itäyihtam.

kītahtawä kā-wāpahtahk sākahikanis, äkutah sisunä nipīhk kā-wāpahtahk asisiyah. utinam, äh-titipinahk. mistahih tahkupitam, äh-nayahtahk, ä-sipwähtät. sīsīpah itah k-āyāyit, äkutah tsīkih äh-pimuhtät, kā-wāpamikut sīsīpah.

ōmis ītwäwak sīsīpak : " hā, kistäsinaw ! " itwäwak ; " käkway kā-nayahtahk ? " äkusi itwäwak.

" mahtih nika-kakwätsimāw, " itwäw awa sīsīp.

" äha' , " itwäwak.

" nistäsä, kīkway kā-nayahtaman ? "

āhtsi pikuh pimuhtäw ; tāpiskōts äkāh äh-pähtawāt, āhtsi pikuh pimuhtäw.

āsay mīnah sīsīp umis ītäw : " nistäsä, kīkway kā-nayahtaman ? " äkuyikuhk nīpawiw wīsahkätsāhk.

" māh, " itwäw, " kīkway kā-nayahtaman ? "

" wāh, pasakwāpisimōwinah ! " itwäw wīsahkätsāhk.

" käkway pasakwāpisimōwin ? " itwäw sīsīp.

wīsahkätsāhk ōmis ītwäw : " nīminānah,[1] *" itäw.*

" nīmihinān, " itwäw sīsīp ; " nka-pasakwāpisimunān ! "

" hay hay ! " itwäw wīsahkätsāhk ; " āh, miywāsin äh-kitimākinawiyäk, nisīmitik ! nam āwiyak ntāpwähtākuh, tä-nīmihitutsik, kayās ä-kīhasutamān ta-nīmihitōwinihkäyān, " itwäw wīsahkätsāhk ; " äkusi päkapāk. "

ta-sipwähtäwak äkwah sīsīpak mīna niskak. kahkiyaw ituhtäwak.

umis ītwäw wīsahkätsāhk : " matsi-kakäpātisak, ninuhtähkatäwa ! mistahi nika-mītsisun ! " itäyihtam wīsahkätsāhk.

äh-apit, äkutah takuhtäyiwah.

" āh, āstamitik, nisīmitik ! " itwäw wīsahkätsāhk.

äkwah ä-sipwähtät, ä-sakāyik äh-ituhtät, mihtah itah äh-mihtsāniyikih, äkutah takuhtäw.

" hā, nisīmitik, utinamuk mihtah, " itwäw.

tāpwä utinamwak mihtsät, äkwah ä-usihtātsik wīkiwāw, äkutah äh-apahkwätsik ōhō asisiyah. apisāsiniyiw iskwāhtämis.

" hā, äkwah, nisīmitik, pīhtukäk, " itwäw ; " nīkān ta-pīhtukäwak niskak äkwah kā-misikititsik sīsīpak, " itwäw ; " tsikämā äyōkunik äh-ukimāwitsik, " itwäw.

wäskwāhtämihk äkusi ōmisi itapiyiwah, äyakunik niskak. nätä iskwāhtämihk, äyakunik äh-apisīsisitsik äkutah apiwak. äkwah kipaham um iskwāhtäm awa wīsahkätsāhk, " äkāh ka-wayawītsik, " äh-itäyihtahk. äkwah mātōw wīsahkätsāhk.

" nisīmitik, kinanāskumitināwāw, ä-kīsihtāyäk ōmah mīkiwāhp. äk āwiyak äh-kitimākinawit, kiyawāw kā-kitimākinawiyäk, " itwäw, äh-mātut.

äkusi pōni-mātōw.

ōmisī itwäw wīsahkätsāhk : " hāw, nisīmitik, ōtah tāwayihk nika-nīpawin ; nika-nikamun. nikamuyānih, ka-nīmihitunāwāw. iyikuhk pōni-nikamuyānih, äkuyikuhk ka-tōhkāpināwāw. kīspin manitōw nipätsimāw, ' hweh hweh hweh ! ' nik-ätwān ; äkutah sōhkih ka-nīmihitunāwāw, pähtawiyäkuh, äkusi itwäyānih. "

" āha' , " itwäwak.

äkwah mistik tahkunam wīsahkätsāhk, nīpiyah ä-kayāsayiwiyikih äh-takupitäyikih, ōmisi äy-isiwäpinahk, ä-säwäpayiyikih, tāpiskōts sasawihyākan, ōhi nīpiyah. äkusi äkwah nikamōw.

ōmis ītwäw :

" pasakwāpisimōwinah
nipätsiwitān ! "

äkus ītwäw, äh-nikamut.

äkwah ōhi kahkiyaw äh-pasakwāpitsik, äh-nīmihitutsik, kītahtawä, " hweh hweh ! " itwäw wīsahkätsāhk, äh-utināt ä-misikitiyit niskah, äh-kīskikwäpitāt. äkus ä-ati-wāsakāmät, tahk äh-nikamut, äh-ati-kīskikwäpitāt niskah ōhi mīna sīsīpah kā-misikitiyit. nätäh skwāhtämihk äh-nīmihitut

---

[1] Unusual word.

sihkihp, äwakuh äh-pähtahk käkway, äh-napatäh-tōhkāpit, äh-nīmihitut, kā-wāpamāt wīsahkätsāhkwah äh-ati-nipahāyit.

" īyahā ! " itwäw, " māka mīnah kimästsihikunaw wīsahkätsāhk ! " itwäw.

äh-tōhkāpitsik kutakak, umis ītwäw wīsahkätsāhk : " käkway ōma itah kä-pätāyān nīmihitōwin, kākäpātisitsik[1] *? ninōhtähkatāh ! " itäw ōhi sīsīpah.*

wayawīyāmuwak kutakak, äh-tapasītsik.

äkusi wayawīw wīsahkätsāhk, äh-pāhpit, äh-miywäyihtahk, " mistahi nika-mītsisun, " äh-itäyihtahk. äkusi pīkunam uma wīkih, ōhi mihtah äh-utinahk, äh-kutawät, ōhih ä-wih-nawatsīt nīpin-āyàh. äkusi äh-nawatsīt, kahkiyaw nawatsīw. äkusi ōsām mistah äh-pōnahk, āpwäsiw.

sipwähtäw, " pitah nika-pōn-āpwäsin ; äkuyikuhk ta-kīsisōwak niniskimak, " äh-itäyihtahk.

tāpwāh wāhyawäs äh-ituhtät, kā-wāpamāt mahkäsīsah ä-wīsakäyihtamiyit uskātiyiw, äh-watiskāyit, äkā äh-kih-pimuhtäyit, ä-wīh-tapasīhikut.

" tsäskwa, nisīm ! " itäw.

" wāh, namuya ! " itik ; " usām māka mīna nānitaw kiwīh-tōtawin, " itik.

" namuya ! " itäw ; " ä-wih-ātsimustātān. īh uma kiwāpahtän tsī mistahi kā-pikihtäk ? "

" äha' , " itik.

" äkutah mihtsät ninipahāwak niskak mīna sīsīpak, äkutah äh-nawatsiyān, " äh-itāt ; " mistahi ka-mītsisunānaw, " itäw ; " mākah pitah kakakwä-nakatunānaw. näma wāhyaw k-äspatinäk äwakuh ka-tätipäwäpahtānānaw. "

" hāh, namuya ! kiwāpamin äkāh äh-kīh-pimuhtäyān, ä-wīsakäyihtamān niskāt, " itwäw mahkäsīs.

umis ītwäw wīsahkätsāhk : " asiniyak niskātihk nika-tahkupitāwak, " itwäw.

" äha' , " itwäw mahkäsīs.

asiniyah utināw wīsahkätsāhk, äh-tahkupitāt uskātihk.

" haw, nisīm, äkwah ! "

äkwah sipwäpahtāwak. nakatäw mahkäsīsah wīsahkätsāhk.

" häy, umīhkawikīh awa mahkäsīs, kā-kitimākaskātak nisīm ! itāp ātiht nik-āsamāw, äyikuhk ta-takupahtātsih, " itwäw wīsahkätsāhk.

mayaw äh-ākawāwät wīsahkätsāhk, kīwäpayiw awa mahkäsīs, namuya ä-wīsakäyihtahk uskāt, ōma kā-pikihtäyik äy-ispayit. äh-takuhtät, niskah sīsīpah mīna kā-wāpamāt äh-kīsisuyit. utināw, äkwah äh-mītsisut, wīsahkätsāhkwah äh-kimutamawāt unawatsīwiniyiwa. kitamwäw kahkiyaw. usitiyiwah pikuh ōhi niskah äkwah sīsīpah, äkunih piku iskutähk astāw, " tawāpahtahk wīsahkätsāhk, " äh-itäyihtah. äkusi tapasīw, " nka-kisiwāhāw, " äh-itäyimāt wīsahkätsāhkwah.

äkwah wīsahkätsāhk iyikuhk äh-takuhtät mistah āpwäsiw ; ayisk mistahi pimipahtäw.

" häy, āstäpwäsiyānih nika-mītsisun, " äh-itäyihtah, " itāp ātiht nkāsamāw nisīm, " itäw mahkäsīsah, " iyikuhk takuhtätsih, " itäyihtam.

---

[1] The ending of the vocative plural is, of course, *-itik*. The sound *ts* for normal *t* appears in diminutives (among the younger generation of speakers, almost universally); less often in other words formed with suffixes containing *s* (as in the present instance); and occasionally in other words, probably always with a diminutive touch.

namuya kiskäyihtam āsay äh-kitamwāyit uniskimah. äkusi äkwan utinam ōm ōsitiyiw. nama käkway niskah.

" hä hä häy, nōsāmih-mästihkaswāw ! " itwäw.

piyis kahkiyaw utinäw ; kahkiyaw nama käkway ; usitiyiwah piku.

" hä hä häy, māka mīn ätsik ānih äh-wayäsihit mahäsihit mahkäsīs, kā-kitamwāt niniskimah ! äkus ätsik ānih kä-nōhtähkatäyān ! " itwäw ; " hā hah, kikisiwāhin, mahkäsīs ! namuya ta-pīhtsāw askiy itä tit-ätāmuwin. niya nikiy-usīhtān askiy ; ka-miskātin ; miskātänih kā-kitamwatsik niniskimak ! " itwäw wīsahkätsāhk, äh-sipwähtät, äh-ntunawāt mahkäsīsah.

namuya wāhyaw äh-ihtāt, kā-wāpamāt, äh-na-nipāyit, mitunih äh-mistatayäyit ; ayisk kīh-kīspuyiwah. asiniyah utinäw, ä-wīh-pakamahwāt.

" yahā ! " itwäw ; " nka-watōkatahwāw,[1] *" itwäw ; " nik-ōtastutinih awa mahkäsīsiwayān ! " itwäw ; " kiyām nka-pasisamawāw, ta-nipahāpasut ōm ōhtsi paskāpahtäw, " itwäw.*

na-nituhtāk, ōm äh-itāt. äkusi kutawäw, wāsakām ä-saskahahk maskusiyah. äkwah äh-kwāhkutäyik, waniskāw awa mahkäsīs. mistahi kaskāpāsōw.

" he' , " wīsahkätsāhk umis ītwäw ; " hihe' , mahti mīnah kitamuk niniskimak ! " itäw.

kuntah wāskāpayihōw awa mahkäsīs, äh-kaskāpahtäyik mistahi. piyisk namuya wāpamäw wīsahkätsāhk. kwaskwäpayihōw awa mahkäsīs, iskutäw uma äh-pāsitsi-kwaskuhtit, äh-tapasīt. namuya wāpamäw wīsahkätsāhk, äh-tapasiyit. piyis misiwä pasitäyiw, äkutah äh-wāskāhtät wīsahkätsāhk.

"tāpwä nikitimahāw, äh-nipahīhkaswak mahkäsīs, " itwäw wīsahkätsāhk ; kā-wāpahtahk pihkuh äh-astäyik, mustusu-mäy itah äh-kiy-astäyik, " tāpwä nikitimākīhkaswāw ! " äh-itwät ; " mahtih k-äskuhkasut, nka-mōwāw, iskuhkasutsih, " äh-itäyihtah ; uma pihkuh ä-wīh-utinahk, " kā-kīsisut iskutäw äs ōmah äwaku mahkäsīs, " äh-iytäyihtah, äh-tsīsihut.

äkuyikyhk namuya kiskäyihtam ä-kīh-tapasiyit.

äkusi äkuyikuhk äwaku ātayōhkäwin.

äh-tah-tahkiskawāt sihkihpah,[2] *" hāw, ōtäh nīkān ayīsiyiniw kit-ōhpikiw ; ka-wāpamik uma kā-nanaputōkanäskātān. ' sihkihp ' kik-äsiyihkātikwak. namuya ka-miyusin ; usām kikisiwāhin äh-wīhtaman, äh-tōhkāpiyan, " itäw.*

äkusi äyōkō.

Once upon a time, as Wisahketchahk was tramping along—as usual he was hungry—as he was tramping along, he saw some ducks and many geese, and ducks.

Then this was what he thought: "How shall I kill them?" he thought.

Presently he saw a little lake, and by the water's edge some weeds. He took them and rolled them up. He tied up a great bundle of them, took it on his back, and went off. When he came walking close to where the ducks were, they caught sight of him.

The ducks said, "Ho, our big brother! What is that he's carrying on his back?" they said.

"Suppose I ask him," said one duck.

---

[1] Error?

[2] This paragraph was added in answer to a leading question. "I did not tell you that part," he explained. This is characteristic of our informant. Notice that even now he does not explain the diver duck's red eyes.

"Yes, do," they said.

"Big brother, what is that you're carrying on your back?"

He kept right on walking; just as if he had not heard, he kept on walking.

Again the duck asked him, "Big brother, what is it you're carrying on your back?"

Only then did Wisahketchahk stand still.

"Say," it said, "what is it you're carrying?"

"Why, Shut-Eye Dances!" said Wisahketchahk.

"What is a Shut-Eye Dance?" said the duck.

Wisahketchahk spoke thus: "A saltatory rite," he told the other.

"Do you give us a dance," said the duck; "Let us dance the Shut-Eye Dance!"

"Splendid!" cried Wisahketchahk; "Oh, it is fine that you have taken pity on me, little brothers! No one has given heed to me until now, and danced, when long ago I had pledged myself to give a ritual dance," said Wisahketchahk; "So then, come ashore."

Off went the ducks and geese. All of them came.

Thus spoke Wisahketchahk: "Hopeless ninnies, I've been starving! I shall have a big meal!" thought Wisahketchahk.

They came to where he sat.

"Ha, come here, little brothers!" said Wisahketchahk.

Setting out and making for a clump of trees, he came to where there was plenty of wood for a fire.

"Ha, little brothers, take up some faggots," he said.

Accordingly they took up a plenty and built themselves a lodge, which they thatched with those weeds. The little doorway was very small.

"Ha, now, little brothers, come inside," he said; "First the geese and the big ducks will come in," he said; "Especially those who are chiefs," he said.

Accordingly these, the geese, sat like this, at the far end, facing the door. Over at the other end, by the door sat the little fellows. Then that Wisahketchahk blocked up the doorway, thinking "So that they can't get out." Then Wisahketchahk wept.

"Little brothers, I thank you for having built this lodge. When no one took pity on me, it was you who pitied me," he spoke, weeping.

Then he ceased weeping.

Thus spoke Wisahketchahk: "Now, little brothers, here in the centre I shall stand; I shall sing. When I sing, you will dance; you will close your eyes. Not until I cease singing will you open your eyes. When I summon the spirit-power, I shall say, 'Hwe, hwe, hwe!' Then you will dance with all your might, when you hear me call thus."

"Very well," they answered.

Then Wisahketchahk took hold of a branch that had old leaves on it which rustled when he swung it, like this, just like a bell, those leaves. Thereupon he began singing.

These were his words:

"Shut-Eye Dances
I bring here!"

were the words of his song.

Then, when they all had closed their eyes and were dancing, presently, "Hwe, hwe!" went Wisahketchahk, taking hold of a big goose and wringing its neck. In this way he kept on circling round, singing all the while, and, as he went, wringing the necks of the geese and of the big ducks. Over yonder by the door danced Hell-Diver, and when he heard something or other, and opened one eye as he danced, there he saw Wisahketchahk killing one after another.

"Yah!" he cried, "It's the same old story, Wisahketchahk is killing us off!"

When the others opened their eyes, Wisahketchahk said, "What sort of a dance would I be bringing you blockheads? I was hungry, that's all!" he said to those ducks.

They fled out of doors, the others, trying to get away.

Thereupon Wisahketchahk went out of the lodge, laughing and rejoicing, thinking, "I shall eat a plenty." So then he tore up that lodge of his, taking the faggots and building a fire to roast those summer creatures. He roasted them whole. Having made too big a fire, he began to feel hot.

He went off, thinking, "First I shall get over feeling hot; by that time my geese will be done."

And so when he had walked a little ways, there he saw Fox, who had a pain in his leg, and was limping and could not walk properly, as he tried to run away from him.

"Wait a moment, little brother!" he called to him.

"Dear me, no!" the other answered; "You are only going to play me some new trick," he said to him.

"No!" he told him; "It is only that I want to tell you some news. Do you see all the smoke rising over here?"

"Yes," said the other to him.

"Over there I have killed a lot of geese and ducks, and there I am roasting them," he told him; "We shall have plenty to eat," he told him; "But first let us race. Let us run around that hill not far from here."

"Oh dear, no! You see I can't walk, with my sore leg," said Fox.

Wisahketchahk spoke thus: "I shall tie stones to my leg," he said.

"Very well," said Fox.

Wisahketchahk took some stones and tied them to his leg.

"There, little brother, come on!"

So they set off at a run. Wisahketchahk left Fox behind.

"Hey, I thought this Fox was a runner, this poor little brother of mine whom I am leaving so far behind! I shall give the poor fellow a few of them when he arrives from his run," said Wisahketchahk.

As soon as Wisahketchahk was out of sight behind the hill, that Fox turned back, and his leg was not sore at all, as he made for the rising smoke. When he got there, there he saw the geese and ducks a-roasting. He took them and ate, robbing Wisahketchahk of his roasts. He ate them all up. Only the feet of those geese and ducks, only those did he put into the embers, thinking, "Let Wisahketchahk see them." Then he made for safety, thinking of Wisahketchahk, "He will be angry at me."

Then, when Wisahketchahk arrived, he was very hot; for he had had quite a run.

"Hah, when I am no longer hot, I shall eat," he thought; "I shall give my little brother a few, too," he said of Fox, "when he gets here," he thought.

He did not know that the other had already eaten his geese. So now he took one of those feet. There was not any goose.

"Oho, I have overcooked him!" he said.

At last he took them all out; every one was gone; only the feet were there.

"Oho, it's surely Fox has been fooling me again, eating up my geese! And so I am to stay hungry!" he cried; "Ho, you have got me angry, Fox! The earth will not be big enough for you to escape. It was I created the earth; I will find you; and when I find you, who ate up my geese!" cried Wisahketchahk, as he went off to look for Fox.

He had not gone far, when he saw him taking a nap, his belly all big; for he had eaten a hearty fill. He took up a stone, to strike him.

"Yah!" he said; "I shall ruin his hide," he said; "I might as well have a cap of his fox-pelt!" he said; "I had better make a fire round him so that he chokes in the smoke," he said.

The other was listening to what he said about him. So then he made a fire, setting fire to the grass round about. When the blaze came, Fox got up. The smoke was getting too thick for him.

"Ha," said Wisahketchahk; "Haha, just you eat up my geese again!" he said to him.

Fox dashed about in a circle, this way and that, as the smoke grew denser. At last Wisahketchahk could see him no more. Up leaped Fox, jumping across the flame, and making for safety. Wisahketchahk did not see how he ran away. At last there was a big fire, and Wisahketchahk kept walking round it.

"I have surely put an end to Fox; burning him to death," said Wisahketchahk; and when he saw the ashes lying, where there had been buffalo-dung, "Surely I have burned him to a sorry end!" said he; "I shall eat what is left of him, if there is any of him left from the fire," he thought; and he was going to take up the ashes there, thinking, "And this must be Fox, burned up in this fire," as he deceived himself.

Even now he did not know that the other had got away.

And so this is the end of this sacred story.

When he kicked Hell-Diver, "Now then, ahead in future time mortal man will grow up; he will see here on you where I have kicked your rump crooked. 'Hell-Diver,' they will call you. You will not be handsome; too much have you angered me by telling this and by opening your eyes," he told him.

So much for this.

(7) Wisahketchahk as a Captain

Louis Moosomin

näh-namiskwäkāpaw.

kītahtawä äsah sa-sipwähtäw ; ayisk misiwä kīh-tōtam wīsahkätsāhk. ahpōh kī-kaskihtāw äh-unōtinikäwukimāwit.

kätahtawä sipwähtäw äsah. ā, papamuhtäw. kītahtawä wāskahikan [1] *kāh-ōtihtahk.*

[1] Properly "stockade"; used of the trading-post forts, and of white men's houses generally. This is the first of many foreign features in this tale: *Wisahketchahk* is here among white people.

" āy, āy-api, ay-api, nistäsä !"

äkwah tapwäh apiw äsah. ntōnikäyiwa iskwäwa, äw-asamikut. hōh, namwāts käkway wāpahtam kit-ōtinamiyit mītsiwin. sōskwāts tāpiskwäkanäkinwah utinäyiwa, uta mītsisuwinähtikuhk äsiwäpinäyit. wāpahtam äkutah nanātuhk mītsiwinah.

māka mīna itäyihtam wīsahkätsāhk ; "nka-kimutin," itäyihtam.

mā-mitunäyihtam tānisi t-äsi-nōhtä-nipäyit ōhi ka-pä-kīwukawāt.

ōmis ītwäw : " hāw, kiyawāw, nisīmitik, näwu-tipiskāw kik-ātsimustātināwāw."

" hā, tāpwä, nistäsä, nimiywäyihtänān äh-ātsimuhk ! " itik ōhih iskwäwah.

nama wīhkāts wāpamäw ta-kīsitäpuwit.

" nika-kimutamawāw, nipātsih, utāpiskākanäkinwah, " äy-itäyihtahk äsah wīsahkätsāhk, äkwah ātsimōw kapä-tipisk.

namuya ōhtsi nipāyiwa. āsay mīna kapä-kīsik ātsimōw. kīhtwām mīna äh-tipiskāyik, āsay mīna käyāpits namwāts nipāyiwa.

" mān äkā nka-kīh-kimutamuwāhtayik ! "

mwähtsi näu-tipiskāw äh-ātsimut, äkuyikuhk nipāyiwa ōhi uskinīkiskwäwa. ntunikäw utasiwatsikaniyihk ; kimutamawäw. äkus īsi sipwähtayimäw ; tapasīw.

näwu-tipiskāw pimipahtäw. äkwah kītahtawä kā-pähtahk ä-matwätsīkahikäwiht.

" uhtsitaw kik-ōtihtitin, " itäyihtam äsah.

äkwah sipwähtäw. āsay mīna äh-wāpaniyik, āhtsi piku pähtam. äkwah piyisk näwu-tipiskāw tāpiskōts päyakwan iyikuhk ä-matwä-tsīkahikäyit, näwu-tipiskāw mwähtsi ä-pmuhtāt, äkuyikuhk wāpamäw kīkisäp, ä-matwäwāskahikanihkäyit. namwāts käkway wāpahtam kita-usīhtayit mihtah, āta näwu-kīsikāw äh-pähtahk. nīsu piku mihtah kiyastäyiwa.

" wāh, nisīm, kayās uhtsi, näwu-tipiskāw aspin, kā-pähtamān ä-nikuhtäyin ! "

äh-ātah-kitōtāt, namwāts ahpōh wīh-kitāpamik. kapä-kīsik pikw īsi ātah äy-isi-kitōtāt, ahpōh namwāts wī-kitāpamik. ntawāts äkwah, ä-wīhtipiskāyik, aspin äh-astāyit tsīkahikaniyiw, äh-āta-nawaswātāt, namuya kiskäyimäw äh-pīhtukäyit. namuya miskawäw ; wanihäw.

misiwä papāmitātsimōw, " nisīm, kikitimahin ! " äh-papāy-itwät, äh-papāmitātsimut, ä-wīh-kakwä-ka-kitutikut, äh-ntawäyihtahk ta-kitutikut.

piyisk ätukä nästuhkwasiw. kawīhkwasiw. sāsay mīna kayahtä äh-waniskāt, kī-nā-nātwāyinihtäyiwa. āsay mīna kapä-kīsik āta, " nisīm ! " pikw īsi äh-āt-ītāt, nama wīh-ka-kitutik. āsay mīna ä-tipiskāyik, aspin āt ä-kīwäyit, ati-mitsiminäw ; äh-ati-pīhtukäyit wīkiyihk, äkutah uhtsi wanihäw. āsay mīna kapä-tipisk papāmitātsimōw, ä-ntunawāt ; piyisk mīna muhtsihk äkusi isi nipāw. kīkisäpä äh-waniskāt, āsay mīna kīh-nikuhtäyiwa mīna kīhtwām.

" anuhts äkwah ōhtsitaw kika-kitusin ! " itäyihtam äsa māka mīna wīsahkätsāhk.

āsay mīna kapä-kīsik āta äh-kitutāt, nama ki-kitutik. āsay mīna atikīwäyiwa. mistahi äkwah pakwātam. kisisin.

" āhpoh ōm[1] ! " ītäyihtam ; " kähtsinaw apiw ! tsīpay äkā kā-wīh-kakitusit ! " itäyihtam äsah.

---

[1] Meaning not clear; record may be wrong.

tāpwä māhtakuskam uskan, äkutah ä-miskahk.

äkwah kīkisäpā kayāhtä äh-päkupayit, " awas, wīsahkätsāhk ! kōtamihin ! nimiywäyihtäh äh-tsīkahikäyān ! " k-ätikut, kayāhtä ä-mātakuskawāt.

" tsäskwa, nisīm ! " itäw ; " nisīm, mistahi kikakwātakihin, āta näukīsikāw äh-kitutitān, äkā äh-kitusiyin. "

" hāw, nstäsä, " itik, " ōtah ä-kīh-nipahisuyān, " itik ; " äwakuh. "

" tānähki māka äkā käkway k-ōh-kaskihtāyin, tahkih ä-nikuhtäyin tahtu-kīsikāw ? "

" ōtah kayās ä-kih-pahkwäkahamān nisit, " itik äsah.

" namuya wīhkāts tsī kimītsisun ? "

" äha', " itwäw awa tsīpay ; " tāntäh māka kīw-ōhtinamān mītsiwin ? " itäw wīsahkätsāhkwa.

" asamikawiyan tsī māka, kikah-mītsisun ? "

" äha', nikah-mītsisun, kīspin asamiyin, " itwäw äsah awa tsīpay.

" hāw, nisīm, kik-āsamitin ! "

äkwah ōma kā-kīh-kimutit tāpiskākanäkin utinam, äh-taswäkiwäpinahk. atōspuwināhtikuhk [1] *pōtih kahkiyaw käkway wāpahtam. tānispihk ätukä ōmītsisuhtay awa tsīpay ! ayisk wīsahkätsāhk k-äsiyīhkāsut kahkiyaw awiya kīh-wayäsimäw.*

mistahi nāspits atamihäw äh-asamāt.

" hā, mistahi kitatamihin, [2] *wīsahkätsāhk, ōma k-āsamiyan ! "*

" hā, nisim, " itäw, " niya nipapāmātsihun. nama nāntaw nik-ätāpatsihtān ōma tāpiskākanäkin. kiya nama nāntaw ka-kīh-uhtinamāsun tamītsiyin, " itäw ōhi tsīpaya.

" äha', " itwäw awa tsīpay, " mistahi kitatamihin, wīsahkätsāhk ! äkwah nama wīhkāts nka-nōhtähkatān, wīsahkätsāhk. mahtih nimistikōwātihk usāwi-sōniyāw äkutah miskawatsih, utinähkan, " itwäw awa tsīpay.

tāpwä wīsahkätsāhk ä-sīhkimiht, ntunikäw usāwi-sōniyāwa.

" wīsahkätsāhk, kakwä-iyinisih māka ! āta wiyah kimōhtsōwin. ōtah kwäski-sakāhk namuya wāhyaw ukimāw mäkwāh kwāpahwäw sōniyāwa. äwaku kik-ätuhtān. kikā-na-ntawāpamāw. ōmisi kik-ätāw : ' niyanān tāpwä miyusiw kā-kwāpahwāyāhk usāwi-sōniyāw, ' kik-ätāw ; ' kiya mistahi māyātisiw. käkāts pisisik nipiy kikwāpahän, ' kik-ätāw ; ' niyanān usāwi-sōniyāw pisisik nkwāpahwāw, ' kik-ätāw ; ' äkwah kiya käkāts pisisik nipiy kkwāpahän. nawats itah sōniyāw k-ōhtinak kīstah päy-ituhtäyin, ' kik-ätāw. äkwah wāhyaw päy-ituhtahatsi, kika-nipahāw. ' k-äsinākusit awa ukimāw, äkusi nika-wīh-sinākusin ! ' kik-ätwān. itāp ka-naspitawāw. "

äkusi sipwähtäw, ä-kīh-kakäskimikut wīsahkätsāhk ōhi tsīpayah, äkwah ukimāwa ä-wīh-ntawi-nipahāt. tāpwäh namuya wāhyaw äy-ituhtät, sīpīsis utihtam, ä-mäkwä-kwāpahwāyit sōniyāwa.

" tāpwä kiya mistahi māyātisiw sōniyāw ka-kwāpahwat, " itwäw wīsahkätsāhk ; " äkwah niyanān mistahi miyusiw sōniyāw ; usāwi-sōniyāw pikuh nōtinānān. "

" tāntä māka mahtih ? " itik ; " ituhtähin. mahti nka-ntawāpahtān, " itik. käkwah āh wāpahtähäw. " nīnān usāwi-sōniyāw pikuh nōtinānān, " itik.

---

[1] The ordinary term is *mītsisōwināhtik ;* the word in the text resembles Ojibwa *adōhpōwin ;* Cree *atōspōw*, Ojibwa *adōhpō :* "he eats on something," initial stem *atōt- :* "on something," transitive verb final *-pw- :* "by mouth," with middle-voice verb derivative *-ō-*.

[2] Literally, "You delight me," the usual formula of thanks.

äkwah tāpwä sipwähtahäw ; itah äh-āyimaniyik atih-ay-ituhtahäw. äkwah wāhyaw äh-ayātsik, mistikwah nīsu äh-tsimasuyit, äkutah ä-säkuyit, ustikwāniyihk pakamahwäw ; nipahäw.

" äkusi nka-wīh-naspitawāw awa ukimāw ! " itwäw äsah wīsahkätsāhk. tāpwä, ayisk wītsihik ōhi tsīpayah ; tāpwä naspitawäw äsah ōhi ukimāwa. " äkwah mahtih sämāk nka-kīwān. mahtih äsinākusiyit wīwah, " itäyihtam.

atsiyaw piku kwāpahwäw sōniyāwa. wawäyīw ; äkus īsi kīwäw. wāhyaw uhtsi pätsāpamik ōhi kā-nipahāt wīwiyiwa.

" tānisi k-ōh-pä-kīwäyin ? nama wīhkāts nōhtaw kipä-kīwān. iyikuhk nīsusāp tipahikan māna kā-pä-āpihta-kīsikāw-mītsisuyin. mistahi kītahtawä kimōhtsōwin ! "

āta wiyah äsa nisituhtawäw. äkwah äkus īsi kīwäw. mīna ntaw-ituhtäw. atsiyaw päy-ōtihtik ōhi kā-kī-kiskinōhamākut tsīpayah.

" kähtsinā wīpats kika-nipahikawin ! usām mistahi pakahkam kiwīh-mōhtsōwin ! namwāts ahpōh kikiskäyimāw pīsimuhkān ! " itik.

äkwah wāpamäw pīsimuhkāna, äkuyāk kā-nisitawäyimāt. äkwah kīwäw, nīsusāp tipahikan äy-ispayiyik. āsay mīna ntaw-ātuskäw, min ä-ntawāpamāt sōniyāwa. äkwah wīpats pōn-atuskäw.

" tāpwä kītahtawä mistahi kimōhtsōwin, " itik ōhi uwīkimākanah, " äkwah wāh-wīpats äh-pä-kīwäyin ! " itik.

" hāh, " ōmis ītwäw ; " kītahtawä wā-wīpats käkway niwāh-wani-kiskisin, " itwäw.

äkw äh-utākusiniyik, masinahikan kā-pīhtukatāyit. namwāts nisitaw-inam. kā-kiskisit anihi tsīpayah ka-kīh-kitimākäyimikut, äkwah wayawīw.

" wahwa, mistahi kimōhtsōwin ! " itik ; " äkus ätsik āna wīpats kā-nipahikawiyan ! "

sā-sāminamiyiwa ōhkwākana, uskīsikwa, utōn : nisitawinam masinah-ikan. äkwah äh-wāpahtahk, masinahikätäyiw, wāpahkih ä-wīh-pä-nōtiniht ; ayisk unōtinikäwah[1] *ōhi ukimāwah kā-nipahāt, äkwah wāh-wīpats äsah māna äh-päh-nōtinimiht. masinahikäw ; ātsimustawäw utīnima.*

tāpwä, " wawäyīk, iyinitik. kiwīh-pä-nōtinikunānaw[2] *wāpahkih. nipäy-itisahamākawin, " itäw, " masinahikanah. "*

tāpwä kikisäpā takuhtäyiwa kā-päh-ntupayīstākutsik. māka wiya wīsahkätsāhk māka mīna ka-kitāpahkäw kuntah.

kītahtawāh ōmis ītik ōh īskwäwah : " tāpwä mistahi kimōhtsōwin ! kitiyinīmak wī-mästsihāwak, " itik ; " kitayōwinisah ta-sīhkihkämuyan kit-ōtinamihk, ta-pusiskaman, mīna kitäm kita-wiyāhpitiht. "

tāpwä wīsahkätsāhk sīhkihkämōw utāmah ta-wiyāhpitimiht. wiyāh-pitimāwa. pustayōwinisäw ; nitawi-nōtinikäw. mistahi māka mīna mōhtsōhkāsōw. kahkiyaw äsah mästsihäw ōhi kā-pä-nōtinikäyit. äkusi päyak pikuh kīwätisahwäw, masinahikan ä-kiw-ōsihtāt.

nätäh äh-takuhtatātsik,[3] *ōmis ītwäwak utiyinisiwak : " māka min ätukä wīsahkätsāhk ! " itwäwak.*

masinahikan usīhtaw : " kīspin kiya wīsahkätsāhk, kiwīh-nipahitin sōskwāts. usām misiwä kitisīhtsikān. "

---

[1] Should be obviative; I may have mis-heard a form *unōtinikäyiwah*, but do not know if such would be the obviative of this preterit.

[2] This would seem to mean "he (or it) will come to fight us"; probably read *kiwīh-pä-nōtinikawinānaw* : "we shall be come to and fought with" (passive).

[3] Why plural actor? The rest of the story is obscure because the persons are not kept distinct.

pōt äkwah äh-pätamāht wīsahkätsāhk, ayamihtāw.

" kiy ätukä māka mīna, wīsahkätsāhk, ōma kā-tōtaman, " itāw.

tapasīw ; namuy āhpōh awiyah wāpahtähäw ōma masinahikan ; äkus īsi äy-isih-tapasīt.

näu-tipiskāw pimāmōw. kītahtawä ä-misāyik sākahikan äw-utihtahk, " äkusi kā-kīh-ititān, ' wīsahkätsāhk māka mīn ätukä kiya, ' kā-kiy-ititān, " itik ayīsiyiniwah, äh-nakiskawāt sisunä sākahikanihk ; " hāw, wīsahkätsāhk, ka-mätawānānaw ! " itik.

äkwah tāpwä kakwätsimäw tānisi kit-äsi-mätawätsik.

" waskits nipīhk ka-pimuhtānānaw, " itik.

" äha' , " itwäw wīsahkätsāhk.

tāpwä ati-sipwähtäw awa wīsahkätsāhkwah kā-mawinähwāt. namwāts ahpō wayiskam nipiy. akāmihk äh-kīh-takuhtät, äkutä uhtsi täpwātäw wīsahkätsāhkwah.

" haw, mwähtsi tāwakām ayātsih wīsahkätsāhk, äkutah ntawi-kihtāpayiw ; māka namuya niwīh-nipahäw. äkutah nipīhk ta-mätsimwātsih-nahapiw ! "

tāpwäh itāmi-nipīhk äkutä nahapiw, itamihk nipīhk. kahkiyaw käkway äh-atutät, nama wiya tāpwähtāk.

kahkiyaw, " nkustānān kā-tōtask, " itik.

kītahtawä mākwah kā-täpäyimut kit-ōtināt wīsahkätsāhkwah. utinik äyakunih. äkusi pimātsihik.

Once upon a time he went from place to place; for Wisahketchahk did all kinds of things. He even managed to become a captain of soldiers.

Once upon a time, the story goes, he set out. Well, he tramped about. Presently he came to a wooden house.

"Ha, stay a while, stay a while, big brother!"

So he stayed there. A woman looked for something to give him to eat. Ho, he saw nothing at all in the way of food that she could take. At once she took out a shawl and threw it on the table. There he saw all kinds of food.

In his usual way, Wisahketchahk thought, "I shall steal it," he thought.

He kept revolving in his mind how he could make his hostesses want to sleep.

He said, "Now, in return, my little sisters, for four nights I will tell you stories."

"Oh, indeed, big brother, we like story-telling!" those women said to him.

He never saw them do any cooking.

"When she goes to sleep, I shall steal her shawl from her," thought Wisahketchahk, and told stories all night.

But they did not go to sleep. All the next day he told stories. When another night came, again they did not sleep at all.

"Could it be that I should be unable to steal it from them!"

When he had told stories for exactly four nights and days, then those young women went to sleep. He searched where they kept their things; he stole it from them. So then he went off with it; he fled.

For four days and nights he ran. Then at one time he heard someone noisily chopping wood.

"I shall do my best to reach you," he thought.

Then he went on. When the next day broke, he still heard it. And at last, when he had heard the other chopping away for four days and nights, apparently always at the same distance, and when he had walked four days and nights, then at last, in the morning, he saw him, noisily working at a wooden structure. He saw no wood at all with which that person could build anything, though he had heard the noise of it for four days. Only two sticks lay there.

"Dear me, little brother, for a long time, ever since four nights ago, I have heard you chopping!"

Although he spoke to him, the other would not so much as glance at him. Although through the day he addressed him in all manner of ways, he would not even look at him. And then, at nightfall, when the other laid down his hatchet and was off and away, he needs ran after him, but he could not make out into what place he had disappeared. He could not find him; he had lost him.

He crawled about, and, "Little brother, you are making me desperate!" he kept crying, to make the other speak to him; desiring to have the other address him.

At last he must have got sleepy from weariness. He fell, overcome by sleep. When he awoke, there was the other already a-splitting of logs. Again, though all day he kept saying to him, "Little brother!" he would not talk to him. When the next night came, when the other made off to go home, he held fast to him, but when he went into his dwelling, from that point he lost him. Again he crawled about all night, looking for him; at last he again slept right there on the bare ground. In the morning, when he got up, this time, too, the other had already started working at his wood.

"Now today I will see to it that you talk to me !" thought Wisahketchahk, as before.

Again, though he talked to him all day, he could not make the other address him. Again the other went home. He was very much annoyed. He landed on something sharp.

"Maybe it is this!" he thought; "Surely he is at home here! He is a dead man, this person who will not converse with me!" he thought.

Accordingly, he threw his weight on that bone and held it down, right there where he had found it.

Then, in the morning he was awakened by the other saying to him, "Get away, Wisahketchahk! You are keeping me back! I was having a pleasant time at chopping!"—for he was holding him down by the weight of his body.

"Wait a bit, little brother!" he told him; "Little brother, you were tormenting me terribly, by not talking to me, when for four days I addressed you."

"Well, brother," the other told him, "It is because in this place I killed myself," he told him; "That is the way of it."

"But why is it you accomplish nothing, when you are always a-chopping every day?"

"It is because of old in this place I chopped off my foot," the other told him.

"Do you never eat?"

"No," said the dead man; "Where could I get any food?" he said to Wisahketchahk.

"But if you were given something to eat, would you eat?"

"Yes, I would eat, if you gave me food," said the dead man.

"Very well, little brother, I shall give you something to eat."

Then he took the shawl he had stolen and spread it out. Look you, on a table he saw all kinds of things. I wonder when that corpse had last eaten! For he who was called Wisahketchahk deceived everyone.

He entirely won him over by giving him the food.

"Hah, you greatly oblige me, Wisahketchahk, giving me food like this!"

"Oh, little brother," he told him, "as for me, I am travelling about. I shall not have any use for this shawl. But you would not have any resource from which to get anything to eat," he told the dead man.

"Yes," said the dead man, "I thank you very much, Wisahketchahk! Now I shall never be hungry, Wisahketchahk. Go see; if you find any gold in my wooden box, just take it," said the corpse.

According as he was bidden, Wisahketchahk looked for gold.

"But, Wisahketchahk, be sensible! After all, you are a crazy fellow. At the other side of these woods a chief is now digging gold. You will go where he is. You will go see him. You will say to him, 'The gold we others are digging is really fine,' you will say to him; 'Yours is very poor. You are scooping up almost nothing but water,' you will say to him; 'But as for us others, I scoop up pure gold,' you will say to him; 'And you, you are scooping up almost nothing but water. You had better come over yourself to where I get gold,' you will tell him. And when you have led him far off, you will kill him. 'As this chief looked, so I shall look!' you will say. Then you will resemble him completely."

Then Wisahketchahk set out, as he had been directed by the dead man, to go and kill that chief. And really, he had not gone far, when he came to a brook where the latter was digging for gold.

"Truly, the metal you are digging up is very poor," Wisahketchahk told him; "But our metal is very fine; we get nothing but gold."

"Now, where is that, pray?" the other answered him; "Take me there. Let me go see it," he told him. He showed him some. "We get nothing but gold," he told him.

So then he led him away; he led him on into rough places. Then, when they had gone quite a ways, as the other got between two trees that stood close, he hit him on the head and killed him.

"So now I want to resemble this chief!" said Wisahketchahk.

And really, for he was being helped by that Deadman, really, he looked exactly like the chief.

"Now I shall go straight home. Let me see what his wife looks like," he thought.

He dug for gold but a short while. He dressed up; right then he went home. From afar the wife of him whom he had killed saw him coming.

"Why are you coming home? You never come home before the regular time. It is always only at twelve o'clock that you come home to eat dinner. You are acting very crazily, all of a sudden!"

He did somehow understand what she was saying. So he went right back. He went back where he had come from. Soon the Deadman who had instructed him came to where he was.

"Certainly you will soon get yourself killed! It is evident that you will act too crazily! You do not even know the clock!" he told him.

Then he looked at a clock, making his first acquaintance with it. Then he went home, when twelve o'clock had come. Then he went back to work, to look for gold. He quit work after a short time.

"Really, of a sudden you have gone altogether insane," that wife of his said to him, "coming home early all the time like this!"

"Why," he said, "my memory has become very short, all of a sudden."

Then, in the evening someone brought in a letter. He could make nothing of it. Remembering that Deadman who had befriended him, he went out of the house.

"Alas, you are a crazy fool!" he told him; "And so it appears you will soon be killed!"

The other touched his face, his eyes and his mouth; he could read. Then, when he read it, it was written that tomorrow people were coming to fight him; for that chief he had killed had been at war, and had been attacked, it seemed, every little while. He wrote; he told his followers the news.

"Get yourselves ready, men. Tomorrow they are coming to fight us. Letters have been sent to me."

And really, in the morning they arrived who were coming to make war against them. But as for Wisahketchahk, of course, he merely looked on in his useless way.

Presently that woman said to him, "Truly, you are entirely foolish! Your men will all be killed," she told him; "You ought to order your clothes to be taken out for you to put on, and your horse to be saddled."

So Wisahketchahk ordered his horse to be saddled. It was saddled. He put on his clothes; he went and fought. Of course he carried on in a crazy way. He killed all those who had come to fight. He sent only one back home, having written a letter.

When they arrived over there, the wise men said, "Doubtless this is Wisahketchahk, up to his old tricks!"

He wrote a letter: "If you are Wisahketchahk, I shall kill you without delay. You are cutting up altogether too much."

When it was brought to Wisahketchahk he read it.

"Doubtless it is you, Wisahketchahk, up to your old tricks, who are doing all this," he was told.

He fled; he did not even show anyone this letter; he fled just as he was, at once.

He ran four days and nights. Then, when he came to a big lake, "I told you so, 'Doubtless you are Wisahketchahk, up to your old tricks,' I told you," said a man to him, whom he met by the shore of the lake; "Now, Wisahketchahk, let us have a contest!" he said to him.

So he asked him in what way they were to contend.

"We shall walk on the surface of the water," the other told him.

"Very well," said Wisahketchahk.

Accordingly he started out who had challenged Wisahketchahk. He did not even ripple the water as he stepped. When he reached the other side, from there he shouted to Wisahketchahk.

"Now, when Wisahketchahk is right in the middle of the water, he will sink under water; but I do not mean to kill him. Let him sit down there for good, there in the water!"

And really, there he sat down, under water. When he called every kind of being to help him, they did not heed him.

Everyone told him, "We fear him who is doing this to you."

At last the loon consented to take Wisahketchahk from where he was. He took him out. So he saved his life.

(8) **Wisahketchahk and the Bear**

Adam Sakewew

sākäwäw

kītahtawä wīsahkätsāhk, " hah, mahtih nik-ōsīhtān ; usām kītahtawä nikā-mākuhikun käkway, " itäyihtam.

usīhtāw misāskwat ; usīhtāw atsusisah.

" käkway kä-kīnikāk äkutah kit-āstāyān, " itäyihtam.

kītahtawä miskam mistik, mihtah ōma tāpiskōts. napakihtak usīhtāw ; tāpihtitāw mihtsät.

" äkusi ! " itäyihtam ; " nik-ōh-minahun kita-mītsisuyān, " itäyihtam ; " ā, kīsāts mīnah tsāpihtsikanis nik-ōsīhtān ; äwaku mīna nik-ōsīhtān, " itwäw.

ä-kīsihtāt, " āh, mīnah napakihkumān nik-ōsihtān ; usām miywāsin awa mistik kit-ōh-usīhtāyān, " itäyihtam.

usīhtāw mōhkumān, napakihkumān.

äkwah ä-wāpahtahk unīmāskwākanah, " ptanä mōskīstawit,[1] *mōskistākawiyān ! " itäyihtam ; " usām miywāsinwa nnīmāskwākana ; nama käkway nika-kustän, " itäyihtam.*

ä-kī-kīsihtāt, sipwähtāw. pasāhtsāhk akāmihk äkutä wāpamäw wākayōsah. hā, kiskäyihtam ä-matsihtwāyit.

" ā, nika-kisīmaw, täpwātak ; äkusi nika-nipahāw ; nika-muwāw, " itäyihtam.

äkwah ōmisi itäw : " awäna nāhā ? " täpwäw, " kā-wāpikiskitsät ! "

äh-pähtahk awa wākayōs, kisīmäw.

" mahtih tānitä kā-täpwähk ! " itäyihtam.

nam āwiya wāpamäw. kāsōw wīsahkätsāhk. kīhtwām äh-mōnahikäyit, " mahtih nka-kakwä-wāpamāw awā kāy-isit, " itäyihtam.[2] *äkwah sīpā ōmisi tōtam, äh-wātihkät ; ōtäh usāpiw. pōtih kā-pimi-sākiskwät. wāpamik āsay.*

" hawīna nāhā kā-wāpikiskitsät ! " itäw.

häw, wāpamäw ayīsiyiniwah ; mōskīstawäw. äkwah awa wīsahkätsāhk pīmakāmipitäw upīhtatwāna. kisiwāk ōtay ä-pä-nakiyit, pimwäw. nātwāhtin ōma mistik. wīpisisah piyisk mästinam.

---

[1] A slip of the tongue; the dictator corrects himself in the next word.

[2] I.e., the bear; the next sentences are obscure because third person and obviative are not kept apart.

" äha', kā-pa-päyakunīmāskwäwinähk kiy-ayīhtiyān, ka-kīh-wawānihih!" itäw.

utinam tsāpihtsikanis; tahkamäw.

äh-tahkamiht awa wākayōs, " mam!" itwäw.

nātwāhtitäw.

" kā-pa-päyakunīmāskwäwinähk kīh-ayīhtiyān, ka-ki-wawānihih!" itäw.

tahkamäw ōm ōhtsi napakihkumān mistik ka-kīh-usihtāt; nātwāhtiniyiw.

äkusi äkwah säkihik, " manitōww!" äy-itäyihtahk. " nika-nipahik!" itäyihtam; " ntsawāts nka-tapasīn," ä-nātāmututahk itah ä-sakāyik.

mituni kisiwāk askōk, äh-tāwatiyit. iyāpasāpitsi, kisiwāk askōk. nīpisiya äh-asaskitäyikih, äkutah itāmōw. äkwah kāsispōkutsin awa wākayōs. tätipäwäpayihōw wīsahkätsāhk. kapä-kīsik äkutah wāsakāmätisahuk. kītahtawä näyawapitwāwi, āyītaw nīpawistātōwak. kītahtawä kā-wāpumāt äskanah, itah kā-pāh-pimipahtāt äkutah äh-mōskatāwahkiskawāt. nakīw. mān āwa wākayōs wīmāskawäw, mana kuntah ä-wākastäyit awa wākayōs.

" pākāhkam awa wākayōs kustäw," itäyihtam awa wīsahkätsāhk.

mistahi nayōwapiw. awa mīna wākayōs nayawapiw. ntsawāts tahkiskawäw wīsahkätsāhk ōhi kā-kustimiht äskanah. piyisk pahkwatsiwäpiskawäw.

nitsawāts äh-wīmāskawāyit, " kustäw!" itäyihtam awa wīsahkätsāhk.

utinäw ōhi äskanah.

" pakahkam awa kustäw!" itäyihtam.

nitsawāts ustikwānihk akunäw, ōmisi äh-itāt ōhi wākayōsah: " hwhw[1]!" äh-itāt, kā-wāki-kwāskuhtiyit.

" mahtih nika-mōskīstawāw! nayawapiw!" äh-itäyimāt. muskistawäw; tapasiyiwa.

iyāpasāpiyitsih ōhi wākayōsa, kisiwāk askōwäw, " hwhw!" äh-itāt.

äkusi māna wīh-kakwä-mīhkawikīw. piyisk wāpamäw wīsahkätsāhk ōhi wākayōsah, pīstäw utōniyihk äw-uhtsikawiyik.

piyisk awa wākayōs, " kiyām nika-wäpahuk!" itäyihtam.

kawipayihōw äkwah awa wīsahkätsāhk.[2] uhtiskawapīstawäw ōmis äh-itināt äskanah, ä-wīh-nipahatāhtamiyit, mayaw kätāpamikutsih, " whwh!" äh-nimisīwihāt.

" pakahkam kustäw!" itäyihtam; " namuy āwa wīhkāts ta-waniskāw, nakatimakih ōhi nitäskanah," itäyihtam.

" hāw, wākayōs! mistahi kitäyimisun, ayīsiyiniw miyākuhatsih. nīsta nitayān käkway kit-ōh-nipahitān."

tāwatiw wākayōs, ispīh äh-päy-itisinimiht ōhi äskanah, wīpitah ä-sāmahamuht.

" tsatsämāsinwa ōhi kīpitah!" itäw wīsahkätsāhk.

" hāw, ntäskan, wäpahwāhkan awa tsatsämāpitsis wākayōs! wäpahwāhkan, mayaw waskawītsih ōtah uhtsi. kanawäyim ta-waskawīt. kuntah nōtamihik; nikīwutäwa! mäyākwām, ntäskan; kinisituhtän uma! wäpahwāhkan!"

---

[1] Undulating velar or palatal spirant, with rounded lips; said to be the noise a buffalo makes when angry.

[2] Slip of informant's tongue, or of my hand, for *wākayōs*: "the bear," and so translated.

äkusi tsimahäw ōh äskanah ätiskwäsiniyit.

" wäpahwāhkan, ntäskan ! niwīh-sipwähtān. wāpum awa wākayōs ! —misawāts kika-wäpahuk. äkusi kika-nipahik, mayaw waskawiyani ! "

äkusi tsimahäw äkutah. nakatäw ; sipwähtäw.

äh-kih-pipuniyik ,kīhtwām äh-nīpiniyik, " mahtih nka-ntawāpamāw nisīm, " itäyihtam.

ituhtäw : awīn ōhi ! kī-sīkwāhkatusuyiwa ōhi wākayōsah.

" heh ! äkusi kā-kīh-ititān : misawāts ki-waskawiyin, sämāk ka-kīh-nipahikuh awa nitäskan ! "

äkusi äkuyikuhk äskwāk ātayōhkäwin.

Once upon a time Wisahketchahk thought, "Well, suppose I make some arrows; sometime something or other will drive me to close quarters."

He prepared a saskatoon willow; he made some arrows.

"I ought to put something sharp on here," he thought.

Presently he found a stick of wood, like this faggot here. He made flat slivers of wood; he put them as tips on many arrows.

"There!" he thought; "With these I shall kill game and have something to eat," he thought; "Why, to be the better prepared, I shall make also a spear; this too I shall make," he said.

When he had finished it, "Why, I shall make a broad-bladed knife, too; for this piece of wood is very good to make it of," he thought.

He made a knife, a broad-bladed knife.

Then, when he looked upon his weapons, "I just wish he—I just wish someone would attack me!" he thought; "For my weapons are very good; I shan't be afraid of anything," he thought.

When he had finished them, he started out. At the other side of a ravine he saw a bear. Ha, he knew him for an ugly customer.

"Ho, I shall make him angry by calling to him; then I shall kill him; I shall eat him," he thought.

Then he called to him, "Who is that creature over there?" he shouted, "That white-rumped one!"

When the bear heard that, he was angered.

"Let me see from where this shouting comes!" he thought.

He saw no one. Wisahketchahk was hiding. When the other was back at his digging, he thought, "Let me try and see him who is saying this to me." Then down underneath there, he did like this, as he dug his pit; from here he looked forth. Sure enough, there he was, sticking out his head. Already the other saw him.

"Who is that white-rump over there? Pshaw!" he called to him.

Well, he saw a man; he made for him. Then that Wisahketchahk pulled round his quiver by the strap. When the other came to a halt close by, he shot an arrow at him. That stick of wood fell broken as it struck. Soon he used up all his arrows.

"Yes, yes, if I were the kind of person who carries only one weapon, you would be the finish of me!" he called to him.

He took his spear; he jabbed at him.

When the bear was hit with the spear, "Mum!" he went.

It broke as he pushed it home.

"If I were the kind of person who carries only one weapon, you would be the finish of me!" he told him.

He made a stab at him with that flat knife which he had made out of a piece of wood; it broke lengthwise under the impact.

At this, he grew afraid of the other, thinking, "He is supernatural!" "He will kill me!" he thought; "I had better run away," and he headed in panic for the woods.

The other was close at his heels, with gaping jaws. Whenever he glanced back, the other was close upon him. He fled to where some willows stood in a clump. The bear just missed as he jumped. Wisahketchahk dashed round the trees. All day long the other chased him round and round. Presently, whenever they were out of breath, they would stand facing each other, at either side. Then at one time, he saw a horn from over which he had kicked loose the ground as he ran by. He stopped. The bear always made a detour round it, taking a crooked course for no evident reason.

"Plainly this bear is afraid of it," thought Wisahketchahk.

He was badly out of breath. The bear, too, was out of breath. Wisahketchahk tried kicking that horn, which was an object of fear. At last he knocked it loose with his foot, as he passed.

When the other with plain intent made a circuit round it, "He is afraid of it!" thought Wisahketchahk.

He seized that horn.

"Plainly he fears it!" he thought.

He tried holding it on his head and saying "Hwoo!" to the bear, and there, the latter jumped off at an angle.

When he thought of the other, "Suppose I go for him! He is tired!" he attacked him; the other ran away.

Whenever the bear glanced back, he was close upon him, saying, "Hwoo!"

So he tried to run faster and faster. At last Wisahketchahk saw the foam dripping from the bear's mouth.

At last the bear thought, "Well, he might as well toss me on his horn!"

And the bear threw himself flat on the ground. He sat down facing him, holding out the horn at him, like this, while the other was almost dead, puffing for want of breath, and every time the other looked at him, he threatened him, going, "Hwoo!"

"Plainly he is afraid of it!" he thought; "He will never get up, if I leave this horn of mine here," he thought.

"Now then, bear! You think a great deal of yourself, when you drive a man to close quarters. But I, too, have something with which I can kill you."

The bear had his mouth gaping, and the horn was stuck out at him till it touched his teeth.

"Those teeth of yours are very short!" Wisahketchahk told him.

"Now, my Horn, be ready to toss this stubby-tooth bear! Toss him as soon as he stirs from this spot. Watch his slightest move. He has delayed me for no reason; I was going visiting! Look sharp, my Horn; you understand what I say! Be ready to toss him!"

With that, he stuck the horn upright in the ground toward the bear's head, as he was lying.

"Be ready to toss him, my Horn! I am going away from here. Watch this bear!—You cannot avoid his tossing you. So then, he will kill you, as soon as you budge!"

So he stuck it upright there. He left it; he went away.

When winter had passed and summer had come again, "Suppose I go have a look at my little brother," he thought.

He went there; what had become of him! That bear had starved to death.

"Heh! That is what I told you: certainly, if you had budged, at once this Horn of mine would have killed you!"

That is the end of this sacred story.

(9) Wisahketchahk and the Rapids

Coming-Day

kā-kīsikāw-pīhtukāw.

" nisīm ! " āh-wāpahtahk pāwistik ; " nisīm ! "

" wāy ! " itik.

" ' tāpwā nisīpwāwāmun ! ' kitāyihtān. kimawinähutin, awīna kiyipa kä-kihtimit, " itäw.

" ā, namuya ! iyikuhk ta-pōn-āskīwik,[1] *äkuyikuhk nikīh-itik kōhtāwīnaw ta-kīskuwäyān, " itik.*

" ā, māka kiwīh-mawinähutin ! "

ōmis ītäyihtam : " pipuhkih ta-kīskuwāw, " äh-itäyimāt.

äkutah nahapiw äkwah wīsahkātsāhk, um äh-pähtākwaniyik. äkwah umis ītwäw wīsahkätsāhk : " blblblbl[2] *! "*

apiw äkutah. piyisk pipuniyiw. āhtsi pikuh äkutah apiw, pisisik äkus äh-itwät, " blblblbl ! "

piyis nīpin. miyuskamiw. äkwah kōnah kahkiyaw nama käkway. äkwah mistahi nipiy ōtah päy-ayāyiw, itah äh-apit. piyisk umayikuhk[3] *iskupäw nipiy. äkuyikuhk pasikōw, päyak askiy, " blblblbl ! " äh-itwät.*

ōmis ītwäw : " wātsistakā nama kih-āyiwākitunāmāw nisīm ! " itwäw.

äkus äh-sipwähtät.

äkusih äkuyikuhk äyakōw.

"Little brother!" when he saw the rapids; "Little brother!"

"Yes, what is it?" it answered him.

" 'Truly, I keep long at my noise!' you think. I challenge you to see which of us will weary first," he told it.

"Oh, no! When the green earth ceases to be, only then did Our Father tell me to cease from my noise," it told him.

"Oh, but I mean to challenge you!"

He thought, "In winter it will stop"; that was what he thought of it.

Then Wisahketchahk sat down there where its sound was heard. And Wisahketchahk said, "Blblblbl!"

---

[1] As *askiy* means not only "earth," but also "summer" and "year," double meaning and misunderstanding are probably essential to the story.

[2] Sound made by pulling tongue back and forth between rounded lips, with voicing.

[3] Gesture to chest.

He sat there. At last winter came. Still he sat there, all the while saying, "Blblblbl!"

At last it was spring. The thawing weather came. Then all the snow disappeared. Then much water came and was where he sat. At last he was up to here in the water. Only then he arose to his feet, having said, "Blblblbl!" for a whole year.

He said, "Incredible, how my little brother cannot be out-talked!"

With that he went away from there.

That is the end of this.

(10) Wisahketchahk and the Magic Headgear

Coming-Day

kā-kīsikāw-pīhtukāw.

kītahtawä wīsahkätsāhk äh-pmuhtät, kā-wāpahtahk mīkiwāhp.

äh-takuhtät, " ham ham ! " itwäw.

māka mīna nōhtähkatäw.

" ahaw, tawāw ! " itik.

äh-pīhtukät, päyakuyiwa nāpäwa. äh-nahapit, nanātawāpahtam käkway ka-mītsit. nama käkway wāpahtam. äkusih apiw.

kītahtawäh ōmis itwäyiwa : " yāh, nistäs unōhtäkhatāh ! " itwäyiwa.

wäskwāhtämihk äkutä kīkway ätukä äh-tahkupitäyik wāpahtam. äwakuh itinamiyiwa, äh-āpahamiyit : pōt ōma astutn, sihkusiwayān uhtsi astutin, mīna kitsuhtsikanis. akwāsiwäpahamiyiwa iskutäw, äh-miyāhkasikäyit, miyāhkasamiyit astutin mina kitsōhtsikanis. ka-kitāpamäw, äh-tōtamiyit. pustastutinäyiwa, äh-yōhtänamiyit, äkwah wīpisisiyiw päyak äh-utinamiyit. äh-kituhtāyit, kiyipa pāpayiyiwa mustuswah päyak, ōt äskwāhtämih äh-pimipayiyit. pimäyiwa ; nipahäyiwa. kāwih kätastutinäyiwa, äh-asiwatāyit, äh-tahkwaskwäpitamiyit apasōhk.

" hāw, nistäsä, ntawi-manisah utäyaniy ; äwaku pikuh ! " itik.

tāpwāh utinam,[1] *äh-nitawi-manisahk utäyaniy.*

" mān äkā nika-kīspuhtān ! " itäyihtam.

äkwah nawatsīw.

wayawīw, " mistahi nk-ōtinän wiyās, " äh-itäyihtahk.

nama käkway mustuswah ; sipwähtäyiwa. kāwih pīhtukäw, äkwah äh-mītsisutsik.

" nisīm, kakikä tsiw umah äkus äy-isi-minahuyin ? " itäw.

" äha'. nama wīhkāts, wāh-minahuyāni, npapāmuhtān. äyakō uma nipustastutinān, wāh-minahuyāni, äh-kituhtāyān, äh-pätsimakik mustuswak, " itwäyiwa.

" kah ! " itäw.

ōmis ītäyihtam wīsahkätsāhk : " nika-kimutamawāw ! " itäyihtam ; " nik-ātsimustawāw, ta-nōhtähkwasit, äkā ta-kiskäyihtahk, kimutamawaki, " itäyihtam.

äkwah äh-tipiskāyik, ātsimustawäw, ä-wīh-kakwä-nōhtähkwastimāt. äh-kiskäyimāt, äh-nōhtähkwasiyit, äkwah kawisimōwak. nama wīh-nipāw. mayaw äh-nipāyit, utinam, äh-wayawīhtatāt ōm āstutin, äh-kimutit, äh-nayahtahk. äkus īsi tapasīw. pāh-pimipahtāw, kuntah äh-wā-wākuhtät,

[1] Probably the word *mōhkumān :* "knife" has dropped out in record.

" äkā ta-mitisit, " äh-itäyimāt. äkwah ä-wīh-wāpaniyik, itah äh-wayahtsāyik, äkutah kawisimōw.

" kīsikāki, pimuhtäyāni, nika-wāpamik, pä-nawaswāsitsih, " itäyihtam ; " iyikuhk tipiskāki, nka-tapasīn, " äh-itäyihtahk, äkutah kā-kawisimut.

mayaw äh-pimisihk, nipāw, mitunih äh-papätikusihk, äh-nayōhtahk ōm astutn.

kītahtawä, äh-mäkwā-nipāt, kuskuskunik, " nistäsä, waniskāh ! kikipiskawin. niwīh-kutawān, " äh-itikut.

äs ōma pīhtsāyihk wīkiyihk, itah kā-kutawäyit māna äkutah äs ōmah kā-nipāt. waniskāw.

" yahō, nisīm, äkus äsi-kīskwähkwasiskiyān ! awah[1] *ätukä kahutinamān kiwīskwähpitākan ! " itäw, äh-kätōwatät, kāwih äh-tahkupitahk.*

" uhtsitaw nka-kimutin, " itäyihtam.

asay mīna äh-tipiskāyik, ātsimustawäw, ä-wīh-kakwä-nästuhkwastimāt. äyikuh mina äh-nipāyit, asay mīna utinam, äh-wīwahut, äh-tapasīt. kapätipis pimipahtāw. " miyāmay wāhyaw nitayān ! " äh-itäyihtahk, ä-wīhwāpaniyik, mistikwah äh-tsimasuyit, ä-sakāyik, " äkutah nka-nipān, " itäyihtam. äkusi nahapiw, mistikuhk äh-aspatisihk. ōmis īsi kīskipitam uskutākay, mistikwah ōhi äh-asitahpitisut. äkus īsi äh-nipāt. aspin pikuh äh-nipāt, kītahtawä kā-kuskuskunikut.

" nistäsä, waniskāh ! kōtamihin ; nitastutin ! niwīh-kakwä-minahuh ! " itik.

äh-tōhkāpit, awīn ōma, pīhtsāyihk kīh-apiw, apasōhk äh-astahpisut.

ōmis ītwäw : " yahō ! äkus ōma māna äh-isi-kīskwähwasiskiyān, pikw ätukä äh-utinamān kiwīskwähpitākan, nisīm ! " itäw, äh-pasikōt, kāwih äh-tahkupitahk.

kiyipah utinamiyiwa, äh-kwayakunamiyit, ä-pustastutinäyit. āsay mīna äh-kituhtāyit, pätsimäyiwa mustuswah. mīn äyakuni pimwäyiwa, äh-nipahāyit.

" hā, nisīm, tānähkih päyak pikuh kāh-nipahat ? " itäw.

" hā, äkuyikuhk ka-kīspunānaw päyak utäyaniy, " itäw.

äkusi tahkupitamiyiwah mīna ōma utastutiniyiw. äkwa wiya ntawihutinam utäyiniy. äkus ä-kīh-mītsisutsik, piyisk mīna tipiskāyiw. iyikuh mīna äh-nipāyit, āsay mīna kimutiw, āsay mīna äh-tapasīt. mitun äkwah wīh-kakwä-mīhkawikiw. wāhyaw mīn äh-ayāt, āsay mīna ä-wīh-wāpaniyik, āsay mīna säskisiw. nīsu mistikwah äh-nīswaskisuyit, äkutah tastawāyihk nahapiw, äh-asitahpitisut, "namuya äkwah äkutä pīhtsāyihk nka-nipān ! " äh-itäyihtahk. äkus īsi nipāw. kītahtawäh äh-mäkwā-nipāt, kā-kuskuskunikut.

" nistäsä, waniskāh ! kikipiskawin. niwīh-pōnän. "

äs ōma itah k-ōh-wayawīhk, iskwāhtämihk äkutah äs ōma k-āsitahpisut.

" yahō, nisīm, kikī-wīhtamātin äh-kīskwähkwasiskiyān. nama tsiy awa kitastutin äwaku, ' nik-āyāwik ! ' äh-itäyimit kitastutin ? " itäw.

mīna äh-tipiskāyik, āsay mīna äh-nipāyit, utinam, äh-wīwahut, mīna äh-tapasīt, äh-sōhkih äh-tapasīt. iyikuh mīna äy-wīh-wāpahk, āsay mīna wīh-nipāw. kīhtsähkusīw ispimihk. äkutah äkwah nipāw, mīna äh-asitahpisut.

---

[1] The animate form *awah :* "this" is a slip of speech or record, since the following verb has inanimate form of object.

aspin ä-nipāt, kītahtawä mistik uhtsi kā-kuskuskuyahkahukut, " waniskāh, nistäsä ! ka-kaskāpasun ! niwīn-pōnän, " äh-itikut, wīkiyihk ispimih äh-akusīt, itah k-ōh-wayawiyāpahtäyik äkutah.

" yahō, nisīm, äkuyikuhk äkus ōma äsih-kiskwähkwasiskiyān ! " itäw, äh-päh-nīhtakusīt, äh-pīhtukät, äh-ta-tahkupitahk, itah kāh-kīh-tahkupitäyik.

ōmis ītik : " wīsahkätsāhk, namuya ka-kīh-kimutamawin nitastutin. äyak ōma näpāyanih äh-pä-kīwähtahikuyan. nawats ta-pōnihtāyan ! " itik.

äkus ä-kīh-mītsisut, sipwähtäw.

äkuyikuhk äskwāk ātayōhkäwin.

Once upon a time, as Wisahketchahk was walking along, he saw a tipi.

When he reached it, he said, "Hum, hum!"

As usual, he was hungry.

"Yes, yes, come in!" someone called to him.

When he entered, there was a lone man. When he sat down, he looked all round for something to eat. He saw nothing. So there he sat.

Presently the other said, "Oh dear, but I am forgetting that my elder brother is hungry!" he said.

He saw that something or other was tied fast in the doorway. The other took that thing and removed the covering: it turned out to be a headgear, a headgear of weasel-skin, and a little flute. The man scattered some embers of the fire and burned incense for the headgear and the flute. He watched the man do it. The man put on the headgear, opened the door-flap, and took one of his arrows. When he blew on the flute, quickly a buffalo came running, and ran right past the doorway. The man shot it and killed it. He took off the headgear, put it back in its covering, and tied it fast to the wood of the tent-poles.

"Now, big brother, go cut out the tongue; only that!" he told him.

So he took it, and went and cut out the tongue.

"It looks as if we should not get our fill!" he thought.

Then he prepared the roast.

He went out of the tent, thinking, "I shall take a lot of the meat."

The buffalo was not there; it had gone away. He went back in, and they ate.

"Little brother, do you always kill game in this manner?" he asked him.

"Yes. I never tramp about when I want to kill game. I put on this head-dress, when I want to kill game, and by blowing the flute, summon buffalos," said the man.

"You don't say!" he answered him.

Wisahketchahk thought thus: "I shall steal it from him!" he thought; "I shall tell him stories to make him sleepy, so that he will not know when I steal it from him," he thought.

Then, when night came, he told him tales, so as to make him get sleepy. When he knew that the other was sleepy, then they went to bed. He kept from going to sleep. As soon as the other slept, he took the headgear, and went out of the tent with it, stealing it and carrying it over his shoulder.

In this way he fled. He ran on and on, making all kinds of turns and twists, with the thought, "So that he may not track me." Then, towards dawn in a hollow place he lay down.

"If I walk on in daytime, he will see me, in case he comes here pursuing me," he thought; "When night comes, I shall continue in my flight," he thought, as he lay down.

As soon as he lay down, he fell asleep, lying all doubled up, with the headgear still on his shoulders.

Suddenly, in the midst of his sleep, someone shook him and roused him, saying to him, "Big brother, get up! You are blocking my way. I want to build the fire."

There he was, inside the other's tipi; he had been sleeping right where the other always built the fire. He arose.

"Dear me, little brother, I am afflicted with sleep-walking like this! And here it seems I have taken your sacred bundle!" he told him, removing his burden and tying it back in its place.

"All the more surely, I will steal it," he thought.

That night again he told him stories to make him sleepy. As soon as the other went to sleep, again he took it, slung it over his shoulder, and made off. All night long he ran. When he thought, "Surely, I am far off," towards dawn, where a tree stood, in a wooded place, "Here I shall sleep," he thought. So he sat down, leaning against the tree. Like this he tore his jacket and tied himself fast to the tree. In this position he went to sleep. Hardly had he gone off to sleep, when suddenly the other shook him awake.

"Big brother, get up! You are delaying me; my headgear! I want to try and kill some game!" the other was saying to him.

When he opened his eyes, what was this? He was sitting inside the place, tied fast to a tent-pole.

He said, "Dear me! This is the way I am afflicted with the habit of walking in my sleep; and it seems that in some way I have taken up your sacred bundle, little brother!" he said to him, and rose to his feet, and tied the thing back where it belonged.

The other at once took it, shook it out, and put on the headgear. Again, when he blew the flute, he called a buffalo. This one, too, he shot and killed.

"Now, little brother, why do you kill only one?" he asked him.

"Oh, one tongue is quite enough to give us our fill," he told him.

With this he again tied up that headgear of his. And Wisahketchahk went and took up the tongue. When thus they had eaten, finally night came again. Again, as soon as the other slept, he stole it, and again made off in flight. He was bound to run fast, now, and far. When again he had gone a great distance, and again dawn was near, again he went into the brush. Where two trees stood side by side, there he sat down between them, and tied himself fast, thinking "This time I shall not be sleeping inside there!" So he went to sleep. Suddenly, in the midst of his sleep, there was the other, shaking him awake.

"Big brother, get up! You are blocking my way. I want to put wood on the fire."

It appeared that in the place where one went out of the tent, right in the doorway it appeared that he was tied fast.

"Dear me, little brother, I told you I was given to walking in my sleep. Are you sure that this headgear of yours has not been thinking 'Let him possess me!' meaning me?" he asked him.

The next night, as soon as the other slept, again he took the thing, slung the bundle across his shoulder, and again made off, fleeing with all his might. When dawn again was near, again he meant to sleep. He climbed high up on a tree. There he went to sleep, after again tying himself fast.

He had gone off to sleep, when suddenly the other was prodding him awake with a stick, saying to him, "Get up, big brother! You will be strangled by smoke! I am going to put wood on the fire," and there he was, perched on top of the other's dwelling, right at the place where the smoke comes out of the tipi.

"Dear me, little brother, just see how terribly I am afflicted with sleep-walking!" he said to him, as he climbed down and came into the tent and tied the thing back into the place where it had been tied fast.

The other answered him thus: "Wisahketchahk, you will not be able to steal my headgear from me. It was this headgear itself which brought you back here whenever you went to sleep. You might as well give it up!" the other told him.

At this, as soon as he had eaten, he went away.

That is the end of the sacred story.

(11) The Bear-Woman

Coming-Day

kā-kīsikāw-pīhtukäw.

kītahtawä päyak ayīsiyiniw itahk äh-wa-wīkit, äh-päyakut, nama wīhkāts wāpamäw ayīsiyiniwah, wiya pikōh äkutah äh-ayāt. kāh-nipātsih kā-tipiskāyik, wiyāpaniyiki mātsīw. wiyāpamātsi mustuswah, nipahäw. päyak utäyiniy utinam, äkwah päyak upäminak, äh-kīwät, ä-takuhtät wīkihk, äkwah manah äh-kīsitäput, kāh-mītsisutsi, äkwah ä-nikuhtät. äkusi äkwah piyisk tipiskāyiw māna. äkwa äy-ay-apit, piyisk kaskäyihtam äh-päyakut. äh-wāpaniyik, mīn äh-mātsīt, mīnah päyak nipahäw mustuswah. kīwäw; apsīs utinam kā-mītsit.

tsīk äy-ihtāt wīkihk, kā-wāpahtak mistah äh-astäyikih mihtah wīkihk. ay-itäyihtam; "awiyak ä-kīh-takuhtät,"[1] äkus ītäyihtam. miywäyihtam. äh-pīhtukät, nam āwiyah wāpamäw, äsah kāh-wähpāhtakahikäyihk. mihtātam äkāh äh-wāpamāt awiyah. ay-apiw. "tānähk ōmah äkā k-ōh-apit awiyak?" itäyihtam. pōtih itah k-āpit maskisinah miskam. mistahi miywäyihtam, "iskwäw māskōts kā-kīh-takuhtät," äh-itäyihtahk; "kīksäpā nika-mātsīn; nika-kakwäh-käsiskawāw, mīnah takuhtätsih," äh-itäyihtahk.

äh-wāpaniyik, kiyipah sipwähtäw, äh-mātsīt. mīnah nipahäw päyak mustuswah. utäyiniy utinam äkwah uspikäkanah äkwah utihtihkusiwah äkwah upäminak. äkus īsi kīwäw, "nika-käsiskawāw," ä-itäyihtah. pāh-pimipahtāw.

tsīk äy-ihtāt wīkihk, wāpahtam äh-pikihtsäsiyik, mīnah mistahi mistah äh-astäyikih. äh-pīhtukät, iyāyaw nanātawāpiw: nam āwiyah wāpamäw.

---

[1] Short, simple speeches are often conjunct.

mistahi mihtātam äkā h-apiyit awiyah. äkwah ä-paminawasut, kītahtawä kā-miskahk maskisinah. utinam, äh-wā-wāpahtahk, äh-miywāsiniyikih.

" māskōts iskwäw kā-tāh-takusihk, " itäyihtam ; " hāh, uhtsitaw nikakakwäh-käsiskawāw. kīkisäpā nika-sipwähtān, " äkusi itäyihtam.

tāpwäh ä-kīh-mītsisut kawisimōw äh-nipāt. kīksäpā waniskāw ; namuya mītsisōw, ä-sipwähtät, ä-mātsīt. pōtih kiyipah nipahäw mustuswah. äkwah ä-kīh-wiyinihāt, uspikäkanah utihtihkusiwah utinam, äh-ati-kīwät. pāhpimipahtāw. tsīk äy-ihtāt wīkihk, kā-wāpahtahk mistah a-pikihtäyik wīkih. mistahi miywäyihtam, " māskōts apiw, " ä-täyihtah.

äh-takuhtät, ä-pīhtukät, awīn ōhih kīh-apiyiwah mistahi äh-miyusiyit iskwäwah ōhtapiwinihk. äkutah nahapiw, ä-wīh-pāhpihikut, ä-kitāpamāt. sāsay äsah kāh-paminawasōyit. sämāk utinamiyiwah umaskisinah, ä-kätaskisinänikut, kutakah ä-wīh-pustaskisinahikut, äkwah ä-kāsītsihtsänikut, äh-kāsīhkwänikut. äkusi äkwah asamik ; äkwah mītsisuwak. ā, mistahi miywäyihtam.

ōmis ītäw aw īskwäw : " tānikhih apisīs kā-pätāyin wiyās ? "

" āh, " itwäw awa nāpäw, " nam āwiyak ntihtatäyimāw ; äyak ōhtsi apisīs k-ōh-pätāyān, " äkusi itwäw awa nāpäw ; " tāntäh māk ōmah äy-uhtuhtäyin ? " itwäw awa nāpäw.

" wāhyaw ōtāh äh-wīkiyāhk, " itwäw aw īskwäw ; " kiyām miyātsiyinih mistahi pätāh wiyāsah ; nōhtähkatäwak, " itwäw aw īskwäw, " nōhtāwiy, " itwäw.

" äha' , " itwäw awa nāpäw.

äkutah uhtsi tahtu-kīsikāw mātsīw. piyisk mistahi nipahäw mustuswah. awa iskwäw mistah ātuskäw, wiyāsah äy-usihtāt.

mistah äh-ayātsik, " nawats ituhtäyahk nōhtāwiy, " itwäw awa iskwäw ; " mistahi nōhtähkatäwak. "

" äha' , " itwäw awa nāpäw.

" wāpahkih, " itwäw aw īskwäw.

" käkway käy-āpatsihtäyahk ta-pimiwitāyahk käkway ? "

" āh, tit-āhtakun ätukä tānisi t-äsi-pihkuhuyahk, " itwäw aw īskwäw.

tāpwä kīksäpā äh-mītsisutsik, " nīkānuhtähkan, " itäw uwīkimākanah ; " itāp mistikwah ka-tsimatān, äkutah ta-kapäsiyahk ; äkutah uhtsi ka-mātsīn, " itäw aw īskwäw unāpämah.

tāpwä ä-kīsi-mītsisutsik sipwähtäw awa nāpäw. äkwah aw īskwäw wawäyīw, ōhi utsayānisiwāwah unīmāwiniwāwah nāh-nāway äh-astāt. äkwah ä-kīsi-wawäyīt aw īskwäw atih-tāh-tähtsi-tahkuskäw unīmāwiniwāwah ; äkusi äh-ati-sipwähtät, nama käkway ihtakuniyiwah ōhōw unīmāwiniwāwa. äkus īs äh-pah-pimuhtät. itäh äh-utākusiniyik kā-miskahk mistikwah äh-tsimatäyikih, äkutah kapäsiw. äkwah ä-tahkiskātsikät aw īskwäw, wīkiwāw äkutah astäyiw. äkwah utinam, äh-mānukät. äh-kīsi-mānukät, pīhtsāyihk āsay mīna tahkiskātsikäw ; kahkiyaw äkutä pahkihtiniyiwa utsayānisiwāwah unīmāwiniwāwa. äkusi äkwah pīhtukäw aw īskwäw, äh-paminawasut.

pōtih äh-ati-kīwät awa nāpäw, kā-wāpahtahk wīkiwāw, " tānisi tiyōtahk ? " äy-itäyimāt uwīkimākanah. äh-pīhtukät, kā-wīh-pāhpihikut uwīkimākanah. äh-itāpit, kahkiyaw wāpahtam utsayānisiwāwa unīmāwiniwāwa. mistahi māmaskātam äh-tōtamiyit.

ōmis ītwäw awa aw īskwäw : " wāpahkih ka-takuhtānānaw itah nōhtāwiy k-āyātsik. mistahi nōhtähkatäwak, " itwäw awa iskwäw.

tāpwāh äh-wāpahk, kīksäpā waniskāwak. ä-kīh-mītsisutsik, wawäyīwak.

" wītsiwōhkamawin,[1] *" itwäw aw īskwäw ; " ' tānisih äh-tōtahk ? ' k-ätäyihtaman, ka-kiskäyihtän tānsih äh-tōtamān, " itwäw away iskwäw.*

" hāha' , " itwäw awa nāpäw.

tāpwä wawäyīwak, nāh-nāway äh-astātsik utsayānisiwāwa unīmāwiniwāwa. äh-kitāpamāt uwīkimākanah, äh-atih-sipwähtäyit, äh-tah-tähtsitahkuskäyit unīmāwiniwāwah, nama käkway wāpahtam awa nāpäw.

äkus īsi pimuhtätsik, mistahi māmaskātäw uwīkimākanah, äh-tōtamiyit. äkus īsi ä-pa-pimuhtätsik, kītahtawä, äh-at-ōtākusiniyik, kā-wāpahtahkik äh-pikihtäyik itah äh-pasahtsāyik, ä-sakāyik ; äkutah ä-sākäwätsik, kā-pämātāwisiyit usīmisah aw īskwäw.

ōmisi itwäyiwah : " āyäyi, misi-pätāw nīmāwinah nimis ! " itwäyiwah. äkus āti-takuhtäwak wīkiyihk.

awa kisäyiniw, " hay hay hay ! " matwä-itwäw.

ä-yōhtänahk aw īskwäw, äh-pīhtukä-tah-tahkiskātsikät, pīhtsāyihk pahkihtiniyiwah unīmāwiniwāwa utsayānisiwāwa. äkusi awah nōtukäsiw äh-at-ōtinahk, mistahi miywäyihtam, " äkwah kä-mītsisuyān, " äh-itäyihtah. nanāskumōw awa kisäyiniw. äkusi pīhtukäwak.

ōmis ītwäw awa kisäyiniw : " äkusi ä-kīh-itäyihtamān, ntānis, ' ituhtä ! ' kā-kīh-ititān, ' äh-pa-päyakut ninahāhkisīm, ' " itwäw awa kisäyiniw.

äkutah ay-ayāw äkwah. pātih kinwäsk ä-kīh-ayāt äkutah, äkwah ämiyuskamiyik, kā-kiskäyihtahk wākayōsah kā-wīwit ōh īskwäwah k-ätäyihtahk, ōhi mīnah kisäyiniwah nōtukäsiwah wākayōsah äs ōhi. äkwah mihtātam äkā tahkih ta-kīh-wītsäwāt.

äkusi äkuyikuhk äwakō ātayōhkäwin.

Once upon a time a man lived all alone and never saw any people, being all alone in that place. When he had slept at night, in the morning he went hunting. Whenever he saw buffalo, he killed them. He would take a tongue and a thigh-bone and go home, and when he reached his dwelling, he would prepare his meal, and when he had eaten, he would gather firewood. So night would come upon him. As he stayed thus by himself, at last he felt lonesome. When daylight came and he as usual went hunting, again he killed a buffalo. He went home; he took a little to eat.

When he was near his dwelling-place, he saw a great pile of firewood by his tent. He wondered about it; "It must be that someone has come," he thought. He was glad. When he entered, he saw nobody, though it was plain that someone had swept the place. He was sorry that he saw no one. He stayed there. "How is it that there is no one here?" he thought. Lo, there where he sat, he found some moccasins. He was very glad, thinking, "A woman perhaps is the one who came here. In the morning I shall hunt; I shall try to come upon her while she is here, if she comes again," he thought.

At daybreak he quickly went off to hunt. Again he killed a buffalo. He took the tongue, the ribs, the kidneys, and a thigh-bone. Then he went home, thinking, "I shall come in time to find her there." He kept running.

---

[1] Error or real variant? The usual form would be *wītsōhkamawin.*

When he got near his dwelling, he saw a little smoke, and a great pile of firewood. When he entered, eagerly he looked about: he saw no one. He was very sorry that no one was there. Then, as he went about his cooking, soon he found some moccasins. He picked them up and examined them; they were very pretty.

"Probably it is a woman has been coming here," he thought; "Now all the harder I shall try to find her here. Early in the morning I shall go," he thought.

After eating he lay down to sleep. He got up early; without eating he went forth to hunt. In a short time he killed a buffalo, and when he had cut it up, took the ribs and the kidneys and went home. He ran as he went. When he was close to his dwelling, he saw much smoke rising from his tent. He was very glad, thinking, "Perhaps she is there."

When he got there and entered, lo and behold, there sat a very handsome woman on his settee. He sat down there, and she smiled at him as he looked at her. It appeared that she had already done the cooking. Without delay she took off his moccasins and put others on his feet, and she washed his hands and face. Thereupon she gave him to eat, and they took their meal. Oh, he was very glad.

Thus spoke that woman: "Why do you bring so little meat?"

"Oh," said the man, "I did not think anyone was here; that is why I brought only a little," he said; "But whence do you come?" he asked.

"A long ways from here we dwell," she answered. "Please, when you hunt, bring much meat; they are in want of food," she said, "my father and his people."

"Very well," said he.

So he hunted every day. In time he killed many buffalo. The woman worked a great deal, preparing the food.

When they had a large amount of it, "Suppose we go to my father's place," said the woman; "They are very hungry."

"Very well," said the man.

"Tomorrow," she said.

"But what are we to use to carry things?"

"Oh, there will be some way we can manage," she answered.

Then, when they ate in the morning, "Go on ahead," she told her husband; "Then you will set up some sticks at the place where we are to camp; from that place you will go hunting," she said to her husband.

So, when they had eaten, the man set out. And the woman made ready, laying their belongings and their food supply in a row. Then, when she had got ready, she went along, stepping each time upon their bundles of food; and when in this wise she set out, not a trace was there of their supplies of food. So then she walked on. Toward nightfall she found the sticks that were set up in the ground; there she made camp. When she kicked the ground, there lay their tent. Then she took the tent and set it up. When she had set it up, inside again she stamped the ground; on that spot fell all their belongings and their supplies of food. Then she went inside and cooked their meal.

There, when the man came back and saw their dwelling, "How did she do it?" he thought concerning his wife. When he entered, there she was, smiling at him. He looked about and saw all their belongings and their supplies of food. He wondered greatly at what she had done.

Thus spoke she: "Tomorrow we shall come to where my father's people stay. They are in great want of food," she said.

So when day broke, early they arose. When they had eaten, they made ready.

"Help me," said the woman; "Since you have been thinking, 'How does she do it?' you shall now know how I do," she said.

"Yes," answered the man.

Accordingly they made ready by laying in a row their possessions and their stored meats. When he watched his wife, as she went forth and stepped on one after another of their bundles, he saw nothing at all there.

So as they walked on, he marvelled greatly at what his wife had done. Then, as they walked on, towards evening they saw smoke rising from a wooded ravine; when they came in sight of that place, the woman's younger sister came forth.

She cried: "Splendid! My elder sister is bringing a great store of meat!"

So they went on and came to the house.

The old man called out, "Splendid!"

When the woman opened the door and, as she entered, stamped repeatedly, then into the lodge fell their stored meats and their belongings. Then when the old woman went on to pick them up, she greatly rejoiced, thinking, "So now I shall eat." The old man gave thanks: "Thus I had it in mind, daughter, when 'Go there,' I said to you, 'where my son-in-law dwells alone', " said the old man.

There he stayed then. When he had been there a long time, and spring had come, then he knew that she, the woman, as it seemed to him, whom he had to wife, was a bear, and that also the old man and the old woman were bears. And he was sorry that he could not always be with them.

That is the end of this sacred story.

(12) The Bearsark Woman

Louis Moosomin

nāh-namiskwäkāpaw.

kītahtawä päyak nāpāw wiya piku äh-päyakukamikisit pisisik māna. kītahtawä namuya wīhkāts apiyiwa uwīkimākana, tahtu-kīsikāw äh-sipwähtäyit, kāh-wāwäsihuyitsih, ayōwinisa äh-miywāsiniyikih tahtu-kīsikāw äh-pusiskahk awa iskwäw. kīspin piyä-kīwätsih, mistahi māna māyātaniyiwa, kunta māna misiwä ä-asiskīwiyikih.

" tānähki ätukä ? " itäyihtam awa nāpäw ; " mahtih nika-kakwä-wāpamāw, " itäyihtam.

tāpwä mātsīhkāsōw. äkwah kīmōts päh-wāh-wīskawahtāw wīkiwāw, mahtih ä-wīh-kiskinawāpamāt uwīkimākanah, tāntäh isi kitah-sipwähtäyit. kā-wāpamāt aspin utah sakāhk äy-isi-sipwähtäyit, kiskäyimäw itäh äh-ituhtäyit. kā-wāpamāt äkutä sakāhk wākayōsah ä-wāh-uwītsimusiyit, mistahi kisiwāsiw, äh-uhtäyimāt ōhi wākayōsah.

" wāpahkih nika-nipahāw ! " itäyihtam.

tāpwä äh-utākusiniyik, ōmisi itwäw awa : " anuhts wākayōs nimisk-awāw itah äh-ōwātit, " itwäw awa nāpäw, äh-kīwät.

äkwah ōmisih itwäw anah iskwäw ; ōmisih äsah kīh-itik ōhih wītsimusah wākayōsah : " kīspin nipahikawiyāni, utināhkan nipahkäkin," kīh-itik äsa ; " äkusi itāp ntawäyihtamani pikw īspihk ayīsiyiniwak mihtsät kikanipahāwak," kīh-itik äsa awa iskwäw ; äkusi ōmisih itäw unāpäma : " äkāya misiwä pīkuswāhkan. tāpiskōts atāwākan käy-isi-pahkuniht, äkusih isīhāhkan," kīh-itäw äsa unāpäma.

" äha'," itwäw awa nāpäw, ä-sīhkimikut wīwa.

tāpwä wīhpi-pahkunäw ōhi, ispīhk äh-ntawi-nipahāt ōhi wākayōsa.

ōmisi itwäw an īskwäw : " namuya katsāts ta-mōwāyahk ! "

" īkamā māka awiyak käh-kīh-muwāt äh-uwītsimusiyit ! " itäw uwīkimākanah.

äkusi tāpwä kīsihäw ōhi wākayōsiwayānah. äkwah utsawāsimisiw awa iskwäw. nīsu nāpäsisah ayāwäw sämāk, nīsōtäwa. äyakuni wākayōsah äsah uwītōsämā. tāpwä āpihtaw wiyawāhk misiwä ōpīwāwak äsa ōki nāpäsisak. äkusi äyiwähk kitimākäyimäw awa nāpäw ; äyiwähk wī-kakwähuhpikihäw, āta namuya wiya utawāsimisah. tāpwä uhpikiwak ōki awāsisak.

äkwah äh-ati-misikititsik, kītahtawä ōmisih itäw : " äkāya wīhkāts tāpwähtamuk, nitawāsimisitik, āhki kiyawāw ' wākayōsak ' itikawiyäku. kiyawāw tāpwä äkutōwahk. äkusi itikawiyäku kīspin, ka-kwäskimunāwāw."

äkusi tāpwä nama wīhkāts äsa tāpwähtamwak ōki awāsisak, äkusi ätihtwāwi.

kītahtawä awa usīmimās, " kiyām wākayōsiwitān mahtih ! " itäw ōhi ustäsah.

tāpwä wākayōsiwiwak. pä-nōtsihäwak awāsisah, äh-pä-pā-paskatayäpitātsik.

äkwah kisiwāk wīkiwāhk kā-pih-nipahihtwāwi[1] *ōki maskusisak, sämāk awa iskwäw kisiwāsiw äsah. unāpäma kīhkāmäw ; wayawī-kwāskuhtiw ; nitaw-ōtinäw ōhi kā-kiy-ōsihāt uskutākayah, ōhi maskwayāna. äkus īsi at-īsi-kwäskīmōw. pīhtukä-kwāskuhtiw kähtsiwāk wīkiwāhk ; unāpäma ati-nipahäw. äkutah uhtsi mituni kahkiyaw ayīsiyiniwah mästsihäw. mituni äsa äh-mīhtsätihk, äwakuni kahkiyaw mituni nipahäw. ōkāwiya piku iskuhäw. ātah äh-pā-pāskisuht, namuya äsa kīh-sākōtsihäw ; namuya kīh-nipahäw, piyisk äkus īsi kahkiyaw ayīsiyiniwah kā-kisi-mästsihāt. äkwah awa uskinīkiw kīwutäw, äwaku awa umisa kā-wākayōsiwiyit. äkwah awa iskwäw ōhtāwiya iskuhäw, ōhtsitaw ä-wīh-kakwātakihāt. tāpwä päyak mistahi kwātakiyäw ukāwiya, mīna usīmisa päyak, äwakuni piku äh-iskuhāt. äkwah māna pikw ītä ä-papāmātsihut, piyä-takuhtätsi piku nayästaw äh-kīhkāmāt, nanātuhk äy-isi-kwātakihāt, kiyäkaw ä-saskahwāt, misiwä äsa umikiwak ōki käht-āyak mina aw īskwäsis. mistahi äsah kitimahäw. kītahtawä awa uskinīkiw kā-takuhtät, " tanähki uma ? " itäyihtam, itah ōma kā-kīh-mihtsätiyit ayīsiyiniwa kahkiyaw äh-mästsihimiht. päyak piku mīkiwāhp wāpahtam, uhpimä äh-tsimatäyik. äkwah kītahtawä usīmisah kā-wāpamāt, äh-ntawi-tāpakwäyit, wāpuswah ä-wīh-kakwä-nipahāyit.*

" tānähk ōma k-ōh-ispayik, nisīmis ? " itäw.

ōmis ītwäw awa iskwäsis : " ä-kih-mästsihtāt kimisinaw. kahkiyaw ayīsiyiniwah kīh-mästsihäw. nayästaw pikuh kōhtāwiyinaw pimātisiw," itwäw aw iskwäsis.

mistahi pakwātam awa nāpäw.

---

[1] Why iterative?

"*äkwah mistahi namuya ä-sākōtsihiht, ātah äh-pāskisuht,*" *itwäw awa iskwäsis.*

äkusi äkwa, "*tānisi kä-kīh-tōtamān?*" *itäyihtam awa nāpäw.*

"*pikw ätsik āna kita-kakwätsimāyäk tantōwihk unipiwin äh-astäyik. kakwätsimāhkäk; mahtih, 'kähtsināh awiyak ä-sīhkimikuyäk!' āta wiya kik-ätikuwāw. 'namuya! usām mistahi äh-manitōwiyin, äkā äh-kīh-nipahikawiyin,' kik-ätāwāw.*"

tāpwä kīwäw awa iskwäsis. nīsu wāpuswa nipahtamāk ōhi ustäsah.

ōmis ītwäw: "*nōhtāh,*" *itäw,* "*nistäs niwāpamāw,*" *itäw ōhtāwiya,* "*äwakuni ōhi ä-nipahtamawit. 'kakwätsimāhkäk tāntōwihk äh-uhtsinipit,' itwäw ana.*"

āh, tāpwä awa mayaw ōhi äh-takuhtäyit, mituni misiwä äsah äh-miswākaniwit awa iskwäw. äkwah tāpwä kakwätsimäwak.

"*tānähki k-ō-nōhtä-kiskäyihtamäk? nama tsī ahpōh kikusisiwāw kākäh-kīwutät niwīh-kakwä-nipahik?*" *itwäw äsa awa iskwäw.*

"*hā, namuya, ntānis! 'māskōts mistahi manitōwiw,' äh-itäyimitān, k-ō-nōhtä-kiskäyihtamān tānimatōwihk t-ōnipōwiniyan.*[1]"

"*hā, nōhtāh, āta nikiskäyihtän äh-wīh-kakwä-nipahikawiyān, k-ōh-kakwätsimiyan!*" *itwäw awa iskwäw;* "*nisitihk tāwāyihk.*"

äkwah tāpwä mayaw ä-sipwähtäyit awa, sämāk ituhtäw awa uskinīkiw, ōhtāwiyah äh-ntawāpamāt mīna ukāwiya.

"*hwā, 'nitāwisitānihk nōnipōwinin; äwak uhtsi äk āwiyak k-ō-kīh-nipahit,' itwäw äsa.*"

äkwah ōmis ītwäw awa uskinīkiw: "*mistikwa ka-kīnīkihkwatamuk.*[2] *äkusi misiw ītah ka-tsāh-tsimatānāwāw. äkusi äkutah kita-kisisin anima. äkusi äkutah kä-nipahāyahk,*" *itwäw äsah awa uskinīkiw.*

mayaw ä-sipwähtäyit, misiwä tsimatāwak mistsikusah.

tāpwä ä-takuhtäyit, "*mahtih asamik!*" *äh-itikutsik, sämāk mātsihkīhkāmäwak.*

"*kähtsināh awiyak äkusi ä-kīh-itikuyäk, k-ōh-kāh-kīhkāmiyäk!*" *itwäw awa iskwäw.*

"*äha'; ōtah kīh-takuhtäw nistäs,*" *itwäw awa iskwäsis.*

iskutäw äsah uhtsi pakamahwäw ōhi umisah. tāpwä pikuh äkus īsi wayawīyāmōwak. äkusi äkwah aw īskwäw utihtināw ōhi uskutākayah, ōhi māna k-ōtināt wāh-nipahtākätsih maskwayānah. mayaw äh-atih-pimipayit awa iskwäw, māka mīna äh-kwäskimut, sämāk utāwisitānihk kisisin. pahkisin äkutah. äkutah äsah kīh-nipahāw äwakuh iskwäw, mihtsät ayīsiyiniwah ä-kīh-nipahāt.

Once upon a time a certain man always dwelt off alone with his family. After a while his wife never stayed at home, but went off every day, after putting on her fine clothes; every day that woman put on her good clothes. When she came back home, they were always in a bad state, muddied all over.

---

[1] The regular formation from *nipiw*: "he dies" would be *nipiwin*: "death" (cf. *unipiwin*: "his death" earlier in this text) and *unipiwiniw*: "he has his death." But the form here in the text is probably recorded right: *nipōwin*: "death" and *unipōwiniw*: "he has his death" are probably relics of the time when "to die" was an irregular verb, cf. Fox *nepwa*, Menomini *nepuah*: "he dies," Fox *nepōweni*: "death."

[2] Normal form probably, *kā-kīnikihkutamuk*.

"I wonder what this means?" thought the man; "Suppose I watch her," he thought.

So he pretended to go hunting. Then he gradually stole up to the lodge, to watch his wife and learn which way she would go. When he had seen her go off into the woods, he knew where she was going . . . .

"Tomorrow I shall kill him!" he thought.

So then in the evening he said, "Today I found a bear's den," said the man, when he came home.

Then the woman spoke thus; for thus she had been told by her lover, the bear: "If I am slain, do you then take my hide," he must have told her; "In this way, later, should you so desire, you may at any time kill many people," he must have told that woman; so now she said to her husband, "Do not cut him up. Just as one skins a fur-bearing animal for sale, do you so prepare him," she told her husband.

"Very well," said the man, in answer to his wife's request.

So he cut the creature out of its hide, when he went to kill that bear.

The woman said, "We do not have to eat him, do we?"

" . . . . " replied the husband.

Then accordingly she prepared that bearskin. Then that woman gave birth. Even then and no later, she had two boys, twins. . . . . And those boys were covered with fur all over half of their bodies. Then that man to some extent took pity on them; he decided to bring them up as best he could, even though they were not his. And so those children grew up.

Then, as they were growing up, at one time he told them, "Never give credence to it, my children, if ever you are called 'bears.' Such, indeed, you are. If that is said to you, you will change your bodily form."

Accordingly, those boys never gave heed when they were called that way.

Then at one time, "Let us turn into bears!" the younger one said to the elder.

So they turned into bears. They came pursuing the children, and when they reached them, tore them open at the belly.

Then when, close to the lodge those bear-cubs were killed, at once that woman grew angry. She upbraided her husband; she sprang out of the lodge; she went and took that mystic dress she had made, that bear-skin robe. At once she thus changed her bodily form. She came bounding right into the lodge; she killed her husband. Then she killed off all the people. Although there were many of them, she killed them all. Only her mother she spared. Although she was shot at again and again, she could not be overcome; it was impossible to kill her, so that at last she thus had exterminated those people. Then that young man went visiting, whose elder sister was the woman who had turned into a bear. And that woman had spared her father, only so as to torture him. Truly, she greatly tormented her mother and her little sister, having spared only them. When she had been going about here and there, when she came back, she would do nothing but scold them, and torment them in various ways, burning them pell-mell, so that those old people and that little girl were all covered with scars. She kept them in a grievous state. Presently, when that young man arrived, "What can be the matter?" he thought, since all the many people there had been killed. He saw only one tipi, standing off to one side. Then presently he saw his little sister going out to snare rabbits.

"How has this happened, little sister?" he asked her.

Said the girl, "Because our sister has killed all in the place. She has exterminated the people. Only our father is alive," said the girl.

The man was deeply shocked.

"And she has not been overcome, even by shooting," said the girl.

Then, "What shall I be able to do?" thought the man.

"It seems that the only way is for you to ask her where is her mortal spot. Ask her. 'Surely someone has put you up to this!' she will say to you. 'No! It is only that you are so greatly endowed with supernatural power, that you cannot be killed,' you will say to her."

Accordingly the girl went home. Her brother killed two rabbits for her.

She spoke thus: "Father," she said to her father, "I have seen my brother; he it was killed these for me. 'Ask her in what spot a wound would cause her death,' he says."

Then truly, as soon as that other had arrived, that woman was wounded all over her body. Then accordingly, they asked her.

"Why do you want to know? Is it not perhaps that your son who visited here wants to kill me?" said the woman.

"Oh, no, my daughter! Because I thought of you, 'Doubtless she is greatly endowed with spirit power,' is why I wish to know in what part you have your vital spot."

"Ho, father, I do know that you are asking me because an attempt is to be made against my life!" said the woman; "It is in the middle of my foot."

Then, as soon as she had departed, the young man came to see his father and mother.

"Ha, 'At the sole of my foot is my vital spot; that is why no one can kill me,' she says."

Then the young man said, "Point the ends of some sticks. Then you will stick them upright in the ground everywhere. Then she will prick herself on them. That is the way we shall kill her," said the young man.

As soon as she had gone away, they stuck the little slivers everywhere into the ground.

And so, when she came and told them, "Give me to eat!" at once they began to revile her.

"Surely someone has told you to do this, that you all insult me!" said the woman.

"Yes; my brother has been here," said the little girl.

And then with a burning brand she struck the woman, her sister. Then at once, they fled out of the lodge. Then the woman seized her mystic dress, the bearskin robe which she always took when she was about to kill. As soon as the woman dashed along, changing, as always, her bodily form, at once she ran a sliver into her sole. She fell to the ground. And so there that woman was slain who had killed so many people.

(13) Little-Snow-Dart

Simon Mimikwas

mimikwās.

kayās äsah nähiyawak, misāw ōtänaw ; wīkiwāwa īntaw-mīkiwahpah. mihtsätiwak awāsisak.

kītahtawä äh-pipōhk mihtsät awāsisak mā-mätawäwak mistikwah ; sōsimäwak,[1] *mitātaht nīsusāp. äkwah sōsimānah äkunih mitihtäwak. awiyak itäh puyuyitsih usōsimānah, äkutä t-ōh-pä-kīwätsik.*

äkusi sipwähtäwak. piyis nīsu pikuh ayäsinwak.[2] *piyisk näwāw nanipāwak ; äh-utäkusihk äkwäyāk utihtäwak usōsimānah, äyakō h-apisīsisit usīmimāw, äyakō nāpäsis usōsimānah. äkusi äyakō iskwäyāts utihtäwak näwāw mwähts äh-nipātsik. äkusi usīhtäwak mistikwah uhtsi wīkiwāw. äkutah ayāwak.*

mwähtsi mitātaht äh-tipiskāk, äkwah mistahi māyi-kīsikāw. näwutipiskāw äkuyikuhk mispun. äkusi nōhtähkatäwak.

kītahtawäh usōsimānah utināw ; wayawīw ; pakamisimäw : " mātsīk ! " itäw.

äkusi āsay äh-wāpahk, kayāhtä apiyiwah pīhtsāyih usōsimānah. äkwah wayawīw : wiyās mistahi wayawītimihk astäw. äkusi äkwah pīhtukatāw. äkusi äkwah awāsisak mītsisōwak.

tahtwāw äh-tipiskāk mispun. äkwah wanihāwak ; wīkiwāhk wanihāwak. kapā-pipun äkutä ayāwak.

kītahtawä äkwah, " kīwätān ! " tāpwä sipwähtäwak. kīwäwak äkwah. äkusi äh-tipiskāk takuhtäwak.

äkusi, " tānt äh-kīh-ayāyin ? "

" ä-kīh-papāh-mätawäyān. "

äkusi kitahamāk uhtāwiyah. " kā-kīh-wītsäwatsik namuya tsī awiyak kimisi-wanātsihāw ? "

" namuya awiyak ; kahkiyaw npäsiwāwak. "

" äkusi kiyām kanawäyimik, " itwäw päyak kisäyiniw.

äkusi nōhtähkatäwān. äkusi wīhtamwak mītsiwin wiyās mistahi äh-ayātsik itä kā-kīh-tuhtätsik. äkusi kutakihk tāpwäw kisäyiniw, ta-nātahkik ayīsiyiniwak mītsiwin, itäh kā-kīh-tuhtätsik awāsisak. äkusi tāpwä sipwähtäwak. tāpwäh mistahi pätāwak.

äh-takuhtätsik, " tānitah, tānisi äsi-kaskihtāyäk mītsiwin mistahi k-āyāyäk ? "

" nisōsimān äh-māh-minahut. "

" hāw, ntawāts k-ōsōsimānisit kik-äsiyihkāsun. "

kītahtawä äh-nīsitsik awāsisak māka minah sōsimäwak. ma-mitihtäwak. äkunih. nikutwāsik äh-nipātsik utihtäwak usōsimāniwāwah. kutakah mīkiwāhpah äkutä kiyōtäwak. tāpwäh pähtākwan äh-takuhtätsik.

ksäyini päyak : " takusin k-ōsōsimānisit. mistahi manitōwiw ; äkā wiyah mawinähuhk ; nama wiya ka-kīh-sākōtsihāwāw. "

---

[1] Throwing the snow-dart, *sōsimān*, animate gender. A Cree friend later made me a pair: the dart consists of a cigar-shaped piece of light wood, about 5 inches long and about 1 inch in diameter, ornamented with burnt pattern, and fixed on a slender reed. These are thrown so as to speed along the ice or hard snow. The sport has gone out of use.

[2] Probably an error.

äkusi äh-nīpiniyik, " äkwah ayīsiyiniw wī-uhpikihitōw. nīkān utäh kik-āpatsihikōwāw äwakō ana kiw-ōhpikit. äkusi kaskihtāw kīw-ōhpikit anah. kik-āpatsihikuwāw äwakō. nama wiya miywāsin kita-mōtōyäk."

ātiht wākayōsak, ātiht mustuswak äwakō ōtänaw mīkiwāhpah, kähtsiwāk äh-nipahitutsik.

" äkusi nanārisk sakāhk ki-ōtaskīnāwāw," itäw wākayōsah. " äkwah kiyawāw paskwāhk kik-ōtaskīnāwāw. maskusiyah ka-mītsināwāw. äkusi māka niwīh-kīwān."

äkusi kīwäwak. takuhtäwak wīkiwāhk.

" tāntäh ä-kīh-tuhtäyin māka mīnah ?"

" āh, ä-kīh-papā-mätawäyān."

" āh, pōnihtāh ; äkāya kīhtwām papā-mätawāh. isām ka-misi-wanātsihāw awāsis, kuntah kā-ppāmātsihuyin ; nama wya tahkih ka-sākōtsihāw ayīsiyiniw."

" namuya. kākikā kahkiyaw äkwah nisākōtsihāwak, äh-mā-mitunäyimakik anikih kā-wīw-ōhpikitsik. usām namuya ta-kīh-miyw-uhpikiwak ayīsiyiniwak, tāpitawih matsi-nōtsihituyäkuh. äkusi kiyawāw ispimihk kik-ōtaskīnāwāw. äkwah niya asinīwatsīhk nik-ōtaskīn. kākikā nkapamihāw ayīsiyiniw anah kāw-ōhpikit. äkusi pikuh t-äsiw-uhpikihitōw ayīsiyiniw. usām nikitimākäyimāw, äkā wīhkāts äh-nahih-papāmātsihut ayīsiyiniw, tahkih äh-astāhāyäk ta-ma-misi-wanātsihāyäk. äku pikōh äh-wāpahtamān, ta-miyupayik ōm āskiy."

äkusi nanānisi-sipwähtäwak. wīstah sipwähtäw ; kiwāpamāw asinīwatsīhk äh-tsimasut ; wīhkimākusiwak ; sīsīhtapihkwanak siyihkāsōwak. äwakō yāhkih kahkiyaw kā-kīh-paskiyawāt tahtōh kā-matsihtwāyit.

äkusi kahkiyaw.

Among the people of old there was a large town; their houses were ordinary lodges of skin. There were many children.

At one time, in winter, many children were playing with sticks; they were throwing snow-darts, twelve of them. They followed the snow-darts. From wherever anyone's snow-dart stopped in its course they would go home.

So they set out. At last only two were left. Four nights they slept on the way; not till the next morning did they reach the snow-dart of the smallest one, the youngest brother, that boy's snow-dart. This one they reached last, after four nights. Thereupon they built a tent for themselves out of sticks. There they stayed.

On the tenth night came a great storm. For four nights it snowed. So they began to be hungry.

Then at one time, he took his snow-darts; he went outside; he threw them on the ground: "Hunt!" he told them.

Thereupon, when daylight had come, there suddenly within the lodge lay his snow-darts. Then he went outside: a great store of meat lay outside the lodge. Accordingly he brought it in. So the children ate.

Every night it snowed. They were lost; at home they were given up as lost. All winter they stayed there.

Then at one time, "Let us go home!" So they set out. They went home. At nightfall they arrived.

Then, "Where have you been?"

"Playing about here and there."

His father forbade him to do that. "You have not brought to grief any of those who went with you?"

"Not one; I have brought them all home."

"Then you may as well take care of them," said an old man.

For his people there were starving. So they told that they had much food over at the place where they had gone. Then the old man called out at the other lodges that the people were to fetch food from the place where the children had been. So they set out. They really brought a great deal.

When they arrived, "But how did you manage to have so much food?"

"Because my snow-dart killed game."

"Very well, then your name shall be Little-Snow-Dart."

Then again, at another time the two children threw snow-darts and followed them. After six nights on the way they reached their snow-darts. There they visited some other lodges. The report went round that they had come.

One old man said, "Little-Snow-Dart has come here. He has great spirit-power. Do not attack him; you will not be able to defeat him."

Then, when summer had come, "Now mortal man is to come into the generations of his life. In the time ahead he will make use of you, that one who is now to come into life. In this way he will be able to live. He will make use of you. It is not good that any longer you should eat one another."

Some were bears and some were buffalo who lived there in the same village of tents but killed each other.

"And so in different places of the woods you shall have your place of abiding," he said to the bears. "And you others shall dwell on the prairie. You shall eat grass and herbs. And now I shall return to my home."

So they went back home. They arrived at their camp.

"And where did you go this time?"

"Oh, I have been playing here and there."

"Now, stop it; never again go about to play. For you will bring the children to grief wandering about in this needless way; not always will you defeat people."

"No. For all time now I have defeated them all, with the thought of those who are to come into life. For mortal men will not be able to live properly, if you continue like this in your evil pursuit of one another. Therefore, you shall have your abode up aloft. And I shall dwell in the Rocky mountains. For all time I shall take care of mortal man, that one who is to come into life. Only so will the generations of man be able to live. For I have taken pity on mortal man, who can never roam about since you affright him with the fear that you will bring him to destruction. Only in this way do I see a good future course for this earth."

Accordingly they departed in various directions. He too departed; you can see him standing in the Rocky mountains; pleasant is their scent; fir-cones they are called. That is he who of yore overcame all the beings of evil power.

That is all.

(14) Little Snow-Dart

Adam Sakewew

sākäwāw.[1]

kītahtawä wīkiwak ayīsiyiniwak, nīsu ukimāwak, päyak matsihkiwis[2] *uhtāwiya. kītahtawä awāsisak mihtsät sōsimäwak.*

" mahtih kakwätsiyawähitutāk ōma kā-sōsimäyahk kahkiyaw, mahtih awīna nähtā-sōsimät, awīna wāhyaw kä-pahkisiniyit, " itwäw päyak awāsis ōhkuma äw-ōhpikihikut.

äkusi sōsimäwak. äkwah ati-utinäwak sōsimāna. piyis päyak usōsimāna ayīsisiniyiwa kōnihk. pimitisahwäwak.

" äkā wiya awiyak nōhtaw kita-kīwäw ! " itwäw.

äkwah piyisk ä-sakāyik äkutah ati-säskipayiyiwa, ä-mitihtātsik ōhi sōsimāna, ä-paskwāyik äkutah wāhyaw, ä-sakāyik äkutä ispisiyiwa.

kītahtawä äw-utākusiniyik, awīn ōma, kī-mihtiskāyiw.[3] *käkāts pahkisimuyiw ; kwayask ōmis īsi tsimasuyiwa usōsimāna. äkuyikuhk yōtiniyiw ; mispuniyiw.*

" ōtah ayātāk. ka-kawatsinānaw. mānukätāk ; mihtikuwāhp usīhtātāk. ātiht maskusiyah kit-ōtinamwak. misīhtāk kīkinaw, " itwäw.

äkusi usīhtāwak. piyisk äh-tipiskāyik, kīsihtāwak. ä-wāpaniyik, käyāpits mistahi māyi-kīsikāyiw.

" äkāya kīwätāk. ka-kawatsinānaw, " itwäw ; " nikuhtāk. äkwah ōtah skwāhtämihk tsāh-tsāhkākunāhamuk. päsīhkuk kisōsimāniwāwak kahkiyaw, " itwäw.

miyāw. kahkiyaw äkwah wīskwāhtämihk tsimahäw kahkiyaw sōsimāna. äkwah kīksäpa wayawīw, äh-utināt kahkiyaw sōsimāna. nikamōw.

" niyāk ! mātsīk ! " itwäw awa, sōsimāna kā-kīh-itisahumiht, ka-kīh-pimitisahumiht.

äkusi āhtsi piku māyi-kīsikāyiw.

äkwah äw-utākusiniyik, " kahkiyaw pīhtukäk. ōtah tawayāk iskwāhtämihk mīna wiskwāhtämihk, " itwäw.

piyis äkusi tōtamwak. kītahtawä awa kā-kīh-mitihtimiht usōsimāna äyuku kā-pīhtukäkutsiniyit usōsimāna. ä-kīh-itaskōtuyit usōsimāniwāwa, äkus īsi itaskōtuyiwa. kahkiyaw mihkōwiyiwa sōsimāna.

" äkāya wayawīk ! " itwäw.

kätahtawä kā-pah-pitihkuhtiniyik kīkwa.

ä-k-īsi-pitihkuhtiniyik käkwah, " äh hāw, äkwah wayawīk ! " itwäw awa kā-kīh-mitihtimiht usōsimāna.

äkusi wayawīwak. awin ōhi, nanātuhk pisiskiwah, ukwāskwäpayihōsah, nanātuhk ähtasiyit pisiskiwah, ōki äh-minahutsik sōsimānak, äwakunik äy-āpuhtätsik, usām ä-manitōwit awa usōsimāna kā-mitihtimiht.

---

[1] When I asked Sakewew to tell me a last story, he said, *nimästātayōhkänasinin* : "I have run entirely out of sacred stories." (Initial stem *mäst-*: "exhaust"; medial *-ātayōhkanä-*, formed from the noun *ātayōhkan* : "prehistoric spirit-animal," with post-medial *-ä-* ; Plains Cree in this way freely forms a medial from any noun; compound final *-hsin*, consisting of pre-final *-ht-* : "come down, fall, lie" and animate intransitive verb final *-in*). At last he produced this story, for which he perhaps delved deep into his memory, since it contains details about the contests of spirit-animals, as well as a number of unusual words.

[2] In this tale the position of this person is much like that of Wisahketchahk. On Star-Blanket Reserve one of my informants identified the two.

[3] Unknown word; translation a guess.

ōmis itäyihtam : " ōki awāsisak ta-wani-kiskisiwak. wīkiwāhk namuya ta-pikiskātamwak ! " itäyihtam.

tāpwä äkusih ispayiyiw.

" hāw, usīhtāk täsipitsikanah kiyām mihtsät ! " itwäw.

äkusi tōtamwak ōki awāsisak. ä-tipiskāyik, āsay mīna ntumäw sōsimāna.

" äkā wiya äkwah mätawākäk ōki sōsimānak. atuskäk. täsipitsikanah usīhtāk kiyikaw. ōtah akutāk kāhkäwakwah pīhtsāyihk, " itwäw.

äkusi tōtamiyiwa ōhi awāsisah. mayaw äh-wāpaniyik, āsay mīna nikamōw kīksäpā, ä-sōsimāt, " mātsīk ! " äh-itāt sōsimāna.

äy-utākusiniyik, " pīhtukäk kahkiyaw ! tawāyāk iskwāhtämihk wiskwāhtämihk mina ! " itwäw.

äkusi tōtamwak. āsay mīna pīhtukäkutsinwak sōsimānak. āsay mīna āpuhtäwak. äkuyikuhk āstä-kīsikāyiw. äkuyikuhk mōtsikäyihtamwak awāsisak, äh-mītsisutsik.

äkusi itahkamikisiw ; päyakwaniyiw äh-tōtahk. piyisk ōma kā-misisakāyik, äwakō wāsakām akutäyiwa wiyāsah, nanātuhk mītsiwinah, wiyawāw äh-atuskätsik. mistahi mīsihtāwak.

kītahtawä awa matsihkiwis kīksäpā kā-wayawīt, ä-ntawi-sikit, äkutä äw-uhtiniyik, kā-pä-paswämākwaniyik. nōsōskam, ä-pasut, ä-paswämākasikät. kīksäpā kisiwāk itäyihtam. päyāhtik pimuhtäw. ōma kā-mahkāskwäyāyik äh-utihtahk, āsay utākusiniyiw. käyāpits paskwāyiw. wayatsāwiw. tahki paskwämākwaniyiw. mituni äh-utākusiniyik, takuhtäw.

" äyahā, kistäsinaw takusin ! mahtih asamihk. nohtähkatäw, " itwäw awa sōsimānah kā-kīh-mitihtimiht.

äkusi kapä-tipisk mītsisōw ; nōhtähkatäw ayisk.

äkwah awa k-ātuskahāt sōsimāna äwaku ōmis īitwäw : " mahtih ta-māyikīsikāw, äkā ta-kīwät awa nistäs, äkā kit-ātsimut ! " itwäw.

tāpwä äh-wāpaniyik, māyi-kīsikāyiw.

äkusih ōmisih itwäw : " mātsīk ! " itäw sōsimānah.

äw-utākusiniyik, " pīhtukäk kahkiyaw ! " itwäw ; " kāy-itapiyäk, äkus īsi tawapik ! " itwäw.

äkusi tōtamwak. kitāpamäw awa matsihkiwis. tāpwä pīhtukäpayiyiwa sōsimāna, kuntah k-ōyātamiyit[1] *awāsisah, äh-miywäyihtamiyit, äh-wiyinihtākäyit. äkusi kitāpamäw.*

" ā, nisīmitik, ka-wītsätināwāw. usām ninōhtähkatān itäh k-ōhtuhtäyān, äkā awiyak ä-kīh-minahut, äh-nōhtähkatähk, pikuh äh-mätawähk, äkus äy-isi-mītsisuhk,[2] *" itwäw.*

" hā, nistäsä, namuya ka-kīh-mwästātitinān. usām nam āwiyak kähtäāyiwiw ōtah ; pisisik awāsisak, " itwäw awa sōsimānah k-ātuskahāt.

päyakwan äh-tōtahk.

kītahtawä ä-wayawīt kīksäpā, " mistahi mīsihtāwak ōki kā-kīh-wanihihtsik awāsisak, " itäyihtam, äh-wiyinut, " nika-kīwān. nka-ntaw-ātsimun, " äh-itäyihtahk.

tkīwäw. äkusi kīwäpahtäw.

tsīkih wīkiwāhk äh-ihtāt, " hāw, mahtih nistäs kā-kīwät, ' nka-ntawātsimun, ' k-ätäyihtahk, ta-wani-kiskisiw ! namuya kit-ātsimōw ! " itäyiham awa sōsimānah kā-kīh-mitihtimiht.

---

[1] Unknown word; translation a guess.

[2] That is, the two chiefs, in person or by proxy, would engage in contests of magic power, each setting as stakes an agreed number of his followers, to be killed and eaten by the other side, in case of defeat.

wani-kiskisiw awa matsihkiwis. ōhtāwiya wīkiyihk äh-pīhtukät, kunta pikw īsi ay-itwäw. äkusi namuya.

kītahtawä mina äh-kawāhkatusut, äkā käkway äh-mītsit, äkusi kīksäpā ä-ntawi-sikit, kā-pä-paswämākwaniyik.

" äyakunik awāsisak kā-mīsihtātsik. nka-ntawi-mītsisun," itäyihtam.

namwāts wīh-wāyōnīw. namuya nōhtä-wīhtam, iyāyaw äh-nōhtähkatät. sipwähtäw. äh-utākusiniyik takusin.

" māka mīna kistäsinaw takusin. asamihk; ta-mītsisōw," itwäw.

äkusi tāpwä asamäw.

" hāw, ōtah ka-wa-wītsätināwāw, nisīmitik," itwäw.

äkwah mistahi ayāwak mītsiwin ōki awāsisak kä-kīh-wanihihtsik.

äkusi iyikuhk mīnah äh-wiyinut, äkuyikuhk mīnah, " nka-ntaw-ātsimun," itäyihtam.

äkusi kīwäw. mitunih tsīki wīkiwāhk äh-ihtāt, " mahtih ta-wani-kiskisiw awa nistäs kā-wīh-ātsimut !" itäyihtam.

tāpwä wani-kiskisiw.

" käkwākanihk[1] *ōma ä-kīh-nātamān ?" itäyihtam.*

äkusi ay-ayāw mīn äkutah. kītahtawä mīna äh-nōhtähkatät, äh-wayawīt, mina kā-pasut, äh-paswämākwaniyik. nitsawāts sipwäpahtāw. āsay mīna ntawi-takusin.

" nisīmitik, namuy äkwah kiwīh-uhtsi-nakatitināwāw," itwäw awa.

ay-ayāw äkutah. iyikuhk mīna äh-wiyinut, kīwäw.

" namuy äkwah nika-wani-kiskisin ; awāsisak mīsihtāwak," itwäw āskaw.

mwähtsi ä-wīh-yōhtänahk wīkiwāw, " awāsisak !" itwäw ; wani-kiskisiw.

äkus īsi ay-ayāw ōhtāwiya wīkiyihk.

kītahtawä mīna äh-kawāhkatusut, mīna kīksäpā äh-wayawīt, käyāpits pä-paswämākwaniyiw.

" äyukunik nisīmak kā-mīsihtātsik !" itäyihtam.

sōskwāts sipwäpahtāw. äy-utākusiniyik, takupahtāw. äkusi ay-ayāw mīn äkutä.

" tānisi awa äsiyīhkāsut, awa kā-tipäyimiyäk, awa nisīm?"

" ' ōtah wiya wāh-wīhiyäkuh, " k-ōsōsimānisiw," kik-äsiyīhkāsināwāw,' kīh-itwäw. äkusi nama wīhkāts niwīhānān," itik awāsisah.

iyikuh mīna äh-wiyinut, " hā, nisīm, tānis ōma äsiyīhkāsuyan ?" itäw.

" ō, nistäsä, uki mānah kā-wītsäwakik, ' k-ōsōsimānisiw,' nitisiyāhkātikwak. äkusi māna itwäwak."

äkwah kīksäpā kā-kīwät, " nisīm k-ōsōsimānisiw mīsihtāw," itwäw āskaw.

wīkiwāhk ä-takusihk, " namuy äkwah ta-wani-kiskisiw ; kiyām kit-ātsimōw nistäs !" itäyihtam.

äkus äh-pīhtukät wīkiwāhk, " nisīm mīsihtāw usōsimānisiw. nikāh-utināw, äh-tāpāhkōmak, nōhtāh," itäw ōhtāwiyah ; " ōtah awa nōhkum-inān kā-wīkit, äwaku ōsisima kā-mīsihtāyit. māka nnitawi-wīhtamōwāw

[1] Unknown word (or phrase?).

nōhkum," itwäw ; "' wāpahkih kita-pä-pitsiw[1] *kōhtāwīnaw nōhkum mīnah. kahkiyaw ayīsiyiniwak ta-pä-pitsiwak,' äh-itwät nisīm k-ōsōsimānisiw," itäw ōhtāwiya.*

äkusi tāpwä miywäyihtam aw ōkimāw, ä-ntuhkämuyit awāsisah.

" kitawāsimisiwāwak kā-kīh-wanihāyäkuk kinitawäyimikuwāwak, äh-mīsihtātsik," itwäw.

tāpwä kīksäpā kahkiyaw pitsiwak, awa kutak mīn ōkimāw. tāpwä mitunih äw-utākusiniyik taku-pitsiwak. ntsawāts ay-āpihtaw ayāwak ōhi wiyāsah.

" kutak aw ukimāw nama nāntaw kik-ätuhtānāwāw. namuya kīkiwāhk kak-äsi-kīwānāwāw. ōtah kik-āyānāwāw kīkināhk. niya nōhkum āskaw wīkihk nik-āpin, āskaw kistäsinaw wīkiwāhk. äkusi kika-tōtänānaw," itwäw.

äkwah päyak mustus utakisiyah ä-kī-pāsahkik, äyakunih ntawi-miyäw ōhkumah.

" nōhku, kanawäyiht ōhi. äkāya wīhkāts utinah," itwäw.

äkwah kiyipa atih-kitānawäwak.

ōmis itwäw nāha kutak ukimāw ; — äh-utākusiniyik päh-tah-tahkiskamwān wīkiwāw matsihkiwis : " äkwah mina kimätawānānaw, nä-mitanaw kit-ähtasihk," itwäw äwak āna ukimāw.

ōhtāwiya tapahtiskwäyiyiwa.

äkusi, " tānisi, nistäsä, äy-isi-mätawāhk ? "

" hā, nisīm, miskwamīhk äh-mätawāhk. äkusi māna kōhtāwiyinaw pikuh ä-nā-nakāhtwāt,[2] *" itāw.*

" hāh, nistäsä, tahtwāw kä-mätawāhk, ta-nāh-nīsinānīwiw," itwäw awa kā-kīh-mīsihtāt.

" ' kitah-nā-nīsinānīwiw,' itwäw nisīm," itäw ōhi.

äkw ä-wāpaniyik, ituhtäwak. äkwah awa k-ōsōsimānisiw ituhtäw. pōti ayänānāw-mitanaw māmawuw ihtasiwak wiyawāw awa äh-āstwātutsik.

---

[1] A preverb particle, such as *päh* : "hither" is freely added to any verb, e.g. *päh-ituhtäw* : "he walks hither." An initial stem, such as *pā-* : "hither," is never added to a word, but appears only before non-itial elements, as in *pāpahtāw* : "he runs hither," where *-pahtā-* : "run" is an element that never occurs in word-initial. Thus,

particle:	initial stem:
papāh	*papām-* : "around, about,"
isih	*it-* : "thither, thus,"
uhtsih, ōh	*uht-* : "thence, therefore,"

and many others.

There is overlapping of two kinds. In central Algonquian certain initial and non-initial stems are alike (except for the difference implied by these names), e.g. Cree *pitsi-* and *-pitsi-* : "move camp," whence *päh-pitsiw* and *pāpitsiw* : "he moves camp hither," probably with some difference of meaning.

The other kind of overlapping is peculiar to Cree, and probably due to phonetic alterations which shifted the boundary between *t* (which occurs at the end of many initial stems) and *ts* (which occurs as the penult of many particles). Thus *pätsāstam-* : "facing hither," as, e.g. in *pätsāstamuhtäw* : "he walks facing hither" looks as though it contained a preverb particle **pätsih* : "hither," which otherwise is unknown in Plains Cree, or else an initial stem *päts-*, a form unparalleled in Cree and in the related languages. The initial stem here was really **pät-* ; Cree *pätsāstam-* is a phonetic or analogic modification of **pätāstam-*, cf. Menomini *pītā'namōhnew* : "he walks facing hither." Similarly Cree *misatim* : "horse" for **mistastim* (or **mists-astim*, or **mis-astim*). Cf. Introduction.

[2] Freely formed secondary derivative *nakāhtwāw* : "he stops people," from a freely formable **nakāhäw*, **nakāhtāw* : "he stops him, it"; cf. *sākuhäw, sākuhtāw* : "he overcomes him, it," and *sākuhtwāw* : "he overcomes people." Yet the actual translation is a guess.

äkus äw-utihtahkik miskwamīhk, äkwah awa kā-manitōwit kutak ukimāw uskinīkīma, äwakuni nätä si-kwāskuhtiyiwa miskwāmīhk. pōtih nikikwah kā-kōkiyit miskwamīhk, äkwah nätä tāwakām äkutä kā-mōskipäyit. kāwih kōkiyiwa, äkwah ōtah itah kā-kīh-uhtsi-kōkiyit, äkutah wäh-pä-pasikōyit ayīsiyiniwah.

äkwah matsihkiwis uhtāwiya äsi-kwāskuhtiyit, pōt āwa sākwäs kōkīw itah kā-kīw-uhtsi-kōkiyit nikikwah. itäh kā-kīh-päkupäyit, äkutä päkupäw awa matsihkiwis uhtāwiya. āsay mīna käw-uhtsi-kōkiyit, äkutah uhtsi pä-pasikōyiwa uhtāwiya.

sākuwäw matsihkiwis, " nāh-nam āwiyak ! " äh-itwät.

" namuya ! kipaskäyākawināwäw. kunt ītah miskwamiyah kīh-pikwāskawāt kōhtāwiy, ' nāh-nam āwiyak ! ' ka-kīh-itwāhtānaw ! " itäw ; " māka tāpi-pimutam,[1] *" itäw.*

äkwah awa kutak misiwä tsah-tsāhkasinahikāsōw. kawipayihōw, kuntah äh-ati-kāh-kwätipipayihut äyīni-kinusäw. namwāts pisuskawäw miskwamiyah. nätäh tāwakām mīna äkutä äh-wayawīt, äkutäh uhtsi papätsāstamuhtäw awa ayīsiyiniw kā-kinusäwit.

äkwah awa k-ōsōsimānisiw nikamōw, äh-pākāskwāhikät usōsimānah.

" nikik misinihāw[2] *! "*

äh-itutāmut,[3] *kawipayihōw : amisk. amiskōwiw. päkamahwātsi miskwamiyah, anta misiwä kā-ma-matwäskupayiyik.*

pāh-pimituhtäw, ä-nikamut, " nīkān ntamiskōwin ! " äh-itwät.

kōkīw. nätä tāwakām kītahtawä miskwamiy kuntah kā-tsimasut, miskwamiy äh-wayawīwäpiskawāt.

kunt äkwah sākuwäw matsihkiwis, ōpispāskwatōwi-pakamākan[4] *äh-tahkunahk. kähtsināhōwak äh-sākōtsihihtsik. hāh, paskiyākäw k-ōsōsimānisiw.*

häw, äkwah äw-utākusiniyik, kisiwāhtwāw matsihkiwis ōhtāwiya.

" nkutwāsu-mitanaw kit-ähtasinäniwiw wāpahkih. ' na-nā-nīsinäniwiw, ' itwäw, " itäw.

" ' äha' , ' itwä, nisīm, " itwäw.

āsay äkusi kīksäpā, " tānisi äy-isi-mätawähk, nistäsä ? " itäw.

" päyak wanaskāt[5] *äh-wīh-pimutamihk. äyaku māna sōskwāts nipaskiyākawinān, " itwäw matsihkiwis.*

kīksäpā ituhtäwak. hā, tāpwä nīsusāpu-mitanaw ayīsiyiniwak ayāwak äkutah.

" äkwah awa nīkān kā-pimutahk nīsutsihts kita-pataham ! " itwäw awa k-ōsōsimānisiw.

pōtih tāpwä äkuyikuhk patahamiyiwa.

ōhtāwiyah äkwah pāmutamiyit, " tsīki nīsutsihts, apisīs ayiwākäsīs tapataham awa ! " itäw uhtāwiya.

tāpwä āsay matsihkiwis sākuwātäwak. äkwah awa kutak āsay mīna pimutam ; min äwaku käkāts tāwaham.

---

[1] The term *pimutam :* "he shoots (it)" is used for taking one's turn in any kind of contest.

[2] Unknown word; translation a guess.

[3] Unknown word; translation a guess.

[4] If correctly recorded, probably some kind of reduplication of *piskw- :* "lump," as in *piskwahtsäw :* "it is lumpy land."

[5] I do not know whether *päyak wanaskāt* is one or two words, i.e. whether the independent word *wanaskāt* is found in Cree or not.

äkwah awa usōsimānah isiwäpinäw. sämāk kunt ītä itakutsiniyiwa. pīs kwaskipayiyiyiwa.[1] *pōtih kwayask kā-mōskistamiyit usōsimāna ; tāwaham. uhtakutsin awa sōsimān, kunta kā-säkuwät matsihkiwas, äh-atipakamahwät ōhi astwākäwinah.*

hāh, äw-utākusiniyik, " āh, ayänānäw-mitanaw äkwah kit-ätasināniwiw, " itāw.

" tānis äkwah, nistäsä ? "

" uma kā-sōskwāk miskwamīhk ä-kakwä-nakatituhk. nama wīhkāts paskiyawāwak, " itwäw.

" hā, äkusi ! "

wiyāpaniyik, ituhtäwak. pōtih āsay ayāyiwa äkutä ; äkwah ay-isisipwähtäwak. ōhtāwiya awa k-ōsōsimānisiw akāmihk wāhyaw uhtsipayiyiwa.

itä täkuhtätsik, " hāw, kimätawāhtānaw ! kikakwä-nakatituhtānaw ! " itāw matsihkiwis uhtāwiya.

kawipayihōw, nikikwah äh-ati-sōskupayihuyit. mähkawikiyiwa.

" hāw, nōhtāh, pimitisahikäh ! " itäw uhtāwiya.

äkwah ōmis ītwäyiwa uhtāwiya : " nama nika-kä-atimāw, nikusä ; nitatsiwihik, " itwäyiwa.

äh-kawipayihut, pōt āwa sākwäs. wīst äyiwähk sōskupayihōw.

äkwah awa k-ōsōsimānisiw wītsi-pakäsah äwakuh, " uskats äh-pawāmiyān, atihkwasiniy[2] *nikīh-kitimākäyimik ! " itwäw, äh-kawipayihut.*

kisīkutsin aw ātihkwasiniy.

äkwah awa k-ōsōsimānisiw, " uskats äh-pawāmiyān, ākwask kik-āpin. āpihtaw miskwamīhk kika-tähkitsäskiwakisinin[3] *! " itwäw ; " uskats äh-pawāmiyān, näyāhtakāw*[4] *nikī-kitimākäyimikun ! " itwäw.*

tāpwä pimitisahwäw.

" k-äspisakutäki mōsasiniyah, äkuyikuhk kik-äspisīn, nisōsimān ! " itwäw.

tāpwä äy-utihtahk upawāmōwin, awīn ōma, kiy-ākwaskīw. pikiwah pasakuskiwah mistahi usäpiyiwa ōhtāwiya ; tsīk äkutah at-āyāyiwa.

" nōhtāh, mitsimīw utäh utahk ! " äkusih itäw.

nawatsi-mitsimīw sōsimānihk, äh-atimāt ōhi nikikwah.

" kikakwä-nakatituhtānaw ! " itäw.

" äya' ! ata wäy āni nitispisipayin ! " itik.

äkwah ōhi atihkwasiniyah. tihtipitsäskiwakisin.

" kikakwä-nakatituhtānaw ! " itäw.

" äya ' ! itāp anih nitispisipayin ! " itäw.

tāpwä nakasiwäwak matsihkiwis uhtāwiya. äkusi äkwah kisiwāhāwak ōki.

" hāw, äyāhtasihk[5] *äkwah ! " itāwak.*

äkwah piku ta-nipahiht matsihkiwis ; nama ta-kīh-sākuhtwātsik.

" äkwah namuya ka-tāpi-pimutänānaw ! " itāwak.

äkwah awa k-ōsōsimānisiw ntawi-ntumäw awāsisah.

---

[1] Probably an error of record; perhaps for *kwäsk-* : "twisting to one side."

[2] Literally "elk-stone," but what is it? *mōsw-asiniy, mōsasiniy* : "moose-stone" is a gun-bullet.

[3] *tähk-* is unknown to me; perhaps an error of record for *tihtip-* : "turning over or round," cf. below. The medial *-tsäskiwak-* means "mud, sticky stuff."

[4] Translation a guess; cf. *näyāw* : "promontory."

[5] The first two syllables may be wrongly recorded.

" hāw, awa kōhkuminaw uhtsīhkamāhk. mituni t-āyāpisāsinwa. tsīsawātamuk ōhi utakisiyah," itwäw.

äkwah wiyāpaniyik, sōskwāts ispitsiwak kahkiyaw sisunä sākahikanihk.

äkwah, " nisīm, kika-sākuhtwān tsī ? " itäw.

" namuya. māskōts usām ayiwāk at-āyimaniyiwa," itāw awa matsihkiwis.

mistahih āyimäyihtam.

äkwah awa nīkān pimutam matsihkiwis uhtāwiya. kā-wītsi-pakäsiyit kā-misikititsik sihkihpak äkutōwiw, pikw ītah äh-pikwāskāwāt miskwamiyah ; äkwah awa matsihkiwis uhtāwiya itōwahk k-āyōtōtsikātihtsik[1] *äkutōwahk. äkwah kāwi itah wäh-päkupäyitsi, äkutah uhtsi-kōkīw awa matsihkiwis uhtāwiya.*

" hā, tāpwä paskiyawāwak ! " itwäyiwa.

ayis tāpi-pimutam. äkwah awa k-ōsōsimānisiw wītsi-pakäsah āsay mīn äyaku nikamōw, " nitamiskōwin niya ! " äh-itwäyit.

mitunih misikitiw amisk. päkamahahahki, usuy uhtsi misiwä mamatwäskupayiyiw. äkusih asawāts itäh uhtsi kōkīw, kunta māna miskwamiyah kā-sähkwäpiyit,[2] *itäh piyäkupäyitsi kätahtawä mitun ōtah sisunä piyäkupäyit.*

ōmis ītäw ustäsah mīn ōhi amiskwah : " iyikuhk takusiniyāni, kikamātahpinatāwāwak, äkā ayiwāk kīh-tōtamāni. iyikuhk takusiniyāni ; misawāts nika-kiskäyihtän, awiyak nīkān kä-pakamahwāt awiya. äkusi namuya kwayask kit-äspayiw, " itwäw.

nikamōw : " niyah niwāpamākōwin[3] *! " itwäw, miskwamīhk äh-pakitsīt.*

papāmuhtäw miskwamīhk, kuntah äh-pā-pimituhtät, piyisk k-ātihsāpupäyit miskwamiyah. tsähkatahwātsih miskwamiyah, kuntah misiwä kā-ma-matwäskupayiyit. āhkami-kituw mākwa. piyisk waskitisik nipīwiyiw, äh-āhkami-kitut. pīsk yōtinipayāstaniyiw. äkuyikuhk sākuwäw matsihkiwis.

" namuya wiyawāw nipiy usīhtāwak ! wiya nisīm nipiy usīhtāw ! māka, ' iyikuhk takuhtäyāni, ' ä-kīh-itwät nisīm ! nīsu niwī-kakäkināwak, ä-wīhmōwakik, äh-wiyinutsik. ayis niya nisīm nkīh-utināw, " itwäw.

kōkīw awa mākwa, akāmihk nätä kāh-matwä-kitut mākwa, äkutä mina. piyis mā-mahkāskāw ōma sākahikan. piyis nama käkway miskwamiy. kītahtawä pä-kōkīw ōtah kisiwāk.

piyäkupät, " hāw, āstamitik ! kahkiyaw äkāya awiyak nipahihk ! āstamitik ! " itäw ; " äkwah ōhi utsakisīsah tahtuh äh-pāpayihtātsik, uhpimäh kit-āti-nīpawiwak. tahtuh äkā äh-pāpayihtātsik mīna äwakunik uhpimä ta-nīpawiwak, " itwäw.

äkwah ātiht pāpayihtāwak.

" ā, kiyīsāhkamikisit,[4] *tahtuh kā-pāpayihtāyäk, mistikwah kik-ōmītsiwināwāw, ātiht maskusiyah. ' ntaw-uyasuwāh ! ' ä-kiy-itikawiyān. kiya, nistäsä, ayīsiyiniwak nihtāwikitwāwi, uhpikitwāwi, ' pahkwatsōw,*[5] *' kik-*

---

[1] The allusion is plainly to the hell-diver duck; the difficulty is that the present passage seems to imply a difference between the "diver-duck" (*sihkihp*) and "the one that is made merry over."

[2] Unknown word; perhaps error of record.

[3] One expects *niwāpimākōwin ;* if the text is correct, it contains an archaic or pseudo-archaic medial stem *-amākw- :* "loon."

[4] Probably red *hk* for the final *t ;* I have so translated.

[5] Allusions to the lynx may be introduced on my account.

äsiyīhkātikwak ; kiya sakāhk kik-ōh-pimātsihun ; äkusi kiya, nistäsä, āsay kikīs-ōyapin. äkwah kiya, nōhtāh, ' sākwäs, ' kik-äsiyīhkātik ayīsiyiniw ; nipīhk kik-ōtaskīn ; māka nanātuhk käkway kika-mītsin, kinäpikusak wiyās ; kā-tahtō-wiyāsiwit kik-ōh-pimātsihun. hā, äkusi nanānis, nanātuhk kik-äsi-pisiskiwinānaw. ayīsiyiniwak nihtāwikitwāwi, kahkiyaw kika-sākōtsihikunawak. niva, ' kihtsi-wāpi-mākwah, ' nik-ätikawin. māka namuy ōtah niwīh-ayān. kā-misāk nipiy äkutä niwīh-ayān ," itwäw.

äkuyikuhk äskwāk ātayōhkäwin.

Once upon a time some people dwelt in a place, and there were two chiefs, and one of them was Silly-Fellow's father. Then at one time many of the children played at throwing snow-darts.

"Let us all try to outdo each other throwing snow-darts, and see who is the best at it, whose snow-dart lands farthest away," said one child, who was being brought up by his grandmother.

So they threw their snow-darts. Then they went and picked up their snow-darts one after the other, as they came to them. At last only one boy's snow-dart was left lying on the snow. They went after it.

"Let no one go home before we have got it!" he said.

At last they found that it had gone into a wood. As they followed the track of that snow-dart, across a far stretch of prairie there, into the woods it had sped.

Presently, as evening came on, they were deep in the woods. It was near sunset; there, standing straight upright in the snow, like this, was the boy's snow-dart. Just then the wind began to blow; it snowed.

"Let us stay here. We might freeze. Let us set up a shelter; let us build a hut of wood. Some of you are to gather grasses. Make our hut big," he said.

Accordingly, they built it. At last, when night came, they had finished it. The next morning it was still very stormy weather.

"Let us not go home. We should freeze," he said; "Gather firewood. And here by the door, dig away the snow. All of you bring me your snow-darts," he said.

They were given to him. Then he stuck all the snow-darts on end into the floor, opposite the doorway. Then, early in the morning, he went out, taking all the snow-darts. He sang.

"Be off! Hunt!" he sang whose snow-dart had been followed to that place, had been pursued across the land.

The storm kept on.

Then, in the evening, "All of you come indoors. Form two lines from the doorway to the opposite wall," he ordered.

Soon they had done this. Then presently the snow-dart of him whose snow-dart had been tracked, came flying into the hut. In the order in which their snow-darts had gone, in that order they now came, one following the other. All the snow-darts were stained with blood.

"Do not go out of the house!" he said.

Presently some things were falling with a repeated thud.

When those things had fallen with a thud, "There, now go out!" said he whose snow-dart had been tracked.

Then they went out. What was there, but all kinds of game-animals, jumping deer, all the game-animals there are? For these snow-darts had killed game, and it was they were supplying meat, so much of a manitou person was he whose snow-dart had been tracked.

Thus he thought: "Let these children forget. Let them not get homesick!" he thought.

Really, it was so.

"Come, set up a great many drying frames!" he said.

Those children did as he had bidden. At dark, again he asked for the snow-darts.

"Do not now play with these snow-darts. Work. Set up drying frames everywhere. Hang up the dried meat indoors here," he ordered.

The children did as he said. As soon as day broke, early in the morning again he sang, as he flung the snow-darts, bidding the snow-darts "Hunt!"

At nightfall, "Come inside, all of you! Form two lines from the door to the opposite wall!" he ordered.

They did so. Again the snow-darts came flying into the house. Again they had supplied meat. By this time the day was done. The children were happy, because they could eat.

That was the way he managed things; it was always the same thing that he did. In time, all over that large grove pieces of meat were hanging, all kinds of food supplies, as a result of their work. They had a big store of meat.

Then at one time, when this Silly-Fellow had gone out in the morning, ..., from the direction whence the wind was blowing there came the smell of fat meat. He set out in the direction of the scent, following the smell of fat meat. In the early morning he thought it was near. He walked slowly. When he reached that big wood, it was already evening. Again he came to open country. He broke into a run. All the while he smelled the scent of fat meat. When it was well on toward dark, he got there.

"Oho, our elder brother has come! Give him something to eat. He is hungry," said he whose snow-dart had been tracked.

Then he ate all night; for he was hungry.

Then the one who made the snow-darts work said, "Let there be stormy weather, so that this big brother of mine may not go home and tell what he has seen!" he said.

Really, the next morning, there was stormy weather.

Then he spoke thus: "Hunt!" he said to the snow-darts.

Towards evening, "Come indoors, all of you!" he said; "As you sat before, sit now, in two rows!" he commanded.

They did so. Silly-Fellow watched them. Really, the snow-darts came flying into the house, and the boys cheered loudly with joy, and set about cleaning the game. He watched them.

"Oh, little brothers, let me stay with you. I go hungry too much in the place whence I come, because no one there can kill any game, and all go hungry and eat only as one eats after a contest," he said.

"Oh, big brother, we could not refuse you. Especially, as there is no older person here, but only children," said he who made the snow-darts work.

He did always the same thing.

Then, early one morning, as he went out of the house, "A great supply of food have these children who have been lost," he thought, and, because he had got fat now, "I shall go home. I shall go tell what I have seen," thought he.

He went home. He ran for home.

When he had got near their dwelling-place, "Now then, let my big brother who is going home thinking, "I shall go tell what I have seen,' let him lose his memory! Let him not tell!" thought he whose snow-dart had been tracked.

That Silly-Fellow lost his memory. As he entered his father's dwelling, he said all kinds of disconnected things. So nothing came of it.

After a time, when he was again starved lean, for he had nothing to eat, ... there came the odour of fat meat.

"That is the boys storing up food. I shall go there and eat," he thought.

He did not even think of going back. He did not want to tell about it, but thought only of his hunger. He started out. Towards nightfall he got there.

"Here comes our big brother again. Give him something to eat; let him eat," said he.

So he was fed.

"Now, let me stay here with you, my little brothers," he said.

By this time, much food had those children who had been lost.

Then, when he had again got fat, again he thought, "Let me go tell what I have seen."

So he went home. When he had got very near their dwelling-place, "Let my big brother lose his memory, who is going to tell what he has seen!" thought he.

Really, he lost his memory.

"What on earth was I going after?" he thought.

So then he stayed there again. After a time, when again he was going hungry, as he stepped out of the tent, again he smelled an odour of fat meat. Off he ran; what else was there to do? Again he reached the place.

"Little brothers, this time I shall not leave you any more," he said.

He stayed there. When he had got fat again, he went home.

"This time I will not forget: the boys have a supply of meat," he said at intervals.

Just as he was about to open the door-flap of their tipi, "The boys!" he said; he had forgotten.

So then he stayed in his father's tipi.

After a time, when he was again lean with hunger, as he stepped out of doors in the morning, again there came the scent of fat meats.

"That is my little brothers laying up a store of meat!" he thought.

At once, off he ran. Towards nightfall, he got there, on the run. So then he again stayed there.

"What is his name, his who directs you, this little brother's of mine?"

" 'When here you wish to call me by name, "Little Snow-Dart," you will call me,' he has said. And so we never call him by his name," the boys told him.

When he was fat again, "Well, little brother, what is your name, really?" he asked him.

"Why, big brother, they who are with me here call me 'Little Snow-Dart.' That is what they always say."

Then, in the morning, when he went home, "My brother Little Snow-Dart has a store of meat," he said at intervals.

When he arrived at their dwelling-place, "Now let him not forget; let my big brother tell what he has seen!" thought he.

So, when he entered their tipi, "My brother, Little Snow-Dart, has a store of meat. I have taken him up, adopted him, father," he told his father; "This grandmother of ours who lives right here, it is her grandson has the store of meat. But I am going to tell my grandmother about it," he said; " 'Tomorrow let our father move his camp here, and my grandmother, too. All the people are to move camp to this place,' says my brother, Little Snow-Dart," he told his father.

Truly, then, this chief was glad that the boys were inviting people.

"Your boys whom you had lost want you to come to them, because they have got a store of meat," he said.

So, in the morning, they all moved camp, including that other chief. Late in the evening they arrived with their camps. They had to share the meat half and half.

"You are not to go anywhere in the precinct of this other chief. You are not to go back to your homes. You are to stay here in our house. As for me, some of the time I shall stay in my grandmother's tent, and some of the time in my big brother's. That is the way we shall do," he commanded.

Then he went and gave his grandmother the entrails of a buffalo, which they had dried.

"Grandmother, take care of these. Do not ever take them," he said.

Then, soon they had eaten up all the food.

Thus spoke that other chief —at nightfall there came a kicking at the tipi of Silly-Fellow and his family: "Now again we shall engage in a contest, to the number of forty," said that other chief.

His father bowed his head.

Then, "In what way, big brother, is it that they contend?"

"Oh, little brother, it is a contest on the ice. And in this our father is always defeated," he was told.

"Now then, big brother, in each contest let there be two instead of one on a side," said he who had made the supply of meat.

" 'There are to be two on a side,' says my brother," he told those others.

Then, the next morning, they went to the place. Little Snow-Dart went there, too. He saw that eighty was the number of them, all together, whom they and the other were staking. Then, when they had come to the ice, the servant of that other chief, who had spirit power, leaped out upon the ice. And behold, there was an otter diving into the ice, and there, out in the middle of the lake, there it came bobbing forth. Again it dived, and back here, whence it first had dived, he rose to his feet in human form.

Then, when Silly-Fellow's father leaped forth, there, a mink was diving where the otter had dived in. Where the other had come to the surface, there Silly-Fellow's father came up. Then, again, where the other had dived in, Silly-Fellow's father rose to his feet.

Silly-Fellow began to cheer, crying, "They are done for!"

"No! You have been defeated. If your father had broken through the ice, no matter where, then we could have cried, 'They are done for!' " he was told; "But he has merely followed the other's lead," he was told.

The second contestant of the other side was speckled all over his body. He threw himself to the ground, and there was a muskalonge flopping about. It did not even touch the ice as it went. Then, when it came forth yonder at the centre of the expanse, from there came walking in human form that man who had been a fish.

Then Little Snow-Dart chanted, pounding with his snow-dart as though on a drum.

"The otter is beaten!"

As he sang, he threw himself to the ground: a beaver. He turned into a beaver. Whenever he struck the ice, everywhere crashing it would break.

He walked in different crosswise ways, singing, and, "First I am a beaver!" were his words.

He dived. Suddenly over yonder, in the middle of the lake, the ice stood pell-mell on end, as he flung it aside in emerging.

At this, Silly-Fellow cheered wildly, and laid hold of his knobbed war-club. They saw beyond doubt that they were defeated. Oh, Little Snow-Dart had defeated the opponent.

That evening Silly-Fellow's father was enviously hated.

"Let the number be sixty tomorrow. 'Let the contestants be in pairs,' says he," he was told.

"Say, 'Yes,' little brother," said he.

Then, early in the morning, "What kind of contest is it, big brother," he asked him.

"One withy is to be shot. In this we are always defeated at once," said Silly-Fellow.

In the morning they went there. Really, there were a hundred and twenty men there.

"Now let him who shoots first miss the mark by two fingers!" said Little Snow-Dart.

Really, by even that much the other missed the mark.

Then, when his father shot, "Close to two fingers, by a tiny bit more, let this one miss it!" he said of his father.

Truly, already Silly-Fellow's side were being whooped at. Then the second opponent shot at it; he too almost hit it.

Then he flung his snow-dart at it. At once it went speeding in every direction through the air. At last it whirled round. Lo and behold, his snow-dart made straight for the mark; he struck it square. Down fell the snow-dart, and wildly whooped Silly-Fellow, as he began to club, one after the other, those who had been set as stakes.

Then, in the evening, "Now, this time let the number be eighty," he was told.

"How is it to be this time, big brother?"

"Over the smooth place on the ice there will be a race. They are never beaten at this," he said.

"Oh, very well!"

The next morning they went there. There, the others were there already; then they started. Little Snow-Dart's father was coming a long ways off, from the far shore.

When they got there, "Oho, do not forget we were to have a contest! Do not forget we were to race each other!" Silly-Fellow's father was told.

He flung himself down, and off went an otter, sliding over the smooth surface. It went very fast.

"Come, father, go in pursuit!" he said to his father.

Then his father said, "I shall not be able to overtake him, my son; he has far outdone me," said he.

When he flung himself down, there was a mink. It, too, as well as it might, went gliding over the ice.

Then the opponent who was paired with Little Snow-Dart, said, "When first I dreamt, the elk-ball took pity on me!" and threw himself on the ground.

Swiftly that elk-ball went speeding.

Then Little Snow-Dart said, "As first I dreamt, on ahead you will stay still. Half-way across the ice you will flounder as though mired!" he said; "When first I dreamt, the treetop took pity on me!" he said.

Truly, he went pursuing the other.

"As swiftly as speeds a bullet through the air, so swiftly will you speed, my snow-dart!" he said.

Truly, when he reached that which had befriended him in dreams, why, there he was in the lead. In pitch, in sticky gum his father was badly stuck; close to that place the others were passing.

"Father, hold fast here, at the rear!" he said to him.

He seized hold of the snow-dart as it passed him, and overtook that otter.

"Do not forget we were racing!" he said to it.

"Yes! Don't you see how fast I am going?" it answered him.

Then that elk-ball. It was floundering in something that held it stuck fast.

"Do not forget we were racing!" he said to it.

"Yes! Can't you see how fast I am going?" it said to him.

Truly, Silly-Fellow's father and his partner were outstripping the others. This made the others angry.

"Come, in full number now!" they were told.

Now there was danger that Silly-Fellow might be killed; they could not possibly defeat the others.

"And this time we shall not do as the other does!" they were told.

Then Little Snow-Dart went and called the boys.

"Now, go help our grandmother. They are to be very small; cut up those entrails," he said.

Then, the next morning, at once they all went in a body to the edge of the lake.

Then, "Little brother, shall you win?" he asked him.

"No. Doubtless the other is too formidable," Silly-Fellow was told. He was very much distressed.

Then Silly-Fellow's father had the first turn. His opponent was in the shape of a great diver-duck, crushing through the ice wherever it went; and Silly-Fellow's father was one of those that are made merry over. Then from wherever the other came to the surface, from there Silly-Fellow's father would emerge after his dive.

"Ho, truly they are beaten!" said the others.

For he was but following the other's lead. Then the opponent who was paired with Little Snow-Dart, he too began to sing, saying, "I am a beaver, I!"

Very large was the beaver. Whenever it struck anything with its tail, in all directions it went crashing. It dived from the other direction, and always the ice went breaking, wherever it came to the surface. Suddenly it came to the surface right there, very close to the shore.

Thus he spoke to his big brother and to that beaver: "When I arrive, you may begin to slay them, in case I cannot surpass what has been done. Not before I arrive; I shall be sure to know it, if anyone before that strike down any other. If that is done, things will not go well," he said.

He sang: "I am a white loon, I!" he sang, as he alighted on the ice.

He walked about on the ice, crossing it in every direction, until at last water began to seep through the ice. Whenever he struck the ice with his beak, on all hands it would move with crashing noise. Unceasingly the loon gave its call. At last the water stood on top of the ice, as he unceasingly gave his call. At last a wind began to blow. Then Silly-Fellow whooped.

"It is not they are making the water to be! It is my brother is making the water to be! But, 'Not before I arrive,' said my brother! Two of them I shall pick out to eat, fat ones. For it was I adopted him as my little brother," he cried.

The loon dived, and lo, yonder on the far shore a loon was giving its call, and over here another. At last the lake ran to high waves. At last the ice was gone. Suddenly he bobbed up right close by.

As he came to the surface from the water, "Now, then, all of you, come here! Let none of you slay anyone! Come here!" he ordered them; "Now as many as cast up these bits of entrail, let them stand off to one side. And as many as do not cast them up, let them too stand to one side," he ordered.

Then some of them threw them up.

"Now then, when the order of things is completed, as many of you as have cast it up, trees shall be your food, and grasses, of some. For, 'Go lay down a law!' I was told. You, my brother, when mortal men grow forth and flourish, 'Lynx,' they will call you; you will find your sustenance in the woods; and so you, my brother, have found your place. And you, my father, 'Mink,' mortal man will call you; by the water you will have your domain; but all kinds of things you will eat, the flesh of little snakes; from whatever creature has flesh you will get your life. So now in different directions, into the form of different animals you will all go. When mortal men come into being, they will overcome you all. As for me, 'Great White Loon,' I shall be called. But not here shall I stay. I shall stay by the Great Water," he said.

This is the end of the sacred story.

(15) Pine Root

Mrs. Maggie Achenam

kā-wīhkaskusahk.

kätahtawä ayīsiyiniwak äh-mihtsätukamikisitsik, kihtimiw äkutah päyak uskinīkiw, kākikä äh-pimisihk. piyis tān-tahtw askiy, piyis watapiyah misiwä ōhpikiniyiwa, iyikuhk äh-kihtimit.

kätahtawä ä-pa-pimisihk, kā-pä-kitōtiht. äh-itāpit, iskwāhtämihk kā-paspāpiyit uskinīkiskwäwah näwu. mistahi māh-miyusiyiwa.

" kītimusinaw, " itik, " kīh-pa-pimisin watapīw-iyin, " itik.

äkusi sipwähtäyiwa. waniskāpahtāw ; paspaskipayihäw uwatapiyimah ; nawaswäw uskinīkiskwäwah. kutakah mīnah päy-atimik uskinīkiwah ; āsa mīna kutakah ; näwiwak nāpäwak, äh-pimitisahwātsik wītsimusiwäwah. wāhyaw äkwah ä-ihtātsik, kätahtawä nakiyiwah.

" nītimusä, watapīw-iyin, nisīm awa kiwīh-wīhtamātn tānisiy äsiyīhkāsut : näm īskuh k-ōsähtsāk pīwanuskwäw isiyīhkāsōw. "

kwa sipwähtäwak. mistahi misi-piwaniyiw. taswäkinäw utakuhpah ; äkutah sīpāh pa-pimuhtäwak. umā k-ōsähtsāyik äh-utihtahkik, āstä-kīsikāyiw.

āsa mīnah pähikwak.

" kutak äkwah nisīm, nītimusä, watapīw-iyin, mistahi kā-kisihk isiyīhkāsōw, " itäw.

äkusi minah sipwähtäwak. mituni kisināyiw ; usitiwäwah mitunih wiy-āhkwatsiwak. ätataw takuhtäwak ; käkäts kawatsiwak.

äkusi äkwah sipwähtäwak. kätahtawä äkwah nāpäwak, täpwātäw iskwäwah.

" tsäskwah ! " itäw ; " awa nisīm ka-wīhtamātin nīstah äsiyīhkāsut : uskātsihku-kimiwan näm īskuh k-ōsähtsāk. "

äkwah sipwähtäwak.

" ī, tāpwä miyuyīhkāsōw kītimusinaw ! "

kway äh-sipwähtäyit, misi-kimiwaniyiw. äkwah sipwähtäwak. āsa mīnah täpwätäw.

" kutak nisīm ōmis isiyīhkāsōw : kīsōpwäw näm īskōh k-ōsähtsāk. "

mituni kīsupwäw ; äkwah ōk īskwäwak mustāpäkasäwak[1] *iskwäwak ispimihk isih. äh-utihtahkik usähtsāw, pōni-kimiwan.*

" hä äy ! " itwäwak ; " tāpwä āyimaniyiw kītimusinaw usīmah äsiyīhkāsōyit ! "

" äkwah niyah, näm īskōh k-ōsähtsāk k-āsä-mōhkituhtäw nitisiyīhkāsun. "

tāpwä mistahä asähtäwak ōki.

" k-āsä-mōhkituhtäw ! tāpwa miywāsiniyiw kītimusinaw uwīhōwin ! "

äkwah nōtukäsiw āh-asawāpamäw utawāsimisah.

---

[1] This feature certainly does not belong here; it spoils the climactic point of the next stroke.

" tānisi ōh käkway äh-isi-mōhtsōwisiyäk ? "

" awas ! nītimusinān uwīhōwin[1]*! " itwäwak.*

wīkiwāw äh-utihtahkik, äkuyikuhk kwayask pimuhtäwak.

kutak äkwah waskāhikanis namuya ä-kīsōwāyik, äkutah asiwasōwak ōkih mōsāpäwak. nama käkway kutawānāpisk. mituni wīh-āhkwatsiwak. äkwah päyak pimutāhkwäw ; pīhtsāyihk äkutah waskāhikanisihk mā-mōminäwak utähiminah, ātah äh-pāh-pāhkatsiyit mistsikusah.

äkwah awa kisäyiniw, " ntawāpam ; t-ōsāmāskatsiwak, " itik uwīki-mākanah.

paspāpiw : kīh-mā-mōminäyiwah mīnisah. kīwäw.

" nääh ! " itwäw kisäyiniw ; " māh-mōminäwak, itah misawāts kiw-ōh-pimātisiwakwä ! " itwäw.

kīhtwām äh-tipiskāyik āsa mīnah ayiwākäs äkwah ksināyiw. āsay mīnah pimutahkwäw. āsa mīnah mōminäwak ayah misāskwatōminah.

" ntawi-paspāpi ! "

ntawi-paspāpiw nōtukäsiw.

" mā-mōminäwak aniki, kisäyiniw. nnōhtähkatāh ! ah, ta-māh-mātsī-wak ! "

äkwah mātsītisahwāwak.[2] *wāpamäwak kwaskwäpayihōsah, äh-mih-kusiyit. nawaswātäwak. pimwäw ; mōhtāskikanähusōw.*

kīhtwām kīskwähkwasiw nōtukäsiw.

" äh-pawātamān nnahāhkisīm iskah äh-nipahāt kwaskwäpayihōsäh āh-mihkusiyit, utah isk äh-pimi'pahtāt, äh-mōwak. "

äkusi äkwah mātsīw ; wāpamäw ; pimwäw äkwah utāhk isih ; nipahäw. kīwätsitāpäw. pīhtukäw wīkiwāhk.

" äōkunih kā-wīh-muwāt nōtukäsiw ! "

äh-yōhtānāhk nōtukäsiw, " hä äy äy ! tāpwä nikakwāhyakihik, nipa-wäkanah ! "

" misi-wīhkuhtuk ; iyawis pakāsimihk , " itwäw.

iyawis pakāsimäwak ; äkwah ä-misi-wīhkuhtutsik, kitamwäwak. äkusi äkwah sākōtsihäw usikusah.

äkwah atsusisah usīhtäw nāō. äkwah ituhtäw uwītsäwākanah itah kā-kīh-nipahimiht. ispāhkäw.

" awas, awas, awas ! ka-pistahutināwāw ! "

kā-tsīpipayiyit, āsa mīna kutak ispāhkäw. käyāpits äkus itäw, kā-pasikusipahtāyit. käyāpit nīsu pimisiniyiwah. āsay mina ispāhkäw ; waniskāpahtāyiwah. äyakw äs āwa kā-waniskāpahtāt matsihkiwis.

" ä-pmātisiyān tsī ? "

" äha' ; äk äh-pimātisiyin, māka k-ōh-pīkiskwäyan, ayiwāk ihkin ! " itwäw äsah.

" tāpwä nimiywäyihtän äh-pimātisiyān ! hay hay hay hay ! " itwäw äsah.

äkwah awa matsihkiwis kīh-kīwähtahiskwäwäw äsah äyukw ānih.

namuy äkuyikuh kinwāw ātayōhkäwin äh-kīsihtāyān.

---

[1] That is, if the old woman discusses their action, she is in danger of unknowingly speaking her son-in-law's name, which, of course, is tabu to her.

[2] From here on the story is badly shortened.

Once upon a time, where some people dwelt, a certain youth was so lazy that he was always lying down. At last, after I don't know how many years, the fibrous roots of the white pine had grown up all round his body, so lazy was he.

Then at one time, as he lay there, someone came and called to him. When he looked, there, peeping in at the door, were four young women. Every one of them was very pretty.

"Our sweetheart," they said to him, "has lain there long enough, has Pine-Root Man," they said to him.

With that they were off. Up he leaped and ran; he ripped through his roots of the pine; he ran after the young women. Another young man came and caught up with him; then still another; four were the men pursuing their sweethearts. Then when they had gone a long ways, presently the women stopped.

"Sweetheart mine, Pine-Root Man, I shall tell you how my younger sister here is called: Up-to-yon-Rise-of-the-Land-Blizzard-Woman she is called."

Then they were off again. There was a terrible blizzard. He spread out his blanket-robe; beneath it they walked along. When they reached that rise in the land, the sky grew clear again.

Again the others waited for them.

"And this other younger sister of mine, Pine-Root, my sweetheart, is called Very-Cold-Weather," she told him.

With that they were off again. It was very cold; their feet very nearly froze. They barely got there; they were frozen near to falling.

Then again they set out. Presently, from the men's party, he called out to the women.

"Wait!" he called to her; "Let me now tell you how this younger brother of mine is called: Rain-of-Awls-up-to-yonder-Rise-in-the-Land."

Then they were off.

"Goodness me, really a beautiful name has our sweetheart!"

Then, when they set out, it rained hard. Again they set out. Again he called to them.

"My other younger brother is called like this: Hot-Weather-up-to-yon-Hill."

It was very hot; then those women went naked as they went upward. When they reached the hill, it stopped raining.

"Oh dear!" they cried; "Really, it is terrible, the way our sweetheart's younger brother is called!"

"Now, as for me, ... I am called."

Truly, at a great rate those persons walked backwards.

". . . . . Truly beautiful is our sweetheart's name!"

Now, the old woman was on the lookout for her children.

"What on earth makes you act this crazy way?"

"Get away! Our sweetheart's name!" they cried.

When they reached their dwelling, only then did they walk properly.

Into another little house that was not heated the lone men were placed. There was no stove. They were very nearly frozen. Then one shot an arrow; in there in the little hut they were eating strawberries from the bush, even though the little trees were snapping in the cold.

Then the old man of that place, "Go take a look at them; they will be freezing too stiff," he was bidden by his wife.

He peeked in; they were eating berries from the bush. He went back.

"Bosh!" said the old man; "They are eating berries from the bush, they will be living on that, no doubt!" said he.

The next night it grew even colder. Again he shot an arrow. Again they ate berries from the bush, saskatoon-berries.

"Go peep in!"

The old woman went and peeped in.

"Those persons are eating berries from the bush, old man. And here am I going hungry! Come, let them go hunting!"

Then they were driven off and away. They saw a jumping-deer, a red one. They chased it. One shot at it; he pierced himself through the chest.

Again the old woman talked in her sleep.

"It was that I dreamt that my son-in-law killed the red jumping-deer that ran by here, and that I ate it."

So then he went to hunt; he saw it; he shot it from behind; he killed it. He dragged it back. He entered their dwelling.

"Here is the creature the old woman wanted to eat!"

When the old woman opened the door, "Dear me! Truly he brings calamity on me! My dream-guardian!"

"Have a big feast; boil it whole," he said.

They boiled it whole; they gave a big feast and consumed it. And thus he overcame his mother-in-law.

Then he made four arrows. Then he went to where his companions had been killed. He shot into the air.

"Away, away, away! I shall be hitting you by accident!"

They twitched a bit, and again he shot into the air. He repeated his words, and the other rose to his feet and ran. Two still lay there. Again he shot into the air; the other jumped to his feet. Now he who jumped to his feet, it seems was Matchihkiwis.

"Am I alive?"

"Yes. If you were not alive, it would be strange that you are talking!" he said.

"Really, I am glad I am alive! Hurrah, hurrah!" he said.

And so now Matchihkiwis took home a woman for himself.

Not so very long is the sacred story which I have finished.

(16) Pine Root

Adam Sakewew

sākäwäw.

awa kisäyiniw äkwah ōsisima uskinīkiwa, nīsiwak pikuh wīkiwāhk. äkwah kitimākäyimäw awa kisäyiniw ōsisima. mātsīw tahkih.

kätahtawä, " hāw, nōsisi, mahtih kit-ōtastutiniyin nika-kakwä-nipa-hāw, " itäw ōsisima.

" äha' , " itik.

" usām awiyak ntastāhik, kit-ōtihtisk, " itäw awa kisäyiniw ōsisima.

tāpwä nipahäw mistāpuswa ; äkwah pahkunäw.

" hāw, nōsisi, nika-kakwä-nipahāw kutak, kit-ōtastutiniyin, " itäw ōsisima.

" äha' , " itik.

äkwah kāhkākiwa nipahäw ; pahkunäw.

" hāw, nōsisi, ōma kā-mātsiyān tahtu-kīsikāw, awiyak utihtiskih, äkā wiya kitāpamāhkan, " itik umusōma.

" nimusō, " itäw, " mahtih kakwä-nipah paspaskiw ; nik-ōwahpihtisin, " itäw.

" tāpwä, nōsisi, miywāsin ōma k-ätwäyin. kik-ōhtsīhkamātin. äkutah asiwahāhkan awa asiniy, pähpäkahākan, " itäw ōsisima.

äkwah usīhtāw tsatsäkahkwāna awa kisäyiniw.

" hāw, nōsisi, kakwä-naskwänamōhkan ōhi tsatsäkahkwāna, kit-āpatsihtāyin, " itik umusōma.

" äha' , " itäw.

" äkwah mahtih, nōsisä, ōtah apih, " itik.

pōtātsik[1] *: pōti asiniy apiw.*

" hā, usām kinäsōwihitin ; māskōts ka-sākōtsihikun ! " itik umusōma ; " mahtih, nōsisä, pimisini ; kwayask sāsakitsisini, " itik umusōma.

pāh-pōtātsik: misiwä utsäpihtah misiwä itamuyiwa, aspin māna itāmāskīhk, äkwah ä-mamāhtsikwahpitikut utsäpihkak uhtsi.

" nōsisi, ōmisi kik-äsiyīhkāsun, " itik ; " watapīw-iyin kik-äsiyīhkāsun. äkā wiya kitāpamāhkan awiyak, " itik umusōma ; " ōhih tsikahkwānah kakwä-nawatinah. iskwāhtämahukanihk äkutah niwīh-tahkupitān ōhi kāmiyitān, awa mīna kāhpihtsis, " itik umusōma ; " äkā wiya kitāpam awiyak, utihtiskih. "

" äha', nimusō, " itäw.

tāpwä namuya käkway wīh-kitāpahtam iskwāhtäm. wäwäkisin ustikwānihk utakuhpah. kītahtawä pä-säwäpayiyiw käkway. pähtam ; wäwäkistikwānäw ; kuntah kā-pä-pāhpiwiht pähtam.

" iskwäwak ōki, " itäyihtam ; " äwakuni k-ätāt nimusōm, " itäyihtam.

pōtih ka-pä-pīhtukäyit.

" häy, äs āwa āt äh-na-nipāt, äkā kā-wi-kitāpamikuyahk kītimusinaw ! " itik.

" kähtsinā miyusiwak ! " itäyihtam aw uskinīkiw.

äkusi kāh-kitutik, nanätuhk äy-itukut ; nama wīh-kitutäw.

" tāpwä kipakwātikunaw kītimusinaw watapīw-iyin ! " itik ; " nyā, kīwätān, ntāyīm ! " itwäyiwa.

pōtih kāwi pä-paskwāpiyiwa päyak, päyak k-āti-pāhpiyit.

" misawāts sipwāhtäwak," itäyihtam ; " pōtih nk-ätāpin iskwāhtämihk, " äh-itäyihtahk ; " misawāts nam āwiyak nka-wāpamāw, " äy-itäyihtahk.

ntsawāts pāskihkwäyiw, iyāyaw iskwāhtämihk äy-itāpit.

" häy, āt ätsik āwa äkā äh-nipāt, äkā kā-wīh-kitāpamikuyāhk ! " äh-itwäyit, k-āti-pāhpiyit.

pasikōpayiw ; kahkiyaw paspaskipayihtāw ōhi watapiyah. äh-pītsitsipayit, ōhih kā-kī-usīhtwākut umusōma naskwänam ; pimiwitāw. päyakwan iyikuhk askōwäw. kahkiyaw tahkunam ōhih kā-kī-usīhtuwāht kitōtastutinit, mīna wahpihtisah, mīna tsikahkwānah.

---

[1] Doubtless *pōtātsikāw* : "he blew," or *pōtātik* : "the other blew on him."

äkusi kätahtawä sākahikan utihtamwak ; namwāts askiy nōkwaniyiw itäh ka-wiy-ituhtāyit päyak wītimusah. " häy häy ! " āskaw ōma wa-wīhtamākäwak.

" tānisi äsiyīhkāsuyin, nītimusä watapīw-iyin ? " itik.

" ha ! namuya niyi nīkān ta-kī-wīhtamātakuk niwīhōwin ! kiyawāw nīkān ta-wīhtamawiyäk kiwīhōwiniwāwa ! " itäw wītimusah.

" äha' ! ntāyīm, kiya nīkān wīhtamaw kītimusinaw kiwīhōwin, " itäw usīma.

" äha', näma iskuh kā-näyāk, äkutä iskuh, ' k-ōskātsihku-mispuhk, ' ntisiyīhkāsun. kik-āskōwinān, " itäw ; " hā, niyāk ! " itäw.

äkwah sōskwāyiw, ä-miskwamīwiyik. utinam utsikahkwān ; saskawuhtäw. kutak utinam ; pähpäkahākan äkutah kikamuhtäw. äh-misākaniyik pimuhtäw. ātah uskātsihkwa äh-pahkihtihkih ustikwānihk, āhtsi pikuh pa-pmuhtäw. wätihtahkik ōma kā-näyāyik, pōti äyāpits pä-wītsäwäwak wītimusiwāwa.

" häy, mākw āwa ka-pahpakwatäyimāhtānaw, ntāyīm ! äkwah māka wiyaskuts kä-wīhisut ! "

" hā, namōya ! kiyawāw nīkān kika-wīhtamawināwāw kiwīhyōwiniwāw. "

" äha' ! nämay isku kā-näyāk, äkutah iskuh 'kā-sōskwāstimäwi-pimuhtäw, ' ntisiyīhkāsun, " itik.

äkwah tā-sōskwāsit. sākahikan tāwakām namuya kaskatin, äkutä kitätāsit awa uskinīkiw. äkwah äh-ati-sipwähtätsik, msi-yōtiniyiw. tsikahkwānah utinam aw ōskinīkiw ; äkwah saskahuhtäw. äh-āta-yōtiniyik, papmuhtäw. piyisk utihtamwak.

" hāw ! "

" häy, āhtsi pikuh kiwītsäkunaw awa kītimusinaw ! äkwah māka wiyaskuts kä-wīhisut. "

" äha, nitimusitik. ninīsuyīhkāsun, " itäw ; " näma kisiwäk ōma kānäyāk, äkutah iskuh, ' kā-kisākamitäwi-kimiwahk, ' nitisiyīhkāsun, animah iskuh kā-näyāk. "

" äkwah niyā māka, nitimusä ; kik-āskōtinān. "

mayaw ä-sipwähtät, āsay mātsih-kimiwaniyiw. tāpiskōts äh-uhtäk nipiy, äkus īsi kisākamitäyiw.

äkwah ōki, " häy, nikīsisun ! " pikw ītah äy-ayinisutsik uk īskwäwak, kätisk äy-utihtahkik.

pōtih, " häy, tāpwä kītimusinaw āyimaniyiw uwīhōwin ! käyāpits päyakwāw ta-wīhisut. "

" äha' ! "

" äkwa māka kiwāskahikanisinawa nōkwanwa. "

" hā, nītimusä, näm īsku wāskāhikan kā-nōkwahk, äkutah, ' kā-nānāhtäwi-pimuhtäw-k-āsä-muhkituhtäw, ' nitisiyīhkāsun. "

äkwah ōk iskwäwak ōtah uskutākāwāwa umis īsiwäpinamwak ōtäh ; äkwah asähtäwak, tāpiskōts ōmisi äh-nawakītsik.

" häy, tānisi māka mīna ōki piyäy-isinākusitsik kīs-kīskwähkāniskwäwak ? "

" häy, näkā, äkāyāh nānitaw itwäh ! ka-pistsi-wīhāw kinahāhkisīm ! ōwīhōwin ōma kā-tōtamāhk, isku kiwāskāhikanihk tāwikiskamāhku ! "

pikunitah awāsisah kā-pähtākusiyit.[1] *äy-asähtätsik, äh-asä-mōhkituhtätsik, tāwikisinwak uwāskāhikanisiwāhk. äkwah pōyōwak.*

---

[1] This is probably the same laconically stated supernatural symbol of the conquest as in Jones' *Fox Texts* 196, 13.

"hääy, nitawāsimisitik, äkutä anah uhtapik, unipäwinik; usām nikīskwähkwasiskin; nika-pa-pistiskākān ninahāhkim," itwäw.

kawisimōwak, äh-tipiskāyik. käkāts äh-wāpaniyik, häy, kītahtawä kā-papāmitātsimut awa nōtukäsiw; mistahi kīskwähkwasiw! piyisk unahāh-kisīma kuspiwäpinik.

"häy, ntawāsimisitik, ōma kā-sākahikaniwik, äkuta ana kā-misikitit amisk ustikwān äh-mītsiyān äkwah usuy," itwäw awa nōtukäsiw, "äkuyikuhk iskah kā-pōni-kīskwähkwasiyān, wāpahki iskah äh-nipahāt nnahāh-kim," itwäw.

ā, pähtam awa ōskinīkiw. kītahtawä äh-wāpaniyik, kīksäpā sipwähtäw, tsīkahikan äh-utinahk äkwah utsikāhkwāna. wätihtahk sākahikan, tāwakām twāhipäw. mistahi twāhipäw.

äkwah, "hāw, nimusō, pä-wayawī! kipäy-asamitin ōma ka-wīhkista-man!" itwäw.

kätahtawä ka-pä-tāwatiyit ä-misikitiyit amiskwah. tsikahkwātäw; nipahäw. ustikwān utinam, usuyiw mīna; kīwähtatäw. pīhtukäwäpinam.

"äyakuni kā-wīh-mītsit kikāwiyiwäw!"

mātōw awa nōtukäsiw, "nipawākan!" äh-itwät; "häy, mätwäwanä ntaw-āsamihkuk ayīsiyiniwak! ōhi ta-mītsiwak; anihi minah kā-nipah-imiht ta-nātäwak; ta-mōwäwak!"

tipiskāyiw āsay mina; kawisimōwak. äkusi āsay mina kīskwähk-wasiw awa nōtukäsiw.

pōtih äh-päkupayit, "iskah ninahāhkim ä-nipahāt ukwāskwäpayihōsa ä-misikitiyit, äwakuni ä-nipahāt nnahāhkisīm, äkuyikuhk iskuh kā-pōni-kīskwähkwasiyān, ä-mītsiyān ustikwān," itwäw.

tāpwä kīkisäpā kuntah kā-pähtākwaniyik, "äwakwā!" äh-itwäyit ayīsiyiniwah. ä-wayawī-kwāskuhtit, pōt ōhi kī-pimi-kwāskwäkutsiniyiwa ōhi apsi-mōsusah. tsikahkwātäw; nipahäw; ustikwān pikuh utinam. pīhtukäwäpinam.

"äwakō anih kā-wīh-mītsit kikāwiyiwäw!" itäw.

āsay mina mātōw awa nōtukäsiw.

"nipawākan äh-mihtātak, ä-nipahiht!" itwäw; "hā, nitawāsimisitik, nitaw-āsamihkuk ayīsiyiniwak!"

"āha'," itwäyiwa.

äkwah mōwäwak kutakak ayīsiyiniwak.

äkwah tipiskāyiw. āsay mina kīskwähkwasiw awa nōtukäsiw.

"häy, ntawāsimisitik, ōtah ä-pimipayit wāwāskäsiw, äyakuni iskah ninahāhkisīm äh-nipahāt, ustikwān iskah äh-mītsiyān, äkuyikuhk kā-pōni-kīskwähkwasiyān," itwäw.

kīkisäpā kā-pähtahk, "hah, namuya äkwah nka-nipahāw!" itäyihtam awa watapīw-iyin.

"äwakwā wāwāskäsiw māmaskāts ä-misikitit!" k-ätwäwiht, wayawīw. päyak pikuh utsikāhkwān utinam. tsikāhkwātäw, äh-pimipahtāyit, watayihk aspin utsikāhkwān äh-kikiskamiyit. kīwäw aw ōskinīkiw. kahkiyaw utinam utsikāhkwānah, utastutinah. pimitisahwäw. pōtih äsa māna itah äh-apiyit. piyisk mituny utākusiniyiw. kāh-kīpa nahapiyiwa. kītahtawä kā-wāpahtahk äh-miywasiniyik sakāw. wāsakām nīpisiyah ayāyiwah. äkwah ati-mispuniyiw.

"ā, namuya misawāts wāhyaw ta-nipiw. ōtah nka-nipān. nika-pōh-pōnän; nika-kutawān," äh-itäyihtahk.

mistahi sakāyiw, pisisik uski-mätusah äkutōwahk, äkwah kayāsi-mistikwah, māyi-mätusah äkutōwank. äkwah pānaham, ä-kutawät. ati-tipiskāyiw.

kisiwāk ōtah äh-tsimasōwit, " mihtih, mätusi-mihtih, ōma nika-pōnän, " äy-itäyihtahk, utinam.

ōmis äh-tōtahk, " hāā ! " k-ätwäyit ōhi mistikwa.

pōnihäw. ntsawāts akāmihk, akāmiskutäw anāskäw nīpisiyah masku-siyah mīna. nama wīh-nipāw. mistahi yōtiniyiw, äkwah äh-mispuniyik. kītahtawä ōtäh nāmawan kīkway kā-pähtahk aw ōskinīkiw. kätahtawä äh-itāpit, kā-pä-pāh-pahkisiniyit. utāsiyiwa ōtä asastäyiwa ; namwāts tahku-pitamiyiwa.

" ähähäy, nōhkum ! wīh-kawatsiw amä nōhkum ! hāhāw, hā, nōhku, äkutäh anih apih. wāwāskäsiw ä-kīh-nawaswātak, ä-kīh-miswak, ninästu-wākunāmun. wāpahkih nka-ntawi-nipahāw, nōhkō. wiyās kika-mītsin-ānaw. "

" hääy, nōsisimis, usām mistah äh-nōhtähkatäyān, ōtäh kā-wīkihk, äkutä äy-ispitsihk, aspin kā-wäpinikawiyān, äh-wanisiniyān. "

" ā, tāpwä, nōhkō, ka-kīwähtahitn ōtäh kā-wīkihk, wāpahki, kä-nipahaki wāwāskäsiw. niwih-nikuhtān ; usām ka-kawatsin. "

ah-iskunamawäw utāsiyiwa, mīnah umaskisiniyiwa äh-tahkupitamwāt. mistahi kitimākäyimäw ōhkumah.

" ā, nōhkō, niwīh-nipān. kakwä-pōnamāsu, " itäw ōhkumah.

" häy, nōsisimis, kaskihtāyāni, nika-pōnän, " itik ōhkuma.

tāpwä nipāw aw ōskinīkiw, namuya ä-nipāt, ä-wīh-wayäsihāt, " äwakōw awa nimanātsimākan, " äh-itäyihtahk.

kītahtawä, " nōsisä, nkawatsin ! " itik.

āhtsi piku tāpiskōts äh-nipāt, " hhhrr[1] *! " äh-itwät aw uskinīkiw.*

kītahtawä awa nōtukäsiw kā-waniskāt, " näy ! mätwäwanih nimistikum nka-takuhā ! " k-ätwäyit.

äkwah ntuhtawäw. āpahamiyiwa ōtäh[2] *isi ; pōtih äh-kaskipitäyik maskihkiy.*

" näy, namayäw ! āpisīnikan ätsik ōma ! " itwäw awa nōtukäsiw.

astäw. kutak ōtäh is āpahikäw, kutak äh-utinahk maskihkiy, " nää, äwaku ! " k-ätwäyit. äkwah mā-mākwahtam mistsikus awa nōtukäsiw. äkwah maskihkiy sāmihtitäw äkutah.

" tsäh, äyakw ätsik ōma mistikwak k-ōh-usīhakik ! " itwäw.

äkwah ōh ōsisima, umis ītisinam, ä-wīh-sāmahwāt ōh ōskinīkiwa. nawatinamwäw uspituniyiw.

" tsä, wänikunä-mahkay ! "

nawatinamiyiwa uma mistsikus.

" äää, nōsisä, tsäskwah pitah ! āsay kisākōtsihin, " itik ; " hā, nōsisä, tsäskwah ayīsiyiniw ta-nihtawikihitōw nīkān ōtäh. yōskihtak kit-ōtinamwak. äkutah kit-ōh-kīsōnak awāsis[3] *wīh-ōhpikitsih, nīstah kit-ōhpikihak. māka pahkisimuhk nk-ōtaskän. ' nōtukäsiw nipawātäw,' itwätsi ayīsiyiniw, kita-tāpwäw. hāw, äkusi, nōsisā, sāmahun. "*

sāmahwäw ōhkumah ōm ohtsi maskihkiy. pōt āwa mistik äh-kīskipayit kīh-nīpawiw. äkusi mistikōw awa nōtukäsiw.

---

[1] Deep breathing (not snoring) is imitated.

[2] Gesture to bosom-fold of garment.

[3] Infants were (and sometimes still are) kept in the "moss-bag" which is filled with crumbly wood.

ākwah ōhih, " ā, " kā-kīh-itwäyit, " ōma kutak maskihkiy āpisīnikan, " k-ätwäyit ōhkumah, äwaku utinam. sāmahwäw mistikwah. pōt ōhi käht-äyiniwah kīh-nīpawiyiwa.

" hwhw ! " itwäyiwa ; " nnästukāpawin ! " itwäyiwa.

kisiwāk äh-tsimasuyit mistikwah sāmahwäw. kākāts wāpaniyiw· kutakah mīna. hāw, pōtih uskinīkiwa kīh-nīpawiyiwa.

" hāw, " itäw ōhi kähtäyiniwa, " ākāya kihtimiyuh[1]*; sāma ōhi ōki mistikwak ōm ōhtsi āpisīnikan k-ätwät nōhkum. niwī-ntawi-nipahāw awa wāwāskäsiw. nika-wītsäkwak mitātaht, misiwä ta-pätōwatätsik, ta-nāh-nawatsiyäk. pimātisiyānih, kä-nīsu-tipiskākih nika-takuhtān, " itäw.*

" äha' , " itik.

ākwah ituhtäw. ōhih wāwāskäsiwah nmuya wāhyaw nipiyiwa. ustik-wān utinam. kīwähtatäw. hā, wīkiwāhk takōhtatäw ; pīhtukäwäpinam.

" äwakw āni kikāwiyiwāw kā-wīh-mītsit ! "

mātōwak ōki uskinīkiskwäwak, ōkāwiyiwāwa ä-mawihkātātsik. käh-tsināhowak ä-sākōtsihimiht.

äh-tipiskāyik, kawisimōwak. kätahtawä aw umisimāw kīskwähkwasiw ; kuspiwäpinäw wītimusah awa watapīw-iyin. äkusi äh-päkupayit awa īskwäw, wīhtam.

" häyäy, kītimusinaw awa iskah ōma wāskāhikanis kā-pisikwastäyik, äkutah päyakutipiskwah äh-ayāt, äkuyihuhk kā-pōni-kīskwähkwasiyān, " itwäyiwa.

hā, ituhtäw äh-wāpaniyik ; nikuhtäw, mistahi wāskāhikanisihk äh-pīhtukātāt ōhi mihtan. äh-tipiskāyik, äh-apit, nama kākway iskwāhtäm. misiwäsiyiwa ōhi mistikwah. mistahi ksiniyiw. ay-awasōw. piyisk mästih-kasam umihtima. ntawāts kawisimōw.

kätahtawä, " hāw, ntastutin, kīsōnin ! " itäw mistah ä-misikitiyit wāpuswah.

mituni kiyīpa kawatsiw awa wāpus. utinäw ; pōh-pōtātäw.

" ' kīsōnin ! ' kititin. "

āsay mina kiyipa kawatsiw. āsay mina utinäw. äkwah kītahtawä kawatsiyiwa. namuy äkwah utinäw ; kutak ulastutina utinäw.

" hāw, nimusō, pawahukä ! " itäw.

äkwah awa kāhkākiw kitōw, äh-pa-pakamahahk ōma waskahikan, misiwä äh-miskwamiwiyik. kiyipa kawatsiw awa kāhkākiw.

" māskōts nika-kawatsin, " itäyihtam awa uskinīkiw.

äkwah ntsawāts utinam utsikahkwān, äh-kawatsiyit ōhi kāhkākiwa. utinam utsikahkwān, iskutäw äh-tsikahkwātahk. mistah iskutäwiyiw. mistahi kwāhkutäw ōma tsikahkwān. kiyipah āstawiw. kāhkākiw awa pimisin, äh-kawatsit. äkwah kutak utinam utsikahkwān ; āsay mina tsikahkwātam ; āsay min äyōkō kwāhkutäw. nimiskōtinäw kāhkākiwah. kākāts wāpaniyiw. āsay mina āstawiw. kutak utinam ; āsay mina tsikah-kwātam iskutäw ; mistahi kwāhkutäyiw utsikahkwān. kätahtawä āstawiyiw. ä-wīh-āstawiyik, utinäw wāhpihtsisah paspaskiwah ; äkwah pakamisimäw.

" pawahukä, naphihts ! " itäw.

utinäw utastutinah. pōtātäw ; pōtih pimātisiyiwah kāhkākiwah. utinäw wāpuswah ; pōtātäw ; pōtih pimātisiyiwa.

---

[1] Probably for *kihtimih :* "be lazy."

äkwah ōhih paspaskiwah " pawahukä ! " itäw.

kītahtawä awa paspaskiw sipwäpahtäw pīhtsāyihk, ōmis äh-tōtahk, ōmis äh-itwät : " nīpin ! nīpin ! nīpin ! " pisisik äh-itwät, äkwah kāhkākiw pisisik äh-kitut, äkwah awa wāpus pikw ītah äh-kawipayihut.

nam äskwa äh-āstawiyik utsikahkwān, " āyiwākäs kit-ātih-kwāhkutäw ōma nitsikāhkwān ! nimusō, nimästinān ntsikahkwānah ! " itwäw.

nähih umusōma kā-kitimākäyimikut, äwakuni kāy-itāt. äkwah kiyipa nama käkway kōnah pīhtsāyihk ; āyiwākäs kwāhkutäw. äkwah awa paspaskiw pīhtsāyihk misiwä ispahtäw, äy-usihtāt nīpin, nīpiyah äh-ntutamāt, ōsisima äh-kanawäyimāt. äkwah käkāts äh-wāpahk, misiwä sākikinwah nīpiyah ; mīnah pīhtsāyihk muhtsihk mīnisah uhpikinwah, utähiminah. ayis awa paspaskiw namuya kipihtuwäw, pisisik " nīpin ! " äh-itwät. äkwah awa nāpäw uskinīkiw kätayōwinisäw ; musäskatäw ōtäh, äh-kīskwäpit.[1] utinam mīnisah, äh-mītsit. mituni kisupwäyāw pīhtsāyihk.

äkwah äh-kīsikāk, āsay pīsim äh-nōkusit, " häy, ntāyīm, ntawih-wayawīwäpin kītimusinaw ! kuntah winskam kitastsikäwikamikunaw. "

ituhtäw päyak. äh-at-ītuhtät, ki-kituyiwa kāhkākiwa. pähtawäw ; mīnah paspaskiwa. pōtih ä-paspāpit, kīh-mā-mōminäyiwa.

" häy, nītimusä, nama tsī kah-kiy-asaminān ōhi kā-mītsiyan utähimina ? "

" ā, tipiskuhk ä-nipāyān, kimis iskah äh-kitāyäk ōhih mīnisah, äkuyikuhk iskah kā-pōnih-kīskwähkwasiyān tipiskuhk. "

" nā, äkā m āyimahk ta-kitāhk, nītimusä ! " k-ätikut.

kīwäw.

" tānisi māka, nitāyīm, tānisi māka ? "

" āpisīs anihi mīnisah utähiminah kitāyahkuh, äkuyikuhk ta-pōnih-kīskwähkwasit kītimusinaw. ä-ma-mōmināt niwāpamāw, piku māka ta-tōtamahk, ntāyīm, " itäw.

tuhtäwak.

" hāw, nītimusitik, pīhtukäk ! iyikuhk kitāyäku ōhi, pōnihtāhkäk. äkuyikuhk ka-wayawīnānaw. "

mistahi miywäyihtamwak ōki kīskwähkāniskwäwak. äkwah mōminäwak. äyātah-itäh-kāh-kitātwāwi, äkutä pimipahtäw awah paspaskiw. kāwih kikamuyiwa utähiminah. piyisk ōk īskwäwak ōmisi itapiwak, usām äh-kīsputsik.

" hääy, nītimusä, kisākōtsihinān ! āpihtā-kīsikāk äkutä isih kīpiyah-kininān. kisākōtsihinān. tāpwä nika-kisäwātisininān. ayīsiyiniwak uh-pikitwāwi, ' nipawātāw äh-kīskwät iskwäw, ' itwätsi, kita-tāpwäw. hāw, nītimusä, kiyipah ! "

" āh, isi-kīpipayihuk ! " itäw.

mayaw äh-kīpipayihutsik, āsay kīh-atimwäwätamwak, äh-āhtuhtätsik ä-sākōtsihihtsik mats-āyak.

äkuyikuhk äskwāk ātayōhkäwin.

---

[1] Or "sat playing?"

This old man and his grandson, a youth, dwelt, the two, alone, in a tipi. The old man was fond of his grandson. He always hunted.

Then at one time, "Now then, my grandchild, I think I shall try to kill some creature that you may use for a hat," he said to his grandson.

"Yes," answered the other.

"For too much does someone frighten me with the foreboding that he will come upon you," said the old man to his grandson.

And so he killed a jack-rabbit; then he skinned it.

"Now then, my grandchild, I shall try to kill some creature, that you may have another hat," he told his grandson.

"Yes," answered he.

Then he killed a raven; he skinned it.

"Now, my grandchild, when I hunt each day, should anyone come to you, do not look at him," his grandfather told him.

"Grandfather," he told him, "Please try to kill a partridge; let me have a tobacco-pouch of it," he told him.

"Indeed, my grandchild, what you say is right. I will help you. Put this stone inside, and you have a slung-shot club," he told his grandson.

Then the old man made a set of darts.

"Now, my grandchild, try to seize these darts on the run, that you may use them," his grandfather told him.

"Yes," he said to him.

"And now, grandchild, sit over here," the other told him.

He blew forth his breath: there lay a stone.

"Ho, I am leaving you too weak; perhaps something will overcome you!" his grandfather said to him; "Do, grandchild, lie down; lie down flat on your back," his grandfather told him.

He blew forth his breath more than once: on all sides roots clung fast, roots from way down under the ground, until he was firmly tied down by the roots.

"My grandchild, this shall be your name," he told him; "Pine-Root-Man will be your name. Do not look at anyone," his grandfather told him; "Try to take with you these darts. Here to the stick of the door-flap I shall tie these things which I give you, and also your tobacco-pouch," his grandfather told him; "Do not look at anyone that may come to you."

"Yes, grandfather," he told him.

Accordingly not at all would he look at the door. He lay wrapped up, with his blanket over his head. Then at one time something came a-jingling. He heard it; he wrapped up his head; he heard someone come near to him, gaily laughing.

"These are women," he thought; "These are the ones my grandfather meant," he thought.

There, they came in.

"Hey, and so there he sleeps, just the same, our sweetheart who will not look at us!" they said to him.

"Surely they must be beautiful!" thought the young man.

Then they kept talking to him, saying all kinds of things; but he would not speak to them.

"Truly, we are disdained by our sweetheart Pine-Root!" they said to him; "Come, let us go home, sister-wife!" they said.

Then, look you, one came back, peeping in, while the other went laughing on her way.

"By this time they have departed," he thought; "Just let me look at the doorway," he thought; "After all, I shall not see anyone," he thought.

He uncovered his head, and eagerly looked at the doorway.

"Hey, and so he is not asleep after all, the one who will not look at us!" she said, and off she went, laughing.

He leapt to his feet; he ripped through all those cedar-roots. As he dashed forth, he seized those things which his grandfather had made for him; he took them along. He did nothing but follow them. He held in his hand all the things that had been made for him to wear as headgear, and his tobacco-pouch, and the darts.

Thus presently they came to a lake; no land was visible there whither one of his sweethearts was headed. "Hey, hey!" they would shout now and then, as a sign.

"What is your name, sweetheart, Pine-Root?" one asked him.

"Ho! I will not be the first to tell you my name! First you must tell me your names!" he told his sweetheart.

"So be it! My sister-wife, do you first tell our sweetheart your name," she told her younger sister.

"Yes. As far as yon point of the land, up to yonder place, 'Rain-of-Awls' is my name. You will follow us," she told him; "There, be off!" she said to the others.

Then it was slippery on the ice. He took one of his darts; he leaned on it as he walked. He took another; he attached the slung-shot club to it. He walked across the expanse of ice. Though awls were falling on his head, nevertheless he kept walking on. When they had reached that promontory, there, again they came and kept their sweetheart company.

"Hey, but surely we had our fun of him, my sister-wife! But now it is his turn to name himself!"

"Ho, no! You first are to tell me your names."

"Very well! As far as yon point of the land, up to yonder place, 'Walks-Blown-on-the-Ice,' is my name," she told him.

And then the wind was to carry him along on the smooth surface. The lake was not frozen shut in the middle, and thither the youth was to be borne by the wind. Then, when they set out on their way, there came a great wind. The youth took a lance; he used it as a cane. In spite of the wind, he kept walking. At last they reached the place.

"There!"

"Hey, in spite of all, our sweetheart is keeping us company! But now it is his turn to name himself."

"Yes, sweethearts. I have two names," he told them; "As far as yon close-by point of the land, up to yonder place, 'Hot-Water-Rain' is my name, as far as yon point of the land."

"But now, sweetheart, be off; we will follow you."

As soon as he started off, at once it began to rain. Like boiling water, so hot was the liquid.

Then those women, "Hey, I am being scalded!" and they dodged hither and thither, and only with difficulty reached the goal.

There, "Hey, truly a dangerous thing is our sweetheart's name! Once more let him name himself."

"Yes, indeed!"

"But now our little wooden houses are in sight."

"Why, sweetheart mine, as far as yon house that we see, up to that place, ... is my name."

. . . . then they walked backwards, stooping over just like this.

"Hey, what is the matter now with these little ones that make themselves look like prairie chickens?"

"Hey, mother, do not speak! Before you know it, you will be speaking your son-in-law's name! It is his name, what we are doing until we bump into your house!"

Then, from no one knew where, was heard the cry of a child. Walking backwards . . . . they landed against their little wooden house. Then they stopped.

"Hey, my children, sit over there with that man, make your bed over there; I am too much given to sleep-walking; I might run into my son-in-law," she said.

When darkness fell, they went to bed. When it was almost daybreak, hey, there was the old woman crawling about; a bad case of sleep-walking! At last her son-in-law shoved her aside.

"Hey, my children, that lake over there, if I ate the head and the tail of the giant beaver that is there," said that old woman, "then, my dream tells me, I should cease to walk in my sleep, if tomorrow my son-in-law would kill it," she said.

The youth heard that. Presently, when day broke, early in the morning he set out, taking an ax and his darts. When he reached the lake, in the centre he made a hole in the ice. He made a great hole in the ice.

Then, "Now, O my grandfather, come forth! I have come to feed you that whose taste you so love!" he said.

Presently, there came with gaping mouth the giant beaver. He threw his dart at it; he killed it. He took its head and its tail; he took them home. He flung them into the house.

"Here are the things your mother wants to eat!"

The old woman wept, crying, "My dream guardian!" Hey, as it is destined, go feed them to mortal men! These things they will eat; and him who has been slain they will fetch; they will eat him!"

Again night fell; they went to bed. Then again the old woman walked in her sleep.

There, when she awoke, "By my dream, if my son-in-law kills the giant jumping-deer, if my son-in-law kills him, that will be the end of my sleep-walking, if I eat its head," she said.

Then really, in the morning, "There he goes!" the people's cry was heard. When he leaped out of the house, lo, that jumping-moose had bounded past. He threw a dart at it; he killed it; he took only its head. He flung it into the house.

"Here is what your mother wants to eat!" he called to them.

Again the old woman wept.

"It is mourning my dream-spirit I am, that has been killed!" she said; "So now, my children, go feed it to mortal men!"

"Yes," they said.

Then the other people ate it.

Then night fell. Again the old woman walked in her sleep.

"Hey, my children, the elk that runs by here, I dreamt that if my son-in-law kills it, and I eat its head, then I shall cease to walk in my sleep," she said.

In the morning, when he heard this, "Oh, I shall not kill him now!" thought that Pine-Root-Man.

"There goes that elk that is so strangely large!" he heard the people cry, and went outside. He took only one dart. He threw the dart at it, as it ran past, and off it went with his dart in its belly. The youth went back. He took all his lances and his head-dresses. He pursued it. There, he kept coming to where it had stopped to rest. At last it was late in the afternoon. At frequent intervals it was stopping to rest. Presently he came to a pleasant grove of trees. Willows stood round about. It was beginning to snow.

"Oh, in any case, it will die not far away. I shall sleep here. I shall keep up a fire; I shall have a fire," he thought.

It was a big grove, all of young poplars, and of old trees, of black-poplars. Then he cleared away the snow and made a fire. It was getting dark.

As a tree stood close by there, "Firewood, a log of poplar wood I shall put on my fire," he thought, and started to take it.

As he did so, "Oh, oh!" cried that tree.

He left it alone. He thought it better at the other side; at the other side of the fire he made his resting place of willow-boughs and grass. He could not sleep. There was a strong wind, and it snowed. Presently, there to the windward, the youth heard something. When he looked in that direction, there came someone falling. Her leggings were gathered down here; she had not tied them up at all.

"Oh dear, oh dear! Grandmother! My poor grandmother will freeze to death! Come, come, grandmother, sit over there. I was chasing an elk which I had wounded and am tired from tramping through the deep snow. Tomorrow I shall go kill it, grandmother. We shall have meat to eat."

"Alas, my dear grandchild, I am terribly starved; when they moved camp to where the people are staying, they went off leaving me behind, and now I have got lost."

"Never mind, grandmother, I will take you back to where they live, tomorrow, as soon as I have killed the elk. I will get some wood; you are too cold."

He pulled up her leggings for her and tied up her moccasins. He treated his grandmother very kindly.

"Now, grandmother, I am going to sleep. Try to keep up the fire to warm yourself," he told his grandmother.

"Alas, my dear grandchild, I if I am able, I shall put wood on the fire," his grandmother answered him.

And so the youth went to sleep, but he did not really sleep, but only meant to deceive her, for he thought, "This is none other than my mother-in-law."

Presently, "Grandchild, I am freezing!" she said to him.

Unheeding, just as if he were asleep, "Hhhrr!" went the youth.

Presently that old woman rose from where she lay, and, "Yah, as it is destined, I shall add him to my trees!" she said.

He listened to her. She took something from here, and it turned out to be some herbs tied in a packet.

"Bah, this is not it! Why, this is the restorer!" said the old woman.

She put it down. From the same place she unfastened another, taking another medicine, and, "Yah, this is it!" she said. Then the old woman chewed a little twig. Then she rubbed some of the medicine on it.

"Faugh, and this is the stuff with which I make trees!" she said.

Then she held it out at her grandson, meaning to touch the youth with it. He caught her by the arm.

"Faugh, you filthy beast!"

He seized the stick she was holding.

"Hey, grandson, wait a moment! You have defeated me," she said to him; "Now, grandson, in future time mortal man will live in successive generations. They will gather crumbly wood. There I shall keep warm the child that is to grow up, so that I too shall have part in bringing him up. But in the place of the setting sun I shall have my home. 'I have dreamt of the old woman,' when a mortal being speaks thus, he will speak truly. So now, my grandson, touch me with it."

He touched his grandmother with that medicine. Lo, there stood a cleft tree. Thus that old woman turned into a tree.

Then he took that of which his grandmother had said, "Oh, this other medicine is the restorer," this he took. He touched a tree with it. Lo and behold, there stood an aged man.

"Whew!" he said; "I am weary of standing!" he said.

He touched with the stick a tree that stood close by. It was almost daybreak. Then another. Then, behold, there stood a young man.

"Well now," he said to the aged man, "do not be idle; touch these trees with this which my grandmother called the restorer. I shall go kill that elk. I shall take ten men with me, so that they can bring all of it, for you to roast. If I live, after two nights I shall arrive," he told him.

"So be it," the other answered him.

Then he went there. The elk lay dead not far from there. He took the head. He took it home with him. He brought it to their house; he threw it into the doorway.

"Here is what your mother wanted to eat!"

The young women were weeping, mourning for their mother. They knew with certainty that she had been defeated.

When darkness fell, they went to bed. Presently the elder one began to walk in her sleep; Pine-Root shoved his sweetheart aside. When thus the woman awoke, she told her dream.

"Hoho, I dreamt that if our sweetheart here stayed one night in that little wooden house that stands empty there, that would be the end of my sleep-walking," she said.

He went there at daybreak; he gathered firewood, bringing a great many faggots into the little wooden house. When night came, and he sat there, the doorway disappeared. The wooden walls were unbroken. It was very cold. He warmed himself at the fire. At last he had burned up all his firewood. He needs went to bed.

Presently, "Come, my hat, warm me!" he said to the very large rabbit.

Very soon the rabbit was overcome by the cold. He took him up; he kept breathing on him.

" 'Warm me!' I told you."

Again very quickly it was overcome by the cold. Again he took it up. Presently again it fell to the ground for cold. This time he did not take it up; he took his other hat.

"Come, my grandfather, beat out the walls of the house!" he told it.

Then that raven croaked, as it beat the wooden house that was covered all over with ice. Quickly the raven was overcome by cold.

"No doubt I shall freeze to death," thought the youth.

So now he needs took one of his darts, when that raven had succumbed to the cold. He took one of his darts, and threw it at the fire. There was a big fire. That dart blazed high. Quickly the flame subsided. The raven lay there, overcome by cold. Then he took another of his darts; again he threw his dart at it; this one, too, blazed up. He held the raven over the fire. It was near dawn. Again the fire went out. He took another; again he threw a dart at the fire; his dart made a great blaze. Presently it ceased to flame. When it was about to go out, he took his tobacco-pouch made of a partridge; he threw it down.

"Beat the walls of the house, my tobacco-pouch!" he said to it.

He took up his hat. He breathed on it; there, the raven was alive. He took up the rabbit; he breathed on it; lo, it lived.

Then to the partridge he said, "Beat out the house!"

Then soon that partridge set out, indoors there, doing like this, crying "Summer! Summer! Summer!" crying it incessantly; and at the same time the raven croaked without ceasing, and the rabbit threw itself down here, there, and everywhere.

Before his dart ceased to flame, "A while longer let this my dart blaze high! My grandfather, I have come to the end of my darts!" he said.

It was that far-off grandfather of his who had cared for him, whom he addressed. Then, at once, there was no more snow within the house; the fire blazed higher. Then that partridge flew everywhere inside there, creating summer, calling for leaves, and serving its grandchild. Then when dawn was at hand, the leaves everywhere sprang forth; and inside there on the ground berries grew up, strawberries. For that partridge did not cease from its call, as all the time it cried, "Summer!" Then that man, that youth, took off his clothes; he was naked there, and sat reeling. He took berries and ate them. It was very hot inside there.

. . . .

One of them went there. As she came near, the raven called repeatedly. She heard it; also the partridge. There, when she peeped in, he was eating berries from the bush.

"Hey, sweetheart, can you not give us some of those strawberries you are eating?"

"Yes, last night when I slept, I dreamt that if you and your elder sister ate up all of these berries, then I should cease to walk in my sleep of nights."

"Why, surely it will not be difficult to eat them all, sweetheart!" was her answer to him.

She went back.

"How now, my sister-fellow-wife, how now?"

"If we eat up the few berries, strawberries, there, then our sweetheart will cease to walk in his sleep. I saw him eating berries from the bush, and that is all we need to do, my sister-wife," she told the other.

They went there.

"Come, my sweethearts, come in! When you eat these up, then stop. Then we shall go out of here."

Those giddy wenches liked the idea. So then they ate berries. Whenever they had in any place eaten them up, thither the partridge would run. The berries would be back on the stalk. At last those women sat like this, having overeaten.

"Hey, sweetheart, you have defeated us! Push us headlong to the direction of the noon. You have defeated us. We promise to be good. When mortal men come into being, if one shall say, 'I have dreamt of a Giddy Woman,' he will be telling the truth. Come, sweetheart, be quick!"

"Well then, fling yourselves over!" he told them.

As soon as they had flung themselves over, at once they went noising it yon way, going to a new abode after their defeat, the evil beings.

That is the end of the sacred story.

(17) Clotkin

Coming-Day

kā-kīsikāw-pīhtukāw.

kītahtawā itah ä-wīkitsik awa mistanask uwīkimākanah sikākwah, nama käkway utawāsimisah. awah sikākuskwäw ustäsah wākayōsah āyimisiyiwa, äh-kāsakäyit, kāh-kiyipah äh-kitāyit umītsiwiniwāwa. äkwah nama käkway nihtah-nipahtāw awa wākayōs. äkwah awa mistanask mistahi nōhtähkatäw ; wīh-nipahāhkatusōw.

ōmis ītwäw awa mistanask : " nutukäsiw, ka-nipahāhkatusunānaw. nawats sipwāhtäyahk, " itäw ; " umisi nik-ätāw kistäs[1]; māskōts wīh-pakitinikuyahku ta-sipwähtäyahk. äkusi pikuh ka-pmātisinānaw. "

" āha' ! "

tāpwä ntumäw wīstāwah ōhi wākayōsah.

äh-pīhtukäyit, " ahāw, ta-tawāw ! " itäw wīstāwah wākayōsah ; umis ītäw : " nīsta, kitsīsimitin ; namuya ka-mītsisuyan kā-ntumitān. nama käkway nitayān ta-mītsiyān ; māka ōmisi ä-wīh-ititān, k-ōh-nitumitān : ahāw, nīsta, kitimākihtawin ; kitimākinawin. kikākīsimutātin ; pakitinin ; nika-sipwähtān ; nika-nitunän ta-mītsiyāhk. kisīm awa ta-nipahāhkatusōw. piyis miskamānih ta-mītsiyahk, nipahakwāwih mustuswak, nika-pä-kīwān, ta-pātäyān wiyās, " itäw wīstāwah ; " usām ōtah kisiwāk nama käkway mustus, " itäw wīstāwah, ä-wīh-wayäsimāt ; usām äh-kitimahikut, äōkō uhtsi k-ō-wīh-sipwähtät.

" āha' , " itwäw wākayōs, " tāpwä, nīstā, ka-miywāsin, nipahatsih mustus. anuhts nama käkway nimītsisun nīsta, " itwäw wākayōs.

---

[1] We are not told what he will say.

tāpwä miywäyihtam awa mistanask, äh-pakitäyimikut wīstāwah. tāpwä äkwah kawisimōwak, äh-nipātsik. äh-wāpahk, äh-kīkisäpāyāyik, wawäyīw awa mistanask, äh-pitsit.

äkwah äh-sipwähtätsik, äkwah ōmis ītwäw awa mistanask : " hāw, ōma kā-wī-sipwähtäyān, ta-māyi-kīsikāw ; ta-mispun ! " itwäw.

äkus ä-sipwähtät, tāpwä, namuya wāhyaw äh-ihtāt, āsay mispuniyiw. namuya kisināyiw. pa-pimipitsiw kapä-kīsik, piyisk nama kākway mäskanaw um ītah kā-pä-pimuhtät. piyis tipiskāyiw. āhtsi pikuh pa-pimuhtäwak ; wāpani-pimuhtäwak uwīkimākanah. äyōku mīnah kapä-kīsik äh-pimuhtätsik, äh-at-ōtākusiniyik, kā-wāpamāt mustuswah.

" hā, nōtukäsiw, äkus ä-pimātisiyahk ; mustuswak ōki nika-minahun, " itwäw mistanask ; " hāw, ōma kā-sakāk äkutah ntawi-kapäsih, " itäw uwīkimākanah.

äkwah wiyah ituhtäw, ōhi mustuswah ä-wīh-kakwä-nipahāt. tāpwä äh-tsikahkwātāt, kahkiyaw nipahäw. miywäyihtam ä-wīh-mästsihāt. äkwah pōni-mispuniyiw. äkwah äh-wiyanihātsik, äh-pāh-pahkwäkiswātsik, kahkiyaw wiyāsah utinamwak ; nama käkway wäpinamwak. tsikämā mistahi kī-nōhtähkatäwak. mistä miywäyihtam awa sikākuskwäw, iyikuhk wiyās äh-wāpahtahk, " namuya nka-nipahāhkatusunān,[1] " äy-itäyihtahk.

äkwah nāhah wākayōs mistahi nōhtähkatäw. äkwah kaṣkäyihtam äkā äh-takusiniyit wīstāwah, " māskōts nipahäw mustuswah, " äh-itäyihtahk. äkwah nōhtä-ntunawäw wīstāwah. " hā, mahtih nka-ntunawāw wiyāh mistanask ; māskōts nipahäw mustuswah, " itäyihtam ō wākayōs, äkwah äh-sipwähtät. namuya wāpahtam itah äh-kīh-pimuhtäyit ; tsikämā kīh-mispuniyiw ; wanihäw mistanaskwah. piyisk kāwih kīwäw, äkā h-miskawāt uwīstāwah.

äkwah awah mistanask āsay mīnah wāpamäw mustuswah ; mīn äyōkuni kahkiyaw nipahäw. mīn äyōkuni kahkiyaw utinäwak ; nama kākway wäpinamwak. mistahi ayāwak ka-mītsitsik.

äkwah awah wākayōs sipwähtäw, āsay mīnah ä-ntunawāt wīstāwah. piyis nīswäw äh-nipāt, äkuyikuhk miskawäw mistanaskwah, mistah äh-ayāyit mītsiwin, äkwah wiyah ä-wīh-nipahāhkatusutsik utawāsimisah uwīkimākanah. mistahi miywäyihtam ä-miskawāt wīstāwah.

ōmis ītwäw : " hay hay hay ! äkwah kä-mītsisuyān, nīstāw äh-utihtak, mistahi äh-ayāt wiyāsah, " itwäw awa wākayōs.

äkwah tāpwä asamäw ; ma-mītsisōw ; iyāta-pōni-mītsisutsi, kiyipah nōhtähkatäw. äkwah äh-kīsitāpuwiht, äh-asamiht, piyisk tipiskāyiw. namuya wīh-nipāw, kapä-tipisk äh-mītsisut ō wākayōs. piyisk wāpaniyiw.

" hāhāw, nīstā, kāhkäwakwah ta-tahkupitam nisīm, ka-kīwähtatāyān. mistahi nōhtähkatäwak kitihkwatimak, kimis mīna, " itwäw.

tāpwä mistahi tahkupitam, ta-nayahtamiyit.

äkwah ä-wīh-kīwät awa wākayōs, ōmisi itäw : " hā, nistā, kīh-nīsutipiskākä nika-pāpitsin, " itwäw wākayās.

äkusi äh-kīwät.

äkwah umisī itwäw mistanask : " äkusi ihtik [2] ānih kā-kitimahikuyahk mīnah, nōtukäsiw, kistäs. hāw, tahtuh äh-miywāsikih kikāhkäwakuma kātāh. takuhtätwāwi, kahkiyaw tit-ōtinam kimītsiwininawa, " itäw uwīkimākanah.

---

[1] In monologue the Cree (like the Fox and the Menomini) use the first person plural in the exclusive form, as if addressing some being not involved in the act.

[2] Probably read *ätsik*.

tāpwäw kātāw ātiht, äh-wātihkät pīhtsāyīhk wīkiwāhk, äkutah äh-asiwatāt umītsiwinah.

äkwah awah wākayōs kā-kīwät wāpani-pimuhtäw. äh-utākusiniyik, takuhtäw uwīkiwāhk. mistahi pätāw ka-mītsiyit tawāsimisah. mistahi miywäyihtamiyiwa.

ōmis ītwäw : " mihtsät nipahäw mistanask mustuswah. kä-wāpahk kik-äspitsinānaw, " itwäw.

ā, miywäyihtamiyiwa utawāsimisah. käkāts wāpanih-mītsisōwak. iyikuhk ōmah kā-pätāwiht, käkāts kahkiyaw kitāwak. äh-wāpaniyik, wawäyīwak, ä-sipwähtätsik, äh-ituhtätsik ōhih mistanaskwah. piyis tipiskāyiw ä-pimuhtätsik ; namuya nipāwak. piyis wāpaniyiw. äkwah äwakō kapäkīsik pimuhtäwak. äh-utākusik, äkuyikuhk takuhtäwak ōh ītahk äh-wīkiyit mistanaskwah. kwayātsih-pānaham awa sikākuskwäw itah ta-kapäsiyit ustäsah, uhpim äkutah ä-sakāyik, äkuta äh-ntawi-kapäsiyit. " ōtäh, " āt äh-itāt awa sikākuskwäw ustäsah, namuya tāpwähtam awa wākayōs, itah äh-kapäsit awa wākayōs.

äh-kīsih-tsimatātsik wīkiwāw, " āh, āstamitik, nitawāsimisitik, nātahtān wiyāsah, " itäw utawāsimisah.

kahkiyaw sipwähtäwak. äkwah awa sikākuskwäw mistahi mākwäyimōw, äh-kiskäyihtahk ä-wīh-utinamiyit unīmāwiniwāw.

" ahā, nīstāh, pīhtukä ! " āt äh-itāt awa mistanask, namuya tāpwähtam awa wākayōs.

kahkiyaw wiyāsah utinam.

" ā, ntawāsimisitik, kīwähtatāk, " itäw utawāsimisah.

ōhu wiyāsah āwatāwak mistahi. kahkiyaw utinam, äh-mästsi-kīwähtatāt wiyāsah. äkwah pīhtukäw awa wākayōs ; kahkiyaw utinam umītsiwiniyiwa mistanaskwah, kahkiyaw äh-maskamāt. äkwah awa sikākuskwäw mātōw, äh-mawihkātahk, unīmāwinah äh-mihtātahk.

umis ītäw : " niwīkimākan, äkus ätsik āni kä-nipahāhkatusuyahk," itwäw, päskis äh-mātut.

" kiyām āpä ! " itwäw awa mistanask ; " ayīsk kakäpātisiw kistäs, " itäw uwīkimākanah.

äkusi mituni nama käkway ayāw ta-mītsit awa mistanask. äkwah wākayōs mistahi ayāw mītsiwin ; pisisik mītsisōwak awa wākayōs. piyis kinwäs nama käkway mītsiw awa mistanask ; wīh-nipahāhkatusōw piyisk. iyātah-wāpamātsih mustuswah, namuya wīh-nipahäw.

" misawāt kahkiyaw tit-ōtinäw awa wākayōs, nipahimakih, " äh-itäyihtahk, äk ōhtsi namuya wīh-nipahäw.

piyis mīnah nōhtähkatäw awa wākayōs, äh-kitāt nīmāwinah. kītahtawä kā-wāpamāt mustuswah. ituhtäw awa wākayōs.

" hāw, nistah, mistanask ! kisiwāk ōtah ayāwak mustuswak. minahōh ; kinōhtähkatānānaw, " itwäw.

äkwah mistanask pasikōw, äh-ati-sipwähtät, äh-tsikahkwātāt. kahkiyaw nipahäw.

täpwäw awa wākayōs, " nitawāsimisitik, mästsihäw kisisiwāw ! āstamitik ! pä-nātamuk wiyās, " itwäw, äh-ati-sipwähtät.

āsay awa mistanask päyak äh-wiyinuwit ōhi mustuswah äkunih wīh-utinäw ; äkuyikuhk kā-takuhtät awa wākayōs.

" tānähki, mistanask ? "

" āh, ä-wīh-ayāwak, äh-umustusumiyān, ä-wīh-uwiyāsimiyān. mistahi nnōhtähkatānān, nīsta, " itwäw mistanask.

umis ītwäw wākayōs : " āyähtān ätukä kiy-ōwiyāsimiyan äh-wiyinut!" itäw.

" ā, māka kisīm nōhtähkatäw, " itwäw.

tāpwä pikuh utinäw awa wākayōs ōhi mistanaskwah, ä-sakipitunänāt, äh-kwāhtsiwäpināt.

" kīwä ! nama käkway kik-āyān wiyās," itäw mistanaskwah.

kīwäw mistanask ; kustäw wākayōsah. kahkiyaw utinam wiyāsah awa wākayōs. äkwah äh-utākusik, ituhtäw awa sikākuskwäw itah ä-kīh-wiyanihtākäwiht. wāpahtam mihkuh. äwakuh utinam ; kīwähtatäw, äh-asiwatāt utaskihkuhk, pahkih äwakō äh-kīsisahk mihku, äh-mītsitsik awa mistanask.

piyisk äh-tipiskāyik, piyisk kawisimōwak. äh-mäkwā-pimisihkik, nam äskw äh-nipātsik, kā-pähtawātsik awāsisah äh-mātōyit. waniskāw awa sikākuskwäw, äh-kutawät, kā-wāpamāt awāsisah askihkuhk äh-asiwasōyit, äh-mātōyit. utinäw, äh-kitimākinawāt, " kik-ayāwānaw, " äh-itāt uwīkimākanah.

ōmis ītwäw mistanask : " namuya ka-kīw-uhpikihānaw. käkway käpustayōwinisät ? ta-nipahāhkatusōw, ä-nōhtähkatäyahk. kiyām wayawīwäpin," itäw.

" nka-kitimahāw, " itwäw awa sikākuskwäw.

" wayawīwäpin kiyām, " itwäw mistanask.

äkwah awa sikākuskwäw utsämäw, äh-wayawīwäpināt, " tāpwä nikitimahāw," äh-itwät.

kā-pä-pīhtukätātsimuyit ōh āwāsisah, " nutukäsiw, utin ; wayawīwäpin."

utinäw away iskwäw, äh-wayawīwäpināt, äh-ma-mawimuwit.

äh-pä-pīhtukäyit, äh-pimuhtsäsiyit, " hā, nutukäsiw, wayawīwäpin, " itwäw.

āsa mīna wayawīwäpinäw.

kā-pä-pīhtukäyit nāpäsisah, " ähā, nōtukäsiw, wayawīwäpin."

äh-āta-ma-mawimuwit, wayawīwäpinäw.

kā-pä-pīhtukäyit uskinīkiwa mistah ä-miyusiyit, äh-wītisiyit, äkusi ōtä wäskwāhtämihk ä-nahapiyit, ä-musäskatäyit, " hāh, nutukäsiw, kitakuhpah awih ; t-akwanahōw. "

äkusi ōmisi itwäw awaw uskinīkiw : " nōhtā, " itäw ōhi mistanaskwah, " kitayān tsī pahkäkinus, apihtsatsikus-pahkäkinus ? "

" aha' , nka-ntunän. "

äkwah nitunam ; miskam.

" hāw, ōm ītah, nikusis, " itwäw mistanask.

ōmisi tōtam : pahpawipayihtäw aw uskinīkiw pahkäkin.

" miskutākay ta-wīh-ihtakun ! " itwäw awaw uskinīkiw.

tāpwä, miskutākay. pustasākäw.

käyāpits, " pätāh pahkäkinus, " itwäw awa uskinīkiw.

mīna miyäw. awa uskinīkiw pahpawipayihtäw.

" t-ōtāsiyān ta-wiy-ihtakunwah ! " itwäw.

tāpwä, mitāsah.

äkwah ōmis ītwäw aw ōskinīkiw, watōw-awāsis : " nōhtāh, mustuswayānis, pāhpākōwäwayānis ! "

utinäw. pahpawipayihäw awa uskinīkiw.

itwäw, " ta-wīh-misäkisiw, tit-ōtakuhpiyān, äskanak ta-kikamutsik, mīnah waskasiyah ta-kikamuyit ! " itwäw awa uskinīkiw.

tāpwäh kikamuyiwa äskanah mīna waskasiyah, mustuswaskasiyah. äkus äkunih akwanahōw aw uskinīkiw.

" hā, nōhtāh, kīspin kitayāwāw nikikwayānis, miyin."

tāpwä nitunawäw awa mistanask ; miskawäw.

" hāw, ītah, nikusis," itäw.

utinam awā uskinīkiw ; pahpawipayihäw.

ōmis ītwäw : " ta-misiwäsiw awah nikikwayān, t-ōtastutniyān !" itwäw aw uskinīkiw. " äkusi, nōhtāh, ntawi-kīskikahah misāskwatwah ahtāpāhtik.[1] *"*

tāpwäh ntawi-kīskikaham awa mistanask. mistahi miywäyihtam uskinīkiwah äh-ayāwāt. äkwah, " tān-tah awah äh-uhtuhtät ?" itäyihtam awa mistanask, ōh ōkusisah. namuya kiskäyihtam. askihkuhk kā-kīh-asiwatätsik mihkuh, äyuk ōhtsi ayīsiyinīwiw aw uskinīkiw, usām äh-kisiwāsit, ōhih äh-kitimahimiht mistanaskwah. äkusi aw uskinīkiw ōmis īsiyīh-kāsōw : watōw-awāsis. tāpiskōts mihkuh kinwäs äh-astäk maskawāw ; äku niyān " watōw " ntisiyīhkātānān. äkutah uhtsih aw uskinīkiw äh-uhtsīt, äkusi watōw-awāsis.

äkwah ōh atsusisah usīhtāwak. piyisk wāpaniyiw, kahkiyaw äh-kīsihtät-sik. äkwah nama käkway mītsisōwak. äh-apitsik kīksäpā, kā-pätuhtät awah wākayōs. umis ītwäw : " hā, nīstāh mistanask, minahuh ōki mustus-wak," itwäw.

äkusi mistanask utinam ōma tsikahkwān, äh-wayawīt. wāpamäw mustuswah. ituhtäw, ä-wīh-kakwä-nipahät. tāpwä tsikahkwätäw ōhi mustuswah ; kahkiyaw nipahäw. äkwah tānihih äh-wiyinuyit, äwakunih tähtapiw awa mistanask.

" nīstāh, aw äkwah niya niwīh-ayāwāw," itäw wākayōsah.

" ayītä ätukä kiyah kiy-āyāwat äh-wiyinut ?" itwäw wākayōs ; " ā, namuya, nistāh !"

" nistah, ōma nnōhtähkatānān kisīm !"

" ā, namuya !" itwäw awa wākayōs.

mākah aw uskinīkiw paspāpiw, äh-kitāpamāt ōhtäwiyah. kītahtawä k-ōtinahk mōhkumān awa wākayōs, ōhi mistanaskwah äh-pakamahwāt ustikwāniyihk ōta ; tsikahkwäwäpahwäw ; utinäw uspituniyihk, wīkiwäyihk äsiwäpināt. aw uskinīkiw watsōw-awāsis kisiwāsiw, ōhtāwiyah äh-tsikahk-wäwäpahumiht ; ati-wayawīw, äh-ati-sipwähtät, ōhtäwiyah ä-ituhtät. tsīk äy-ihtāt, äkuyikuhk waniskāyiwah ōhtäwiyah ; kipistanähumāwah. äh-wāpamāt awa wākayōs ōh ōskinīkiwah äh-pätuhtäyit, " yāh yahāh, nitihkwā, äkusi māna ntōtawāw äh-pa-pāhpisihak kōhtāwiy, ätamihitsih, mihtsät näpahātsi mustuswah !"

ōmis ītwäw awa mistanask, uskiwanihk uhtsi mihkuh äh-wāh-wäpinahk : " namuya äh-pa-pāhpisihiyan, nīstāh, mistahi äh-kwatakihiyan, nīstāh !"

tsämāk aw ōskinīkiw pīkiskwäw, " tāpwä mistahi kikitimahāw nōhtā-wiy !" itäw, uhtsāhtsāpiyah uhtsi äh-pakamahwāt ōhi wākayōsah.

mituni tāskiwäpahwäw, uspiskwanihk ōtä äh-ākōpayihuyit ōhtäwiyah mistanaskwah, äh-kwäskipayihut. āsa minah ōmis īsi māmawōpayiyiwah wākayōsah ; pä-mōskīstāk. āsa mīna pakamahwäw ; tāskiwäpahwäw mīna.

" ā, nuhtā, päyak äyōkō utihtin !" itäw ōhtäwiyah aw uskinīkiw.

---

[1] This sounds like "bow-tree" (*ahtsapiy* : "bow").

mina wīsta napatä utihtinäw ; äh-māh-maniswāt, nipahäw. äkwah awah wākayōs utawāsimisah, ustäsimāw awa pä-mōskīstawäw ōh ōskinīkiwah.

ōmis ītwäw: " tāpwä kikitimahin, watsōw-awāsis, nōhtāwiy kā-nipahat, " itwäw.

äh-pāpayiyit, aw uskinīkiw pimwäw ; nipahäw. kutakah minah pämōskīstāk ; äkunih mīnah nipahäw, äh-pimwāt. piyis kahkiyaw mōskīstāk ; kahkiyaw mästsihäw ōhi wākayōsah. miywäyihtam awa mistanask äh-mätsihimiht, äh-kīh-kitimahikut. mistahi äkwah ayāw wiyās, äkutah uhts äkwah aw uskinīkiw äh-māh-mātsīt, äh-māwatsihtamawāt ōhtāwiyah mītsiwin.

mistah ä-kīh-ayāt, ōmis ītwäw : " ā, nōhtah, kika-nakatitin. ōtäh nik-ätuhtān kā-wīkihk," itwäw awa watsōw-awāsis.

" wāh ! "

mihtātam awah mistanask ä-wīh-sipwähtäyit ukusisah, sām äh-sākihāt.

" nōhtāh, namuya ä-wīh-wäpinitān ; nika-takuhtān, " itwäw aw ōskinīkiw.

" āha', " itwäw mistanask.

tāpwä pasikōw, äh-utsämāt ōhtāwiyah äkwah ukāwiyah. äkus īsi wayawīw, ä-sipwähtät. mayaw äh-ākawäwät, utinam atsusis, äh-pimutāhkwät.

" ā, nīpisis ōma, äkutah nika-nīpawin ! näkih ayīsiyiniwak kā-wīkitsik, āstam-itah äkutah nka-pahkisinin ! " itwäw.

tāpwä äkutä pahkisin. äkutah utinam wīpisis. äkusi ituhtäw mīkiwāhpihk ; päyak nōtukäsiwah mistahi äh-ktimākisiyit, äh-päyakuyit, äkutah pīhtukäw.

" ay-apih, nōsisimis ! " itik.

äyak ōma utänaw mistah ä-āyimisit wākayōs äkutah äh-ukimāwit. nä ōtawāsimisah, nīsw īskwäwah, nīsu näpäwah. kīspin äh-kiskäyihtahk mustuswah näpahimihtsih, kahkiyaw äh-utinahk wiyinwah awa wākayōs kā-ukimāwit, äkwah mäkwāts nōhtähkatäwak, äkut äh-ay-ayāt awa watsōw-awāsis. namuya kiskäyihtam awa watsōw-awāsis. äh-wīhkwästäyikih mīkiwāhpah, tawāyihk äh-astäyik pīhtukahān.

äkwah ōmisī itik ōhkumah awa watsōw-awāsis : " nōsisä, mistah ōmah äh-nōhtähkatähk ; iyātah-natunawātwāwih mustuswah uskinīkiwak, namuya miskawäwak ; namuya wāpamäwak. äkusi aw ōkimāw, awiyah pīhtukäpayihāyitsih mustuswah, utänisah ä-wīh-miyāt, mistahi ä-miyusitsik uskinīkiskwäwak. " äkusi ōmis ītäw : " mākah iyātah-nipahimihtsih mustuswah, kahkiyaw wiyinwah äh-utinahk ō wākayōs, itah kā-miywāsik wiyās äh-utinahk, namuy āwiya ä-kīhnipahikut, äh-āyimisit."

" hāh hāw, nōhkōh, nika-nātsipahān itsi, " itäw ōhkumah.

" äkāyah ! " itik ; " namuya misawāts äh-miywāsik wiyās ka-kīh-mītsinānaw, " äh-itikut ōhkumah.

piyisk kawisimōwak. kīksäpā äh-waniskāt awah watsōw-awāsis, käyāpits nipāyiwah ōhkumah. äkus īsi wayawīw, ä-sipwähtät, mustuswah ä-nātāt. wāhyaw äh-ayāt, mustusu-mäyah māwatsihtāw, ä-nāh-nāwayōstāt, umis īsi, mustusu-mäyah.

umis ītwäw : " pasikōk ! pasikōk ! pasikōk ! " itwäw.

pasikōyiwa mustuswah mihtsät.

" tsäskwa ! tsäskwa ! " itäw.

ituhtäw ; wāpamäw päyak äh-wīnuwit ; äwukunih māh-manipitam upīwayah.

" hāw, kika-kawāhkatusun, " itäw ; "hāw, uma kā-wīh-kīwähtahitakuk ka-pīhtukäpayināwāw pīhtukahānihk. kiyah, " itäw, " namuya ka-pīhtukān. ōt äsi natimihkisihk kik-äsi-ituhtān. atimwak ka-māmawōhkākwak ; mīn awāsisak ka-pāh-pimukwak. kunt ītä ayāw nōhkum wīkih ; ka-wāpahtān ; äkutah iskwāhtämihk ka-nipahikwak awāsisak, " itäw ōhi mustuswa. äkusi, " ā, niyāk äkwa ! pimipayik ! "

äkwah tāpwä sipwäpayiwak mustuswak, äkwah ōtä nāway ä-pimipahtāt, mustuswah ōhih ä-sīhkitisahwāt. äh-pōn-āpihta-kīsikāyik, takusinwak ōki mustuswak. äkwah awō mustus päyak äh-kawāhkatsusut, äwakō kunt ītäh ispayiw. äkus ōki ayīsiyiniwak äh-wāpamātsik äh-kawāhkatsusuyit, namuya pisiskäyimäwak. atimwak māmawōhkawäwak, piyisk nāpäsisak ä-pāh-pimwātsik, awa nōtukäsiw wīkihk äy-ispayiyit. äkutah nipahik awāsisah awa mustus.

awa nōtukäsiw mistahi miywäyihtam, " äkwah wiyās nikah-ayān, " äh-itäyihtahk.

äkwah awa watsōw-awāsis ākawāyihk ayäw ; namuya wāpamik ayīsiyiniwah, " tāpiskōts awāsis äh-kitimākisit, äh-māyātisit, äkusi nik-äsinākusin ! " äh-itwät awah watsōw-awāsis.

äkusi kīwäw ; ōhkumah, äh-takuhtät, mäkwāts wīnihtakäyiwah.

" hāy hāy hāy, nōhkō ! äkwah wiyās kik-ayānānaw ! " itwäw.

" äha', " itik ōhkumah.

äkwah näkih kutakak mustuswak, äkunih kahkiyaw nīpahäwak ōk ayīsiyiniwak. māka mīnah awa wākayōs k-āyimisit kahkiyaw ōtinam wiyinwah, äh-kitimahāt ōwītsäwākanah. äkwah awah watsōw-awāsis äh-pīhtukatāyit ōhkumah wiyāsah, kahkiyaw pīhtukatāyiwa.

" nōhkō, akwanahah kiwiyāsimah ! " äkwah awa nōtukäsiw ä-kīh-akwanahahk, " nōhkō, ntawi-kīskatahah nāwō nīpisīsah. "

tāpwä awa nōtukäsiw ntawi-kīskataham ; pätāw.

" ōh, ītä, nōsisä, " itwäw.

" nōhkō, wayawīh ! wayawītimihk ōtah nīpawih ! "

tāpwä äkwah awa watsōw-awāsis pāh-pasastäham wiyāsah, " paskunä, paskunä ! " äh-itwät.

tāpwä wiyinōwiyiwa.

" a, nōhkō, pīhtukä ; äkwah pakāhtākuhkä ; mītsisutān ! "

awa nōtukäsiw äh-pāskinahk uwiyāsima, äh-wāpahtahk äh-wiyinuwiyikih, kāwiy akwanaham.

" nōsisä, nōsisä ! namuya kik-āyānānaw ōhi. kiskäyihtahkih aw ōkimāw, ta-pä-nātam, " itwäw.

" ā, nōhkō, mītsisutān, " itwäw.

tāpwäh äkwah paminawasōw awa nōtukäw. awa watsōw-awāsis misiwäw ōtōnihk uma wiyin sinikuhtitāw, äh-tōmisit. äkusi äkwah wayawīw.

" nōhkō, pānsāwäh ; akutāhkan kiwiyinuma. niwī-ntawi-ma-mätawān. "

" nōsisä, kāsīhah kitōn ! "

" āsay, nōhkō ! "

äkus īsi sipwähtäw, ōhi k-āyimisiyit wākayōsah äkuni ōkusisiyiwah äh-ntawih-wītsi-mätawāmāt. kā-wāpamikut mistah äh-tōmisit utōnihk watāhk mīnah, äkusi kīwäyiwah ōhi nāpäsisah, äh-ntawi-wīhtamawāyit ōhtāwiyiwa.

ōmis ītwäyiwa : " nōhtāh, mistah äh-tōmisit ōtah aw awāsis kā-kitimākisiyit ōhkumah ! "

" wāh, namuya ! " itwäw wākayōs ; " nkīh-wāpamāw äh-kawāhkatusuyit, " itwäw.

äkusi kīwäpahtāw aw watsōw-awāsis ōhkumah wīkisiyihk. äh-apit pīhtsāyihk, kā-pä-paspiskwäyiyit ōhi nāpäsisah. wāpahtamiyiwah wiyinwah. kīwäyiwah.

ōmis ītwäyiwah ōhkumah : " nōsisä, āta kikīh-kitahamātn ä-wīh-ituhtäyan. kahkiyaw ōhi ta-päw-utinam anā wākayōs, " itwäyiwa.

nāhā nāpäsis ātsimustawäw ōhtāwiyah. " mistahi wiyinwah ayāwak mīna kāhkäwakwa äh-wiyinōwiyikih, " äkus ītäw.

pasikōw aw ōkimāw, äh-ituhtät ; äh-yōhtänahk, äh-itāpit, kāh-wāpahtahk.

" ā, mästatäw-awāsis, nipä-nātän kōhkum ukāhkäwakumah, mīnah wiyinwah. "

" aha' , utinah, " itäw.

utinamiyiwa kahkiyaw, äh-maskamikutsik, äh-kīwähtatāyit. mātuyiwa ōhkuma ä-mawihkātamiyit uwiyinumiyiwa.

ōmis ītäw : " kiyām apä, nōhkō ; nika-nātän kiwiyinuma, " itäw.

" äkā wiya, nōsisä ; kika-nipahik. "

" namuya, nōhkō ; niwīh-nātän ! "

äkus āti-pasikōw, äh-ituhtät.

äh-yōhtänahk, umis ītwäw : " māski-maskwah, npä-nātän nōhkum uwiyinuma. "

" aha' , äha' , utinah."

pīhtukäw ; pasikōyiwa ä-sakipitunänikut, äh-wayawīwäpinikut. āsa mina pasikōw. pīhtukäw, " nipä-nātän nōhkum uwiyinuma," äh-itāt.

" hä' !"

āsay awah awa māski-maskwah ukusisah ōmisi itwäyiwah : " nōhtāh, äkāyā pisiskäyīm ! nama wīhkāts awiyak äkusi kitōtāk. äh-manitōwit ätukw āwa ! nitakis ätukw āwa kä-mantōwit ! kākāts awa pāskatayäpayiw, ä-mistatayät. "

ä-wīh-utinahk uwiyinuma, ōhkumah, āsay mīnah kā-pasikōyit ōh ōkimāwa. nawatinamwäw uspituniyiwa, äh-nāh-nātwānamwāt ōhō wākayōsah ; mīna utōniyiw tāwāpiskanäpitäw. äkusi nama käkway kīh-mitsiminamiyiwa. äkusi äkwah kahkiyaw ōwiyinumiyiwa ōhkumah, ukāhkäwakumiyiwa kīwähtatāw, aspin äh-ma-mawimuyit ōhih wākayōsah, " wāh, wāh ! " äh-itwäyit.

pätāw wīkiwāhk. äkus āy-apiw äkwah.

äkwah awa wākayōs ukusisah ōmisiy itik : " äkusi kā-kīh-ititān, nōhtāh ; namuya kitāpwähtawin, " itik ; " hāw, kakwäh-iyinihkāhisuh kispitunah mina kitōn, " itik.

" āha' . "

äh-ātah-wīh-kakwä-iyinihkahisut, namuya kaskihtāw. piyisk wīhnipiw.

" hāw, " itik ukusisah, " hā, nōhtā, nisīmah ōhi "—ōk ōskinīkiskwäwak —" ä-isi-nīsiyit miyih. kika-pimātsihik ta-wīkimāt. "

" āha' , "

tōpwä awa nōtukäsiw ituhtäw, äh-ntawi-miyāt utānisah ōhi watsōwawāsisah.

umisiy ītäw: "hāw, äyukunik ntānisak kimiyikawin, ka-kakwä-pimātsihat kisäyiniw," itwäw.

"hāha'," itwäw watsōw-awāsis, "hā, nya, kīwä," itäw ōhi nōtuk-äsiwah.

tāpwä ituhtäw. äh-pīhtukät, pōtih mistahi tāwatäyiwah. äkusi äkwah sōskwāts uspituniyiwah utinam, ä-sinikunamawāt. kāwih miywāsiniyiwa. mīnah utōniyiw äwaku mīnah ä-sinikunamwāt, äkusi miyw-ayāyiwa. äkusi kīwäw ōhkumah wīkiyihk; äkutä ayāw. piyis tipiskāyiw. äh-wāpaniyik uhpimäh mānukäyiwa ōh ōskinīkiskwäwa. äh-kīsi-mānukäyit, pä-nitumäw. ituhtäw. äh-pīhtukät, sämāk wāpamäw ōh ōskinīkiskwäwa äh-umisimāwiyit; kiskäyihtam äh-pakwātikut, äh-wīnäyimikut äyōkunih. nahapīstawäw; tahkih uhpimä ispayihuyiwa. namuya kisiwāk wītapimik, äh-pakwātikut. piyisk äh-tipiskāyik, äh-kawisimutsik, namuya wīh-akwanahik, usām äh-māyātisit, äh-itäyimikut. piyisk ä-wīh-kakwä-akwanahut, namuya tāpwäh-tāk. piyisk äkus īsi nipāyiwah. äkwah utanaskāniyihk sikiw. äh-kiskäyih-tahk aw īskwäw, waniskāw.

"yipātsihäw nitanāskānah," itwäw aw īskwäw.

äkusi utinäw; kawisimōw aw iskwäw. ä-wih-āta-kawisimut awa watsōw-awāsis, pakwātik. ntawāts pasikōw. ōhi kutakah usīmimāwah äkutah kawisimōw. äwakunih akwanahuk; namuya pakwātik. piyisk äh-nipāyit, āsa min äyakunih sikitäw. kiskäyihtamiyiwa.

waniskāyiwa, "tsäskwah, waniskā!" äh-itikut; "awa nika-utināw kā-sāpupät!" äkusi itwäyiwa.

äkusi utinäyiwa kutakah, äh-ahāyit. äkusi kawisimōwak. äkwah akwanahik. äwakunih namuya pakwātik; kitimākäyimik äwakuni.

piyis wāpaniyiw. äh-waniskātsik, kätāpamātsih ōh ōmisimāwa, kis-käyihtam äh-pakwātikut.

ōh ōsīmimāwa kā-wītapimāt mīnisah äh-usīhtāyit, äh-asamikut, wāh-mītsisutsih, umis ītwäyiwa ōh ōmisimāwa: "nisīm, tāpwä namuya kipak-wātāw awiyak äh-wīninākusit!" äh-itwäyit.

äkusi äōkō äh-tipiskāk, äkwah äh-nipātsik, ōmis ītäw ōh ōwīkimākanah: "hāw, kitāpatsihun äkā kā-pakwāsiyan," itäw; "namuya äkusi ta-isinākusiyān ōma kā-wāpamiyan äsinākusiyān. kä-wāpahk nika-nātāwak mustuswak. wīhtamawāhkan kōhtāwiy äkā wiyah kā-kitimahāt ayīsiyini-wah; kāy äkwah äkusi tit-ōtinam wiyinwah; äkusi itāhkan. hāw, pāsi-wakwāwi mustuswak, nika-pä-nīkānuhtān. pahkäkin nik-ōskutākān; äkutō-wahk nik-ōtāsin; äkwah mustuswayān nik-ākwanahun; äskanak ta-kikamōwak mīnah waskasiyak. mīnah nikikwayān nik-ōtastutinin. niy äwakō. nika-pīhtukān pīhtukahānihk. nik-āskōkwak mustuswak. wäsk-wāhtämihk uhtsi nika-kīhtsäkusīpayihun; äkutäh nik-ākusīn. kika-päy-ituhtān; mīnisāpuy ka-pätān. äkutä ka-mītsinānaw; ka-nīsu-mītsisun-ānaw. kīspin kitayān äh-miywāsikih kitayōwinisah, äwakunih kika-pustayō-winisān, wīh-päy-ituhtäyini," itäw uwīkimākanah.

äkusi nipāwak. äh-mäkwä-nipāt aw uskinīkiskwäw, kītahtawä päku-payiw. namwāts nipāyiwa unāpäma, āsay ä-sipwähtäyit, äh-nātäyit mus-tuswah. kiyipa wāpaniyiw. äkusi ä-kīh-waniskātsik, umisah ä-kīh-mīt-sisutsik, wayawīw, ōhtāwiyah äh-ituhtät.

ōmisiy itäw: "nōhtāh, aspin kīksäp ä-sipwähtāt kinahāhkisīm."

"āh yahāw, ntānis, tānähkih äkā kā-kitahamawat? ta-kawatsiw nnah-āhkisīm," itwäw.

"ōmisi mākah kitik kinahāhkisīm, nōhtāh : ' päsiwakwāwi mustuswak, äkāya kā-tōtahk, k-ōtinahk wiyinwah, ōhi utiyinīmah kā-maskamāt wiyinwa,' kitik kinahāhkisīm, ta-wīhtaman tsit-āsawāpamātsik mustuswah. äkusi kīh-itwäw kinahāhkisīm."

" āha', ntānis, nika-pōnihtān ; k-ätwät nnahāhkisīm nka-tōtän."

äkusi kīwäw aw uskinīkiskwäw.

äkusi wayawīw awa kisäyiniw, ōmis äh-itwät : " uskinīkītik, asawāpik. kayās kīksäp äsah kī-sipwähtäw ninahāhkisīm, äh-nātāt mustuswah," äh-itwät awa kisäyiniw.

äkusi tāpwäw kapä-kīsik ay-asawāpiwak ōk ōskinīkiwak. äh-pōn-āpihtā-kīsikāyik, kā-pāpayiyit mustuswah. sāsay aw uskinīkiskwäw mīnisah kīsisam, " māskōts takuhtätsih," äy-itäyimāt unāpäma. pōtih kisiwāk äh-päy-ihtāyit, uskinīkiwak ōki kā-wāpamātsik mistah äh-miyusiyit uskinīkiwah, nīkān äh-pä-pimipahāyit mustuswah, äh-askōkuyit. namwāts nisitawäyimäwak ōh ōskinīkiwah. sämāk pīhtukäw uma pīhtukahān ; äkutah ōhtsi wäskwāhtämih kīhtsäkusīpayihōw ōw uskinīkiw ; äkuyikuhk äkwah pīhtukäpayiyiwa ōhi mustuswah. sämāk kā-wāpamāt äh-miyusiyit uskinīkiwah : äwakunih unāpämah. sämāk wāsakām uhtsi kīhtsäkusīwak uskinīkiwak iskwäwak mīnah, ä-wīh-wāpamātsik ōhi mustuswah. äkusi äkwah äh-pāh-pāskiswātsik ōhi mustuswah, aw ōskinīkiskwäw mīnisah wiyākanihk ä-kīh-astāt, kā-ntaw-asamāt uwīkimākanah. wāpamäw awa umisimäw kā-kīh-pakwātāt ; äkwah miywäyimäw äh-miyusiyit, äh-wāpamāt āsay usīma kā-ta-kīhtsäkusiyit, ä-wīh-miyāyit ōhi mänisah, " nah ōhi utinah," äh-itāyit. ōtinam aw ōskinīkiw. kahkiyaw awiyah miywäyimik aw ōskinīkiw. äkusi äkwah kīwäpahtäw awa ōmisimäw kā-kīh-pakwātāt.

ōmisi itäw ukāwiyah : " nākāh, pātāh mīnisah !"

miyik. äkwah kīsisam. namuya mistahi kīsisam, " käkā kä-pä-kīwät nnāpäminān," äy-itäyihtahk, usām äh-miywäyihtahk. äh-wāpamāt usīmah äh-wītsi-mītsisōmāyit, " nīst äkutä nika-mītsisun," äh-itäyihtahk, tāpwä sipwähtatäw umänisimah, äh-takuhtatāt.

" nah ōh ōtinah," itäw.

aw uskinīkiw ōmisiy itäw : " pä-āmatsiwähtatāh," itäw ōhi kā-kīh-pakwātikut.

tāpwäh āmatsiwäw aw īskwäw. mwähtsih tsīki äh-ayāt, kā-sōskuskawāt mistikwah ; nīhtsipayiw ; sīkipayiyiw umänisāpōm ; usit napatä mitsimōtäw ; kusāwäkutsin. kahkiyaw awiyak mistahi pāhpiwak, iskwäwak, awāsisak. piyisk mātōw aw uskinīkiskwäw, äh-näpäwisit, ä-nīhtsipayit. äkusiy isī äh-pihkuhut. kīwäw, äh-mātut. äkwah ōki, āsay kahkiyaw äh-nipahimiht mustuswah, kīwäw awah watsōw-awāsis.

ä-pīhtukätsik wīkiwāhk, awa kā-kīh-pakwātāt, " nisīm, nistah päyak umaskisin nika-kikamuhtāwān ; nika-pustaskisinahāw napatäh," äh-itwät ; " namōwya !" itwäw aw uskinīkiw.

wīst äkwah pakwātäw, ä-kīh-pakwātikut ōh ōmisimāwa. äkusi ay-ayāwak äkutah. pisisik mātōw awa ōmisimäw, äh-näpäwisit, ä-kīh-nīhtsipayit. papāmuhtäw tahkih. piyisk, " tānähkih ?" äh-itikut nanātuhk awiyah, " tānähki k-ōh-mātuyan ?"

" äh-näpäwihit watsōw-awāsis, äh-pakwāsit," äkusi äh-itwät.

" a nōsisä, kahkiyaw awiyah kitimākäyimik watsōw-awāsis," äh-itiht aw īskwäw, tahkih äh-papāh-mātut.

kītahtawä päyak nōtukäsiwah kā-wāpamāt, " tānähkih, nōsisim, pisisik ä-mātuyan ?" äh-itikut.

"äh-näpäwihit watsōw-awāsis," äh-itāt.

"äh, tsäskwah, nistah ta-näpäwisit nka-tōtawāw," itäw awa nōtukäsiw.

kītahtawä äh-papāmuhtät awa watsōw-awāsis, apisīs sīpīsis kā-wāpahtahk. äkutäh ituhtäw akāmihk aw ōskinīkiw kā-miyusit.

äh-ati-kīwät, kā-wāpamāt nōtukäsiwa, "nōsisäh, nayōmin; nama nikīh-āsōwahän," äh-itwäyit.

"a nōhkō, āsukanis nik-ōsīhtān, ta-pimuhtäyan."

"nōsisä, nika-pakastawäpayin," itwäw ō nōtukäsiw.

piyisk, "äha'," itäw.

nayōmäw, äh-āsuwahōhāt.

"hā, nōhkō, äkutah äkwah," äh-itāt, namuya wi-nīhtakusīw awa nōtukäsiw.

ä-wīh-kakwä-pahkwatināt ōhi nōtukäsiwah, nama kīh-pihkuhäw; tāpiskōts pīwāpisk uspituniyiwa uskātiyiwah mīna. äkwah namuya wīh-kīwäw, ä-näpäwisit, nōtukäsiwah äh-nayōmāt. piyisk ōmisi ōtah wīh-kipihkitunänik. piyisk kīwäw.

äh-wāpamāt aw ōmisimāw, mistahi pāhpiw, "tānähki ukistäyimuh watsōw-awāsis, nōtukäsiwah kā-päh-nayōmāt?" äh-itwät.

aw ōskinīkiskwäw äh-wāpamāt unāpämah, mistahä pakwātäw. äh-ātapakamahwāt, namuya kīh-nipahäw. kahkiyaw ayīsiyiniwak äh-āta-pakamahwātsik, namuya kīh-nipahäwak ōhi nōtukäsiwah. piyisk wīh-nipiw awa watsōw-awāsis. piyisk ōmisi tōtam, ōmisi, äkā ä-kīh-pīkiskwät. äkwah watōwah äyakuni äh-māwatsihimiht, äkutah äh-kawipayihut. awa nōtukäsiw ōhi watōwah äkunih pikōh mitsiminäw. awa wiya watsōw-awāsis uhpimä uhtsih pasikōw.

awa nōtukäsiw ōmisiy itwäw: "nōsisä, kiyām nika-pimātisin!" itwäw.

"äha'," itwäw watsōw-awāsis.

äkusi utinäw ōhi nōtukäwah, usitiyihk ä-mitsiminät.

ōmis ītwäw: "hā, nōtukäsiw, tsäskwah ōtäh nīkān ayīsiyiniwak titāyāwak; ōmisi tit-ätwäwak,"—pakamisimäw; usit pikō umah nōkwaniyiw awa nōtukäsiw,—"'kōhkōhkō-wiyaman[1]' tit-ätwäwak!"

"āstam!" itäw ōhi kā-kīh-pakwātikut iskwäwah.

äh-āta-mātuyit, utinäw; mistik äh-tsimasuyit, äkutah pakamisimäw.

"äkutah kiyah ka-kikamun; 'wasaskwätōw' kik-ätikwak ayīsiyiniwak. nama nāntaw kik-ätāpatisin; usām kikistäyimun—hā, āstamitik kahkiyaw ayīsiyinītik! hāw, nimanātsimākan, kiyah kitawāsimisak kiwīkimākan, ā, sipwähtäk! niyak! kiyawāw ōtäh nīkān ayīsiyiniwak 'wākayōsak' kāsiyihkātikōwāwak,—äkwah kiyawāw,"—kutakah,—"kiyawāw mahīhkanak, äkwah kutakak kiyawāw mahkäsīsak, äkwah kutakak kiyawāw pisiwak, kiyawāw kīhkwahākäsak!"

äkusi kahkiyaw pisiskiwah äkwah usīhäw. äkwah sipwähtäw; kīwäw; uwīkimākanah mīnah wītsäwäw. nistwäw äh-nipātsik, utihtäw ōhtäwiyah mistanaskwah. miywäyihtam awa mistanask äh-utihtikut ukusisah.

äkusi päyak tipiskāw äkutah äh-ayāt, ōmisiy itäw: "hā, nōhtah, usām kikīh-miyu-pimātisin. hā, kiyah ōtäh nīkān ayīsiyiniwak 'mistanask' kit-ätwäwak äyakunik ayīsiyiniwak. kika-mōwikwak, usām ä-kīh-miyupimātisiyan. —äkwah kiyah,"—ukāwiyah,—"'sikāk' kit-ätwäwak; mis-

---

[1] I do not know what this substance is.

tahi kā-miyu-pimātisin ; nama wīhkāts ka-tahkwamāwak ayīsiyiniwak. hā, niya ! ' wīntsuyäsīs ' kik-ätikwak ayīsiyiniwak ; kika-mōwikwak."

sipwähtäw.

" äkwah niyah watōw ; mihkuh uma, watōw niyah. äkusi äkwah nama käkway."

äkusi äkwah nama käkway ātsimuwin. äkuyikuhk äh-iskwāk ātayōhkäwin.

Once upon a time there dwelt somewhere Badger and his wife, Skunk, and they had no children at all. This Skunk-Woman's elder brother was Grizzly, and he was a terrible glutton, who always in a jiffy ate up all their food. And this Grizzly was not good at killing anything. So Badger went hungry much of the time; he nearly starved to death.

This is what Badger said: "Wife, we shall be starving to death. We had better go away from here," he said to her; "I shall tell your brother so; perhaps he will be willing to let us go. Only in this way can we stay alive."

"Yes, do that!"

So he called his brother-in-law, Grizzly.

When he came into the tent, "Good, come in!" said he to his brother-in-law, Grizzly; thus he spoke to him: "Brother-in-law, I am disappointing you; it is not to a meal that I am calling you. I have nothing to eat; it is only to tell you something, that I have called you: now, brother-in-law, hear me with pity; take pity on my plight. I beg this of you; let me go; let me go away from here; let me look for something to eat. Your sister here is almost dead from hunger. If, in time, I find something for us to eat, if I kill some buffalo, I shall come back here and bring meat," he told his brother-in-law; "for hereabouts there are no buffalo at all," he told his brother-in-law, meaning to deceive him; because the other too cruelly abused him, was why he wished to go away.

"Very well," said Grizzly; "Indeed, brother-in-law, it will be well if you kill a buffalo. At present I too have nothing to eat," said Grizzly.

Truly, glad was Badger that his brother-in-law gave him leave to go. So then they went to bed and slept. In the morning, at early day, Badger made ready to move camp.

Then, as they set out, then Badger spoke thus: "Now then, when I set out, let there be foul weather; let it snow!" he spoke.

So when he departed, really, he had not gone far, and already it was snowing. It was not cold. He went along with his camp all day, until there was no trail at all in the place where he marched. At last night came. Still they marched on; they tramped on till dawn, he and his wife. When they had marched all of that day, too, as evening came on, he saw some buffalo.

"There, old woman, now we can live; I shall make a killing of these buffalo," said Badger; "There, go camp over in that grove," he told his wife.

And he went to try and kill the buffalo. Indeed he threw his spear at them and killed them all. He was glad when he saw that he was going to get all of them. Then it stopped snowing. Then they cleaned them and took off the hides and took all the flesh; they wasted none of it. No wonder, for they had suffered much from hunger. Skunk-Woman was happy to see so much meat, thinking that, "Now we shall not starve."

Then that Grizzly in yonder place got very hungry. He grew restless when his brother-in-law failed to arrive, thinking, "No doubt he has killed buffalo." He wanted to look for his brother-in-law. "Ho, suppose I go look for Badger; no doubt he has killed buffalo," thought Grizzly, and went forth. He could not see where the other had gone by; for, of course, it had snowed; he lost Badger's trail. At last he went back home, unable to find his brother-in-law.

Then that Badger again saw some buffalo; these too he killed, all of them. These, too, they took entirely; they threw nothing away. They had much to eat.

Then Grizzly set out to look again for his brother-in-law. At last, after two nights on the road, he found Badger, found him in possession of much food, while he and his wife and children were starving. He was very glad to have found his brother-in-law.

He cried, "Splendid! Now I shall eat, now that I have come to my brother-in-law, who has so much meat," said Grizzly.

And so, really, he was given food; he ate and ate; even though he finished meal after meal, right off he was hungry again. So, as he was cooked for and served, night came on. He felt no need of sleep, but ate all through the night, that Grizzly. At last day broke.

"Hoho, brother-in-law, let my sister tie up dried meat for me to take home. Your nephews are very hungry and your sister," he said.

So she tied up a great amount of it, for him to carry on his back.

Then, when Grizzly was ready to go home, he spoke: "Now, brother-in-law, two nights from now I shall move my camp to this place," said Grizzly.

So then he went home.

Then thus spoke Badger: "So it is in this way that your brother will again reduce us to misery, wife. Now, do you hide the best of your dried-meats. When they come here, he will take away all our supplies of food," he said to his wife.

Accordingly, she hid some, digging a pit within the tent and putting in her store of food.

And that Grizzly, going home, marched all night. In the evening he arrived at his camp. He brought a great deal for his children to eat. They were very glad.

This is what he said: "Badger has killed many buffalo. Tomorrow morning we shall move camp to that place," he said.

Very glad were his children. They ate almost till dawn. As much as this was, which had been brought for them, they devoured nearly all of it. The next morning they made ready and set out to go to Badger's. Night fell while they were on the march; they did not stop to sleep. Day broke. All that day, too, they marched. In the evening they arrived there where Badger was camping. Skunk-Woman beforehand had cleared away the snow where she planned for her brother to camp, off to one side in a grove, off where he was to go and camp. Although Skunk-Woman said, "Over here!" to her brother, that Grizzly paid no heed, but camped right there.

When they had set up their tent, "Now, come here, children, let us fetch meat," he told his children.

They all went forth. Then that Skunk-Woman felt very sad, when she knew that he was going to take their food-supplies.

"Well, brother-in-law, come in!" said Badger, in vain, to him, but Grizzly paid no heed.

He took all the meat.

"Come, children, bring it home," he bade his children.

They carried off the meat in great quantity. He took all, carrying home the meat to the last bit. Then Grizzly went inside the tent; he took all of Badger's food supplies, robbing him of all. And Skunk-Woman cried, grieving for it, lamenting her store of food.

She said, "Husband, and so we are to starve to death," she said, weeping.

"Stay still where you are!" said Badger; "Your brother is incorrigible, and that is the end of it," he told his wife.

And so Badger had absolutely nothing to eat. And Grizzly and his household did nothing but eat. At last Badger had eaten nothing for a long time; at last he was almost dead from hunger. Although he would see buffalo, he did not care to kill them.

"In any case that Grizzly will take them all, if I kill any," he thought, and that was why he did not care to kill them.

At last Grizzly also was hungry, when he had eaten up the supplies. Then once he saw some buffaloes. Grizzly went there.

"Listen, brother-in-law, Badger! Close by here are some buffaloes. Make a killing, we are all hungry," he said.

Then Badger rose to his feet and went out to spear them. He killed them all.

Grizzly hallooed, "Children, your uncle has got them all! Come here! Come fetch the meat," he cried, and started out.

By this time Badger was on the point of taking one of those buffaloes, a fat one; just then up came Grizzly.

"What is the idea, Badger?"

"Why, I wanted it, seeing that I have some buffaloes, I wanted to have some meat. We are very hungry, brother-in-law," said Badger.

Grizzly cried: "And so you are going to have a fat one for your share of the meat, are you, indeed!" he said to him.

"Oh, but your sister is hungry," said he.

In truth, Grizzly merely took hold of Badger, seizing him by the arm, and flung him off to one side.

"Go home! You shan't have any meat at all," he told Badger.

Badger went home; he was afraid of Grizzly. Grizzly took all the meat. Then, in the evening, that Skunk-Woman went to the place where the butchering had been done. She saw some blood. She took this; she took it home and put in it her kettle, and heated a part of it, of that blood, for herself and Badger to eat.

Then, when night came, they went to bed. As they lay there, before they had gone to sleep, they heard a child crying. Skunk-Woman got up and lit a fire, and there she saw a child in the kettle, crying. She took it up, looking upon it with tender pity, and saying to her husband, "Let us keep him."

Badger said, "We shall not be able to raise him. What is he to wear? He will starve to death, seeing that we go hungry. Throw him out of doors, do," he told her.

"I shall be destroying him," said Skunk-Woman.

"Do throw him out of the house," said Badger.

Then Skunk-Woman kissed him as she threw him out, saying, "Truly, I am destroying him."

Into the tent the child came crawling, and, "Old woman, pick him up; throw him out."

The woman picked him up and flung him outside, as he cried.

When he came in, toddling, "Ho, old woman, throw him out," he said.

Again she threw him out.

Into the lodge came a boy, "Haha, old woman, throw him outside."

Although the child wept, she threw him out.

In came a youth, very handsome, with long hair, and sat down in the place of honour, opposite the door, naked as he was, and "Hah, old woman, lend him your blanket-robe; let him wrap himself in it."

Then thus spoke that youth: "Father," he said to that Badger, "have you a little scrap of leather, of kid-leather?"

"Yes, I shall look for it."

He looked for it and found it.

"Now, here you are, my son," said Badger.

This is what he did: the youth shook the piece of leather.

"Let there be a coat!" said the youth.

And really, there was a coat, which he put on.

Again, "Bring a scrap of leather," said the youth.

He gave him another. The youth took it.

"Let there be breeches for me!"

Truly, there were some breeches.

Then this youth, Clot-Child, spoke thus: "Father, a bit of buffalo hide, a bit with the wool on it!"

He took it; he shook it in the air, that youth.

He said, "Let it be a whole fur, for my blanket-robe, and let the horns be on it, and the hoofs!" said the youth.

Truly the horns were on it and the hoofs, the buffalo-hoofs. So then the youth wrapped himself in it.

"Now, father, if you have a bit of otterskin, give it to me."

So Badger looked for it; he found some.

"Here, son," he said to him.

The youth took it; he swung it up and down.

He said, "Let this otterskin be whole, that I may have it for a hat!" said the youth. "And now, father, go cut some saskatoon willows, for a bow."

So Badger went out and cut some. He was very glad that he had the young man. And, "Whence did he come?" thought Badger of his son. He did not know. From the blood that they had put in the kettle that youth had taken shape as a human being, because he was too angry at the way Badger was being abused. Therefore, this youth was named Clot-Child. Just as blood that has been standing long grows hard; this we call "a clot." And from this it was that the youth sprang; therefore, he was Clot-Child.

Then they made those arrows. At last morning came, and they had finished them all. Now they had nothing to eat. As they sat there, early in the morning, up came that Grizzly. He said, "Ha, brother-in-law Badger, make a killing of those buffalo."

So Badger took a lance and went out. He saw some buffalo. He went there to kill them. He hurled his lance at those buffaloes; he killed them all. Then Badger sat down on whichever one was the fattest.

"Brother-in-law, this one, now, I want to have," he said to Grizzly.

"And do you really suppose you can have the fat one?" cried Grizzly; "Oh, dear, no, brother-in-law!"

"Brother-in-law, even now your sister and I are hungry!"

"Oh, no!" cried Grizzly.

But that youth was peeking out of the tent, watching his father. Suddenly Grizzly seized a knife and struck Badger here, on his head; he knocked him headlong; he grabbed him by the arm and flung him toward his tent. The youth Clotkin flew into a rage, when his father was knocked down; he came out and started toward his father. When he got near, his father got up; he was bleeding at the nose from the blow. When Grizzly saw the youth approaching, "Yoho, nephew, this is the way I treat your father, just by way of teasing him, whenever he makes me glad by killing buffalo!"

Thus spoke Badger, as he kept throwing blood from his nose: "Not by way of teasing me, brother-in-law, but because you sorely torment me, brother-in-law!"

At once the youth spoke up, "In truth, you are cruelly abusing my father!" he said to Grizzly, and struck him with his bow.

He struck a big gash in the other's body; his father, Badger, stayed behind his back, and he faced about. Again Grizzly, like this, pulled himself together, and came attacking the youth. Again he struck him; again he cleft him with the blow.

"Come, father, take hold of him on one side!" the youth bade his father.

He himself took hold of him on the other side; he kept slashing him until he killed him. Then the oldest of Grizzly's sons came attacking the youth.

He cried, "Truly, you ruin me, Clotkin, in killing my father."

As he drew near, the youth shot him; he slew him. Another also came attacking him; this one, too, he killed with a bowshot. Finally all of them attacked him; he did away with all of those bears. Badger rejoiced that they were exterminated, who had tormented him. He had much meat now, for now that youth used to hunt and collect food for his father.

When he had much of it, he spoke as follows: "Now, father, I shall leave you. I shall go where people dwell," said Clotkin.

"Oh, dear!"

Badger was sorry that his son was going away, for he loved him.

"Not that I mean to abandon you, father; I shall be coming back," said the youth.

"Very well," said Badger.

Thereupon he arose and kissed his father and mother. Then he went out and departed. As soon as he was round a bend, he took an arrow and shot it.

"Now, on this arrow of mine let me stand! Where yon people dwell, there let me fall to earth!" he said.

Really, there he came to earth. Then he took his arrow. So he went to a lodge; where a poor old woman dwelt alone, there he entered.

"Be seated, my grandchild!" she said to him.

In that village a most terrible bear was the chief. He had four children, two women and two men. Whenever he learned that a buffalo had been killed, that bear who was chief would take all the fat meat, so that now they were starving, there where Clotkin was staying. Clotkin did not know that. Where the tents stood in a circle, there in the centre was a buffalo-close.

Then thus did Clotkin's grandmother speak to him: "Grandchild, there is great famine here; even though the young men look for buffalo, they find none; they see none. And the chief, if anyone drives buffalo into the corral, the chief will give him his daughters, and very handsome young women they are." Then she also told him: "But even when buffaloes are killed, that bear takes all the fat meat, whatever meat is at all good, and nobody can kill him, so terrible is he."

"Well then, grandmother, I shall make a round-up, never fear," he told his grandmother.

"Do not!" she answered him; "Even if you did, we should not be allowed to eat any good meat," she told him.

In due time they went to bed. In the morning, when Clotkin got up, his grandmother still slept. Thus he went out of the lodge and away, to fetch buffalo. When he was far off, he gathered . . . . and laid them in a row, like this.

He spoke: "Arise ye! Arise ye! Arise ye!"

A great herd of buffalo arose from the ground.

"Stop! Stop!" he cried to them.

He went up to them, he saw one that was fat; he pulled a few hairs from it.

"Now then, you will be very lean," he said to it; "Now, when I take you all home with me, you will run into the corral. But you," he said to the one, "you will not go in. You will go over this way, a little ways up the river. The dogs will set upon you; and the children will shoot at you. Somewhere thereabouts is my grandmother's lodge; you will see it; there in the doorway the children will kill you," he said to that buffalo. And then, "So now, off with you! Run!"

Then really, the buffalo ran off, and he ran along behind them, driving the buffalo. After mid-day those buffalo arrived. The one buffalo that was lean ran off by itself somewhere. When the people saw that it was entirely lean, they paid no attention to it. The dogs set upon it, and at last the boys kept shooting at it, as it ran toward that old woman's lodge. There the boys killed that buffalo.

The old woman was very glad, thinking, "Now I shall have meat."

Now Clotkin was behind some obstacle; the people did not see him, and, "Like a poor, ugly child let me look!" said Clotkin.

Then he went home; as he walked up, his grandmother was busy skinning and cutting up the carcass.

"Splendid, grandmother! Now we shall have meat!" he cried.

"Yes," his grandmother answered him.

But those other buffalo, the people killed them all. And, as usual, that terrible bear took all the fat meat and left his followers in want. Clotkin's grandmother brought the meat into the lodge, all of it.

"Grandmother, cover up your meat!" And when the old woman had covered it, "Grandmother, go chop four willow-withes."

So the old woman went out and chopped them off; she brought them.

"Here they are, grandson," she said.

"Grandmother, go out of doors! Stand there, outside the lodge!"

Then that Clotkin whipped the meat, saying "Be fat, be fat!"

Truly, the pieces turned into fat meat.

"Grandmother, come in; now do your cooking; let us eat!"

When the old woman uncovered her meat and saw that it was fat, she covered it again.

"Grandchild, grandchild! We shall not keep these. If the chief learns of this, he will come and get it," she said.

"Oh, grandmother, let us eat," he said.

So then the old woman set about cooking. Clotkin smeared the fat meat all round his mouth, greasing his face. Then he went out of the lodge.

"Grandmother, make dried meat; hang up your fats. I am going to play a bit."

"Grandchild, wipe your mouth!"

"So I have, grandmother!"

Thus he went off to play with the sons of the terrible bear. When those boys saw him with grease all over his face and his belly too, they went home to tell their father.

They said, "Father, that child whose grandmother is so poor is all greased, here!"

"Dear me, no!" cried the bear; "I saw him, and his beast was entirely lean."

Now Clotkin ran back to his grandmother's tiny lodge. When he sat down inside, there came those boys sticking their heads into the door. They saw the fat meat. They went back.

His grandmother said, "Grandchild, didn't I tell you not to go there? That bear will come and take it all," she said.

That boy told his father. "They have much fat meat and much dried meat of the fattest," he told him.

The chief rose to his feet and went there; when he opened the door and looked in, there he saw it.

"Come, Pot-Belly Child, I have come to get your grandmother's dried meat and the fats."

"Very well, take them," he answered him.

He took it all, robbing them, and carried it home. The boy's grandmother wept over the loss of her fat meats.

He said to her, "Sit still, grandmother; I will fetch your fat meats."

"Do not, grandchild; he will kill you."

"No, grandmother; I will fetch them!"

So he got up and went there.

When he opened the door he cried, "Cripple-Bear, I have come to get my grandmother's fat meats."

"Yes, yes, take them."

He entered; the other rose to his feet, seized him by the arm, and flung him out of the lodge. He got up again. He entered, saying to the other, "I have come to fetch my grandmother's fat meats."

"Yes!"

Already that Cripple-Bear's sons spoke thus: "Father, do not heed him! Never does anyone deal thus with you. I suppose this creature has some unusual power! Not by a long ways will he have mystic power! He is nearly bursting at the belly, so pot-bellied is he."

As he was about to take his fat meats, that is, his grandmother's, there again that chief rose to his feet. He took hold of the bear's arms and broke first one, then the other; and he tore his mouth way open. So now the other could not hold anything. Thereupon he took home all his grandmother's fat meats and slices of dried meat, while back there the bear was howling, "Oh dear, oh dear!"

He brought them to their lodge. Then he stayed there.

Then the bear's sons said to him, "This is what I told you, father; you did not listen to me," they told him; "Now then, try to cure your arms and your mouth," they said to him.

"Yes."

Vainly he tried to cure himself; he was not able. At last he was near to death.

"Now then," his sons said to him, "now, father, my sisters here"—those young women—"my two sisters here do you give to him. He will restore you to life, if he can marry them."

"Very well."

Accordingly the old woman went there to give her daughters to Clotkin.

She said to him, "Now, these daughters of mine are being given to you, that you may try to save the old man's life," she said.

"Very well," said Clotkin, "be off, go home," he told the old woman.

He went there. When he entered, there was the other, with his mouth hanging wide open. Then he at once took hold of the other's arms and rubbed them. They were well again. Also his mouth he rubbed for him, and he got well. Then he went back to his grandmother's lodge; there he stayed. At last night fell. In the morning, off to one side those young women built a lodge. When they had finished, he was sent for. He went there. When he entered, at once he saw the elder of the young women; he knew that she disliked him, that she thought him disgusting. He sat near to her; always she moved away. She did not sit close to him, for she hated him. . . . .

When the younger one, by whose side he sat, prepared some berries and gave them him to eat, as he began to eat them, the elder sister said: "Sister, truly you do not mind if a person looks dirty!"

Thereupon, the next night when they went to bed, he said to his wife: "There, you did well by yourself in not rejecting me," he told her; "Not thus shall I look, as now you see me. Tomorrow I shall bring in some buffalo. Do you then tell your father not to deprive the people; he is not to take the fat meats; tell him this. Now, when I bring the buffalo, I shall come walking at the head. I shall be wearing a leather coat; I shall have breeches of the like; and a buffalo-robe I shall have for my blanket; there will be horns on it and hoofs. And an otterskin I shall have as my headgear. That will be I. I shall enter the buffalo-pound. The buffalo will follow at my heels. Opposite the entrance I shall climb up on the hurdle; up there I shall stay. You will come there; you will bring stewed berries. There we shall eat; we two shall eat together. If you have good clothes, you shall put them on when you are about to come there," he told his wife.

Then they went to sleep. Presently that young woman woke up from her sleep. Her husband was not sleeping there; he had already gone away to fetch the buffalo. Soon day broke. And so, when they had got up and she and her elder sister had eaten, she went out of the lodge, to her father.

She said to him, "Father, your son-in-law departed early this morning."

"Oh, dear me, daughter, why did you not stop him? My son-in-law will freeze," said he.

"But this is what your son-in-law says to you, father: 'When I bring the buffalo, he is not to do that way, to take the fat meats, to rob his followers of the fat meats,' your son-in-law tells you, and that you are to announce that they shall watch for buffalo. This is what your son-in-law said."

"Very well, daughter, I shall stop; as my son-in-law says I shall do."

Thereupon the young woman went home.

Then that old man went outside and said, "Young men, be on the lookout. Early in the morning, I hear, my son-in-law went out to fetch buffalo," said the old man.

Accordingly the young men kept watch all day. After the day had reached noon, there came the buffalo. Already that young woman was cooking berries, thinking that doubtless her husband would soon arrive. Behold, as the herd approached, those young men saw a very handsome youth leading at a run the buffalo, who followed at his heels. Not at all did they recognize that youth. He promptly entered the pound; then at a point opposite the entrance that youth flung himself climbing to the top of the hurdle; at that moment the buffalo ran in. At once she saw the handsome youth: he was her husband. At once the young men and the women climbed up from all sides to see the buffalo. And while they were shooting at the buffalo, that young woman went to give her husband the berries which she had placed in a bowl. The elder sister, who had scorned him, saw him; now that he was handsome, she liked him, as she saw her younger sister climbing up to give him the berries, saying to him, "Here, take these." The youth took them. Everyone liked the youth. So then the elder sister, who had scorned him, ran home.

She said to her mother, "Mother, let me have some berries!"

Her mother gave her some. Then she stewed them. She did not stew them long, for she thought, "It is almost time for our husband to come home," and was happy over the thought. Because she had seen her younger sister eating with him, and thought, "I want to eat there, too," she went off to take her berries there.

"Here, take these," she said to him.

The youth told her, "Bring them up here," he said to her who had scorned him.

So the woman went up. Just as she came near, she slipped on one of the logs; down she went; her berry-stew spilled; one of her feet was caught; she hung there in the air. Everybody laughed, women, children, and all. Soon the young woman wept with shame at having fallen down. At last she got herself free. She went home weeping. As for the others, when all the buffalo were killed, Clotkin went home.

When they entered their tent, she who had scorned him, "Sister, let me help him on with one of his moccasins; let me put one of his moccasins on his foot," she said, but, "No!" answered the youth.

Now it was his turn to scorn the elder sister, who had scorned him. So thus they dwelt there. The elder sister unceasingly wept for shame at having fallen. She was always wandering about. Then it came to the point that all kinds of people asked her, "Why? Why do you weep?"

"Because Clotkin put me to shame and scorns me," she would say.

"Child, everyone is fond of Clotkin," that woman would be told, as she went about and wept.

Then at one time she saw an old woman who asked her, "Why, grandchild, do you always weep?"

"Because Clotkin put me to shame," she told her.

"There, wait a bit and I shall put him to shame," the old woman told her.

Presently, as Clotkin went about, he came upon a little brook. The handsome youth crossed it and went somewhere on the other side.

On his way back, he saw an old woman, who said, "Grandson, take me on your back; I cannot get across."

"Grandmother, I shall make a little bridge so you can walk."

"Grandson, I should fall into the water," said the old woman.

At last he consented.

He took her on his back and carried her across.

But when he said to her, "Now, grandmother, here you are!" that old woman would not get down.

When he tried to pull the old woman off, he could not get her free; like iron were her arms and legs. So then he did not care to go home, for he was ashamed to be carrying the old woman on his back. But in time, here, like this, she had him almost strangled. So at last he went home.

When that elder sister saw him, she laughed much, saying, "What was he so proud about, this Clotkin who comes with an old woman riding on his back?"

When the young woman saw her husband, she was greatly distressed. Although she clubbed her, she could not kill her. Though all the people clubbed her, they could not kill that old woman. Finally Clotkin was near to death. At last he did like this, like this, being unable to walk. Then, where the lumps of clotted blood had been laid in a heap, thither he flung himself. The old woman was holding fast to nothing but a clot of blood. But Clotkin rose from the ground off at one side.

The old woman said, "Grandson, please let me live!"

"Yes," said Clotkin.

With that he took the old woman, holding her by the feet.

Thus he spoke: "Now, old woman, off in the future there will be mortal men; this they will say"—and he flung her down; only one foot could be seen of that old woman—" 'Pig-vermilion,' they will say!"

"Come here!" he said to the woman who had scorned him.

Weep as she might, he took hold of her; where a tree stood, he flung her against it.

"This is where you will stay fast; 'Glowing fungus,' the people will call you. You will not be good for anything; you are too conceited.—Now, come hither, all you people! Now then, my father-in-law, you, your children, and your wife, now, depart! Be off! Off in the future mortal men will name you 'Bears.'—And you"—to the others—"you they will call wolves, and you others foxes, and you others lynxes, and you coyotes!"

So in this wise he made all the animals. Then he went from there; he went home; he took his wife with him. When they had been two nights on the way, he came to his father, Badger. Badger was glad that his son had come to him.

Then when he had been there one night, he said to him, "Now, father, you have been too good a creature. So now, mortal men in the time to come will say of you, 'Badger,' these mortal men. They will eat you, because you have been a good creature.—And you"—to his mother—" 'Skunk,' they will say; a very good creature you will be; never will you bite people. There, go! 'Polecat,' mortal men will call you; they will eat you."

She departed.

"As for me, a blood clot, blood am I. And, therefore, nothing at all."

And so there is nothing at all of my tale. This is where the sacred story ends.

(18) **Fisherskin-Hat**

Coming-Day

kā-kīsikāw-pīhtukāw.

kītahtawā päyak awa nāpäw kwah päyak iskwäw, uwīkimākanah, nīsiwak. kītahtawā awāsisah ayāwäwak. ākutā äkwah äh-ay-āyātsik, pisisik mātsīw awa nāpäw. piyisk wāpamäwak awāsisah, nāpäsis. äkwah äkutah ay-ayāwak. piyisk misikitiw awa nāpäsis. pōti miyusiw awa nāpäsis. miywäyimäwak; sākihäwak ukusisiwāwa. namuya käkway atuskäw awa nāpäsis. tahkih miywāsiniyiwa utayōwinisa, ä-kaskikwātahk aw iskwäw ukusisah utayōwinisiyiwa. äkusi piyisk uskinīkiw aw āwāsis.

äkwah awa uskinīkiw ōmis ītwäw: " mahtih kakwä-nipah utsäk," itāw ōhtāwiya.

miyākīkih[1] *awa nāpäw wīh-kakwä-wāpamäw utsäkah. kītahtawā wāpamäw utsäkah; nipahäw. äwakunih usīhäw aw ōskinīkiw. äh-kīsihāt, utastutiniw. mīna atsusisah ayāw, nikikwayānah äh-upīhtatwānit, äkutah*

[1] Apparently a particle; meaning?

äh-āsiwatäyikih uwīpisisah aw ōskinīkiw. uskutākay pahkäkin äh-pīmikitäyik ; utāsah mīna ä-pīmikitäyikih. nama wīhkāts mātsīw.

kītahtawä ōmis ītwäw : " nōhtāh, kiyānaw tsī pikuh äh-ayīsiyiniwiyahk ? " itäw.

" namuya. misiwä ayāwak ayīsiyiniwak. māka namuya äh-miywātisitsik, pisisik äh-mätawätsik. kīspin sākōtsihitutsik, misi-wanātsihituwak ; namuya miywātisiwak."

" kah ! " itwäw aw uskinīkiw ; " mahtih nika-kakwä-wāpamāwak kutakak ayīsiyiniwak," itwäw aw uskinīkiw.

mihtātam awa kisäyiniw mīn āwa iskwäw, ukusisiwāwa ä-sākihātsik.

" māskōts ta-misi-wanātsihōw," äh-itäyimāt ukusisiwāwa, mātōw aw īskwäw.

äkusi namuya kī-kitahamawäwak ä-wīh-sipwähtäyit ukusisiwāwa.

" wāpahkih nika-sipwähtān," itwäw aw uskinīkiw.

" hähähäy ! " itwäw awa nāpäw ; " nikusis, äkā wiya āpihtaw-kīsikāhk isi ituhtä ! " itäw ukusisah.

" āha' , " itwäw awa uskinīkiw.

tāpwä äh-wāpaniyik, sipwähtäw aw uskinīkiw.

umis ītwäw : " nōhtāh, näkā, nika-takusinin, äkā misi-wanātisiyānitāpiyāhk ä-wīh-wāpamakik ayīsiyiniwak," itwäw aw ōskinīkiw, ä-pustastutināt. " hāw, utsäkiwayānah-k-ōtastutinit nitisiyihkāsun," itwäw, äh-ati-wayawīt.

mātōyiwa ukāwiya, äh-atamiskākut. äkusi sipwähtäw, äh-pimuhtätkapä-kīsik pimuhtäw, äkā ä-pīsimuwiyik itähkäy isih äh-ituhtät. kītahtawä äh-pimuhtät, äh-utākusiniyik, kā-wāpamāt pihyäwah. pimwäw ; nipahäw, " nika-mōwāw, itah kapäsiyāni," äy-itäyihtah. äkusi äh-kīh-utināt, ati-papaskupitäw.

äy-āyapāskwäyāyik ä-pimuhtät, kītahtawä kā-wāpahtahk wīstäpahkwāyikamikus. äkutah ituhtäw, " mahtih käkway ōma itah äh-ayāt ? " äyitäyihtah.

äh-takuhtät skwahtämihk, " pīhtukä, nōsisimis ! " k-ätwät nōtukäsiw.

äh-pīhtukät, pōt ōhi kī-päyakuyiwa.

" ta-tawāw ! " itwäyiwa ; " nähä uhts-āpi," itik.

ōhi pihäwah kā-tahkunāt miyäw ōhkuma.

" kitatamihin, nōsisimis ; äkutōwahk nnōhtä-mōwā ! " itwäyiwah. äkusi äkwah ōmis ītik : " nōsisimis, āyiman ōma itä k-ätuhtäyin. nawats wāpahkih kīwäyin. āyimisiwak ōma ayīsiyiniwak," itik ōhkuma.

" namuya, nōhkō ; usām āsay nipä-sipwähtān," itäw.

" kah ! " itik ; " awahä māka, nōsisä ! " itik.

tāpwäw paminawasōyiwa, päyak mīnis äh-pakāhtāyit äkwah päyak tsīsāwānis.

ä-kitāpamāt, " kähtsinā namuya nika-kīspun ! " itäyihtam.

ōmis ītwäw awa nōtukäsiw : " nōsisimis, kika-kīspun ōma," itäw.

" yahä ! " itäyihtam aw uskinīkiw, " namuy ätsik āwa kä-kī-mā-mitunäyimak ! " itäyihtam.

" āha' , nōsisimis ! katāt tsī ka-mā-mitunäyimin ? " itik.

kiskäyihtamiyiwa äh-mā-mitunäyimāt.

äkusi äkwah asamik ; äkus īsi pakitinamāk utaskihkuyiwa. äkwah äh-mītsisut, kahkiyaw māna äh-utinahk, ä-saskamut, ätāpitsih askihkusihk, käyāpits nīsu kiy-astäyiwa. piyisk āhkamäyimōw äh-mītsisut. piyisk kīspōw ; namuya kīh-kitāw ōhi k-āsamikut ōhkumah. itisinamawäw.

" namuya nikīh-kitān, nōhkō, " itäw.

" nah, nōsisimis tāpwä äh-īkitsikāwit äh-mītsisut, äkā kā-kīh-kitāt nimīnisimah, nikīsitäpōwinah ! " itik.

piyisk mistahi tipiskāyiw.

" nōsisä, kinästuhtā ; kawisimuh, " itik.

kawisimōw ; wīsta kawisimōw awa nōtukäsiw. äkusi äh-wāpaniyik, ä-waniskātsik, mina mītsisōwak.

ä-kīsi-mītsisutsik, " ā, nōsisä, äkāy ōm ōtah äh-uhtsi-sākāstäk, äkāy ītuhtä ! āyimisiw äkutah äh-ayāt, " itik ; " ōtäy isi nātakām is ītuhtä, " itik.

" äha' , " itwäw, äh-sipwähtät, äh-pimuhtät.

wāhyaw äh-ihtāt, " mahtih tānähk ōma k-ōh-kitahamawit nōhkum ? " itäyihtam.

äkutä isi waskīw. kītahtawä, käkāts äh-āpihtaw-kīsikāyik, kā-wāpamāt ayīsiyiniwah ispatinähk äh-apiyit. uhpimäh äkutah wīh-at-ītuhtäw, äh-pasikōwit, äkutä k-äsi-waskīt. äk āt äh-wīh-ituhtāt, māka äkutä isi ispayiw. piyisk āmatsiwäw, äh-wāpamāt. pōt ōhi mistahi māyātisiyiwa ayīsiyiniwa, äh-māskāwikanäyit, äh-āpisīsisiyit, maskwayānah äh-kikasākäyit, äh-päh-nātikut, kuntah ä-päy-ustustutamiyit, umis äh-itikut : " utsäkiwayānah-k-ōtastutinit, māna kipä-mätawā ! " itik ; " kayās, ' wīh-papā-mätawäw, ' kik-īh-itikawi ! "

" namuya ä-papā-mätāwäyān," itäw.

" hā, namuya ! pikuh ka-mätawäyahk ! " itik.

"namuya ! " itäw.

" īh näma kā-sakāk kiwāpahtän tsī kā-pikihtäk ? "

" āha' ! "

" mistah ānik äkutah ä-miyusitsik uskinīkiskwäwak nīsu äh-ayātsik. äyōkunik kik-āstwātunānaw," itik.

" ā, namuya ! " itäw.

" ā, kiyām māsihitutān ! " itik.

piyis, " äha' ," itäw.

äkwah astäw utakuhp minah uwīpisisah, kahkiyaw utayōwinisah ; utastutinah pikuh namuy āhyäw.

" hā, kitastutin mīna ahih," itik.

" hwā, namuya ! "

äkus īsi māsihitōwak. namuya kīh-sākuhäw. mwähtsih äh-nayawapit, ātsikäwäpahwäw ; kawiwäpinäw.

" āh, utsäkiwayānah-k-ōtastutinit, nipisuhän kiskāt, k-ō-sākuhiyin. päyakwāw ! " itik.

" ā, namuya ! āsay kisākuhitin, " itäw.

" namuya ; päyakwāw ! "

" āha' ! "

māsihitōwak. äh-mäkwā-māsihitutsik, kwāskwäwäpinäyiwa utastutinah. äkusi äkwah sākuhik ; kaskāwikanänik, ä-sāpuskākut, ä-maskamikut umiyusiwin. kā-kī-wāpamāt äy-isinākusiyit, äkus īsinākusiw aw uskinīkiw. äkuh ōhi kāh-māyātisiyit miyusiyiwa. äh-kitāpamāt, " mistahi pikō uma äh-miyusiyān, kā-kīsinātsihit, ä-maskamit nimiyusiwin ! " itäyihtam. utayōwinisah utinamiyiwa, ä-pustayōwinisäyit, utastutinah mīna.

" äkunih anih kitayōwinisah, maskwayānätās ! " itik.

utayōwinisiyiwa äkwah pustayōwinisäw. wiyaskuts äkwa pisisik ustustutam. ayisk namuya tāpwähtam kā-kīh-itikut ōhkumah.

" hāw, maskwayānätäs, ntawi-wīwitān ! " itik.

tāpwä sipwähtäwak, äh-ituhtätsik ōh ōskinīkiskwäwah. tsīk äh-īhtātsik, kā-pä-wayawiyit ōh ōskinīkiskwäwah. tsīk äh-īhtātsik, kā-pä-wayawiyit ōh ōmisimāwa.

wāpamikwak, " nisīmis ! " kā-matwäy-itwäyit ; " pä-wayawī ! mātsikōtitān ōk ōsikinīkiwak kā-päts-ästamuhtätsik ! "

äh-wayawīt ōw ōskinīkiskwäw, kā-wāpamāt äh-pätsāstamuhtäyit.

" ā, nsīmis, kakwäts-āsiskamātutān ! awiyak nakasiwätsih, anihi kā-miyusiyit kit-unāpämiw, " itwäw aw ōmisimāw.

" äha', " itwäw aw ōsīmimāw.

wayatsāwiwak ōk īskwäwak. mwähtsih wāh-nakatikutsih usīmisa, utihtināw äh-asäwäpināt ; piyisk aw ōmisimāw ōhi kā-miyusiyit uskinīkiwah nawatinäw, " awa niya nika-wīkimāw ! " äh-itwät.

māka aw ōskinīkiskwäw usīmimāw äyaku miyusiw.

äkwah, " na kināpām ! " itāw aw ōsīmimāw, ōhi kā-māskāwikanäyit k-ōstustutaskäyit.

kīwähtahäwak. äh-pīhtukätsik, awa k-ustustutaskät nätä iskwāhtāmihk äkutah nahapiw. awā wiya kā-miyusit uskinīkiw tahk äh-ākwaskitiniht, äh-utsämikut uwīkimākana, mistahi miywäyihtam. äkutah ayāwak, mīnisah pikuh äh-mītsitsik ōk īskwäwak. piyisk tipiskāyiw, äh-apitsik. iyikuhk ä-kawisimutsik, päyakuhkwāmiw awa kā-māskāwikanät.

piyis wāpaniyiw. äh-wāpahk, kīkisāpā äh-waniskātsik, äh-kīh-mītsisutik, wawäyīw, ä-wīh-mātsīt awa kā-miyusit. ä-wīh-ati-wayawīt, tahkiskawäw ōhi ka-māskāwikanäyit.

" tān ätapiyin, maskwayānätās ? kinahāhkapihtānaw ! "

äh-ati-wayawīt, kīpiwāpiskawäw, kuntah äh-ustustutamipayiyit.

äkusi äh-waniskāt, umis ītäw : " pätā pīsākanāpiy, " itäw ōhō uwīkimākana.

miyik pīsākanāpīs. äkus āti-wayawīw, äh-at-ōstustutahk, wīst äh-mātsīt.

" käkway ätukä kä-nipahtāt ! " itäw aw ōmisimāw wītimwa.

äkusi äkwah kapä-kīsik mātsīwak. äh-utākusiniyik, takusin awa kā-miyusit. pōtih āpuhtäw nikikwah päyak. äkusi namuya takusin awa k-ōstustutaskät.

piyis äh-tipiskāyik, " namuya tsiw uyā kōh-wāpamāw nāntaw ? " itäw unāpäma.

" äha' ; namuya nōh-wāpamāw. tāntä kä-kawatsikwä ! " itäw, ayisk äh-pipuniyik.

kītahtawä kā-pä-saskahuhtäyit, äh-pä-takuhtäyit.

" nī, mīnah täkuhtät ! " itwäw awa umisimāw.

äh-pä-pīhtukät, äkutah iskwāhtämihk nahapiw, äh-itisinamawāt pīsākanāpiy ōh ōwīkimākanah. äh-utsipitahk aw ōskinīkiskwäw, kā-pä-pīhtukäpitāt päyak paspaskiwa pihyäwa.

ōmisi kih-itwäw aw ōmisimāw, unāpäma äh-pāsiwāyit nikikwa : " nisīmis, namuya kik-āsahtunānaw. kiwīkimākaninawak äy-isi-nipahātsik, ka-mōwānawak, " itäw usīma, " namuya ta-kih-nipahtāw käkway, " äh-itäyimāt usīmah uwīkimākaniyiwa.

äkusi tāpwä namuy āsahtōwak, ōki kā-miyusit awa nikikwa äh-mōwätsik. äkwah awa usīmimāw paspaskiwa mōwäwak. äkusi piyis kawisimōwak. käyāpits päyakuhkwāmiw awa maskwayānätās.

iyikuhk mīna äh-wāpaniyik, kīksäpā äh-waniskātsik, āsay mīna wayawīw, äh-mātsīt awa kā-miyusit. āsay mina tahkiskawäw.

" tāniy ätapiyin ? kōskiskwäwāhtānaw, maskwayānätās ! " itäw, äh-kīpiwäpiskawāt, tāpiskōts ta-nipiyit, iyikuhk äy-ustustutamiyit, kunta māna mistah äh-pāhpit aw ōmisimāw, wītimwa kiyīpiwäpiskāmihtsih. āsay mīn äyakō sipwähtäw, äh-mātsīt. äyakō kapä-kīsik papāmuhtäw. iyikuhk äh-utākusik, āsay mīna takuhtäw awa kā-miyusit ; asay mīna nikikwah päsiwäw.

" ä, äkwah kä-miywäyihtahkik nistäsak, tit-ōtastutinitsik ōhi nikikwayānah ! " itwäw aw ōmisimāw.

iyikuhk mistah ä-tipiskāyik, kītahtawä kā-pä-ustustutamiyit.

" hīhīyī, mīnah wāh-takuhtät ! " itäw wītimwa, äh-wīnäyimāt.

äh-pä-pīhtukäyit, ä-kih-nahapiyit, k-ätisinamōwāt pīsākanāpiy ōwīkimākana.

" māka mīn ätukä paspaskiwa ! " itwäw aw ōmisimāw.

äh-utsipitahk, kā-pīhtukäpitāt amiskwah.

" hay hay hay ! äkwah kä-miyu-mītsisuyān ! " itwäw aw uskinīkiskwäw.

äkwah äh-wiyinihāt, mituni wiyinwäyiwa, äkunih äh-kīsiswāt, āpihtaw usuy min ōma äh-kīsisahk.

umis ītwäw aw ōmisimāw : " nisīmis, asamin usuy anima pahkih ; nīsta nik-āspahtsikān ! " itäw.

" namuya ! ' ä-isi-nipahtātsik kināpäminawak, ka-mītsinānaw, ' kikīh-itwān ōma. "

äkwah akāwātamawäw usīmisa, amiskwa äh-mōwāyit.

piyisk mistah ä-tipiskāyik, " āstam-itah nawats ! ōtah nitanāskānihk apih ! " itāw awa k-ōstustutaskit maskwayānätās. aspin, " āstam itah nitanāskānihk api, " k-ätiht, aw uskinīkiskwäw äh-miywäyihtahk amiskwah äh-päsiwāyit ; äyakō uhtsi k-ōh-itāt.

äkusi äkwah ayāw äkutah. äkwah äh-nipātsik, "kisiwāk ōtah nipā," itik ōh ōskinīkiskwäwa, maskwayānätās äh-itiht.

äkusi umis ītwäw aw ōmisimāw : " hīhī ! " itwäw ; " utanāskānihk wäsāmihk äkwa ä-wīh-nipähāt ! " itwäw, äh-wīnäyimāt ōhi wītimwa.

äkusi nipāwak. äh-wāpahk, āsay mīna äh-waniskātsik, mīna mītsisōwak. äh-kīsi-mītsisutsik, āsay mīna wawäyīw, ä-wīh-mātsīt awa kā-miyusit uskinīkiw. äh-ati-wayawīt, tahkiskawäw.

" tān ätapiyin ? kinahāhkapīhtānaw ! " itäw.

kīpiwäpiskawäw. pāhpiw aw ōmisimāw, ōh äh-tōtāmiht wītimwa.

äkusi ä-kīh-waniskāt, " pätāh pīsākanāpiy, " itäw.

äkusi äkwah ä-kīh-miyiht, wīstah mātsīw.

" haw, nisīmis, kōskiskwäwāniwihtānaw, pikuh ta-nikuhtäyahk, " itäw.

äkusi nikuhtäwak, äh-awatātsik mihtah.

äh-āpihtā-kīsikāyik, " pita ka-mītsisunānaw, " itwäwak ōk ōskinīkiskwäwak.

äkwah kīsitäpōwak ; paminawasōwak, aw ōsīmimāw amiskwah äh-nawatsīt. äkwah aw ōmisimāw akāwātamawäw usīmisah.

ōmisiy itäw : " nisīmis, mahtih pahkih pä-manipitamawin. apisīs nista nika-mōwāw, " itäw.

" nāh ! äkus āni ! kīst ānah kiwīkimākan kīh-nipahäw nikikwah, tamōwat. ' ka-pāh-päyakuh-mītsisunānaw, ' kikīh-itwān, ' nama käkway ta-kīh-nipahtāw, ' äh-itäyimat niwīkimākan, " itäw.

" nāh ! ä-kīh-pa-pāhpisimitān, nisīmis ! " itäw.

" āha' ! namuya ka-kīh-asamitn, " itäw umisah.

äkusi äkwah ōki kā-mātsītsik, iyikuhk äy-utākusik, takusin awa kā-miyusit. nikikwah nīsu päsiwäw. iyikuhk mistah äh-tipiskāyik, äkuyikuhk kā-päw-ustustutahk awa maskwayānätās. äh-pīhtukät, pīsākanāpiy itisinamawäw uwīkimākanah.

ōmis ītäw : " käkway mīnah kā-wīh-atamihit ? " itwäw aw uskinīkiskwäw.

äh-utsipitahk, nīsu amiskwah kā-pīhtukäpitāt.

" hāy hāy ! äkwah äwakuni nka-kanawäyihtän usuyah, nōhtāwiy nikāwiy ka-mītsitsik ! " itwäw. " hāw, ōtäh uhtsi apih, " itäw, itah ä-kīh-miyu-nahastāsut.

" āh, namuya ! " itwäw maskwayānätās, äh-wīnäyimisut.

" ōtäh kiyām apih ! " itik.

piyisk äkutä nahapiw, äkwah awa uskinīkiskwäw ōt äskwāhtämihk äh-wiyanihāt amiskwah. äkusi äh-kīsi-wiyanihāt, äkwah paminawasōw, amiskwah äh-kīsiswāt.

ōmis ītwäw ōw ōmisimāw : " nsīmis, asamin päyak usuy, " itäw.

" nāh, äkus āni ! kīstah kiwīkimākan kāh-nipahāt usōyiwa äwaku mītsih ! " itäw umisah, äkā ä-wīh-asamāt.

wiyawā piku miyusiyiwa äh-mōwātsik ; ayisk awa kā-miyusit kā-nipahāt nikikwah namuya wīnuyiwa. äkusi piyisk äh-kīsi-mītsisutsik, mistah äh-tipiskāyik, kawisimōwak. äkwah aw ōsīmimāw ōh ōnāpäma akwanahäw, äh-nīsōhkwāmitsik.

ōmis ītwäw aw ōmisimāw : " wāwāts ätukw āwa äkwah ä-wīh-wīhpä-māt ! " itäw.

" nāh ! ahpōh kiya wiyīhpämat kiwīkimākan, äkāh äh-miywāsik käkway äh-nipahtwāsk ! " itäw.

äkusi nipāwak. kīkisäpā mīnah ä-waniskātsik, mīna ä-kīh-mītsisutsik, kiyipahk pasikōw awa kā-miyusit, ä-kisiwāsit, ä-wīh-mātsīt, äh-ah-ayiwīhi-kut maskwayānätāsah. āsay mīna äh-ati-wayawīt, āsay mina tahkiskawäw.

ōmis ītäw : " tān ōm ätapiyin ? kinahāhkapīhtänaw ! " itäw, äh-kīpiwäpiskawāt, äh-ati-wayawīt.

" pätāh pīsākanāpiy, " itäw uwīkimākanah.

ä-kīh-miyikut, äkusi wayawīw, wīstah äh-mātsīt.

wāhyaw äh-ihtāt, ōmis ītwäw : " matwān tsī äh-kikih-maskamit nimin-ahōwin kā-maskamit nimiyusiwin ? " itwäw maskwayānätās.

äkus äh-sipwähtät, ä-kikasāmät māna, kītahtawä kā-wāpamāt apisi-mōsusah. nīsu nipahäw unītsāniwa, mitunih äh-wiyinuyit. äkuyikuhk kīwäw, äh-utāpät ōhi nīsu. kītahtawä mitun äh-utākusik, kā-takusihk awa kā-miyusit. päsiwäw iyāpäw-āyisah apisi-mōsusah ; namwāts nisitusiyiwa.

äkwah äh-tipiskāk, kā-wayawīt ōw ōskinīkiskwäw, " äsah nama mayaw takuhtäw, " äh-itäyimāt ōwīkimākanah.

" isk ōyāh äh-kōtawäyimāt unāpäm isk äsah ! " k-ätwät aw ōmisimāw, äh-pāhpihāt usīmah.

kītahtawä wayawītimihk äh-nīpawit aw ōskinīkiskwäw, kā-pähtahk wāhyaw äh-pä-nikamuyit awiya. miywäyihtam äh-nikamuyit. ā, mituni kiyipah kisiwāk kā-pä-nikamuwit. pīhtukäw, " äwaku ! " äh-itäyimāt uwīkimākana, ōm ōkīsitäpōwin äh-kīsisahk, kiyipah kā-pätwäwitamiyit, ä-päw-ustustutamiyit.

"yīh! mina tākusihk!" itwäw aw ōmisimāw, tsikämā äh-wīnäyimāt wītimwa.

äh-pä-pīhtukäyit, itisinamawäw pīsākanāpiy. äh-utsipitahk aw ōskinīkiskwäw, namuya kaskihtāw. pasikōw awa maskwayānätās; äh-utsipitahk, nīsu apisi-mōsusah kā-pīhtukäpitāt.

"hāy hāy! äkwah nīsu nk-āyāwāwak apsimōsusiwayānisak!" itwäw.

äkusi nahapiw, äh-utinahk maskisinah ä-miywāsiniyikih, ä-pustaskisinahāt unāpäma.

"nāh, wäsāmihk äkwa kā-pustaskisinahāt awa umaskisinihkäwinah!" äh-itāt usīma.

"nah, ahpōh kiya pwästaskisinahat māna, äkā äh-miywāsiniyik käkway äh-nipahtāt kināpäm!"

äkusi äkw ä-kīh-mītsisutsik, äkwah wiyanihtākäw aw ōskinīkiskwäw. ä-kīsi-wiyanihāt, äyikuhk äkwah kawisimōwak, äh-nipātsik. kīkisäpā äh-waniskātsik, ä-kīh-mītsisutsik mīna, wawäyīw awa kā-miyusit, äh-kisiwāsit, ä-wīh-mātsīt, ä-ah-ayiwihikut ōhi maskwayānätāsah. sōskwāts wayawīw.

ōmis ītwäw aw ōskinīkiskwäw: "nāh, tānähk āwah utahkiskawāh māna, wāh-wayawītsih? näpäwisītukä, äh-āh-ayiwīhikut!" itäw.

äkusi äkwah wīstah wawäyīw maskwayānätās, äh-mātsīt, piyisk wāhyaw äh-ayāt. kītahtawä äh-pōn-āpihtā-kīsikāyik, äkuyikuhk kā-wāpamāt mōswah. nipahäw äkunih, kahkiyaw äh-utāpāt, äh-kīwät. äkwah awah kā-miyusit wawāskäsiwah päyak nipahäw, iyāpäw-āyah äh-sīhkatsiyit. äy-utākusiniyik, takusin. mistahi miywäyihtam aw umisimāw, wawāskäsiwah äh-wāpamāt.

"hāy hāy! äkwah äyakō kiy-ōmaskisiniyāhk!" itwäw.

piyisk mistah äh-tipiskāyik, äh-wayawīt ōw ōsīmimāw, āsay mīna kā-pāhtahk äh-pä-nikamuwit awiya, äkwah kisiwāk kiyipah kā-pä-nikamuwit, äh-na-nīpawit, äh-miyuhtawāt ōhi kā-nikamuwit. kisiwāk äh-päy-āyāyit, kā-pīhtukät; maskwayānätās äsā awah kā-pä-nikamuwit māna utasāmah. äh-pīhtukät, itisinamawäw pīsākanāpiy. äh-utsipitahk, namuya kaskihtāw; äkwah awa maskwayānätās kā-pīhtukäpitāt nīsu mōswah.

"hāy hāy! tāpwä nimiywäyihtän, päyak kit-ōmaskisiniyāhk, äkwah nōhtāwiy nistäsak päyak tit-ōmaskisinitsik!" itwäw.

namwāts äkwah pīkiskwäw aw ōmisimāw, äh-ayiwihimiht unāpäma. äkusi äkwah iyāyaw asamäw aw ōnāpäma uskinīkiskwäw. ä-kīh-mītsisutsik, äkwah wiyinihtākäw aw uskinīkiskwäw: pōt ōhi kā-wiyinuyit ōhi mōswa.

"nisīmis," itwäw aw ōmisimāw, "päyak anima uskāt miyin; nkapāstasun," itäw.

"nāh, äkus āni! namuya ka-kīh-miyitin; kipakwātāw awa kītim; namuya ta-kīh-wīhkasiniyiw äh-nipahtāt käkway," itäw umisah.

äkusi piyisk mistahi tipiskāyiw. piyisk kawisimōwak. äh-wāpaniyik, āsay mīna ä-kīh-mītsisutsik, āsay mīna mātsīwak.

ōmis ītwäw awa maskwayānätās: "pätā kipīsākanāpīm," itäw uwīkimākana.

äh-mātsīt, wāhyaw äh-ihtāt, npahäw wākayōsah mitunih äh-wiyinuyit. äkwah awa kā-miyusit takwāhnāwa nipahäw. käyāpits namuya wiyinōw awa takwāhnāw. iyawis māna äh-utāpätsik käkway kā-npahtātsik, äkusi äkwah äy-utākusik, takusin awa kā-miyusit takwāhnāwa kā-nipahāt. äkwah mistah äh-tipiskāk, kā-takusihk awah maskwayānätās, äh-pīhtukät. āsay miywäyihtam aw ōskinīkiskwäw, äh-pīhtukäyit. pīsākanāpiy äh-utsipitahk, namuya kaskihtāw.

ōmis ītwäw : " käkway mīnah kā-wīh-atamihit niwīkimākan ? " itwäw äkwah.

" yīy, " āsay itwäw aw ōmisimāw, " wäsāmihk äkwa 'niwīkimākan,' äh-itāt ! " itwäw.

" nāh, tsikäma namuya äkusi nititāw, äh-māh-miyu-nipahtwäwit ! " itwäw aw ōsīmimāw, awa maskwayānätās äh-sākihikuyit uwīkimākanah. äh-utsipitahk, wākayōsah kā-pīhtukäpitāt.

" hāy hāy hāy ! " itwäw aw ōskinīkiskwäw ; " tāpwä mistahi wīh-miywäyihtam nōhtāwiy, mistahi pimiy äh-wīh-ayāyān, masku-pimiy ! " itwäw.

äkusi pitah pustaskisinahäw uwīkimākana maskisinah. äkusi äkwah äh-asamāt, äh-mītsisutsik, tahk äh-kitāpamāt aw ōmisimāw usīmah, äh-akāwātamawāt äh-miyu-mītsisuyit. äh-kīsi-mītsisutsik, äkwah wiyinihtäk-äwak. äh-kīsi-wiyanihātsik, äkuyikuhk mistahi tipiskāyiw. piyisk kawisi-mōwak.

ōmis ītwäw maskwayānätās : " hāw, " itäw uwīkimākana, " kä-wāpahk namuya nika-mātsīnān, " itäw, " ta-matutisiyāhk, " itäw ; " kitāpatsihun äkā kā-pakwāsiyin, " itäw ; " namuya äkus äsinākusiyān ; aw āwa kītim k-äsinākusit, äkus äsinākusiyān, ä-maskamit nimiyusiwin, äh-wayäsih-sākōtsihit. wiy ōma utisinākusiwin ōma k-äsinākusiyān, " itäw ; " äkuyi-kuhk mistahi māy-isīhtāw nitayōwinisah, anihi kā-kikiskahk. wāpahkih matutisānihkähkan. äkusi pikuh nka-sākōtsihāw, " itäw ; " ōtah waya-wītimihk ōtah, awa kisiwāk nikīh-wāpamāw asiniy äh-misikitit, " itäw ; " äwakō ka-kisāpiskiswāw. äkwah awah maskō-wiyin äwaku kik-āpahkwān. äkwah wiyākanihk pimiy kika-tihkisān, pimiy kit-ōsīhtāyin, äwakō uhtsi ta-sīkahāhtawak aw āsiniy, " itäw ; " kīspin matutisiyāhkuh, kīsisutsi, ' pāskinah ! ' itwätsi, äkā tāpwähtawāhkan ; kimis wīh-pāskinahkih, mamät-simināhkan, " itäw.

" äha' , " itwäw aw uskinīkiskwäw.

äkusi nipāwak.

äh-wāpahk, kīksäpā ä-waniskātsik, äh-ma-mītisutsik, ōmis ītwäw maskwayānätās : " nītsi-nahāhkis ! " itäw.

" tānähki ? "

" pita namuya ka-mātsīnānaw. pitah k-ayiwäpinānaw ; kinästusin-ātukä, " itäw.

" āha' , ninästusin, " itwäw.

" ka-matutisiyahk, ka-säsāwihkasōyahk, " itäw.

" äha' , mitunih nnōhtä-matutisih, " itwäw.

āsay ōmis ītwäw aw ōmisimāw : " namuya kika-matutisin ; usām kika-wīnihkasun, " itäw uwīkimākana.

" hā, ninästusin uma. kiyām nka-matutisin, " itwäw.

äkusi ä-kīh-mītsisutsik, äkwah wayawīw aw ōskinīkiskwäw, äw-usīhtāt matutisān, äkwah äh-pōnahk.

äh-nātāt asiniyah ōhi kā-misikitiyit, äkwah ä-wāskāskawāt, " asiniy, yāhkīstawin ! " itäw.

āt äh-misikitiyit, sākuhäw, äh-uhpināt, äh-kīwāhtahāt ; äyakuni ä-kisāpiskiswāt. äkwah äh-kisāpiskisuyit, apahkwäw ōhi wiyinwah itāmihk, masku-wiyinwah, äkwah waskits utakuhpiwāwa. äkwah mīna pimiw uma usīhtāw, äyuku mīna ä-wīh-uhtsi-sīkahāhtawāyit asiniyah.

"sāsay ākwah nikīsihtān, niwīkimākan," itäw.

"hāw, nītsi-nahāhkis, kiwīh-matutisīhtānaw!" itäw.

"nāh!" itwäw umisimāw; "namuya! usām ka-wīh-miskutōnamawin niwīkimākan, äh-miyusit!" itäw usīmah.

"nāh! tānisi k-äsi-miskutōnamātān ä-nihtā-minahut niwīkimākan?" itäw.

"nītim," itwäw maskwayānätās, "pīsākanāpiy tahkupitamaw kiwīkimākan, ta-mitsiminaman pīsākanāpiy, äkā kā-maskamikawiyan kiwīkimākan."

"äha'!"

tāpwä käiayōwinisäwak äkwah, äh-pīhtukätsik ōm ītah kā-matōtisutsik äkwah tāpwä aw ōmisimāw pakwahtähäw uwīkimākana, äy-uhtsi-sakāpäkināt uwīkimākana, ä-kustahk ka-maskamiht. äkusi äkwah mituni kipahwäwak äkwah.

äkwah pīkiskwäw awa maskwayānätās, äh-itwät, "haw, ä-nästusiyān k-ō-matutisiyān, māka ä-pakwātamān ōm äsinākusiyān!" itwäw; "kāwih nimiyusiwin nik-āyān!" itwäw, pimiy äw-uhtsi-sīkahāhtawāt asiniyah ōhi.

kīsisōw awa kā-miyusit uskinīkiw.

ōmis ītwäw: "pāskinamuk! nikīsisun!" itwäw.

namuya tāpwähtam awa uskinīkiskwäw. āhkamäyimōw ä-sīkahāhtawāt asiniyah.

mīn āwa āhkamäyimōw, "pāskinamuk! nikīsisun!" äh-itwät.

namuya tāpwähtam aw ōskinīkiskwäw.

ōmis ītwäw: "niwīkimākan, pāskinā!" itäw.

ä-wīh-pāskinahk, umisah awah mamätsiminäw.

"awas! niwīkimākan kīsisōw!" itäw.

namuya tāpwähtawäw, umisah äh-mamätsiminät.

piyisk ōmis ītwäw awa maskwayānätās: "hāw, niwīkimākan, pāskin äkwah!" itwäw.

āsay maskamäw umiyusiwiniyiw, kāwiy äy-utinahk ōma kā-kīh-miyusit. äh-pāskināt awa ōmisimāw, äwakunih ōhi maskwayānätāsah kā-mitsimināt pīsākanāpiw uhtsi.

"nā, nisīmis, äsah kāh-miskutāhpitsitutsik kiwīkimākaninawak!"

"ā, namuya!" itäw awa kā-miyusit uskinīkiw; "äwakw āna kiwīkimākan, nītim, ä-kīh-maskamit nimiyusiwin. äkuyikuhk äy-ihkäyihtamān, nitayōwinisah iyikuhk ä-sōsawīhtāt, ä-sōsawiskawāt nitastutinah," itwäw.

tāpiskōts ayiwākäs äh-miyusiyit, mistahi miywäyihtam aw ōskinīkiskwäw, unāpämah äy-isinākusiyit. aw ōmisimāw mātōw, äh-māyātisiyit unāpäma. namuya pisiskäyimäw, tahk äh-ustustutamiyit, äh-māskāwikanäyit, ōhpimä äh-nīpawit, äh-mātut.

"tānähkih, nītim, kā-mātuyin? kuy-utsämā māna kiwīkimākan! utsäm äkwäyāk!" itäw.

namuya wīh-utsämäw, äh-wīnäyimāt unāpäma, tahk ä-mātut.

"nisīm, kiyām nista nik-ōnōpämin kināpäm!" itäw.

"āh, namuya! nītim kōnāpämin ōma!" itäw.

äkusi äh-pāh-pahpawipayihtāt utayōwinisah aw ōskinīkiw, kāwi miywāsiniyiwa. äkwah ä-pustayōwinisätsik, awa maskwayānätās ä-kīsi-pustayōwinisät, kā-sipwähtät; ayis pakwātam äh-pakwātikut uwīkimākana. sipwähtäw. äkwah awa äkutah ayāw. äkwah mistahi miywäyihtam aw ōsīmimāw.

" tāpwä ntāpatsihun äkā ä-kīh-ātawäyimitān ! " itäw uwīkimākanah.

äkwah awah umisimāw, " nisīmis, nīstah, nka-wīkimāw kināpäm, " itäw.

" namuya ! nītim kikīh-wīnäyimik, " itäw.

äkusi äkwah pōyuwak. tahtu-kīsikāw äkwah mātsīw, mustuswah äkwah äh-nōtsihāt, āh-iyawis äh-pätsitāpät mustuswah ; piyisk mistahih ayāwak mītsiwin. kītahtawä äh-ati-miyuskamiyik, äkwah utsawāsimisiw ; nāpäsisah ayāwäw. äkwah usām mistah äy-itäyihtahk, iyikuhk äh-ayātsik mītsiwin, namuya tahtu-kīsikāw mātsīw. kītahtawä ä-sākäwät, käwät, kā-pätsāstamuhtäyit uskinīkiwah nīsu. kīwäw.

äh-pīhtukät, " hā, nīsu pätāstamuhtäwak uskinīkiwak ! " itwäw.

" nāh, äkunik ätukä nistäsak ! " k-ätwäyit.

äkusi paminawasōw aw īskwäw, " ta-mītsisōwak nistäsak, " äh-täyihtahk.

pōtih ä-pä-sākäwätsik ōk ōskinīkiwak, kā-wāpahtahkik wayawītimihk mistahi äh-akutäyikih wiyāsah.

" hay hay ! " kā-päy-itwäyit ; " tāpwä nimiywäyihtän äy-isi-wāpahtamān ! " k-ätwäyit.

äh-pä-takuhtäyit, " ahā, ta-tawāw ! " itäw wīstāwah.

äh-pīhtukätsik, " hahā ! " miywäyimäwak wīstāwa. päyak namwāts unāpämiyiwa usīmiwāwa.

" iya, " itwäw, " tānihk ätukä päyak äkā k-ōnāpämit ? " itäw.

" yāah, āt āna kisīm kīh-unāpämiw ; māka kī-sipwähtäyiwa unāpäma, äh-pakwātāt muystas. kinwäsk āta kīh-unāpämiw, māka äkā tāpwä ä-nihtāminahuwit. kikiskäyimāwāw ätukä : maskwayānätās äsiyīhkāsut. "

" ä ä ha' ! äyakw āna kikīh-uwīstāwināwaw ! " itäw.

näpäwisiwak ōk ōskinīkiwak, äy-isinākusiyit, ä-kīh-uwīstāwitsik.

ōmis ītwäwak : " anuhts ōma k-ōtākusik ōtah ta-kapäsiw nōhtāwiyinān, äh-päy-ispitsiyāhk uma, mistah äh-nōhtähkatähk ; māka ä-kiskäyihtahk nōhtāwiy ōm ōtah äh-ayāyin, nīstāh, k-ō-päy-ispitsiyāhk. äkusi ä-kīh-itäyihtāhk nōhtāwiy, ōtah kā-kīh-pä-nakatāt nisīma, ' māskōts äkā awiya ātawäyimikutwāwi, wīkimikutwāwi, ta-nipahtāyit käkway pisiskiwah, ' ä-kīh-itäyihtahk nōhtāwiyinān, " itwäwak ōk ōskinīkiwak ; " mistahi ta-miywäyihtam, ōmisi wāpahtahkih, " itäw.

miywäyihtamuk ōk ōskinīkiskwäwak ä-wīh-pāpitsiyit ōhtāwiyiwāwa. äkusi tāpwä kätahtawä kā-pä-pīkiskwäyit ōhtāwiyiwāwa, ä-pä-sākäwäyit.

ōmis ītwäyiwa : " miyāmay ōhi wiyāsah ! " itwäyiwa ; " ninōhtähkatāh ! " itwäyiwa, kā-wayawīt aw ōskinīkiskwäw, " āha' , wiyāsah māka ! " äh-itāt ōhtāwiyah.

ta-nanāskumōw awa kisäyiniw, ä-miywäyihtahk, äkwah " äkusi ä-kīh-täyihtamān, ntawāsimisitik, ōtah k-ōh-kīh-pä-nakatitakuk, " äh-itāt utawāsimisah.

isi wayawīw aw ōskinīkiskwäw ; ōmis ītwäw : " äkunih māk ōhi niwiyāsimah, pikw animah äh-miywāsikih äy-itäyihtaman, nōhtāh, äkutah kapäsih, " itäw.

äkwah tānihi äh-miywāsiniyikih wiyāsah, äkutah pānahikäyiwah tawāsimisah.

" hāw, ntīnīmitik ! " itäw ōhi ; " itah äsi-miywäyihtamäk wiyāsah, kapäsik, " itäw ayīsiyiniwah.

äkusi kapäsiwak. äkuyihuhk äkwah ntawi-pīhtukäw utānisah wīkiyihk, äh-wāpamāt unahāhkisīmah. pōtih ōsisimah mīna āsay misikitisiyiwa, äh-utinät, ä-wiy-utsämät ōsisimah. mistahi miywäyihtam. kahkiyaw ayīsiyiniwak miywäyihtamwak. piyisk kinwäsk äkutah ayāwak, iyikuhk ä-misikitiyit ukusisiwāwa.

kītahtawä ōmis ītwäw awa kisäyiniw: "ntānis, namuya tsī wīhkāts kipähtawāw ninahāhkisīm, awiya ta-pimātisiyit ta-wāhkōmāt?"

"āta wiy āna, 'nōhtāwiy mīna nikāwiy,' itwäw māna, 'kayās äkwah kā-nakatakik,' itwäw māna."

"hah, äha', ntānis, kaskäyihtamōtukänik aniki nitähtāwāw. ituhtähkäk; kiyāskuts ntawi-pamihāhkanik kisikus mīnah kisis," itäw utānisah; "äkuyikuhk nimamāhtākusin, iyikuhk käkway äh-nipahtāt ninahāhkisīm, äh-mītsiyān," itäw.

"häha', nka-wīhtamawāw," itik utānisah.

äh-kīwät, ōmis ītäw uwīkimākanah: "'ituhtähkäk ōhtāwiyah ninahāhkisīm,' äh-itwät nōhtāwiy," itäw.

"äha', wāpahkih ka-sipwähtānānaw. kitimākisitukänik; māka kayās kā-pä-nakatakik," itäw.

tāpwä iyikuhk äh-wāpaniyik, wawäyīwak, äh-wīh-sipwähtät, tāpwä kahkiyaw awiyah ayīsiyiniwah äh-atamiskākutsik. äkus ä-sipwähtätsik, nīswāw äh-kīh-kapäsitsik, äkuyikuhk wāpahtamwak wīkiwāw tah k-ätuhtätsik.

"hāw, nika-nīkānipahtān; nka-wīhtamawāw ntawih nōhtāwiy ä-wīhtakuhtäyahk," itäw.

"äha'!"

äkwah sipwäpahtāw. äh-takuhtät, pōtih namwāts mamīhk käkway wāpahtam, ta-mītsiyit.

ä-pīhtukät, pōt ōhi ay-apiyiwah ōhtāwiyah ukāwiyah, "hāy hāy! nikusis takusin!" äh-itwäyit, ä-atamiskākut, kunt äh-mātuyit ukāwiyah, iyikuhk äh-miywäyihtamiyit äh-wāpamikut.

äkusi nanāskumuyiwah.

"ā, ksiwāk päy-ihtāw äh-pä-wītsäwak iskwäw, mīnah kōsisimiwāw," itäw.

nanāskumōw awa kisäyiniw.

"mahtih!" itwäw awa nōtukäsiw, äh-wayawīt, äh-ntawi-nakiskawāt ustimah äkwah ōsisimah. itah ä-nakiskawāt, utsämäw.

"nistim!" itäw; "päsiw nōsisimis!" itäw.

miyik, min äkunih äh-uy-utsämät. äkus ä-ati-sipwähtätsik, ōsisima ä-nayōmāt. äh-takuhtätsik, ä-pīhtukahāt, sämāk awa kisäyiniw ntumäw ōsisimah, äh-uy-utsämāt. äkusi äkutah äkw ä-ay-ayātsik, äkwah mīnah äh māh-mātsīt aw uskinīkiw, äkwah awah uskinīkiskwäw mistah äh-atuskät, äh-pamihāt umanātsimākanah. kitimākäyimäw mituni, iyikuhk äh-miyupamihāt usikusah usisah mīna.

aspin äkuyikuhk äh-iskwāk ātsimuwin ätayōhkäwin. äkuyikuhk.

Once upon a time there were two people, a man and his wife. Presently they had a child. There where they dwelt the man would always hunt. And so, in the course of time, they had a child, a boy. They stayed in that place. In time the boy grew big. He turned out handsome. They loved him; they were fond of their son. The boy did no work at all. His clothes were always good, for the woman sewed her son's clothing. So in time the child became a young man.

Then that young man spoke as follows: "Pray, try to kill a fisher," he said to his father.

And so that man tried to get sight of a fisher. Presently he saw a fisher; he killed it. The youth prepared it. When he had finished it, he wore it as a hat. He had arrows, too, and used an otterskin for his quiver, to put his arrows in, that youth. His coat was a hide ornamented with quill-work; and his breeches, too, were worked with quills. He never went hunting.

Then at one time he spoke thus: "Father, are we the only human beings there are?" he asked him.

"No. Everywhere are people. But they are not good, they always contend. When they defeat one another, they destroy each other; they are not good."

"Just think of it!" said the youth; "I should like to try and see the other people," said the youth.

The old man was sorry at this, and the old woman, for they cherished their son.

"Surely he will go to his undoing," thought the woman of their son, and wept.

And so they were not able to keep their son from going forth.

"Tomorrow I shall go," said the youth.

"Dear me!" said the man; "My son, do not go in the direction of noon!" he told his son.

"Very well," answered the youth.

Accordingly, when day broke, the youth departed.

He said, "Father, mother, I shall come here, if I am not destroyed. It is only that I want to see the people," said the youth, as he put on his hat. "Now then, Fisherskin-Hat is my name," he said, as he stepped out of the house.

His mother wept as she said farewell to him. So he set out and walked along. All day he walked, walking in the direction where there is no sun. Presently, as he walked along, in the evening, he saw a partridge. He shot it and killed it, thinking, "I shall eat it when I camp for the night." So he took it and plucked it.

As he walked by a place where there were clumps of trees, presently he saw a little lodge of smoked-up leather. He went there, thinking, "I wonder what sort of person stays there."

When he reached the doorway, "Come in, grandchild!" said an old woman.

When he went in, there she was, all by herself.

"Come in!" she said; "Sit over there!" she told him.

He gave his grandmother the partridge he was holding.

"Thank you, my grandchild; this is exactly what I was wanting to eat!" she said. Then she told him thus: "Grandchild, it is a hard place to which you are going. It would be better if you went home tomorrow. Hard to deal with are the people there," his grandmother told him.

"No, grandmother; for now I have already set out this way," he answered her.

"Dear me!" she said to him; "Then be careful, grandson!"

And so she set about cooking a meal, putting in the pot a single berry and a single bit of chopped meat.

When he observed her, "Surely I shall not eat my fill!" he thought.

Thus spoke his grandmother: "My grandchild, you will eat your fill of this," she told him.

"Goodness me!" thought the youth, "Plainly, I shall not be able to think about her!" he thought.

"No, my grandchild! Why should you have to think about me?" she said to him.

She knew that he had taken her as his object of meditation.

So then she gave him to eat; she gave him her cooking-pot, just as it was. As he ate, whenever he took up the whole contents and put it into his mouth, when he looked at the little pot, there lay the two morsels again. At last he ate all the faster. At last he had enough; he was not able to eat up the things his grandmother had given him to eat. He handed it back to her.

"I cannot finish it, grandmother," he said to her.

"Dear me, truly my grandchild merely pecks at his food, seeing that he cannot finish my little berries, my bits of cooked meat!" she said to him.

By now it was deep night.

"Grandson, you must be tired from walking; lie down," she told him.

He lay down; the old woman, too, lay down. When dawn came, when they got up, they ate again.

When they had eaten, "Now then, grandson, do not go in this direction whence comes the morning light! Hard to deal with is he who dwells there," she told him; "Go this way, toward the north," she told him.

"Very well," said he, as he departed and continued his journey.

When he had gone a long ways, "I wonder why my grandmother warned me away from this place?" he thought.

He turned in that direction. Presently, when it was almost noon, he saw someone sitting on a knoll. He was going to walk on, leaving the place to one side, when the other arose, in the very direction toward which he had turned. Although he tried not to go there, yet he landed in that direction. At last he went up the hill where he saw the other. There he saw that that man was very ugly, hunchbacked and small, and clad in a bearskin coat; this man came to meet him, and as he came, had a fit of coughing, and said to him: "Fisherskin-Hat, you always were coming here to play!" he told him; "Of old, 'He will go about engaging in contests,' was said of you, you know!"

"It is not going about to engage in contests I am," he told him.

"Oh, don't say that! Only do let us have a contest!" the other said to him.

"No!" he answered him.

"Do you see that clump of trees right over there, where the smoke is rising?"

"Yes!"

"Very beautiful are the two young women who live there. They will be the prize," the other told him.

"Oh, no!" he said to him.

"Oh, please do let us wrestle!" the other said to him.

At last he said, "Yes," to him.

Then he put down his blanket-robe and his arrows, and all his clothes; only his hat he did not put down.

"Ho, set down your hat, too," the other told him.

"Oh dear, no!"

So then they wrestled. He could not overcome him. At last, just as he was getting out of breath, he tripped the other and threw him; he got him down.

"Ho, Fisherskin-Hat, I stumbled over your leg, that is why you have got the better of me. Once more!" the other said to him.

"Oh no! I have beaten you now," he answered the other.

"No; once more!"

"Very well!"

They wrestled. While they were at grips, the other knocked his hat up into the air. Thereupon the other overcame him; he broke his back and entered his body, taking away his good looks. As he had seen the other to look, such was now the appearance of that youth. And that other, who had been ugly, was now handsome. When he looked at him, "Greatly has he injured me as to my good looks, robbing me thus of my beauty!" thought he.

The other took his clothes and put them on, and his hat as well.

"These here are your clothes, Bearskin-Breeches!" the other told him.

Then he put on the other's clothes. And now he, instead of the other, was incessantly coughing. Well, he had not followed his grandmother's advice.

"Well now, Bearskin-Breeches, let us go take our wives!" the other told him.

So they set out to go to those young women. When they were near the place, out came the elder sister.

She saw them and at once cried out, "Little sister! Come out! Here are these young men coming!"

When that young woman came out, there she saw them walking up.

"Come, little sister, let us see who gets there first! Whichever runs the faster, let her have the handsome one for her husband," said the elder sister.

"Very well," said the younger.

The woman started to run. Whenever her younger sister was about to pass her, she seized hold of her and flung her back; in the end that elder sister grabbed hold of the handsome youth saying, "This one I shall wed!"

But it was the younger woman who was handsome.

Then, "There's your husband!" they said to the younger one, pointing to the hunchback who had a cough.

They took the men home with them. When they entered the lodge, the one who had the cough took his seat yonder by the doorway. But the handsome youth, whose wife kept hugging and kissing him, thought it very fine. There they dwelt, and those women had only berries to eat. At last night came, as they sat there. . . . .

Morning came. In the morning, when they got up, when they had eaten, the handsome one went out to go hunting. On his way out, he kicked the hunchback.

"Why are you sitting like that, Bearskin-Breeches? Didn't you know we were staying at our wives'?"

On his way out he upset him with a kick, so that he reeled about and coughed.

When he arose, he said to his wife, "Bring me a rawhide rope."

She gave him a little leather thong. Thereupon he left the house, coughing as he went, to go a-hunting, he too.

"I can't imagine what he will kill!" said the older sister of her brother-in-law.

So all day they hunted. At nightfall the handsome man arrived. His booty turned out to be one otter. Meanwhile he who had the cough did not arrive.

At last, when it was dark, "Did you not see him anywhere?" the one asked her husband.

"No; I did not see him at all. I daresay he will be freezing to death somewhere!" he answered her, for it was winter-time.

After some time, there came the other, leaning on a stick; at last he arrived.

"Why, he really has come!" said the elder sister.

When he entered, he took his seat there by the door, and handed his wife the rawhide. When the young woman pulled at it, in she pulled a partridge or a prairie-chicken.

This was what the elder sister had said, when her husband brought the otter: "Sister, we shall not invite each other to eat. Whatever our husbands kill we shall eat," she had told her sister, for she thought that her sister's husband would not succeed in killing anything.

So now, accordingly, they did not share their food, but the handsome man and his wife ate the otter. And the younger sister and her husband ate the partridge. So in time they went to bed. . . . .

And again, when day broke and they got up, the handsome man went out to hunt. Again he kicked the other.

"Why are you sitting like that? Didn't you know we were newly married, Bearskin-Breeches?" he said to him, kicking him over, so that he coughed as if he were going to die, the elder sister meanwhile laughing and laughing at her brother-in-law being kicked about. The latter, too, went off to hunt. All that day he tramped about. When night fell, again the handsome man arrived; again he brought an otter.

"Hey, now my big brothers will rejoice, when they get these otter-skins for hats!" said the elder sister.

When it was entirely dark, then came the other a-coughing.

"Well, well, well, there he is again!" she said of her brother-in-law, for she abhorred him.

When he entered and had taken his seat, he handed his wife the raw-hide rope.

"I suppose, another partridge!" said the elder sister.

When the woman pulled at it, into the lodge she drew a beaver.

"Splendid, splendid! Now I shall have good eating!" said that young woman.

When she skinned it and cut it up, it was very fat; and she cooked it, cooking also half of the tail.

This is what the elder sister said: "Little sister, give me part of that tail to eat; let me, too, have something good with my meal!" she asked her.

"No! 'Whatever our husbands kill, we shall eat,' you said not long ago."

Then she envied her sister the beaver which she was eating.

* * * * * * * * * * * * * * * * *

So they slept. In the morning, when they got up, they ate again. When they had eaten, the handsome young man again made ready to go hunting. On his way out of the lodge, he kicked the other.

"Why are you sitting there like that? Didn't you know we are staying at our wives' house?" he said to him.

He kicked him headlong. The elder sister laughed at what was done to her sister's husband.

Then, when he got up from where he lay, "Bring me a leather thong," he told her.

And so, when he was given it, he too went hunting.

"Come, sister, don't forget we are newly married; we must fetch wood," said the elder sister to the younger.

So they fetched firewood, and hauled the faggots.

When it was noon, "Let us stop and eat," said the young women.

Then they cooked; they prepared their food, the younger woman roasting some beaver-flesh. The elder envied her for it.

She said to her: "Sister, do tear off a part for me. Let me too eat a bit of it."

"Pshaw! So that is the way of it! You have a husband too, and he has killed an otter, and you can eat it. 'We shall each eat separately,' you said, when you thought of my husband, 'He won't be able to kill anything,' " she told her.

"Nonsense! I was teasing you, sister!" she answered her.

"Never mind! I shall not by any chance give you any," she told her elder sister.

Then, of those two who were hunting, at nightfall the handsome one arrived. He brought two otters. When it was quite dark, Bearskin-Breeches came a-coughing. When he came into the lodge, he handed his wife the leather rope.

She said to him, "What sort of a treat is he bringing me now?" said that young woman.

When she pulled at it, she drew two beavers into the house.

"Splendid! Now I shall save up these tails for my father and mother to eat!" she said. "Come, sit over here," she told him, pointing to where she had neatly arranged her part of the tent.

"Oh, no!" said Bearskin-Breeches, disgusted with his own person.

"Please sit here!" she told him.

At last he took his seat there, while that young woman by the doorway skinned and cut up the beavers. When she had finished them, she cooked a meal, she cooked beaver-flesh.

Thus spoke the elder sister: "Little sister, give me one tail," she said to her.

"Pshaw, just you eat the tails of the things your husband killed!" she told her elder sister, and would not give her any.

Only they had good meat to eat, for the otters which the handsome man had killed were not fat. Then, in time, when they had finished their meal, when darkness had fallen, they went to bed. . . . .

So they slept. In the morning, when they got up, and had eaten again, the handsome one rose to his feet without delay, for he was angry that Bearskin-Breeches had outdone him every time in hunting. Again, on his way out of the lodge, he kicked the other.

He said to him, "Why are you sitting there like that? Don't you know we are staying at our wives'? " he said to him, kicking him headlong, as he left the lodge.

"Bring me a leather rope," he said to his wife.

When she had given it to him, he too went out to hunt.

When he was far off, he spoke as follows: "It can't be, can it, that he robbed me of my hunting power when he took away my good looks?" said Bearskin-Breeches.

So he went from there, on snowshoes, as always, and presently he saw some dwarf moose. He killed two cows, very fat ones. Then he went home, dragging the two. Presently, late in the evening, the handsome man arrived. He brought a young bull of the dwarf moose; it was by no means a good specimen.

Then, after nightfall, the young woman went out of doors, thinking of her husband, "It seems he is not coming home on time."

"It really seems as if that person who has just gone out were lonesome for her husband!" said the elder sister, sneering at the younger.

By and by, as the young woman stood outside there, she heard someone far off who came singing. She was glad that he was singing. Oh, very quickly he came near, as he sang. She went indoors, thinking, "It is he!" of her husband, and heated her cooked food, while he quickly came with noise, but now of coughing.

"Faugh! He's back!" exclaimed the elder sister, for truly she felt disgust at the thought of her sister's husband.

When he came in, he handed her the rawhide. When the young woman tugged at it, she could not get it in. Bearskin-Breeches got up; when he drew it in, into the tent he pulled two dwarf moose.

"Splendid! Now I shall have two skins of dwarf moose!" she said.

Then she sat down, taking some pretty moccasins, and put them on her husband's feet.

"Fie, she is even putting her fancy-work moccasins on his feet!" she said of her younger sister.

"Why, even you are in the habit of putting moccasins on your husband's feet, when he doesn't kill anything good!"

Then, when they had eaten, the young woman set about her butchering. When she had cleaned the animals, they went to bed and slept. In the morning, when they had got up and breakfasted, the handsome man went out, angry because, when he tried to hunt, Bearskin-Breeches kept outdoing him. He went straight out of the tent.

Then said that young woman, "Hoho, how now? Did not he always use to kick him as he went out? He must be ashamed at being outdone!" she called to him.

Then Bearskin-Breeches, too, got ready and went hunting, and after a while he was far off. Presently, in the afternoon, he saw some moose. He killed some, and dragged them home. And the handsome man killed one deer, a male that was very lean. At nightfall he arrived. The elder sister was very glad when she saw the deer.

"Splendid! Now we can use it for moccasins!" she said.

When at last it was quite dark, the younger sister went outside, and then she heard someone who came a-singing. And quickly he came near with his song, while she stood there and listened with pleasure to him who sang. When he had come near, she went inside; it seems that it was Bearskin-Breeches' snowshoes that always came singing. When he came in, he handed her the rawhide. When she tugged at it, she could not manage it; then Bearskin-Breeches drew in two moose.

"Splendid! Truly, I am glad that we can have moccasins from one, and my father and my brothers from the other!" she said.

The elder sister now spoke not at all, as her husband was outdone. Then the young woman with zeal prepared her husband's food. When they had eaten, the young woman skinned and cut up the game: look you, those moose were fat.

"Little sister," said the elder, "Give me one of those leg-bones; let me eat the marrow," she asked her.

"Oho, so that is where we are! I certainly shall not give you any; you hate your brother-in-law here; anything he has killed cannot possibly taste good," she told her sister.

Then in time it was night. Finally they went to bed. When morning came, and they had eaten breakfast, again they went hunting.

Thus spoke Bearskin-Breeches: "Bring your rawhide rope," he told his wife.

As he hunted, when he was far off, he killed a very fat bear. And the handsome man killed a bull buffalo. This time too, the buffalo was not fat. They always dragged home entire whatever they killed; so now, in the evening, there came the handsome man, who had killed a bull buffalo. And when it was all dark, there came Bearskin-Breeches, and entered the tent. The young woman was happy as soon as he came in. When she pulled at the rawhide rope, she could not manage it.

She said, "What new treat has my husband in store for me?"

"For shame," the elder one cried at once; "She even goes so far as to speak of him as 'husband'!" she said.

"Well, and certainly there is no reason why I should not call him so, seeing that he always makes good killings for me!" said the younger, for Bearskin-Breeches' wife loved him.

When he drew it in, he brought in a bear.

"Splendid!" cried the young woman; "Truly, my father will be very glad, that I am to have plenty of fat, of bear's-fat!" she said.

Then first she put moccasins on her husband's feet. Then she gave him his meal, and they ate, and all the while the elder sister kept watching the younger, because she envied her the good things she was eating. When they had eaten, they cleaned the game. When they had cleaned it, it was dark night. Then they went to bed.

Bearskin-Breeches spoke as follows: "Now," he said to his wife, "tomorrow he and I shall not hunt," he told her, "but we shall take a steam-bath," he told her; "You have done well by yourself in not disdaining me," he told her; "This is not the way I really look; the way your sister's husband there appears, that is the way I really look, for he has taken my good looks from me, overcoming me by treachery. But the way I now appear is really his bodily form," he told her; "Moreover he is greatly defiling my garments which he is wearing. Tomorrow prepare a hut for the steam-bath. Only thus shall I overcome him," he told her; "Right outside here, close by, I saw a large stone," he told her; "You will heat it. And this bear's-fat you will use to cover the hut. Also in a bowl you will melt fat, you will prepare fat for me to pour on the stone," he told her; "When we are in the steam, and he feels the heat, and says, 'Open up!' then pay him no heed; and if your sister starts to open the hut, hold her fast," he told her.

"Very well," said the young woman.

So then they went to sleep.

In the morning, when they had got up and eaten, Bearskin-Breeches spoke: "Brother-in-law!" he said to the other.

"What is it?"

"Let us not hunt now. Let us rest a while; you must be tired," he said to him.

"Yes, I am tired," said he.

"If we took a steam-bath, the heat would refresh us," he said to him.

"Yes, I should very much like to take a steam-bath," said he.

At once the elder sister said, "You shall not take a steam-bath; you will get too dirty and sweaty in the heat," she said to her husband.

"Yes, but I am tired. Do let me take a steam-bath," he said.

Accordingly, when they had eaten, the young woman went out and built the hut for the steam-bath, and made a fire.

When she went to get that large stone, she walked round it and said to it, "Stone, be light for me!"

Big as it was, she managed to lift it and take it back with her; that was the stone which she heated. When the stone was hot, she covered the hut with fat underneath, bear's-fat, and with their blanket-robes on the outside. Then she prepared the grease with which he was to sprinkle the stone.

"Now I have finished, husband," she told him.

"Now then, brother-in-law, we were going to take a steam-bath, you know!" he said to the other.

"Goodness!" cried the elder sister; "No! You are too likely to take out my husband instead of yours, my handsome husband!" she said to her sister.

"Nonsense! How could I want to exchange my husband for yours, my husband who is a good hunter?" she answered her.

"Sister-in-law," said Bearskin-Breeches, "tie a rawhide rope to your husband; then you can hold fast to the rope, so that your husband shall not be taken from you."

"Very well!"

Thereupon they took off their clothes and went into the structure where they were to take the steam-bath. Then the elder sister really did tie something round her husband's waist by which to hold him on the line, in her fear that she would be robbed of him. Then they closed them in tightly.

Then Bearskin-Breeches spoke, saying, "Now, because I am weary I am taking a steam-bath, but, besides, I hate the way I now look!" he said; "Let me have back my good looks!" he said, as he poured fat on the stone.

The handsome youth felt too hot.

He said, "Open it up! I am hot!" he cried.

That young woman paid no heed. He sprinkled the stone all the more.

He cried all the more, "Open it up! I am too hot!"

The young woman paid no heed to his noise.

He cried, "Wife, open it up!" to her.

When she wanted to open it, the younger sister held the elder back.

"Get away! My husband is being scalded!" she said to her.

She paid no heed to her elder sister, but held her firmly.

At last Bearskin-Breeches said, "There, wife, now open it!"

By this time he had taken away the other's comely appearance, and regained his former good looks. When the elder sister opened the hut for him, it was that Bearskin-Breeches whom she was holding on the rawhide thong.

"Dear me, sister, it seems our husbands have changed places as to the rope!"

"Oh, no!" the handsome young man told her; "This person here is your husband, my sister-in-law, who had robbed me of my good looks. But now I have had enough of his defiling my clothes and my headgear," he said.

It seemed as though he were even handsomer than before; the young woman was very glad to see her husband looking like that. The elder sister wept because her husband was ugly. She paid no attention to him, for he coughed incessantly, and was hunchbacked, but she stood to one side and wept.

"Why are you weeping, sister-in-law? You might be kissing your husband, you know! At least give him a kiss!" he said to her.

She would not kiss her husband, for he disgusted her, and she kept weeping.

"Little sister, please let me have your husband!" she begged her.

"Oh, no! It is my brother-in-law who is your husband!" she told her.

Then, when that youth gave his clothes a good shaking, they were pretty again. Then they put on their clothes, and when that Bearskin-Breeches had put on his, he departed; for he did not like his wife's disdain. He went away. But the other stayed there. Then that younger sister was very happy.

"Truly, I did well by myself when I did not scorn you!" she said to her husband.

Then the elder sister said to her, "Little sister, do let me be married to your husband!"

"No! My brother-in-law was disgusted with you," she told her.

Then they ceased. He went hunting every day, and chased buffalo, and brought them home entire; in time they had much food. Presently toward spring, they had a child; a little boy. Then, when he thought that they had too much food, he no longer hunted every day. Then at one time, as he went to an outlook, there were two youths coming that way. He went back.

As he entered the tent, "Ho, two youths are walking hither!" he said.

"Dear me, those must be my brothers!" was what she said.

Thereupon that woman began cooking, for she thought, "My brothers shall eat."

There, when those young men came into view of the place, they beheld a great amount of meat hanging outside the tent.

"Splendid!" was what they said as they approached; "Truly, I am glad to see things like this!" they said.

When they reached the place, "Hello, come in!" he said to his brothers-in-law.

When they entered, "Hoho!" they liked their brother-in-law's looks. But one of their sisters had no husband at all.

"Hey," said the one, "Why is it that one has not a husband?"

"Oh, why, this sister of yours did have a husband, but her husband went away; he took a dislike to her after a time. She was married quite a while, but the man was not really much of a provider of game. Perhaps you know him: his name is Bearskin-Breeches."

"Heavens, yes! So we had that person for a brother-in-law!" the one answered him.

Those young men were ashamed that such a looking man had been their brother-in-law.

They spoke as follows: "Today, at nightfall, our father will camp here, for we are moving camp to this place, on account of great famine; because our father knew, after all, that you were here, brother-in-law, is why we are moving camp this way. This, in fact, was our father's thought, when he came and left my sisters here, for, 'Perhaps some man or men will not disdain them and marry them, and then kill something in the way of game,' was what our father thought," said those youths; "He will be very glad, when he sees the way things are," the one told him.

The young women were glad that their father was coming with his camp. Then really, in time, came the sound of their father's speech, as he came in sight.

He said, "Surely that is all meat!" he said; "And here was I starving!" he said, and out went that young woman, saying to her father, "Yes, meat, indeed!"

The old man gave thanks, for he was glad, and then, "This was what I had in mind, my children, as my reason for coming and leaving you in this place," he told his children.

Then the young woman went out of doors and said, "But as to these my stores of meat, whichever you think is the best, father, by it pitch your tent," she said to him.

Then by the best stores of meat, there his children cleared away the snow.

"Now, my men," he said to the others; "Camp wherever you like the look of the meats," he told the people.

So then they pitched camp. Thereupon he went and entered his daughter's tipi, to see his son-in-law. There he beheld also his grandson, who by now was quite a lad; he took him and kissed him again and again. He was very glad. All the people were glad. They continued to stay there for a long time, until their son was big.

Then at one time the old man spoke thus: "Daughter, do you never hear my son-in-law say that any of his relatives are alive?"

"To be sure, he often speaks of his father and mother, and says, 'It is a long time since I left them'."

"Yes; so there, daughter, surely my son-in-law's father and his wife must be lonesome. You had better go there; do you now, in turn, take care of your husband's mother and father," he told his daughter; "I am sufficiently well off now, so long as I eat the things my son-in-law has killed," he told her.

"Very well, I will tell him this," his daughter said to him.

When she went home, she said to her husband, " 'Go you to my son-in-law's father,' is what my father says," she told him.

"Very well, tomorrow we shall depart. No doubt they are in want; after all, it is a long time since I left them to come here," he answered her.

Accordingly, when day broke, they made ready for his departure, and truly, all the people bade them farewell. So they departed, and when they had camped twice on the way, they came in sight of his people's home to which they were going.

"Here, I shall run ahead; I shall go tell my father that we are about to arrive," he said to her.

"Very well."

Then he ran on. When he got there, behold, he saw nothing at all of things to eat.

When he entered the lodge, there sat his father and his mother; "Splendid! Our son has come!" they cried, as they greeted him, and his mother wept for no reason at all, except that she was so glad to see him.

And so they gave thanks.

"Now, close by on her way hither is a woman who has come here with me, and also your grandchild," he told them.

The old man spoke his thanks.

"Oh, I must!" exclaimed the old woman, and went out of the lodge, to go meet her daughter-in-law and her grandchild. When she met her, she kissed her.

"My daughter-in-law!" she said to her; "Give me my grandchild!" she said to her.

The other gave her the child, and him too she kissed many times. Then they left that spot and went on, and she carried her grandchild. When they arrived, and she took him into the house, at once the old man called his grandson, and kissed him repeatedly. So then they stayed there, and the young man always hunted, and the young woman worked hard, taking care of her parents-in-law. She was very kind to them and took good care of her mother-in-law and of her father-in-law.

And this is the end of the story, of the sacred story. That is all.

(19) Wampum-Head and His Nephews

Coming-Day

kā-kīsikāw-pīhtukāw.

päyak ōtänaw äh-misāk, kayās äsa äh-mōtutsik. äkusi awa iskwäw äh-ukimāwit, piyäsiw-iskwäw, napatä ōtänaw äh-tipäyihtahk, äkwah napatä ōtänaw äh-tipäyihtahk äwakō ukimāw mahīhkan; nāpäw äōkō. utōskinīkīmiwāwa äh-astwätutsik, äh-mätawätsik, äh-manitōwi-mätawätsik, päyak siyākōtsihihtsih, äkusi uwītsäwākanah äh-nipahimiht, äh-mōwimiht, äkusi piku 'äh-mōtutsik' isiyīhkätäw. nanātuhk, ōki ayīsiyiniwak kā-itwähk, nanātuhk pisiskiwak äyōkunik. äkus äōkō.

äkwah awa mahīhkan k-ōkimāwit, äkutah uhtsi päyak uskinīkiskwäw, usīmisah, nāpäsisah äh-apisīsisiyit, ä-kitimākäyimāt, ä-sākihāt, ōhtāwiya ukāwiya kutakah wītsisāna kahkiyaw äh-nipahimiht, wiyawā piku nīsu ä-pimātisitsik usīmisa, ōmis ītäyihtam: "nika-sipwähtān; nisīmis awa māskōts wīh-pimātisitsih," äh-itäyihtahk; "usām kitimākisiw, äh-apisīsisit," itäyihtam; "hāw, anuhts kā-tipiskāk, mistahi ta-māyi-kīsikāw! tamispun!" itwäw; "nika-sipwähtān, äkā ta-kiskäyimikawiyān itä kā-wīh-ituhtäyān." äkusi itäyihtam.

tāpwä, äh-tipiskāk, mistahi māyi-kīsikāw, äh-mispuhk. äkwah miywäyihtam aw ōskinīkiskwäw. mayaw mistah äh-tipiskāk, wawäyīw, wīkiwāw äh-manisahk, ispimihk itah äh-māyātahk äh-wäpinahk. äkwah utanāskānah, utakōhpah, kahkiuaw ta-kīh-āpatsihtāt kākwayah utinam, äh-kīsi-wawäyīt, mustuswayān äkutah äh-wäwīkahpitahk utsayānisah. äkus īsi ä-sipwähtäw, äh-utāpät ōh ōtsayānisah, tāpiskōts nipakitāpānāsk, äkus īsi äh-utāpät, äkwah usīmisah äh-nayōmāt. si mistahä māyi-kīsikāyiw. kapä-tipisk māyi-kīsikāyiw, äh-pimuhtät. piyisk wāpaniyiw; āhtsi pikuh māyi-kīsikāyiw. iyikuhk äh-utākusik, äkuyikuhk astä-kīsikāw. āhtsi pikuh pimuhtäw. piyis tipiskāw. äkutah äkwah kapäsiw. nama käkway mītsiw, äkutah äh-nipāt. äyikuhk äh-wāpaniyik, mīna sipwähtäw. äh-wāpaniyik, äkwah mātuyiwa usīmisa, äh-nōhtäkatäyit. äkusi nitsawāts wawäyīw, ä-sipwähtät. äyikuhk äh-miskahk itah äh-ayapāskwäyāyik, äkutah päyak mistah äh-sakāyik, äkutah ituhtäw, äh-nanātawāpahtahk, "itah ä-miywāsik ta-wīkiyān," äh-itäyihtahk. tāpwä miskam sakāhk äy-ihkatawāyik, äh-nipīwiyik, wāsakām mistah äh-sakāyik. äkutah kapäsiw. pānaham, äkutah ä-wīh-wīkit; äkwah kutawäw. āhtsi pikuh mātuyiwa usīmisah, ä-nōhtähkatäyit. ä-kīh-kutawät, äkwah usīhtäw ä-wīh-tāpakwät.

tāpwä äh-nipāyit usīmisa, tāpakwäw, "māskōts wāpus nipahakih," äh-itäyihtak; "nisīmis ōka-mōwā," äh-itäyihtahk.

äkwah mihtah äh-utinahk, äkutah k-ōtinahk mihtah, tapasiyiwa äkutah uhtsi wāpuswah. äyakunih tāpakwāsuyiwa päyak. nipahäw.

"hāy hāy! äkwah nisīmis kä-mītsisut!" itäyihtam.

kīwähtahäw; iyāyaw usīhäw, ä-wīh-kīsiswāt, ä-wīh-asamāt usīmisah. äkusi äh-kīsiswāt, päkupayiyiwa usīmisa. äkusi äyakuni asamäw. äkwah wiya pasikōw, äh-āwatät mihtah, ä-wīh-usihtät wīkiwāw. piyis mistahih utinam mistikwah. ikuyikuhk wīh-mātuyiwa usīmisah, äkwah ä-nahapīstawät, äh-kākītsihät. äkwah äkutah ay-ayāw. iyikuhk äkā äh-mātuyit āsay, usīhtāw wīkiwāw, maskusiyah äh-manisahk, äyakunih mīna äh-apahkwät wīkiwāhk, mīna äh-anāskät. äkuyikuhk ä-wīh-tipiskāk, āsay t-äsi-kīsōwāyik äy-īsīhtät wīkih, äkwah pīhtukahäw usīmisa, äkwah äh-kutawät pīhtsāyihk. mwähtsih äh-pahkisimuyik, kāh-matwä-ma-mawimuyit wāpuswah. ituhtäw : pōtih päyak. nipahäw. miywäyihtam.

" äkusi namuya ta-nōhtähkatäw nisīmis, " itäyihtam.

ay-apiw.

äkwah ä-tipiskāyik, mā-mitunäyihtam, " pitanä äkā uhtsih awiyak miskawit ! " äy-itäyihtahk ; " kahkiyaw ayīsiyiniwak äkus is āyāwak ätukä ? " äh-itäyihtahk ; itä k-ōh-ituhtät ōhi ayīsiyiniwah kāy-itātisiyit, kā-nāh-nipahituyit, äh-mōtuyit, " äkusi ätukä kutakak mīna is āyāwak ? " äy-itäyihtahk, äyaku uhtsi k-ōh-itwät.

tāpwä miywäyihtam äh-päyakut, " äkusi māskōts nk-ōhpikihāw nisīmis, " äh-itäyihtahk.

äkutah tahtu-kīsikāw mihtah äh-utinahk, mīna äh-tāpakwät äh-mihtsātiyit wāpuswah, tāpwä täpiskāyikih, kāh-nipātsih, wiyāpahk äh-nātät wāpuswah, mituni miywäyihtam māh-mihtsät äh-nipahät. piyisk usīhtāw wiyawitimihk itah ä-wīh-akutät wāpuswah, usām mihtsät äh-nipahät.

" hāw, äkus ätsik ōma äkā mayaw kä-nōhtähkatäyāhk nisīmis ! " itäyihtam.

nama käkway kutak atuskātam, nayästaw äh-tāpakwät äkwah mihtah äh-utinahk, äkutah uma k-āy-ayāt, " pitan ōma äkā uhtsih miskawit awiyak ! " äh-itäyihtahk.

kītahtawä äkwah, kinwäsk itah äh-ayāt äkwah, usīmisah äkwah misikitiyiwa. äkwah usīhtāw atsusisah, usīmisah äy-usīhtawät, ä-wīh-kakwä-nihtāh-pimutahkwähät. tāpwä piyisk nihtāh-pimutahkwäyiwa ; piyisk nakatsihtāw käkway ta-wīh-kakwä-nipahät awa nāpäsis. kītahtawä sakāhk äh-papāmuhtät awa nāpäsis, wāpamäw wāpuswah. ä-wīh-kakwä-nipahät, tāpwä nipahäw. ha, miywäyihtam, äh-pīhtukahät.

" hāy hāy ! " itwäw awa uskinīkiskwäw ; " äkus ätsik āni äkā kä-kīh-nipahāhkatusuyāhk, āsay äh-nipahät nisīmis wāpuswah, " itäyihtam.

äkwah tāpwä kutakah usīhtāw atsusisah, nawats äh-misāyikih, " käkway tsit-ōh-miyu-nipahtät, " äy-itäyihtahk. piyisk äh-kīsihtät, äkwah äyakunih äh-āpatsihtät awa nāpäsis, tāpwä māh-mihtsät nipahäw wāpuswah. äkwah aw īskwäw pīkunam apāhkwāsun, äy-usihtät usīma tsit-ōtāsiyit, mīna t-ōskutākayit. äkwah kākāts uskinīkiw awa nāpäsis. mistahi miyusiw awa nāpäsis. äkwah äkutah ōm äh-ay-ayātsik, kītahtawä wāpuswah ä-wīh-kakwä-wāpamāt, ä-papāmuhtät, kāh-mātāhāt päyak apisi-mōsusah.

" kīkway awa ? " itäyihtam ; " mahtih nika-kakwä-wāpamāw, " itäyihtam.

kītahtawä kā-wāpamāt.

" käkway awa ? " itäyihtam ; " mahtih kä-kīh-nipahak, " itäyihtam.

tāpwä pimwäw ; tāpwä nipahäw. äh-utihtät, namuya nisitawäyimäw kīkwayah ōhi.

" mahtih nika-kīwähtahāw ; mahtih kä-nisitawäyimāt nimis " itäyihtam.

kīwähtahäw, äh-utāpät, äh-takuhtahät wīkiwāhk.

"*nimisä, mātsikōtsitān kīkwayah awa?*" *itäw.*
äh-wayawīt aw ōskinīkiskwäw, sämāk nisitawäyimäw.
"*hāy hāy! äkwah kä-miyu-mītsisuyahk, nisīmis! apsi-mōsus awa,*" *itik.*
"*hāh!*"
miywäyihtam.
"*äkwah äwakunih kiy-umaskisinit nisīmis,*" *itwäw aw uskinīkiskwäw, äh-wiyinihāt.*

tāpwä äyakunih mōwäwak äkwah. äkusi nama käkway äkwah wiyah tāpakwäw aw īskwäw; ayis usīma äkwah nāh-nipahäyiwa wāpuswa. tāpwä ōhi usihäw aw īskwäw, ä-wih-utsit-ōmaskisiniyit[1] *usīma. äh-kīh-nipātsik, äh-wāpahk, äh-waniskāt aw uskinīkiskwäw, āsay namwāts nipāyiwa usīma, äh-mātsiyit. äh-pōnih-āpihtā-kīsikāk, āsay usīmah takuhtäyiwa; nīsu apisi-mōsusah päsiwäyiwa.*

"*hāy hāy!*" *itwäw aw uskinīkiskwäw;* "*äkus ätsik ōma äkā kä-kīh-nōhtähkatäyahk!*" *itäyihtam;* "*äyakuni nisīmis äkwah t-ōtāsiw,*" *itäyihtam.*

äkusi ä-kīh-kīsi-wiyininihāt, äkwah iyāyaw asamäw usīma. nama wiya wīhkāts äkwah kitutik usīma, usām äh-näpäwisiyit ta-kitutikut, äkwah äh-uskinīkiyit.[2] *tāpwä mīna äh-wāpaniyik, kiksäpā äh-waniskāt, sāsay äsah kā-sipwähtäyit usīma, äh-mātsiyit, äkwah wiya ōhi iyāyaw apisi-mōsuswayānah äy-usīhāt, mitāsah ä-wīh-usīhtāt. äh-utākusiniyik, äh-kīsihāt, apisi-mōsuswayānah, kā-takusiniyit usīma. āsay mīna nīsu päsiwäyiwa apsi-mōsusah. miywäyihtam aw uskinīkiskwäw. piyis mīna tipiskāyiw. äkuyikuhk äh-kīsi-atuskātāt ōh apisi-mōsuswayānah, äh-pāswāt. äkusi täpiskāyikih äh-kaskikwāsut, usīma äy-usīhtuwāt ayōwinisah.*

piyisk mīna mustuswah nipahäyiwa päyak, äh-pāsiwāyit, "*kīkway ätukä?*" *äh-itäyihtahk aw ōskinīkiw.*

aw ōskinīkiskwäw äh-wāpamāt, "*hāy hāy hāy!*" *itwäw;* "*äkwah nisīmis äwakuni kiy-utanāskānit.*"

äkusi itäyihtam; māka nama wīhkāts äkwah pīkiskwātitōwak, pikuh atsiyaw äh-kitāpamāt aw īskwäw usīma, "*tāpwä mistahi miyusiw nisīmis,*" *äh-itäyihtahk;* "*tāpwä miywāsin ä-kīh-pä-sipwähtahak nisīm,*" *äy-itäyihtahk.*

tahtu-kīsikāw äh-mātsīt aw ōskinīkiw, pisisik mustuswa māh-misiwä äh-pätsitāpät, hāh, mīna mayaw piyäsiwātsih mustuswah, wiyāpahkih äsay äh-kīsihāt aw īskwäw mustuswayānah, äh-utanāskānitsik, mīna äh-utakuhpitsik usīma, kītahtawä kīkisäpā äh-waniskāt aw īskwäw, käyāpits nipāyiwa usīma. ä-kiskäyimikut äh-kīsi-paminawasut, waniskāyiwa. ākusi äkwah ä-mītsisutsik. ä-kīsi-mītsisutsik, äkuyikuhk wayawīw aw ōskinīkiw, äh-nitawi-kīskatahwāt asāmāhtikwah, ä-wīh-usīhāt asāma, mīna äh-wanīhikät, nīsu äy-usīhtāt wanīhikanah. iyikuhk äh-takuhtät, äh-wāpahtahk aw īskwäw mistikwah äh-pīhtukatāyit, ä-kīh-asamāt, äkwah utinam ōhi mistikwah aw īskwäw, äh-tīhkisahk.[3] *äh-kīsi-mītsisut aw ōskinīkiw, äh-mōhkutahk, asāma äy-usihāt, äkuyikuhk kiskäyihtam aw īskwäw äh-usīhāyit asāma. äkwah usīhtäw ōma pahkäkin, ä-wīh-wāskāsahk aw iskwäw. tāpwä äh-wāpahk,*

---

[1] The prefix *utsit-* is probably an error.

[2] The tabu against naming and speech between brother and sister seems to have lost its force on Sweet Grass; it is violated below in this story. The tabu is maintained on Star Blanket Reserve.

[3] If the verb is really *tihkisam*: "he melts it," the object would seem to be the sticks.

äh-ntawāpahtahk uwanihikanah, päyak tasōhäw kihīwa, äkwah päyak nikikwa.

" äh ! "

äwakuni mīkwanah kahkiyaw utinäw. äkwah ōhi kihīwa[1] *pahkunäw aw īskwäw, äh-pāswāt.*

" māskōts ä-wīh-utastutinit nisīm, " itäyihtam.

piyisk äkwah usīhäyiwa asāma. äh-kīs-ōsīhāt, äkwah awa iskwäw utinäw, äh-askimātät uh āsama, äh-pāswāt. äkusi äh-kīsi-pāsōyit, kīksäpā iyikuh mīna äh-waniskāt, kayāhtä māka mīna namuya nipāyiwa usīma, āsay äh-mātsiyit, ä-wīh-āy-atuskät wayawītimihk, pahkäkinwah äh-ay-usīhtāt, " äh-miywāsik nik-ōsīhtān nīkinān, " äh-itäyihtahk. iyikuhk äh-utākusihk, wayawītimihk äh-nīpawit, kīkway kā-pähtahk. äh-ntutahk, pōti kā-pä-nikamuyit awiya ; itäyihtam.

" nisīm ätukä, " itäyihtam.

äh-pīhtukät, kiyipah āsay kisiwāk kā-pätwäwītamiyit. kisiwāk äh-päy-ayāyit, kīskōwäyiwa. pōtih usīma kā-matwä-takusiniyit. mihtah itah äh-astäyikih, äkutah äh-tähtsiwäpināyit utasāmiyiwa, kā-kitōyit.

" äyōkunik ätsik ōki kā-pä-nikamutsik ! " itäyihtam aw īskwäw.

pōtih äh-wayawīt, pisisik askäkin kā-pätāyit. äh-utināt, äh-wā-wāpah-tahk, pōt äs iyāpäyisah kā-wāpamāt, äskana äh-kikamuyit, äkwah waska-siyiwa. äyakunih māh-maniswäw, uhpim ä-ahāt. askäkin min uma mih-tihk tähtastāw.

" ä-wīh-utakōhpit ätukä, " itäyihtam.

äskanah ōhi mīnah uwaskasiyiwa pīhtukahäw, äh-ahāt. äkwah äh-kīsi-mītsisut aw ōskinīkiw, utinäw ōh äskanah, iskutähk tsīk äkutah äh-ahāt, ä-wīh-kätsikwahahk anih ōskanah. piyis kahkiyaw utinam anih ōskanah. piyis kawisimōw. äh-wāpahk päyakwanuhk apiw ; namuya mātsīw, äh-usīhāt äskanah.

äkwah aw īskwäw ōhi mustuswayānah äh-usīhāt, ähwah, " nōhtähk-atätukä ! " äy-itäyimāt usīma, ōhtapiwinihk k-ōh-pasikuyit usīma.

äkusi äkutah, " tānähk ätukä ? " itäyihtam.

äkwah aw ōskinīkiw ä-kīh-wīh-kimutamawāt umisah mīkisisah.

äkusi, " kīkway ätukä ? " itäyihtam aw īskwäw.

piysk kīsihäw ōh äskanah aw usinīkiw, mīn ōhi waskasiyah. äh-tipiskāk kīsihäw aw īskwäw mustuswayānah. iyikuhk äh-wāpahk, äkuyihuhk kikamu-häw aw ōskinīkiw ōh äskanah, mīn ōhi waskasiyiwa, ä-wih-utakuhpit aw uskinīkiw.

ōmis ītäw ōmisa : " nimisä, mīkisisak tsī kitayāwāwak äh-wāpiskisit-sik, äkwah ä-askähtakusitsik ? " itäw.

" äha' . "

äkusi aw īskwäw utinäw, äh-itisinamawāt. äkwah aw uskinīkiw ä-sīkahut, äh-kīsi-sīkahut, ōhi mīkisisah äh-pāh-pōtātāt, māh-mihtsätiyiwa kā-wāpiskisiyit ōhi mīkisisah ōtah ustikwānihk, napatä wästsakāsah kahkiyaw ä-tāpiskahwāt mīkisisah, tāpiskōts äh-wāpistikwānät napatä, äkwah napatä ōhi k-āskīhtakusiyit mīkisisah äh-itamuyit ustikwānihk, äh-mīkisistik-wānät. äkwah tāpwä miyusiw aw uskinīkiw, uskutākay äh-pīmikitäyik, sihkusiwayānah äh-kikamuyit, mīna utāsihk äh-kikamuyikih, äh-pīmikitäyikih, mīn äkutah sihkusiwayanah äh-kikamuyit, äkwah ōhi nikikwayānah äh-utastutinit, utakuhpah äskanah äh-kikamuyit äkwah

---

[1] Doubtless slip of the tongue for *nikikwa;* so translated.

waskasiyiwa äkutah äh-kikamuyit. äkwah tāpwä miyusiw aw ōskinīkiw, äkusi äkwah äh-kīsi-nānapātsihisut. äkutah äkwah tahtu-kīsikāw äkwah äh-mātsīt, tahtu-kīsikāw päyak äh-nipahāt mustuswah, piyis mistahi mītsiwin ayāwak.

kītahtawä kinwäsk äkwah itah äh-ayātsik, kītahtawä nama wiyah wīh-mātsīw aw uskinīkiw, päyakwanuhk äh-apit. iyātah-asamātsi usīmah, namuya wīh-mītsisōw aw ōskinīw, tahk äh-kamwātapit.

ōmis ītäyihtam aw īskwäw : " kähtsināh wīsakäyihtam nisīm, " itäyihtam.

piyisk nīsu-kīsikāw namuya nāntaw ituhtäw aw uskinīkiw, tahkih äh-kamwātapit.

kītahtawä ōmis ītäw aw īskwäw : " a nisīmis, äh-wīsakäyihtaman tsī ? kikaskäyihtamihin, äkā äh-mītsisuyan, " itäw.

" namuya, " itwäw aw uskinīkiw.

äkusi namuya wīhtamawäw käkway.

äh-wāpahk, mīnah äh-waniskātsik, äh-kīsi-mītsisutsik, " hāw, nimisä, ōma k-äsinākusiyān, k-äsīhuyān, äkusi tst-äsinākusiw uskinīkiw ; mīna utasāma äkusi ta-isinākusiyiwa. ōma k-āpihtā-kīsikāk, äkutä tit-ōhtuhtäw uskinīkiw. ōtah iskwāhtämihk äkutah kit-āhäw utasāmah. ' hāw, niwīkimākan, äh-pä-nātitān ! ' kik-ätik. äkus ītiskih, äkāya kitutāhkan. ä-wīh-pä-mawinähut äyakw āwa uskinīkiw, " itäw umisah ; " niwīh-mātsīn ōtäh isi äkā äh-pīsimuwik ; äkutä kākikä k-äsi-mātsiyān, äkutä nk-ōhtuhtān, " itäw ōmisah ; " kīspin kitutatsi, nka-sākōtsihik ; māka äkā kitutatsi, äkusi nka-sākōtsihāw, " itäw ōmisah ; " kwayask āpihtā-kīsikāki, äkuspi kā-wih-takuhtät, " itäw umisa.

äkusi äh-wawäyīt, äh-mātsīt.

äkwah aw īskwäw ōmis ītäyihtam : " māskōts kinwäsk äh-nīsiyāhk nisīmis, māskōts aw äkwah äh-akāwāsit, " itäyimäw usīma ; äh-mōhtsōwit aw īskwäw, kāy-itäyimāt usīma.[1]

äkusi aspin kā-mātsiyit usīma. äkwah ä-kskäyihtahk ä-wih-āpihtā-kīsikāyik, pīhtukäw, äh-paminawasut aw īskwäw. ä-wīh-mītsisut, mwähtsih äh-kīsi-paminawasut, kītahtawä käkway pähtam ; āpihtā-kīsikāhk itähkäy isi kā-pähtahk äh-pä-nikamuyit awiya. piyisk kisiwāk.

" äkusi māna k-ätihtākusiyit nisīm utasāma," itäyihtam.

kisiwāk äh-päy-ihtāyit, kiskuwäyiwa. äkwah musis äkwah pä-pimuhtäyiwa. päyakwanuhk apiw. ōtäskwāhtämihk äh-pä-takuhtäyit, utasāmiyiwa äkutah āsusimäyiwa. äh-pä-pīhtukäyit, mituni naspitawäyiwa usīma.

" yāhkīh ay-apiw awa niwīkimākan ! äh-pä-nātitān uma ! " k-ātikut.

usīmah ōhi k-äsinākwaniyikih utayōwinisiyiwa, äkus isinākwaniyiwa utayōwinisiyiwa. mīn ōm ōstikwāniyiw äkus īsinākwaniyiw. namuya kitutäw aw īskwäw.

āsay mīna, " wawäyī ! äh-pä-nātitān ōma ! ä-wīh-wīkimitān ! " k-ätwäyit.

ōmis ītwäw aw īskwäw : " namuya äkusi äh-itäyihtamān, kā-wīh-kakwä-uhpikihitān, nisīmis ! " itwäw aw īskwäw.

äkusi k-āti-pasikōt awa nāpäw.

" hāw, kä-wāpahk āpihtā-kīsikāki, nika-takusinin, ta-pä-mawinähwak nītsi-mīkisistikwān, " k-ätwäyit ; " tsikäm āni itah awiyak nama nikitutik, "

---

[1] This motif accords with the existence of the tabu.

k-ätwäyit, äh-ati-wayawiyit, äh-ati-utināyit utasāmiwa, äkus äh-ati-papustasāmäyit. mayaw äy-ati-sipwähtäyit, k-āti-nikamuyit asāma. mistahi mihtātam aw īskwäw ōhi äh-kitutāt nāpäwa, āta äh-kīh-wīhtamākut usīma. pōtih āpihtaw äh-utākusik kā-pähtawāt nātakām uhtsi äh-pä-nikamuyit asāma. äkunih äkwah usīma, māka mīna äh-āpuhtäyit. māka mīna utasāmiyiwa äh-tähtsiwäpināyit, kā-kitōyit asāma. äh-pä-pīhtukäyit, mistahi mihtātam ä-kīh-kitutāt ōhi nāpäwa. ä-kīh-nahapiyit usīma, asamäw. äkwah äh-mītsisuyit, wiya atuskātam ōhi wiyāsah kā-pätāyit usīma, äy-āhakutāt wayawītimihk. äyikuhk ä-kīs-atuskät, äh-pīhtukät, äkwah nahastāw utuyākaniwa, āsay ä-kīsi-mītsisuyit.

" nimisä, tāpwä kikitimahin, kā-kitutat ana nāpäw," itwäyiwa ; " namuy āna ä-wīh-wīkimisk," itik ; " häw, takuhtätsi, wāpahki, pämawinähutsi, ōtah nik-uh-kutāwaskamikīn ; wiya mīn äkus ta-tōtam. pīhtukätsi, wīh-mawinähutsi, ' kiya nīkān ! ' nik-ätāw ani. tāpwähtawitsi, äkutah t-ōh-kutāwaskamikīw ; ōmiy utah k-āpiyān, äkutah tsit-ō-sākiskwäw. äkusi nika-kīskikwäwäpahwäw. ustikwān uhpimä ta-pahkihtin. utinamōhkan anim ustikwān. äkus ōma miyaw ōma nika-mitsiminīn. māka, äkā ōtinamani ōma mistikwān, kāwi ta-tāpiskōpayiyiw ustikwān. äkusi nikasākōtsihik. hā, äkusi, nimisä ! "

ā, säkisiw aw īskwäw.

" piyisk niya mīna äkusi nika-tōtän, ta-kutāwaskamikiyān. nīst äkusi nika-tōtāk. äkusi sämāk tit-ōtinam nistikwān, t-āti-wayawīhtatāt. kīspin äkus īspayikih, sākōtsīhitsih, itäh kā-pahkisimuhk, äkutä tit-ōhtuhtäw nāpäw. kahkiyaw utayōwinisah ta-mihkwahikätäyiwa. äyakw ana ä-wihpä-nātisk, ä-wīh-wīkimisk. tāpwähtawāhkan äwaku, äh-miywātisit," itik usīma aw īskwäw ; " hāh, äkusi, nimisä ! "

piyis äkusi tipiskäyiw. piyis kawisimōwak. äh-wāpahk, ä-kīh-waniskāt, äkwah äh-kīh-mītsisutsik, mitunih nānapātsihōw aw uskinīkiw, äh-wawäsit. pīsk käkäts āpihtā-kīsikāyik, namuya käkway atuskātam aw īskwäw, äh-kaskäyihtahk ; ōm ōsīma, " māskōts nka-sākōtsihik, " k-ätwäyit, äwakō tahkih äh-mā-mitunäyihtah. piyisk āpihtā-kīsikāyiw, āsay kāpätwäwītamiyit, äh-pä-nikamuyit asāma.

" häh, " itäyihtam, " mitun ätsik ōma äh-kakäpātisiyān, ' nisīm ätukä, ' kā-kīh-itäyihtamān ! " itäyihtam.

ōtah ä-pä-takuhtäyit uskinīkiw, ōtah iskwāhtämihk āsusimäyiwa tasāmiyiwa.

äh-pä-pīhtukäyit, " yah, nītsi-mīkisistikwān, äh-pä-mawinähutān ! " k-ätwäyit.

" āha' ! " itwäyiwa usīma.

äh-kitāpamāt, tāpiskōts päyak ayīsiyiniw äkus īsinākusiyiwa.

" hā, kiya nīkān, nītsi-mīkisistikwān ! " itimāwa usīma.

" āh ! namuya ! kiya nīkān ! kiya kipä-mātawān, " itwäyiwa usīma.

" āha' ! "

kitāpamäw. itah äh-apiyit, äkutah wäh-kutāwaskamikiyit, usīma itahk äh-ōhtiskawapiyit, äkutah wä-sākiskwäyit, usīma umōhkumāniyiw uhtsi kīskikwäwäpahwäyiwa. itäh k-āpit aw īskwäw, äkutah pahkihtin ōma ustikwān. utami-tapasīw aw īskwäw ; namuya utinam. ōm ōstikwān kāwi äkutah tāpiskupayiyiw. äkusi pimātisiyiwa. pä-wayawiyiwa ; kāw äkutä nahapiyiwa.

" häw, kiyäskuts māka ! " k-ätimiht usīma.

wawäyiyiwa ; itah k-āpiyit usīma, äkutah wäh-kutāwaskamikiyit usīma. nähi kā-pä-mätawäyit itah k-äs-ōhtiskawapiyit, äkutah kā-sākiskwät usīma. äh-kiskikwäwäpahumiht usīma, itäh äh-pahkihtiniyik utinam aw uskinīkiw, äh-ati-wayawīt.

" itah nāh awiyak kiy-ō-sākōtsihit ! " itwäyiwa, äh-ati-sipwähtäyit, ä-sipwähtatāyit ōhō mistikwān.

äkwah ma-mawimōw, äh-mātut, usīma ustikwāniyiw ä-sipwähtatāwiht. utinam usīma wiyawiyiw, äh-astāt uhtapiwiniyih. namuya nipiw, äh-ātah-sipwähtatāwiht ustikwān. yähyäyiwa, ä-pa-pimisiniyit uhtapiwiniyihk. äkwah tahk äh-mātut aw īskwäw, piyisk kinwäsk äkutah ayāw, tahkih äh-yähyäyit usīma ; māka nama käkway ustikwān.

äkusi kītahtawä kā-takuhtäyit nāpäw, pahkisimōtāhk äy-uhtuhtäyit.

ä-pīhtukäyit, tāpwä piku uhtapiwinihk nahapiyiwa, " äh-pä-nātitān ; ä-wīh-wīkimitān, " äh-itikut.

sämāk nisitawäyimäw äwakuni kā-kih-itikut usīma.

" äha' , " itäw ; " pitah ka-mītsisunānaw, " itäw.

tāpwä paminawasōw. äh-kīsi-paminawasut, äkwah mītsisōwak.

äh-kīsi-mītsisutsik, " hāw, wawäyiy äkwah, " itik.

äkusi wawäyīw.

" tsäskwa pitah, " itäw ; " pitah nika-pōnän, äkā tit-āhkwatsit nisīm, " itwäw aw īskwäw, äh-wayawīt, näō äh-utināt yōskīhtakwah, äyakunih äh-pōnāt.

" haw, " itwäw, äh-pakitināt, " äkāya wīhkäts āstawih ! —hāw, äkusi ! " wayawīw. kahkiyaw pīhtsāyihk uma wīkiwāw k-āstäkih nakatam aw īskwäw, ä-sipwähtätsik, äh-kīwähtahikut. äkusi nätä, käkāts äh-tipiskāk, takusin wīkiwāhk awa nāpäw. pōtih misāyiw wīkih awa nāpäw, kahkiyaw äh-mihkwahikātäyik.

" āh, äkutah ayā äkwah ! "

tāpwä miywäyihtam aw īskwäw äh-wītsäwāt nāpäwa. mistahi kakāy-awisiw awa nāpäw, pisisik äh-mätsīt, awa mīna iskwäw kahkiyaw käkway äy-usīhtāt. piyis kinwäsk äh-uwīhtsähtutsik, kītahtawä kiskäyihtam aw īskwäw äh-wīh-ayāwāt awāsisah, piyisk ä-misikitit. äkuyikuhk awa nāpäw kiskäyihtam.

" hāw, namuya nika-mätsīn, " itwäw ; " usām mistahi kik-ātuskān. äkwah awāsis ä-wīh-ayāwat, namuya nintawäyihtän t-ātuskäyin. māskōts wih-uhpikitsih aw āwāsis kā-wīh-ayāwāyahk, " itäw.[1]

" äha' , " itäw aw īskwäw.

tāpwä namuya mistahi ōh-atuskäw, äkā ta-misi-wanātsihāt ōh āwāsisah. piyisk kītahtawä äkwah āhkusiw aw īskwäw, ä-wīh-wāpamāt awāsisah. tāpwä piyisk tawāsimisiw, pōtih nāpäsisah.

kītahtawä, " tāpiskōts kutak, " itäyihtam.

" miyāmay mīna päyak, " itäw unāpäma.

tāpwä min äyakuni wāpamäwak. min äyaku nāpäsis. nīsōtäwak ayāwäwak. miywäyihtam awa nāpäw, mīn āw īskwäw. äkwah nama wīh-käts mätsīw awa nāpäw, pāh-päyak äh-pamihātsik utsawāsimisiwāwa. piyisk kinwäs itah äy-ayātsik, piyisk misikitisiwak awāsisak ōki. äkwah äh-pimuhtätsik awāsisak ōki, utōskwanisiwāhk mōhkumānah sākikiniyiwa ōki nāpäsisak. mituni māmaskātamwak utawāsimisiwāwa äh-mōhkumān-

---

[1] Rationalized or rudimentary couvade?

itōskwanäyit. kiyipa misikitiwak. äkwah atuskäwak, awa nāpäw äh-māh-mātsīt. awa mīna iskwäw atuskäw äkwah. äkwah ōk āwāsisak pisisik ma-mätawäwak, atsusisah äh-ayātsik, äw-uhtsi-mätawätsik. kītahtawä māna namuya wāpamäw awa iskwäw utsawāsimisah kā-kapä-kīsik. äyikuhk wä-tākusiniyikih, äkuyikuhk takuhtäyiwah utsawāsimisah.

kītahtawä, " ka-wanisinināwāw ! " itäw utsawāsimisah.

piyisk misikitiwak ōki nāpäsisak. kītahtawä māka mina äh-īkatäh-täyit, äh-ākawäwäyit, wīh-kakwä-wāpamäw aw īskwäw ukusisah.

ōmisi k-ätwäyit : " hāh, nisīmis ! mahti mīna nitawāpamātān kisisin-aw ! " k-ätwäyit.

äkuyikuhk kā-kiskisit usīma, aspin kā-kīh-kīskikwäwäpahumiht. äh-pimutahkwäyit, aspin wīpisisiyihk kīh-ati-nīpawiyiwa. äkus īsi kīwäw. namuy äkwah wīh-atuskäw, äh-ay-apit, äh-mā-mitunäyihtah aspin äh-kitimahimiht usīma. äyikuhk ä-wīh-tipiskāyik, kā-takuhtäyit uskusisah.

" käkway uma māna äh-nātamäk, kā-kapä-kīsik äkā kā-takusiniyäk ? "

māka kiskäyimik äh-kitāpamāt ukusisah, aspin kā-sipwähtäyit, k-ōti-nīpawiyit wīpisisiyihk.

ōmis ītik : " näkā, ōtäh uma māna äh-ituhtäyāhk, päyak mīkiwāhp äh-ayāk, ayīsiyiniw äh-päyakut, äkā äy-ustikwānit, äkw āna māna äh-ntawāpamāyāhk, äkāw ōma k-āpiyāhk, " itik.

mātōw aw īskwäw.

iyikuhk äh-pōni-mātut, ōmis ītäw : " ntsawāsimisitik, kisisiwāw ana ; nisīmis ana ; mistah āna ä-kīh-miyusit, ä-kīh-mīkisiwiyik ustikwān, māka ä-kīh-mawinähukut wītsi-mīkisistikwāna, aspin ä-kī-sipwähtatāyit ustikwān. käyāpi tsīh [1] yähyäw ? "

" äha' ; käyāpits yähyäw, " itik ukusisah.

ōmis ītwäw aw ōsīmimās : " nistäsä, äyakw ätsik ānimah ōtäh ōtänaw k-āyāk, anah pīhtäyask kā-wīkit, äyakw ätsik ānima ispimihk k-ākutäk, itah kāhkākiw k-ākusīt, " itwäw aw ōsīmimās ; " hā, kä-wāpahk mīna ka-nitawāpamānaw kisisinaw, " itwäw aw ōsīmimās.

" äha' . "

tāpwä äh-utākusik, takusin awa nāpäw, ä-kīh-mātsīt. uwīkimākanah ka-kamwātapiyiwa.

" tānähki, niwīkimākan ? " itäw.

" nā, ōk ōki kitsawāsimisinawak kā-kapä-kīsik äkā k-āpitsik, k-ätitān māna, äs ōki usisiwāwa äh-mān-ituhtätsik, äyakuni äh-ātsimustawitsik, k-ōh-kamwātapiyān, " itwäyiwa.

äkusi tāpwä äh-tipiskāyik, äh-nipātsik, äh-wāpahk, kīksäpā āsay mīna sipwähtäyiwa utsawāsimisiwāwa. äkwah namuya wīh-kitahamawäw aw īskwäw utawāsimisah.

äh-ntawāpamātsik ōki awāsisak usisiwāwa, äkutä äh-takuhtätsik, ä-kīh-pōnahkik, ōmis ītwäw aw ustäsimās : " hā, nsīmis, mahti niya nīkān nika-kakwä-nātän kisisinaw ustikwān, " itäw.

" äha' . "

" hā, nsīmis, kīspin pätāyāni, kakwä-waniskāpitāhkan kisisinaw, " itäw.

" aha' . "

äkus ä-ati-wayawīt aw ustsäsimās, äkutah skwāhtämihk äh-ayāt, " hāw, uskats ä-kīh-itäyihtamān tit-ōmitsaskusīsīwiyān ! "

---

[1] For *käyapits tsīh* ; so usually in close-knit phrases of rapid speech when final and initial *ts* come together.

tāpwä ʌnpihyāw, äh-pimihāt äkutä kā-kīh-wāpahtahk usisah ustikwāniyiw. äkutä äh-takuhtät, tsīki mwähtsi äh-ihtāt, kā-kituyit ōhi kāhkākiwa.

äkus āwa kā-mīkisistikwānät wayawīw, äh-täpwät, " kiwīh-maskamikawinānaw nikāhkwāskwahikan ! " äh-itwät.

äkusi tapasīw awa umītaskusīs, äkwah ä-nawaswātiht, äh-kīwä-mākuhiht, ayis atimihtsih ta-nipahiht. äkusi piyisk takusin usīmisah itah k-āyāyit. äkusi pōnihāw.

äkwah aw ōsīmimās ōmis ītäw : " tānsi tiyōtaman ? " itäw ustäsah.

" hā, mayaw tsīkih äh-ayāyān, āsay kitōw ana kāhkākīw ; nimōsihikawin. "

" kah ! ā, mahti niya ! " itwäw aw ōsīmimās.

äkwah aw ōsīmimās wayawīw.

" hāw, uskats ä-kī-htäyihtamān ta-kähkähkuwiyān ! " itwäw.

tāpwä kähkähkōwiw ; uhpihyāw, äy-ispihāt. äkutä äh-takusihk, ispimihk uhtsi mōskīstawäw ōhi kāhkākiwah. kāhkākiw awa ispīh äh-wāpamāt, namuya wīh-kitōw, äh-kustāt kähkähkwah. ōma ustikwān manipitam awa kähkähk, äkus äh-tapasīt. äyikuhk wāhyaw äh-ihtāt, äkuyikuhk kituyiwa. iyātah-wayawīpahtāt awa, āsay wāhyaw kīh-atimihāyiwa.

" ähähä ! " itwäw ; " nawaswäk, nawaswäk ! kimaskamikawinānaw nōstikwānim ! " itwäw.

nanātuhk itōwiwiwak, äh-nawaswätsik. mīhkawikiw kähkähk ; nakatäw kahkiyaw ōhi kā-pimihāyit.

tsīk äh-ihtāt, ōmis ītwäw : " nistäsäh, yōhtäwäpinah ! kakwä-waniskāpis kisisinaw ! " itäw.

tāpwä ä-yōhtäwäpinahk, äkwah ōhi ä-wīh-kakwä-waniskānāt, äkuyikuhk kisiwāk äkwah ayāw.

" äwakwä, nistäsä ! sinikuhkitunäpis ! " itäw.

tāpwä tāpiskupayiw um ustikwān, äkwah aw ōstäsimās ä-sinikuhkitunānāt. äkusi pimātisiw. kā-nawaswätsik ōki kahkiyaw kīwäwak. miywäyihtamwak ōki nāpäsisak äh-pimātisiyit usisiwāwa.

" haw, kīwätān äkwah ! kīwāhtahātān kisisinaw ! "

ā, wayawīwak. uwīpisisah äkwah utastutinah, äyakunih piku utinam awa kā-mīkisiwiyik ustikwān, äkus äh-wayawītsik.

" ā, nisīmis, niya nka-pimiwihāw kisisinaw. "

" äha' . "

hā, äh-pimutahkwät, " hāw, nisis, ōtah nk-āti-nīpawinān. kā-wīkiyāhk āstam-itah kā-sakāk, äkutah nika-pahkisininān. "

tāpwä pimih-nīsukāpawiwak wīpisisihk. äh-utākusik, äkutah pahkisinuk, äkutah uhtsi ä-pimuhtätsik. aw īskwäw wayawitimihk äh-atuskät, kītahtawä kā-pä-sākäwäyit usīma äkwah utawāsimisah, āyītaw äh-pä-pmuhtätsik ōk āwāsisak usisiwāwa.

sämāk aw īskwäw, " hāy hāy ! nisīmis pimātisiw ! " itäw, ä-takuhtäyit, äh-atamiskawāt, äkwah äh-pīhtukätsik, äh-ati-kīsitäput aw īskwäw. kītahtawä kā-pīhtukäyit uwīkimākana.

" hay hay hay ! " itäw ; " tāpwä āyimāts niwāpamāw nīstāw ! " itwäw awa nāpäw.

äkusi äkutah ayāwak. pisisik äh-mätawākätsik usisiwāwa, namuya äkwah wīhkāts kunt ītä ituhtäwak ōki awāsisak, usisiwāwa ä-wītsi-mätawämātsik pīhtsāyihk.

" *äkā tōtāhk kisisiwāw ! mistahi kimätawākānāwāw !* " *äh-itāt aw īskwäw utsawāsimisah,* " *hā, namuya !* " *itwäw aw ōskinīkiw ;* " *kiyām nka-mätawākātikwak nitähkwatimak ; äwakunik k-ōh-pimātisiyān,* " *itäw umisah.*

äkusi piyisk kinwäsk ayāwak. awa nāpäw pisisik mātsīw. kītahtawä namuya takusin. äh-wāpahk, äkā äh-takusihk, " *mahtih, nitähkwatimitik, nka-nitunawāw kōhtāwiyiwāw,* " *itäw.*

" *aha'.* "

tāpwä nitunawäw. itah äh-mātāhāt mitihtäw ; pōt äsah kāh-mātāhāyit mōswa ; äyakunih mitihtäyiwa wīstāwa. pōtih wāpahtam äy-usätināyik, ä-pasāhtsāyik äkutah, mōhkitsiwanipäk äh-ayāyik. äkutah äsa kā-kītuhtäyit wīstāwa. äh-utihtahk, itah uhtsih kā-wayawītsiwaniyik, kā-päsākiskwäyit misi-kinäpikwah, äh-tāwatiyit, äh-utatāmikut, ä-misiwäpayihikut. awän ōhi, äkutäh kīh-apiyiwa wīstāwa, namuya äh-nipiyit. wīstah namuya nipiw. wītapimäw wīstāwah, piyis ätukä äh-tipiskāyik.

äh-wāpaniyik, äka äh-takusihk, ōki nīsōtäwak, aw ōstäsimās, " *mahtih nka-ntunawāw ksisinaw !* "

" *awahä, nistäsä !* " *itwäw aw ōsīmimās.*

äkusi sipwähtäw aw ustsäsimās. pōtih itah äsah k-āti-mitihtāyit mōswah, äkutah at-ay-ituhtäw. piyisk utihtam ōma mōhkitsiwanipäk. tsīk äh-ihtāt, kā-pä-sākiskwäyit misi-kinäpikwa, äh-tāwatiyit, äh-utatāmikut. äh-papätikupayihut, ōhi utōskwanihk mōhkumānah kā-sākikiniyikih, " *äwakuni nik-ōh-mātiswāw,* " *äy-itäyihtahk, naspāts isiwäpinam ōhi, ä-misiwäpayihiht. pōt ōhi usisah kiy-apiyiwa, äkwah ōhtāwiyah.*

äkusi mīna tipiskāyiw. äh-wāpahk, aw äkw ōsīmimās kā-sipwähtät, äh-ntunawāt ustäsah. pōtih äsa kā-mitihtāt mōswah. wīstah mitihtäw. mōhkitsiwanipäk äh-utihtahk, tsīki äh-ayāt, ōm ītah k-ōh-pä-sākiskwäyit misi-kinäpikwah, māka mīna pä-sākiskwäyiwa.

" *äwakuni kā-misi-wanātshikutsik,* " *itäyihtam.*

äh-tāwatiyit, ä-wih-utatāmikut, pāyakwanuhk nīpawiw. iyāta-tāwatiyitsi, namuya kīh-ispayiw.

" *sōhkih, misi-kinäpik ! tāwatih ! pä-wayawīh !* " *itäw.*

iyātah-itwäyitsih, ä-wīh-utatāmikut, namawya kaskihik. tahkih ayiwākäs äh-pä-wayawiyit, " *sōhkih !* " *äh-itāt, sōhk äh-tāwatiyit, papätikōpayihōw, ōmis īsi āyītaw ä-isiwäpinahk utōskwanah. mituni tāskiswäw ōhi misi-kinäpikwah. awän ōhi, ustäsah usisah ōhtāwiya äkutah uhtsi päwayawiyiwa. nipahäw ayisk ōhi ; äkusi kīwähtahäw. kīwäwak ; äh-tipiskāyik takusinwak wīkiwāhk.*

äkwah äh-wāpahk, ōmis ītwäw usīmimās awa : " *hāw, usām kimōhtsōwin, nistäsä. namuya äs āni kimanitōwin ; pisisik kisākōtsihikawin. ntsawāts äh-itäyihtamān niya kik-ätitināwāw.* "

" *aha'.* "

" *hāw, nōhtāh, kiyawāw nikāwiy : tsäskwah ayīsiyiniwak tit-ähtāwak ; nīkān ōtäh watsīhk kikāw-ayānāwāw ; ka-misikitināwāw ; ukiniyak k-äsiyīhkāsunāwāw,* " *itäw ōhtāwiyah äkwah ukāwiyah,* " *usām äh-miyu-pimātisiyäk. — äkwah kiya, nisisä, ōtäh äh-pahkisimuhk, äkutä kik-ōtaskīn. ' äh-mīkisistikwānät ayīsiyiniw nikitimākäyimik, ' tit-ätwäw ayīsiyiniw ; äh-nipāt, kika-wāpamik, nisisä. — äkwah niyanān : ōtah nīkānäs isi tit-āpisīsisiwak atsāhkusak ; tsāh-tsīkih tit-āyāwak ; nik-äkutōwiwinān niyān nistäs,* " *itäw ;* " *hāh, äkusi, niyāk !* "

äkusi ōki sipwähtäwak. watsiy äh-utihtahkik awa ōwīkimākana, kawipayihōwak ; ukinīwiwak. äkwah ōki nāpäsisak ispimihk ituhtäwak, äh-atsāhkusiwitsik.

äkusi äkuyikuhk äh-iskwāk ātayōhkäwin.

There was a certain large town, of old, when, as we are told, they ate each other. And there a woman was chief, a Thunderbird-Woman, who ruled over one-half of the town; and over the other half there ruled as chief a Wolf; a man was this one. They used their followers as prizes of the contest, of their manitou contests, so that, whenever one was defeated, then his followers were killed and eaten; that is what is called "eating each other." Various kinds, those who were called men, various kinds of beasts they were. That is the way this was.

Then in the part where the Wolf was chief, a young woman from there, who had a small brother whom she cared for and loved, when her father and mother and all her other brothers and sisters had been killed, and only the two, she and her little brother were left alive, then thus she thought: "I shall go away; perhaps it will be possible for my little brother here to live," she thought; "He is too pitiful, the little fellow," she thought; "So then, tonight let there be very bad weather! Let it snow!" she said; "I shall go away and no one shall know whither I go." So she thought.

Really, when night fell, there was very bad weather, and it snowed. Then the young woman was glad. As soon as it was very dark, she made ready; she cut down her lodge and threw it aloft into the storm. And her sleeping-mats and her blanket-robes and all the things she would have occasion to use, she took, when she had made ready, and she wrapped all her possessions in a buffalo robe. In this way she set out, dragging her belongings, dragging them as if on a flat sled, and carrying her little brother. There was a bad storm. The storm kept on all night, while she walked on. At last day dawned; the bad weather did not abate. All that day it stormed. Only towards evening the day grew clear. She kept on walking. At last night fell. At that point she camped. She had nothing to eat, there where she slept. When day broke, she went on. Then, when day broke, her little brother cried, because he was hungry. Yet she needs made ready to go on. When she had found a stretch of country that was dotted with clumps of trees, where there was one larger grove, thither she went, to look it carefully over, thinking, "I shall try to find a good place to live." Really, she did find in the wood a hollow place where there was water and dense forest round about. There she pitched camp. She cleared off the snow where she meant to dwell; she built a fire. Her little brother still was weeping with hunger. When she had built the fire, she made something to use as a snare.

And so, when her little brother had gone to sleep, she set a snare, thinking, "Perhaps I may kill a rabbit; my little brother could eat it."

Then, as she gathered faggots, from the place where she gathered faggots, some rabbits scampered forth. One of them got caught in the snare. She killed it.

"Splendid! Now my little brother shall eat!" she thought.

She took it back with her; eagerly she prepared it to cook, that she might give her brother to eat. When she had cooked it done, her little brother awoke. So she gave him food. Then she got up and fetched sticks to build their lodge. In the end she had got many sticks. By this time her little brother was again on the verge of crying, so she sat down by him and consoled him. There she remained. As soon as he had ceased to weep, she built their lodge, cutting grasses, with which she thatched the lodge and made matting for underfoot. By this time darkness was at hand, but she had built her lodge so that it would be warm; and now she took her little brother inside, and built a fire within. Just at sunset she heard a rabbit squeal. She went there: there was one. She killed it. She was glad.

"So my little brother will not go hungry," she thought.

She sat there.

Then, in the night she meditated, thinking, "Would that no one might ever find me! Are all persons, I wonder, even so?" she thought; the way those people were in the place whence she had come, they who always killed and ate each other, because she thought, "Are others, I wonder, that way too?" was why she spoke thus.

Truly, she was glad to be alone, for she thought, "In this way, perhaps I shall bring up my little brother."

There every day she gathered firewood and snared many rabbits; and truly, after each night, when she had slept and in the morning fetched the rabbits, she was very glad that she continued to kill many of them. At last she built out of doors something on which to hang the rabbits, having killed so many.

"Well, and so now my little brother and I shall not too soon be hungry!" she thought.

She worked at nothing but snaring rabbits and bringing wood, and concerning that place where she was, she thought, "Would that no one might ever find me!"

Then in time, when she had been there a long while, her brother grew larger. Then she made arrows for her brother, meaning to teach him to be a good marksman. Really, in the end he was a good shot; in time the lad became skilled to the point where he wanted to try to kill something. Presently, as he walked about in the wood, he saw a rabbit. When he tried to kill it, really, he killed it. He was glad, and brought it into the lodge.

"Splendid!" said the young woman; "And so now there will be no danger of our starving, now that my little brother is killing rabbits," she thought.

And so she made some more arrows, larger ones, thinking, "So that he can do well at killing things with them." At last, when she had finished them, and the lad was using them, really he killed many and many rabbits. Then the woman tore pieces from the tent-covering and made something for her brother to wear as breeches and as a shirt. By this time the lad was almost a young man. He was very handsome. Then, as they dwelt there, presently, as he was walking about, trying to get sight of rabbits, he came upon the track of a dwarf moose.

"What kind of creature is this?" he thought; "Suppose I try to get a look at him," he thought.

Presently he saw it.

"What kind of creature is this?" he thought; "Let me see if I can kill him," he thought.

So he shot an arrow at it; really, he killed it. When he went up to it, he did not know what manner of beast it was.

"Let me take him home; let me see if my big sister knows him," he thought.

He took it home, dragging it, and brought it to their dwelling.

"Big sister, come, see; what sort of creature is this?" he said to her.

When the young woman came out, at once she recognized it.

"Splendid! Now we shall have good eating, little brother! This is a dwarf moose," she told him.

"Ho!"

He was glad.

"And from this creature my brother can have moccasins," said the young woman, as she set about skinning it.

So then they ate it. And now the woman no longer set snares; for now her brother continued to kill rabbits. So now the woman prepared that creature, that her brother might have moccasins of it. When they had slept, in the morning when the young woman got up, her brother was by no means still asleep, but had gone hunting. In the afternoon her brother arrived; he brought two dwarf moose.

"Splendid!" said the young woman; "And so now we shall never need to go hungry!" she thought; "Now of these creatures my brother shall have breeches," she thought.

So, when she had finished skinning them and cutting them up, with zeal then she gave her brother his food. Never now did her brother address her, for he was too bashful to speak to her, now that he was a young man. Then, the next morning early, when she arose, she saw that again her brother had already gone away to hunt; she, for her part, set zealously to work preparing the hides of the dwarf moose, to make breeches. Toward evening, when she had finished tanning the dwarf-moose skins, her brother arrived. Again he was bringing two dwarf moose. The young woman rejoiced. Soon night came. By this time she had finished working the hides of the dwarf moose, and was drying them. So then, of nights she would sew, making clothes for her brother.

At last he killed also a buffalo, and brought it home, thinking, "What kind of beast is this?"

When the young woman saw it, "Splendid! Splendid!" she exclaimed; "Now my brother can have this one for his sleeping mat."

So she thought; but now they never spoke to each other, only that the woman would look for a moment at her brother and think, "Truly, my brother is very handsome," and, "Truly, it is well that I brought my brother off here."

The youth hunted every day, and dragged home buffalo always entire; as soon as he would bring a buffalo, by the next morning the woman had already prepared the buffalo hide, for sleeping robes and robes to wear, for her brother and for herself. And then one morning, when she got up, her brother was still asleep. When he knew that she had finished cooking, he got up. So then they ate. When they had eaten, the youth went out of doors, to cut sticks for snowshoes which he intended to make, and to set traps, two traps which he had built. When he came back, when the woman saw that he was bringing sticks of wood, after giving him his meal, the woman took the sticks, and melted some fat. When the youth had eaten, and was whittling the sticks to make snowshoes, then the woman knew that he was making snowshoes. Then she prepared that rawhide for cutting round the edge. Then, the next morning, when he went to look at his traps, he had trapped an eagle and an otter.

"Ha!"

He took all the feathers. And the woman skinned the otter, and dried the skin.

"No doubt my brother wants a head-dress," she thought.

Then he made also his snowshoes. When he had done making them, the woman took the snowshoes and threaded them with the thongs, and dried them. And so, when they had dried, when in the morning she got up, again her brother no longer slept, but had gone hunting; so she went about her work outside the lodge, tanning hides, thinking, "I shall improve our dwelling." Towards evening, as she stood outside the door, she heard something. As she listened, it appeared that someone was singing as he came; so it seemed to her.

"I wonder if it is my brother," she thought.

When she went inside, quickly from close by came the sound of that person. When he had come near, he broke off his song. It was her brother, coming home with song. Where the faggots lay, on top there he threw his snowshoes, and as he did so, they gave a call.

"And so it is they who came a-singing!" thought the woman.

When she went out, he was bringing nothing but fresh hides. When she took it, and looked at it, she saw that it was the skin of a young bull, with the horns and the hoofs. These she cut off, and laid them aside. The hide she laid also on top of the firewood.

"Doubtless he wants a blanket-robe," she thought.

The horns and the hoofs she brought indoors and put them down. Then, when the young man had eaten, he took the horns and placed them close to the fire, to take out the bone. At last he took all the bone. Then he went to bed. The next morning, he sat in one place; he did not hunt, but prepared the horns.

And the woman, preparing the buffalo robe, just as she thought of her brother, "He must be hungry!" even then her brother rose from his settee.

Then, "I wonder what is the matter!" she thought.

But it was because that youth meant to steal his sister's wampum-beads.

So, "What can it be?" thought the woman.

At last the youth finished preparing the horns and the hoofs. By nightfall the woman finished the buffalo robe. When the next day dawned, the youth attached to it the horns and the hoofs, to make him a blanket-robe.

He said to his sister, "Sister, have you wampum beads that are white, and some that are blue?" he asked her.

"Yes."

Accordingly, she took them and handed them to him. Then the youth combed his hair, and when he had combed it, breathed upon those beads, whereupon a great many of those white wampum-beads were on his head there; he had threaded all the hairs on one side of his head with the beads, just as though his hair were white, and on the other side the blue beads were strung on his head: he was a Wampum-Head. Then truly handsome was that young man; his coat was ornamented with quill-work and with tassels of weasel-skins, and some were on his breeches, and they, too, had quill-work, and they had weasel-skins on them, and he had a headgear of that otterskin, and on his robe were horns, and hoofs were on it. Then truly handsome was that youth, when in this guise he had decked himself. Then, as he hunted each day, and each day killed a buffalo, in time they had a plenty of food.

Then at one time, when they had long dwelt there, then presently the youth did not care to hunt, but sat still in one place. Although she gave her brother food, the youth would not eat, but sat listlessly there.

The woman thought, "Surely my brother is in pain."

At last two days passed and the youth had not gone anywhere, but sat all the time inactive.

Then the woman asked him, "Brother, are you in pain? You make me sad, not eating," she told him.

"No," said the youth.

Thus he did not tell her what it was.

The next morning, when they got up and had eaten, "Now then, my sister, even as I look, even as I am dressed, so a young man will look; even his snowshoes will look so. From the direction of noon that youth will come. Here by the door he will place his snowshoes. 'Come, my wife, I have come to fetch you!' he will say to you. When thus he speaks to you, do not address him. One who comes to challenge me is that youth," he told his sister; "I shall hunt over here, in the direction where the sun never goes; from this direction, where always I do my hunting, from this direction I shall come," he told his sister; "If you speak to him, he will defeat me; but if you do not speak to him, then I shall defeat him," he told his sister; "Exactly at noon, that is when he will come," he told his sister.

With that he went out of the lodge, on his hunt.

Then the woman thought thus: "Perhaps because my brother and I so long have been alone together, perhaps now he has fallen in love with me," she thought concerning her brother; because she was silly, she thought thus of her brother.

So her brother was off hunting. When she knew that noon was at hand, she went indoors, and prepared her meal. As she was about to eat, just as she had done cooking, she heard something; in the direction of noon she heard someone who came a-singing. At last he came near.

"Even so my brother's snowshoes always sound," she thought.

When he had come near, he ceased from his song. And now he was in sight, walking hither. She sat still. When he came to the doorway, there he leaned up his snowshoes. When he came inside, greatly he resembled her brother.

"From of old my wife sits here! It is to fetch you I have come!" he said to her.

As looked those clothes of her brother's, so looked this person's clothes. His head, too, looked exactly so. The woman did not speak to him.

Again, "Get ready! It is to fetch you I have come! It is to marry you!" he said.

Thus spoke the woman: "It was not with the like of this in mind that I did my best to bring you up, my brother!" she said.

At that the man rose to his feet.

"Very well, tomorrow at noon I shall come to challenge my fellow Wampum-Head," he said; "Seeing that everywhere else no one ever speaks to me," he said, and went out of the lodge, taking his snowshoes as he went, and putting them on. As soon as he started away, the snowshoes began to sing. Very sorry was the woman that she had spoken to this man in spite of her brother's instruction. Then, in the middle of the afternoon she heard snowshoes come singing from the north. It was her brother, bringing, as always, a treat of game. When he threw his snowshoes, as always, on the wood, the snowshoes gave a call. As he came into the lodge, deeply she regretted that she had spoken to that man. When her brother had sat down, she gave him his meal. While he ate, she worked at the meats which he had brought, hanging them out of doors. When she had finished her work, she went indoors and put away her brother's dishes, for he had done eating.

"Sister, truly, you have brought me to an evil pass by speaking to that man," he said; "His purpose is not to marry you," he told her; "Now then, when tomorrow he comes to challenge me, at this spot I shall sink into the ground; he, in turn, will do the same. When he comes into the lodge to challenge me, 'You first!' I shall say to him. If he complies, there he will sink into the ground; and right here where I sit he will stick out his head from the ground. At that I shall slash off his head. His head will fall to one side. Do you then take his head. I shall hold fast to the body. But, if you do not take the head, his head will fly back into place. In this way he will overcome me. There, that is the way of it, sister!"

Oh, the woman was frightened.

"Then I, too, shall do the same, I shall sink into the ground. He will do the same thing to me. Then at once he will take my head with him out of the lodge. If this happens, if he defeats me, then from the direction of the setting sun will come a man. All his garments will be made of red. He will come to fetch you; he will marry you. Give credence to him, for he is good," her brother told her; "There, that is the way of it, my sister!"

At last night came. At last they went to bed. In the morning, when he got up and when they had eaten, the youth made a careful toilet and put on his finery. It was almost noon, but the woman did not work at anything, for she was unhappy; she brooded without cease on her brother's words, "Perhaps he will defeat me." At last it was noon, and already that person came noising it, snowshoes a-singing.

"Alas," she thought, "It is plain that I was most stupid to think, 'Perhaps it is my brother!' " she thought.

When the youth arrived there, he leaned up his snowshoes in the doorway.

When he came into the lodge, "Ha, my fellow Wampum-Head, I have come to challenge you!" he said.

"Yes!" spoke her brother.

When she looked at them, they looked like one and the same person.

"Ha, you first, my fellow Wampum-Head!" her brother was told.

"Ha! No! You first! It is you have come to play," said her brother.

"Very well!"

She watched him. There where he sat, there he sank into the earth, and there, in front of her brother as he sat, there he came sticking out his head, and her brother with his knife slashed through the other's neck. Toward where the woman sat fell that head of his. She was taken up with fright; she did not seize it. That head of his went back into place. Thereupon he was alive. He emerged from the earth; he sat down again in his place.

"There, but now it is your turn!" her brother was told.

He made ready, from where her brother sat, he sank into the earth. In front of where he sat who had come to play, there her brother stuck out his head from under the earth. When her brother's head had been slashed off, that youth took it from where it fell, and started out of the lodge.

"There is the one who, of all anywhere, could defeat me!" he said, as he started to go away, taking with him that head.

Then she lamented, weeping, because her brother's head was taken away. She took up her brother's body, and placed it upon his settee. He did not die, even though his head had been taken away. He breathed, as he lay there, on his couch. Then, weeping without respite, at last a long time that woman stayed there, her brother all the while breathing; but he had no head.

Then, at one time, there arrived a man who came from the region of the setting sun.

When he came into the lodge, really, he sat down directly upon her couch, saying to her, "I have come to fetch you; I mean to marry you."

At once she recognized him as the one of whom her brother had told her.

"Yes," she said to him; "But first let us eat," she said to him.

Accordingly she cooked a meal. When she had prepared her meal, they ate.

When they had eaten, "Come, make ready now," he told her.

So she made herself ready.

"Wait a bit," she said to him; "First I must put fuel on the fire, that my brother may not freeze," said the woman, and went out of the lodge; she took four sticks of crumbling wood and put them on the fire.

"There," she said, as she set them down, "Never go out!—Well, I am ready!"

She went out. The woman left behind in their lodge all the things that were there, and they departed, that man taking her with him to his home. Accordingly, over yonder, at nightfall, that man arrived at their dwelling. She saw that his lodge was a large one and that it had been made entirely red.

"Now dwell here!"

Truly, the woman was glad to be with the man. The man was very industrious, hunting all the time, and the woman, too, made all manner of things. At last, when they had been married for a long time, she knew that she was going to have a child; . . . . Then the man knew it.

"Very well, I shall not hunt," he said, "You would be working too much. Now that you are going to have a child, I do not want you to work. Perhaps the child we are to have will grow up," he told her.

"Yes," the woman answered him.

Accordingly, from that time on she did not work much, so as not to injure that child. Then in time the woman fell ill, as she was about to see her child. Then, finally, she bore her child, and it turned out to be a boy.

Presently, "It seems as if there were another," she thought.

"Surely there is one more," she told her husband.

Really, they saw this one, too. This one, too, was a boy. They had twins. The man was glad, and the woman too. Then the man never hunted, each of them taking care of one of their children. At last, when they had been there a long time, those children grew bigger. Then, when those children had begun to walk, knives grew forth from the elbows of those boys. They wondered greatly at their children's having knife-elbows. Quickly they grew up. Then they worked, as the man hunted. The woman, too, now worked. And those children always played, having arrows with which to play. Then, in time, the woman would not see her children all day. Only just before evening her children would come home.

Presently, "You will get lost!" she told her children.

At last those boys grew to full size. Then at one time, when in their usual way they had walked off and out of sight, the woman decided to try to observe her sons.

One of them said, "Come, younger brother! Let us go again to see our uncle!"

At that she remembered her brother, who had had his head cut off, the last she had seen of him. Her sons shot arrows, and off they sailed, standing on their arrows. Thereupon she went home. She did not care now to work, but sat there, thinking of how her brother had been undone when last she had seen him. Not until nightfall did her sons come home.

"What is it you always go after, when all day you do not come home?"

But her sons knew that she had observed them as they went off standing on their arrows.

Thus they answered her: "Mother, because we always go off there, to where there is a solitary lodge, where one man stays alone, who has no head—because we visit him, that is why, as you say, we do not stay at home," they told her.

She wept.

When she stopped weeping, she said to them, "My children, he is your mother's brother; he is my younger brother; he was very handsome, and beaded was his head, but his fellow Wampum-Head challenged him to a contest and carried off his head. Is he still breathing?"

"Yes; he still breathes," her sons told her.

The younger brother spoke as follows: "Elder brother, plainly it appears that it is none other than that which, in the town over there, hangs aloft over the dwelling of him who lives in the centre, there where the raven sits aloft," said the younger brother; "Come, tomorrow let us again visit our uncle," said the younger lad.

"Very well."

At nightfall that man arrived from his hunt. His wife was sitting and brooding.

"What is the matter, my wife?" he asked her.

"Dear me, when these children of ours, as I always am telling you, stay out all day, it seems that they always go to where their uncle is, and now they have told me it, and that is why I sit and grieve," she said.

Then, when night came, and they had slept, then in the morning early, again their children went off. And now the woman did not care to stop her children.

When those children went to see their uncle, and had come there and built up the fire, the elder boy said, "Now, younger brother, let me first try to go get our uncle's head."

"Very well."

"Well then, brother, if I come bringing it, try to pull our uncle to his feet," he told him.

"Yes."

Then, as the elder brother was going out of the lodge, as he stood in the doorway, "Now, at the very first I did think that I should be a swallow!"

Really, he rose into the air and flew to where he had seen his uncle's head. When he got there, just as he was near, that raven croaked.

At that the wampum-headed one came out of the lodge, and hallooed, crying, "Someone is trying to rob us of my lodge-emblem!"

Then that swallow fled, and was pursued and close pressed on his way home, for if he were overtaken, he would be killed. At last he arrived where his younger brother was. Then he was left alone.

Then the younger lad spoke to him; "How did you fare?" he asked his elder brother.

"Ho, just as I got close, that raven croaked; my coming was perceived."

"Well! Now, let me try!" said the younger lad.

Then the younger brother went out of the lodge.

"Now, at the very first I did think that I should be a hawk!" he said.

So he turned into a hawk; he rose into the air, flying high. When he came to that place, from on high he attacked the raven. When the raven saw him, it would not croak, for it feared the hawk. The hawk snatched that head and made off in flight. Not until he was far on his way did the raven croak. Though that person came running forth from the lodge, by this time the other had flown far off on his course.

"Alas!" he cried; "Go in pursuit! We have been robbed of my head!" he cried.

They turned into all manner of creatures, as they went in pursuit. The hawk was swift; he left behind all that fly in the air.

When he came near, he cried, "Brother, open the door! Try to pull our uncle to his feet!" he told him.

When, accordingly, the other threw open the door and made ready to pull him to his feet, by that time he was close by.

"Here it comes, brother! Rub his mouth!" he told him.

Truly, that head flew into place, and the elder lad rubbed his mouth. So he came to life. All those who had given chase went back. Those boys rejoiced that their uncle had come to life.

"Now then, let us go home! Let us take our uncle home!"

They stepped out of the lodge. His arrows and his head-dress, only these he took whose head was beaded, as they stepped forth from the lodge.

"Now, younger brother. let me be the one to take our uncle."

"Very well."

Then, shooting an arrow, "Come, uncle, on this we others shall stand as we go. In the grove this side of where we live, there we shall come to earth."

Truly they went along, two of them standing on his arrow. Toward evening they came to earth there, and from that point walked on. As that woman was at work out of doors, presently she beheld coming forth her brother and her children, the children walking at either side of their uncle.

At once that woman said to him, "Goodness! My brother is alive!" and went to welcome him, and they went indoors and she set about preparing a feast. Presently her husband came in.

"Splendid, splendid!" he said to him; "Truly, after long delay I see my wife's brother!" said that man.

So there they stayed. Those children did nothing but play with their uncle, and now never went off anywhere, but played with their uncle indoors.

"Do not thus with your uncle! You treat him too much as your playfellow!" said the woman to her children, but, "No!" said that youth; "Let my nephews treat me as their comrade at play; it is to them I owe my life," he told his sister.

So at last they were there a long time. That man was always hunting. Then at one time he did not come home. When he had not arrived by the next morning, "Now, my nephews, I shall look for your father," he told them.

"Very well."

So he sought him. Where he came upon his trail, he tracked him; it appeared he had come upon the trail of a moose; this moose his brother-in-law had tracked. At last he saw a hill over a ravine in which was a spring of water. To that place it seemed that his brother-in-law had gone. When he came to it, then from where the spring flowed forth, a Great Serpent thrust out its head with gaping jaws, and drew him in and swallowed him bodily. Whom did he see but his brother-in-law sitting there, alive. He, too, did not die. He sat with his brother-in-law, until it must have been night.

When he did not come home by next morning, of those twins the elder, "Let me go look for our uncle!"

"Be on your guard, my brother!" said the younger lad.

Accordingly, the elder brother set out. There where it appeared that his father had trailed the moose, there he walked on. At last he came to that spring. When he came near, the Great Serpent thrust forth its head, gaping, and sucked him in. When he doubled himself up, thinking of the knives that grew forth from his elbows, "With these I shall cut him to pieces," he swung them awkwardly, and was swallowed whole. There sat his uncle and his father.

Thus came another night. In the morning the younger brother set out to look for his elder brother. He came to where it appeared that he had trailed a moose. He too trailed it. When he came to the spring, as he got near to where the Great Serpent had thrust forth its head, again it thrust out its head.

"This is the one who destroyed them," he thought.

As it opened wide its jaws to draw him in, he stood still in place. No matter how much it opened its jaws, it could not make him come that way.

"Courage, Great Serpent! Open your jaws! Come out a bit farther!" he said to it.

Though he continued to encourage it to draw him in, it could not get hold of him. It kept coming out farther and farther, and he said to it, "Courage!" and it stretched its jaws as far as it could; he doubled himself up and swung his elbows out at both sides, like this. He cut the Great Serpent all to strips. Whom did he see but his brother, his uncle, and his father, coming out from there! For he had slain that creature; so now he brought them home. They went home; at nightfall they arrived at their dwelling.

Then, the next morning, thus spoke that younger lad: "Now then, you are too foolish, my elder brother. It seems that you have no manitou power; you are always being defeated. It will be better if I tell you what I have planned."

"Very well."

"Well then, my father, as for you and my mother: soon there will be mortal men; in future time you will stay on the hills; you will be tall; thorn-trees you will be called," he told his father and his mother, "because you are good beings.—And you, my uncle, over here in the place of the setting sun, there you will have your habitation. 'The man with the beaded head has taken pity on me,' a man will say; in his sleep he will see you, my uncle.—And as for us: here, a little ways ahead there will be small stars; they will be near to each other; such will we be, my elder brother and I," he said to them; "There, that is the way of it; be off!"

Accordingly, those others went off. When they came to a hill, he and his wife, they threw themselves upon the ground; they turned into thorn-trees. And those boys went up aloft and turned into stars.

And so this is the end of the sacred story.

(20) Flute-Bearer

Coming-Day

kā-kīsikāw-pīhtukāw.

päyak äs ōma ōtänaw äh-misāk, äh-māh-mätawätsik, äh-mōtutsik. kītahtawä päyak awa iskwäw pakwātam, äh-kitimākäyimāt usīmisah.

"nka-sipwähtahāw; ta-kakwä-uhpikiw," itäyihtam.

äh-tipiskāyik, sipwähtäw, äh-tapasīt.

"māskōts, — nōhtāwiy nikāwiy äh-nipahihtsik, äkwah nipäyakun nisīmis, — asitsi māskōts mätawähkih, äkwah nika-nipahikawin," itäyihtam; äyakō uhtsi k-ō-sipwähtät.

nistwāw äh-nipāt, äkutä miywāsiniyiw askiy, misiwä ä-sakāyik.

"āh, māskōts ōta nam āwiyak nik-ōtihtik," itäyihtam; "äkusi tit-ōhpikiw nisīmis," itäyihtam.

tāpwä äkutah usīhtāw wīkih. kiyipa kīsihtāw wīki. äkwah usīhtāw astis uhtsi tāpakwāna, ä-wīh-kakwä-nipahāt wāpuswa, "äkutōwahk piku nik-ōh-pimātisinān nisīmis," äh-itäyihtah. tāpwä tāpakwäw. äkwah mihtah mistahih āwatāw. äkw äh-tipiskāyik, ä-kīh-nipātsik, äh-wāpahk, nātam utāpakwānah. nīsu nipahäw wāpuswah.

"hāy hāy! äkwah nisīmis kä-mītsisut!" itwäw, äh-kīwähtahāt.

tāpwä miywäyihtam awa nāpäsis, äh-päsīmiht wāpuswah. äkwah kīsiswäw aw īskwäw, äy-asamāt usīmisah. ä-kīsi-mītsisut, kutakah mīna usīhtäw, āsa mīna äh-ntawi-tāpakwät; äkuyihuhk māna kāh-kīwätsih, äh-atuskātahk mihtah, itah äh-ay-ayāt.

piyisk misikitiyiwa usīma, äkwah äy-usīhtāt atsusisah, ä-kiskinōhamawāt ta-pmutahkwäyit usīmisah. tāpwä kaskihtāw ä-pimutahkwät awa nāpäsis. "māskōts kīkway wäh-nipahtātsih uskinīk-itsih," äh-itäyimāt, k-ōh-kiskinōhamawāt. wiya tahtu-kīsikāw äh-nipahāt wāpuswah, äyaku piku äh-atuskät, äkwah awa nāpäsis pisisik äh-mätawät pīhtsāyihk, āskaw wayawītimihk, awa piku iskwäw äh-atuskät, mituni kitimākäyimäw usīmisa, itah ä-wiy-ōhpikihāt. kītahtawä äkwah ä-misikitiyit usīma, usīhtāw utayōwinisiyiwa, wīki äh-pīkusahk, äyakō uhtsi uskutākayiw äw-usīhtāt, mīna utāsiyiwa. äkwah wäskwāhtämihk uhtapiw awa, äh-at-ōskinīkit; äkwah päyakwanuhk apiw awa, äh-at-uskinīkit. namuya äkwa papāmuhtäw wayawītimihk, nayästaw äh-mītsisut, wāpuswah piku äh-mōwātsik umisah. nama wīhkāts kitutitōwak.

piyisk uskinīkiw. kītahtawä utinam umōhkumān, ä-ntawi-kīskikahahk misāskwatwah, äkwah ahtsāpiyah, äh-pīhtukatāt, ä-wīh-usīhtāt, äh-mōhkutahk, ōhi mīna ahtsāpiyah, atsusisah ä-wīh-usīhtāt. äkwah namuya tāpwä kīh-nipahäw aw īskwäw wāpuswah. äkwah nōhtähkatäwak. pakwātam aw īskwäw äh-nōhtähkatätsik, usām päyakwanuhk äh-apiyit usīma. äkwah awa uskinīkiw k-ōsīhtāt ōhi misāskwatwah, utinam tsīkahikan, ä-ntawiwanähikät mistikwah uhtsi, mistiku-wanähikan. nīsu usīhtāw. äkusi äh-kīwät, päyak piku nipahäyiwa ōmisah wāpuswah. pōti äh-wāpahk, ä-ntawāpahtahk uwanihikanah, nipahäw kīhīwa, äkwah ōhōwa; äkusi nīsu. äwakuni mīkwanah uhtsi usīhtāw wīpisisah. äh-kīsihtāt, äkwah umisah astis miyik, äy-usihtāt, ahtsāpīhk äh-tahkupitahk. äkwah mīna äh-ntawāpahtahk uwanähikanah, tasōhäw nikikwah äkwah utsäkah, äkwah utsäkiwayānah ä-wīh-upīhtatwānit, nikikwa ä-wīh-utastutinit, nikikwayānah. äkwah ōhi kihīwa, uskan ōtah umatōwahk, utihtsimanikanis utinam, kitsuhtsikanis äh-usīhtāt. äh-kīs-ōsīhtāt, utinamiyiwa umisah kāwiyah, ä-wīh-kikamuhāyit kitsuhtsikanisihk. äh-kīsihtāyit, akutäw.

äkusi miywäyihtam aw īskwäw, "äkwah käkway ta-nipahtāw nisīm!" äh-itäyihtahk.

pōtih nama wiya wīh-mātsiyiwa usīma, päyakwanuhk äh-apiyit. āskaw nama käkway nipahtāw wāpuswah aw īskwäw. äkusi nama käkway mītsiwak. pakwātam aw īskwäw äkā ä-wīh-mātsiyit usīma; äkā käkway äh-asamāt usīma, äyak ōhtsi k-ōh-pakwātahk. mīna äh-wāpahk, äh-nātahk utāpakwāna, nama käkway nipahtāw.

äh-takuhtät wīkiwāhk, umaskisina äh-pahpawahahk, äh-kōniwiyikih, "hä ä äy!" itwäw aw īskwäw; "tāpwä nimihtātän äkā käkway äh-asamak nisīm!" itwäw; "äkwah äy-uskinīkit, wiyaskuts ätukä käkway ta-nipahtāw, ta-mītsiyāhk, nitäyihtäh, äkā k-äspayik," itwäw aw īskwäw, äh-utinahk mihtah, ä-wīh-pōnahk. "nka-pähtāk nisīm," äh-itäyihtahk, ōma k-ōh-itwät.

äkus āti-pīhtukäw, äh-pōnahk. nahapiw. äh-pa-pimisihk ōw uskinīkiw, waniskāw, äh-utinahk kitsuhtsikanis mīna wīpisisah. äkwah maskusiyah utinam, iskutäw äh-akwāsiwāpahahk. äkutah astāw maskusiyah, äh-kaskāpahtäyik, kitsuhtsikanis ōma äkutah äh-itisinahk, äh-miyāhkasahk.

äkusi ōmis ītwäw : " hä äy, nimisä, äh-kitimākinātān, äkā käkway k-ō-wih-nipahtāyān, usām mistahi t-ātuskäyin, äy-itäyimitān, " itäw umisah[1]*; " yōhtäwäpinah ! "*

yōhtänam aw īskwäw, äkwah aw ōskinīkiw äh-kituhtsikät. äh-kīsi-kituhtāt, akutāw. kiyipah kā-pāpayiyit apisi-mōsusah, äh-mihtsätiyit, äkutah iskwāhtämihk ä-pimipayiyit, äwakuni äh-pāh-pimwāt. iyikuhk äh-mästinahk wīpisisah, äkuyikuhk pōyōw. ähtsi pikuh mihtsät mistahi nipahäw. äkuyikuhk tapasiyiwah äyakuni.

" äh, nimisä, ntaw-utinah nīpisisah. mihkōwikwāwi, kāsīhamōhkan. "

tāpwä wayawīw aw īskwäw. äh-itāpit, mihtsät apisi-mōsusah nipahäyiwa.

" hāy hāy ! äkwah kä-mītsisut nisīmis ! " itwäw, atsusisah ōhi äh-wāh-wīhkwatinahk, äh-ati-kāsīhahk.

äh-pīhtukatät, pōti kī-musäskatäyiwa usīma, äh-wäwäkinamiyit utakuhpiyihk. ä-kih-utinamiyit atsusisah, ōh ōtayōwinisiyiwa, " nimisä, wayawīwäpinayi ! "

äh-wayawīwäpinahk, äkwah umōhkumān utinam, äh-wayawīt. äh-nanātawāpahtahk ōhi kā-wayawīwäpinahk, namuya wāpahtam. äkusi äkwah äh-wiyanihtākät. ōh apisi-mōsusah ä-kīsi-wiyanihāt, iyāyaw paminawasōw. äh-kīsi-mītsisut, äkwah ōw āpisi-mōsuswayāna nāō utinäw, ä-wīh-pāswāt. äkus uwiyāsima pīhtukäyāwatāw. äkwah ātiht wayawītimihk astäyiwa, sām mihtsät kāh-nipahāyit. äh-kīsi-nahastāt, äkwah pīhtukäw, päskis mīna äh-paminawasut, āskaw äh-atuskātāt ōh āpisi-mōsuswayāna. äh-utākusiniyik, āsay kīsihäw, äkwah äh-kaskikwātahk usīma äh-utayōwinisiyit. käkāts ta-kawisimutsik, äh-ispayiyik, kīsihtāw. itisinamawäw usīma. pustayōwinisäw aw uskinīkiw. āsay mīna kutakah pāswäw. äkusi ä-kawisimut awa uskinīkiw, awa wiy īskwäw atuskātäw apisi-mōswayāna. piyis ä-nōhtähkwasit, kawisimōw. kīksäpā äh-päkupayit, āsay usīma simatapiyiwa. äkusi paminawasōw. ä-kīsi-mītsisutsik, āsay mīna aw uskinīkiw iskutäw utinam, mīna äh-miyāhkasahk ukituhtsikanis.

"yōhtäwäpinah, nimisä ! " itäw.

ä-ki-yōhtänahk, kituhtāw. äkwah wāwāskäsiwah äyakō pätsimäw, äyakunih äkwah äh-nōtsihāt. iyikuhk mīna äh-mästinahk wīpisisah, äkuyikuhk mīna tapasiyiwa.

" ā, nimisä, utina nīpisisah ! "

äh-wayawīt aw īskwäw, ā, mihtsāt äkwah wawāskäsiw.

" hāy hāy ! mahtiy äkwa äk äh-nōhtähkatäyān ! " itwäw aw īskwäw, ōhi äh-wāh-wīhkwatinahk atsusisah.

äh-pīhtukatät, āsay mīna kīh-musäskatäpiyiwa usīma.

" hā, nimisä, äyakunih anih wayawīwäpinah ! " itäw.

wayawīwäpinam. äkwah umōhkumān utinam aw īskwäw, ä-wīh-wiyanihtākät. nama käkway wāpahtam usīma utayōwinisiyiwa, ayis äh-wäpinamiyit. äkusi äkwah mīna wiyinihtākäw. äh-kīsi-wiyinihtākät, äkuyikuhk äkwah kīsitäpōw, ä-wīh-mītsisutsik. piyisk mītsisōwak. ä-kīsi-mītsisut, iyāyaw äkwah usīhäw pisi-mōswayānah, äkwah päyak wāwaskäsiwa, wawāskäsiwayāna. iyikuhk äy-utākusik, kahkiyaw kīsihtāw, äkwah pitah äh-paminawasut. äh-kīsi-mītsisutsik, äkwah kaskikwāsōw. äkwah kīsihtāw utayōwinisiyiwa usīma. iyāyaw äkwah pāsam pahkäkinwah. piyis mistahi tipiskāyiki, äyikuhk kawisimōw. iyikuhk äh-päkupayit,

[1] A good instance of bravado: one lets a bad situation go far, and then, before acting, belittles the danger by giving a trivial reason for the delay.

äkuyikuhk sāsay waniskāyiwa usīma. kakwäyāhōw äh-paminawasut. mayaw äh-kīsi-mītsisutsik, āsay mīna miyāhkasamiyiwa ukitsuhtsikanisiyiw.

" yōhtäwäpinahk ! "

ä-yōhtäwäpinahk, kituhtāw. āsay mīna pätsimäw mōswah, äkwah äyakunih mīna äh-nōtsihät. iyikuhk mīna äh-mästinahk wīpisisah, pōyōw.

" ā, nimisä, ntaw-ōtinah nīpisisah ! "

äh-wayawīt, mihtsät äkwah mōswah.

" hāy hāy hāy ! äkwah äkā mayaw kä-nōhtāhkatäyāhk ! " itwäw aw īskwäw, äh-āt-utinahk atsusisah.

äh-pīhtukät, āsay mīna musäskatäpiyiwa.

" ā, nimisä, äkunih anih wayawīwäpinah ! " itäw umisah.

wayawīwäpinam ; äkuyikuhk umōhkumān äh-utinahk, äh-wayawīt, ä-wāh-wiyanihtākät. äkwah wiyanihtākäw. ä-kīsiyinihtākät, äkuyikuhk äkwah paminawasōw. ä-kīsi-mītsisutsik, äkwa mīna äh-usīhät apisi-mosuswayāna, päyak mīnah wāwāskäsiwäkin, " tsit-ōtakuhpit, " äy-itäyihtah, käkāts äh-ati-tipiskāyik, kīsihtāw, pita min äkwah äh-paminawasut, ä-wīh-asamāt usīma. tāpwä ä-kīsi-mītsisutsik, äkwah kaskikwāsōw, ayōwinisah äw-usīhtāt. maywäs kawisimuyit usīma, āsay kīsihtāw, äkwah kutakah äh-pāswāt apisi-mōswayānah äkwah mōswayānah. iyikuhk iskuh ä-nōhtähkwasit, pōn-ātuskäw, ä-wīh-nipāt. äh-wāpahk, ä-waniskāt, āsay kīsimatapiyiwa usīma. äkusi äkwah ati-paminawasōw, ä-wīh-mītsisutsik. mayaw ä-kīsi-mītsisutsik, mīna miyāhkasamiyiwa kituhtsikanis. yōhtäwäpinam aw īskwäw, ä-kituhtāyit usīma. äkwah mustuswah pāpayiyiwa, äkunih mīna äh-nōtsihät. äyikuh mīna äh-mästinahk wīpisisah, äkuyikuhk pōni-nipahäw.

" äkusi, nimisä ! utinah nīpisisah ! " itäw.

äh-wayawīt aw īskwäw, āsay mīna miywäyihtam.

" hāy hāy ! äkus ätsik ōma äkā wīhkäts kä-kōta-mītsiyān ! " itwäw aw īskwäw, äy-āh-utinahk atsusisah.

äh-pīhtukät, āsay mīna kī-musäskatäpiyiwa usīma.

" ā, nimisä, äyakunih wayawīwäpinah ! " itik ; " äh-manāh-mistahātuskahitān, äkā k-ōh-ma-mātsiyān, " itäw.

äkusi wayawīwäpinam aw īskwäw, äh-utinahk umōhkumān, ä-wayawīt, äh-wiyanihtākät. iyāyaw iyāpäsisah wiyanihäw.

" äyakunih äkwah t-ōtakuhpiw nisīm, " itäyihtam.

ä-kīsi-wiyanihät, pit äwakuni pīhtukahäw, itah ta-pāsōyit äh-kikamuhät. äkuyikuhk äkwah ä-ntawi-wiyanihtākät. äh-ay-āpihtā-kīsikāyik, pit äkwah paminawasōw, ä-wih-asamāt usīma. ä-kīsi-mītsisut, äkwa mīna usīhäw pisimōsuswayānah, äh-kīsihät, äkwa mīn ōhi mustuswayānah. äh-utākusik, kīsihäw. pit äkwah mīna paminawasōw, äh-mītsisutsik. ä-kīsi-mītsisutsik, äkwah mīna äh-kaskikwāsut, mistahīs äh-tipiskāyik, kīsihtāw ayōwinisah, äkwa mīn āwa uskinīkiw äh-pustayōwinisät, awa wiy iskwäw äh-ay-atuskātahk uwiyāsima. äyikuhk mistah äh-tipiskāyik, kawisimōw. äyikuhk äh-pākupayit, käyāpits nipāyiwa usīma, iyāyaw ä-paminawasut, ä-wīh-asamāt usīma. äyikuhk ä-kīsi-paminawasut, waniskāyiwa usīma, äkwah äh-mītsisutsik. ä-kīsi-mītsisutsik, namuya äkwah miyāhkasamiyiwa. äkwah wiya wayawīw, äy-usīhtāt itah ä-wīh-akutāt uwiyāsima, täsipitsikan. äkusi äkwah ä-sākaskinahtāt äwaku täsipitsikan, kutakah mīna usīhtāw täsipitsikana, äkutah t-āstāt uwiyāsima. piyisk kinwäsk atuskātam, ä-nahastāt wiyāsah. iyikuhk äh-kīsihtāt, äkwah usīhtāw pahkäkinwa, ayōwinisa äkwah ä-wiwusīhtuwāt usīma, tāpwä äh-kīsihtāt, äh-pāh-pīmikitahk.

kinwäsk äkwah äh-ayātsik, ōmis ītwäw aw uskinīkiw : " hāw, nimisä, kiyānaw tsī pikuh ōma k-äsinākusiyahk ? " itäw.

" ä ä ä, nisīmis, mihtsätiwak ōma ayīsiyiniwak, tāpiskōts kiya äkwah niya äkutōwahk äy-ihtātsik ; māka namuya kwayask äy-itātisitsik, äh-māh-mawinähututsik, siyākōtsihitutwāwi, äh-nipahitutsik. äywaku äh-pak-wātamān, kā-kīh-pä-sipwähtahitān, äh-apisīsisiyan, ' māskōts wīh-ōhpikit-sih, ' ä-kīh-itäyimitān. ōtä isi āpihtā-kīsikāk isi mihtsätiwak ayīsiyiniwak, māka ä-matsi-nōtsihtātsik, " itäw ; " iskwäwak watsistwanihk äh-akusītsik, awiyak uskinīkiw äkutä täkuhtātsi, āsay ä-sīhkimiht ta-kīhtsäkusīt, utihtātsi awiyak ta-wīkimāt. māka nōhtaw nīhtsipayiwak uskinīkiwak, äh-nipah-isihkik. äkusi äyakunik äh-ati-mōwātsik. äwaku namuya miywāsin. äkwah ōtä māmihk, äkutä misāw ōtänaw ; äwakunik äh-kā-kakwä-nakatit-utsik, awiyak näkatihtsih, ä-misi-wanātsihiht, mīn äyakunik äh-mōtutsik. äyakō uhtsi, ' pitanä uhpikihak ! ' k-ō-kih-täyimitān. āyiman nānitaw ta-kīh-ituhtäyin, " itäw usīma.

" hā, nimisä, wāpahkih nka-sipwähtān, " itäw.

mātōw aw īskwäw, äh-pakwātahk ä-wī-sipwähtäyit usīma, " māskōts ta-misi-wanātsihāw, " äh-itäyihtahk.

äkusi äkway ä-tipiskāk, kawisimōw. kīksäpā waniskāw aw īskwäw, ä-wi-sipwähtäyit usīma, äh-kīsitäput. äh-kīsi-mītsisut, wawäyīw aw uskinī-kiw, ä-pasikōt, ukituhtsikanis ōma äh-tāpiskahk, ōtäh äh-astāt uspisk-wanihk kitsuhtsikanis.

" ā, nimisä, awiyak wāh-wīhitsih, ' upipikwan-kā-nayahtahk ' nik-äsiyīhkāsun, " itwäw aw uskinīkiw, äh-ati-wayawīt, ä-sipwähtät.

āpihtā-kīsikāhk isi sipwähtäw, äkutä watsistwanihk k-ākusiyit iskwäwah, äkunih äh-ntawāpamāt. nīswāw äh-nipāt, äkuyikuhk utihtam ōtänaw.

äh-takuhtät, " äwahō-ō-ō, upipikwan-kā-nayahtahk takusin ! " itwäwān.

hā, päyakwayak ntumāw. mistahi miywäyihtamwak ōk āyīsiyiniwak, " äkwah kä-mītsisuyāhk ! " äh-itäyihtahkik.

äkutah ayāw wīsahkätsāhk,[1] *ōh ōkimāwa äh-uy-ōhtāwīhkāt, ōh ōskinīk-iskwäwa äh-usīmit. tāpwä äh-tipiskāyik, ituhtäw wīsahkätsāhk. äh-pīhtu-kät, apiyiwah ōhi uskinīkiwa.*

" upipikwan-kā-nayahtahk, māna kipä-wīwih nisīmak, " itäw.

" namuya ! " itik.

" ā, namuya ! wāpahkih ka-ntaw-wīwin nisīmak. utihtatwāwi, kika-wīwin, watsistwanihk äh-akusītsik nisīmak, " itäw.

" āha' , " itik.

tāpwä kīwäw wīsahkätsāhk.

" āh, nōhtāh, äh-pä-wīwit äs āni upipikwan-kā-nayahtahk, " itäw.

" äaha' ! " itwäyiwa.

piyis wāpaniyiw. wayawīw kīkisäpā, äh-kīsi-māh-mītsisōwiht awa wīsahkätsāhk.

" hāw, hāw, iyiniwitik, pä-wayawīk, pä-wayawīk ! upipikwan-kā-nayahtahk pä-kitāpamik, ä-wīh-nitawi-wīwit ! " itwäw, äh-ati-sipwähtät.

ā, kahkiyaw ayīsiyiniwak tuhtäwak, äkwah ä-wīhkwäpitsik tāwāyihk äkutah äh-tsimasut awa mistik. äh-kīsi-apitsik, kā-pä-takuhtät upipikwan-kā-nayahtahk. äh-kitāpamāt, tsapasis ayāyiwa watsistwanihk, äh-takuhtät, sämāk äh-ati-mātsikiyit. äkusi ä-wīh-utihtāt watsistunihk, pa-pakamah-

---

[1] In the succeeding episode Wisahketchahk seems to play merely the role of one of the spirit-animals. At the end of the story he is more in character. The same is true of a version obtained on Star-Blanket Reserve.

wäyiwa mistikwah ; kāwi kinwāskusiyiwa. äkwah äkuta wīpisisah āpatsihtāw, äh-uhtsi-kīhtsäkusīt. miyästinahkih, äh-pa-pakamahwāt upīhtatwānah, kāwi sākaskinäyiwa wīpisisah.

äkusi takhih ä-sipwäyāhtawit, wiy āwa wīsahkätsāhk tahk äh-itāpit, " asawāpamihk, ta-pätakutsihk upipkwan-kā-nayahtahk ! " äh-itwät wīsahkätsāhk.

piyisk näwāw ä-yahkīmuyit ōhi mistikwah, namuya äkwah wāpahtam askiy. hāw, utinam umistanipiwayān, äh-pōtātahk.

" utäh tahkuhts watsistwanihk nika-pōnāsin, ōk īskwäwak itah k-āpitsik ! " itwäw.

tāpwä äkutä pōnāsiw.

" äkusi māka kä-wīkimitāhk ! " itik iskwäwah.

" äha' ! "

utinäw ōh ōsimimāwa, äh-nīhtsiwäpināt.

tahk äh-asawāpit wīsahkätsāhk, kītahtawä kā-pätisāpamāt, " hywww ! "[1] *äh-sākōwät ; " äkwah piyätakutsihk upipikwan-kā-nayahtahk ! "*

itah äh-s-ōhtsiskawapit wīsahkätsāhk, äkutah pahkisiniyiwa. awīn ōh, ōsīma ! mituni wanātsipayiyiwa.

" wass ! " itwäw wīsahkätsāhk.

kutakah mīn ōhi nīhtsiwäpinäw. piyätisāpamātsih wīsahkätsāhk, āsay äh-sākōwät, " äkwah piyätakutsihk upipikwan-kā-nayahtahk ! " äh-itwät, māka piyākisiniyitsi, namuya kwayask isi-wāpamäw usīma. näpäwisiw. äkwah awa upipikwan-kā-nayahtahk pōtātam uma mistanipiwayān.

" wāhyaw ōtä nka-nīhtāsin ! " itwäw.

äkusi wīsahkätsāhk ōmis ītwäw : " hä hah ! tāpwä nikakwayakihik, nisīma kit-äsi-näpäwisiyān k-äsiwäpināt ! " itäw ; " tāntä kä-pīhtsāk askiy t-ätāmuyin ? niyah kiwīh-ntawi-nipahitn, upipikwan-kā-nayahtahk ! kinäpäwihin ! "

äkusi äkwah äh-ntunikät, äh-wāh-wāskāpahtät, ōmis īsi, tāntäh tanīhtakusiyit äh-ntunahk. kītagtawä miskam itah äsah äy-ōh-tapasiyit. äkwah mitihtäw.

" namuya ka-kīh-wanihitin, niya ka-kih-usīhtāyān askiy ! " itäw, äh-mitsihtsipayīstawāt.

kītahtawä wīh-atimik.

äkwah äh-pätwäwitamiyit wīsahkätsāhkwah, " hāw, ōtah ta-wīh-kāyās-āyiwiw atsusis ! " itwäw awa upipikwan-kā-nayahtahk, äh-kä-kätaskisināt, " ā, nimaskisinitik, tapasīk ! " äh-itwät.

" yahō ! " itwäw wīsahkätsāhk, äh-wāpahtahk ōm ātsusis ; " ā, kiy ōma upipikwan-kā-nayahtahk ! " itam atsusis, äh-wā-wāpahtahk ; " yā, māk āwa k-ātimiskanawät ! āh, kayās nimusōmipanak ōtah kā-kīh-nōtinitutsik, äkuspīh ōmah ä-kīh-patahututsik um ātsusis ! " itwäw.

äkus īsi äh-īkatawäpinahk, äkwah mīna äh-nawaswät. mayaw äh-ākawäwät, kunt ītä isi tapasīw äkwah awa upipikwan-kā-nayahtahk. wīsahkätsāhk iyikuhk itäh äh-pōnihtiniyikih maskisinah, pä-kīwäw.

" yōh ! ayōkw ätsik āna upipikwan-kā-nayahtahk k-ayīsīhut ! " itwäw ; "namuya äkwah kika-wanīhin ! " itäw.

äh-takupahtät, awänipan atsusis, äsa kāh-tapasiyit !

" wīnikunämahkay ! " itwäw wīsahkätsāhk, āsay mīna äh-nawaswät.

[1] Call made with palm alternately pressed over mouth and removed.

kītahtawä mīna äkwah ä-wīh-atimāt, käkāts äkwah t-ātimāpamāt, äkuyikuhk äh-askōwāt, ōmis ītwäw aw ōpipikwan-kā-nayahtahk : " hāw, nik-äskwäwin ! nka-pwāwīn ! "

tāpwä äkus īsinākusiw. ä-sākäwät, awīn ōhi, iskwäwah ka-papāmuhtäyit.

" namuy äkwah kika-wayäsihin ! kiy ōma, upipikwan-kā-nayahtahk ! sōskwāts kiwīh-pakamahutn ! "

mätōw aw īskwäw.

" mīn ätsik ān äwaku äkā kä-kitimākinawit ! ōtah kā-pimpahtāt, ' äkāya nakasin ! ahpōh ka-wīkimitin ! ' äh-āt-ītak, äkā kā-tāpwähtawit ! kayās äh-ntawi-mōnahikähk ä-kīh-wanisiniyān, " itwäw aw īskwäw ; " äkus äh-āt-ītak, ' hāw, usām wīsahkätsāhk ninawaswātik, ä-wīh-nipahit ! ' nitik, " itwäyiwa.

" ā, namuya ! namuya kika-wayäsimin ! kiy ōma, upipikwan-kā-nayahtahk ! " itäw.

" kiyām kitimākäyimin ! äkā wiya nakasin ! ahpōh ka-wīkimitn ! " itäw wīsahkätsāhkwa.

" mahti māka nīpaw ōtahk ! " itäw wīsahkätsāhk.

äkwah ōmisi tōtam, ä-wīh-tāhkināt.

" kah ! tāpwä äs āni kiya iskwäw ! " itäw ; " pähin ōtah ; nikantawi-nipahāw upipikwan-kā-nayahtahk ; mituni ōma ninäpäwihik, nisīma ä-nīhtsiwäpinamawit. äkāya nāntaw ituhtä ! " itäw.

" äha' ! kiyipah māka takuhtähkan, " itik.

" äha'. äkutah pähin, niwīkimākan ! " itäw.

äkusi ä-sipwäpahtāt, mayaw äh-ākawäwät, tapasiyiwa. māka mīna wāhyaw äh-ayāt, umaskisiniyiwah piku kiy-astäyiwa.

" ähähä ! äkuta māna kah-kisiwāyit upipikwan-kā-nayahtahk ! namuy äkwah kika-wayäsihin ! itah äkwah kä-wāpamitān, äkwah ka-pakamahutin ! ka-nipahitn ! kikisiwi-näpäwihin, nisīmak äkā kwayask äh-isiwäpinamawiyin ! " itäw.

äh-takupahtāt, awīnipan ōh īskwäwah, äsa kāh-tapasiyit.

" hā hah ! äkutah māna kāh-kisiwāhit upipikwan-kā-nayahtahk ! namuy äkwah ka-wanihin ! äkuyikuhk mistahi äh-pimipahtäyān, usām äh-kisiwi-tsīsihiyin, iskwäw äh-itäyimitān ! "

kītahtawä äh-pa-pimipahtāt, āsay mīna kisiwāk askōk.

" hāw ! " itwäw, mistikwah äh-utinahk, tāpiskōts wāskahikan äh-itastät ; " hāw, ta-kayās-āyiwiw wāskahikan ! " itwäw.

nīsu mīna mistikwah utinäw, äh-pōh-pōtātāt.

" hāw, kiyawāw iskwäwak kik-äkutōwināwāw, āpihtawikusisāniskwäwak ! äkwah niya nika-kisäyiniwin āpihtiyukusisān ! mituni nka-kawikihkān ! " itwäw.

tāpwä kisäyiniwiw. pīhtsāyihk ayāwak. kītahtawä wīsahkätsāhk kasākäwäpahtāt. wāpahtam wāskahikanis.

" hāw, uhtsita piku kika-pakamahutin ! kiy ōma, upipikwan-kā-nayahtahk, k-äsihuyin ! " itäw.

äh-at-takupahtāt, kā-pä-wayawiyit uskinīkiskwäwa.

" kikih-kisiwi-näpäwihin ! sōskwāts äkwah kika-nipahitn, upipikwan-kā-nayahtahk ! " itäw.

" nā, mīn ätsik ān äyakō äkā kä-tāpwähtākuyāhk ! ' awiyak utihtikuyahku, wīkimāhkäk, ' ä-kīh-itikuyāhk nōhtāwīnān, usām äh-kisäyiniwit, äkā

äh-kīh-pamihikuyāhk, äh-āt-āyākuyāhk. ' usām wīsahkätsāhk nnawaswātik, ä-wīh-nipahit, ' k-ätwät aw ōtah kā-pimāmut, kiya käkuts kitimākihtawinān ! ahpōh ä-isi-nīsiyāhk ka-wīkimitnān ! " itik.

" yahōh ! tāpwä nnōhtä-wīwin āpihtäyukusisāniskwäwak ! usām nnästusin. pita nika-kapäsin. wāpahk iyikuhk, nka-ntawi-nipahāw. kīh-nipahakih, äkuyikuhk ka-pä-pamihitināwāw, " itäw.

" pīhtukä māka ! " itik.

äh-pīhtukät, awīn ōhi, kisäyiniwānäsah kīh-apiyiwa.

" äy, tāpwä kitimākisiw kōhtāwiyiwāw ! "

" häha' . "

" ka-pamihitnāwāwan, k-äsi-nitawäyihtahk kōhtāwiyiwāw, " itäw.

āh, apiw nipäwinihk, tahk äh-māsihikut, āyītaw uhtsi äh-apiyit.

piyis ä-tipiskāyik, " nnästusin, nīwitik. pita nipātān, " itäw.

äkwah kawisimōwak. päyak wähtiskawisinōstawātsi, kwäskipitik ōhi päyak, " pä-kwäskisinih ! " äh-itikut. piyisk kapä-tipisk äkus äh-tōtākut, nama kīh-nipāw. iyikuhk käkāts äh-wāpaniyik, äkuyikuhk mituni nästuhkwasiw. mayaw kā-nipāt, tapasiyiwa ōhi kisäyiniwānäsah.

ōmis ītäw kāhkākiwah aw ōpipikwan-kā-nayahtahk : " ōtah mītusihk akusī ! ' waniskāh, wīsahkätsāhk ! ' itāhkan ; ' kkī-nawaswāh ! ' itāhkan ; ' " māk ān äkwa nikisiw-itisahuk ! " kitik, ' itāhkan ; ' " itah atimitsih, äkwah nka-nipahāw ! " kitik, ' itāhkan. "

äkus īs äh-sipwähtät.

" ta-wih-nama-käkwayiw ōma wāskahikanis ! " itwäw, äkus äkus äh-sipwähtät.

kītahtawä kā-kāh-kitut kāhkākiw. päkumik wīsahkätsāhk. äh-tōhkāpit, awīn ōma, wayawitimihk kīh-nipāw ! āyītaw ōtah mistikwah kīh-pimisiniyiwa ; äwakuni " iskwäw " kā-kīh-itäyimāt.

" wīnikunämahkay ! tān-tahtwāw äkwah ka-wayäsihit ! " itäw wīsahkätsāhk.

äh-kituyit kāhkākiwa, " ā, wīsahkätsāhk ! ' nikisiwāhik äkwah ! ' kitik aw ōpipikwan-kā-nayahtahk ; ' itah äkwah atimitsih, nika-nipahāw äkwah ! ' kitik anih upipikwan-kā-nayahtahk, " itik.

" yahō ! " itwäw wīsahkätsāhk ; " ta-wīh-ta-tāpwäw ōyā ! " itwäw wīsahkätsāhk ; " āsay ōma nistwāw niwayäsihik. namuya wīhkāts äkuyikuhk awiyak niwayäsimik ! " itwäw ; " hā, nika-pōnihā ! nika-kīwān, " itwäw ; " äkus āni ä-pimātisiyin, upipikwan-kā-nayahtahk ! " twäw wīsahkätsāhk.

äkuyikuhk äh-iskwāk ātayōhkäwin.

The story goes that there was this big town where they always had contests and ate each other. Then at one time a certain woman took a dislike to this, because she loved her little brother.

"I shall take him away from here; I shall try to have him grow up," she thought.

In the night she went away, fleeing.

"Perhaps—since my father and my mother have been killed, I am now alone with my little brother—perhaps, if there is another mass contest, I now shall be killed," she thought; that was why she went away.

After two nights' journeying, she was at a place where the land was good, with woods everywhere.

"Oh, perhaps here no one will come upon me," she thought; "In this way my little brother will grow up," she thought.

So there she set up her dwelling. She quickly built her lodge. Then she made snares of sinew, meaning to try to kill rabbits, thinking, "Only from these shall my little brother and I be able to get our sustenance." So she set her snares. Then she gathered a great amount of firewood. Then, when night had come and they had slept, in the morning she went to look at her snares. She had killed two rabbits.

"Good! Now my little brother will eat!" she said, as she took them home.

The little boy was glad when the rabbits were brought. Then the woman cooked them and gave her little brother to eat. When she too had eaten, she made some more snares and went again to lay them; and then, whenever she went home, she tended to the firewood, and stayed there.

In time her brother grew big, and then she made arrows and taught him to shoot. So the boy learned to shoot. Because she thought, concerning him, "Perhaps he will kill something when he comes to adolescence," was why she taught him. As she killed rabbits every day, she was the only one of them to work; as the boy was always playing in the lodge, or sometimes out of doors, and only the woman worked, she was very good to her little brother, there where she was trying to raise him. Then, presently, when her brother grew big, she made clothes for him, cutting pieces from the tent, from which she made him a coat and breeches. And he sat in the place opposite the door, as he came to the age of approaching manhood; he stayed always right there, as he came to adolescence. He did not go about now out of doors; he did little more than eat his meals, and rabbits were all they had to eat, he and his sister. They never spoke to each other.

At last he was a young man. Then at one time he took his knife and went to cut some saskatoon sticks, and wood for a bow, and brought them inside the lodge to work at them, whittling them, and the bow as well, to make arrows. And then the woman was no longer well able to kill rabbits. Then they hungered. The woman was grieved that they should hunger because her brother always stayed right there. When the youth had prepared those saskatoon sticks, he took an ax and went to set a trap of boughs. He made two of them. Then when he came home, his sister had killed but one rabbit. In the morning, when he went to look at his traps, he had killed an eagle and an owl; one in each trap. He made his arrows with those feathers. When he had finished them, his sister gave him a sinew, which he prepared and fixed on his bow. The next time he went to look at his traps, he had trapped an otter and a fisher; and now he meant to make a quiver of the fisherskin, and of the otter a hat, of the otterskin. And from the eagle he took the bone here, like this, from the upper part of the wing, and made a flute. When he had made it, his sister took some porcupine-quills to attach to the little flute. When she had finished it, he hung it up.

Then the woman was glad, thinking, "Now my brother will kill something!"

But she found that her brother would not hunt, and did not stir from the spot. Often enough the woman did not kill any rabbits. Then they had nothing to eat. She was grieved that her brother did not care to hunt;

because she had nothing to give her brother to eat, was why she disliked it. The next morning, when she went to her snares, she had not killed anything.

When she came to their dwelling and was shaking out her moccasins, for they were full of snow, she cried, "Oh dear, oh dear! Really I am sorry I have nothing to give my brother to eat!" she said; "Now that he is a young man, he in his turn ought to kill something for us to eat; so I thought, at least, but it has not turned out that way," said the woman, as she took up some faggots to put on the fire. "My brother will hear me," was her idea in speaking so.

Thereupon she went inside and put fuel on the fire. She sat down. The youth arose from where he lay, and took the flute and his arrows. Also he took some dried incense-grass and pushed back the fire. There he placed the grass, and when it began to make smoke, he held the little flute over it, perfuming it with the incense.

At the same time he spoke as follows: "Dear me, sister, it is because I feel sorry for you that I have not been killing anything, because I thought you would have too much work," he told his sister; "Throw open the door-flap!"

The woman opened the doorway, and the youth played on his flute. When he had done playing music, he hung it up. At once there came running dwarf-moose in great number, and as they ran past the doorway, he kept shooting them. He stopped only when he had used up his arrows. He killed a great many of them. Then they ran away.

"There, sister, go get my arrows. If they are bloody, wipe them off."

Accordingly, the woman went outside. When she looked to see, he had killed many dwarf-moose.

"Splendid! Now my brother will eat!" she said, as she kept pulling out the arrows and wiping them.

When she brought them indoors, there was her brother undressed, wrapped up in his blanket-robe. When he had taken back his arrows, then, of his clothes, he said, "Sister, throw them out of the lodge!"

When she had thrown them out, she took her knife and went out. When she looked about to see the things she had thrown out, she did not see them. Then she set about skinning and cutting up the game. When she had cleaned those dwarf-moose, she set eagerly about her cooking. When she had eaten, she took four of the skins of the dwarf-moose to dry. Then she brought in her meat. But some was left outside, for he had killed too many. When she had arranged it all, she came in, and again attended to her cooking, even while working the hides of the dwarf-moose. Towards evening, she had finished tanning them, and began sewing clothes for her brother. When it was almost time for them to go to bed, she had finished them. She handed them to her brother. The youth put on the clothes. Then she dried some more. Then, when the youth went to bed, the woman kept on working the moose-hides. At last, when she grew sleepy, she went to bed. Early in the morning, when she awoke, her brother was already sitting up. Accordingly, she cooked. When they had eaten, the youth again took some fire and burned incense to his little flute.

"Open the door-flap, sister!" he said to her.

When she had opened it, he blew on his flute. This time he brought deer to his call, and gave chase to them. Again, only when he had used up his arrows, did they flee.

"There, sister, take up my arrows!"

When the woman went out, there were many deer.

"Splendid! Now, surely, I shall not go hungry!" she said, as she went about pulling free the arrows.

When she brought them in, again her brother sat without his clothes.

"There, sister, throw these things out!" he said to her.

She threw them out. Then she took her knife, to clean the game. Not a thing did she see of her brother's clothes; he had cast them off. Then, accordingly, she again cleaned game. When she had finished cleaning game, she cooked, that they might eat. Then they ate. When she had eaten, she eagerly went about preparing dwarf-moose skins and one deer-skin. By evening she had finished it all, and then she stopped to cook. When they had eaten, she sewed. Then she finished her brother's clothes. Then, with zeal she went about drying hides. At last, when it was quite dark, she went to bed. When she awoke, her brother had already got up. She worked quickly, cooking the meal. When they had eaten, he again burned incense under his flute.

"Open the door!"

When she had opened it, he played. As before, he made moose come by the sound, for these he now sought. Again, when he had exhausted his arrows, he ceased.

"Now, sister, go take up my arrows!"

When she went out, there were many moose.

"Splendid, splendid! Now we shall not for a long time go hungry!" said the woman, as she set about taking the arrows.

When she went indoors, again he sat undressed.

"Now, sister, throw those things out!" he told his sister.

She threw them outside; then she took her knife and went out and began to clean the carcasses. She skinned them and cut them up. When she had finished cleaning them she set about her cooking. When they had eaten, then she again prepared skins of dwarf-moose, and a deer-hide, with the thought, "That he may have it for a blanket-robe," and just as darkness was coming on, she had them done, and stopped to cook again, to feed her brother. So, when they had eaten, she sewed and made clothes. Before her brother went to bed she had them done, and already was drying other skins of dwarf-moose and of moose. When she got sleepy, she ceased work and went to bed. The next morning, when she arose, her brother was already sitting up. So then she cooked, that they might eat. As soon as they had eaten, he again burned incense to his flute. The woman threw open the door-flap, and her brother played the flute. Then buffalo came running, and he made a killing of these too. Again, only when he had used up his arrows did he cease killing them.

"So there, sister! Take up my arrows!" he told her.

When the woman went out, again she was glad.

"Splendid! So now, it appears, I shall never be at a loss for something to eat!" she said, as she went on taking the arrows.

When she went in, again her brother sat without his clothes.

"Now, sister, throw these out of the lodge!" he told her; "It was because I hesitated to give you too much work, that I never used to hunt," he told her.

So the woman threw them out of the lodge, and took her knife, and went out and cleaned the game. She eagerly set about skinning a young bull-calf.

"Now my brother shall have a blanket-robe of this one," she thought.

When she had skinned it, she first brought it inside and fastened it to dry. Then she went again to cut up game. When noon came, she stopped to cook a meal, to give her brother to eat. When she had eaten, again she prepared skins of dwarf-moose, and tanned them, and also that buffalo-robe. By evening, she had tanned it. Then she stopped, to cook, and they ate. When they had eaten, and again she sewed, then, when it was quite dark, she finished the garments, and the youth put them on, while the woman went on preparing the stores of meat. When it was entirely dark, she went to bed. When she awoke, her brother was still asleep, and eagerly she set about cooking, that she might give her brother to eat. When she had finished cooking, her brother arose, and they ate. When they had eaten, this time he did not burn incense. She went out and set up a drying-frame, on which to hang her meats. Then, when she had filled that drying-frame, she set up other drying-frames, on which to place her stores of meat. She worked a long time at placing the meat. When she had done, she prepared hides, intending to make clothes for her brother, and she finished them and ornamented them with quill-work.

When they had stayed there a long time, the youth spoke as follows: "Now, sister, is it only we who look like this?" he asked her.

"Dear me, little brother, in truth there are many people who exist in the same form as you and I; but they are not of decent character; they always challenge each other to contend, and when they have defeated each other, they kill each other. It was because I hated this, that I took you away and brought you here when you were small, thinking of you, 'Perhaps he will grow up.' Here, in the direction of noon are many people, but they are of evil purposes," she told him; "Women are poised aloft in a nest, and whenever any youth arrives there, he is urged to climb up, being told that if anyone reaches them, he may marry them. But before they reach the goal, the youths fall down, falling to their death. Then those people eat them. This is no good thing. And here, in the east, yonder is a great town; the people there run races, and when anyone is outrun, he is destroyed, for these people, too, eat each other. That is why, 'Would that I might bring him up!' was my thought concerning you. It will be no light thing for you to go anywhere," she told her brother.

"Now then, sister, tomorrow I shall go forth," he told her.

The woman wept, for she hated her brother's going forth, thinking, "Perhaps he will be destroyed."

So, when night came, she went to bed. Early she arose to cook for her brother's departure. When the youth had eaten, he made himself ready and rose to his feet, hanging his little flute round his neck, placing it to hang on his back.

"Now then, sister, whenever anyone is to name me, 'Flute-Bearer' I shall be called," said the youth, as he stepped out of the lodge and went forth.

He set out in the direction of noon, toward where the women were poised aloft in the nest, for them he was going to see. When he had slept twice, he reached the town.

When he arrived, "Yohoho, Flute-Bearer has come!" was said of him.

Then he was called to one lodge. Those people rejoiced in the thought, "Now we shall eat!"

In that place dwelt Wisahketchahk, having adopted the chief as his father and those women as his sisters. And so, at night, Wisahketchahk came there. When he entered the lodge, there sat the youth.

"Flute-Bearer, it would seem that you have come to take my younger sisters to wife," he said to him.

"No!" the other answered him.

"Oh, yes! Tomorrow you will come to take my sisters to wife. If you reach them, you shall have them to wife, my sisters who are poised aloft in the nest," he told him.

"Oh, very well," the other answered him.

So Wisahketchahk went home.

"Why, father, it seems that Flute-Bearer has come to take wives," he said to him.

"Oh, yes!" said the other.

The next day came. In the morning, when his people had eaten, Wisahketchahk went out of the lodge.

"Now, now, ye men, come forth, come forth! Come look at Flute-Bearer, who is going to take wives!" he cried, as he went out.

Then all the people came and sat in a circle round where that tree stood upright in the ground. When they had seated themselves, there came Flute-Bearer. When he looked at them, they were quite low with their nest, but as he came nearer, at once they began to rise. And when he was about to reach them in their nest, they would beat the tree; it would grow longer again. Then he used his arrows, climbing by their means. Whenever he had used them up, he would beat his quiver, and it would be full of arrows.

Then, as he went climbing on and on, and Wisahketchahk was always looking up, the latter cried, "Watch for him, all of you, for Flute-Bearer to come tumbling!"

At last, when four times the tree had lengthened, he no longer saw the earth. Then he took a wisp of fur and blew on it.

"There to the nest let me be blown, there where those women are!" he said.

Truly, he was blown to that place.

"And so now you will marry us!" said the women to him.

"Indeed, yes!"

He took hold of the younger one and threw her down.

Wisahketchahk was all the while on the alert, and there suddenly he saw her coming, and whooped, "Hoyoyoyoyo! Here comes Flute-Bearer, tumbling!"

Right in front of Wisahketchahk, as he sat, she fell to the ground. Why, it was one of his sisters! . . . .

"Fie!" cried Wisahketchahk.

He threw down the other one as well. When Wisahketchahk saw her coming, again he whooped and cried, "Here comes Flute-Bearer, tumbling!" but when she hit the ground, in no seemly way, he saw his sister. He was ashamed. Then Flute-Bearer breathed upon the hair of fur.

"Far yonder let me be blown to earth!" he said.

Then Wisahketchahk said, "Heavens! Truly, he has given me a shock, throwing my sisters in a way to cause me shame!" he said of him; "Whereto in all the extent of the earth will you flee? I shall go out to kill you, Flute-Bearer! You have put me to shame!"

Then he made search, running round about, like this, looking for where the other should come to earth. Presently he found the place from which the other apparently had started to flee. Then he tracked him.

"Not by any chance shall I lose track of you, I who created the earth!" he called to him, as he pursued the trace of him.

Then, in time, he was about to overtake him.

Then, when Wisahketchahk came noisily near, "Now, let there be an old arrow here!" said Flute-Bearer, taking off his moccasins, and saying, "Now, my moccasins, flee!"

"Yoho!" cried Wisahketchahk, when he saw that arrow; "Ho, it is you, Flute-Bearer!" he said to the arrow, as he examined it; "Yah, but there go his tracks yon way! No, when my grandfathers fought here of yore, they must have missed a shot with this arrow!" he said.

So he threw it aside, and went on with his chase. As soon as he was over the hill, Flute-Bearer ran off in some other direction. Wisahketchahk, as soon as he had got to where those moccasins had come to rest, turned about and came back.

"Oho! So this was the way Flute-Bearer disguised himself!" he cried; "You shall not again get away from me!" he told him.

When he got there on the run, there was no trace of the arrow, it was plain that he had fled!

"Filthy scab!" cried Wisahketchahk, and again gave chase.

Presently, when again he was about to overtake him, and was close upon his heels, Flute-Bearer said, "Now, let me be a woman! . . . . ."

Truly, he took that form. When he came over the hill, there was a woman walking about.

"This time you shall not deceive me! It is you, Flute-Bearer! Now I shall club you!"

That woman wept.

"So it seems that this one, too, will not take pity on me! That one who ran by here, even though I said to him, 'Do not leave me! I will marry you, if you like!' yet he gave me no heed! A long time ago, when we went to dig tubers, I got lost," said the woman; "Even though I said this to him, he said to me, 'No, Wisahketchahk is too hot in pursuit of me, to kill me!' " Thus spoke the woman.

"Oh, no! You shall not deceive me! This is you, Flute-Bearer!" he told him.

"Do take pity on me! Do not leave me! If you like, I will marry you!" he said to Wisahketchahk.

* * * * * * * * * * * * * * * * * *

he said to him; "Wait here for me; I am going off to kill Flute-Bearer; the fact is, he has greatly shamed me by throwing down my sisters. Do not go off anywhere!" he told him.

"Very well! But come soon," he answered him.

"Yes, wait here for me, my wife!" he said to him.

Then, when he ran off, as soon as he was round a bend, the other fled. Again, when he had gone a long ways, there lay only the other's moccasins.

"Dear me! This is the way Flute-Bearer always gets me angry! You shall not deceive me this time! Wherever I see you, I will strike you down! I will kill you! You made me furious with shame, when you threw my sisters down to me in unseemly wise!" he cried to him.

When he came there on the run, where was that woman! Plainly, the other had fled.

"Hoho! This is the way Flute-Bearer always gets me angry! This time you shall not escape me! Now I have done enough running, and letting you fool me to the uttermost rage, thinking you a woman!"

Presently, as he ran on and on, again he was close upon his heels.

"Now!" he said, taking up some sticks and laying them in the shape of a wooden house; "Now, let there be an old wooden house!" he said.

Then he took two saplings and breathed upon each.

"Now, you, you are to be women, half-breed women! And I shall be an old man, a half-breed! I shall be very old!" he said.

Truly, he turned into an old man. They were inside the house. Presently Wisahketchahk came running over the hill. He saw a little wooden house.

"Ha, I shall club you all the more surely! This is but your disguise, Flute-Bearer!" he called to him.

When he came a-running, out from the house came the young women.

"You have angered me by putting me to shame! Now I shall kill you at once, Flute-Bearer!" he said to them.

"Gracious, and so this one, too, will pay no heed to us! 'If anyone comes to where we are, do you marry him,' our father told us, for he is so very old, he cannot care for us, though he is with us. One man who ran by here said, 'Wisahketchahk is too hot on my trail; he wants to kill me.' So do you at least hear us with pity. If you like, the two of us will marry you!" they told him.

"Really, I do fancy taking half-breed women for wives! And I am very tired. Suppose I do stop here till tomorrow. Tomorrow I shall go kill him. When I have killed him, then I shall come here and provide for you," he told them.

"But do come in!" they said to him.

When he went in, who was that? An old man was sitting there.

"Dear me, your father is really to be pitied!"

"Yes, indeed."

"I shall take care of you both for him, in whatever way your father desires," he told them. * * * * * * * * * * *

Thus spoke Flute-Bearer to a raven: "Perch here on the poplar! 'Get up, Wisahketchahk!' do you say to him; 'Don't forget you were giving chase!' do you say to him; ' "But now he has got me angry, chasing me!" he says to you,' do you say to him: ' "Wherever he overtakes me, there I shall kill him!" he says to you,' do you say to him."

With that he made off.

"Let this little wooden house disappear!" he said, and off he went.

Presently there the raven gave its call. It awakened Wisahketchahk. When he opened his eyes, what was this? He had been sleeping out of doors! At either side of him lay a stick of wood; it was these he had taken for women.

"Filthy brute! How many times has he cheated me!" Wisahketchahk said of him.

Then the raven called: "Ho, Wisahketchahk! 'He has got me angry now!' says Flute-Bearer to you; 'Wherever he overtakes me now, I shall kill him!' is what Flute-Bearer says to you," it told him.

"Yoho!" said Wisahketchahk; "The fellow might be telling the truth!" said Wisahketchahk; "The fact is, he has fooled me three times now. Never has anyone fooled me as much as that!" he said; "Well, I will leave him alone! I will go home," he said; "So now you have got away with your life, Flute-Bearer!" said Wisahketchahk.

That is the end of the sacred story.

(21) Sun-Child

Coming-Day

kā-kīsikāw-pīhtukäw.

kītahtawä, ayīsiyiniwak äh-pimipitsitsik, iskwäwak paskäwak, nānitaw nikutwāsik iskwäwak, ä-wīh-mōnahikätsik mistaskusīmina. äkutah päyak miyusiw iskwäw ; namuy āwiya unāpäma ōhtāwiya ukāwiya pimātisiyiwa. äkusi wītsihiwäw äyaku. äkwah tahki pimuhtäwak, äh-mōnahikätsik.

kītahtawäh ä-pasāhtsāyik, äkutah awa kā-miyusit iskwäw mihtsät miskam mistaskusīminah, äh-mōnahahk. piyisk usām kinwäs ayāw. namuya kiskäyihtam äh-nakatiht. iyikuhk äh-kiskäyihtahk, āsay pahkisimōw. äkwa äh-sipwähtät, nam āwiya uwītsäwākana. äkus īsi sipwähtäw. namuya kiskäyihtam tāntäh äy-ituhtäyit uwītsäwākana.

kītahtawäh uskinīkiwa ka-pätsāstamuhtäyit. nīpawiw. utihtik.

" tānähk ōma ? " itik.

miyusiyiwa ōh ōskinīkiwa.

" äh-wanisiniyān, " itaw ; " niwītsäwākanak äh-nakasitsik, " itäw.

" kah ! kīspin kintawäyihtän ta-kīwähtahitān, ka-kīwähtahitin. "

" äha'. namuya māka nikwayask[1] nika-kīh-ituhtahisun, " itwäw aw īskwäw.

namuya ayisk kwayask isi-nisituhtawäw, " nīkināhk ä-wīh-isih-kīwähtahit, " äh-itäyihtahk ; māka namuya : ōhōw uskinīkiwah wīkiwāyihk ä-wīh-ituhtahikut.

äkusi kīwähtahik, äh-pa-pmuhtätsik. piyisk äh-tipiskāyik, mistah ähtipiskāyik, kītahtawäh kā-wāpahtahk mīkiwāhp äh-misāyik. äkuyikuhk kiskäyihtam namuya wīkiwāhk äh-ituhtät aw īskwäw. äkusi takuhtäwak.

äh-pīhtukät, " ähähähähä ! " k-ätwäyit pīsim ōhtāwiya ä-kisäyiniwiyit ; " tsäskwah, nikusis ! pitah nika-miyāhkasikān, " itwäyiwa.

äh-miyāhkasikät, " hāw, äkwah nistim ta-pīhtukäw, " itwäyiwa.

pīhtukäw aw īskwäw. pōt ōhi kīh-wāpistikwanäyiwa kisäyiniwa ähapiyit, kā-wāpahtahk wäskwāhtämihk nanātuhk käkway äh-astäyikih, ayōwinisah, mīnah uspwākanak, asinīw-uspwakanak, mina wiyākanihk äh-astäyikih mīnisah äh-kīsitäyik.

---

[1] The speaker starts to compound *kwayask:* "properly" with the following verb. This is contrary to habit; he corrects himself by starting the verb all over again. I have often observed the same thing in Menomini, where a similar "incorporation" is permitted but awkward.

äkusi, " ähähäy ! " itwäw awa kisäyiniw ; " āyiman, nikusis, kā-päsiwat nistim ! " itwäyiwa ; " kīkway kiy-āsamāyahk ? pikuh mīnisah, " itwäyiwa.

äkwa mīnisah asamik. äh-kīsi-mītsit, kawisimōwak.

äh-mäkwā-nipāt, äh-waskawiyit[1] *unāpäma, āsay kā-pähtahk, " nikusä, waniskā ! asāy wīh-kīsikāw ! kipamihtā kīsikāw ! " k-ätwäyit kisäyiniwa.*

isi-waniskāyiwa. wīstah waniskāw, mīna mīnisāpuy äh-utinamiyit, äh-asamikutsik ōhi kisäyiniwa. kaskihtäwäkin utinamiyiwa, äkwah mihkwäkin iyikuhk ka-täpipayiyik iskwäw t-ōtāsit ; äkwah papakiwayānäkin manipitamiyiwa.

" hā, nikusis, äyakunih ani nistim ta-kaskwātamāsōw,[2] *" itäw.*

äkusih äh-kīsi-mītsisutsik, ati-wayawīw awa uskinīkiw. äkwah awa aw īskwäw usīhtāw uskutākay, kapä-kīsik äh-kaskikwāsut. mwähtsi äh-pahkisimuyit, kīsikwāsōw, kā-pä-pīhtukäyit uwīkimākana. yāh, miywäyihtam äh-pīhtukäyit.

äkusi utah ayāw, nayästaw mīnisah äh-mītsitsik. tāpwä kīkisäpā māna äh-sipwähtäyit unāpäma, kā-kapä-kīsik namuya äh-takusiniyit, äyikuhk pähkisimuyiki, äh-pihtukäyit. äkusi namuya kiskäyihtam käkwayah ōhi unāpäma mīn ōhi usisah. mistahi māna kaskäyihtam, äkā wīhkāts kutakah awiya äh-wāpamāt.

kītahtawäh, äh-apit, äh-tipiskāk, " nikusis, kiyīsikākih ta-kīh-papāmuhtäw nistim. miyāmay kaskäyihtam, " itäw ukusisah.

" äha' , " itwäwiwa.

" ayisk kiyāna mīna kikīh-isih-pakitinikunaw kā-tipäyihtahk kahkiyaw käkway, ta-pamihtāyan askiy. niya äh-kīh-āyimäyihtamān ta-pamihtāyān, ' kiyām wiya äy-usk-āyiwit t-ātuskawäw, ' kā-kīh-itäyimitān, ' kōhtāwīnaw ksä-manitōw, ' " k-ätwāyit ukusisah.

" hāw, niwīkimākan, äkā äpiyāni, kika-papāmuhtān ōtah. ōma mīna wāsakām ay-ihtakunwa mistaskusīmina, " itwäyiwa.

tāpwä äkusi tōtam ; kā-sipwähtäyitsi uwīkimākana, äkusi wīstah äh-papāmuhtät, äh-mōnahahk mistaskusīminah. piyätätsih, wätākusiniyikih, kāh-pāh-pīhtunahkih, itäh äh-apiyit usisah, äkutä äh-pakitinahk. utinam māna awa kisäyiniw, äh-nanāskumut.

" kākikä ntakāwätä ōmatōwahk, usām wāh-wīhkāts äh-asamikawiyān, " itwäyiwa.

iyikuhk pähkisimuyiki, äh-pīhtukäyit unāpäma, äkusi äh-asamāt, mistaskusīmina mīna mīnisāpuy äh-mītsitsik, nama käkway pītus äh-mītsitsik.

kītahtawä täpiskāyiki, " hā, nikusis, miyāhkasikä ! " äh-itwäyit, kā-pä-yōhtänamuht, māna mihkwäkin, āskaw kaskitäwäkin, āskaw papakiwayān, kikih-mīnisāpuya, äh-pīhtukätisinamuht, äkus äh-utinahk aw uskinīkiw.

kītahtawä kiskäyihtam aw īskwäw awāsisah ä-wīh-ayāwät.

" hāw, äkāya wīhkāts äkwah papāmuhtä ; māskōts kwayask wīh-wāpamāyahkuh awa awāsis, " itik uwīkimākanah.

tāpwä päyakwanuhk äkwah ayāw ; namuy äkwah mōnahikäw aw īskwäw ; ayisk kitahamāk uwīkimākana. tāpwä piyisk nōhtä-wāpamäw utsawāsimisah, äh-āhkusit, äkwah ä-wīh-wāpamāt utsawāsimisah. äh-tipiskāyik, kāh-wāpamätsik, uwīkimākana äh-pamihikut. pōt ōhi nāpäsisah.

---

[1] One should expect "when he budged" to follow the father's call.

[2] For *kaskikwātamāsōw*.

äkusi miyupayiw. äkwah, ā, mitunih ayōwinisah mihtsät ayāwak ; ayis namuya kōtaw-āpatsihtāw aw īskwäw, ōhi utsawāsimisah äw-isi-pamihāt ; ayisk wäyōtisiw awa kisäyiniw. mistahi miywäyihtam awa kisäyiniw äh-uyōsisimit, äwaku pāskats äh-kanawäyimāt ōsisima, iyikuhk äh-miywäyihtahk äh-uyōsisimit, āskaw piku äh-kanawäyimāt aw īskwäw utsawāsimisah, äh-papāmuhtät, äh-papāmuhtahāt, äh-kaskäyihtahk māna aw īskwäw, äkā wīhkāts kutakah awiyah äh-wāpamāt.

kītahtawä äkwah äh-misikitiyit ukusisah, äkwah äh-papāmuhtsäsiyit, kītahtawä māka mīna kīksäpā ä-sipwähtäyit unāpäma, wīstah sipwähtäw, kuntah äh-papāh-sā-sākäwät. kītahtawä kā-wāpahtahk mīkiwāhpis. ituhtäw.

äh-takuhtät, " ta-tawāw, nōsisimis ! " k-ätwäyit nōtukäsiwa. pīhtukäw.

" ääāy, nōhkum ätsik āwa itah äh-ay-ayāt, kā-kaskäyihtamān māna ! " itäw ; " kayās kīh-kiskäyimitān, ōtah äh-wīkiyin, kah-päh-kāh-kiyōkātin, nōhkō, iyikuhk kā-kaskäyihtamān māna, " itäw.

" hääy, nōsisä, kikiskäyihtän tsī ōm ītah k-āyāyan ? "

" nama wiya, " itäw.

" ōtäh ōma nīhtaskamik ä-kīh-uhtuhtäyan, kikiskäyimā tsī āna kā-wīkimat ! " itik.

" namuya, " itäw.

" k-āyisiyinīwiyin, ' pīsim, ' k-ätwäyin, äkutōwahk ana. äyakw anim ōhtsi kā-kapä-kīsik äkā k-ōh-apit ; äh-pamihtät askiy, ōtäh nihtsāyihk äh-kīsikāstäskamawāt ayisiyiniwah. äwakunik aniki kitōtämak kītahtawä māna ka-pīhtukätisinahkik mīnisāpuyah äkwah ayōwinisah, äh-miyihtsik kiwīkimākan, " k-ätikut.

" hääy, nōhkō, kah-kīh-tsi-pihkuhin ? "

" yā, nōsisä, wiya miskaman mustusu-mäy sisunä sakāhk äh-astäk, kīspin miskaman, kah-kīh-pihkuhitin. äkutah anima äh-pakunäyāk ōma kīsik, äkutah anima äh-uhtsi-pihkuhut māna kiwīkimākan, " itik ; " nitunah, " itik.

äkusi wayawīw, äh-ntunahk. namuya kinwäs nōtsihtāw, äh-miskahk. nitawāpamäw ōhkuma.

" nōhkō, nimiskän ! " itik awa nōtukāsiw ōsisima.

" äkus āni, nōsisä, kika-pihkuhun. nah ōma, " itäw, upīsākanāpīm, " nōsisä, mistikuhk tahkupitamōhkan. äkwah kik-ōsīhtān watsistwan, itah t-āpiyäk kikusis, " itik ; " itāp anih nōhtäpayikih nipīsākanāpīm, ta-sīpäkipayiw, " itik ōhkuma ; " äkwah nätä kitaskiy utihtamani, k-āpihkunän anim itah kā-wīh-pōsiyin. ' nōhkō, äwakwä kipīsākanāpīm ! ' kik-ätwān. ka-pä-uhpiwäpinän. itāp anih ta-pahkihtin ōtä tahkuhts, " itik.

äkusi sipwähtäw, äkwah äh-ntawih-usīhtāt watsistwan.

āsay kiskäyihtam awa pīsim ä-wīh-sipwähtäyit ōwīkimākana ; āsay pakwātam. māka nam äskwah kīsi-tätipäwäw ōm āskiy.

äkwah awa iskwäw äh-kīsihtāt, äh-takupitahk mistikuhk, äh-pakitāpä-kinisut, āta äh-nōhtäpayiyik, tahkih sīpäkipayiyiw pīsākanāpiy.

äkuyikuhk äh-kīsi-tätipäwät awa pīsim. ituhtäw itah k-ōh-pinasiwäyit uwīkimākana. utinäw asiniyah.

" hāw, täpiyāhk niwīh-pa-pāhpisihāw niwīkimākan ! " itäw, äkutah ä-nahikāpawit ōma kā-pakunäyāyik ; " hāw, ustikwānihk ta-pahkisiniyiwa ōh āsiniya niwīkimākan ! namuya nika-pistahwāw pīsimōwāsis nikusis ! " itwäw äsah, äh-pakitināt asiniya.

äkus īsi kīwäw, äh-pīhtukät.

" *nikusis, kimiskawāw tsī, itäh äh-ituhtät nistim?* "

" *äha', nikīh-mātāhwāw itäh äh-ituhtät, äh-kīwät,* " *itäw.*

" *kah! matwān tsī kwayask ta-päsiwäw nōsisima!* " *itäw.*

" *häha'!* "

äh-kīkisäpāyāyik, mwähtsih äkwah ä-wīh-pōnäsihk[1] *aw iskwäw, äkuyikuhk k-ātimikut ōh āsiniya. pahkisiniyiwa ustikwānihk. paskipayiyiw pīsākanāpiy; pahkisin muhtsihk; nipahisin.*

äkusi äkutah pa-pimisin. äkwah awa awāsis äkutah ay-ayāw, äh-nāh-nōnihtahisut,[2] *āta äh-nipiyit ukāwiya. namuya kiskäyihtam äh-nipiyit ukāwiya, pisisik äh-ma-mätawät äkutah, itah ukāwiya ä-pimisiniyit. piyisk kinwäsk äkutah ayāw. piyisk atih-sīkōnäsiniyiwa ukāwiya.*

kītahtawä äh-papāmi-ma-mätawät, kā-miskahk itah äh-ayāt awa päyak nōtukäsiw, kā-wāpahtahk ukistikānisiyiwa, nanātuhk käkwayah äh-kistsikäsiyit. namuya kiskäyihtam käkwayah ōhi awa äwäsis, äkutah māna äh-ma-mätawät, ōhi kistsikānisah äh-māh-manipitahk, äh-mätawākät, namuya äh-mītsit, kuntah äh-mätawākät. ätuhtätsih ukāwiya, äkuyikuhk māna awa nōtukäsiw utihtam ukistsikānisah, kunta māna kā-pimastäyikih, äh-māh-manipitamiyit awāsisah, kā-mātāhāt māna.

" *pitan āwa wāpamak!* " *itäyihtam, äh-wawiyatäyimāt, äh-apisīsisiyit pakahkam, äh-itäyihtahk.*

kītahtawä äkwah askamawäw, kītahtawä kā-pāpahtāyit awāsisah. mistahi wawiyatäyimäw, äh-kitimākinawāt. äh-pāpahtāyit, äh-utihtamiyit ukistsikānisah, mannakisk māh-manipitamiyiwa, äh-atiwäpinamiyit. ka-kitāpamäw, äh-wawiyatäyimāt. piyisk kisiwāk päyayāyiwa, ōtah äh-pätakuhtäyit, ōhi äh-māh-manipitamiyit. mōskīstawäw awa nōtukäsiw. iyikuhk äh-kiskäyimikut, ä-wīh-tapasiyit, āsay nawatinäw, äh-mamawimuyit äh-kustikut.

" *nōsisimis, nōsisimis!* " *äh-itāt, äh-uy-utsämāt,* " *tāntāh ōmah äh-uhtuhtäyin?* " *itäw.*

" *ōtah kisiwāk,* " *itik.*

" *nōsisimis, nama wiya kikisiwāhin, ōhi nikistsikānisah kā-misi-wanātsihtāyin. nawats nimiywäyihtän ä-miskātān,* " *itäw.*

äkusi äh-pakitināt; sipwäpahtāyiwa. äkwah ay-askōwäw. pōtih kā-wāpahtahk itah äh-pimisiniyit awiya. äkutah takuhtäyiwa.

" *käkway awa, nōsisä?* " *itäw;* " *äwaku tsī awa 'nikāwiy' k-ät-wäyan?* "

" *häha'! kutak māk āwiyak namuy āwiyak; äwakw āwa piku äh-nīsiyāhk nikāwiy,* " *itäw.*

" *hääy, nōsisimis, mistah ätsik ōma äh-kitimākisiyin, nōsisä! ka-kīwähtahitin. kik-āyātin. namuy āwa äh-pimātisit kikāwiy, ayis āwa ä-kīh-nipit. misawāts piyisk ōtah ka-misi-wanātisin, äkā nakatatsih. aspin k-āskīwik nama wīhkāts äkus īspayiw, äkā äh-pimātisit ta-kīh-wīts-āyāmiht,* " *itäw;* " *ka-kīwähtahitin,* " *itäw.*

" *āha'!* "

---

[1] Plainly so heard; perhaps *pōnäsin* is a different word from the transparent *pōnisin*, formed with initial *pōn-*: "cease," final *-sin*: "come down, fall," and connective *-i-*.

[2] Informant first said *äh-na-nāh-nōhisut*, where the *-na-* is a slip of the tongue; in correcting this he substituted the longer derivative verb in the text.

tāpwä kiwä-wītsäwäw ōsisima. takuhtahäw wīkihk. hay, kitimākäyimäw ; kitimākinawäw, äh-asamāt. miywäyihtam awa nāpäsis, äkwah äh-wītsäwāt nōtukäsiwa. äkusi äkwa pōnäyimäw ukāwiya.

kītahtawäh itah äh-ay-ayātsik ōhkuma, " nōsisä, tahk ōma māna nipapāmuhtān. kāya wīhkāts nānitaw ituhtä. kanawäyihtah māna kīkinaw, āskaw kit-ätuhtäyin nikistikānisihk, " itäw ōsisima.

tāpwä kītahtawä äh-kīsikāyik, " nōsisä, niwīh-papāmuhtān, " itäw, " äh-ntunamān māna ta-mītsiyān, " itäw, " mīna āskaw äh-ituhtäyān ōtä uskinīkiwak äh-wīkitsik wāhyawäs, " itik.

äkusi mān ä-sipwähtäyit, äkwah māna wiya äkutah äh-kīskwät, āskaw ukstikānisiyihk äh-ituhtät, kāh-ituhtätsi kuntah äh-māh-manipitahk māna ukistsikānisiyiwa.

wätākusiki, täkusihki awa nōtukäsiw, " nōsisä, kikīh-ituhtān tsī nikistsikānisihk ? " " äha' , " ätikutsih, äkus äh-ituhtät, kunta māna kā-pimastäyikih ukistsikānisah, äh-māh-manipitamiyit.

" nōsisimis tāpwä ä-kākäpātisit ! " itwä māna awa nōtukäsiw, äh-pāhpit māna, äh-mōskinahk, äh-kīwähtatät. piyīhtukätsi, k-ōtināt māna, äh-uy-utsämāt, " nōsisimis, nōsisimis ! " äh-itāt māna.

kītahtawä kā-kakwätsimāt ōhkumah, äkwah äh-misikitit.

" nōhkō, käkwayah ōhi ? " itäw, nīswayak wīhkwāhk äy-asiwatäyikih, äh-tahkupitäyikih apasōhk.

" hā, nōsisä, kunt ānihi, " itik.

namuya wīh-wīhtamawäw käkwayah ōhi k-āsiwatäyikih. māka kiskäyihtam awa pīsimōwāsis äh-waskawipayiyikih mān ōhi wīhkwayah. äkusi äkuta äh-ay-ayātsik, kītahtawäh äkwa māka mīna ä-sipwähtäyit ōhkumah, kā-kimutamawāt utsastsisimisiyiw, äy-usihtāt tāpakwānan. äh-kīsihtāt, tahtwayak äh-pīkupayiyik uwīkisiwāw, akutah äh-tāpakwät, äkwah ispimihk äh-kipahahk wīkiwāw. äkwah päyak ōma wīhkway kā-pōskusahk, kuntah kā-sākaskinäyit tsahtsahkayiwah. äkutōwahk äs ōhi k-āsiwasuyt. kunt ä-sākōwät, äh-nōtsihāt, hātah kā-wīh-wayawīhāyit, kahkiyaw tāpakwātäw. mästsihäw, kuntah äh-tatāhpit, äkwah äh-mätawākät äyakunih. iyikuhk, " ta-takuhtäw, " äh-itäyimāt ōhkumah, äkwah päyakwayak asahäw, äh-akwanahwāt, " äkwah kä-mōwāyāhkuk, " äh-akwanahāt,[1] äh-itwät ; " äkwah kā-mōwāyāhk nōhkum, " itwäw.

iyikuhk äh-takuhtäyit, äh-utākusiniyik, äh-pīhtukäyit, ōmis ītäw : " nōhkō, äkwah ka-mītsisunānaw, " itäw.

" kīkway awa kā-wih-ayātamihit nōsisimis ? " itik.

" äyakw ānima pāskinah, nōhkō. "

äh-pāskinahk, awīn ōhi tsāhtsāhkayōwa !

mātōyiwa ōhkuma, " tāpwä nikitimahik nōsisim ! " äh-itwäyit ; " tāpwä kakäpātisiw nōsisim ! " äh-itikut.

äh-kīskwäyit äyikuhk, äkwah utinäyiwa, äh-paskupitäyit. äh-kīsihāyit, äkwah pakāsimäyiwa.

äh-kīsiswāyit, " nōsisä, kiya piku mītsisuh, " itik.

tāpwä wiya piku ma-mītsisōw. iyikuhk äh-kīsput, pōni-mōwäw. ahäyiwa.

---

[1] If this is correctly recorded, informant was hesitating between two words, *akwanahäw* (for older *-ahyäw*) : "he places him covering" and *akwanahwäw* : "he covers him with something, or by tool." The latter is attested by the occurrence of the corresponding form with inanimate object, *akwanaham*, and of other derivatives; not so the former, whose inanimate would end in *-astäw*.

" wap kīhtwām mīna ka-mōwāwak, " itik.

äkus äh-ay-ayātsik mīn äkutah, tahtu-kīsikāw ä-sipwähtäyit ōhkumah, iyikuh mīna äh-kitamwāt ōhih tsahtsahkayōwa, āsay mīna tāpakwäw. äkwah mīna ispimihk äh-kipahahk wīkiwāw, āsay mīna ōma wīhkway pōskusam, kuntah kā-kitōyit ōmītsaskusīsah, kunta māna kā-sākōwāt, äh-nōtsihāt. tahtuh kā-wīh-wayawiyāmutsik, tāpakwātäw. mästsihäw māka mīna. āsay mīna päyakwanuhk asahäw, äh-akwanahwāt. äkuyikuhk kā-takuhtäyit ōhkumah.

ōmis ītäw : " nōhkō, äkwa mīna ka-mītsisunānaw, " itäw.

" kīkway awa kā-wīh-atamihit nōsisim ? " itäw awa nōtukäsiw.

" äyakw ānima pāskinah, " itäw ōhkuma.

äh-pāskinahk, sämāk äkwa mātuyiwa.

" hā, nōhkō, kiyām api ! kunta māna kimātun ! " itäw.

äh-kīskuwäyit, ōmis ītik : " nōsisä, tapwä mistahi kikakäpätisin. äh-kitimākisiyin kōh-kitimākäyimitih, äkwah kā-mästsihatsik nitawāsimisak ! ntawāsimisak ōki, nōsisä. sipwähtä. ntsawāts piyisk nāntaw ka-kīh-tōtātin. kikisiwāhin, äkwah äh-āta-kitimākäyimitān, iyikuhk kā-kīsināt-sihiyin, nikistsikānisah mīna mistah ä-misi-wanātsihtäyin ; äkwah mīna nisākihāhtayak nitawāsimisak, kā-mästsihatsik. niyā, sipwähtä ! kimanā-kitimahitin, äh-kitimākisiyin, " itik.

äkusi pasikōw, äh-wayawīt, ä-sipwähtät. kuntah pikw ītä isi sipwäh-täw. itah äh-tipiskāyik, kuntah kawisimōw. äh-wāpaniyik, sipwähtäw. äh-āpihtā-kīsikāyik, kāh-wāpahtahk mīkiwāhp, itah mituni äh-ay-āhkwat-sāwahkāsiyik. äkutah ituhtäw. pōt ōma kī-masinahikātäyiw mīkiwāhp.

äh-takuhtät, " hāhā, tawāw, tawāw, pīsimōwāsis ! " kā-matwä-itwäyit uskinīkiwa.

äh-pīhtukät, awīn ōhi, kī-wāsakāmäpiyiwa uskinīkiwa, mituni ä-māh-miyuhuyit, usām piku pähpāsāpuwayāna äh-wiyāhtamiyit.

" ōtäh uhtsi ! " äh-itikut, namuya tāpwähtawäw.

" ōtah kiyām ! " itäw, skwāhtämihk ä-nahapit.

kītahtawä, " hayā, wäsā nama mayaw kitasamāwāw pīsimōwāsis ! miywāsinōpan äh-utihtikuyahk ! " k-ätwäyit.

" yahā, kīkway māka kī-kīh-asamayah ? "

" tsäh, kīpah ta-kīsitäk wīnāstakay nawatsīk ! kīpah ta-kīsitäw. "

tāpwä nawatsīw. kiyipah akwānamiyiwa.

" yahō, matwān tsīw uma kīsitäw ! " itwäyiwa ; " mahtih kutsih-paskähtah ! namuya pakahkam kīsitäw mātsikōtitan ! "

äyōku mīna paskähtam.

" namuya kīsitäw, " itwäw mīn äyaku, " mātsikōttān ! "

kutakah miyäw, uhpimä äh-ati-paskähtahkik. piyisk wāsakāmä-paskähtamwak ōkō uskinīkiwak.

āsa nāha nōtukäsiw pä-sipwähtäw, awa pīsimōwāsis ka-päh-nakatāt nōtukäsiwa, ä-kiskäyihtahk äh-utihtäyit utawāsimisah pīsimōwāsisah. äyukw äs āna nōtukäsiw ōhih utawāsimisah uskinīkiwa kā-mitātasiyit.

piyisk kahkiyaw ōk ōskinīkiwak paskähtamwak.

" kīsitäw ōma, " itwäwak.

" āh, äkus īsi asamihk ! " itäwak pīsimōwāsisah.

utinam mōhkumān, wāsakām äh-wāskasahk uma wīnāstakay. äh-kīsi-manisahk, sisikuts matustäwäpinam. äkus īsi wayawiyāmut, " kimäst-sihikunaw pīsimōwāsis ! " k-ätwäyit. tāpwä kahkiyaw nipahäw. sīsīk-

wäyiwa äs ōhi. mästsihäw.[1] *äkusi tapasīw.*

äkusi nāha nōtukäsiw pä-nawaswäw, pīsimōwāsisah äh-pimitisahwāt.

" *äkwah anih kikisiwahin, pīsimōwāsis, mituni kā-kitimahiyin, nitawāsimisak äkwah äh-mästsihatsik !* "

äkus īsy äkwah nawaswātik äkwah nōtukäsiwa, pikw ītä äh-itāmut. kītahtawä kisiwāk äkwah äh-askōkut, äkwah säkihik.

umis ītwäw : " *nōhtāh, kisiwāk pimuhtä ! niwīh-nipahik sīsīkwäw nōtukäsiw !* " *itäw.*

tāpwä tsapasis pimuhtäyiwa ōhtāwiya pīsimwa. mistahi kisitäyiw, piyisk ä-wīh-kīsisut awa nōtukäsiw. pōyōw.

" *äkus ānih ä-pmātisiyin, pīsimōwāsis ! kipōnihitin,* " *itik ;* " *māka äkutah uhtsi äkā wiya, äkāya wīhkāts mustāhtak nahapih !* " *itäw awa nōtukäsiw pīsimōwāsisah.*

tāpwä nawats ispimihk pimuhtäyiwa ōhtāwiya. kīwäw awa nōtukäsiw. äkwah awa pīsimōwāsis ä-pimuhtät, miskawäw asiniya äh-napakāpiskisiyit. utinäw äyakuni, itah ä-wīh-nahapit, äkutah äh-ahāt, äh-anāskasut ōh āsiniyah. tahkih äkusi tōtam, mīna ä-wīh-nipāt, äh-anāskasut asiniya, wiyāpaniyiki, säpwähtätsi, äh-pimiwihāt asiniya.

kītahtawä ōma äh-papāmātsihut, kītahtawä kā-wāpahtahk ōtänaw. äkutah takusin. ispatināhk nīpawiw, äh-kitāpahtahk ōhi mīkiwāhpah.

" *yahō, pīsimōwāsis takusin !* " *itwäwān.*

āsay päyak päy-ituhtäyiwa, äh-pä-ntumikut.

" *hā, pīsimōwāsis, kiwīh-päy-ituhtān !* "

" *äha' hä .* "

wītsäwäw.

äh-pīhtukät mīkiwāhpihk, " *nhā, ta-tawāw !* " *itāw.*

äh-nahapit, " *hā, asamihk kiyipa ! nōhtähkatätukä !* " *itāw.*

" *ähähähäy, haha, pīsimōwāsis ! āyiman ani itah kā-takuhtäyin pisisik äh-mätawähk, äh-manitōwi-mätawähk. äkusi niyanān tahkih ä-sākōtsihikawiyāhk. āsay ōma kīsäyihtamōtukä, ä-wih-mawinähusk pīwāpisku-mustus.*[2] *āyimisiw ani ; nama wīhkāts nisākōtsihānān. äkusi āta sākwäyimuyāhkuh, ōhtsitaw nika-misi-wanātsihikunān,* " *itwäyiwa.*

" *namuya äh-papā-mätawäyān,* " *itäw.*

" *māskōts uhtsitaw ka-mawinähukwak. awiya mastaw kā-takusiniyit, sämāk mawinähwäwak,* " *itäw ;* " *māka utākusin anuhts. wāpahki māskōts ka-mawinähukwak,* " *itäw.*

äkusi äkwah asamäw. piyisk tipiskāyiw. äyukō kīksäpä, ä-kihmītsisutsik, sāsay kā-täpwäwiht.

" *hahāw hahāw hahāw ! wawäyīk ! päh-ntawāpahkäk ! wīh-mätawāniwiw ! äh-papā-mätawät, äh-itwähk, kā-takuhtät utākusihk pīsimōwäwāsis, wīh-mätawäw pīwāpisku-maskwa ! pä-wiyawīk !* "

āsay pä-tuhtäyiwa.

---

[1] Characteristic obscure passage of the type not due to extraneous difficulties of dictation or recording. One or more causes may be at work, such as laziness, fatigue, impatience at the slow pace of dictation, obstructive attitude toward the recorder, desire to withhold information from the foreigner, actual tabu, or traditional omission. Probably the last-named was here operative; informant had heard the story told in this way and would not add to it. For he could not be induced to dictate the explanation which he voluntarily gave: The rattlesnake-youths have left each a poison-fang in the edge of the maw, to kill Sun-Child when he eats. By throwing their fangs into the fire he kills the rattlesnakes.

[2] Error; the beast is a bear, below.

" hāw, pīsimōwāsis, kiwīh-wawäyīn, pīwāpisku-maskwa ä-wīh-mawinähusk."

äkusi, " hāw, äyiwähk wawäyī. misawāts āta äkā tāpwähtamani, uhtsitaw ka-kakwä-misi-wanātsihik," itik ōhi wīkiyihk kā-pīhtukät, ōm ītah k-āpit.

" äha'. namuya nōh-papā-mätawān," itwäw; " äyiwähk māka," itwäw.

äkus äh-wawäyīt. sāsay itah ä-tahtakwahtsāsiyik, äkutah äy-ituhtäyit.

" hā, kiyipa pä-wayawī!" itäw.

äkusi wayawīw, äh-ituhtät. sāsay wīhkwäkāpawiyiwa.

äh-takuhtät, " haw, pīsimōwāsis, kipapā-mätawān, kitikawin. kiya māka nīkān ka-pimutän."

" namuya! kiyawāw nīkān! äka mā niya wäh-mätawäyān."

" ää'," itwäw awa wākayōs.

āsay ōmis ītäyihtam: " hāw, nōhtā, kisiwāk uhtsih kanawäyimin!" itwäw, ōmisi äh-itäyihtah: " māskōts kisāstäkih, ta-nayawapit," äh-itäyihimāt ōhi wākayōsa.

tāpwä ati-kisitäyiw, äh-ati-kisāstäyik.

" haw, nätä nika-päw-uhtuhtān. näwāw ka-wāyōnistātn; mwähtsi näwāw äkutah nka-pimakutsinin," ä-wih-utihtinikut, ä-wih-kakwä-nipahikut.

māka kisitäyiw. mistahih ati-sipwähtäw awa wākayōs, äkutä äy-uhtsipä-sipwähtät, äh-pä-nātät pīsimōwāsisah. tāpiskōts äh-yōskahtsāyik, äh-pä-pimuhtäyit, äyikuhk äh-kutāwahtsinamiyit. kisiwāk äy-ihtāyit, wayōniyiwa. mīna äkutäh uhtsi pä-sipwähtäyiwa. ayiwākäs äkwah iskuskiwäyiwa. mīna kisiwāk äy-ihtāyit, wayōniyiwa. āsay mīna pä-sipwähtäyiwa, tahk āyiwāk äy-iskuskiwäyit. käyāpits wayōniyiwa äkwah, äkutah äkwah ka-kakwä-nipahikut. māka sāsay mistahi nayawapiyiwa. ispih kisiwāk äkwah äh-ayāyit, pisisik pīwāpisk isinākusiyiwa.

kuntah ä-sākōwäwiht, " äkwah miyāmay wi-pä-kwaskwäpayihōw!" äh-itäyihtahk, ōhih uwītsäwākanah itah kā-kīh-pīhtukät äyakuni, " āhkamäyimuh!" tahkih äh-itikut, äkwah äh-pä-kwaskwäpayihuyit, kawipayihōw. nama wāpamik. iyätah-isi-kwāskwäpayihōyit, itah kā-kīh-nīpawit, āsay itäh k-ōhtuhtäyit, äkutä āsay nīpawiw awa wākayōs,[1] äh-kwäskipayihut. pōtih kīh-nīpawiyiwa. äkus ä-mōskīstawāt. wāh-utihtātsih, äh-kawipayihuyit, namuya wāpamäw, kunta māna kā-sākōwäwiht uwītsäwākana pīsimōwāsis, äh-miywäyihtamiyit ōhi äh-mätawākätāt. piyisk wīh-nipahatāhtamiyiwa. ōki mīna ayisiyiniwak mākōhkasōwak, usām kisiwāk äh-ayāyit pīsimwa. piyisk päyakwanuhk nīpawiw awa wākayōs, ä-wīh-nipahatāhtahk. piyisk äkwah utinam wīpisisah, nähi nōtukäsiwa kā-kīh-uhpikihikut äwakuni ä-kīh-usīhtwākut. äh-tāwatsiyit awa wākayōs, ä-wīh-nipahatāhtahk, äyakuni kā-pimwāt utōniyihk; ayisk äkutah pikuh namuya pīwāpiskōwiyiwa. aspin äh-pīhtukāhāyit kähkähkwah, ä-sāpuwäyawīhāyit, utähiyiw äh-atitahkunamiyit, ka-sākōwäwiht uwītsäwākanah pīsimōwāsis.

" hāw, pīsimōwāsis, ōtäh āpihtaw-kīsikāhk isi kwahkunin. äkutä, 'äh-pīwāpiskōwit wākayōs nkitimākäyimik,' itwätsi ayisiyiniw tsäkwah kā-wih-uhpikit, ta-tāpwäw," itwäw.

" häy, isi-kawipayihō!" itäw.

äkus isi-kawipayihōyiwa.

---

[1] Slip of tongue; it is Sun-Child who stands there; so translated.

ōmis ītwäw : " niwītsäwākanitik, äkā wiya nipahihkuk k-āstwākawiyäk, " itäw ; " tahkih äkusi tōtamäku, namuya ta-kīh-uhpikiw ayisiyiniw, " itäw ; " äkusi ka-pōnihtānāwāw kā-mätawäyäk, " itäw.

" äkusi tāpwä ! " itwäyiwa uwītsäwākana.

utiyinīmiwāwa äs ōki māna ä-kīh-astwātutsik, māka ä-sākōtsihāt, k-ōh-kitahamawāt, tāpwähtāk. äkwah kustik ; namuy āwiya äkwah ta-kīh-mawinähukut, äkunih piku äh-mantōwiyit kā-sākōtsihāt. äkusi wätinah äkwah äh-ayātsik ōk āyisiyiniwak.

kītahtawä äh-sipwähtät, ispatināhk ä-nahapit, wani-kiskisiw asiniyah māna äh-anāskasut. kītahtawä kā-mōsihāt äh-kwayasitäyit ōtäh, itah k-ōh-mīsīt, kinäpikwah sīsīkwäwa, nähi kā-kīh-mästsihimāt utawāsimisiyiwa nōtukäsiwa, äyakuni äh-tōtākut. ayis, " äkäya wīhkāts mustāhtak apih ! " kīh-itik. äkwah äh-āta-kakwä-pihkuhāt, nama kīh-pihkuhäw. piyisk uwītsäwākanah utihtik. ōma äh-mākuhikut, ä-wīh-nipahikut, piyisk mihtsätiwān itah uma k-āyāt, tahkih ä-sīhkimikut ta-kakwä-nipahāt ōhi sīsīkwäwa, usām äh-miywäyimikut ōh āyisiyiniwa. tahkih ispimihk at-ītuhtäyiwa ; ōtä piyisk ustikwānihk asiwasuyiwa. äkwah ōtä äkwah wīh-kāhkīskwäw, ä-wīh-nipahikut. käkway umōhkumān ntutam. miyāw. äkwah äh-manisahk ōtah, ä-wīh-kakwä-pakunähahk ustikwān, piyisk pakunäham.

" hāw, nōhtā, nimākuhik ; niwīh-nipahik sīsīkwäw ! kisiwāk pimuhtä !" itäw ōhtāwiya.

tāpwä kisiwāk ayāyiwa. ōki ayisiyiniwak pinasiwäwak, usām mistah äh-kisisutsik. kītahtawä ka-wayawiyāhtawiyit, äh-nipayihkasōyit. äkusi pimātisiw. äkwah ōma ustikwān ōmis isi sinikunahk, iyiniwiw.

äkuyikuhk ōhtāwiya äkutah kā-nīpawiyit, " ähähähä haha ! " äh-itikut ; " ayisk kīh-kakäpātisiw kikāwiy, kā-kīh-sipwähtahisk, äkā awiyak k-ōh-kakäskimisk, kā-papā-misi-wanātahkamikisiyin, k-ōh-kakäpātisiyin. tahk āyiwākäs kik-āti-misi-wanātahkamikisin, nikusis. nitsawāts ka-kīwähtahitin. usām kikakäpātisin. tahk äkusi papā-tōtamanih, namuya ta-miywāsin. namuya äkusi nitisi-nōtsihtān, " itik.

äkus äh-kīwätsik, ispimihk wīkiyihk äh-ituhtahikut, aspin umusōma äh-wīkimāt.

äkuyikuhk äskwāk ātayōhkäwin.[1]

Once upon a time, when some people were on the trek, some women left the band, about six women, to dig wild turnips. Among them was one beautiful woman; none of her people, husband, father, or mother, was living. She went along, now, with the others. They kept on walking and digging roots.

Then presently, in a valley, this handsome woman found many wild turnips, and dug them up. In the end she stayed too long. She did not notice that she was left alone. By the time she noticed it, the sun was setting. So, when she went away from there, she had no companions. So she set out. She did not know whither her companions had gone.

Then at one time she saw a young man coming toward her. She stood still. He came to where she was.

"What is the matter?" he asked her.

This youth was handsome.

---

[1] Informant adds that Sun-Child was turned into the Morning Star.

"It is that I have lost my way," she told him; "that my companions have left me," she told him.

"Is that so! If you want me to take you home, I will take you home."

"Yes. But I shall not be able to find the way very well," she said.

For she did not understand him aright, and thought he was going to take her home to her dwelling; but no: it was to his people's home that the youth meant to take her.

So he took her home with him; they walked on and on. At last, at nightfall, when it was quite dark, she saw a large lodge. Only then did she realize that it was not to her people's dwelling that she was going. So they reached the place.

When he entered, the Sun's father, who was an old man, said, "Dear me! Wait a bit, my son! Let me first burn incense," he said.

When he had lit the incense, "There, now let my daughter-in-law come in," said he.

She entered the lodge. There she saw that white-headed was the old man who sat there, and she saw many kinds of things placed at the far end of the lodge, garments, and pipes, stone pipes, and stewed berries in the bowl.

Then, "Dear me!" said the old man; "It is no easy thing, my son, that you have brought me a daughter-in-law!" he said; "What can we give her to eat? Nothing but berries," he said.

Then she was given berries to eat. When she had eaten them, they went to bed. While she was asleep, as her husband stirred, already she heard the old man call, "My son, get up! Day is at hand! Do not forget that you take care of the day!"

At this her husband arose. She too got up, and again the old man took some berry stew and gave it them to eat. He took some black cloth, and enough red flannel to make a woman's leggings; and he tore off a length of cotton cloth.

"There, my son, even these let my daughter-in-law sew into garments for herself," he told him.

Then, when they had done eating, the young man went out. Then the woman made a dress for herself, sewing all day. Just as the sun set, she finished her sewing, and there, her husband came into the lodge. Oh, she was glad when he came in.

So she stayed there, and they ate only berries. And truly, her husband, leaving always in the morning, all day he would not arrive, but only at sunset would he come into the lodge. She did not know what manner of men were her husband and her father-in-law. She often felt very lonely, for she never saw anyone else.

Then at one time, as she sat there at nightfall, "My son, do allow my daughter-in-law to walk about during the day. Surely she must feel lonely," said the old man to his son.

"Very well," he answered.

"After all, as for you and me, we were created and set down by Him who orders all things, that you might take care of the earth. When I found too hard the task of caring for it, 'Let him, who is still young, do the work,' I thought concerning you, 'for our Father, the Great Manitou'," said he to his son.

"Well then, my wife, when I am not at home, you may walk about here. Here too, round about there are wild turnips," said he.

Then really she did so; when her husband had gone away, she too would walk about, digging wild turnips. When she brought them home in the evening, after peeling them, she would put them down where her father-in-law sat. The old man would take them up and give thanks.

"Always, you must know, I have longed for the like of these, for very seldom am I given them to eat," he would say.

At sunset, when her husband came into the lodge, she would give him food, and they would eat wild turnips and berry stew, nothing else.

Then at times, when night had come, the old man would say, "Now, my son, burn some incense!" and the door of the young man's lodge wou.d be opened, and red flannel, and sometimes black cloth, sometimes muslin, together with dishes of berry stew, would be projected into his lodge, and the young man would take them up.

In time the woman knew that she was going to have a child.

"Well, now never walk about; let us hope that we may without mishap have sight of this child," her husband told her.

Then really she stayed in one place; no longer now did that woman dig roots; for her husband had forbidden it. Really, in due time, she felt the need of having sight of her child, for she grew ill, being about to see her child. In the night they saw it, she and her husband, who was caring for her. It turned out to be a boy. Then she was well. Now, they had, oh, many clothes; for the woman did not lack whatever she would use in caring for that child of hers; for rich was that old man. The old man was very glad to have a grandchild and even tended the child himself, so glad was he to have a grandson, and the woman only now and then took care of the child, walking about, taking the child about, for she was mostly sad at heart because she never saw any other people.

Then at one time, when her son had grown larger and was already walking a bit, then at one time, when her husband, as always, had gone forth early in the morning, she too went out, mounting at random over the crests of the hills. Presently she saw a little lodge. She went there.

When she came to it, "Come in, my grandchild!" said an old woman.

She entered.

"Goodness me, and so here is my grandmother living here, and I lonesome and sad all the while!" she said to her; "Long ago, if I had known that you were living here, I should have been coming to see you, lonesome and sad as I have been all the while," she said to her.

"Dear me, grandchild, and do you know what place this is where you are?"

"No," she answered her.

"And down there on the earth below, did you know who he was whom you have married?" the other asked her.

"No," she answered her.

"That which you as a mortal call 'Sun,' even such is he. This is the very reason why all of each day he is away from home; because he is taking care of the earth, shedding in his course the bright light of day upon the mortal men below. It is they, your kinsfolk, who ever from time to time are sending into his lodge cookings of berries, and clothing, gifts which your husband and his family receive," the other told her.

"Alas, grandmother mine, will you be able to bring me back?"

"Yah, my grandchild, if you find the buffalo-dung which lies by the grove, if you find it, I shall be able to bring you back. That is where this sky is pierced, and whence your husband always makes his way," she told her; "Look for it," she told her.

And so she went out and looked for it. It did not take her long to find it. She went to see her grandmother.

"Grandmother, I have found it!" the old woman was told by her granddaughter.

"Now, grandchild, I can help you to escape. Take this," she told her, giving her her rawhide thong, "and tie it, later, to a tree. But first you will make a nest in which you and your son will sit," she told her; "And then, later, when my rawhide thong is too short, it will stretch," her grandmother told her; "Then when you reach yon earth of yours, you will untie that in which you will be riding. 'Grandmother, here is your rawhide thong!' you will say. You will fling it aloft towards this place. Then it will come falling here," she told her.

So she went away, first to make the nest.

The Sun by this time knew that his wife intended to go away; already he felt the grief of it. But he had not yet completed his circuit of this earth.

Then when the woman had made the thong and had tied it to a tree, and had let herself down by the rope, even though it proved too short, the rawhide thong each time stretched to new length.

By this time the Sun had finished his roundabout course. He went to the place from which his wife had let herself down. He took up a stone.

"Now then, I shall at least turn the joke on my wife!" he said of her, standing close to that opening; "Now then, let this stone come down upon my wife's head! Let me not by chance injure Sun-Child, my son!" he said, as he let go the stone.

Thereupon he went home and into the lodge.

"My son, have you found where my daughter-in-law has gone?"

"Yes, I have found her tracks, where she went on her homeward way," he answered him.

"Why! I wonder if really she will succeed in bringing my grandchild safely to her home!" he said to him.

"Yes!"

When early morning had come, just as the woman was about to alight from her fall, even than that stone overtook her. It came down on her head. The rawhide thong broke; she fell upon the bare ground; she was killed by her fall.

There she lay. The child stayed there, sucking from time to time at her breast, even though his mother had died. He did not know that his mother was dead, but kept playing about that place where his mother lay. For a long time, in the end, he was there. In time his mother's body began to decay where it lay.

Then at one time, as he went about at his play, he found the place where dwelt a certain little old woman, and he saw her little garden, where in a small way she raised different plants. The child did not know what they were, but merely would play round there, pulling up the little plants and playing with them, not eating them, but at purposeless play. When he had gone back to where his mother was, only then would the old woman come to her garden, and there would be her plants lying round, where the child had plucked them up, and then she would see the tracks of him.

"I wish I could get sight of this rascal!" she thought, finding him droll, seeing that surely he must be a tiny fellow.

So then she lay in wait for him. Presently the child came running. She thought him very droll, and he touched her heart. As he came running and reached her little plants, without hesitation he began to pluck them up and throw them about. She kept observing him, and found him lovably droll. At last he had come quite near, walking closer, as he kept uprooting the plants. The old woman made a dash for him. By the time he perceived her and tried to escape, she had hold of him, as he cried in fear of her.

"My little grandchild, my little grandchild!" she said to him, kissing him again and again; "Where do you come from?" she asked him.

"Right near here," he told her.

"My dear little grandchild, I am not angry at you for having spoiled these plants of mine. I am too glad I have found you," she told him.

Then, when she set him down, off he ran. Then she followed him. There she saw someone lying. To that place the child went.

"What person is this, my grandchild?" she asked him; "Is this the one of whom you speak as your mother?"

"Yes! There is not anyone else; there are just we two, my mother and I," he told her.

"Alas, my dear little grandchild, I see that you are in a woeful plight, my grandchild! I shall take you home with me. I shall keep you as my own. Your mother here is not alive; she has died. You will surely perish here, in the end, if you do not leave her. Never since this earth began has it been so, has it been possible for one not living to be stayed by," she told him; "I shall take you home with me," she told him.

"Yes!"

Really she took her grandchild home with her. She brought him to her dwelling. Oh, she felt sorry for him; she pitied him and gave him food. The little boy liked being with the old woman. And so he ceased thinking of his mother.

Then, presently, as he and his grandmother were living there, "Grandson, I am in the habit of always walking about here. Do you never go off anywhere. Always stay and take care of the house, and from time to time go to my garden," she told her grandson.

And really, when day came, "Grandson, I am going to walk about," she told him, "to look for things to eat," she told him, "and to go, as I do from time to time, to where some young men live, not very far from here," she told him.

So she would always go away, and he would play there, going sometimes to her garden, and when he went there, pulling up his grandmother's plants.

In the evening, when the old woman came, "Grandchild, did you go to my garden?" and when he said "Yes," she would go there, and there her plants would be lying scattered about, where he had pulled them up.

"Truly my little grandson is naughty!" the old woman would say, and she would laugh, as she picked them up and carried them home. When she came into the lodge, she would pick him up and kiss him again and again, saying, "My dear little grandson, my dear little grandson!"

Then at one time he began to ask his grandmother questions, when he had grown larger.

"Grandmother, what sort of things are these?" he asked her, of some things that were enclosed in two separate bladders that were tied to the lodge-poles.

"Why, grandson, never mind what they are," she answered him.

She would not tell him what things were in there. But Sun-Child knew that those bladders were always twitching and moving. And so, as they lived there, once when his grandmother had gone off in her usual way, he filched her little sinew strings and made some snares. When he had made them, wherever their little dwelling was broken, he set a snare, and at the top he closed up the smoke-hole of their lodge. Then, when he had cut open one of those bladders, there, it was full of blackbirds. So these it was were in there. He whooped and yelled, and chased them, and try as they might to fly out of the house, he snared them all. He killed them all, laughing loud and amusing himself with them. When he thought his grandmother was about to arrive, he piled them up in one place and threw something over them, and as he put them under the covering, "Now we shall eat them," he said; "Now we shall eat them, my grandmother and I," he said.

When she arrived, in the evening, and came into the lodge, he said to her, "Grandmother, now we shall eat."

"What will this dear little grandchild of mine be giving me as a treat?" she asked him.

"Just uncover this here, grandmother."

When she uncovered it, what did she see but the blackbirds!

His grandmother wept, saying, "Truly, my grandson has done me grief!" and telling him, "Truly, my grandson is naughty!"

When at last she ceased her lamentation, she picked them up and plucked them. When she had got them clean, she set them to cook.

When she had cooked them done, "Grandson, do you alone eat," she told him.

Accordingly, he alone partook of the meal. When he had his fill, he quit eating them. She put them away.

"You will eat some more of them later," she told him.

So, as they continued to live there, and his grandmother went off every day, when he had eaten all of those blackbirds, again he set snares. Again he closed up their lodge at the top, and again he cut open a bladder, and the place was filled with the twittering of swallows, as he whooped and yelled and gave them chase. As many of them as tried to escape from the house, he snared. He killed them all, this time too. Again he piled them up in one place and covered them up. Then his grandmother came home.

He said to her, "Grandmother, now we shall eat again," he told her.

"What treat is this grandson of mine about to give me?" the old woman asked him.

"Uncover this here," he said to his grandmother.

When she uncovered it, at once she began to weep.

"Oh, grandmother, be quiet! You are always weeping for no reason at all!" he said to her.

When she ceased crying, she said to him, "Grandson, surely you are very naughty. It was because you were in a miserable state that I took pity on you and befriended you, and here you are doing away with all my children! These are my children, grandson. In the end I may be led to do you some harm. You have angered me, even though I felt pitying kindness for you when you did me harm and greatly laid waste my garden-plants; I loved and cherished these my poor children whom you have all destroyed. Be off; go away! I do not want to bring you to ruin, poor creature that you are," she said to him.

Accordingly, he arose, went out of the lodge, and departed. He went off in some direction, he knew not whither. Wherever he was at nightfall, he lay down, not choosing where. When day broke, he went on. At noon he saw a tipi in a place where there were many small ravines. Thither he went. He saw that the tipi was covered with painted symbols.

When he reached it, "Oho, come in, come in, Sun-Child!" a young man called out to him.

When he entered, what did he see but some youths sitting round the sides of the lodge, splendidly dressed, but wearing only striped robes!

When "Over here!" they said to him, he did not heed their invitation.

"This will do, right here!" he answered them, seating himself by the door-flap.

Then soon, "Dear me, we are indecently slow about serving food to Sun-Child! And just now we thought it so glad an event that he came to us!" said one.

"Goodness, but what can we give him to eat?"

"Why, quickly roast a buffalo-stomach to be served well done and piping hot! Quickly roast it done."

So one put on the roast. Very soon he took it from the fire.

"Dear me, surely it cannot be done?" said another; "You had better bite off a piece to try! Surely you will find it can't be cooked done!"

He too bit off a piece.

"It is not done," said this one too; "Just see for yourself!"

He gave it to another, and each took a bite next to where the other had bitten. When they got through, these youths had bitten off morsels all round the edge of the gizzard.

By this time yonder old woman had set out to come here, the old woman from whom Sun-Child had parted when he came, for she knew that Sun-Child had reached her sons' abode. For these ten youths were that old woman's sons.

At last all these youths had taken bites.

"It is cooked done," they said.

"Ho, so now let him eat!" they said of Sun-Child.

He took his knife and cut all around the edge of the stomach. When he had pared off the edge, suddenly he threw the trimming into the fire. At once he fled out of the lodge, as they cried, "Sun-Child is killing us all!" Indeed, he had killed them all. For they were rattlesnakes. He had done away with them all. And so he fled.

And now yonder old woman came in pursuit, chasing Sun-Child.

"Now you have really angered me, Sun-Child, doing me so many griefs and now destroying all my sons!"

So now he was chased by the old woman, and fled he knew not where. In time, when she was close upon him, he became frightened.

He cried, "Father, come near in your course! The Old Rattlesnake Woman means to kill me!" he said to him.

Truly, low in his course came his father, the Sun. It grew very hot, until at last the old woman felt herself about to be roasted. She gave up.

"And so you have saved your life, Sun-Child! I give you up," she said to him; "But owing to this, do not, do never seat yourself on the bare ground!" said the old woman to Sun-Child.

Accordingly, his father went higher in his course. The old woman went home. And Sun-Child, as he walked on, found a stone of flat shape. He took it up, and wherever he meant to sit down, there he placed it, using that stone as a seat. He did this every time, putting the stone under him also when he went to sleep, and in the morning, when he went on, taking the stone with him.

Then at one time, as he wandered about, he came upon a town. He reached it. He stood on a rise in the land and looked at the tents.

"Oho, Sun-Child has arrived!" was said in his hearing.

Soon one came to him, to invite him in.

"Ho, Sun-Child, you are to come!"

"Oh, very well."

He went along with him.

As he entered the lodge, "Oh, come in!" he was told.

When he sat down, "There, quickly give him food! Surely he must be hungry!" was said of him.

"Why, gracious heavens, it is Sun-Child! Truly it is no light thing that you have come here, where unceasing are the contests, the contests of spirit-animals. And indeed, it is we who are always defeated. By this time doubtless he has already decided to challenge you, the Iron Bull. Most dangerous is he; never have we defeated him. And so, no matter how unwilling we are to contend, he is determined to destroy us completely," the other explained.

"I do not happen to be going about in search of contests," he told him.

"Doubtless they will challenge you none the less. They challenge at once any new arrival," he was told; "But it is evening now. Tomorrow probably they will challenge you," he was told.

Then he was given food. At last darkness fell. Then, the next morning, when they had eaten, already he heard the announcing call.

"Hear ye, hear ye, hear ye! Make ready! Come to look on! There will be a contest! Last night arrived Sun-Child, who, it is said, is going about seeking contests; he is to contend with the Iron Bear! Come forth!"

Already the other had come.

"Come, Sun-Child, you are to come forth, as the Iron Bear is to challenge you."

Then, "At any rate, go forth. In any case, even if you pay no heed, none the less he will seek to destroy you," he was told by him into whose lodge he had come, where now he stayed.

"Very well. It is not true that I am going about seeking contests," he said; "But never mind," he said.

Accordingly, he made ready. Already, where there was a stretch of level land, thither the other had gone.

"Ho, quickly, come forth!" he was told.

Accordingly, he went out and proceeded to the place. They were already standing about in a circle.

When he arrived, "Now then, Sun-Child, you are going about engaging in contests, it is said concerning you. You shall have the first shot."

"No! You first! Seeing it is not of my own will I am contending."

"Very well," said that bear.

Already he thought as follows: "Now, O my father, watch me from close by!" he said, thinking this: "Perhaps, if the weather is hot, he will tire," thinking this of the bear.

Really, it grew hotter and hotter, as the bright glow of the sun increased.

"Now then, from yon place I shall come. Four times I shall start for you; and on the fourth time I shall spring," meaning that he would seize him, that he would try to kill him.

But it was very hot. The bear went off a long ways, starting from a good distance to come running at Sun-Child. Just as if the ground were soft swamp, when he came, he sank deep into it. When he was near, he turned back. Again he started from the same place. This time he sank even farther into the ground. Again, when he had come near, he turned back. Again he started hither, always sinking deeper into the earth. Now he turned back once more, and now was when he would try to kill him. But by this time he was very tired. When he was near, he looked as though all of iron.

Those on his side were yelling wildly. "Now surely he will come leaping!" he thought. His comrade at whose house he was staying kept telling him to take heart. And then, as the other came leaping, he flung himself down on the ground. The other did not see him. In vain the other tried to hurl himself to the spot whence he had stood; already he stood there whence the other had come, throwing himself from place to place. Then he saw the other stand still. At once he attacked him. When the other, as soon as he was upon him, flung himself down, he could not see him; wildly all this time his companions were whooping for Sun-Child, happy that he was giving that other a fight. At last the other was helpless from want of breath. Those men, too, were oppressed by the heat, for the Sun was too near. At last he stood still in one place, that bear, almost dead from want of breath. So then he took his arrows, which that little old woman who had raised him had made for him. Where that bear stood with open mouth, helplessly panting, he shot him in the mouth; for only there was the other not of iron. In flew a hawk, flying clear through the creature's body, seizing his heart, while Sun-Child's companions cheered him.

"Very well, Sun-Child, throw me into the direction of noon. There, when mortal man, who in time is to grow forth, says, 'The Iron Bear has taken pity on me,' he will speak true," said he.

"Ho, throw yourself to the ground facing so!" he told him.

So the other threw himself to the ground, facing that way.

Thus he spoke: "My comrades, do not kill those who have been given as stakes by your opponents," he told them; "If you always do thus, mortal man will not be able to grow forth," he told them; "In this wise you are to cease from your contests," he told them.

"Truly, that is right!" said his companions.

For in fact these people were accustomed to stake their followers; but now that he had overcome them and prohibited it, they obeyed him. For they feared him; there was no one now who could challenge him, since he had defeated the one among them who had most spirit power. So now these people lived in peace.

Then at one time, as he went forth and sat down on a hilltop, he forgot to follow his custom of using the stone as a seat. Presently he felt something crawl in here, ... a rattlesnake; it was yon old woman whose children he had wiped out, was doing this to him. For, "Never sit on the bare ground!" she had told him. Then, try as he might to get the creature out, he could not get it out. At last his comrades came to where he was. As thus he was tormented by that creature which was trying to kill him, at last many came to where he was, urging him to try to kill that rattlesnake, for dearly those people loved him. The creature kept going higher and higher; at last it got into his head here. And when it was here, he began to be delirious, as it was killing him. He asked for something to use in the way of a knife. It was given to him. Then he cut a piece away from here, trying to make a hole in his head, and at last succeeded.

"Here, father, the rattlesnake is tormenting me and means to kill me! Come near to me!" he said to his father.

Really, the latter came near. Those people went down from the hilltop, because they were too hot. Presently it came climbing out, forced to extremity by the heat. So his life was saved. Then, when he rubbed his head like this, it healed.

Then, there stood his father, saying to him, "Alas and alas! No wonder, seeing how foolish was your mother who took you away with her, so that there was no one to instruct you, no wonder that you went about making a ruin of things at large, and that you are a fool. You will continue to make a greater and greater mess of things, my son. It will be better if I take you home with me. You are too much of a fool. If you continue to go about as you have, no good will come of it. I do not wish such things to be," his father told him.

So they went home, his father taking him aloft to where he dwelt; and from that time on he stayed with his grandfather.

That is the end of the sacred story.

(22) He Who Carried the Old Woman

Sakewew

sākäwäw.

kītahtawä nistiwak ayīsiyiniwak, nīsu nāpäwak. ōhi nāpäwa usīmiw aw īskwäw. äkwah päyak namuy ātuskäw usīmimāw. misāskwat utinam; ayāw, ä-saskahuhtät uhtsi. äkwah ustäsa mātsiyiwa, mītsiwin äh-tōtamākutsik.

kītahtawä awa nāpäw ustäsimāw, mistah äh-ayātsik mītsiwin, "hā, nisīm, mahtih nka-ntunawāw awiyak kit-ōwīstāwiyahk, kimisinaw kit-

ōnāpämit. äwaku uwīstāwiyahku, namuya kika-näpäwisinānaw, nāpäw ōtah ayātsi.[1]"

" *äha'* , " *itik.*

kītahtawä sipwähtäw, äh-pa-pmuhtät. päyakwāw ä-kīh-nipāt, wāpahtam mīkiwāhp. āpihtā-kīsikāhk itskwāstawästäyiw. äkusi pōtih kā-wāpamāt kāhkākiwa äh-ukāhkwāskwahikaniyit.[2] *pōtih äh-utihtahk, kā-kitōwiyit ōhi k-ākutsiniyit mīkiwāhpihk.*

" *tawāw !* " *itik.*

pīhtukäw. kīh-päyakuyiwa nāpäwa. pōtih äh-kīsi-mītsisut, nāpäwa kā-takusiniyit, kutakah uskinīkiwa.

äkwah ōmis ītwäw : " *käkway äh-papā-nātaman, kā-papāmuhtäyin ?* " *itik.*

" *ā,* " *itwäw,* " *ōmis äh-täyihtamān k-ō-papāmuhtäyān : ' mahtih nikōwīstāwih, ' äh-itäyihtamān ; ' nka-miyāw nimisah, ' äh-itäyimitān, änayähtawiyān, äkā wīhkāts äh-pīkiskwät nimis,*[3] *k-ōh-pä-miyitān.* "

" *äya'* , " *itik ;* " *niya wiya nisākwäyimun ; wiya māka nahā nisīm māskōts ta-täpäyimōw,* " *itik.*

" *hā, usām nam äskwa nnihtāh-nipahtān käkway, ta-kīh-wīwiyān wāwis niya ; ahpōh kiya käkway kinihtā-nipahtān, äkā tiyäpäyimuyin.*"

" *ahahäy !* " *itwäw aw ustäsimāw ;* " *ōtah kisiwāk wīkiwak nisīmak ä-nīsitsik,*[4] *päyak nistäs, äh-näwitsik äwakunik, nistu usīma äh-pamihikut. usām nihtāh-nipahtāwak käkway äyakunik,* " *itik ;* " *äkusi äkutä kikätuhtān,* " *itik ;* " *äyakunik ka-ntawāpamāwak. māskōts päyak kitatäpäyimōw,* " *itik.*

ituhtäw. pōtih ä-sākäwät ōm äspatināyik, wāpahtam mīkiwāhp. pōtih kāhkwāskwahikanah wāpamäw, ōhōwa, äsay kā-kituyit. ituhtäw.

mayaw äy-utihtahk, " *tawāw, wäskinīkiyan !* " *itāw.*

äkusi ituhtäw. pīhtukäw. asamāw. ä-kīsi-mītsisut, ist ōskinīkiwa pīhtukäyiwa. pīhtatwānah ah-akutäyiwa.

" *hāw, tānisi ätiskāyan, ōma kā-päh-ituhtäyin ōtah ?* " *itwäw aw ustäsimāw.*

ōmis itäw : " *āh, nimis äh-pä-miyitakuk päyak.* "

" *niya wiya täpiyāhk äh-asamitsik nisīmak. nama käkway nnihtānipahtān. namuya ta-kī-wītsäwak iskwäw,* " *itwäw ; äkwah,* " *hāw, nisīmitik, nikutwāw päyak ituhtäk kiyawāw !* "

itik : " *hāh, iyika mā tsäskwah käkway nihtāh-nipahtāyāhk ! namuya niya nka-kä-ituhtān,* " *itwäwak kahkiyaw.*

" *ahäy, wäskinīkiyan ! ōma k-ōsähtsāk awasāyihk äkutah wīkiw nōhtāwiy. māwatsih wäwustäsimāwiyit ukusisah näwu wīkimäw, äkā tsäskwah äh-wīwitsik äwakunik nisīminānak, äkwah nīsu uskinīkiskwäwak nisīminānak,* " *itäw ;* " *äkutä ituhtä. māskōts nōhtāwiy wīh-miyikuyäkuh utawāsimisah nistu, nīsw īskwäwa äkwah päyak nāpäw, wīh-miyisk nōhtāwiy,* " *itäw.*

äkusi tāpwä wayawīw. iyāyaw äkutä ituhtäw kā-kiskinōhamāht itāh. äkwah äy-ati-sākäwät, pōtih tāpwä mīkiwāhp wāpahtam āpihtā-kīsikāhk

---

[1] On account of the brother-and-sister tabu; the sister's husband would make communication possible.

[2] English-speaking informants could not tell what *kāhkwāskwahikan* was. Literally, it is "thing for tightening (?) sticks."

[3] On account of the brother-and-sister tabu.

[4] He means *ä-nistitsik*, and I have so translated. Informant is given to slips of the tongue as regards numbers and opposites.

äh-itiskwāstawästäyik. äkwah mayaw ä-wāpahtahk, wāpamik kāhkwāskwahikanah, kihiwa. sämāk kitōw awa kihiw. takuhtäw mīkiwāhpihk.

" hāw, tawāw ! " itäw.

pīhtukäw. awīn ōhi, kisäyiniwa, nōtukäsiwa, namwāts awiya wāpamäw, näyästaw itah äh-uhtapiyit umatōwahk, uma nōhtapiwin äkutōwahk ayihtahk, " hāw, tawāw ! " k-ätiht.

ä-kīh-pīhtukät, " hāw, nōtukäsiw, asam ! ta-mītsisōw ! " itäw.

ha, kätahtawä asamāw. ä-kīsi-mītsisut, kā-pä-tatwäwitamiyit, pä-pāpīkiskwäyit iskwäwa. piyä-pīhtukäyit, awīn ōhi, uskinīkiskwäwa. ä-kīsinahapitsik, kutakak mīna piyä-pīhtukätsik näwu nāpäwak.

äkwah ōmis ītik : " hāw, wäskinīkiyan, tānisiw ōma k-ōh-pä-ay-ituhtäyan ? " itwäw awa kisäyiniw ; " ōtah tsiw ōki ntawāsimisak kikīh-pä-āhutihtāwak ? "

" äha', " itäw.

" käkway māka kā-uhtsi-papāmuhtäyan ? "

" ā, äyakunik kitawāsimisak, ' maht äkutah ituhtä, ' äh-isitsik. ä-nayähtawiyāhk nimisinān, pikuh ä-wītsäwāyāhk, äkā wīhkāts äh-pīkiskwät nimis, äkwah päyak nisīm uskinīkiw, anuhts äw-uhtsi-wītsäwāyāhk. ' māskōts päyak kik-ōwīstāwin äkuta ; nōhtāwiy ta-sīhkimäw tawāsimisah, ' äh-itwät awa kikusis, kā-kīh-pä-utihtitakuk. "

" hāw, wäskinīkiyan, ōki ntawāsimisak iskwäwak nam äskwa nihtāwikwāsiwak, ta-kīh-unāpämitsik, mäkwāts kaskikwāsōwin äh-nōtsihtātsik. hāw, äkus īsi nama kikä-miyitin, " itik ; " hāw, kiyawāw, ntawāsimisitik, päyak kit-ätuhtäw, " itäw ōhi nāpäwa näwu.

pikw ānah, " tsä ! äkā mā tsäskwa ä-nōhtä-wīwiyān niya mina ! " itik kahkiyaw ōhi nāpäwa.

" hä ä ay, wäskinīkiyin ! ayis nama tāpwähtamwak tawāsimisak. ntsawāts ōtaw uhtsi kīwäh. aw, äkāh tāpwähtamani, täpiyāhk ōtäh isi äkā wiya ituhtäh, " itik.

äkus īsi wayawīw. ōma itäh kā-kitahamäht, äkutä ituhtäw. pōtih äh-ati-pa-pmuhtät äh-usähtsāyik, ä-säkäwät, pōtih ka-wāpahtahk wistäpahkwayikamik. ituhtäw. iskwāhtämihk äh-ihtät, ispimihk itāpiw apasōhk : pōtih apisīs kā-pimāpahtäyik. äkusi mwähtsi ä-wīh-pīhtukät, äh-paspāpit, awīn ōhi, mituni nōtukäsiwah. ōmisi kīh-tōtamiyiwa, äh-nōhtä äh-nipahāyit utihkumiyiwa. uhtsikwanihk ayiwakäs mōhkitapiw awa nōtukäsiw. äkusi asähtäw aw ōskinīkiw. äh-iy-asähtät, nahikuhtākanämōw, " khhr ! " äh-itwät, " awa nōtukäsiw ōmisi kita-tōtam ; uskutākay ta-yāsäkinam, " äh-itäyihtahk aw ōskinīkiw. ayiwākäs iskunamiyiwa uskutākayiwa.

" tawāw māka, nōsisä ! " itäw.

" ā, misawāts nōtukäwiw. ta-yāsäkinam uskutākay, " itäyihtam. pīhtukäw. kwäskipayihōw awa nōtukäsiw.

" käkway ä-papā-nātaman ? " itäw.

" äh, nāpäw ä-papā-ntunawak, kit-ōwīstāwiyān, " itik.

" āta tsī kikī-wāpamāwak aw ōtah kā-wīkit nimanātsimākan ? " itik.

" äha'. "

" kitayāwāw tsī iskwäw ? "

" namuya. "

" āta tsī kkī-wāpamāwak ntāhkusak ! "

" äha'. "

" äwakunik aniki ä-kiskinōhamawakik kaskikwāsōwin. nihtāwikwāsutwāwi, iyikuhk kit-ōnāpämitsik, " itäw ; " niya nōtsihkawin, " itwäw awa nōtukäsiw.

" āh, usām kinōtukäwin, nōhkō," itäw.

" häy ! äkwäyāk ani ayīsiyiniw päkwāsit ! kahkiyaw aniki kā-päwutihtatsik, nnāpämak aniki, äkā kā-tāpwähtaman ta-wīkimiyan ! "

" hā, nōhkō, usām kinōtukäwin ! "

äkusi ati-pasikōw, äkus äh-itāt. kwāskwäpayihōw awa nōtukäsiw, ōtah äh-itināt, äkwah uskātah ä-wäwakipayihtāt, ōtah äkwah äh-ākwaskitināt. äkwah nōtukäsiw wäw-utihtinikäw. äh-āta-pahkwatināt, nama kaskihäw, usām ä-maskawisiyit ōhkuma. papāmōwatäw, mīna awa nōtukäsiw nipiy äh-wäpinahk, äh-sikitāt. näpäwisiw aw uskinīkiw. äkwah kunta papāmuhtäw. ituhtäw kisäyiniwa wīkiyihk, itah äh-käh-pawāmit aw uskinīkiw. mituni kisäyiniwiw. äy-ati-takuhtät, kā-pä-wayawiyit.

" äyahā ! tānisih k-ōh-pätōwatāmikawiyin, nōtukäsiw ? " itik.

" nāh, ä-pakwāsit awa, ' nōtsīhkawin, ' äh-atiy-itak, äh-pakwāsit, ' ntsawāts nka-nayōmik, ' k-ōh-itäyimak. näki kikusākak, äwakunik ä-māh-miyusitsik, nam āwiyak npakwātik. äkāya nānitaw isin. nikisiwāyik awa, äh-pakwāsit. "

" häy ä äy, wäskinīkiyan ! ōtäh sākahikaniwiw. äkutä maht ītuhtä. äkutäh anih ayāwak nīsu nōsisiminānak, ä-kitimākäyimāt awa kā-nayōmat. niy āni wiya nikustāw niwīkimākan, " itwäyiwa.

sipwähtōwatäw. tāpwäh utihtam sākahikan, kuntah kā-päh-pāhpiyit uskinīkiskwäwa nīsu.

" häy, tānisih māka mīna k-ōh-awāsisīhkāsuyin, kā-pä-nayōmikawiyin ? "

" hāh, äkāya nāntaw itwäk, nōsisimitik ! ä-pakwāsit awa, ä-kisiwāhit, ' ntsawāts nika-papā-nayōmik, ' k-ätäyimak. "

itah näpātsih, täpiskāyiki, käyāpits nayōmäw ; kikōwatäsin. äkusi nama nāntaw itwäwak ōk ōskinīkiskwäwak.

" ntsawāts mahtih npawāmōwinihk nk-ätuhtahāw, " itäyihtam.

äkwah papāy-itōwatäw.

täkuhtätsi upawākanah, " ähähäy, nōsisä, nikustāw ! " itāw.

nama nāntaw kīh-tōtāmāwa ta-pahkwatinimiht. äkusi piyis kahkiyaw upawāmōwinihk nama käkway. äkwah ayāw.

" pikw äkwah ta-nipahit, ta-nipahāhkatusuyān, " itäyihtam.

kätahtawä ay-ätataw takusin itah ätuhtätsi. piyisk utisinākwaniyiw itah kāh-nipātsi, ä-na-nayōmāt nōtukäwa. kītahtawä wāpahtam sīpīsis, äw-utākusiniyik, amiskwa ä-kīh-kipahamiyit. äkutah ituhtäw. nätä akāmihk wāpahtam ahkāpaskwah[1] *äh-ayāyikih ; āspīs mistikwah äh-uyāskwaniyikih ayāyiwa.*

" hā, äkutä akāmihk nka-ntawi-pimisinin. kiyām äkutä nka-nipin, " itäyihtam.

pōtih ätataw pītsitisin.[2]

" ntsawāts nka-pimitātsimun. ōhtsitaw ōma niwīh-nipahik awa nōtukäsiw, " itäyihtam.

kītahtawä ati-sipwähtäw. nahisin sisunä kipahikanihk. āsay tipiskāyiw. ati-pimitātsimōw. käkāts äh-kapāt, nōhtäsin.

" āh, wāpahkih nik-ōtihtän, " itäyihtam.

---

[1] A water-weed, not identified. I do not understand this passage.

[2] If the record is right, the word is analysable as initial stem *pītsit-* : "draw toward one"; connective *-i-* ; animate final *-sin* : "come down, lie"; one would expect *ts* for the *t*. Meaning?

kītahtawä kā-wāpamāt ayīsiyiniwa ; mōyāpitasäkuyiwa ; namahtsiyiwa[1]; *pakamākan äh-päh-tahkunamiyit, kuntah kā-tsā-tsīpipayit ōhi kā-nayōmät.*

" ntsawāts āstam, nīstāh ! " itwäw awa kā-nayōmāt nōtukäsiwa.

äkusi päy-ituhtäw. kiskäyihtam äh-kustāyit äyakunih.

" yāh, tānisi ōma, nistāh, k-ōh-nayōmat awa nōtukäsiw ? "

" ōwa, nīsta ! mahtih kakwä-pihkuh ! "

" ā, nista ! piku māka kita-pakamahwak, äkā wī-pakitiniski ! "

" häy, nōsisä, kitimākäyimin ! kiyām nika-pimātisin ! käyāpits päyakwāw wīh-mätawäw kīstāw. kit-āpatsihtāt nka-miyāw. äkusi kit-ōhsākōtsihtwāt kā-wīh-miyak. kiyām nka-pimātisin, nōsisä ! " itäw.

tāpwäh, " äya' ! äkā wiya kakwä-tsīsi nīstāw. kīspin kakwä-tsīsihatsi, misawāts nka-pähtän. hāw, pakitin ! "

pakitinik.

äkusi, " hā, nistah ! hāw, ōma mītsih ! " itik wīstāwa.

mīnis päyak mītsiw ; kāwih wiyinōw ; maskawisiw kāwih. äkwah miyik nīsu sāpunikanah, äkwah nīsu uskātsihkwah, äkwah asiniyah äh-apisīsisiyit ; nistu.

" hāw, nōsisä, äyāpits päyakwāw kika-mätawān ! " itäw awa nōtukäsiw kā-kīh-nayōmikut.

" hā ! "

äkusi kīwäw awa nōtukäsiw. äkwah awa kā-namahtsīt ntawi-wīwiw umisiyiwa ōhi kā-utihtāt.

äkusi sipwähtäw, äh-wāpaniyik. ä-tahtakwahtsāyik, ä-paskwāyik äh-at-ōtihtahk, kītahtawä ä-mäkwā-pimuhtät, kā-pä-sākäwäyit iskwäwa nīsu.

" häy, nītimusä, äkutah nīpawih ! awiyak āsiskamātsi, äwaku kika-wīwin ; awiyak nakatihtsi, kisīma kit-unāpämiw, " itäw.

nīpawiw. äkwah näki uskinīkiskwäwak pä-wäyatsäwiwak. äkusi nam āwiyak nakatäw.

" häy, äkwah nīkināhk ituhtätān ! " itäw.

äkwah ituhtäwak. pōt ōma mäkiwāhp wistäpahkwayikamik. utihtamwak. pīhtatwānah nayōmäw aw uskinīkiw. ä-takuhtätsik ōtah wistäpahkwayikamikuhk, pīhtukäwak ōk iskwäwak äh-māh-miyusitsik. äh-pīhtukätsik, ōtäh isi, minamahtinihk iskwāhtämihk kīh-apiyiwa uskinīkiskwäsisah, utakikumiyiwa ä-sākamuyit, äkwah ä-pikiwaskāpiyit, kuntah misiwä uhkwākanihk ihkwah kā-papāmāhtawiyit aw iskwäsis, wāwīs ustikwānihk, misiwä wiyawihk, uskātihk, usitihk misiwä äh-ayāyit ihkwah. wāpamäw.

äkwah ä-kīh-mītsisut aw uskinīkiw, " käkway ōma ä-papā-nātaman ? " itäw.

" hā, ä-papā-ntunawak nīsw īskwäwak, nisīm päyak kita-wīwit, äkwah päyak niya. āsay wiya nikī-miskawāw kit-ōwīstāwiyāhk. "

" kāh ! kiy ätsik āhi k-ātsimikawiyin, ' papāh-ntunawäw kita-wīwit, ' k-ätikawiyan ! " itik ōh ōskinīkiskwäwah, tahkih äh-pāhpiyit.

" äha' , niya ! "

" nāhah wīwih, " itwäwak, ōhi k-ōtihkumiyit.

kitāpamäw.

" usām utihkumiw. namuya nika-kīh-wīwin, " itwäw awa.

" hāh ! "

tāpwäh unāpämiwak ; wā-wīkimäwak.

kītahtawäh kunita kāh-papāmitātsimut awa k-ōtihkumit.

---

[1] Perhaps, "He was left-handed"; the meaning in the text is common.

" hāh ! "

kuspiwäpinäwak.

" tānisi māka mina äs-iyinihkäyit[1]*? " itwäw awa k-ōtihkumit ; " häy, ntawāsimisitik, iskah äh-atuskäyān, äkuyikuhk iskah kā-pōni-kīskwähkwasiyān, äh-usīhimak nnahāhkim kit-ōtakuhpit. mistahi nnōhtäh-atuskān, " itwäw aw īskwäsis k-ōtihkumit.*

äkusi kīksäpā mātsīw ; ukwāskwäpayihōsa päyak nipahäw. päsiwäw misiwä.

" hā, äkwah, ntawāsimisitik, pahkwäkisuhk ! " itäw.

pahkwäkiswäwak.

" ntawāsimisitik, ntawi-nitumihk ntäm ! " itwäw awa k-ōtihkumit.

tāpwä ntawi-ntumäw utäma awa k-ōtihkumit. pōt ōhi atimwa misiwä äh-pīwāpiskōwiyit.

" ntäm, ntawi-mītsisuh. nnahāhkim äh-nipahtwāsk kita-mītsiyan. "

mōwäw atim awa kwāskwäpayihōwisa. āsay misikitiw aw ātim, päyakwāw äh-mītsisut.

" niyā ! " itäw ; " kīwäh ! " itäw utäma ; " äkusi, ntawāsimisitik, nātamuk nisīhkipitākanäyāpiyah ! " itäw.

äkusi nātamwak ; pätāwak. usāwāpiskāyiwa pīsākanāpiya. sīhkipitäw. ä-kīsāhpitāt, äkus īsi kīsihäw ; pīhtukäwäpinäw. awīn ōhi, kī-miyusiyiwa utakuhpah aw ōskinīkiw kit-ōtakuhpit.

äkusi min äh-tipiskāyik, āsay mīna kīskwähkwasiyiwa.

iyikuhk min äh-āpisīhkwasit, āsay mīna, " häy, ntawāsimisitik, äh-nōhtäy-atuskäyān ! äkuyikuhk kā-pōni-kīskwähkwasiyān ! "

kīksäpā mātsīw ; wāwāskäsiwa nipahäw. hā, päsiwäw misiwä.

äkusih āsay mīna, " häy, nitawāsimisitik, pahkwäkisuhk ! " itwäw.

pahkwäkisamawāw.

" äkwah ntäm ntawi-ntumihk. kita-mītsisōw, " itwäw.

mītsisōw aw ātim. kitamwäw. äkwah tāpwä mistahi misikitiw äkwah aw ātim. nama kīh-pīhtukäw mīkiwāhpihk. āsay misikitiw.

" häy, ntawāsimisitik, ay-āskaw ōma tāh-takuwāts pikuh äh-atuskäyān, k-äsi-miyusiyān, " itwäw.

äkusi mīna kīsihäw ōhi akuhpah. äh-tipiskāyik āsay mīna kīskwähkwasiw. kiyipa āpahkawisiw. äkusi kīksäpā mātsīw. takwāhnawah nipahäw. nōhtähkatäw aw uskinīkiw ; äkwah apsis wāskitōhk uhtinam wiyāsis, ä-nawatsīhisut, äh-mītsit.

kā-kīsi-mītsisut, " ' ōma k-äsi-maskawisiyān kit-äsi-maskawisiw awa nōsisim ! ' nikih-itikuh nōhkum ! mahtih nika-sākuhäw awa mustus, ä-wīh-utāpäyān ! " itwäw, ōhi kā-kīh-nayōmāt ä-kīh-itikut.

äkusi kīwätsitāpäw, " t-ātuskäw äkwah ! " äh-itäyihtahk. äkus äh-takuhtahāt.

" häy, äkwah kä-pahpakwatsīwayān[2]*! " itwäw awa k-ōtihkumit.*

äkusi ä-kīsi-pahkwäkisumiht, " ntäm ntawi-ntumihk ! " itwäw.

ntawi-ntumimāwa.

piyä-takuhtäyit, " mītsisuh, ntäm ! " itwäw.

äkwah aw ātim atsiyaw kāh-miyāmāt, kuntah wāsakāmäskawäw ; nama wīh-mōwäw.

---

[1] I take this to be *äs-iyinihkahit :* "the way he cures me," but it does not make sense.

[2] If an intransitive verb can be formed with *-īwā-* (from *pahpakwat- :* "amuse"), this form is intelligible. More likely it is either an error of record or a nonsense form, starting as a verb, but ending with the nominal final *-wayān :* "hide of fur."

" tānähk āwa äkā kā-wīh-mītsisut, näkā, kitäm !"

" näh, nitawāsimisitik, nama tsī māka käkwah kōtawäyihtam !" itwäw äkusi, " nama tsī käkway kiwäpinän ?" itäwak unāpämiwāwa.

" apisīs wāskitōhk nikīh-maniswāw, äh-mōwak," itwäw.

" näh, ayīsiyiniw ätukä k-ōnahāhkimiyān, nikīh-itäyihtäh ! ätsik āni wīhtikōw ! äyiwähk mōh iskwastsikan !" itäw.

mōwäw. kitamwäw. äkwah tāpwä misikitiw aw ātim.

äh-tipiskāyik kīsihäw ōhi mustuswayāna.

" äyakw ana kit-ōtanāskāniw ninahāhkim," itwäw.

äkwa mīn ä-tipiskāyik, āsay mīna kīskwähkwasiw, äh-nōhtäy-ātuskät. ā, sipwähtäw kīksäpā. tay ä-watsīwiyik äkutah ituhtäw. wāpahtam wäkayōsi-wātih. takuhtäw äkutah.

" nimusōh, nipä-nātän kiyaw, ā-mawinäwukawiyān !" itäw.

" tsäskwah, nōsisä ! ōma nipahiyini, nīsu utinamōhkan nimihistōwānah. ispisi takuhtäyini kīkiwāhk, päyak matsustähamōhkan. ' pä-kakwämisk ōmah !' itāhkan. äkwah anih kä-mawinähwisk manitōwiw. wāpahkih nīkān utihkumah ka-kakwä-miskāmawah. päyak miskāmatsi, äkus āni kika-paskiyawāw utawāsimisah ta-kīwähtahimat," itik ōhi wākayōsah.

äkusi pä-wayawiyiwa. nipahäw. ā, kīwätsitāpäw. utinam ōhi nīs upīwāyiwa. päyak, äh-pīhtukät, matsustäham. päyak kanawäyihtam.

äkwah äh-takuhtät, " hāw, ntawāsimisitik, ntawi-pahkwäkisuhk äyakunih. nnahāhkim kit-ōtakuhpiw," itäw unahāhkisīma.

äkwah äh-kīsi-pahkwäkiswātsik, māka mina atim ntawi-ntumāw. äkusi mōwäw ōhi wākayōsa ; kitamwäw. äkwah kīwätisahwäw utāma. äkusi äkwa ōhi wākayōsiwayāna ōm ōhtsi k-ōsāwäyik upīsākanāpīm ātay ä-sīhkipitāt, ä-kīsahpitāt, käyāpits askäkinōwiyiwa. namuya kīsihäw anihi wākayōsiwayānah. kāw āpihkunäw.

" kutak nātamuk, nitawāsimisitik !" itwäw.

pätāwak kutak pīsākanāpiy ä-kaskitäwāyik. äy-ata-sīhkipitsihkākät, nama kä-kīsihäw ; käyāpits askäkinōwiyiw. piyis āpahwäw.

" mahti kutak, ntawāsimisitik !"

pakaskih-askähtakwāpäkaniyiw ; pätāwān. nama käh-kīsihäw äyāpits. äkuyikuhk käkäts wāpaniyiw. āsay mīna āpahwäw.

" nitawāsimisitik, maht ānima kā-mihkwāpiskāk nipīsākanāpīm äwakuh nātamuk, äkwah ntahkāmasiniy, äkwah ntsīkahikan, äkwah niyiwahikanāpisk, äyakunih. kakwä-mamiyōk. äkāya wanāpäkinamuk. wäsā nkakwātakihik, äkāya kīh-kīsihak awa, nnahāhkim kit-ōtakuhpit !" itwäw.

tāpwä äy-āta-pätwāwiht, uhtsitaw nama käh-kīsihäw. āpihkupitäw, kunt ītäh äy-isi-wäpināt. itāmihk uhtsi astäw upīsākanāpīm. āsay wāpaniyiw.

" nitawāsimisitik, maht äkwah utinihk nnahāhkim ka-wīh-utakuhpit."

iyāt-ōtinātsik, käyāpits askäkinuwiyiwa.

äkusi, " häy, äkwah māka päyakwäw āsay nisākōtsihik nnahāhkim ! käyāpits päyakwäw !" itwäw ; " māka wiya nnahāhkim wiya nīkān kitapmutahk !" itik.

hāh, utinam ōma wākayōs upīwāyiw.

" wāpaht ōma ! kīspin äkā miskamanih, kitawāsimisak nika-kīwähtahāwak," itäw.

wäpinam. äh-āta-nitunahk aw īskwäsis, nama kīh-miskam.

kītahtawä, " häy, mahti kit-ōtinākaniwiw !"

wāpahtam ; wiy āwa uskinīkiw utinam.

" ōm ītah ! "
tāpwä.
" hā, māka äkwah māka nnahāhkim kä-kakwä-miskawāt ntihkumah päyak ! "
astäyiwa utsīkahikan, utahkāmasiniy, pīwāpiskwah pisisik.
äkwah, " hāh, ōtah māka kit-āspiskwäsimōw ! " uhtsikwanihk.
mayaw ä-nahisihk aw īskwäsis, nama käkway utihkumah. mi-misiwä tah äh-āta-ntunawāt aw uskinīkiw, nama kīh-miskawäw.
" haw, nnahāhkim,[1] *ayis nama kikī-miskawāw ; äkwah māka kä-pakamahutān ! " itäw.*
" ä' ! iyikuhk ōhi sākuhtäyani, äkuyikuhk kika-pakamahun ! "
sāpunikanah tsimatäwäpinam. pōt ōhi ä-misāyikih pīwāpiskwah aspin itām, ispimihk, mīn ōtä muhtsihk.
" häy, nnahāhkim, iyikuh māka sākuhtāyāni ōhi, äkuyikuhk kä-pimitis-ahutān ! "
äyāta-tsīkahahki, piyisk mästsihtitäw utsīkahikan. äkwah utahkām-asiniy mästsihtitäw mīn äwaku.
äkwah, " häy, tāpwä nikisiwāhik nnahāhkim ! ntäm, āstam ! " itäw utäma ; " hāw, ntäm, mīts ōhi ! " itäw.
mayaw ä-sāmahtahk aw ātim, tāpiskōts wiyās. kiyipah kitäw.
" nyā, ntäm, kīwäh ! niwīh-ntawi-pakamahwāw ōyā nnahāhkim ! "
pimitisahwäw ; tsīkahikan pikuh tahkunam. kisiwāk äh-askōkut, utāhk isiwäpinam uskātsihk.
" ōtah misiw-ukāminakasīwāhtikwak kit-ōhpikiwak ! " itwäw aw uskinī-kiw.
ōtāhkimihk tānōtāni misw-ōkāminakasiyak ! wätihtahk awa, iyāta-tsīkahahk, kiyīskikahwātsi, wätsipitātsi, pōtih nama pihkuhōw, ta-kīh-tawinahk. utäma täpwātäw. tāpwä takusiniyiwa.
" hāw, ntäm, mōw ōki ! " itäw.
āsay mīna ati-mōwäw ōhi mistikwah ukāminakasiya. mīn äyakuni kitamwäw.
" niyā, kīwä, nitäm ! " itwäw.
kīwäw awa ātim. nawaswäw aw īskwäsis k-ōtihkumit. käyāpits utsīk-ahikan pimiwitäw. kisiwāk äh-askōkut, ōhkumah ka-kīh-miyikut asiniyah ispāhkäwäpinäw.
" ōtah utasinīwatsiyiw ! itāmihk äkutä nik-āyān ! " itwäw.
äkwah iyātah-wä-kakwä-pīkinikahwāt ōh asiniyah, piyisk mästsi-misi-wanātsihtāw utāpatsihtsikana.
" hāw, nitäm, pä-sipwähtä ! " itwäw, äh-täpwät.
tāpwä kiyipa takusiniyiwa.
" ntäm, nāhah itāmihk kā-pimisihk ntawi-nipah ! " itäw.
äkwah atim awa asiniyah ati-mōwäw. piyis utihtäw.
" äkāya pīkupis, nitäm ! täpiyāhk kaskikwän ! "
äkusi tōtam. nipahäw.
äkwah nāhah ayīsiyiniw kā-kihtimit, usīmah awa äyaku, äsah wīstäwa kā-sipwähtäyit, umisah piku nīsiwak. äkwah nāha misāskwat ayāw äskusit äy-iskwāyik, nanātuhk äy-itasinahikātäyik. ispimihk tahkupisuyiwa mäk-wanah päyak. äkwah äyaku pik ōtinam. umisah kāmwātapiyiwa, äh-pīkiskātäyit usīmiyiwa.

---

[1] Her sudden violation of tabu in addressing him directly implies that he no longer counts as a person; it is all up with him.

"hāw, nimisä," itwäw, "mahtih nistäs nka-ntunawāw!" itwäw; "äkwah awa pōnih-wäpāpīhkäpayitsih, 'äkuyikuhk äsa mäsi-wanātsihut nisīm,' kik-ätäyihtän," itwäw, äh-wayawīt, äh-wäpāpīhkäwäpināt upīhtatwānah.

wa-wäpāpīhkäpayiyiwa. sipwähtäw. misāskwatsus tahkunam. ksīkutsin, kā-sipwähtät. äkwah tāpwä utihtäw ustäsah, äh-pimisiniyit, äh-nipiyit. ōhi mīkwanah ōmis īsi yāyahwäw, ōm ōhtsi ōmistsikumis.

"nstäsä, waniskāh!" itäw.

waniskāyiwa. äkusi tāpwä pimātisiw awa kā-yāyahuht. wītsäwäw ustäsah. ituhtäw.

ä-takuhtät, "hā, nstäsä, kä-wāpahk pä-ituhtähkan," itäw.

"äha'," itik.

äkwah ituhtäw ōhih kaw-utihkumiyit, kā-pä-sākäwäyit uskinīkiskwäwa.

"häy! äkutäh ayāh!" itik; "awiyak āsiskākätsi, äwakuh kikawīwin," itäw.

pāpahtāyiwa. nam āwiya nakatimāwa; tāpiskōts takupahtāyiwa.

"äkwah nīkināhk ituhtätān!" itik.

ā, tāpwä ituhtäwak. hāh, ä-pīhtukätsik, käyāpits äkusi isinākusiw aw īskwäsis.

"häy, käkway um äh-papā-nātaman?"

"ā, iskwäw äh-ntunawak, ä-wīh-wītsäwak," itwäw.

"äkwah naha wīwih!"

kitāpamäw.

"usām utihkumiw," itäw.

"häy, nitawāsimisitik, kiyawāw ätukä äh-itäyimut! kiyawāw unāpämik!" itik.

äkwah ä-tipiskāyik, kawisimōw. kīskwähkwasiw aw iskwäsis.

"mitunih nnōhtäy-atuskān! mistahi ninōhtäh-atuskān! ätukä ä-kihtimit awiyak kāh-pä-nahāhkapit!" itwäw aw iskwäsis.

sämāk kīksäpā sipwähtäw. mituni kiyipa utihtam ustäsa itah kā-kīh-uhtsih-nipahäyit wākayōsah. äkutah takuhtäw.

"nimusō, kipä-nātitin, äh-mätawiyān anuhts kā-kīsikāk!" itäw.

"aha', nōsisä! tsäskwa nīsu nimīstōwanah utinamōhkan. mwiy āta wiya kinäsōwäyimitin. wayäsiyawāw kistäs. äkusi mayaw takuhtahiyini, sämāk utämah ta-nätisahwäw, utāpatsihtsikanah," itäw; äkusi, "hāw, äkwah!" itik.

pakamahwäw; nipahäw. kīwätsitāpäw. kīksäpā mitunih takuhtahäw. mayaw äh-pīhtukät matsustäham uma päyak; päyak pimiwitäw.

äkwah äh-pahkwäwisumiht, "nitawāsimisitik, nātamuk ntsīkahikan, nimihkihkwan, nimānihtwiyāsk,[1] nitahkāmasiniy, nisäkipitākanäyāpiyah, ähtahtikih ntāpatsihtsikanah. äkwah kiya, ntānis, papā-ntunaw nkusis kstäs," itäw; piyisk, "hāw, ntawi-ntum kiya ntäm," itäw utānisa päyak; "äkwah, 'usām utihkumiw,' ukīh-itwāh!"

ayis kisimäw, k-ōh-nātitisahwāt ukusisah. äkwah äh-pä-takuhtät aw ātim, iskwāhtämihk ispayihōw awa uskinīkiw. nam äskw ä-sīhkipitimiht ōhi wākayōsiwayāna, āsay kā-pä-takusihk aw ātim. äkusi äh-pīhtukät, kuntah kā-pä-patapāyōwäyit, kā-pä-sasawāpikiyit, tāpiskōts käkway ä-kustahk.

äkwah ōmis ītäw awa misaskwatsus k-āyāt ōhi; ōmis ītäw ōhi atimwah: "awa tsī ä-mamisiyin?" itäw, ä-sāmahwāt ōh atimwah.

---

[1] Some tool; the final is *-āskw-*: "wood, stick."

pīkupayiw aw ātim ; iyawāpiskipayiw.

ōhi mīna äy-āsastäyikih, " ōhi tsī ä-mamisiyin ? " itäw, utāpatsihtsikaniyiwah akinä äh-atih-sāmahamwāt. äkusi äh-atih-pīkupayiyikih, nama käkway aw īskwäsis iskuhtāwān ; mästsihtāwān tahtuh kā-mamisīt.

" hāw, äkwah kitihkumak nka-nōtsihāwak. päyak miskawakih, äkusi kitawāsimisak nika-kīwähtahāwak, " itäw.

" äha' , " itwäw aw īskwäsis.

ä-kitāpamikut, misiwä uhkwākanihk ihkwah ; äkwah pisinäy ä-päyutihtapiskwäyit, āsay sāmahamwān ustikwān ; nama kī-kutāwiyiwa utihkumah. mānnakisk takwāpiskatahwäw ihkwah. kītahtawä käh-kwätipiskwänäw ; pikw ītä ätāpitsih ihkwah pisisik. kītahtawä kā-pakitsītutākut ihkwah awa mistsikus k-āyāt. äkw ä-kwāhkutäyik äkutah itisinam uma mistsikus. kwahkutäyiw, äkwah ōhi kā-pakitsiyit ihkwah äkutah ōmistikumihk kā-matwätayähkasuyit. mäkwāts äkus äh-tōtahk, kītahtawä kā-takusihk aw uskinīkiw, wīpats kayahtä kā-wāpamāt ukāwiya ä-nōtsihimiht utihkumiyiwa.

" häy, käkway ōma ä-kīh-nātaman, awa kīstāskīs kā-mästsi-misi-wanātsihtāt ntāpatsihtsikanah ? " itik.

tāpiskamiyiwa kitsuhtsikanis, äkwah mōhyāpitsiskānis ukitsōhtsikanisihk äh-tahkupitäyik ; äkwah pīwāpiskus äh-apisāsiniyik pämakāmäskamiyiwa.

äkwah, " hāh, nākā, kitōsāmi-mästsihāwak kitihkumak, käswān äkā sākuhikawiyahkuh, äyakunik ta-mäkinawiyin. ayīs nkī-pä-ntumikawin, ayīsiyiniw ä-kitimākäyimiht, nīsta äh-wīhtamawak, äkwah äkā ma-mayaw k-ōh-pä-kīwäyān. usām, näka, kimatsi-nōtsihtān, " itik ukusisah.

awāsis awa ä-mistatayät, ä-musäskatät, mästatäw-awāsis awa ; ukusisah awa k-ōtihkumit.

" hāw, nīstah, äkwah māka niya ! " itwäw.

äkusi pōni-pakitsiyiwa ihkwah. äkusih utinam muhyāpitsiskanis. äkwah äkuyikuhk kā-takusihk awa atimwa kā-kīh-nipahikut.

" hā, nstäsä, wāhyaw nispiskwanihk ayā ! "

äkus isiwäpinam.

" nawatahaman ōma, äkusi kä-paskiyawiyin ! " itik.

iyāta-wā-kakwä-nawatahwātsi kamāmakusa äh-wāpiskisiyit, āskaw nama wāpamäw, kayahtä māna kisiwāk kā-pmakutsiniyit māna.

" nka-sākōtsihikuh ! " itäyihtam.

kītahtawä ä-wāpiskāyik um ōmistsikumis yāyinam ; wāpiskāyiw. ōtah ä-pimakutsiniyit, ākwask itisinam. äkutah akuhkäw awa kamāmakus. utinäw. utinam ; kunt itastāw.

" äkwah uma ! " itik.

āpahamiyiwa pīwāpiskus ; nätäh isiwäpinam awa mistatäwāsis ; misāyiw pīwāpisk äh-nōtimāyik.

" sākuhtāyanih ōma, kä-paskiyawiyin ! " itik.

äkwah ä-wīh-kakwä-āhtastāt, nama kaskihtāw. kätahtawä ä-nayawīt, ä-wā-wāpahtahk uma mistik, kā-wāpahtahk äh-askihtakwāyik. sāminam ; äkutah utsihtsīhk misiwä ayīsihtitāw. utinam uma pīwāpisk ; sōskwāts uhpinam tāpiskōts ä-yāhkasiniyik.

" hā, nīstāh, äkwah māka kä-māsihituyahk, ta-wītsäwāyahkuk, tantōmāyahkuk. awiyak sākuhihtsih kit-ōtahwāw utāpatsihtsikanah. — nākā, kahkiyaw tsī kitāpatsihtsikanah ? "

"namuya. äyāpits aniki upahtsāwiyak,[1] *itah kita-nīpawiyin," itäw ukusisah.*

"hāw, kiya nīkān ntum kita-wītsäwatsik!"

kituhtāw awa mistatäw-awāsis; misahtsi-pätsimäw kiyikaw muhtsihk uhtsi. äkwah awa mitsāskwatsus k-āyāt äyaku misiw ītä itwahikākäw kīkaw muhtsihk. äkwah uwītsäwākaniwāwa äh-akimātsik, pōtih awa misāskwatsus k-āyāt päyak āyiwākipayiyiwa upawākanah. itāmihk k-āyātsik askīhk utsapīhkäsīsak ä-wāpiskisiyit, ayiwākipayiyiwa päyak äyakuni. äkwah māsihitōwak wīstāwa, aspin ispimihk ä-yāhkīmukih ōhi itah kā-nīpawitsik.

kītahtawä nāh äkwah pīhtatwān mistahi wäpāpihkäpayiw. äkwah nāhah, "äkwah äsah nisīm miyätawät!" itäyihtam; "āta wiya pakahkam manitōwiw; kahkiyaw käkway kīh-wīhtamawāw," itäyihtam.

kätahtawä, "näkā, niwi-sākuhik. kimästinän tsī?"

"namuya ninayawīn," itwäw awa k-ōtihkumit iskwäsis.

"maht äwaku pätāh! nka-tähtsikāpawin."

"namuya äkutōwahk, nkusis!" itwäw.

mistikwak äskusitsik, äkuyikuhk äh-päy-āyātsik, kāw-utinahk upīway awa k-ōtihkumit, ōmatōwihk wahtsīhk[2] *äh-utinahk. pakamaham uma mistsikus. nama käh-yahkīmōw.*

äkwah nāha pwāstawāts wäpāpihkäpayiw.

"häy, uskats ä-pawāmiyān, utsapīhkäsīs, misiwä kīsikuhk askīhk tapapāmāpäkamōwa kipīsākanāpīma!" itwäw.

mākuhāw äkwah. hā, papāmāmōw äkwah, äh-nawaswātiht. äkwah nāh īskwäw pähpäkahākan ayāw, äkwah äy-āpisāsiniyik ahkāmasinīs. pakamaham.[3] *piyisk pīwāpisk tāpiskōts äh-āti-misāyik, tähtsikāpawiw.*

"uskats äh-pawāmiyān, näyäwats ta-pimakutsihk, ta-sipwähtahit awa kā-mākuhāt nisīma! äkutōwahk nikī-wīhtamāku! äkwah niwīkimākan upakamākan kit-ōh-pasastähwak awa kā-tähtsikāpawiyān, ta-kisīkutsihk!" itwäw.

pakamaham.

"itäh nisīm umistsikumis k-āyāyik, äkutä ituhtahin!" itwäw.

pimakutsin. mäkwāts namuya kwayask ihtiw; utāsiyāniw aw īskwäw, äw-utihtāt usīma.

"häy, utihkumiw-iskwäw! mästatäw kā-nayawihāt nisīmah nikitimākäyimimāh!" itwäw.

āpihkunäw utāsiyāna; pasastähwäw ōhi käwiyah.

mästatäw-awāsis pahkisin, ōki mina käwiyak.

"häy, nīstah, k-ōtahun ntāpatsihtsikanah. äyāpits päyakwaw kiwīhmätawān. äwakunih nikäwiy utihkumah äyakuni kik-āpatsihāw,[4] *äkwah ōhi pīwāpisk. ati-miyuskamiki, mituni nīpihki, äkutah kā-wīh-mätawäyin."*

äkusi kīwäwak. takusinwak wīkiwāhk.

"hā, äkwah wāwīs mistahi manitōwiw!" itäyihtam awa nōtukäwa kā-kih-nayōmāt.

[1] Animate plural noun; meaning? The translation is surely wrong. Later in the story it seems that the things, whatever they are, consist of *käwiyak*: "porcupine quills."

[2] As *pīway* is "body-hair" this word is probably "armpit" or "pubes." It is evidently a dependent noun, i.e. one which always has a possessive prefix.

[3] He does not tell what it was she stood on and struck.

[4] Out of construction; he should have said *kik-āpatsihimāwa*, since the object is obviative. Similarly, though *ōhi*: "these" is plural, only one of the objects, the iron, is mentioned, the thong omitted.

äkus ä-nīpiniyik, käkāts äkwah wīstāwa ta-takusiniyit, kītahtawäh ä-pitsitsik, itäh ä-kapäsitsik, kītahtawä kā-pä-sākäwäyit ayīsiyiniwah mituni äh-kawāhkatusuyit, mistsikus k-āyāt, nāh-nāway kā-tahkupitäyikih ä-kaskipitäyikih, äkwah awa kayahtä mistsikus k-āyāt.

äkwah äh-pä-takusihk, "tawāw!" itāw.

äkwah, "ā, tānisi ōma? tāntä äw-uhtuhtäyin!" itäw aw ustäsimāw.

"msāskwatsusīhk."

"tāntä māka?"

"misāskwatsusīhk, ntitwān!"

"käkway māka ä-papā-nātaman?"

"nipä-wīwin. tāntäh awa k-āpit[1] kimisiwāw? usām kīstāwāw kipapāmaskatikuwāw."

"namuya ka-kīh-wīwin."

"ōtah nisīmak kisiwāk päy-āyāwak, kiyawā mīna äyakunik ta-wīwiyāk."

hā, nama tāpwāhtamwak.

"ntsawāts kika-mätawānānaw!" itwäw awa kā-kawāhkatusut äwaku.

"hāw, kiya nīkān!" itāw awa ihkwah k-āyāwāt.

kiyām mamitunäyihtam, ihkwah ta-pakitsiyit. pakitsītutāk awa kā-kawāhkatusut. ntsawāts kwāhkutähk itisinam ōma mistsikus kā-tahkunahk, äkwah ä-kīsisutsik ōk īhkwak, nanātuhk matsi-pisiskiwak, mōhtäwak, ayīkisak, äyakunih äh-utihkumit awa. äkusi käkāts ä-mästsihimiht, pōyōw. äkwah ōma muhyāpitsiskān; sämāk ōmis īsiwäpinam; akuhkäw äkutah. uma pīwāpisk nätä isiwäpinam; sämāk awa kā-kawāhkatusut utinam päyak utsihtsīhk, ä-sinikunahk ōma pīwāpisk; nätä äh-isiwäpinahk, kiy-apisāsiniyiw. äkwah awa ntumäwak kit-uwītsäwākanitsik. pōtih awa kayahtä k-āyāt misāskwatsus päyak ayiwākipayiyiwa, itāmihk askīhk k-āyātsik mōhtsäsah ä-wāpiskisiyit.

"äkutāh ätsik ānih kiy-ätāmuyān, kiy-ätāmuyāhk!" äh-itäyihtahk, kītahtawä pah-kisimuhk äkutä, "hääy, nīstāh, tawayāk! nakatamuk kimistikumiwāwa! niwīh-takuhtān!"

käkway ätukä kā-pätōwākutäyik, kā-pahkihtihk ōma kaskipitsäsah, kā-tahkupitäyikih äwaku. pahkihtin muhtsihk. äkwah ōma käyāpits tsimatäw uma mistsikus, kā-pä-takusihk, hāw, awa kā-namahtsīt, ka-muhyāpitasäkut.

"ōmah tsäskwah ayīsiyiniw kit-ōtinam utsäpihk. 'maskihkiy,' kit-äsiyīhkātam, k-ōh-päh-kitimākäyimāt nīstāw. äkwah ōmah, nīstāw k-āyāt ayīsiyiniw, 'misāskwat, nīpisis,' t-äsiyīhkātam, t-ōh-pimātsihut. hāw, kīwäh, nīstāh. iyinīnāhk ituhtäh. äkā wiya kākäpātsi-tōtah. äkā wiya nipahtākäh," itik wīstāwa; "äkwah kiya kā-pä-mätawiyin, nātakām ituhtäh. äkwah kisīmak iskwäwak ōtäh āpihtā-kīsikāhk kit-äsi-sipwähtäwak. usām tahkih kiwīh-papā-mätawān, äh-uyasuwähk ta-miywāsik askiy, ayīsiyiniw ta-sākaskinät askīhk," itwäw; "äkwah niya ōtah muhtsihk nik-äsikīwān. kahkiyaw nika-kitimākäyimik ayīsiyiniw kikih niwīkimākan. äkwah kiya, nīstāh, āpakusīsak kā-kinwāyuwätsik kik-äkutōwiwin. äkwah niya, 'tsipustsuwiyākanisīs,' k-ätwätsik ayīsiyiniwak, äkutōwahk niya!"

kīpipayihōw; āpakusīsiwiw uwīkimākana kikih; mituni apisīsisiwak. äkuyikuhk äskwāk ātayōhkäwin.

---

[1] Literally, "In which place is this one who sits your sister?"—there being three seated women. Questions of identity are often put in this form.

Once upon a time there were three people, two men and one woman, two men. The men were the younger brothers of the woman. The youngest one did not work. He took a stick of saskatoon willow; he kept it, walking with it as a cane. His elder brother hunted, providing them with food.

Then at one time, when they had a big supply of food, the elder man said, "Well now, brother, suppose I look for someone to be our brother-in-law, so that our sister may have a husband. If we have him for brother-in-law, we shall not be embarrassed, when a man is here."

"Very well," the other answered him.

Presently he set out and tramped along. After one night on the way, he saw a tipi. It stood with the door facing the direction of noon. Then as he looked, he beheld a crow holding together the tips of the tent-poles. When he came there, that creature at the top of the tent gave a call.

"Come in!" it called to him.

He entered. There was a man all alone. When he had eaten, a man arrived, another youth.

He said, "What are you seeking, that you wander about?" he asked him.

"Why," he said, "my idea in wandering about is this: 'Suppose I get a brother-in-law,' is my thought; 'I shall give him my elder sister,' is my thought, concerning you, for I am inconvenienced by my sister's never speaking; that is why I have come to give her to you."

"Yes," the other answered him; "As for me, I do not care about it; but perhaps my younger brother right here will like the idea," he told him.

"Oh, as yet I am not good enough at killing things, to be able to marry, I above all, seeing that even you, who are good at killing things, do not like the idea."

"Dear me!" said the elder; "Near by here live three of my younger brothers and one elder brother, four of them; his three younger brothers take care of him. They are very good at killing game," he told him; "So you had better go there," he told him; "You had better go see them. Perhaps one of them will take to the idea," he told him.

He went there. As he came over the crest of the hill, there he saw a tipi. He saw what held the tips of the tent poles together, an owl, which already was giving its call. He went there.

Just as he reached the place, "Come in, young man!" he was told.

So he went there. He entered. He was given food. When he had eaten, look you, a young man came into the tent. He hung up some quivers.

"Hello, what is your errand, that you come here like this?" asked the eldest of the brothers.

He told him, "Oh, it is that I have come to give one of you my sister, elder than I."

"As for me, I am only given food by my younger brothers. I am no good at killing any kind of game. I could not have a wife," he told him; and then, "Now, brothers, some one of you go there!"

They answered him, "Ho, as if we were any good as yet at killing game! I shall not be able to go there," said all of them.

"Dear me, young man! At the other side of this hill lives my father. He lives with his four eldest sons, and these our elder brothers are not yet married; nor are the two young women, our younger sisters," he told him; "Go there. Perhaps my father will give you three of his children, two women and one man, if my father wishes to give them to you," he told him.

Accordingly, he left the tent. Eagerly he went to the place that had been indicated to him. And as on his way he came over the crest of a hill, there really he saw a tipi that stood with its doorway toward noon. As soon as he saw it, he was seen by the creature which held together the tips of the tent-poles, an eagle. At once the eagle gave its cry. He reached the tipi.

"Ho, come in!" he was told.

He entered. Whom did he see but an old man and an old woman, and no one else he saw but them, sitting alone on a thing like this blanket, like this on which I am sitting now; and, "Come in!" he was told.

When he had come in, "Now, old woman, give him food! Let him eat!" was said about him.

In due time he was given food. When he had eaten, suddenly there came some people with loud noise, two women, talking both at once. When they had come in, he saw that they were young girls. When they had taken their seats, some more people came in, four men.

Then the other said to him, "Now then, young man, how is it you have come tramping all the way here?" asked the old man; "Have you come to be with my children here?"

"Yes," he answered him.

"But what is the aim of your wandering about?"

"Oh, because those children of yours told me, 'You had better go there.' The fact is, we are in a difficult position with our elder sister, because we are alone with her, so that my sister never speaks; that is, I and my one younger brother, a young man, we are alone with her now. 'Perhaps you will find a brother-in-law in one of them there; my father will urge his children,' said your son, and that is why I have come to you."

"Well now, young man, these women children of mine have not yet learned to sew, so that they could take a man; in fact, they are even now engaged in learning to sew. Well, so I cannot give them to you," he told him; "Now then, as for you, my children, let one of you go there," he said to those four men.

Each and every one, "Nonsense! I too am a long ways from wanting to marry just now!" all those men said to him.

"Dear me, young man! You see that my children will not hear of it. You had best turn back from here and go home. If you will not do that, at least do not go in this direction here," he told him.

So he left the tipi. He went in the direction against which he had been warned. As he tramped along and came over the crest of a hill, there he saw a little lodge of smoked leather. He went there. As he stood in the doorway, he looked up at the tips of the lodge-poles: he saw a little smoke coming forth. Just as he was about to enter, as he peeked in, whom did he see, but a very old woman? * * * * * * * * * * *

"But do come in, grandchild!" she said to him.

"Well, at any rate she is an old woman. * * * * * * * * * * he thought. He went in. The old woman turned to face him.

"What are you going about for?" she asked him.

"I am going about looking for a man to be my brother-in-law," he told her.

"But have you seen my father-in-law who lives close by?" she asked him.

"Yes."

"Have you a wife?"

"No."

"But have you seen my sisters-in-law?"

"Yes."

"They are the ones I am teaching to sew. As soon as they are good at sewing, they are to take husbands," she told him; "I am the one for you to woo," said the little old woman.

"Oh, you are too old, grandmother," he answered her.

"Why! So now for the first time a mortal man rejects me! All those whom you saw on your way here are my husbands, and here you refuse to marry me!"

"Oh, grandmother, you are too old!"

He rose to his feet as he said this to her. The old woman made a leap, and took hold of him here, and threw her legs round him, and clasped him here round the neck with her arms. The old woman kept a tight hold. Though he tried to pull her free, he could not move her; his grandmother was too strong. He carried her about like a pack-load, * * * * * * * The youth was ashamed. Then he wandered helplessly about. He went to the tipi of an old man, a place of which he had dreamt, the youth. He was a very old man. When he arrived, the other came forth from the lodge.

"Dear me! Why are you being carried here like a pack, wife?" he asked her.

"Yah, because this person rejected me when I told him, 'Woo me!' Because he rejected me, is why I thought, 'Then let him at least carry me on his back.' Those fellow-husbands of yours, handsome as they are, every one, none of them refused me. Do not argue with me. This person has angered me by refusing me."

"Alas, young man! There is a lake close by here. You had better go there. For there stay two of our grandchildren, whom she you are carrying indulges. But as for me, I fear my wife," said the old man.

He went off with his pack. Really, he came to a lake, and there came two young women, laughing gaily.

"Hey, why are you again acting like a child, being carried here on someone's back?"

"Oh, do not reason with me, my grandchildren! When this person rejected me and angered me, I decided, 'Then at least let him carry me round on his back'."

Wherever he slept of nights, still he had her on his shoulders; he lay with his pack. So those young women said nothing.

"I shall have to take her to my dream-guardians," he thought.

So he carried her round to these places.

Whenever he reached a dream-guardian of his, "Alas, grandson, I fear her!" he would be told.

Nothing could be done to her, to shake her loose. At last he had gone to all of his dream-guardians without avail. So there he was.

"There is nothing in sight but that she will kill me, that I starve to death," he thought.

Then in time he would scarcely reach any place for which he was bound. At last, what a sight it was, when he slept anywhere, as he kept carrying the old woman on his back! Then at one time he saw a brook, towards evening, a brook which beavers had dammed. He went there. Over on yonder bank he saw some water-weeds; here and there were sticks of wood that had been shaped.

"Oh, I shall go lie on yonder bank. I may as well die over there," he thought.

He found that he could barely move as he lay.

"I had better crawl. It is plain that this old woman means to kill me," he thought.

Presently he started. He lay down by the side of the dam. It was dark now. He kept crawling. When he had almost reached the bank, he could go no farther.

"Oh, tomorrow I shall get there," he thought.

Then he saw a man; he wore his clothes with the fur on the outside; he was clumsy in his movements; as he came, carrying a club in his hand, she whom he was carrying on his back, suddenly began to wriggle and squirm.

"Pray do come here, brother-in-law!" said he who was carrying the old woman.

He came. He knew that she feared this person.

"Ho, how is it, brother-in-law, that you carry this old woman on your back?"

"Alas, brother-in-law! Do try to free me!"

"Why, brother-in-law! But all you have to do is club her, if she will not let go of you!"

"Oh, grandchild, take pity on me! Please let me live! Your brother-in-law will be engaging in contests again. I shall give him things to use. He will defeat people with what I shall give him. Please let me live, grandchild!" she said to him.

Accordingly, "Yes! Do not try to deceive my brother-in-law. If you try to deceive him, without fail I shall hear it. Now then, let him go!"

She let go of him.

Then, "Here, brother-in-law! Eat this!" his brother-in-law said to him.

He ate one berry; he was in flesh again; he was strong again. Then she gave him two needles, and two awls, and a small stone; three gifts.

"There, grandchild, you will be engaging in contests again!" the old woman told him who had carried her about.

"Thanks!"

Thereupon the old woman went back home. And he who was clumsy in his ways went to marry the elder sister of him he had met.

So the latter went on, the next morning. When he came to a place where the land was level and wooded, presently, as he was walking along, two women came into sight.

"Hey there, sweetheart, stand still! Whichever gets there first, her you will marry; whichever is beaten, will have your younger brother for husband," he was told.

He stood still. Those young women over there broke into a run. Neither one was beaten.

"Well, let us go to our dwelling!" he was told.

They went to the place. He saw it, a tipi made of bits of old leather. They reached it. The youth was carrying a quiver. When they reached the tipi of old leather, the two pretty women went in. When they entered, over here, at the left of the door-flap, sat a little girl with mucus hanging from her nose, and her eyes all sticky; and lice were climbing about all over this little girl's face, and more, of course, on her head, and all over her body and legs and feet, all over were lice. He looked at her.

When the youth had eaten, "What are you about seeking?" he was asked.

"Why, I am going about looking for two women, one for my younger brother to marry, and one for me. I have already found a man to be our brother-in-law."

"Indeed! So you are the one of whom they say, 'He is seeking about for a wife,' you are the one of whom this is said!" the young women told him, and laughed without cease.

"Yes, it is I!"

"Here is one for you to marry," they said, pointing to the lousy girl.

He looked at her.

"She is too lousy. I cannot marry her," he said.

"Hoho, children, do you take him for your husband; he refuses me."

"Good!"

Really, they took him for their husband; they both married him.

Then presently, for no reason at all the Lousy One suddenly crawled about.

"Ho!"

They threw her back.

"How is it he always cures me?" said the Lousy One; "Why, children, I dreamt that I was working; I dreamt that I should stop walking in my sleep as soon as I made something for my son-in-law to use as a blanket-robe. I long greatly to work," said the little girl, Lousy One.

Accordingly, in the morning he went hunting; he killed a jumping-deer. He brought it whole.

"Here, now, my children, skin it!" she told them.

They skinned it.

"My children, go call my dog!" said Lousy One.

The Lousy One called her dog. That dog turned out to be entirely of iron.

"My dog, go eat. My son-in-law has killed something for you to eat."

The dog ate the jumping-deer. At once the dog grew big, when he had eaten that single meal.

"Begone!" she said to it; "Go home!" she said to her dog; "So now, my children, go get my thongs for stretching hides!" she told them.

Accordingly, they fetched them; they brought them. The thongs were of yellow metal. She stretched the hide. When she had tied it, she finished it; she flung it inside the lodge. Look you, very handsome was the youth's blanket that he was to have for his robe.

Then, when night came again, again she walked in her sleep.

When she awoke from her trance, again, "Oh, my children, it is because I am longing for work! Then I shall stop walking in my sleep!"

In the morning he hunted; he killed a deer. He brought it entire.

Then, again, "My children, skin it!" she said.

It was skinned for her.

"Now go call my dog. He is to have a meal," she said.

The dog ate its meal. It ate all. Then truly very large grew that dog. It could not get into the tent. It had grown large, now.

"Oh, my children, it is because only now and then I work, and little at a time, that I am so beautiful," she said.

Then she finished this robe, too. In the night again she walked in her sleep. Quickly she came out of her trance. So in the morning he hunted. He killed a bull buffalo. The youth was hungry; so he took a small bit of meat from the fleshy part of the leg and roasted it for himself and ate it.

When he had eaten, " 'Even as strong as I am, so strong let this my grandchild be!' my grandmother did say of me! Let me now be strong enough to handle this buffalo which I wish to drag!" he said, remembering what she had said to him, whom he had carried on his back.

So he dragged home his load, thinking, "Now she will have work!" So he got it there.

"Oho, now I shall have a jolly time!" cried the Lousy One.

So, when it had been skinned, "Go call my dog!" she said.

It was gone for and called.

When it came, "Eat, my dog!" she said.

Then the dog, sniffing at it a little, merely walked in a circle round it; it would not eat it.

"Why will not this creature eat, mother, this dog of yours?"

"Yah, my children, does he not miss something?" she asked.

Then, "Did you not throw away anything?" they asked their husband.

"I cut a little from the fleshy part of the thigh and ate it," he said.

"Yah, and here was I thinking, 'Doubtless a human man is he whom I have as son-in-law!' So he is a Windigo! At any rate, eat the leavings!" she said to it.

It ate it. It finished it. Then truly big was that dog.

By dark she had finished the buffalo-robe.

"This let my son-in-law have as his sleeping-robe," she said.

This night again she walked in her sleep, because she longed for work. In the morning he set out. He went to a hilly place. He saw a bear's den. He went up to it.

"Grandfather, I have come to take your body, for I am being challenged!" he said to it.

"A moment, my grandchild! When you now slay me, then take two bristles from round my mouth. When you reach your dwelling, then throw one into the fire. 'Come try to find this!' say then to her. Indeed, she who will challenge you has spirit power. Tomorrow, taking the first turn, you will try to find her lice. If you find one, then you will have won from her the right to take her daughters home with you," the bear told him.

With that it came out from its lair. He killed it. Oh, he dragged it home. He took those two bristles. One, as he entered, he threw into the fire. One he kept.

Then, as he arrived, "Now then, my children, go skin that creature. My son-in-law shall have a blanket-robe," she said of her son-in-law.

Then, when they had done skinning it, as usual the dog was sent for and called. Then it ate the bear; it ate it all. Then she sent her dog back whence it came. But then, though she stretched that bearskin with her yellow thong, when she had got it all tied, it turned back into an undressed skin. She could not tan that bearskin. She untied it.

"Fetch another, my children!" she ordered.

They brought another thong, a black one. Though she worked at the stretching, she could not tan it; it turned back into an undressed hide. At last she untied it.

"Come, another, my children!"

It was a bright green thong; it was brought for her. Still she could not finish the hide. By this time it was nearly dawn. Again she untied it. "My children, fetch now that thong of mine that is of red metal, and my pounding-stone, and my ax, and my meat-pestle, all these. Do your best. This thing is actually tormenting me, this thing I cannot tan, that my son-in-law may have a blanket-robe!" she said.

Truly, though the things were brought for her, yet she could not finish the hide. She undid the tying, and flung it away, she cared not where. She placed her thong down below. By this time it was daylight.

"My children, take this now, which my son-in-law is to have for a blanket-robe."

When they took it up, it was back in the state of an undressed skin.

Then, "Dear me, so now once my son-in-law has beaten me! Let us try again!" she cried; "But it is my son-in-law who is to try first!" she said of him.

He took that bear's bristle.

"See this! If you do not find it, I shall be free to take your daughters home with me," he said to her.

He threw it away. Although the little girl looked for it, she could not find it.

Presently, "Ho, let it be found!"

She saw it; it was the youth who took it into his hand.

"Here it is!"

Truly, there it was.

"Ho, but now let my son-in-law try to find one of my lice!"

There lay her ax, her pounding-stone, and all the things, all iron.

Then, "Very well, but let her lay her head here!"—on his knee.

As soon as the little girl lay down in position, gone were her lice. Though vainly the youth sought them all over, he could not find them.

"Now then, my son-in-law, since you have not been able to find one, now I shall club you!" she said to him.

"Oho! When you get over these, then you shall club me!"

He threw the needles so that they stood on end. There, they turned into huge iron things, going deep into the ground and high aloft and over the earth.

"Hey, son-in-law, but when I have got past these, then I will chase you!"

Vainly she chopped at them; at last she had worn out her ax. Then she wore out also her pounding-stone.

Then, "Hey, truly my son-in-law is driving me into a rage! My dog, come here!" she called to her dog. "Here, my dog, eat these!" she called to it.

As soon as the dog had touched them with its snout, they were like meat, and quickly it devoured them.

"Be off, my dog, go home! I am going off to club my son-in-law who has just now left!"

She pursued him; she had only her ax in her hand. When she was close upon him, he threw an awl behind him.

"Here let great thornberry-trees grow forth!" said the youth.

Behind him, what numbers of great thornberry-trees! When she reached them, though she hewed at them and split them with her ax, and pulled them up, yet she could not get through, could not make an opening through them. She hallooed for her dog. Truly, it came.

"Now, my dog, eat these!" she told it.

Again it went eating, this time the thornberry-trees. These too it ate up.

"Be off, go home, my dog!" she cried.

The dog went back home. The Lousy Little Girl went in pursuit. Again she was carrying her ax. When she was close at his heels, he flung up into the air the stone his grandmother had given him.

"Here is a place of rocky mountains! Underneath there I shall be!" he cried.

Then, though she tried to smash those rocks with her ax, at last she wore out every one of her tools.

"Ho, my dog, come here!" she cried, shouting.

Truly, quickly it came there.

"My dog, go kill the one that lies down yonder below!" she told it.

Then that dog went eating the rock. At last it reached him.

"Do not tear him to pieces, my dog! Only strangle him!"

So it did. It killed him.

Then that lazy man off yonder, this one's younger brother, was all alone with his sister, for it seems that his brother-in-law had gone away. He had a saskatoon stick which was as long as he was tall, with all kinds of designs on it. At the tip a feather was fastened. Only this he took. His sister was sitting there, moodily, longing for her absent brother.

"Now, sister," he said, "suppose I go look for my brother!" he said; "And when this thing ceases to sway as it hangs, then, 'Now it appears that my brother has gone to destruction,' you will think," he said, and went out of the tent, after setting his quiver a-swinging by a push of his hand.

It kept swaying as it hung. He went away. He held the saskatoon stick in his hand. As soon as he had left, he went with great speed. Then really, he reached his elder brother, where he lay dead. He stroked him, like this, with that feather, with that stick of his.

"Brother, arise!" he said to him.

He arose. So he really came back to life, when he had been stroked with the stick. He went with his elder brother. He went there.

When he arrived, "Now then, elder brother, tomorrow do you come here," he told him.

"Very well," the other answered him.

Then he went toward where that Lousy One was, and there from over the hill came the young women.

"Hey! Stand still where you are!" they said to him; "The one who outdistances the other, her you will take to wife," he was told.

They ran toward him. Neither was left behind; at the same time both reached him.

"Now let us go to our dwelling!" they said to him.

So they went there. There, when they entered, that little girl again looked as she had looked before.

"Hey, what are you going about seeking, like this?"

"Oh, the fact is, I am looking for a woman to marry," he said.

"Then marry this one here!"

He looked at her.

"She is too lousy," he said of her.

"Oho, my children, it must be you he has in mind for himself! You take him to husband!" she said of him.

Then, when night came, he lay down to sleep. That little girl walked in her sleep.

"Greatly I am longing to work! Much I am longing to work! It seems as if some lazy person has come here to stay as son-in-law!" said the little girl.

In the morning at once he went off. Very quickly he came to where his elder brother had found and killed the bear. He walked to the spot.

"Grandfather, I have come to fetch you, for I am engaging in a contest this day!" he said to it.

"Yes, my grandchild! But first do you take two hairs from round my mouth. To be sure, I do not think you lacking in power of your own. Your elder brother was deceived by an unfair stroke. Now, as soon as you have brought me there, she will send for her dog, who is an instrument of her power," it told him; and so, "Very well, come now!" it told him.

He clubbed it; he killed it. He dragged his burden home. Very early in the morning he arrived with it. As soon as he entered, he threw one of those things into the fire; one he kept on his person.

Then, when the game had been skinned for her, "My children, go get my ax, my hide-scraper, my stick for treating hides, my pounding-stone, my thongs for stretching hides, as many as are my tools. And you, my daughter, go round and look for my son, your elder brother," she told them; and then, finally, "Now, do you call my dog," she told one of her daughters; "For I do not forget that he said, 'She is too lousy!' "

For she had been angered by the speech; that was why she was sending for her son. Then, when that dog arrived, the youth threw himself toward the door. The bearskin had not even been stretched, when the dog arrived. Then, when it came into the tent, though no harm had been done to it, it had its tail between its legs, and cringed as it came, just as though it feared something.

Then He Who Had the Saskatoon Stick spoke of it thus; thus he spoke of that dog: "Is it on this creature that you rely?" he said of that dog, and touched it with the stick.

That dog broke into bits; it crumbled into tiny bits of metal.

And of those things that lay there in a pile, "Is it on these things that you rely?" he asked her, and touched her tools one after another with the stick. When then, one after another, they fell to pieces, that little girl had nothing left her; all the things on which she relied had been destroyed.

"Well, now I shall hunt your lice. If I find one, then I shall be permitted to take your daughters home with me," he said to her.

"Very well," said the little girl.

When he looked at her, all over her face were lice; then, at the very moment when she sought to lower her head, already her head had been touched with the stick; her lice had no time to disappear. Without mercy he smashed the lice against the stony ground with his long stick. After a while he turned her head to the other side; wherever he looked, it was full of lice. Then suddenly some lice came and settled on Him Who Had the Saskatoon Stick. At that he pointed his stick toward the blazing fire. A flame leaped up on the stick, and the lice that had settled on him were there on the stick, roasting until their bellies burst with a pop. While he was doing all this, in time that young man arrived, and at once saw to his surprise how his mother's lice were being hunted down.

"Hey, on what errand were you off, while your brother-in-law here was destroying my tools to the very last one?" she called to him.

The son wore a little flute round his neck; the flute was tied with a small hide thong with the fur turned out; and a small piece of iron he wore across his shoulder.

Then, "Why, mother, too greatly are you wasting your lice. It happens that even if we are not defeated, you are to give them up. For I have been called here to be present at the blessing of mortal man, that I too may give him mystic knowledge; and that is why I was so slow about coming home. You have gone too far in your evil pursuits, mother," her son said to her.

He was a pot-bellied child and went naked; Pot-Belly Child was he; he was Lousy One's son.

"Now then, brother-in-law, now is my turn!" he said.

Then the lice ceased coming down. Then he took the little thong with the fur on it. Then he arrived who had been killed by the dog.

"Ho, elder brother, stay far behind my back!"

He flung the thing like this.

"If you catch this on the fly, you have won it from me!" he told him.

Though he tried to hit it in the air with his stick, in the form it had taken of a white butterfly, yet from moment to moment he could not see it, and then again, suddenly right close there it would be in the air.

"He will surely defeat me!" he thought.

Then presently he rubbed the white part of his stick; it was white. As the thing flew past, he held it in front of it. There the butterfly clung to it. He took it into his hand. He took the thing, now lifeless; he laid it down carelessly.

"Now try this!" the other said to him.

He untied the little piece of iron; over yonder Pot-Belly Child threw it; it was a huge round block of iron.

"If you can handle this, you have won it from me!" he told him.

Then, when he tried to move it from the spot, he could not budge it. Presently, as he grew tired, as he looked at that stick, he saw that it turned green. He touched it with his hand; he placed it against every part of his hand. He took hold of the iron bar; at once he lifted it up, as though it were light.

"Ha, brother-in-law, but now we shall come to grips, and we shall call to us whatever beings are to be on our side. Whichever of us is beaten shall lose the instruments of his power.—Mother, are all your implements gone?"

"No. There are still those instruments of levitation upon which you may stand," she told her son.

"Now then, do you first call those who are to be on your side!"

Pot-Belly Child blew his whistle; with his call he brought in great number all manner of beings from the earth. And He Who Had the Saskatoon Stick pointed in every direction all over the ground. Then, when they counted their supporters, it turned out that He Who Had the Saskatoon Stick was by one follower ahead. Of the spiders that dwell under the ground, a white one of them was the odd one. Then he and his brother-in-law contended, as those things on which they stood stretched up into the air.

Then, at this time, that quiver off yonder began to sway greatly. And yonder woman thought, "Now, it appears, my brother is contending! However, by all means he has spirit power; all manner of mystic knowledge has been communicated to him," she thought.

Presently, "Mother, he is about to defeat me. Have you used it all up?"

"I am not yet weary," said the little girl, Lousy One.

"Then bring me what you have! Let me stand on it."

"It is not of that kind, my son!" she said.

They were aloft now at the height of the trees, when the Lousy One took one of the hairs from here, on her body. With it she struck that stick. It could no longer grow in length.

Then that thing off yonder barely swayed a bit as it hung.

"Hey, as first I dreamt, spider, everywhere in the sky and on the earth, your strings would be tied about!" he cried.

He was now being close pressed. He fled about, and was pursued. And that woman off yonder had a stone mallet encased in leather and a small pestle-stone. She struck them. With them she beat something. At last, when, like iron, it widened out, she stood on it.

"As first I dreamt, through the air he is to fly, and to take me hence, he who presses close upon my brother! It was the like of him, after all, that gave me mystic knowledge! And let it be with my husband's war-club that I strike this being on which I stand, that it may speed fast through the air!" she spoke.

She beat it.

"There where is my brother's stick, thither take me!" she said.

She sped through the air. * * * * * * * * * * * *

"Hey, Lousy-Woman! Do not forget that I love my brother whom Pot-Belly is tiring!" she cried.

* * * * * * * * with it she beat those porcupine quills.

Pot-Belly Child fell to the ground, and so did those quills.

"Ho, brother-in-law, you have won from me my implements. Again some time you will be engaging in a contest. These, my mother's lice you will have for your use, and also these things, the iron and the other. As the warm weather comes on, well on into summer, that is when you will be contending."

Thereupon they went home. They came to where they dwelt.

"Ha, now he is more of a manitou than ever!" thought He Who Had Carried the Old Woman on His Back.

Then, when summer came and it was almost time for his brother-in-law to arrive, then at one time, as they moved camp and were stopping for the night, there came into sight a very lean man carrying a stick to which at intervals covered-up bundles were tied; they were surprised that this person, too, carried a stick.

Then, as he came to where they were, "Come in!" they said to him.

Then, "Why, what is this? Whence do you come?" the elder brother asked him.

"From the willow-wood."

"But whence?"

"From the willow-wood, I say!"

"And what are you seeking, as you go about?"

"I have come to take a wife. Which of the women sitting here is your sister? For your brother-in-law leads you too much of a chase, always going away."

"You cannot have her to wife."

"My younger sisters have come with me and are staying close by here, so you may marry them in return."

They did not accept this offer.

"Then we shall have to settle it by a contest!" said the lean one.

"Very well, you first!" he was told who had the lice.

He merely fixed his thought on the idea that lice were to come down. They came down and settled on the lean man. He pointed the stick which he was carrying toward the blazing fire, and the lice burned up, all the different evil animals, such as worms and toads, which he had as lice. So when they had been almost all destroyed, he quit. Then he tried the string with fur on it. At once he moved his stick like this, and there, the thing clung to it. Then he threw the piece of iron over yonder; at once the lean man took it up into one of his hands and rubbed it; when he threw it back yonder, it was small again. Then they summoned those who were to be their followers. It turned out that he who had surprised them by also having a saskatoon stick had one follower more, a white worm of those that stay under the ground.

Then, just as he was thinking, "And so I must flee; we must flee!" suddenly from the west came the call, "Hey, brother-in-law, make room! Let go your sticks! I am coming!"

Then something came a-flying with noise, and down fell the little bundles that were tied fast to that stick. It fell to the ground. And that stick stood upright in the ground again, when he arrived, none other than that awkward man, who wore his garments with the fur turned out.

"In time to come, mortal man will take up this root. 'Medicine,' he will call it, with which my brother-in-law has blessed him in the hither course of time. And this which my brother-in-law has here, mortal man will call 'saskatoon willow,' and with it will preserve his life. Now then, go home, my brother-in-law. Go to the land of mortals. Do not act wantonly. Do not kill," his brother-in-law said to him; "And as for you, who have come here to engage in contest, go to the wooded country of the north. And let your sisters set out toward the south. For you are ever too eager to engage in contests, now that it has been arranged that the earth is to be good, so that man may be plentiful upon earth," he said; "And as for me, I shall return here to the ground. All mortal men shall take pity on me and on my wife. And you, my brother-in-law, the long-tailed mice, of these you shall be. And I, those whom men call 'sharp-nosed mice,' such a one I shall be!"

He threw himself down; he turned into a mouse, and so did his wife; they were very tiny.

That is the end of the sacred story.

(23) Thunderbird and Winter

Mrs. Maggie Achenam

kā-wīhkaskusahk.

äkwah kutak.

kītahtawä äsah nōtukäsiw utānisah wīkimäw. äkunik uyah[1] *nähiyawak. äkwah nōhtähkatäwak, ukiniyah pikōh äh-māwatsihäyit utānisah, nipīhk äh-pakāsimāyit, äyōkunih pikō äh-mōwātsik ; wi-npahāhkatusōwak.*

kītahtawä sipwähtäw uskinīkiskwäw, ukiniyah äh-ppā-māwatsihāt, kā-wāpamāt äh-minahuyit. ituhtäw. namuy āhpoh wīh-kitāpamik. sōskwāts kahkiyaw wiyāsah ōsihtāyiwah. sipwähtäyiwah äkwah. wiya kutak mōsahkinäw watōwah, ä-wīh-muwāt. kīwäw. äkwah äyakunih ōkinīsah mītsimāpōhkäw, mītsimāpuy äyakō äh-mītsitsik, äyaku pikuh.

äkwah äh-wāpahk sipwähtäw ; mīnah sipwähtäw. āsa mīnah mustuswah nipahäw nāpäw. mituni kisināw. uskinīkiskwäw äh-papāmuhtät, ōkiniyah äh-papā-mōsahkināt, ituhtäw ōhi nāpäwah.

" kimäkwāskamān äh-minahuhk, " itäw nāpäw awa ; " manisāwäh pikw iyikuhk. "

äkwah uskinīkiskwäw miywäyihtam.

" äkwah nikāwiy ta-mītsiw mistahi wiyās ! " täyihtam.

sōskwāts päyak mustuswah miyik. kīwäw ; iyawis wiyās kīwähtatäw. äkwah äh-takusihk wīkiwāhk, mistahi mītsisōwak. miywäyihtam nōtukäsiw.

" mīnah sipwähtähkan ; māskōts mīnah ka-wāpamāw ta-nipahāt. "

sipwähtäw. wāpamäw äh-nipahäyit mustuswah. āsay mīnah iyawis miyik. miywäyihtam.

äkwah äkutah, " kōnāpämin tsī ? "

" namuya, " itäw.

" äkusi mākah kah-wīkimitin. "

" tsäskwa pitah, " itäw ; " nikāwiy pitah nka-wīhtamawāw. täpäyimutsi, ka-wīkimitin. wāpahki ka-wīhtamātn. "

" äha' , " itwäw nāpäw ; " nimiywäyihtän. "

äkusi sipwähtäw. äkwah äh-wāpahk, nōtukäsiw utānisah kakwätsimik.

" nka-wīkimäw äyōkō nāpäw, " itik.

---

[1] For *wiyah?*

" äha' ," itwäw nōtukäsiw.

äkwah sipwähtäw uskinīkiskwäw ; wāpamäw nāpäwah.

" äkwah kiwīh-wīhtamātin : ' äha' ,' itwäw nikāwiy ta-wīkimitān. "

kīwähtahäw nāpäwah. takuhtäwak wīkiwāhk. unāpämiw. tahtukīsikāw minahuyiwa. äkwah ä-kāh-kīsupwäyīk, kāmwātsīw uskinīkiskwäw.

" tānis ōmah ä-kāmwātisiyan ? " itäw ōwīkimākanah.

" käkāts äkwah mānah kā-takuhtät niwīkimākan, " itwäw uskinīkiskwäw.

" äkwah nāpäw awa äh-unāpämiyan ätsik ānih ! " itäw ; " kīh-kiskäyihtamān, namuya kah-wīkimitin. tānisi äsinākwahk kīsik, wāh-takusihkih kiwīkimākan ! " itäw uskinīkiskwäwah.

" kīspin wāh-takusihki, wāpaskwäw ; usāwipäskwäw. äyaku niwīkimākan, kisiwāk pä-ayātsih. kisiwāk äkwah, kisiwāk päy-ayāw. tapasī ; ka-nipahik. "

äkwah nāpäw, " namuya ; ōtah nik-āyān. "

kätahtawä kāsōw pīhtsāyihk nāpäw. pä-misi-kitōwak.

" äyōkō niwīkimākan, " i'wäw uskinīkiskwäw.

kisiwāk pä-pōnīsiniyiwah ; pä-pīhtukäyiwa.

" waniskāh, nikusāk ! " itik nāpäw awa.

äkwah waniskāw.

" ka-mätawānānaw, " itik.

" äha' ; kiya nīkān. tānisi t-äsi-mätawäyahk ? kiya nīkān, " itäw awah piyäsiw.

äkw ānih kāh-kitōw. misi-kimiwan ; miskwamiy pahkisin. äkwah awah nāpäw kwäskämōw. asām ay-apiw, äh-ati-misi-kimiwaniyik, miskwamiy mīnah äh-pahkisihk. kätahtawä pōyōw ; pä-pīhtukäw.

" kiyaskuts äkwah, nikusāk ; pimutah, " itäw uskusākah.

" äha' , " itwäw ; " äkwah ta-misi-kisināw ! " itwäw ; " mituni tawāsäskwan ; ta-wāsäskwani-kisin ! "

mistahi kisināw. äkwah misi-pīwan ; mtuni yōtin, mistsikusak äh-pāh-pakatsitsik. mituni wīh-kawatsiyiwa ukusākah asām.

" äkuyikuhk, nikusāk ! kīwinaw wīwih kiyām, " itäw.

äkusi kīsōpwäw kāwi mitunih.

" kiyām kīwinaw wīwih ; kisākōtsihin, " itwäw.

äkusi wiy äōkō päyak minah nikīsihtān ātayōhkäwin.

Now another story.

Once upon a time an old woman dwelt with her daughter. They were Cree. They suffered hunger, for the woman's daughter merely gathered thornberries, which she boiled, and that was all they had to eat; they were almost dead of hunger.

Then at one time the young woman went off to go about gathering thornberries, when she saw someone who had killed game. She went near. That person would not even look at her. Quickly he prepared all the meat. Then he went away. But she, the other, picked up the clots of blood to eat. She went home. Then she made a broth of the poor thornberries, and this broth they ate, only this.

On the next day she went out again. Again that man killed a buffalo. It was very cold. The young woman, as she went about, picking thornberries here and there, went to where that man was.

"You have come just in time to where game has been killed," the man said to her; "Cut off for yourself as much as you please."

The young woman was pleased.

"Now my mother will eat much meat!" she thought.

At once he gave her one buffalo. She went home; she took home the meat entire. When she arrived at her home, they had a big meal. The old woman was glad.

"Go out again; perhaps you will see him again making a killing."

She went. She saw him killing a buffalo. Again he gave her the entire carcass. She was pleased.

And then, "Are you married?"

"No," she answered him.

"Then let me marry you."

"Only wait," she told him; "Let me first tell my mother. If she is content, I will marry you. Tomorrow I will tell you."

"Very well," said the man; "I am very glad."

Then she departed. On the next day the old woman's daughter asked her.

"Let me marry this man," she asked her.

"Yes," said the old woman.

Then the young woman went; she saw the man.

"Now I shall tell you: 'Yes,' says my mother; I may marry you."

She brought the man home with her. They arrived at the lodge. She had him as her husband. Every day he killed game. But when the weather was hot, the young woman became listless.

"Why are you so listless?" he asked his wife.

"Because this is the time, always, when my husband is about to come," said the young woman.

"And so you mean to say you have a husband, this man!" he said to her; "If I had known that, I should not have married you. How looks the sky when your husband is about to come?" he asked the young woman.

"When he is about to come, there is white sky; and yellow clouds are in the sky. That is when my husband has come near on his hither way. And close now, close has he come. Flee; he will kill you."

Then the man, "No; here I shall stay."

Presently the man hid indoors. There came a great thunderstorm.

"That is my husband," said the young woman.

Close by the other came to earth; he came into the lodge.

"Get up, my fellow-husband!" he said to that man.

Then he got up.

"We shall have a contest," the other said to him.

"Very well; you first. What sort of contest shall we have? You first," the Thunderer was told.

Then he roared. There came a great rainstorm; it hailed. Then that man changed his form. A snowshoe lay there during the great storm of rain and hail. Presently he ceased; he came inside the lodge.

"Your turn now, my fellow-husband; shoot your arrow," he told his fellow-husband.

"Very well," said he; "Now let there be intense cold!" he spoke; "Let there be very clear sky; let there be a clear cold sky!"

It grew very cold. And there was a great flurry of snow; there was a strong wind, until the branches snapped and crackled in the cold. The Snowshoe's rival husband froze almost to death.

"Enough, my fellow-husband! Keep you our wife, as you please," he told him.

Thereupon the weather again grew very hot.

"Keep you our wife, as you please; you have defeated me," he said And so now I have finished this story too.

(24) The Ten Brothers

Coming-Day

kā-kīsikāw-pīhtukāw.

iskwäwak äyōkō : mitātaht iskwäwak, piyäsiwak, iskwäwak, äkwah ōhtāwiyiwāwa minah ukāwiyiwāwa ōk īskwäwak, äh-ukimāwiyit ōhtāwiyiwāwa.

äkwah ōtah, askīhk utah, äkutah uskinīkiwak mīna mitātaht, mīn äyakunik uwītisānihtutsik, māka nam āwiya ukāwīwāwa ; ōhtāwīwāwah minah nam āwiya. äkusi päyak piku mīkiwāhp ; nam āwiya kutakah ayīsiyiniwah ayāyiwah kisiwāk.

äkwah ōki ispimihk iskwäwak, itäh k-ayātsik, misāw ōtänaw äwaku. äyukunik ōki iskwäwak, päyak umisimāw matsihkihkwäwis isiyīhkāsōw. äkusi awa usīmimāw, aw ōskinīkiskwäw miyusiw.

äkusi äkwah kutakak ōk ōskinīkiwak mitātaht k-āhtasitsik, äwaku ustäsimāw matsihkiwis ; käyāpits aw ōsīmimāw, aw ōskinīkiw miyusiw. äkusi uskinīkiwak ōki namuya kiskäyimäwak iskwäwa nānitaw kit-āyāyit, mīnah kutakah ayīsiyiniwah. päyakwanuhk äy-ayātsik ōk ōskinīkiwak, pisisik mātsīwak kahkiyaw ōk ōskinīkiwak. kītahtawä ōma äh-mātsītsik māna, äka āwiyah äh-apiyit, aw ōskinīkiw usīmimāw äyaku mānah nīkān takusin. äkusi kahkiyaw nāh-nāway takusinwak.

kītahtawä äh-takuhtät aw ōskinīkiw, kā-wāpahtahk mistah äy-astäyikih mihtah. tāpiskōts awiya ä-kīh-takuhtäyit, itäyihtam, äh-takuhtät. mistahi miywäyihtam, " māskōts awiyak pīhtsayihk tit-apiw, " ä-täyihtahk.

äh-pīhtukät, nam āwiyah wāpamäw. äkusi wayawīw, ta-papāmuhtät, ka-wāpahtahk itah äsah ä-kīh-pimuhtäyit iskwäwah. äkwah mitihtäw itäh äh-kīh-nikuhtäyit ; nam āwiya wāpamäw. kāwih kīwäw ; pīhtukäw, äkwah äh-kutawät, ä-wīh-paminawasut. äh-kīsi-kutawät, uhtapiwinihk äh-apit, kītahtawä käkway kā-kiskäyihtahk itāmihk äh-astäyikih utanāskānihk. äkusi äh-pāskinahk, kā-wāpahtahk maskisinah. utinam, äh-wā-wāpahtahk ; mistahi miywāsiniyiwah. miywäyihtam ; nahastāw.

umis ītwäw : " iskwäw ätsik ānih kā-kīh-takuhtät ! " itäyihtam ; " namuya ta-wāpahtamwak nistäsak, " itäyihtam.

äh-kutsih-pustiskahk, pōtih miyuskam. äkusi äkwah kutakah ustäsah kā-tah-takuhtäyit, piyisk kahkiyaw takuhtäyiwah ustäsah ; mākah namuya wī-wīhtamawäw.

äkusi mīnah ä-kīh-nipātsik, äh-wāpahk, kīkisäpā sipwähtäw ōw uskinīkiw, äh-mātsīt. kutakak mīnah āsk-āskaw sipwähtäwak, namuya māna äh-wītsähtutsik ōk ōskinīkiwak kā-mātsītsik, kahkiyaw äh-pā-päyakutsik, miyātsītwāwi.

äkusi äkwah aw ōskinīkiw, " māskōts ä-wīh-wīkimit awa iskwäw kā-kīh-takusihk, " itäyihtam.

itäh äh-nipahāt mustuswah, äkwah utäyaniy, äkwah itah äh-miywāsiniyik wiyās, äkwah päyak upäminak, äwaku utinam, äkwah umāw, äh-kīwät.

" māskōts takuhtätsih ana iskwäw, ta-mītsiw ōmah umāw ; mīnah tapāstaham um upäminak, ta-mītsit, " äy-itäyihtahk, kīwäw.

äkwah kisiskāhtäw, ä-wīh-kakwä-käsiskawāt uskinīkiskwäwah, äy-itäyihtahk. pōtih äh-utākusiniyik, äh-takuhtät, āsay mīnah mihtah wāpahtam mihtsät äh-astäyikih. wāpahtam äh-pikihtäyik wīkiwäw.

" māskōts apiw, " itäyihtam.

äh-pīhtukät, nam āwiyah wāpamäw, äsah kāh-wäpāstakahikäyit.[1] *miywäyihtam. äkwah pōnam, ä-wīh-paminawasut. äkwah äh-apit, äh-paminawasut, āsay mīna käkway itäyihtam itah kā-kiy-astäyikih maskisinah. äh-utinahk, mīn äyakunih maskisinah. āsay mīna miywäyihtam, äh-wāwāpahtahk. mistahi miywāsiniyiwa, äh-pīmikitäyikih. äkusi astāw, " namuya ta-wāpahtamwak nistäsak, " äh-itäyihtahk. äkwah ōki uskinīkiwak äh-tāh-takuhtätsik, wāpahtamwak mihtah mihtsät. miywäyihtamwak, " tāpwä kiyipah mistahi nikuhtäw, " äh-itäyimätsik usīmiwāwa.*

awah ustäsimāw, äwaku matsihkiwis, umis ītwäw ! " tāpwä nimiywäyihtän mihtah mistahi äh-astäkih, " itwäw.

" äha' , " itwäwak uskinīkiwak.

äkusi namuya wīh-wīhtam aw uskinīkiw. äkusi äkwah tipiskāyiw mīna. ä-kīh-mītsisutsik, äh-ay-apitsik, kuntah äh-āh-ātsimutsik, piyisk kawisimuwak.

" hāw, kiyipah nika-waniskān, " itäyihtam aw uskinīkiw ; " nika-sipwähtān kiyipah, " äh-itäyihtahk.

tāpwäw kiyipah waniskāw, ä-wīh-mātsīt. tāpwä ä-kīh-mītsisut, wawäyīw, äh-mātsīt. mitunih miywäyihtam.

" māskōts ä-wīh-wīkimit away iskwäw kā-takusihk, " itäyihtam.

äkusi itä äh-nipahāt mustuswah, äkwah utinam itah ä-miywāsiniyik wiyās. äkwah äh-kīwät, pāh-pimipahtāw, " māskōts nika-wāpamāw, " äh-itäyihtahk. tsīki äh-ihtāt wīkiwāhk, kā-wāpahtahk mistah äh-pikihtäyik wīkiwāw. ä-takuhtät, mistahi wāpahtam mihtah äh-astäyik. äh-pīhtukät, nam āwiya wāpamäw, äsah mitunih kāh-wäpahtakahikäyit, mīnah utanāskāniwāwa äsah äh-pahpawahamiyit; mīn äsah kāh-paminawasuyit astäyiwa. sōskwāts mītsisōw. āsay mīna kā-wāpahtahk käkway äh-astäyikih. äw-utinahk, āsay mīnah maskisinah. mtuni miywäyihtam.

" hāw, namuya nka-wīhtamawāwak nistäsak, " itäyihtam.

pōtih äh-utākusihk, kā-tāh-takuhtäyit ustäsah.

äkwah umis ītwäw aw ustäsimāw : " tāpwä kikiyipīn, mihtah äh-utinaman, " itäw usīma.

" äha' , ayisk kiyipah nikīh-takusinin, " itäw.

äkusi kutakak mīn ōki ä-kīh-mītsisutsik, äkusi atih-tipiskāyiw. äkwah ay-apiwak, äh-ātsimutsik, ōmah kā-kīh-mātsītsik äwaku äh-ātsimutsik, äh-pā-pāhpitsik.

" äkusi mīnah wīpats nka-sipwähtān, " itäyihtam aw ōskinīkiw.

kiyipah kawisimōw. äkusi kahkiyaw kawisimōwak, äh-nipātsik. pōtih kiyipah waniskāw aw uskinīkiw, äh-paminawasut. äkusi kahkiyaw waniskāwak, äkwah äh-mītsisutsik. mayaw äh-kīsi-mītsisutsik, wawäyīw,

---

[1] Error, for *kā-wäpahtakahikäyit*, or a different word?

äh-mātsīt aw uskinīkiw. äh-kīh-sipwähtät, äkuyikuhk kahkiyaw sipwähtäwak, äh-mātsītsik. itäh äh-minahut aw usīmimāw, mistahi wiyās kīwähtatāw, kiyipah ä-wīh-kakwä-takuhtät wīkiwāhk. tāpwä tsīk äy-ihtät, wāpahtam mistah äh-pikihtäyik wīkiwāw ; äkwah tāpwä mistahi wāpahtam mihtah. äh-ati-takuhtät wīkiwāhk, kā-matwä-kituwähtāyit pīhtsāyīhk awiyah.

äh-pīhtukät, äh-nanātawāpit, kā-wāpamāt iskwäwah. pōtih mituni miywāsiniyiwa utanāskāniyiwa äh-pätāyit. miywäyihtam äh-nahapīstawāt. sämāk umaskisinah kāh-kätikunamiyiwa, kutakah äh-pustaskisinahikut, äh-itikut, " tāpwä mituni yāhkih kikaskäyihtän, ä-wīh-wāpamiyin, ä-kiskäyihtaman ōtah ä-kīh-nakatamān ta-kikaskisinäyan, " äh-itikut.

" äha' , " itwäw awuh uskinīkiw ; umisi itwäw : " ayisk namuya kiyipah kitakuhtān, kayās äh-takuhtäyin ta-kī-kisātaman sämāk, " itäw ; " kuntah kikīh-kāh-kīwān, " itäw.

" āyisk, ' pitah ntaw-āh-atuskä, ' äy-isit nōhtāwiy, " äkusi itwäw aw ōskinīkiskwäw.

äkusi äkwah mītsisōwak. äh-kīsi-mītsisutsik, kā-takuhtätsik ōki kutakak uskinīkiwak, piyīhtukätwāwi, wiyāpamātwāwi ōh ōskinīkiskwäwah, mistahi miywäyihtamwak. nanāskumōwak äh-ōwītimutsik. aw ōstäsimāw matsihkiwis nāway takusin. äh-pīhtukät, äh-wāpamāt ōhiy iskwäwa, mistahi nanāskumōw.

" hay hay ! " itwäw ; " äkwah, äkā äkwah kä-kaskikwātisōyahk ! " itwäw.

äkusi miywäyihtamwak. äkutä tahtu-kīsikāw mātsīwak.

umis ītwäw aw īskwäw : " hāw, nītimutik, kā-nipahāyäkuk mustuswak, mistahi pätāk wiyās. mīna askäkinwah äkā wiya wäpinamuk ; äkwah nama käkway kik-ōmaskisinināwāw, " itäw aw īskwäw.

" āha' , " itwäwak ōk ōskinīkiwak.

miyātsītwāwi, āh-iyawis päsiwäwak, ōmah wiyās. miywäyihtam ōw ōskinīkiskwäw äh-atuskät, pahkäkinwah äy-usīhtät, mīna kāhkäwakwah äh-nīmāwinihkät, piyisk kahkiyaw ōhi nāpäwah umaskisiniyiwa äh-usihtät, piyis mīnah utayōwinisiyiwa äh-usihtät pahkäkinwa uhtsih, māka mīkisah äh-kikamuhät utāsiyihk mīnah uskutākayihk. mistahi miywäyihtamwak ōk ōskinīkiwak, iyikuhk äh-pamihikutsik wītimōwāwah. mistahi kitimäkäyimäwak ōh īskwäwah. mistahi atuskäw aw īskwäw.

äkwah kinwäsk äh-ayät awa iskwäw, kītahtawä awah matsihkiwis akāwātäw ōhih uskinīkiskwäwah. kiskäyihtam aw uskinīkiskwäw äh-itäyihtamiyit ōhi wītimwah. piyis kinwäsk ayāw äkutah.

äkwah kahkiyaw äh-mātsītsik, matsihkiwis awa kā-tätipäwät itah māna äh-nikuhtäyit wītimwa, ōmisi äh-itäyihtahk : " nik-ōwītsimusin nītim, " äy-itäyihtah, äkutah ä-kāsōhtawāt.

äkwah awa aw īskwäw äh-ntawi-nikuhtät, kā-wāpamāt wītimwa äh-päw-utihtikut.

" hāw, nītim, miywäyimin ! " itwäw matsihkiwis.

" kimiywäyimitin, " itwäw aw iskwäw ; " māka k-ätäyihtaman wiy äwaku nisākwäyimun ; usām nisākihāw kisīm, " itäw.

ōmis ītwäw awah awah matsihkiwis : " hä, nītim, päyakwāw pikuh ka-wītsätin. itāp namuya ka-wīhtamawāw nisīm, " itäw.

" nisākwäyimun, nītim, " itik ōh iskwäwah.

äkusi nawatinäw, ä-māsihāt, ä-wīh-kakwä-kawipitāt. namuya sākuhäw ōh iskwäwah. piyisk pimwäw uskātiyihk, " nka-sākuhāw, " äh-itäyihtahk. māka namuya sākuhäw. piyisk äkus īsi pōnihäw, äh-sipwähtät, äh-mātsīt.

äkusi awah iskwäw äkutah uhtsi sipwähtäw, äh-kīwät, äh-näpäwisit, wītimwah ōmah äh-tōtākut. hāta namuya ä-sākuhikut, māka näpäwisiw ; äk ōhtsi k-ō-sipwähtät.

äkwah ōk ōskinīkiwak, äh-takuhtät awa wiyīwit, pōtih āstawiyiw wīkiwāw. namuya wāpamäw uwīkimākanah.

" tānähkih ätukä äkā k-ōh-apit ! " itäyihtam.

äh-ntunawāt, namuya miskawäw. piyisk ituhtäw itäh mānah kānikuhtäyit. wāpahtam äsa nāpäwah äh-kīh-takuhtäyit, äsah ä-māsihituyit, kā-wāpahtahk ustäsah wīpisisiyiw äy-astäyik ä-mihkōwiyik, kā-wāpahtahk itah äsah äh-ati-pimuhtäyit ōwīkimākanah, äh-sipwähtäyit. mihkuh äh-atah-astäyik, ma-mitihtäw. piyisk nōhtaw tipiskāyiw. äkus īsi kīwäw, äh-takuhtät wīkiwāhk. äkwah kutawäw, äh-ay-apit. mistahi mihtātäw uwīkimākanah, ä-nakatikut. piyisk takuhtäwak kahkiyaw uskinīkiwak ; namuya takuhtäw awah matsihkiwis. uskinīkiwak namuya wāpamäwak ōhi wītimuwāwa.

ōmis ītäw : " nisīm, tāniwā nītim ? " itwäwak.

" namuya nikiskäyimāw, " itwäw aw ōskinīkiw ; " kayāhtä äh-takuhtäyān, namuy āpiw ; äkwah äh-ntunawak, namuya nimiskawāw. äkwah itäh kā-nikuhtät māna nitituhtān ; pōtih niwāpahtän äsah äkutah ä-kih-takuhtät kstäsinaw, äsah kāh-māsihāt wītimwa. piyisk niwāpahtän kstäsinaw uwīpisis äh-astäyik. ma-mihkōwiw. äkusi äsa kā-sipwähtät kītimuwāw. nikīh-mitihtäw ; mihkuh at-āh-astäw, itah äh-pimuhtät, piyisk kā-pä-kīwäyān, " itwäw awa uskinīkiw.

" hähähäy ! " itwäwak ōk ōskinīkiwak ; " māka mīn ätsik ānih äkāh katawah tiyōtahk kistäsinaw ! " itwäwak.

mihtātamwak ä-sipwähtäyit ōh īskwäwah. äkwah apiwak ; namuya wīh-mītsisōwak, ä-sipwähtäyit ōh īskwäwa. mistahi äh-tipiskāyik, äkuyikuhk kā-takuhtät awa matsihkiwis. äh-pīhtukät, wāpamäw äh-kāmwātapiyit kahkiyaw usīmah.

" nisīm, tanähki äkā k-ōh-apit nītim ? " itwäw.

" ā, tānihk ätukä ? māskōts nānitaw äh-ituhtät, " itwäw aw uskinīkiw.

" ähähäy hähe ! " itwäw matsihkiwis ; wīsta mihtātam, tāpiskōts äkā nānitaw äh-kīh-tōtahk ; ayīsk muhtsōwiw awa matsihkiwis.

piyisk namuya nipāwak, äh-mihtātätsik ōh īskwäwa. piyisk wāpaniyiw. wawäyīw aw uskinīkiw.

" āh hāw, nistäsitik, niwīh-nitunawāw kītimuwāw, " itwäw.

" äha' , " itwäwak uskinīkiwak.

äkusi äkwah sipwähtäw ōw uskinīkiw, äh-mitihtät uwīkimākanah, äh-pimuhtät. äkwah ōki uskinīkiwak päyakwanuhk apiwak ; namuya wīh-mätsīwak, äh-pakwātahkik ä-sipwähtäyit ōh īskwäwah, äh-mihtātätsik. äkwah aw ōskinīkiw kā-ma-mitihtät uwīkimākanah, piyisk namuya wāpahtam itah äh-pimuhtäyit äsa ; tāpiskōts äh-uhpihāyit itäyihtam. pōtih äkutah nīpawiw, äh-nanātawāpit. tānitah ta-kīh-ituhtäyit uwīkimākanah namuya kiskäyihtam. nitawāts utinam umistanipīwayān, äh-pōtātahk.

" hāw, tāntäh niwīkimākan äh-ituhtät, äkutä nik-ätāsin ! nik-ōmistanipīwayāniwin ! " itwäw.

tāpwä ispimihk itāsiw. kītahtawä kā-wāpahtahk äh-asinīwatsīwiyik. äkutä tahkuhtsāyihk kā-pōnāsit. äkusi äkutah äh-pasikōt, kā-wāpahtahk itah äsah ä-kīh-pimuhtäyit uwīkimākanah. äkwah äh-mitihtāt, äy-ispatināyik äh-ati-takuhtäyit, ä-sākäwāt, kā-wāpahtahk ä-misāyik ōtänaw. wāpamäw ä-mihtsätiyit ayīsiyiniwah. äkutah nahapiw. piyisk kinwäs äkutah apiw, ä-ka-kitāpahtahk ōhi mīkiwāhpah. kītahtawä kā-pätsāstamuhtäyit iskwäwah. kisiwāk äh-päy-ihtāyit, kā-nisitawäyimāt uwīkimākana. mistahi miywäyihtam äh-pä-takuhtäyit.

sämāk utsämik, " tāpwä nimiywäyihtän äh-takuhtäyin, " äh-itikut ; " ayīsk kakäpātisiw kistäs, k-ōh-pä-sipwähtäyān, " itik.

" tānisi äh-tōtāsk nistäs ? " itwäw.

" anima kā-mātsiyäk, ä-ntawih-nikuhtäyān, äkutah kā-pä-takuhtät kistäs, umis äy-isit : ' äh-miywäyimitān, ' äy-isit. ' nīstah kimiywäyimitn, ' nititāw ; ' māka k-ätäyihtaman namuya wiy äwaku ta-kīh-äkus-īspayiw, ' nititāw. ' päyakwāw täpiyāh ka-wītsätin, ' nitik ; ' itāp namuya ta-kiskäyihtam nisīm, ' itwäw. ' nisākwäyimun, ' äh-itak, kā-päw-utihtinit, äh-māsihit. māka namuya nikī-sākuhik. piyisk äkāh ä-kīh-sākuhit, kā-pimut ōtah nipwāmihk. äkusi aspin ä-sipwähtät. äkusi ä-kīh-utinamān anima atsusis ; äkutah aspin ntastān. ' nisākihā niwīkimākan, kā-näpäwihit nītim, ' nitäyihtän, nitsawāts kā-pä-kīwäyān, " itwäyiwa.

" hāw, äh-pä-nātitān, " itik.

äkusi äkwah kīwäwak. äh-takuhtätsik mīkiwāhpihk, miywäyihtamiyiwah ōh äyīsiyiniwa. pōtih pīhtäyisk äh-tsimatäyik äh-misāyik mīkiwāhp, äkutah kā-takuhtätsik, äh-pīhtukätsik, kā-wāpamāt uskinīkiskwäwa ä-mihtsätiyit.

" ä ä iy ! " itwäyiwah ; " kītimunaw takusin ! " k-ätwäyit, äh-nahapit.

äkwah ah-ātamiskāk.

umisi itwäw awa kisäyiniw : " ähähäy ! " itwäw ; " āyisk, ninahāhkisīm, kakäpātisiw kistäs, ōhih kā-tōtawāt wītimwa, ōh-päh-kakwātakihtayin, äh-päy-ituhtäyin, " itwäw ; " hāw, äh-kitimākisiyäk, äkāh awiyak äh-pamihikuyäk, kā-kīh-itisahwak nitānis, ' ntawi-pamis ōk ōskinīkiwak, ' äh-itak, kā-kīh-ituhtät, kā-kakäpātisit kistäs, " itwäw awa kisäyiniw ; " māka nimiywäyihtän ä-takusiniyan, " itwäw.

äkutah ay-ayāw aw uskinīkiw. kätahtawä mānah sipwähtäw, ispatināhk māna äh-ay-apit, ä-ka-kitāpahtahk mīkiwāhpah. piyis māna takuhtäyiwa uwīkimākanah äkutä ispatināhk. piyis kaskäyihtam, ustäsah äkā h-wāpamāt, usām kinwäs äkutäh äh-ayāt.

kītahtawä kunitah ä-sa-sipwähtät, kītahtawä kā-wāpahtahk, itah äh-pasahtsāyik, ä-sakāyik, äkutah kā-wāpahtahk mōhkitsiwanipäk, äh-miywāsiniyik asiskiy, tāpiskōts wiyaman k-äsinākwaniyik. utinam, äh-miywäyihtahk, uskutākāhk äh-āh-ayīsihtitāt, äkwah ustikwānihk, tāpiskōts äh-tōmihkwät äh-itäyihtahk. äkus īsi äh-kīwät. äh-takuhtät wīkiwāhk, äh-pīhtukät, ä-kitāpamikut ōh īskwäwah wītimwah, tsämāk kā-pāhpiyit, " mnā ! " äh-itikut, " māmaskāts awa iyikuhk wīh-mihkōwiw, äh-piyasīh-minahut ! " k-ätikut.

" hay hay hay ! " itwäw awa kisäyiniw.

ōmis ītwäw ōw uskinīkiw : " namuya kākway ninipahāw, " itwäw.

" nāh, äh-minahuyan, ōma mistahi kā-mihkōwiyan ! " itik wīwa.

äkusi utinamiyiwa nipiy, ä-kisīpäkinamiyit um uskutākay mīnah ustikwān.

" māmaskāts awa iyikuhk ä-wīh-mihkuwit ! " itwäyiwa.

äkusi k-āti-wayawīt awa kisäyiniw.

" hāw, hāw, nitōskinīkīmitik, wawäyīk ! nikwatisutān ! ninahāhkisīm nipahäw unītsāniwa ä-wītsäwāyit utsawāsimisiyiwa ! " itwäw awa kisäyiniw.

äkusi wawäyīwak.

" hāw, nitānis, ta-kiskinōhtahiwäw ninahāhkisīm, " itwäw.

äkusi aw uskinīkiw ōmis ītwäw : " namuya käkway ninipahāw, " itāw uwīkimākana.

" ōmah, " itik, " tānitah äy-ōhtinaman, ōmah ' asiskiy ' k-ätwäyin, äkutah k-ätuhtäyin ? " itik uwīkimākana ; " ayīsiyiniwak tsīw uma äh-itäyimiyāhk ? " k-ätikut uwīkimākana.

" äha' , " itwäw aw uskinīkiw.

" namuya, " itik uwīkimākanah ; " kiyawāw ōtäh nihtsāyih k-āyāyäk ōmisi : ' piyäsiwak, ' k-ätwäyäk, niyān äkutōwa, " itik ; " awa kā-nipahat k-ätikawiyan, ' misi-kinäpik, ' k-ätwäyäk, äkutōwa. itah äh-ayāt ōm āsiskiy kā-pätāyan, umihkuh niyān nititwānān, " itik uwīkimākana.

äkusi äkwah sipwähtäwak, äkutä äh-ituhtahāt ōh āyīsiyiniwah. kahkiyaw wītsäwäw uwītimwah.

ä-takuhtätsik äkutä, ōmisi itwäyiwa usisah : " hāw, nitān, ninahāhkisīm kanawäyim, äkāh ta-säkihikut ōhih kā-wīw-utināyit uminahōwina, " itwäyiwa.

äkusi uwīkimākana utinik, tāpiskōts äh-apisīsisit, äkus ä-tōtākut, utihkōkaniyihk äkutah äh-ahikut.

äkuyikuhk, " äkwah namuy āyīsiyiniwak ! " itäyihtam, kahkiyaw äh-papāmihāyit ; " äkwah piyäsiwak ! " uwīkimākanah mīna, äh-misi-kimiwaniyik, mistah äh-kitōyit piyäsiwa, tāpiskōts käkway äh-pāskisamiyit, mistah äh-na-namipayiyik askiy, äh-itäyihtahk. äh-pōni-pähtākusiyit, äkwah äh-utinikut ōwīkimākanah, kā-wāpamāt ä-misikitiyit kinäpikwah äkwah päyak äh-āpisīsisiyit. māmaskātam itah äy-ōhtināyit muhkitsiwanipäkuhk, ä-kīh-wāpamāt.

" nitānis, kīwähtah ninahāhkisīm, " itwäw awa kisäyiniw ; " kapakwātam, kinwäsk kitāpamātsih ōhi kinäpikwah, " äh-itäyihtahk awa kisäyiniw.

äkusi kīwähtahäw uwīkimākanah aw iskwäw, aspin äh-wiyinihtākäyit. äkusi wiyawāw wīkiwāhk takuhtäwak. mīnisah mītsisōwak uwīkimākana. kītahtawä kā-takuhtäyit, äkwah äh-pätāyit wiyās, itäyihtam.

" hā, ntānis, spatināhk ntawih-ay-apik, " itwäw awa kisäyiniw, ōmisi äh-itäyihtahk ; " kīsitäpuwihkih, wīh-mītsisuwihtsih, ta-pakwātam ninahāhkisīm, " äh-itäyihtahk ; ayisk ōhi misi-kinäpikwah ä-wīh-mōwātsik, äyuk uhtsi k-ōh-itāt unahāhkisīma.

piyisk kinwäsk äkutä ayāw aw uskinīkiw, piyäsiwah äh-wītsäwāt.

äkwah ōmis ītwäw awa kisäyiniw : " nitānis, äkwah kīwäk. ninahāhkisīm mistahi kitimākisiyiwa ustäsah, äh-kaskäyihtamiyit, äkā äh-wāpamikut. usām kinwäs ōtäh ayāw. kikīh-itikunaw kā-tipäyimikuyahk, äkā īn-āyīsiyiniwa ta-wītsäwāyahk ōtäh ispimihk, " itwäw awa kisäyiniw.

miywäyihtam aw uskinīkiw.

" hāh, wāpahkih ka-kīwānānaw. "

" hahāw, nitawāsimisitik, wawäyīk ; kiyawāw mīna ntawih-wīkimihkuk kītimuwāw ustäsah. äh-isih-askōwīskutātōyäk, ka-wītsäwāwāwak, " itwäw.

mistahi miywäyihtam ä-wīh-ntawih-unāpämit awa matsihkihkwäwis matsihkiwisah, kunta tahkih äh-pāhpit, " pitanä kiyipah wāpahk ! " äh-itäyihtahk matsihkihkwäwis, ä-nōhtä-unāpämit. äkusi äkwah äh-tipiskāyik, äh-kīh-nipātsik, äh-wāpaniyik, ä-kīh-mītsisutsik, äkwah sipwähtäwak. awa matsihkihkwäwis mituni äh-miywāsiniyik uskutākay, kunt ä-säwäpayiyik, mitun äh-miyuhut. itah äh-asiwatātsik utayōwinisiwāwa umaskisiniwāwa,[1] *äkunih tahkunamwak, ä-sipwähtätsik. piyis takuhtäwak ōm ītah kā-kīh-uhtsi-pimuhtät aw uskinīkiw. namwāts wāpahtam askiy, nīhtsāyīhk äh-itāpit. äkutah nīpawiwak.*

" hāw, niwīkimākan, " itik, " āstam ! "

äh-nahikāpawistawāt, utinik, tāpiskōts äh-āpisīsisit äh-tōtākut, utihkōkaniyihk äkutah äh-ahikut, kā-pähtawāt äh-kā-kitōyit piyäsiwah. äyakunik ōk ōskinīkiskwäwak, äkwah äy-uhpihātsik, äh-pimpahtsi-pähtākusitsik, piyäsiwak. piyisk nīhtsāyīhk takusinwak. itah kā-wīkitsik uskinīkiwak, tsīk äkutah äh-twähutsik, kāwi ayīsiyiniwiwak ōk īskwäwak. äkusi äkwah äh-pimuhtätsik, mistahi miywäyihtam aw uskinīkiw, " äkwah nistäsak tsitāyāwäwak iskwäwah, " äh-itäyihtahk.

äkusi äh-pimuhtätsik, käkāts äh-takuhtätsik, ōmis ītwäw aw uskinīkiw : " ōtah pita ayāk ; wawäsīk ; tōmihkwäk. nka-nitawih-ātsimustawāwak nistäsak, " äh-itāt ōh iskwäwah ; " itāp ka-pä-wīhtamātināwāw, " itäw.

äkusi äh-ati-sipwähtät, wawäsīwak ōk iskwäwak. awa matsīhkīhkwäwis mistahi wawäsīw. awah uskinīkiw äh-takuhtät wīkiwāhk, pōtih nam āwiyah itäyihtam. äh-pīhtukät, kahkiyaw ustäsah kā-pimisiniyit.

" waniskāk, nistäsitik ; nitakusinin ! " itäw.

äw-uhpiskwäyit awa matsīhkiwis, kā-wāpamāt usīma äh-apiyit.

" waniskāk, nisīmitik ; kisīminaw takusin ! " itwäw.

tāpwä waniskāwak, äh-wāpamātsik usīmiwāwa. mistahi nanāskumōwak. " māskōts kīh-misi-wanātisiw, " ä-kīh-itäyimātsik usīmiwāwa, namuya uhtsih nānāpātsihōwak.

" hā, nstäsitik, kāsīhkwäk ; kīh-kāsīhkwäyäku, nānāpātsihuhkäk ; wawäsīhkäk ; iskwäwak nipäsiwāwak, ōyā kītimuwāw wītsisānisah. uma k-ähtasiyahk, äku-tahtuh ihtasiwak iskwäwak. ä-is-ōma-askōwiskutātōyahk, äkusi kik-äsi-nahapīstākōwāwak pīhtukätwāwi, " itwäw.

hā, mistahi miywäyihtam awa matsihkiwis, iskwäwah ä-wīh-ayāwāt. äh-kīsi-nānapātsihuyit, kā-wayawīt aw uskinīkiw, äh-ntawih-nitōmāt ōh īskwäwah.

äh-utihtāt, " tāpwä nama mayaw kitakuhtān, " itik uwīkimākana.

" äha', ayisk nistäsak utamih-nānāpātsihōwak. aspin kā-sipwähtäyān, äkuspi uhtsih päyakwanuhk äh-apitsik, namuya nānāpātsihōwak, ' māskōts misi-wanātsihōw, ' ä-kīh-itäyimitsik, äkā mayaw äh-wāpamitsik, " itäw uwīkimākanah ; " hāw, nītim, " itäw ōh ōmisimāwa, " ōtä skwāhtämihk uhtapiw nistäs ; äku kiya kā-wīh-wītsäwat. nāway kiyah kika-pīhtukān, kahkiyaw pīhtukätwāwi ōkih kisīmak. äkāya mayaw pīhtukähkan. äkutah wayawītimihk pāh-pimuhtähkan. ta-kakwä-ihkäyihtam nistäs, " itwäw ō uskinīkiw.

" äha', " itwäw matsihkihkwäwis.

" hāw ! "

äkwah sipwähtäwak, tahk äh-pāhpit awa matsihkihkwäwis, äh-miywäyihtahk ä-wīh-unāpämit. äkwah ōk ōskinīkiwak äh-apitsik, matsīhkiwis awa tahk äh-paspāpit, kītahtawä kā-pätisāpamāt, päyak kā-wāpamāt äh-miyusiyit äkwah äh-miyuhuyit. piyisk takuhtäyiwa, kā-pähtahkik ä-säwäpayiyit awiyah.

---

[1] Narrator avoids the word *asiwatsikan.*

ä-pīhtukäyit usīmimāwa, ä-nahapiyit, kā-pä-pīhtukäyit wītimuwāw. "*hay hay hay hay!*" *itwäwak uskinīkiwak, ä-nisitawäyimātsik wītimuwāwa. äkutah äkwah kutakah kā-pīhtukäyit, awa uskinīkiw tsīk-ōsīmimāw ä-nahapīstākut. äkutah uhtsi āskaw pīhtukäyiwah, äh-ati-nahapīstākutsik. piyisk kahkiyaw pīhtukäwak. awa pikuh matsihkihkwäwis namuya wīhpīhtukäw. äkwah awa matsīhkiwis äh-āyiwākipayit, tahk äh-itāpit iskwāhtāmihk, äh-asawāpamāt, ta-pīhtukäyit iskwäwah mätwä-āhtuhtäyitsih kāsäwäpayiyit. piyisk pīhtukäyiwa. wahwā, miyuhuyiwa! äh-nahapīstākut matsihkiwis, mistahi miywäyihtam. kahkiyaw äkwah ayāwäwak iskwäwah, kuntah äh-pā-pīkiskwätsik, äh-ātsimutsik, äh-pāhpitsik.*

kītahtawä umisi k-ätwät matsihkiwis: "*yāw, nisīmitik, tān um ätapiyäk? kinahāhkapihtānaw!*" *itwäw.*

utinam kaskaskisiw, ä-sikwatahahk, äh-tōmihkwät, äkw ä-kaskitäwikanakāpit ōtah uskīsikuhk. utinam upakamākan, äh-ati-wayawīt, utah kisiwāk äh-piskwahtsāyik, äkutah äh-pa-pakamahikät; kuntah kā-matwä-mamawimuwit wākayōsah, nipahäw. kīwähtahäw; pīhtukahäw.

"*hāw, äyakw ānah, niwīkimākan! ōmis ätukä kiwīh-ay-itahtsikān ätukä, äh-täyihtaman, k-ōh-pä-wīkimiyin,*" *itwäw matsihkiwis.*

"*hay hay! tāpwä nimiywäyihtän wākayōs ä-wīh-mōwak,*" *itwäw matsihkihkwäwis.*

äkusi äh-wiyinihtākät äkwah äh-pakāsimāt wākayōsa, kahkiyaw äyakunik äh-mōwātsik. äkwah äh-kīh-mītsisutsik, äkuyikuhk tipiskāyiw, ä-kīh-nipātsik.

äkwah tahtu-kīsikāw mātsīwak, äh-pätātsik wiyās. mistahi ka-kāyawisiwak ōk īskwäwak. mistah äh-atuskätsik, kiyipah wīkiwāwa kīsihtāwak; kahkiyaw äkwah pāh-päyakukäwak. āyisk mitātasiwak iskwäwak; mitātaht usīhtāwak wīkiwāwa. äkusi aspin äh-wā-wīkitsik.

äkuyikuhk äh-iskwāk ātayōhkäwin.

This is about some women: ten women, Thunderer-Women, and their father and mother; and their father was a chief.

And here on earth were also ten youths, who, in the same way, were brothers, but these had no mother; and they had no father. So they had only one tent; no other people dwelt near there.

And up above, where those women dwelt, that was a large town. Among those women, the oldest of the sisters was called Silly Maiden. And the youngest was a pretty maid.

And likewise, among those others, those ten young men, the oldest was Matchihkiwis; and, again, the youngest brother was a handsome youth. Now, those young men did not know that there were anywhere any women, or any other people at all. Those youths stayed always in that one place, and all of them did nothing but hunt. Then, as time went on, and they hunted, and none of them stayed at home, then that youngest brother was always the first to get home. After him they would all come, one after the other.

Once upon a time, when that youth came home, he saw a great amount of firewood lying there. Exactly as if someone had come there it seemed to him, as he approached. He was very glad, thinking, "Perhaps there will be someone within."

When he went inside, he saw no one. So he went out and walked round the place, and there he saw that a woman must have gone by. Then he followed her tracks to where she had gathered wood; he saw no one. He went back again; he went indoors and built his fire, to cook the meal. When he had made his fire and was sitting on his couch, soon he knew that there were some things under his mat. When he uncovered them, he beheld some moccasins. He took them and looked at them; they were very pretty. He was glad; he put them carefully away.

He said, "And so a woman has come here!" he thought; "My brothers had better not see them," he thought.

When he tried them on, why, they fitted him well. And then his brothers began to arrive, one after the other, until all of them had come; but he did not care to tell them about it.

Then, when they had slept, on the next day, early in the morning that youth went out to hunt. The others, too, one after the other at intervals, set out, for those young men did not keep each other company when they hunted, but did their hunting each by himself.

Then that youth thought, "Perhaps it is because she wants to marry me that this woman has come here."

Where he killed a buffalo, he took the tongue, and the best parts of the flesh, and one thigh-bone, and the smallest stomach, and went home.

"Perhaps, if that woman comes, she will eat this stomach; and she will split this thigh-bone and eat it," he thought, as he went home.

He walked fast, thinking to come upon the young woman while she was there. Then, towards evening, when he arrived, again he saw a great amount of firewood lying there. He saw smoke rising from their tipi.

"Perhaps she is there," he thought.

When he entered, he saw no one, but it was plain that someone had swept. He was glad. Then he fed his fire, to cook their meal. Then, as he sat there while cooking, it seemed to him that again there was something where the moccasins had been. When he took it out, this too was a pair of moccasins. Again he was glad, as he looked at them. They were very pretty, embroidered with quill-work. He put them away, thinking, "My brothers had better not see them." Then, when those young men arrived, one after the other, they saw a great amount of firewood. They were glad to think of their young brother, "Truly, in a short time he gathers a great deal of wood."

The oldest one, Matchihkiwis, said, "Truly I am glad that there is so much firewood."

"Yes, indeed," said the young men.

Then that youth did not care to tell what had happened. Then it grew dark again. When they had eaten, and had sat a while, telling all kinds of stories, they went to bed.

"Now then, I shall get up early," thought that youth; "I shall set out early," was his thought.

So he got up early, to go hunting. When he had eaten, he made ready to go hunting. He was very happy.

"Perhaps it is because she wants to marry me that this woman has come here," he thought.

So then, where he killed a buffalo, he took the best parts of the meat. When he went home, he kept running, for he thought, "Perhaps I shall see her." When he had got close to their tipi, he saw that much smoke was rising from it. When he arrived, he saw that much firewood lay there. When he entered, he saw no one, though it was plain that someone had swept the place clean, and had brushed out their mats; and there was a meal which she must have cooked. He ate right away. When again he saw some things lying there, and took them up, again it was moccasins. He was very glad.

"Now, I shall not tell my brothers about it," he thought.

Toward evening his brothers arrived, one after the other.

Then the oldest brother said, "Really, you are very quick about getting faggots," he said to his brother.

"Yes, for, you see, I got home early," he told him.

Then, by the time the others had eaten their meal, it was getting dark. Then they sat there a while, telling stories, telling about the hunting they had done, and laughing.

"This time, too, I shall set out early," thought that youth.

Quickly he went to bed. Then they all went to bed and slept. That youth got up early, and cooked his food. Then they all arose and ate. As soon as they had eaten, that youth made ready to go hunting. When he had departed, then they all went out to hunt. From where he killed his game, the youngest brother took home a great deal of meat, and he meant to try to get home quickly. And truly, when he got near, he saw much smoke rising from their tipi; and truly, he saw much firewood. When he went on and approached the tent, there was someone noisily carrying on within.

When he entered, as he looked about, there he saw a woman. Lo, very beautiful were her mats which she had brought. He was happy to go and sit by her.

At once she took off his moccasins and put others on his feet, and said to him, "Truly, you were very sad, of late, with longing to see me, when you knew that I had left those moccasins here for you to wear."

"Yes," said the youth; "For indeed, not promptly have you come, seeing that you might have stayed at once, when long ago you arrived," he told her; "Needlessly you have been going back and forth," he told her.

"It was because my father told me, 'First go there several times to work'," said that young woman.

Then they ate their meal. When they had eaten, then, when those other young men arrived, as they entered and saw that young woman, they were very glad. They gave thanks that they had a sister-in-law. That oldest brother, Matchihkiwis, came last. When he entered and saw the woman, he was delighted.

" Splendid!" he said; "So now we won't have to sew for ourselves!" he said.

So they were happy. Then every day they went hunting.

Thus spoke that woman: "Now, my brothers-in-law, when you kill buffalo, bring home much meat. And do not throw away the hides; otherwise you will have nothing for moccasins," she told them.

"Very well," said the young men.

When they hunted, they always brought the animals entire, for meat. The young woman was happy at her work, preparing leather, and making stores of dried meat, and in time making moccasins for all those men, and clothes out of the hides, and, what was more, putting beadwork on their leggings and their coats. Those young men were very glad to have their sister-in-law take such good care of them. They were very fond of the woman. She worked very hard.

. . . .

. . . . Time passed; she had been there a long while.

Then, when all were hunting, Matchihkiwis went circling about the place where his sister-in-law was wont to gather firewood, and this was his thought: . . . . he thought, as he hid from her there.

Then, when that woman went to gather faggots, there she saw her husband's brother coming toward her.

. . . . that was why she went away.

Then, as for those young men, when he came home whose wife she was, lo, their tent was without a fire. He did not see his wife.

"I wonder why she is not here?" he thought.

When he looked for her, he could not find her. At last he went to where she used to gather faggots. . . . . and then he saw his brother's arrow lying there, covered with blood, and he saw where his wife had walked, as she went away. He followed her trail where the blood at intervals was on the ground. At last it grew dark before he had done. So he went back and came to their dwelling. Then he built a fire and stayed there. He grieved much for his wife, who had left him. Finally all the young men arrived; only Matchihkiwis did not arrive. The young men did not see their brother's wife.

One said to him, "Brother, where is my sister-in-law?" Thus they asked.

"I do not know," said that youth; "To my surprise, when I came home, she was not here; and when I sought her, I did not find her. Then I went to where she is in the habit of gathering wood; there I saw that our oldest brother had come . . . . At last I saw an arrow of our brother's lying there. It was covered with blood. Then, it appeared, your sister-in-law had gone away. I trailed her; there was blood every little ways, where she had walked, but at last I came home," said that youth.

"Heavens and earth!" said those young men; "And so again our eldest brother has been guilty of unseemly conduct!" they said.

They were sorry that that woman had gone away. They sat there; they did not care to eat, because that woman had gone away. When it was entirely dark, then Matchihkiwis arrived. When he came in, he saw that all his brothers were sitting in dejection.

"Brother, why is my sister-in-law not here?" he asked.

"I wonder why. Perhaps she has gone somewhere or other," said that youth.

"Heavens and earth!" cried Matchihkiwis; he was too sorry, just as though he had had nothing to do with it; for this Matchihkiwis was a crazy sort of person.

When the time came, they did not sleep, what with their grief for that woman. At last day broke. That youth made himself ready.

"So now, brothers, I am going to look for your sister-in-law," he said.

"Yes," said the young men.

So then that youth set out to track his wife, and walked on. And the other young men stayed where they were; they did not care to hunt, for they were grieved that that woman had gone away and were sad at her absence. But that youth who was tracking his wife, at last came to a point where he could not see the signs of where she had walked; it seemed to him just as if she had risen from the ground and taken wing. He stood there and looked about him. He did not know where his wife had gone. Knowing no other way, he took a hair of fur and blew upon it.

"Now, whithersoever my wife is bound, thither shall I be wafted! I shall be a hair of fur!" he said.

And truly, he was borne aloft by the wind. Presently he saw where there was a rocky cliff. There, at the summit, he was put down by the breeze. Thereupon, when he rose to his feet, he saw again where his wife had walked. Then, when he trailed her, and came to a rise in the land, as he came round to the other side, there he beheld a large town. He saw many people. There he sat down. He sat there for a long time, looking at all the tipis. Presently a woman came walking his way. When she had come nearer, he recognized his wife. He was very happy when she came.

At once she kissed him, and, "Truly, I am glad that you have come," she said to him; "You must know, it is because your eldest brother is senseless that I went away and have come here," she told him.

"What did my eldest brother do to you?" he asked.

"At that time, when you were hunting, and I was going out to gather wood, to that place came your brother, and said to me, ... Then, off he went. So then I drew out that arrow; I laid it there, as I went away. 'I love my husband,' was my thought, 'but his brother has put me to shame,' and so I needs came back here," she said.

"And now, I have come to get you," she told him.

Then they went to her home. When they reached the tipi, those people were glad. It was a large tipi which stood in the centre of all, to which they came, and, when they entered, there he saw a great many young women.

"Why!" they cried; "Our brother-in-law has come!" they cried, as he took his seat.

Then they all greeted him.

Thus spoke that old man: "Dear me!" he said; "Surely, your oldest brother is foolish to have treated his sister-in-law in this wise, so that you had to suffer much hardship in coming here," he said; "See, because you were pitiable, having no one to care for you, was why I sent my daughter there, saying to her, 'Go take care of those young men,' and so she went, and then your brother played the fool," said the old man; "But I am glad you have come to us," he said.

There stayed that youth. Then, in time, he would go away and sit on a hilltop and look at all the tipis. After a while his wife would come to him there on the hilltop. At last he grew sad, because he did not see his brothers, having been there so long.

Then at one time, when he went off at random, he came to a wooded ravine and there saw a spring, and some good clay which looked exactly like vermilion. He took some, because he liked it, and placed it here and there on his coat, and on his head, thinking to himself that it was just as though he were painting his face. In that guise he went home. When he reached their dwelling, when he entered, and those women, his wife's sisters, looked at him, at once they burst out laughing, and "Goodness!" they said to him, "A strange sight, the way he gets himself full of blood, when he has killed all the game he likes!" they said to him.

"Splendid! Splendid!" exclaimed the old man.

The youth said, "I have not killed any kind of creature."

"Why, surely it was in killing some game that you got yourself all full of blood like this!" his wife told him.

Then she took some water and washed his coat for him and his head.

"A strange sight, the way he gets himself covered with blood!" she said.

Then the old man went out of the tipi.

"Come, come, my followers, make yourselves ready! Let us fetch meat from the killing! My son-in-law has killed a dam with her young!" cried the old man.

At that they made ready.

"Come, daughter, let my son-in-law show the way," he said.

Then that youth said, "I have not killed any kind of creature," he told his wife.

"But this," she said to him, "where did you get it, this, which you call 'clay,' at the place to which you went?" his wife asked him; "And do you think we are human beings here?" she asked him.

"Yes," said that youth.

"No," his wife told him; "When you who dwell there below, say 'Thunderers,' even such are we," she told him; "That creature which they tell you you have slain, when you say 'Great Serpent,' such it is. That clay which you have brought from where it is, we call it that creature's blood," his wife told him.

So then they set out, that mortal man leading them thither. All his wife's sisters went with him.

When they got there, his father-in-law said, "Now, daughter, take care of my son-in-law, that he be not frightened by those who are about to take up the game he has killed," said he.

Thereupon his wife picked him up; as if he were but a small creature she handled him, and placed him under her arm.

At that, "No, they are not mortals!" he thought, as they all began to fly about; "And so they are Thunderers!" as his wife joined them, and there came a great rain, and the Thunderers roared loud, as if they were shooting some object, and the earth trembled much, as it seemed to him. When they had ceased their noise, and his wife took him forth, there he saw a Great Serpent and a small one. It seemed strange to him that they had got those creatures from the spring, when he saw them.

"Daughter, take my son-in-law home," said the old man. "It will not agree with him to look too long at these serpents," was the old man's thought.

So that woman took her husband home, as the others began to cut up the kill. So they arrived at their dwelling. He and his wife ate berries. Presently the others arrived, bringing meat, as it seemed to him.

"Now, daughter, go you two, and stay on the hilltop," said the old man, thinking, "When the cooking is being done, and when we eat our meal, it will be painful for my son-in-law," for they were going to eat that Great Serpent; that was why he said this of his son-in-law.

For a long time, finally, that youth stayed there, with the Thunderers.

Then thus spoke that old man: "Daughter, now go home. My son-in-law's brothers are very unhappy with grieving because they cannot see him. He is staying here too long. He told us who is our Master, that we are not to have mortal men for our companions here above," said the old man.

The youth was glad.

"There, tomorrow we shall go home."

. . . .

The Silly Maiden was very glad that she was to go take to husband that Matchihkiwis; she kept laughing a foolish laugh, and she thought, that Silly Maiden, "I wish tomorrow would hurry up!" for she was eager to have a husband. So then, when night came, when they had slept, in the morning, after they had eaten, they set out. Very fine was Silly Maiden's coat, jingling with bells all over, for she had put on much finery. Those things into which they put their clothes and their moccasins, they carried in their hands, as they set out. In time they came to the place from which that youth had walked. He could not see the earth, when he looked down below. There they stood.

"Now then, my husband," she said to him, "come here!"

When he came and stood close to her, she took him up, handling him as though he were but a small creature, and placed him under her arm, and then he heard the Thunderers' repeated call. It was those young women, who now rose and took wing, and as Thunderers went speeding on with noise. Soon they arrived below. When close to the dwelling place of those young men they landed from their flight, those women again took human form. Then they walked on. That youth was very glad to think, "And now my brothers will have wives."

Then as they walked along, when they had almost come to their destination, that youth said, "Stay here a while; deck yourselves out; paint your faces. I shall go and tell my brothers," he said to those women; "I shall come back and tell you," he said to them.

So then, when he had gone on, those women put on their ornaments. That Silly Maiden decked herself out splendidly. When the youth reached their dwelling, at first he thought there was no one there. When he entered, there were all his brothers lying on their beds.

"Arise, brothers; I have come!" he said to them.

When Matchihkiwis raised his head, there he saw his brother.

"Get up, brothers; our brother has come!" he cried.

They arose, and saw their youngest brother. They were very thankful. Because they had thought of their brother, "Likely he has gone to his destruction," for that reason they took no care of themselves.

"Come, brothers, wash your faces; when you have washed your faces, tidy yourselves; put on your good clothes; I am bringing women, the sisters of your sister-in-law who went away. As many as you are, so many are the women. In the order of our ages they will take their seat by your sides, when they enter," he said.

Oh, very glad was Matchihkiwis that he was to have a woman. When they had groomed themselves, that youth went out to go call the women.

When he came to where they were, "Truly, you are late in coming back," his wife said to him.

"Yes, for my brothers had much to do, grooming themselves. Ever since I went away, they have been staying in that one spot and have taken no care of their appearance, because, when they did not see me in time, they thought of me, 'No doubt he has gone to his destruction,' " he told his wife; "Now then, sister-in-law," he said to that eldest sister, "There by the door sits my oldest brother; he is the one with whom you will keep company. You will enter last, when all your sisters here have entered. Do not enter promptly. Walk back and forth outside the door. Let us try to make my eldest brother suffer from hope deferred," said that youth.

"Very well," said the Silly Maiden.

"Come!"

Then they set out, Silly Maiden laughing all the while, glad that she was to have a husband. And as those young men sat there, and Matchihkiwis kept peering out through the door, in time he saw them approach, and one he saw who was beautiful and wore the finest clothes. At last they arrived, and they heard how some one of them jingled as she moved.

When their youngest brother entered and took his seat, in came their sister-in-law.

"Splendid, splendid!" cried the young men, when they recognized their sister-in-law. And then another came in, and she took her seat by the side of the youth who was next to the youngest. After that they came in at short intervals, and each one sat down by a young man. At last they had all come in. Only that Silly Maiden would not come in. And so Matchihkiwis was left as the odd one, and he kept looking at the doorway, looking out for the woman to enter, who could be heard walking up and down with her clothes a-jingling. At last she came in. Hah, she was beautifully clad! When she sat down by Matchihkiwis' side, he was delighted. So now all of them had wives, and they talked and talked and jabbered, and told stories, and laughed.

Presently Matchihkiwis said, "Why, brothers, why do you sit here like this? Do not forget we are newly married!" he said.

He took some charcoal, ground it up, and painted himself, blackening his face round the eyes. He took his club and went out of the tipi, and where, close by, there was a small knoll in the land, he knocked with his club; then he heard the growling of a bear; he killed it. He took it back to the lodge with him; he brought it inside.

"Here, this is for you, my wife! I daresay you were looking forward to this kind of food when you decided to come here and marry me," said Matchihkiwis.

"Oh, fine! Truly, I am glad that I am to eat bear's meat," said the Silly Maiden.

So then she cut up the bear and put it in the kettle, and they all ate of it. When they had eaten, it was dark, and so they went to bed.

Then they hunted every day and brought home the meat. Very industrious were those women. They worked hard and soon had made their tipis; so then they lived each in a separate tent. For there were ten women; they made ten tipis. And so they lived there from that time on. This is where the sacred story ends.

(25) Burnt-Stick

Louis Moosomin

nāh-namiskwäkāpaw.

kītahtawä yāhkih māh-mästsihtāsōw wīhtikōw. tapasīwak äsah mitātaht uskinīkiwak. āyītaw ä-uhkwākanit awa wīhtikōw, mihtsät ātah mīkiwāhpah äh-ihtakuhkih, äsa māna äh-māh-mästsihtāt.

mitātaht äsa äy-ihtasitsik ōki uskinīkiwak, " tapasītān ! " itwäwak äsa ; " kiyānaw pikuh kik-äskwahikunaw, " itwäwak äsah.

tāpwä wawäyīwak ; mīkiwāhp wāhyaw watsīhk ntawih-usīhtāwak. äkwah kītahtawä kīwäwak ; nātäwak usīmisiwāwa. äkutä nikwatis uwīkiwak. äkutä kītahtawä äh-wa-wīkitsik, kītahtawä nāpäsis māna äh-kanawāpukät, kītahtawä äsah äh-pōnahk, kā-kisisihk. mistsikus wīhkwatsipitam. ōmah mistsikus usitihk kā-kisisihk iskwāhtämihk äh-wäpinahk, kā-pähpīhtukätātsimuyit iskwäsisah.

utinäw äsah, " misawāts namuya nika-kīh-uhpikihāw, " äh-itäyihtahk äsa.

äkwah kā-pä-pīhtukäyit, āsay mīna ä-kīh-wayawīwäpināt, āsay mīna kīhtwām wayawīwäpinäw.

äkwah kīhtwām äh-pä-pīhtukäyit, " nistäsä ! " k-ätikut äsah.

" ah, mahti mīnah ! ahpōh ätukä kit-ōskinīkiskwäww, kīhtwām wayawīwäpinakih ! " itäyihtam äsah. äkwah ōmisih itwäw : " kita-wīh-uskinīkiskwäwiw, ahpōh ätukä äh-wītsihikuwisiyān ! " itwäw äsah.

äkwah kā-pä-pīhtukäyit uskinīkiskwäwa, " ay-apih, nimisä ! " itwäw äsa awa nāpäsis.

pihkahtäwāhtik isiyīhkātäw äsah ōhi uskinīkiskwäwah. äkusi äkwah miywäyihtam äh-umisit ; mīnah äh-mihtsätiyit ustäsah, miywäyihtam kitapamihikutsik ōhi uskinīkiskwäwah.

äkutah äsah māka mīna wīkihkämōw wīsahkätsāhk ōhih uskinīkiwah ; äwaku uhtsi, k-ōh-kiskäyihtamiyit kit-äsih-tapasiyit ōhih wīhtikōwa. ayīsk kih-mahpinäw wīsahkätsāhk ; äwak ōhtsi kā-wīsāmāt ōhi uskinīkiwah.

" mātsikah, nisīmis ! " itwäw äsah.

nīkān äsah māna pīhtukäw awa wīsahkätsāhk.

" tānisi kah-itäyihtän, " itwäw awa nāpäsis, " uskinīkiskwäw kit-āyāwāyahk ? " itwäw äsah.

äkwah wiya wīsahkätsāhk, " kik-ōsīminānaw ! " itwäw ; kahkiyaw käkway kīh-usīmiw ayisk äsah wīsahkätsāhk.

kītahtawä äkwah mistahi kā-kāyawisiyiwa ōhi usīmiwāwa, äh-kaskikwātikutsik, mīnah äh-paminawasuyit. mituni äsah kwayask pamihikwak, äkwah mistahi wīstawāw äsah äh-kitimākäyimātsik. äkwah äh-māh-mātsītsik, tsämāk wīpats äsah māna äh-atih-kīsihtāyit pahkäkinwah, äkwah māna utayōwinisiwāwa äw-usīhtāyit, mituni kwayask äsah äh-pamihikutsik.

kītahtawāh ōmisih itwäw äsah wīsahkätsāhk : " āh, āsay kiskäyihtam ōtah äh-ayāyahk āyītaw k-ōhkwākanit wīhtikōw, " itwäw äsah ; " pikuh nika-kīwōtānān," itäw ; " *äkwah mīna käkway pähtamanih, äkāya wīhkāts nākatōhkäh, näkuhtäyani,"* itäw äsah ōhi uskinīkiskwäwah, pīhkahtäwāhtik k-äsiyihkāsuyit ; äkwah äsah, " äkāya wīhkāts, wāpahtamanih käkway, utin," ītäy äsah, " utinah. äkutah uhtsi äkwah mina nika-kīwōtānān. käkway mīna pähtamanih, äkā apiyāhkuh, mistahi manitōww k-äyītawihkwākanät wīhtikōw. äkusi niya wiya wīsahkätsāhk nikustäw," itwäw äsah wīsahkätsāhk ; " äkwah mīna tāpiskōts niyānān kik-ätihtawinān," itwäw äsah ; " tāpwä näwu-tipiskāw nika-kīwōtānān. mitun āni kitakisināw. äkwah ka-pähtawinān ; äkā yōhtänamōhkan," itäw äsah ōhih uskinīkiskwäwah.

tāpwä ä-kīh-kakäskimiht awa uskinīkiskwäw, äkwah mātsi-nikuhtäw, mayaw kahkiyaw ä-sipwähtäyit ōhi ustäsah. äkwah kahkiyaw mīna kīsāts nāh-nätwaham ; mīn äsah kīsāts kahkiyaw pīhtukatäw ; äkwah äsah mīna kutak kīskatahwäw ä-misikitiyit mītusah. äkwah sōhkih mitunih kipaham wīkiwāw. mistah äsah kisināw.

äkwah kītahtawä kā-matwä-itwäwiht : " nisīmis, nitakusininān ! " kāmatwäh-itwäwiht äsah.

äkwah ayisk kī-kakäskimäw ; namuya äsah wih-waskawīw. piysk wāsakām äkutah wīkihk matwäh-nipahatsiyiwa. waniskāw kīkisäpā ; äh-ātah-wayawīt, namwāts ahpōh awiyah kita-mātahāt. māmaskātam.

" tāpw ätsik ānih ! " itäyihtam awa uskinīkiskwäw.

näu-tipiskāw äh-kīh-ispayik, takuhtäwak ōki uskinīkiwak. äkwah māna kah-kapä-kīsik äh-nikuhtät piku awa uskinīkiskwäw, nama wīhkāts käkway utinam, ātah nanātuhk käkway wiyāpahtahkih. kītahtawä äsa mistahih äh-miyusiyit mäkwanah wāpamäw äsah.

äkwah utinäw, " mätukätah äkā kika-wayäsihitih ! " k-ätikut, kayahtä ōtah äy-uhtsi-pasikōyit ōhi wīhtikōwa āyītaw k-ōhkwākaniyit.

ōmisih äsah itwäw awa wīhtikōw : " tāpwä niwīh-miyu-mītsisun, pihkahtäwāhtik ä-wīh-muwak ! hāw, pīhkahtäwāhtik, pitah ka-kīwähtahitin ; kika-wīnōwitin. "

äkusi awa wīhtikōw nayōmäw äsa ōhi uskinīkiskwäwa. kīwähtahäw, mistahi äsa äh-kakwātakihāt nōtukäsiwa äh-ayāwāt, tahtu-kīsikāw äh-kwayātsi-pakahtamākut, äh-kwayātsi-kīsisamākut, tahtu-kīsikāw äsah māna nīsu ayīsiyiniwah uhtsih äh-muwāt, äkwah māna ayīsiyiniw utakisiyah, täkuhtätsih, pita nīkān äyakunih äsah māna äh-mītsit.

äkwah, " nōhku, " itwäw äsah ; " kikīh-kwayātsi-pakahtān tsī utakisiyah ta-mītsiyān ? mistahi äkwah miyusiw uskinīkiskwäw kā-päsiwak, tamuwak. āhkamäyimuh äh-kakwä-wiyinuwat, " itwäw äsah.

tāpwäh, " äha' , " itwäw äsah awah nōtukäsiw.

mistahi miywäyimäw ōhi uskinīkiskwäwa awa nōtukäsiw, pihkahtäwāhtik k-äsiyīhkāsuyit.

äkwah äsah, " nōsisä, tāpwä mistah iyākwāma ta-nipahitān nipakwātān," itwäw äsa ; " mahtih kiyām kakwä-tsīsih ; niya nipahin," itwäw äsa awa nōtukäw ; " äkwah äkusi kika-pakāsimin, " itwäw äsa awa nōtukäw.

tāpwä awa uskinīkiskwäw miywäyihtam äy-itikut ōhi nōtukäsiwa.

" tānisi māka kä-tōtamān ta-nipahitān ? " itwäw äsah awa uskinīkiskwäw.

" ōmisi, " itwäw awa nōtukäw ; " tsīkahikan kik-ōtinān ; nistikwānihk ka-pakamahān, " itwäw awa nōtukäw ; " ōtäh äkā äh-pīsimōwik näō usätināwa, ōm ōtah nistam usähtsāw kik-āmatsiwān. äkutah uhtsi mīnah kutak *spatināw ka-täpāpahtän. näō ispatināwa miyāskamani, äkutä kakwätakwāmōhkan pīwāpisku-wāskahikan. äwakunih äkutä äh-sākutsihikut. kīspin äkutä takwāmuyani, äkusi kika-pimātisin," itik äsah; " takwāmuyani äkutä, ōmisi itwähkan: ' nistäsä, niwīh-nipahik āyītawihkwākan wīhtikōw!' kik-ätwān. itāp anah kika-yōhtänamākuk."*

tāpwä äh-kih-kakäskimikut awa pīhkahtäwāhtik ōhi nōtukäsiwah, pakamahwäw ustikwāniyihk. äkwah äkus īsi wiyanihäw, ä-kih-nipahāt. pakāsimäw. äh-kih-kīsiswāt, äkus īsi sōhkih tapasīw. pimipahtāw mituni sōhkih. kītahtawā ispatināw ntawāpahtahk, äh-atih-kapä-tipisk äh-pimipahtāt.[1] *āsay mīna kutak ispatināw wāpahtam; āsay mīna äwakuh miyāskam. mīna kutak ispatināw wāpahtam; äwaku mīna miyāskam. kutak spatināw äh-āmatsiwāt, āsay äkwah kā-matwä-täpwātikut ōhi wīhtikōwa.*

" namuya misawāts kitah-pīhtsāw askiy kit-ätāmuyan!" kā-matwä-isi-täpwātikut.

mistahi äsa kisiwāsiw awa wīhtikōw, ōhkumah äh-muwāt. äkwah tapinasiwäw; kutak äw-usähtsāyik äh-āmatsiwāt, ōtah nīhtsāyihk kīh-astäyiw pīwāpisku-wāskahikan. nāwiy äh-itāpit, kīh-pätisāpamäw äsah wīhtikōwa; sōhkih äsah äkwah tāpwä tapasīw. äh-utihtahk, wani-kiskisiw tānisi kā-kīh-isi-kākäskimikut ōhi nōtukäsiwa ka-kīh-nipahāt.

" tawinamawin! āyītawiskīsik niwīh-nipahik, nistäsä!" itwäw äsah.

pikw īsi ātah äh-itwät, mwähtsih äkwah ä-wīh-pä-sakinikut, kā-kiskisōpayit anihi nōtukäsiwa kā-kīh-si-kākäskimikut.

" nistäsä," itwäw äsah mīna kīhtwām, " tawinamawin!" itwäw äsah; " āyītawihkwākan niwīh-nipahik!" itwäw äsah.

yōhtäpayiyiw ōma pīwāpisku-waskahikan. pīhtukäw äsah. wāpamäw äkutah pīhtsāyihk äh-uwīkiyit uskinīkiskwäwah mīn uskinīkiwah.

ōmisi äsa itik ōhih uskinīkiskwäwah: " ntsāhkus, ay-apih!" itik äsah.

kītahtawä wayawītimihk ōtah kā-matwä-takuhtäyit ōhi wīhtikōwah.

" tawinamawin, pīwāpisku-wāskahikan k-ōwīkit!" itwäyiwah äsah.

äkusi äsah yōhtänam awa uskinīkiw, äh-atih-kīskikwätahwāt ōhih wīhtikōwa.

äkwah awa uskinīkiskwäw äkutah ay-ayāw. ayisk mistahi kitimākäyimik ōhi uskinīkiskwäwah mīn ōhi nāpäwah. kītahtawä kā-pīmuyuhikut käkway uhtsih kitah-manitōwit. tāpwä mistahi sōhkisiwin ayāw; mistahi äkwah mīn äyaku manitōwiw äsah. äkwah usīhtāyiwa nāpäw-ayōwinisah, äkutōwa äkwah äh-pusiskahk, mīna unāpäwin äh-usīhtāyit. tāpwä papāmātsīw.

kītahtawä ōmisi itik ōhi: " mistahi kistäsak kipīkiskātikwak. mistahi kakwātakihtāwak, nawats kakwä-wāpamatsik," itik; " ih, tāpwä wiya ōtah namuya wāhyaw ispatināw kik-ōtihtän. äkutah mīkiwāhp ka-wāpahtän, mitunih ä-misāk, äkutah ayīsiyiniwak uhtsitaw äh-kakwātikihāt, äh-watsistwanihkät, äkwah māna ayīsiyiniwah äh-tāh-tähtsi-kwāskuhtit, äkutah mitunih äh-sākaskinätsik ayīsiyiniwak, nanātuhk äy-isi-kakwātakihtātsik, pikw ītōwihk äh-ati-pah-pīkuskawāt anah äkutah k-āyāt mats-āyīsiyiniw," itik äsah; " äwaku piku äh-āyimahk, māka pikuh uskinīkiskwäwa äkunih pikuh k-ōtināt wiya; nāpäwa namuya pisiskäyimäw. mayaw pimāpamiskih,

[1] Inclusion of other words between prefixed particle and verb is very uncommon; somewhat more common is the start, as here, toward such inclusion, which is then annulled by forming the verb all over again.

ōmisi kik-ätik : ' mahtih sikitān, awīna wāhyaw kä-pahkihtiniyik'," itik äsah ; " äkusi kik-ätik."

äh-kīsi-kakäskimiht awa uskinīkiskwäw, wayawīw, äh-utinahk kit-sinīmāt. sipwähtäw äsah. äkwah kītahtawä, mayaw äh-at-īspi-kīsikāyik, kā-wāpahtahk. āt äsah wāhyaw äh-wīmāhtät, äsah wāpamik ōhih mats-āyīsiyiniwah, kā-kapä-kīsik kā-tāh-tähtsi-kwāskuhtiyit, uhtsitaw äsah mituni mihtsät ä-kākwātakihāt awah uskinīkiskwäwah.

kā-pä-nakiskākut, ōmisi äsah itik : " mahtih sikitān, awīna wāhyaw kä-pahkihtiniyik, nīstsās ! "

itāhkōmik äsah. mwähtsi ä-wī-sikit, kā-manipitamiyit ōma ustäsah kā-kīh-usīhtāyit.

" ' nīstsās, ' nitayītāw ; pīhkahtäwāhtik ätsik āwa ! "

äkus īsi kīmōts utinam mistik, misāskwatus ; saskawuhtäw. äh-atihkīwäh-sakiniskänikut, pīhtukahik. pōtih äsah misiwä kā-wāpamāt uskinīkiskwäwa pikw ītōwihk äh-nā-nātwāskikāsuyit.

ōmisi itwäwak ōkih uskinīkiskwäwak : " m ānih kiyānaw mīna äkusi äh-kīh-isi-miyusiyahk, awa uskinīkiskwäw k-äsi-miyusit ! " itwäwak ōki kā-mā-māskisitsik.

hāw, ästāyit äsah tähtapiwin, kiyīhtsäkusiyit mistikwa ōtah äh-tsimasuyit, utinam ōmah kā-kīh-manahut ōmah mistik.

" ta-wīh-pīwāpiskōww ! " itwäw äsah ; " pä-kwāskuhtitsi, kita-wīh-kisisin ! " itwäw äsah.

tāpwä awa äh-kwāskuhtit, kisisin awa mats-āyīsiyiniw kā-nāh-nipahāt ōhih uskinīkiskwäwah. äkusi nipahäw awa pīhkahtäwāhtik ; nipahäw ōhih mats-āyīsiyiniwah.

ituhtäw ustäsah aspin itäh kā-kiw-uhtaskatāt.

hawīna kīh-wāpamäw, äh-mātuyit, wiyah äh-mawihkātikut, äh-at-isītwätsik, " kisīminaw ukih-kitamōkuh wīhtikōwa ! " äh-itwäyit, mäkwāts ustäsah kā-pähtawāt.

" äkuyikuhk pōni-mātuk, nistäsitik ! nitakuhtān ! " itwäw äsah.

mistahi miywäyihtamuk ōki uskinīkiwak. mitātaht iskwäwah kakäkinäw äh-pimātsihāt, äw-utinamuwāt ōhih iskwäwah. äkwah mistahi miywäyihtamuk ōki nāpäwak, äh-wīwitsik.

kītahtawä nanātuhk pīsk,[1] *" namuya tāpwäh niya ayīsiyiniw, " itwäw äsah awa uskinīkiskwäw ; " nnatawäyimik äkwah nōhtāwiy. ntawāts äkwah niwīh-wawāskäsiwin. äkuyikuhk kahkiyaw kimiyu-tōtātināwāw, uskinīkiskwäwak äh-miyitakuk. "*

Once upon a time, long ago, a Windigo carried on his work of extermination. Ten youths took flight. That Windigo, with a face on either side of his head, no matter how many tents there were, always killed off all the people.

Then those youths, who were ten, said, "Let us flee! We alone shall not be killed," they said.

So they made ready; far off on a mountain they went to build their tipi. Then, after a time, they went back; they fetched their little brother. They had their tent off there alone. Then, at one time, as they continued

[1] These two words have no place here. Perhaps the informant was going to say *nanātuhk pisiskiwah :* "various animals."

to dwell off there, and the little boy always stayed to keep the house, then presently, as he was feeding the fire, he ran a splinter into himself. He pulled out the sliver of wood. When he threw out of the door that sliver of wood which he had run into his foot, there came crawling in a little girl.

He lifted her up, thinking, "It is no use, I should not be able to bring her up."

When she came into the tent, after he had twice thrown her out, again he threw her out.

Then, when again she came in, she called to him, "Big brother!"

"Ho, I had better do it again! I should not be surprised if she were to turn into a young woman, if I threw her out again!" he thought. Then he spoke thus: "Let her be a young woman, since it seems that I am being aided by the Powers!" he said.

Then, when there entered a young woman, "Be seated, my big sister!" said the boy.

"Burnt-Stick" it seems that he called the young woman. And now he was glad to have a big sister; and he was glad that all his elder brothers would have this young woman to do their household work for them.

And now it appears that in his usual way Wisahketchahk was staying with these young men; it was because they knew in which direction that Windigo would take flight. For Wisahketchahk was badly frightened; that was why he had asked hospitality of these young men.

"You will see, little brother!" he must have said.

Wisahketchahk was always the first to come into the tipi.

"What would you think," asked the boy, "of our having a young woman?"

And Wisahketchahk, for his part, said, "We shall have her as our younger sister!" for it seems that Wisahketchahk had every manner of creature for his younger brother or sister.

Then this younger sister of theirs was very diligent, sewing for them, and doing their household work. It seems that she kept them very well, so that they, in turn, became very fond of her. When they did their hunting, without delay, it seems, she always tanned the hides and made clothes for them, taking in every way excellent care of them.

Presently Wisahketchahk spoke as follows: "Oh, by this time the Windigo with a face on either side of his head knows that we are here," he said; "But we shall go visiting," he told her; "And then, if you hear anything, never listen to it, when you are gathering wood," he must have told the young woman who was called Burnt-Stick; and, "Never, when you see anything, take it up," he told her; Never take it up. Then we shall be off visiting again. If then again you hear anything, when we are not at home, great manitou power has that two-faced Windigo. So great that even I, Wisahketchahk, fear him," Wisahketchahk must have said; "Then, again, you will hear exactly, as it will seem, the sound of our voices," he said; "Really, for four nights we shall be off visiting. And it will be very cold weather. Then you will hear our voices; do not open the door," he must have told the young woman.

Accordingly, when the young woman had been instructed, she started to gather firewood, as soon as all her brothers had gone away. And she split all the wood, so that it should be quite ready for use; and she brought it all indoors ready for use; and she cut a big poplar tree besides. Then she closed up their tipi solidly. It was very cold weather.

Presently she heard someone call, "Little sister, here we are!" seemed to be spoken for her to hear.

But, after all, she had been warned; she did not stir from the spot. At last all round the lodge there was the sound of them dying of cold. In the morning she arose; when she went outside, she found not even a footprint. She wondered.

"So it really is thus!" thought the young woman.

When four nights had passed, the young men arrived. Then, when the young woman always gathered wood all day, she never picked up anything, although she saw all manner of things. But then at one time she saw a most beautiful feather.

She picked it up, when, "Of course I could not get the better of you!" said the two-faced Windigo, suddenly rising from the feather.

Thus spoke the Windigo: "Truly, I shall have good eating, when I eat Burnt-Stick! Now, Burnt-Stick, first I shall take you home with me; I shall make you fat."

With that the Windigo took the young woman on his back and carried her. He took her home with him, to where he had an old woman whom he led a dreadful life; every day this old woman had his stew ready for him, cooking it done before he got home, for every day he ate two men, his habit being, as soon as he got home, first to eat their entrails.

So now, "Grandmother," he said; "have you boiled the entrails ready for me to eat? Now very pretty is the young woman I have brought home to eat. Do not spare your pains to fatten her," he said.

Then, "Very well," said the old woman.

The old woman became very fond of the maid, Burnt-Stick.

Then, it seems, "Grandchild, surely I hate the very thought of killing you," she said; "Do try to deceive him; do you, instead, kill me," the old woman said; "And then you will set me to boil," said the old woman.

Truly, the maid was pleased at what the old woman told her.

"But how must I do to kill you?" asked the young woman.

Thus spoke the old woman: "You will take an ax; you will strike a blow on my head," said the old woman; "Yonder, in the direction where there is no sun, are four hills, the first and nearest of which you will climb. From there you will see the second hill. When you have crossed four hills, there try to reach in your flight an iron house. The one who dwells there will overcome him. If you manage to get there in your flight, then you will live," she told her; "When you reach the place in your flight, speak thus: 'Big brother, the both-side-faced Windigo wants to kill me!' you will say. Then they will open the door for you."

Accordingly, even as the old woman had directed Burnt-Stick, she struck her on the head. Then she skinned her and cut her up, whom she had slain. She put her in the kettle to boil. When she had cooked her done, she ran away as fast as she could. She ran with all her might. Presently she saw a hill, and all night long she ran. Then she saw another hill; she crossed it, too. She saw another hill; this, too, she crossed. When she climbed the next hill, already she heard the Windigo shouting to her.

"It is no use! The earth will not be large enough to give you refuge!" he shouted to her.

It appears that the Windigo was very angry at having eaten his grandmother. Now she was running down-hill; as she climbed the next rise, there down below was the iron house. When she looked behind her, already she saw the Windigo coming; then really she fled with all her might. When she reached it, she forgot the instruction she had been given by the old woman whom she had killed.

"Open the door for me! Both-Side-Eyes wants to kill me, big brother!" she cried.

Although she called in all manner of ways, he was even about to seize her, when she remembered what the old woman had told her.

"Big brother," she cried again, "open the door for me!" she cried; "Both-Side-Face wants to kill me!" she cried.

The door of the iron house swung open. She went in. She saw those who had their dwelling inside there, a young woman and a young man.

Then the young woman said to her, "Sister-in-law, sit down!"

Soon with noise the Windigo arrived outside.

"Open for me, Iron-House-Dweller!" he cried.

Then the young man opened the door and chopped off the Windigo's head.

Then the young woman stayed there. For that young woman and that man were very good to her. Then in time, they gave her something to keep in the bosom-fold of her garment, to give her manitou power. And really, she had great strength; she too had now manitou power. Then they made men's clothes, which she put on, * * * * * * * * * * Then really, she went about hunting.

Then at one time they said to her, "Your brothers miss you very much. They are suffering greatly; you ought to try to see them," they told her; "Now, not far from here you will come to a hill. There you will see a very large tipi. He who lives there is intent on tormenting people; he builds a nest from which he jumps on people. That place is full of people who suffer from all kinds of injuries, since that evil person who lives there breaks different parts of their bodies as he comes down on them," they told her; "This is the only difficulty, but, after all, he takes only young women; he pays no attention to men. As soon as he sees you, he will say to you, " * * * * * * * * * * * * * * * * * * *" they told her; "That is what he will say to you."

When the young woman had been instructed, she went out of the house, taking provision for the journey. She set out. Presently, just as the day had reached noon, she saw the place. Although she walked far round to avoid it, she must have been seen by that evil man who all day jumped down on young women, taking pleasure in tormenting them.

When he had come and met her, he said to her, " * * * * * * "

So it seemed he was her cousin. * * * * * * * * * * * * *

" 'My male cousin,' I have been calling her; why it is Burnt-Stick!"

Thereupon she secretly took up a stick of saskatoon wood; she used it as a cane. He led her home by the hand and took her into his tipi. And there she saw nothing but young women whose bodies were broken in every way from having been jumped upon.

These young women said, "Only to think that we, too, were as beautiful as this young woman!" Thus spoke those crippled ones.

Then, when he had placed a seat, and had climbed up on a tree which stood there, she took that stick which she had picked up.

"Let it turn into iron!" she said; "When he comes leaping, let him impale himself!" she said.

And truly, as he jumped, he impaled himself, that evil man who used to kill the young women. So Burnt-Stick killed him; she killed that evil man.

She went to where she had left her brothers when she departed.

What did she see, they were weeping, mourning for her, and all the while saying, "Our little sister was eaten by the Windigo!" Thus spoke her brothers as she listened to them.

"Enough; cease weeping, brothers! I have come!" she said.

Those young men were very glad. She had picked out ten of the women she had restored to life, and taken them for her brothers. Then those men were very glad to have wives.

Then at one time, "I am not really a human being," said the young woman; "And now my father wants me. So I shall turn into a deer. I have completed my benefaction to all of you, in giving you young women."

(26) The Thunderer's Brother-in-Law

Louis Moosomin

nāh-namiskwäkāpaw.

kītahtawä yāhkih mīna mitātasiwak nāpäwak.

āsay mīna tapasīwak, " usām kika-mästsihikunaw awa wīhtikōw, " äh-itwätsik äsah.

päyak uskinīkiskwäsisah sipwähtahäwak, usīmisiwāwa. nikwatis äsa ntawih-usīhtāwak wīkiwāw. äkwah äkutä ay-ayāwak. äkwah kinwäs äkutä äsah uy-ōhpikihäwak ōhih usīmisiwāwa. piyisk ispimihk äsa mistikwah tsimahäwak, äkutah äh-mānukawātsik, äh-watsistwanihkätsik, itah äh-uwīkiyit. kītahtawä kahkiyaw kākway äsah pawātam awa kanāts-ōskinīkiskwäw. äkwah kītahtawä kā-kiskäyihtahk kitah-pimihāt. äkwah kutakah nāpäsisah minah usīmisiw äsah awa uskinīkiskwäw.

äkwah ōmisi k-ätät usīmisah : " niwīh-ntāmisun, " itwäw äsah.

" nimisä, tānitäh māka kä-kīh-miskaman mīnisah ? pipun ōma, " itwäw äsah awa nāpäsis.

" nisīmis, namuya nika-kīh-pwātawihtān, " itwäw äsah ; " ayisk nika-pimihān, " itwäw äsah awa uskinīkiskwäw.

äkwa tāpwä wawäyīw, ä-sipwähtät, kutak askiy äy-isi-pimihāt awa uskinīkiskwäw. tāpwä äkutä äh-takuhtät akāmaskihk, mātsi-mawisōw. katisk äsah äh-āpihtā-kīsikāyik äkutä takuhtäw. āsay mātsi-mawisōw misāskwatōminah. päyak mwähtsi ä-sākaskinahtāt umawiswākan, āsay mīna kutak äh-atih-sākaskinahtāt, kītahtawä piyäsiwah kā-pähtākusiyit. kayahtä nāspitsi-säkimik. äh-pākupayit, kayahtä kā-wāh-waniskānikut uskinīkiwa. mistah äkwah äkutah miywäyihtam. māh-māsihitōwak ; uwītsimusiw ōhi uskinīkiwah.

äh-utākusiniyik iyikuhk, kīwäw. tāpwä mīnisah kīwähtatāw. wīkiwāhk äh-takuhtät, mātsih-kīsisam ōhih mīnisah. mistah äkwah miywäyihtamiyiwa ustäsah ä-kīsisamōwāt.

"tānitä ätukä wähtinahk kisīminaw ōhi mīnisah?" itwäwak ōki uskinīkiwak.

māmaskātamwak; uski-mīnisah äh-mītsitsik äh-pipuniyik uhtsih, k-ōh-māmaskātahkik, äkwah wiyah kākikä ispimihk watsistwanihk awa uskinīkiskwäw äh-uwīkit. āsay mayaw äh-waniskātsik, sipwähtäwak ōki uskinīkiwak, wiyah tahtu-kīsikāw pikuh äh-mātsītsik, äh-is-ātuskätsik, kahkiyaw käkway äh-mātsītutawātsik. āsay mīna uskinīkiskwäw nīhtakusiw.

āsay mīna ōmis ītäw usīmisah ōhi nāpäsisah: "mīnah niwīhntāmisun," itwäw äsah awa uskinīkiskwäw.

tāpwäh āsay mīna sipwähtäw awa uskinīkiskwäw, äh-pimihät. āsay mīna akāmaskihk takuhtäw. āsay mīna äkutä itah kā-kīh-uhtinahk mīnisah mātsi-mawisōw mīna. pōtih āsay mīna päyakwäw ä-sākaskinahtät umawiswākan, āsay mīna piyäsiwa kā-pähtākusiyit. mīna nāspitsi-säkimik. kay-ahtä piku mīna sāsay kā-wāpamät, äh-āpahkawisit ōhi uskinīkiwah kā-kīh-wāpamät. āsay mīna māh-māsihitōwak. äkutah kapä-kīsik ay-ayāwak. ayisk miywäyimäw ōhih uskinīkiwah.

äy-utākusiniyik āsay mīna wawäyīw ä-wīh-kīwät. kīwäw, mīna äh-atih-pimihät. käkāts äsa äh-tipiskāyik, wīkiwāhk takuhtäw. āsay mīna mātsi-kīsisam mīnisah. āsay mīna āmatsiwäw. mistahi miywäyihtamwak māna ōki uskinīkiwak, mīnisah miyītsitwāwi.

äkwah mayaw äh-wāpaniyik, āsay mīna mātsīwak. mayaw ustäsah äh-kī-sipwähtäyit, āsay mīna pä-pinasiwäw aw ōskinīkiskwäw, äh-pi-nānapātsihtawāt utayōwinisiyiwa, umaskisiniyiwa mīna.

"päyakwäw mīna niwīh-ntāmisun," itäw äsah usīmisah.

tāpwä sāsay mina wawayīw. äkwa äsah mina äkutä takuhtäw; mātsi-mawisōw itäh kā-nā-ntamisut. āsay mīna päyakwäw ä-sākaskinahtāt umawiswākan, āsay mīna sōhkih kā-pähtākusiyit piyäsiwah. kayahtä piku mīna kā-kiskäyihtahk, iyikuhk äh-āpahkawisit, äkutah mīna māh-māsihitō-wak.

äw-utākusiniyik, sāsay mīna kīwähtatäw mīnisah. äkwah mīna mātsi-kīsisam. ä-kīh-kīsisahk mīnisah, kāwi āmatsiwäw uwatsistwanihk. ä-takuktätsik, māmaskātamuk ōki uskinīkiwak, tahtu-kīsikāw äh-mītsitsik uski-mīnisah.

ōmisih äsah itwäwak: "tāntäh ätukä äh-uhtinahk awa kisīmisinaw uski-mīnisah?" itwäwak äsah.

ā, āsay mīna mayaw äh-wāpaniyik, sipwähtäwak, ä-kīh-mītsisutsik. kahkiyaw sāsay mīna äh-kīh-mästsi-sipwähtäyit, awa uskinīkiskwäw āsay mīna wīhtamawäw usīmisah mīn ä-wīh-sipwähtät. tāpwä sāsay mīna ati-sipwähtäw äsah, äh-ati-pimihät. äkutä äh-takuhtät itäh mānah kāy-isi-ntāmisut, mwähtsih äh-mātsih-mawisut, āsay äsah mīnah piyäsiwah kā-mātsi-pähtākusiyit. āsay mīna nāspits-säkimik awa uskinīkiskwäw. äkwah äh-āpahkawisit, kayahtä kīh-wāpamäw mīna äkutä uskinīkiwa. miywäyih-tam mistahi aw uskinīkiw, äh-wäw-utihtikut ōhi uskinīkiskwäwa.

matsikah atsiyā pikuh äh-kīh-māh-māsihitutsik, āsay mīna kīwäw aw ōskinīkiskwäw. ātah ä-takuhtät wīkiwāhk, namwāts kaskihōw kita-ki-kīhtsäkusīt kā-wīkit uwatsistwanihk. ātah wāh-kīhtsäkusītsih, pwātawihōw. ntawāts nahapiw tsīkih iskwāhtämihk. "tānähk ōma?" itäyihtam. ayisk uhtsitaw ätukä tōtākōwisiw awa uskinīkiskwäw, usām mistahih äh-kiht-säyimikut ōhih ustäsah, äh-kikiskawāwasut äsah. mayaw awa ustäsimāw äh-takuhtät wīkiwāhk, äsah äh-paspāpit, awīna ōhih, kīh-wāpamäw usīmi-wāwa äh-apiyit, äh-kikiskawāwasuyit. namwāts ahpōh pīhtukäw, iyikuhk äh-näpäwisit awa uskinīkiw. mistahi pakwātam. ayisk mituni kanawäyimäwak usīmimāwa ; namuya kiskäyimäwak wīhkāts nāpäwa kita-kīh-wāpamāyit. kutak mīna äh-takuhtät, täpiyāhk äh-wāpamāt, äkus īsi wāyunīw. kahkiyaw äsah kīh-nakatäwak ōki uskinīkiwak, usām äh-näpäwihikutsik äh-tōtamiyit. käkāts äsah äh-wāpaniyik, utsawāsimisiw aw uskinīkiskwäw. äkwah äkutah ay-ayāw ; ōhi pikuh usīmisah, nāpäsisah, äyakunih piku wīts-āyāmäw.

mwähtsi nīsusāp tipiskāw äh-päyakutsik, äkwah ōmis ītäw ; ayisk aw īskwäw k-ōtsawāsimisit nāpäsisah ayāwäw : " kanawäyim kitihkwatim ; niwīh-nikuhtān, " itäw äsah usīmisah.

kahkiyaw utayōwinisiyiwa utinamwäw ; nāspits ispimihk akutawäw, ōmisih āsah äh-itäyihtahk : " nka-kakwä-sipwähtān, " äh-itäyihtahk äs āwa uskinīkiskwäw.

tāpwäh it äh-sakāhk äh-takuhtät, wanakwayah kikamuhäw mistikuhk ; tsīkahikan äkutah astāw ; ayīsiyinīhkānah usīhäw.

" awa ōtah nāpäsis k-āyāt, ' nimisä ! ' itiskih, ' hā ! ' kik-ätāw, " itäw ōhi ayīsiyinīhkānah.

tāpwä äkus īsi isi-wäpinäw[1] *ōhi utawāsimisah, namuya kayās ä-kīh-nōkuhāt. äkwah kītahtawä kinwäs äh-wā-wäwäpitōt, kītahtawä mah-mātōyiwa. täpwäw awa nāpäsis.*

" nimisä, ntihkwatim mātōw ! " itwäw äsah.

" tsäskwah ! nimäkwā-nikuhtān ! " itik äsa ōhi ayīsiyinīhkānah kā-kīh-usīhimiht.

piyisk äkwāh tipiskāyiw. piyisk äkwah wīh-kawatsiwak. māh-mātōwak ōhi usk-awāsisah kā-kiki-wäpiniht. äh-kīh-näwu-tipiskāyik, kītahtawä piyäsiwah mistahi kā-pähtākusiyit. kayahtä piku ōtah kīh-apiyiwa.

" tāpwä mistahi kikitimākisin, nīstāh, " itik äsa ōhi piyäsiwa ; " āsay anih mīnah unāpämiw kimis, " itik ōhi piyäsiwa ; " māka wiya nipänātāw awa kitihkwatim. namuya misawāts ka-kīh-pamihtwāsun, " itik äsah.

äkwah utayōwinisah ispimihk kā-kīh-akutāwiht nāh-nīhtinamāk ōhi piyäsiwah. mayaw ä-kīh-pustayōwinisät, äkusi atih-utinäyiwa ōhi apisisawāsisah. wist äkwah wayawīw. utasāmah ä-kīh-utināt, kā-wāpahtahk äsa itäh umisah äy-isih-sipwähtäyit. kapä-kīsik pimipahtāw. kītahtawä äsah äh-at-ōtākusiniyik, ōtah wayāhtsāhk kīh-täpāpahtam maskusīwakān.[2] *at-ītuhtäw.*

" hwā, äwakw ätukä nimis wīkih ! " itwäw äsah.

pīhtukäw. pōnam. äh-kīh-pōnahk, pa-pimisin. äsah äh-ayītāpit, kītahtawä umisa tōhtōsimiyiwa kā-wāpamāt, äsah ä-kīh-maniswāyit.

" wahwā, tāpwä nikīsinātsihik ! " itäyihtam äsah ; " äkwah äwakunih nika-kīh-uhtsi-kākītsihāhtay nitihkwatim ka-pi-maskamikawiyān ! " itäyihtam äsa.

---

[1] Hyphen is used, because the meaning is here *isi* : "thither, thus" plus *wäpinäw* : "she abandons him." By contrast, the very common unit word *isiwäpinäw* : "he throws him that way or there" has *-wäp-* : "throw" as a non-initial stem. This illustrates the difficulty of drawing a clear line between simple words and compounds; for a native speaker it would be easy.

The repetition of *isi* is worth noting; it is perhaps due to the existence of the much commoner homonym; as homonymy is rare in Cree, the combination *isi-wäpinäw* is inadequate and disturbs the speaker.

[2] Normal form doubtless *maskusīwikān* , and below, the diminutive, normal: *maskusīwikānis*.

äkwah äkutah kapäsiw. kākisäpā mīna sāsay sipwähtäw. aspin äsah umisah itah ä-kih-at-ītuhtäyit, kapä-kīsik ati-mātahäw. āsay mīna äh-utākusiniyik, kutak mīna kā-wāpahtahk maskusiyukānis. pīhtukäw. pōnam. āsay mīna äh-pa-pimisihk, kutakah kā-wāpamāt umisah tōhtōsimiyiwa. āsay mīna mihtātam ä-kīh-pä-nātimiht utihkwatima. sipwähtäw kīkisäpāh. kītahtawä äh-pi-pmuhtät, kītahtawä kā-sākäwät, ōtah mīkiwāhp, kā-wāpamāt umisah pahkäkin ä-mäkwāw-usihtāyit. äkus īsi täpwātäw.

ōmis ītäw : " nimisä ! " itäw ; " nitakusinin ! "

äkwah ōmisih itwäw aw ōskinīkiskwäw : " namuy āwiyak nōh-usīmisin. äkus ōma pikuh äh-kiy-isi-päyakuyān, " itwäw äsah aw ōskinīkiskwäw.

" tāpwä niya nikīh-pä-maskamikawin ntihkwatim, " itwäw äsah.

sämāk kisiwāsiw awa uskinīkiskwäw. mōskīstawäw ōhi nāpäsisah, tsīkahikan äw-uhtsi-pakamahwāt, äh-nipahāt. mitunih pīkinatahwäw.

māka wiya ä-kisäwātisitsik sawäyimäwak āpakusīsak, ä-wīh-kakwä-pimātsihātsik ōhi kā-nipahimiht nāpäsisah.

äkwah tāpwä, " niya nik-āwatāw ! " itwäw äsa itōwāhk kā-misikititsik āpakusīs.

tāpwä äsah nanāpātsihäwak. ayisk kayās kih-ayīsiyiniwiwak ; usām kahkiyaw käkwayih äh-wītsihikōwisitsik, äyak ōhtsi k-ōh-īspayik. tāpwä pimātsihäwak.

äkwah kīkisäpā awa nāpäw kā-wīwit ōhih uskinīkiskwäwa kā-mōht-sōwiyit, usīmisiyiwa kā-nipahāyit, ōmis ītäw : " ntaw-āsamik ōki āpakusīsi-nōtukäwak, " itäw äsah.

äkwah tāpwä ntaw-āsamäw awa uskinīkiskwäw. äh-pīhtukät, kā-wāpamāt ōhih ka-kīh-nipahāt nāpäsisah.

" āsay ätsik ōki mīna äh-kīh-pimātsihātsik matsi-nōtukäsiwak ! " itwäw äsah.

äkwah ōmisih itwäw awa nāpäw : " kiyām äkāyah nipah, niwīkimākan. käyiwähk anah nka-wītsäwāw miyātsiyāni, " itäw.

äkusi pōnihäw aw ōskinīkiskwäw. äkwah tāpwä ōki nōtukäwak waway-īhäwak ōsisimiwāwa, ta-mātsiyit.

tāpwä awa nāpäw ä-wīh-mātsīt, " āstam, wäskinīkiyin ! iskäkānä nahāhkapiyani,[1]*" itäw aw āwāsis.*

äkwah tāpwä wawäyīw awa awāsis, äkwah ä-sipwähtätsik, ōhih äh-wītsäwāt ōhi nāpäwah, äh-mātsiyit.

iyātah-mātahātwāwi, " namuy äwaku, " itik māna ; " usām apisīsisiw, " itik māna.

äkwah tāpwä kutakah mitunih äh-māh-māhkiskamiyit, äwakunih äti-pimitisahwāyit mis-iyāpäw-wawāskäsiwah, wīpats äti-nipahāyit. nāway äh-takuhtät, āsay käkāts kīsi-wiyanihäyiwa.

äkwah ōmisi itik : " nawatsī ōma utakisiy, " itik.

tāpwä nawatsīw.

äkwah äh-kīsisahk, ōmisi itäw : " hāyītaw uhtsih kika-mītsinānaw, " itäw.

äkwah, " tānähki k-ōh-itwäyin ? " itwäw awa nāpäw ; " kiy ōma kitawāsisin, mistahi kā-ntawäyihtaman kita-mītsiyin, " itäw äsa.

" māka ayisk namuya nikaskihtamāsun käkway, " itwäw awa nāpäsis.

" äha' , " itik.

---

[1] The verb *nahāhkapiw* : "he is staying, as son-in-law, with his wife's people"; it applies here only in so far as during this stay a son-in-law is supposed to show himself a good worker. Irony.

tāpwä äh-kīsisahk ōma mayaw utakisiy, tāpwä āyītaw uhtsih mitsiminamwak, äh-mītstsik. äkwah käkāts äh-kitātsik, maskamäw.

" hāw, ōma mītsih, piyäsiw ! " itwäw äsah.

" ōh, käkway itah kä-kitimākäyimikuyin ? " itik äsah ōhi nāpäwa ; " kakwäyahōw ! " itik äsah ; " ati-pasikōw ! " itik äsah.

tah kisiwāk ustikwān uhpimä äh-astäyik, utinamiyiwa itäh isi k-äsikāsitäskanäyit ; nayahtahik. kawiskōsōw.

" kakwäyāhuh ! " itik ; " pasikōh ! " itik : " m āni ātah äh-manitōwakäyimuyin, itah wiya at-ātimitāni, kika-nipahitin ; kik-āti-patakwākimatitin.[1] "

tāpwä ati-sipwähtäw awa nāpäsis. tsīki wīkiwāhk äh-at-āyāt, āsay kisiwāk kā-pätsāstamuhtäyit, äh-atimikut. äkus īsi sā-sākwākimātik. äkwah äsah nipahik ; äskanah kā-kīhtsitāskamāk. äkwah mistahi miywäyihtam awa uskinīkiskwäw, nōhtaw äh-pä-nipahimiht.

äkwah āsay mīna ōki nōtukäsiwak kā-kīh-pimātisihātsik mīna itwäwak, " päyakwāw ta-kakwä-pimātsihātsik ! "

tāpwä awa kā-misikitit nōtukäw āpakusīsi-nōtukäw āwatäw äwaku. tāpwä āsay mīna pimātsihäwak. äsa māna wāh-pimātsihātwāwi, matutisiwak.

äkwah āsay mīna kīkisäpā, " ntaw-asam kōhkuminawak, " itwäw äsah awa nāpäw.

tāpwä äh-ituhtät awa uskinīkiskwäw, kīh-pimātisiyiwa ōhi nāpäsisah.

" āsay ätsik ōki mīna kīhtwām ! nikīh-miywäyihtamwah äh-nipahimiht ! " itwäw äsah.

" kiyām äkus āna päyakwāw mīna nika-wītsäwāw, " itwäw awa nāpäw.

tāpwäh pōnihäw awa uskinīkiskwäw. äkwah wawiyīw awa nāpäsis. mātsīwak. pä-wīsāmik ōhi nāpäwah. āsay mīna sipwähtäwak ; āsay mīna mātahäwak wawāskäsiwah.

" awa tsī ? " äh-ātiy-itāt, " namuya ! usām apisīsisiw, " itik.

mitunih nāspits ä-māh-māhkiskamiyit, äwakunih pämitisahwāyit, " itāp kika-päy-ātimin, " itik.

tāpwä mwästas äkutä äh-takuhtät, āsay käkāts kīsi-wiyanihäyiwa.

āsay mīna, " hāw, awāsis, ōma nawatsī ; mītsīhkahk ōma utakisih, " itik äsa.

tāpwä, " āyītaw uhtsih mīna kika-mītsinānaw, " itäw äsa.

tāpwä, " nīswāw äkwah äkusi kititwān, " itik äsa.

" ayisk niya nikitimākisin, " itwäw äsah awa nāpäsis.

" äha', " itwäw äsa awa nāpäw.

äkwah tāpwä, " itäh niya k-äsi-misāk, äkutä isi niya nik-äsi-mītsin, " itwäw awa nāpäsis.

piyisk mīna sākōtsimäw. äkwah tāpwä āyītaw uhtsi mitsiminamwak äh-mītsitsik. apisīs äy-iskwahtahkik, ispimihk isiwäpinam awa nāpäsis.

" haw, ōma mītsih, " itwäw äsah, " piyäsiw ! " itwäw äsah.

äkwah āsay mīna uhpimä astäyiw ōma ustikwān, āsay mīna äwakuh k-ōtinamiyit, ä-nayahtahikut. āsay mīna pasikōtisahuk, " kakwayahuh ! " äh-itikut. äkwah ati-sipwähtäw. mitunih papāsimik.

" kīspin itah atimitāni, kik-āti-mātakuskātn ntasāmak uhtsi ! " itik äsah.

---

[1] The medial stem is -ākimä- : "snowshoe" (verbal), cf. Ojibwa āgim, Menomini ākim (animate): "snowshoe." The word used in Cree is asām (animate): "snowshoe." I did not catch the word when dictated, but succeeded in making informant repeat it. As a result it is not used in the recurrence of the incident, below.

tāpwä sipwähtäw. kisiwāk äkwa wīkiwāhk äh-at-āyāt, kā-päh-atimikut.

ōmisi itwäw äsah ä-wīh-pä-nipahikut: " piyäsiw, äyakw āna nipahtamawin! niwīh-nipahik!" itwäw awa nāpäsis.

äkwa tāpwä piyäsiwak sōhki pähtākusiwak. nipahäwak ōhih nāpäwah, awāsisah kā-wīh-nipahāyit. äkusi pä-wayawī-kwāskuhtiw aw ōskinīkiskwäw. āsay mīna kīhtwām nipahäw ōhi usīmisah.

" kīhtwām äkwah pimātsihāyäkuh, ka-mähtsihitināwāw!" itäw ōhi nōtukäsiwah.

" haw," itwäwak ōki nōtukäwak, " misawāts namuya ta-kīh-nipahikunaw. kiyām käyāpits päyakwāw pimātsihātān," itwäwak.

tāpwä mīna sāsay usīhtāwak ōma māna itah kā-pimātsihātsik. tāpwä kīsihtāwak. āsay mīna kikisäpāh ä-ntawāpamāt, äh-pimātisiyit ōhi nāpäsisah awa uskinīkiskwäw, kakwä-nipahäw.

mwähtsi ä-wīh-nipahāt, " awa niwīh-nipahik, piyäsiwitik!" āsay mīnah itwäw awa nāpäsis.

tāpwä mistahi pähtākusiwak piyäsiwak.

" hāw," ōmis ītik; " ntawāts ōtäh ispimihk kit-äsi-kīwähtahitān," itwäw awa piyäsiw; " āsay nikis-ōhpikihāw kā-kīh-kīwähtahak kitihkwatim. ōma k-äsinākusiyān, äkusi wīstah isinākusiw," itik ōhi piyäsiwa.

tāpwä sipwähtahik; ati-wäpinik piyäsiwatsistwanihk. äkwah äkutah tahtwāw äh-kīh-näwu-tipiskāyik, äkuspihk äsa ōhi kīs-ōhpikiw äh-piyäsiwit.

äwaku päyak ātsimōwin.

Once upon a time, of old, there were ten men.

Again, they fled, saying, "That Windigo would destroy us all."

As they went away, they took with them a young girl, their younger sister. Off alone somewhere they went and built their dwelling. And off there they stayed. And there for a long time they must have been bringing up their sister. Finally they set up in the ground a tall tree, and in it they built a lodge, making a kind of nest, in which she then had her dwelling. Then in time that pure maiden must have seen all manner of things in her dreams. Then, presently, she knew that she could fly. And there was a little boy, a brother still younger than this young woman.

Then she said to her younger brother, "I shall gather berries."

"Big sister, but where will you find any berries? It is winter," said the little boy.

"Little brother, not by any chance shall I fail," she said; "For I shall fly," said the young woman.

Then really the young woman dressed herself and set out and flew to another land. Really, when she arrived there across the sea, she began to gather berries. She arrived there exactly at noon. She began to gather saskatoon berries. When she had filled one of her berrying baskets and was setting about filling the other, suddenly a Thunderer's roar was heard. It frightened her out of her senses. When she awoke, to her surprise, a youth was raising her to her feet. She was very glad. * * * * * *

Towards evening, she went home. So really, she brought berries. When she arrived at their dwelling, she set about stewing the berries. Her elder brothers were very much pleased when she gave them the stewed berries.

"Where can our sister have got these berries?" asked the youths.

They marvelled at this, that in winter they were eating fresh berries, and because that young woman always had her dwelling up aloft in the nest. As soon as the young men got up, they went away, for every day they did nothing but hunt, for this was their work, to hunt every kind of creature. Again the young woman came down.

Again she said to the boy, her brother, "I am going berrying again," said the young woman.

Accordingly, again the young woman set out, flying. Again she arrived in the land across the sea. Again in the place from which she had taken berries, she set about her berrying. Behold, when again she had filled one berrying basket, again the Thunderer's noise was heard. Again he frightened her out of her senses. Again she saw, when she came to, that youth whom she had seen. * * * * * * * * * * * * * * They stayed there all day, for she liked that youth.

Towards evening again she made ready to return home. She went home, again flying. When it was nearly dark, she came to their dwelling. Again she set about stewing berries. Again she went up aloft. Those young men were always very glad when they had berries to eat.

As soon as the next day broke, again they went hunting. As soon as her elder brothers had departed, the young woman came down again, to attend to their clothes and their moccasins.

"Once more I shall go a-berrying," she must have told her little brother.

Accordingly, again she went forth. Again she arrived at yonder place; she set about berrying where twice before she had found berries. Again when once she had filled a berry-basket, again the Thunderer made himself loudly heard. And when again suddenly she had regained her senses, when she had come to, * * * * * * * * * * * * * * *

Towards evening, again she took home berries. Again she set about stewing them. When she had stewed the berries, she went back up into her nest. When they arrived, the young men marvelled that every day they ate fresh berries.

They said, "Whence does our sister get fresh berries?"

Again, as soon as day had dawned, they set out, having eaten. Again, when every one of them had departed, the young woman told her little brother that she was going off once more. Accordingly, once more she set out and flew. When she arrived there where she had been gathering berries, just as she began to pick, again the Thunderer began to give his sound. Again the young woman was frightened out of her senses by his sound. And when she came to, once more she saw there the youth. That youth was very glad that the young woman always came there to him.

* * * * * * * * * * * Though she arrived at their dwelling, she was not at all able to climb up to the nest in which she lodged. Whenever she tried to climb, she failed. She needs sat down by the door. "What can be the matter?" she thought. The fact was, no doubt, that this young woman was so treated by the Higher Powers of purpose, because she was thought too much of by her elder brothers; * * * * * * As soon as the eldest brother arrived at their lodge, he must have peeped in, and what did he see but their young sister sitting there, * *

* * * He did not even go in, so shamed was that youth. He was deeply grieved. For they kept their sister very carefully; * * * * * * * * * * * * * * When the next one arrived, as soon as he saw her, he turned back. All those young men left her, because she had too much shamed them by what she had done. When dawn had almost come, the young woman bore her child. Then she stayed there; she had with her only her little brother, that boy.

When they had been alone twelve days and nights, she spoke to him as follows; for that woman's child was a boy: "Take care of your nephew; I am going to gather wood," she told her little brother.

She took from him all his clothes; she hung them up high, out of his reach, for, "I shall try to go away," that young woman must have been thinking.

So, when she came to the grove of trees, she fastened her sleeve to a tree; she placed an ax there; she made an effigy of a human being.

"When that boy who is here says to you, 'Sister!' then, 'Yes!' you will say to him," she told that effigy.

And so in this wise she abandoned her child which not long before she had borne. Then presently, when for a long time he had rocked the babe, it began to cry. The boy called.

"Sister, my nephew is crying!" he called.

"Wait a bit! I am in the midst of gathering wood!" he was answered by that effigy which had been made.

At last darkness came. In time they were almost freezing. They wept, he and the babe with which he had been abandoned. When the fourth night had passed, suddenly the Thunderer's loud roar was heard. Suddenly, there he sat.

"Truly, you are in a sorry plight, my brother-in-law," the Thunderer said to him; "Your sister by this time has taken another husband," the Thunderer told him; "But I have come to fetch this your nephew. In any case you would not be able to take care of him," he told him.

Then that Thunderer took down for him his clothes which had been hung high. As soon as he had put them on, the other took away that infant. He too went forth. When he had taken up his snowshoes, he saw the way along which his sister must have departed. He ran on, all day. Presently, towards evening, there in a hollow of the land, he spied a grass hut. He approached it.

"There, this must be my sister's dwelling!" he said.

He went inside. He built up the fire. When he had built up the fire, he lay there. As he looked about him, presently, there he saw his sister's breast, which she must have cut off.

"Alas, truly she brings me to grief!" he thought; "Now with this I could have consoled my nephew that has been taken from me!" he thought.

Then there he spent the night. In the morning he set out again. Along the path that his sister had taken from there, he tracked her all the day. Again, towards evening, he saw another little lodge of grass. He entered it. He fed the fire. Again, as he lay there, he saw his sister's other breast. Again he lamented that his nephew had been fetched away. He set out in the morning. Presently, as he went on, he came out upon a place where was a lodge, and there he saw his sister tanning a hide. At once he called to her.

"Sister!" he called to her; "I have come!"

Then that young woman said, "I have never had any younger brother. I have always been alone, as I am," said the young woman.

"As for me, truly, my nephew was taken away from me as I came," he said.

At once the young woman grew angry. She ran at the boy and struck him with an ax, killing him. She chopped him to bits.

But some kind mice took pity on him, deciding to try to revive that boy who had been killed.

Then, accordingly, "I, I shall take him away!" said a mouse, one of those which are large.

Accordingly, they attended to him. For of old they had human form; because by all the Higher Powers they were aided is why it could happen so. Really, they restored him to life.

Then, in the morning, that man who had to wife the young woman who was so mad and had slain her brother, spoke thus to her: "Go feed those Old Mouse Women," he told her.

Then, accordingly, the young woman went to give them food. When she entered, there she saw the boy she had killed.

"So it seems that these evil old women have brought him back to life!" she said.

Then the man said, "Never mind, do not kill him, my wife. After all, I can take him with me when I hunt," he told her.

So the young woman left him alone. Then, accordingly, the old women made their grandchild ready, that he might hunt.

So, when that man was ready to go hunting, "Come here, young fellow! It would seem you are staying with people," the child was told.

Then the child made himself ready, and they set out, as he accompanied that man on his hunt.

Although they would come upon some creature's trail, "Not this one," the other would say to him; "He is too small," the other would say to him.

Then really, when they saw the trail of another whose tracks were of enormous size, then the man went off pursuing this giant stag, and soon off there slew him. When the boy later arrived, the other had almost finished preparing the carcass.

Then the man told him, "Roast this tripe," he told him.

So he roasted it.

When he had cooked it done, he said to the man, "Let us eat it from either end."

Then, "What makes you say that?" said the man; "You, you are but a child, to be wanting to eat so much," he told him.

"But since I have no power of any kind!" said the boy.

"Yes, very well," the other said to him.

Accordingly, as soon as he had cooked done that tripe, they each took hold of an end, and ate it. Then, when they had almost eaten it up, he snatched it away from the man.

"Come, eat this, Thunderer!" he said.

"Ho, what sort of thing will give its aid to you?" the man said to him; "Get to work!" he told him; "Up with you!" he told him.

Close by there, off to one side, where lay the stag's head, the man took it up by the beast's pointed horns; he put it on the boy's back, for him to carry. He sank to the ground under the weight.

"Look lively!" he told him; "Get up!" he told him; "Believe it or not, though you think yourself of manitou kind, if I overtake you on the way, I will kill you; I will stamp you under my snowshoes."

So the boy started off. When he had got close to their lodge, the other had already come near, and now overtook him. At once he crushed him under his snowshoes. He killed him; he jabbed the horns into him. Then the young woman was very glad that he had been killed before reaching the place.

Then again those old women who had restored him to life said, "Let them try once more to bring him to life!"

Then, accordingly, that big old woman, that Old Mouse Woman took him off with her. They succeeded in bringing him again to life. It seems that they took a steam-bath whenever they were about to bring him to life.

Then again, in the morning, "Go feed our grandmothers," said the man.

When, accordingly, the young woman went there, the boy was alive.

"And so they have done it again! I was glad he had been killed!" she exclaimed.

"Never mind, I shall simply take him with me again," said the man.

Then the young woman left him alone. Then the boy made ready. They went hunting. The man came to take him along. Again they set out; again they came upon the trail of a stag.

"Is this the one?" he asked him, but, "No! He is too small," the other answered.

When one had left hoofprints of enormous size, this one the man pursued; "You will catch up to me later," he told him.

Truly, later, when the boy got there, he had already nearly finished cleaning the carcass.

Again, "Come, child, roast this; let us later eat this tripe," he told him.

Then, "Let us eat it again from either end," he told the man.

Then, "Now for the second time you say thus," the other answered him.

"After all, as for me, I am but a poor creature," said the boy.

"Yes, very well," said the man.

Then, "Let me have the big end, let me eat from the big end," said the boy.

At last he talked the man into it. So then they took hold of it at either end and ate it. When they had but a little uneaten, the boy flung it aloft.

"Come, eat this," he said, "O Thunderer!"

Now again, off to one side lay the head, and again the man took it and put it on the boy's back. Again he drove him to his feet, telling him, "Look lively!" He started out. The man hurried him on with shouts.

"If anywhere I catch you, I will stamp you flat with my snowshoes!" he called to him.

He went off. When he had got near the lodge, the other overtook him.

As the other was about to come upon him and kill him, he cried, "Thunderer, kill this one for me! He wants to kill me!" said the boy.

Then truly the Thunderers made themselves loudly heard. They killed that man who was going to kill the child. Then the young woman came leaping out of her dwelling. Again she slew her little brother.

"If you again restore him to life, I will kill you all!" she said to those old women.

"Now," said those old women, "in any case she will not be able to kill us. Let us revive him once more," they said.

Accordingly, again they built that in which they always revived him. They completed it. When the young woman went to see them in the morning, and the boy was alive, she tried to kill him.

Just as she was about to slay him, "This one means to kill me, O Thunderers!" the boy said again.

Truly with great noise the Thunderers were heard.

"Now then," they said to him; "I shall needs take you home with me aloft," said the one Thunderer; "I have already brought to maturity your nephew whom I took. Even as I look, so looks he too," the Thunderer said to him.

So he took him away from there; he dropped him into a Thunderer's-nest. And there, when four nights had passed, by that time he had grown to maturity as a Thunderer.

That is one tale.

(27) Why the Dead are Buried

Louis Moosomin

nāh-namiskwäkāpaw.

kayās ayīsiyiniwak ōmisi kīh-pakitinikōwisiwak : kahkiyaw käkway kīh-kitimākäyimikwak, tahtuh käkway kā-wāpahtamihk, mīna äkā kā-wāpahtamuht. kahkiyaw käkway kīh-pawātamuk. ahpōh wākayōsah kīh-kiskinōhamākwak käkway. awäk ōhtsi kayās ayīsiyiniwak k-ōh-kih-manitōwitsik.

äkwah nik-ātayōhkān.

kītahtawä yāhkih päyak nāpäw päyakuyiwa utawāsimisah, äkwah mistah äsah äh-kitimākäyimāt, mīna äh-miyu-pamihāt. äkwah kītahtawä, wayawītimihk uwīkimākanah äh-atuskäyit, kītahtawä kā-wanihātsik utawāsimisiwāwah. namuya kīh-kiskäyihtamwak tānisi isi äh-isih-wanihātsik. äkwah äsah mistahi pakwātamwak, äkwanih äh-wanihātsik ōhi utawāsimisiwāwah. nāpäsisah äsah äwakw ani nistam äsah utawāsimisihtāwāw, äyakuni pikuh. nama kiskäyihtamuk tānisi äy-isi-wanihātsik. äkwah pikw ītä ātah äh-kakwätsihkämutsik, äkwah piyisk pōnäyimäwak.

äkwah awa awāsis nik-ātsimāw, tānisi äh-kīh-isih-pimātisit. äkutah ätukä takuhtäw ; wākayōs äkwah anihih awāsisah äsah kīh-kimutiw. äkwah piyisk papāh-wītsäwäw, niyīpiniyikih.

äkwah kītahtawāh itwäw awa nāpäw : " ahpōh ätukä nikusis pimātisiw ! " itwäw māna.

pawātam āskaw māna äh-wāpamāt ukusisah.

kītahtawä päpuniyikih māna kanawäyimik ōhi wākayōsah. äkusi tahtuh pikw ītä ayīsiyiniwak kā-māmustsikäyit, āsay kiskäyihtam awa wākayōs. ahpōh k-ōyaskinahtwākut kiskäyihtam.

ōmisi äsah māna itäw ōhi awāsisah : " nōsisä, āsay mīna ninatumik-awin, " itwäw äsah.

tāpwä äkutah kiy-ōhtsih-pimātisiw anah awāsis. piyisk tāpiskōts ayīsiyiniwah kīh-itäyimäw äsah wākayōsah, äh-uwītsäwākanit.

äkusi piyisk mihtsät askiy äh-uhpikiyikut, äkwah kākāts äh-nāpäwit, ōmisih itik wākayōsah : " äkwah kākāts kikīs-ōhpikin. wīpats äkwa kitah-wayawīn, " itik äsah ; " kōhtāwiy, anuhts kā-wīh-nīpihk, kākāts mästih-kasutsih kōnah, äkuspih nika-nipahik, " itik äsah ; " äkutah sämāk wayawīh-kan. ' kiyah ätsik ōma, nōhtāh ! ' itāhkan, mayaw wāpamatsih ; ' nōhtāh, näwu-tipiskāw namuya ayīsiyiniw nika-wāpamik, iskwäwak tāpiyāk. kiy-awāw mīna namuya ka-wāpaminäwāw. kīspin wāpamitwāwi iskwäwak, äkusi nika-kutāwaskamikin. kakwä-tōtah, ' kik-ätāw kōhtāwiy, wāpamat-sih, " äkusih itwäw awa wākayōs.

" wāpahkih ka-takuhtäw kōhtāwiy, " itwäw äsah awa wākayōs ; " māka niwīh-nipahik, " itäw äsah ōhi ; " sämāk takuhtätsi, kīh-nipahitsi, way-awīhkan, " itwäw äsah.

tāpwä wiyah kisäyiniw awa äh-pä-mātsīt, miskawäw wākayōsa, itah äh-apiyit.

" tāpwä nimiskawāw wākayōs, " itwäw äsah.

äkwah tāpwä nitawi-nipahäw. äkutäh mistikwah utinäw, ä-si-sik-wātakahikät. tāpwä pä-wayawiyiwa ōhi wākayōsah. äkwah äkus īsi nipa-häw. mayaw ōhih wākayōsah äh-nipahimiht, aw ōskinīkiw wayawī-kwāsk-uhtiw.

" äwakw ätsik āwa nōhtāwiy ! " itwäw äsah.

äkwah, " tānähki, uskinīkiw, k-ōh-isiyin ? "

" niy ōma, nōhtāh ! " itwäw äsah ; " wākayōs ä-kīh-kimutamāsk, k-ō-kih-wanihiyin, " itwäw äsah awa uskinīkiw.

äkusi äh-itwät, awa kisäyiniw, " āyimāts niwāpamāw nikusis ! " itwäw äsah.

" nōhtāh, ōm pikuh pītsi-nayōmiyin,[1] *" itwäw äsah awa uskinīkiw.*

tāpwä kisäyiniw ukusisah wīwahōw äsah, äh-nayōmāt.

" äkwah äkutä näwāw piku kik-āh-ayiwäpin, " itäw äsa ōhtāwiya awa uskinīkiw.

tāpwä awa kisäyiniw näyawiskōsutsih ayiwäpiw ä-nayōhtsikät.[2] *mitunih mistahi kusikwatiyiwa, pāskats äsa ustikwānihk äh-tahkupisut, iyikuhk äh-miywäyihtahk ukusisah äh-wāpamāt. uhpimä wāhyaw mānukäw äsah.*

" näu-tipiskāw namuya nika-wāpamikwak ayīsiyiniwak, " itwäw äsah.

tāpwä kisäyiniw usk-āyah papāh-ntāhtāmōw apahkwāsun mīna apasuyah näu. äkwah äsah uskinīkiwah utinäw, äkā tsäskwa iskwäwah äh-āpatsih-āyit ; ayisk äsah kayās kī-kanātisiw ayīsiyiniw, nayästaw kanāts-āskīhk

---

[1] The prefixed particle is doubtless wrong; perhaps read *kitsi-*, which seems to be an allegro variant of (*a*) *kitah-isi-*, *kit-äsi*, i.e. *kitah-*, *tah-* : "that, in order that," plus *isih-* : "thither, thus," and (*b*) *kitisi-*, i.e. *isih-* with personal prefix *ki-*, *kit-* of second person.

[2] The normal forms seem to be *nayōmäw* : "he carries him on back," *nayahtam* : "he carries it on back," and, derived from the latter, *nayahtsikäw* : "he carries on back"; but we find also *nayōhtam*, *nayōhtsikäw*. Menomini has *nayōmäw*, *nayōhtam*, but for the former also *nayāhäw*.

äh-kīh-ayāt. māmaskāts äkwah kanawäyimäw uphimä ukusisah awa kisäyiniw ; näō-tipiskāw ayisk itik kita-ka-kanawäyimāt.

mwähtsi nistu-tipiskāw äh-kanawäyimāt, äh-nipāt, kayahtä, " nōhtāh, äkus ätsik āna äkā wīhkāts kä-wāpamiyin ! " itwäw awa uskinīkiw.

āsay apisīs pikuh kī-sākiskwäw, askīhk äh-kutāwaskamikīt.

äkusi äsa mīna kīhtwām, " äkusi äs ānih namuya wīhkāts kitah-āpisisin ayīsiyiniw ! " itwäw äsa awa uskinīkiw ; " itāmaskamik kita-nahināw ayīsiyiniw, ispīhk uhpikihitutsih ! " itwäw, iskwäyāts äh-pīkiskwät awa uskinīkiw.

māka wiya awa iskwäw[1] *namuya äsa uhtsi wāpamäw ukusisah, äkus äh-isih-nipiyit.*

äwaku päyak ātayōhkäwin.

Of old men were placed here on earth by the Powers in this wise: they were pitied and befriended by every kind of thing, by as many things as are seen, and by the things that are invisible. They dreamt of every kind of thing. Even the bears taught them things. That is why the old-time people had manitou power.

Now I shall tell a sacred story.

Once upon a time, long ago, a certain man had one child, and it seems that he dearly loved him and took good care of him. Then at one time, as his wife was working out of doors, suddenly they lost their child. They could not make out how they had lost track of him. They were greatly distressed at having lost their child. The little boy had been their first child, and the only one. They did not know how they had lost him. Having made inquiry everywhere in vain, at last they gave him up.

Now I shall tell of the child, how he managed to stay alive. He came to some place or other; it appears that a bear had stolen the child. Soon he went about with the bear in summer-time.

Then at one time that man said, "Perhaps after all my son is alive!" he would always say.

Every now and then he would dream that he saw his son.

Then in winter-time the bear would take care of the child. As often as anywhere men performed their worship, at once the bear knew it. He knew even when a pipe was filled for him.

This was what he must have said always to the child: "Grandchild, again I am being invited," he must have said.

So in this way the child stayed alive. In time he looked upon the bear, his companion, as a human person.

Then finally, when the latter had brought him up through many years and he was near to manhood, the bear said to him, "Now you have almost grown up. Soon now you will go outside," he must have told him; "Your father, this coming spring, when the last of the snow is about to melt

[1] i.e., it was his mother who had violated the command; either the tale is laconically told or I missed a sentence above.

away, then your father will kill me," he must have told him; "Then at once do you go outside. 'And so it is you, my father!' do you then say to him, as soon as you see him; 'My father, for four nights let people not see me, women at least. You and my mother, too, I shall not see. If women see me, I shall sink into the earth. Try to do this,' you will say to your father when you see him," spoke that bear.

"Tomorrow your father will come," the bear must have said; "But he will kill me," he must have told the lad; "As soon as he arrives and has killed me, then do you go outside," he must have said.

Then truly, the old man, for his part, as he came that way on the hunt, found the bear where it was staying.

"Truly, I have found a bear," he must have said.

Accordingly, he went to kill it. There he took a long stick and prodded the hole that was in the ground. Truly, the bear came forth. Then, accordingly, he killed it. As soon as the bear had been killed, that youth leaped out from the hole.

"And so this is my father!" he must have cried.

Then, "What do you mean, youth?"

"It is I, father!" he must have said; "Because the bear stole me from you, is why you lost me," the youth must have said.

When he said this, then the old man must have said, "At last I see my son!"

"Father, there is only this, that you must carry me on your back," said the youth.

So the old man took his son on his back and carried him.

"And until we get there, only four times you are to stop and rest," said the youth to his father.

So whenever the old man wearied under his burden, he rested, with his load on his back. The latter was very heavy, the more so, as the old man had tied the strap round his head, so glad was he to see his son. Then far off to one side he set up a tipi.

"For four nights people are not to see me," he said.

So the old man went about borrowing unused tent-covering and four unused tent-poles. * * * * * * * * * * * * * * * In a way to cause wonder then the old man guarded his son, away from the camp; for he had told him to guard him for four nights.

When he had guarded him for exactly three days and nights, as he slept, suddenly, "Father, and so you are nevermore to see me!" called the youth.

Already his head was but a short way above the earth, into which he was sinking.

Then once more, "And so then, it appears that never again shall a mortal man come back to life!" said that youth; "Under the ground man shall be laid away, as the generations go on!" said the youth, speaking for the last time.

But as for the woman, she never again saw her son, who in this wise now had died.

That is one sacred story.

(28) The Origin of Horses

Coming-Day

kā-kīsikāw-pīhtukāw.

kītahtawā ä-mihtsätitsik ayīsiyiniwak, päyak ukimāw utawāsimisah nistuh, nāpäwak. nīsu ayāwäwak iskwäwah. usīmimāw ōw uskinīkiw miyusiw. äkusi namuy āwiya ayāwäw iskwäwa ; māka mistahi kitimākäyimik kahkiyaw ustäsah, wītimwah ; tāpiskōts awāsis äkusi pamihāw, usām äh-kitimākäyimiht, nistu mīkiwāhpah mā-mäskuts äkutah äh-pīhtukät.

äkusi kītahtawäh,—ustäsimāwa ōh ustäsah mistahi kitimākäyimik ōhi wītimwah,—äkwah mituni äh-uskinīkit, kītahtawäh äh-pīhtukät ōh ōstäsah ustäsimāwa wīkiyihk, pōtih päyakwapiw aw iskwäw.

äkusi ä-wīh-wayawīt, " tsäskwa ! " itik wītimwa ; " mītsisuh, " itik.

äkusi asamik. ä-kīsi-mītsisut, ä-wīh-sīkahukut, pasikōw, ä-wīh-wayawīt.

" kiwī-sīkahutih ōma ! " itik wītimwah.

" usām kipäyakwapin, " itäw.

äkusi pasikōw aw iskwäw, iskwāhtämihk äh-nīpawit, äh-kipiskawāt wītimwa.

ōmis ītäw : " nītim, k-ōh-kitimākäyimitān, ä-wīh-wīhtamātān, kit-ōh-uwītsimusimiyin, " itäw, " ayōwākäs ka-kitimākäyimitin, " itäw.

" namuya ! " itwäw aw uskinīkiw ; " usām tāpiskōts nikāwiy nitäyihtān tahtuh k-ōwītimuyān. nisākwäyimun, " itäw wītimwah ; " kiyām nika-wayawīn ! "

äkusi wayawīw aw uskinīkiw.

äkusih ōmis ītäyihtam aw īskwäw : " māskōts wīhtamawātsih ustäsah, ta-kisiwāsiw niwīkimākan, " itäyihtam ; " nitsawāts nka-wīhtamawāw niwīkimākan, " itäyihtam ; " nitsawāts maywäs wīhtamawāt ustäsah, niya nka-wīhtamawāw, " itäyihtam.

äh-pīhtukäyit uwīkimākana, ōmis ītäw : " niwīkimākan, namuya äkus ä-kīh-itäyihtamān, kisīm k-ōh-kitimākäyimak. anuhts äh-pīhtukät, nkakwätsimik ta-nōtsīhkawit, " itäw ; " mitunih nimāmaskātän äy-isi-kitusit, k-ōh-wīhtamātān. äkusi namuya äkwah nika-kīh-kitimākäyimāw kisīm, " itäw.

sämāk pakwātam awa nāpäw.

" namuya äkusi ä-kīh-täyihtamān, ' kakwä-kitimākäyim nisīm, ' k-ōh-ititān māna, " itäw.

äkusi aw ōskinīkiw näpäwisiw ä-kīh-itikut wītimwa. namuya wīh-ayituhtäw.

" tāpwä ätukä äkus äh-itäyihtahk nisīm, äkwah äkā kā-pīhtukät, " itäyihtam aw ōstäsimāw.

māka kisiwāsiw ōma k-ätikut uwīkimākana. kītahtawä wīhkäts äh-ituhtät aw ōskinīkiw, ä-wīh-pīhtukät, wāpamik ustäsah. mōhkumān utinam, " nika-nipahāw nisīm, " äh-itäyihtahk. ä-pä-pīhtukäyit, ä-wīh-tahkamāt, asäpayihōw aw uskinīkiw. täpiyāhk apisīs pikwāhuk. namuya mituni pikwatayähuk. äkus īsi wayawiyāmōw aw uskinīkiw, äh-ma-mawimuyit wītimwah ōhi kā-misimikut. kutakak iskwäwak äh-wayawītsik mōskīstawäwak ōhi nāpäwa, äh-nawaswātäyit usīmiyiwa. nawatināw awa nāpäw, ä-mitsiminiht. äkusi pōyōw. kīwähtahäw. ä-pīhtukät wīkiwāhk, kutakak nāpäwak pīhtukäwak, äh-kitahamāht.

" tänähki k-ōh-tōtawāt usīma, äh-kiskäyimiht äh-kitimākäyimāt ? "

ātsimōw : " äh-kakwätsimāt wītimwah äh-wīh-ōwītsimusit, äyak ōhtsi k-ōh-tōtawak, " itäw.

äkusi aw ōskinīkiw ōhtāwiyah wīkiyihk äkutä pīhtukahäw, äh-nanātawihiht. piyisk kinwäsk ayāw, ä-wīsakäyihtahk, ōh ōsīmimāwa ustäsah äh-pamihikut äkwah uwītimwah. nīsu ayāwäyiwa iskwäwah. äwakunik mistahi pakwātamwak äh-tōtāmiht ōh ōskinīkiwa wītimuwāwa, usām tāpiskōts utawāsimisiwāwa äy-isi-kitimākäyimātsik ōhi. " māskōts ahpōh tanipiw, " itäyihtākusiw aw uskinīkiw. äh-ātah-nanātawihiht, piyisk kinwäsk āhkusiw. piyisk kīwähtahäw awa usīma wīkiwāhk, ä-wīh-pamihāt, " usām äh-kwatakihtāt nōhtāwiy mīna nikāwiy, äh-pamihātsik nisīma, " äh-itäyihtahk ; " māka äkutä wätinahk nka-pamihānān, " äy-itäyihtahk. tāpwä pamihäwak usīma. awa kā-kīh-tahkamāt usīma nama wīhkāts nitawāpamäw, mīn uwīkimākana. napāwihk kaskäyihtam, äh-nōhtä-wāpamāt aw iskwäw kā-kīh-misimāt wītimwah. " nik-ätuhtān, " ätātsih uwīkimākana, äkus äh-pakamahukut, äh-kāhkwäyihtahk awa, k-ōh-tōtawāt usīmah.

piyisk ati-miyw-āyāw aw uskinīkiw.

" kähtsināh miyw-āyāyāni, ahpōh nika-nipahik nistäs. miyw-āyāyāni, nika-sipwähtān. kiyām pikw ītä wī-misi-wanātisiyāni, " itäyihtam aw uskinīkiw, äh-ati-miyw-āyāt.

iyikuhk äkwah äh-miyw-āyāt, māka namuya wīhkāts nipāyiwa ōhō wītimwah äkwah ustäsah, mā-mīskuts äh-kanawäyimikut, täpiskāki äkāyah äh-nipāyit. kītahtawä ōhi usīmimāwa wītimwah, ä-wīh-wāpaniyik, äkā äh-na-nipāyit, kiskäyimäw ä-nōhtähkwasiyit.

ōmis ītäw : " nītim ! "

" tanähkih ? "

" mahtih pahkäkinus pätāh äkwah astis äkwah uskātsihk. "

" tanis ä-wīh-tōtaman ? " itik.

" nimaskisin äh-pīkupayik, ä-wīh-mīsahamān, " itäw.

" pä-kätsikunah ; niya nka-kaskikwātän. namuya wīhkāts kika-kaskikwātisun, ahpoh äh-miyōmahtsihuyin ; wāwīs tsiy äkwah ka-pamihisun, āyimāts äh-pimātisiyan ? " itäw ; " misawāts apisīs ōma, " itäw.

māka mistahi nōhtähkwasiw aw usiknīkiskwäw. piyisk miyäw ōhih kā-nāh-ntutamākut wītimwah. äkwah manisam aw uskinīkiw, äh-uyisahk ōma pahkäkinus. kā-wāpamāt wītimwah äh-nipäyit, kahkiyaw äwakunih utinam ; upīhtatwānah utinäw.

äkus īsi äh-wayawīt, ä-sipwähtät, " kiyām nāntaw itä nika-misi-wanātisin. misawāts tahkih nika-pakwātik nistäs, " äh-itäyihtahk.

äkusi pikunt ītäh isi sipwähtäw.

iyikuhk äh-päkupayit awa nāpäw, namwāts wāpamäw usīmah.

ōwīkimākana kuskunäw, " tāniwā nisīm ? " äh-itāt.

" aspin ōma, 'nika-kaskikwātän nimaskisina, ' äh-itwät, äh-ātah-nahntutamōwak, äkā ä-wīh-miyit, piyisk nimiyāw tsit-āpatsihtāt. äkus äh-isinahisiniyān, äkus ätukä ninipān, äkā k-ōh-kiskäyimak äh-wayawīt, " itäw.

kiskäyihtam äh-sipwähtäyit awa nāpäw usīma. ntawi-wīhtamawäw ōhtāwiya, ta-ntunāmiht usīma, äh-itäyihtahk, ayisk ōhtāwiya äh-ukimāwiyit, äh-tipäyihtamiyit ōtänaw. äkusi wayawīw awa kisäyiniw, äh-wīhtahk ä-wanihātsik ukusisah, ta-māmawō-ntunāmiht, ä-sīhkihkämut.

aw uskinīkiw āsay wāhyaw ayāw. itah mistah ä-sakāyik, äkutah säski-

siw. mäkwā-sakāhk äkutah nahapiw. piyisk kawisimōw, "äkā nikamiskākawih[1] *! " äh-itäyihtahk.*

äkwah ōki ayīsiyiniwak misiwä ntunikäwak. kiyikaw sakāhk äh-ntunāht, nama miskawäw. piyisk tipiskāyiw.

iyikuhk mistah äh-tipiskāyik, äkwah sipwähtäw ōw ōskinīkiw. namuya kiskäyihtam tāntäh k-äsi-sipwähtät. äyikuhk mīnah ä-wīh-wāpaniyik, itah ä-pasahtsāyik, ä-sakāyik, äkutah mīna kawisimōw.

sakāhk äkwa ōki mīna ntunikäwak ayīsiyiniwak ; māka āsay wāhyaw ayāw aw uskinīkiw. nāh-nōhtaw uhtsih wayōniwak kā-ntunawātsik.

kapä-kīsik nipāw aw ōskinīkiw. iyikuhk äh-utākusik, äkuyikuhk päkupayiw. kītahtawä kā-pähtahk ä-matwä-mātōwiht. äkwah ä-wīh-kakwäwāpamāt kā-mātōyit, kā-nisitawäyimāt ustäsah, äkutah äh-ispatināyik äh-na-nīpawiyit. äkusih āhtsi pikuh kāsōhtawäw. wiy uhtsi k-ōh-mātōyit, äh-wanihikut. piyisk ä-wīh-tipiskāyik, aspin äh-kīwäyit, iyikuhk äkāy äh-pähtawāt, wīst äkwa sipwähtäw, äh-tipiskāyik. äyaku mīna kapä-tipisk pimuhtäw. äyikuyk ä-wīh-wāpaniyik, kunt ītah kawisimōw, " misawāts wāhyaw ntayān äkwah, " äy-itäyihtahk ; " misawāts namuy āwiyak nkawāpamik, " äh-itäyihtahk. iyikuhk äh-päkupayit, āsay spi-kīsikāyiw. " kiyām äh-kīsikāk äkwa nika-pimuhtān, " itäyihtam. tāpwäh sipwähtäw. nama wīhkāts mītsisōw, aspin kā-sipwähtät. kapä-kīsik äh-pimuhtät, iyikuhk äh-ati-tipiskāyik, mīna kunt ītah kawisimōw. āsay nōhtähkatäw. mīna äh-wāpaniyik, āsay mīna sipwähtäw. namuya māka kiskäyihtam tāntäh t-ätuhtät. nama wīhkāts kīh-papāh-wāpahtam ōm āskiy. äkusi mistahi nōhtähkatäw. nama wīhkāts äh-tipiskāyik äkwah pimuhtäw, pikw äh-kīsikāyik. piyisk ätukä wāhyaw äkwah ayāw, wiya tahtu-kīsikāw äh-pimuhtät.

kītahtawä kiskäyihtam äh-yīkitsikāwit, äkw äs ānih mistah äh-kawāhkatusut. nama wīhkāts ayisk mītsisōw, uhtsitaw äkā ä-wīh-nipahāt käkway ta-mītsit.

" yahōh, tāpwä miyāmay kuntah niwīh-nipahāhkatusun. nawats käkway ta-nipahikuyān, äkusi ta-miywāsin. mīna äkā käkway nipahikuyāni, niya kīkway ahpōh nipahtāyāni, mīna kutak käkway miskamāni ta-kīh-āpatsihtāyān, nikah-kīwān, nānitaw uhtinamān, " äh-itäyihtahk ; " ntsawāts äkwah käkway wāpahtamāni ta-kīh-mītsiyān, nka-kakwä-nipahtān, " itäyihtam.

māka nama käkway kīh-wāpahtam. kītahtawä äkwah namuya kīh-mīhkawikiw, usām äh-kawāhkatisut, pikuh mistik uhtsi ä-saskahuhtät, äh-nisōwāhkatusut äkwah.

kītahtawä nīswāw ä-kīh-nipāt, äkuyikuhk kā-wāpamāt pihyäwa, " nkakakwä-nipahāw, äkwah kä-mītsisuyān, " äh-itäyihtahk. tāpwä pimwäw ; nipahäw. utinäw äkwah, ä-pa-paskupitāt. kisiwāk ōtah ispatināyiw ; awasitah wāpahtam ä-sakāyik.

" äkutah nka-kakwä-kapäsin, " itäyihtam, ä-sipwähtät.

äh-ati-sākäwät, kā-wāpahtahk mīkiwāhpis äh-tsimatäyik.

" tāpwäh nimiywäyihtän ayīsiyiniwak ta-wāpamakik, " itäyihtam.

namwāts mā-mitunäyihtam ta-misi-wanātsihikut, " iyāyaw äkwah käpimātisiyān ; niwīh-nipahāhkatusuh, " äh-itäyihtahk.

---

[1] Preterit with future particle prefixed. This is not inconsistent with the meaning of the preterit: past intent unaccomplished, or past act no longer true; but the combination is not common enough for me to know its value.

ituhtäw äkutah. äh-takuhtät, nama käkway wāpahtam wayawītimihk, kā-matwä-pīkiskwäwiht, " ta-tawāw, nōsisimis ! pīhtukā ! " kā-matwäh-itwäyit nōtukäsiwa.

äh-pīhtukät, awīn ōhi kīh-päyakuyiwa.

" nōsisimis, nōsisimis, " äh-itikut, " mānih äh-āyimaniyik täh k-ätuhtät ! " k-ätikut ; " nätä uhts-āpih, " itik.

äkwah miyäw ōhi pihäwah.

" nōhkō, awa mōwāhkan, " itäw.

" tāpwä, nōsisimis äh-atamihit ! " itik ; " äkusi nōsisimis unōhtäh-katāh ! nika-paminawatāw, " itik.

äh-apisīsisiyit askihkusah k-ākutāyit, äkwa nīsu äh-apisāsiniyikih wiyāsisah äh-pakastawähamiyit, nīsu mīna mänisisah, " ninōhtähkatāh, apisīs kā-pakāhtākuhkät[1] *nōhkum ! " itäyihtam.*

äkus ōmis ītik : " nōsisä, āyiman itäh k-ätuhtäyin. namuya wīhkāts pä-kīwäw awiyak, äkutä ätuhtätsih. āta māna nikitahamawāwak uskinī-kiwak, " itwäyiwa ; " nōsisä, nawats ta-kīwäyin, wāpahkih. āyiman ōma täh k-ätuhtäyan, " itik.

" yahā, nōhkō, usām āsay wähyaw nitayān. ahpōh ōma kuntah kä-nipahāhkatusuyān, māka wiya äkutä takuhtäyāni, misi-wanātsihikuyāni kīkwayah, ta-miywāsin. ispīhtsih kuntah ta-nipahāhkatusuyān, namuya nka-kīh-kīwān, " itäw.

" hāw, nōsisimis, näwutipiskwah ōtah ayāh, māka ka-kiskinōhamātān kīkway, tānsi tit-āyīhtiyan, " itik.

" aha' ! "

äkuyikuhk äkwah äh-asamikut ; äkwah ma-mītsisōw. namuya kīh-kitāw ōh iyikuhk k-āsamikut. äkāy ä-kīh-kitāt, itisinamawäw ōhkumah.

" näy ! tāpwä yīkitsikāwiw äh-mītsisut nōsisim ! " itik.

äkwah äh-kakäskimikut, ōm ītäh kā-wīh-ituhtät, äyakuh ä-wīhtamākut, piyisk äkwah ä-nikamuhikut.

kītahtawäh ōmis ītik : " nōsisä, kinästusinōtukä ! kiyām pitah nipāh, " itik.

äkusi kawisimōw.

iyikuhk äh-päkupayit, " nōsisä, waniskāy äkwa ! mītsisuh ! nikīsi-paminawasun, " itwäyiwa.

äkwah waniskāw. äkusi äh-pä-pakitinamākut ōh ōtaskihkusiyiwa, äkwah äh-mītsisut.

piyisk kīspōw, " tāpwä äh-apisīs mītsisōw nōsisimis ! " äh-itikut.

" äkuyikuhk nōhkō, äh-kīspuyān māna, " itäw.

äkusi kapä-kīsik äkutah ay-ayāw. wätākusiniyikih, kāh-mītsisutwāwi, äkus äh-nikamuhikut, iyikuhk ähkäyimikutsih, " kawisimuh ! " äh-itikut.

ä-kīh-näyu-tipiskāyik, " hāw, äkwah, nōsisä, äkwah ka-sipwähtäyan, " itik.

āsay näma kā-kiy-isi-miywamahtsihut, sayāw[2] *näwutipiskwah äh-asamikut ōhkumah, āsay mitun tāhtsipōw ; namuy äkwah kawāhkatusōw.*

ōmis ītik ōhkumah : " nōsisä, āt ōma äkus ä-isi-kiskinōhamawakik uskinīkiwak, māka namuya nitāpwähtākuk, k-ō-māh-misi-wanātisitsik. tāpwähtawiyini, kika-miyupayin ; māka sākōtsimiskih awa kā-wīh-utihtat, ka-misi-wanātsihik, " itik ; " käyiwähk awa pimiwih, " äh-itikut, äh-miyikut

---

[1] One would expect a different formation, but the word is common: *pakāhtākuhkäw* : "he sets food to boil."

[2] Unfamiliar particle; perhaps wrongly recorded.

ämiskōhōsiwayānisah[1]*; " äwakw āwa, nōsisä, näutipiskwah kik-āyān. äkā misi-wanātsihiskih, nōhtähkwasiyini, ' nimusō, pita nika-pimisinin ! ' kik-ätāw. ' aha' , ' itiskih, awa kāskikanihk kik-āhāw. ' haw, nimusōm kätusitsih, kitus ! niwīh-nipān. wīh-wāpahkih, kuskunihkan ! ' kik-ätāw awa. äkwah awa, " itik, " itāmihk kika-saniskamāsun, " itik, äh-miyikut utāsiyāniyiwa ōhkumah ; " äkusi piku ka-kī-sākōtsihāw, tōtamanih, ana kisäyiniw. äkwah tsīkih ihtāyanih, mistik kik-āt-ōtinän, namuya äh-misāk mistik, ōma kiy-āti-pimuhtäyin.*[2] *nīswāw nipāyini āsay kika-wāpahtän nipiy. namwāts kika-wāpahtän tāntä äh-kisipākamāk, " itik ; " äkusi pōn-āpihtākīsikāki, äkuyikuhk kisiwāk kik-ōtihtän anima sākahikan. ta-tahtakwahtsāw. kika-wāpahtän apisīs äh-ispatsināsik. äkutah kik-ätuhtān ; äkutah kanahapin. kī-nahapiyini, äkutah tsīki sākahikanihk ka-wāpamāw ta-päsākäwät ayīsiyiniw äh-misikitit. tāpiskōts iskwäw tit-äsihōw. namuya kawāpahtän usitah. pä-takuhtätsi, ' hā, nōsisä, kīwäh ! kā-pä-nātat kikakīwähtahāw, ' kik-ätik. äkuyikuhk ta-pä-sākäwäw ä-wāpiskisit misatim äh-miyusit. ' hāw, äyakw āwa kimiyitin. kīwäh ! ' kik-ätik. äkaya tāpwähtawāhkan. ōmis ītāhkan : ' namuya äyakuh kā-ntawäyimak, ' kik-ätāw. äkusi, ' yāh, tapwäh äkwah, nōsisä ! ' kik-ätik. itäh k-ōhtuhtät kikäsi-kīwähtahik. ' pä-nātah aspapiwin, uhtsitaw ta-kīwä-tähtapiyin, ' kik-ätik, takuhtäyäkuh wīkihk ; ' nōsisä, ntaw-ōtnah ! pīhtukä ! äh-mīkisiwik aspapiwin, ' kik-ätik. utinamani, sakōtsimiski, ta-pä-ituhtäw anih ana misatim. ' utin ; wiyāhpis, ' kik-ätik. uyāhpitatsih, ' tähtapi ! ' kik-ätik ; ' kīwäh ! ' kik-ätik. sākōtsimiskih, tähtapiyini, wīh-ātah-sipwähtäyini, iyāyaw sākahikanihk kik-äsi-sipwähtahik ana misatim. nama ka-kīhsākuhāw. piyisk ta-pahkupäw. äkuyikuhk kä-pä-päkupät kutak misatim ; äyakw āna ka-misi-wanātsihisk, " itik ; " äkā tāpwähtawāhkan, " itik ; " näyutipiskwah äkutah kik-āyān. kīspin tāpwähtawiyini ōma k-ätitān, äkus āna ta-sākōtsihat, kīspin näutipiskwah äkutah ayāyani. māka anima k-äspatsināsik nahapiyini, pätsāstamuhtätsih, äk ānima tāpwähtawatsi ōma k-ätitān, ka-kīhkīhkimik. ' nyā, pīhtukä ! ' kik-ätik. ' kiya nīkān pīhtukä ! ' kik-ätāw. ispih sākōtsimatsih, wīh-pīhtukätsih, ati-pīhtukätsih, ōm ōhtsi mistsikus kik-ōhpāskwahamwān uskutākay. ka-wāpahtän usitah. tāpiskōts misatim usitah k-äsi-wāpahtamwān. ' wäy ! tānis āwa nimusōm äy-isinākwaniyikih usitah ! ' kik-ätāw. ' tānisi äsinākwahkih, nōsisä ? äh-tsī-wāpahtaman ? ' kik-ätik. ' äha' ! tāpiskōts misatimuskasiyah äsinākwahkih kisitah, ' kik-ätāw. nōsisä, mäyākwām kakwä-wāpahtam usitah. kīspin wāpahtamatsi, äkus āni ka-sākōtsihāw. māka äkā wāpahtamani, kika-sākōtsihik, " itik ; " māka wāpahtamani usitah, äkus āni ka-sākōtsihāw. äkwah äyaku näwutipiskwah kīh-ayāyanih, äkusi tahtu-kīsikāw päyak misatimwah kika-miyik. ' kīwä ! ' kik-ätik. namuya ka-tāpwähtawāw. āta wiy āni ōhtsitaw sākōtsihatsih, kika-miyik äwakuni misatimwah. kīhnäu-tipiskākih, äkutah ayāyini, ' hā, nimusō, kitäm ana nāpästim äyōkw āna kā-pä-nātak, ' kik-ätāw. ' äha' , ' kik-ätik. iskwāhtämihk kit-āstāw äh-māyātahk aspapiwin ; äkwah pīsākanāpiy ka-māyātan kit-āh-āniskōpitäk. äyakunih kika-ntutamawāw. ' ōhi kutakah ä-māh-miywāsikih aspapiwinah, pīsākanāpiyah, äwakuni, ' kik-ätik. äkāya tāpwähtawāhkan. äkutah anim ōhtsi ta-sākōtsihisk, āta näutipiskwah paspiyini, " itik ; " mīn äyuku*

---

[1] Later in the story we have the transparent form *amisk-ōhōsiwayānis* pointing to a word **amisk-ōhōw :* "beaver-owl," but I dare not correct the present form, because vowel-change in the initial syllable is archaic in Central Algonquian in several noun-formations.

[2] The *kiy-* is probably an error of record.

sākōtsimatsi, 'hāw, äkwah, nōsisä, ntäm kā-pä-nātat,' kik-ätik. t-ātiwayawīw. äyakw ānima kā-māyātahk aspapiwin pīsākanāpiy tit-ōtinam. äkusi k-āt-āskōwāw. sisunä sākahikanihk ta-nīpawiw. 'ntäm, pä-kapā!' tit-ätwäw. kiyipah nipiy mistahi ta-tsimatäw; tāpiskōts äh-uhtäk t-äsinākwan. piyisk äkutah tit-ōh-päkupäw nāpästim ä-mihkwawät. ta-pä-kapäw. usuy tit-ōtāpäw, ta-sāmaskähtitāt. mīn ōhi wästakayah käkāts ta-sāmaskähtiniyiwa. pä-kapātsih, 'nah, nōsisä, utin!' kik-ätik. äkāya tāpwähtawāhkan. 'utinamawin!' kik-ätāw. kih-utinātsi, 'wiyahpitamawin,' kikätāw. wiyahpitātsi, äkuyikuhk äkwah, 'nah, nōsisä!' kik-ätik. äkāya tāpwähtawāhkan. 'tähtahin!' itāhkan. kīspin äyōku tōtamani, kika-pimātisin; ka-sākōtsihāw. māka maywäs tähtahiskih utinatsi, kika-misiwanātsihik äyukw āna misatim; kika-mōwik," itik; "māka tähtahiskih, äkus āni ta-pä-kīwäyin. näwutipiskwah anima kiy-āyāyin, äkusi nä-mitanaw misatimwak ta-paskiyawat ana kisäyiniw. āt āni kätimākinawakwāwi uskinīkiwak, äkus ōma äsi-kiskinōhamawakik, māka namuya nitāpwähtākwak. misahkamik uskinīkiwak äkā k-ōh-pä-kīwätsik, äh-ati-misi-wanātsihikutsik," itik; "mistahi kaskäyihtam kōhtāwiy kikāwiy kistäs kītimwak aniki kā-kitimākäyimiskik," itik.

äkwah sipwähtäw äkwah, ä-kīh-miyikut ōhi kā-wīh-miyikut. kā-sipwähtät, "nīswāw kika-nipān," ka-kīh-itikut, nīswāw ä-kīh-nipāt, äkuyikuhk wāpahtam sākahikan. namwāts täpāpahtam t äh-kisipikamāyik. piyis tsīk äkwah ay-ihtäw ōma sākahikan. piyis ä-pōn-āpihtā-kīsikāk, ōma k-äspatsināsiyik wāpahtam. äkutah nahapiw. äh-ātay-itāpit, nama käkway wāpahtam. piyisk kā-pä-sākäwäyit sākahikanihk uhtsi ayīsiyiniwah, ähpäh-ituhtäyit. "tāpiskōts iskwäw," itäyimäw, äh-kinwāyik uskutākayiw.

äkusi, "kīwäh," itik, "nōsisä!" itik.

"hā, namuya! äh-pä-ntawāpamitān," itäw.

"hā, nōsisä, kā-pä-nātat ka-kīwähtahāw!" äh-itikut, āsay ka-pätsāstamuhtäyit, ä-pä-sākäwäyit äh-wāpiskisiyit misatimwa.

"namuya äyōkō kā-pä-nātak. kitäm kā-pä-nātak!"

"yā, äyuku māka ntäm ä-sākihak kā-miyitān!"

"namuya äyuku!" itäw.

"kah! äkwah māka uma k-ōhtuhtäyān, äkutah ituhtäh! niyā!" itik.

"namuya, nimusō! kiya nīkānuhtä!" itäw.

kīhkīhkimik. piyisk, wīstah äh-kīhkīhkimāt, piyis tāpwähtāk, äkwah ä-sipwähtäyit, "hā, nōsisä, ut äsi nawats pimuhtä!" äh-itikut. "pimuhtäwaki, ta-wāpahtam nisitah," äh-itäyimikut, äyakw ānima k-ōh-itikut.

äkus äh-ati-sākäwätsik, awīn ōma, ki-misāyiw mīkiwāhp.

ä-takuhtätsik, "ā, nōsisä, pīhtukä! ōtä isi ka-wāpahtän aspapiwin ähmīkisiwik, mīna pīsākanāpiy äh-miywāsik, tit-ōtinaman, tsi-t-āpatsihtāyin ō ka-miyitān ntäm, ta-kīwäyin."

"hā, namuya! namuya niwīh-kīwān! kutak kitäm kā-pä-nātak!" itäw.

piyisk kīhkīhkimik, "kiya nīkān pīhtukä!" äh-itikut. wīstah kīhkīhkimäw. piyis mīna sākōtsimäw. äh-ati-pīhtukäyit, uhpāskwaham uskutsākāsiyiw; wāpahtam äh-misatimusitäyit.

äh-ati-pīhtukät, "tānisy āwa nimusōm äsisität?" itäw.

"nōsisä, ä-wāpahtaman tsī nisitah?" itik.

"āha'."

"tānisi äsinākwahkih?"

" *tāpiskōts misatimwak kitay-isisitān !* "

" *kah ! tāpw äs āni kiwāpahtän nisitah !* " *itik.*

äkusih ati-ta-tipiskāyiw.

äkwah äkutah äh-ayāt, ispih mistahis äh-tipiskāyik, " *nōsisä, namuya ka-nipānānaw, kik-āy-ātsimuyahk,* " *itik.*

" *äha' ! pita nka-wayawīn,* " *itäw umusōma.*

äkusi wayawīw. äkwah ōhkumah utāsiyāniyiwa itāmihk ōtä ä-sakan-iskamāsut, äkwah anihi amisk-ōhōsiwayānisah äyakunih wāskikanihk säkuyahkinäw. pīhtukäw äkwah. äkusi äkwah apiw.

äkwah, " *äkwah ātsimuy !* " *itik.*

äkwah ay-ātsimōw. ōma kā-pä-pa-pimuhtät äyakw äh-ay-ātsimut ; namuya ātsimäw anihi nōtukäsiwa. piyisk uma k-äsi-wāpamāt äyōkw ātsimōw. piyisk pōn-ātsimōw.

äkusi, " *äkwah niyay !* " *itwäw awa kisäyiniw, äkwah äh-ātsimut.*

kapä-tipisk äkwah äyakw ātsimōw, " *häha' !* " *äh-itāt māna aw ōskinī-kiw.*

piyisk nōhtähkwasiw.

" *nimusō, nika-pa-pimisinin ! äkusi k-äsi-nituhtātān !* " *itäw.*

" *äha' !* "*—nipātsih, ayis ta-nipahikut ōhi kisäyiniwa.*

äkusi äkwah pimisin.

" *hāw,* " *itäw ōhi ōtah kā-säkuyahkināt ; ōmis ītäw :* " *nnōhtähk-wasin ! niwīh-nipān ! kāh-kitus awa kisäyiniw, kätutiski ! wīh-wāpahkih, kuskunihkan !* " *itäw.*

" *äha' !* "

äkusi äkwah äh-nipāt wiya. äkwah awa kisäyiniw äh-ay-ātsimut, " *nōsisä !* " *ätātsih,* " *wäy !* " *äh-itikut ōhi amisk-ōhōsiwayānisah,* " *āta wiya tsī kimiyuhtawin ?* " " *äha' !* " *äh-itikut.*

na-nipāw wiy āw ōskinīkiw. iyikuhk ä-kiskäyihtahk ä-wīh-wāpahk, aw ōskinīkiw ōmatuwihk ōkwāskuniyihk [1] *ōhi äh-tsāh-tsāhkatahukut. äkus īsi päkupayiw ; waniskāw.*

äkusi wāpaniyiw. ā, māninakisk wāy-apihtawāw [2] *umusōma.*

iyikuhk käkāts āpihtāh, äkuyikuhk kutak aspapiwin miyik.

" *hā, nōsisä, kā-pä-nātat ntäm ōtah wayawītimihk nīpawiw, kaskitäw-astim,* " *itik.*

" *hā, namuya äyakō kāh-pä-nātak !* " *itäw.*

" *kah !* "

äkusi kāw äh-astāyit ōm aspapiwin, äkwah mīna äh-ātsimustākut, äkā ta-nipāt, äh-itäyimikut. piyis mīna tipiskāyiw, pisisik äh-ātsimuyit.

äyikuh mīna ä-nōhtähkwasit, " *nika-pa-pimisinin,* " *itäw.*

kawisimōw mina, āsay mīna ōh äkutah äh-ahāt.

" *kāh-kitus ! niwīh-nipān ! wīh-wāpahkih, ka-kuskunin !* " *itäw.*

äkusi äh-nipāt, " *nōsisä !* " *ätikutsi,* " *wäy !* " *äh-itāt away kā-kanaw-itipiskwät.*

iyikuhk ä-wīh-wāpaniyik, äkuyikuhk mīna kuskunik. äkusi äh-wanis-kāt.

iyikuhk äh-ākwā-kīsikāyik, äkuyikuhk kutak mīna aspapiwin miyik.

---

[1] If correctly recorded, this shows us the form of the preterit corresponding to indicative *kwāskunik :* "the other rouses him." The lengthened form of the stem, *kwāskw-* for *kuskw-*, would be normal for archaic reduplication, *kakwāskw-*.

[2] Perhaps read *uyapihtāwāw ;* one expects *utāy-apihtāwāw*, *ht*-preterit with subject "they."

" hā, nōsisä, äyōkw āni ! kīwä ! äkwah wāwāskäsiwipīwayäw kimiyitin. kīwä ! mistahi kwatakihtāwak kitōtämak, äh-pīkiskātiskik, " itik.

" namuya ! " itäw.

äkusi kāw ōtinamiyiwa aspapiwin. äkusi mīna äh-ātsimustākut, äkā ta-nipāt, äh-itäyimikut. kapä-kīsik ātsimustāk. piyisk tipiskāw, tahkih äh-ātsimustākut. piyis mistahi tipiskāyiw.

iyikuh mīna ä-nōhtähkwasit, āsay mīna kawisimōw, " nah-naskum ! " äh-itāt ōhi kā-wāyōskīsikusīsiwayānisah ; " kāh-kitus ! niwīh-nipān ! iyikuh māna kā-kuskuniyin, äkuyikuhk ka-kuskunin ! " itäw.

äkusi äh-kawisimut. namuya kiskäyihtam awa kisäyiniw äh-āh-ātsimustawāt ōhi amisk-ōhōsiwayānah, " äyakw āwa uskinīkiw kā-kāh-kitusit, " äh-itäyihtahk ; " tāpwä nama mayaw nipāw, " äh-itäyimāt ōh ōskinīkiwa, " nistutipiskwah äkāy äh-nipāt, " äh-itäyihtahk, tahkih äh-ātsimut.

iyikuhk mīna ä-wīh-wāpaniyik, āsay mīna kuskunik. äkus äh-waniskāt, äkwah tāpwä äh-ātsimut awa kisäyiniw.

äti-kīsikāyik, piyis äh-ākwā-kīsikāyik, āsa mīna päyak aspapiwin utinam.

" hāh, äyakw anih, nōsisä ! kīwä ! äkwah usāwisiw ntäm. äyakw ätukä kā-pä-nātat. kīwä äkwah ! mistahi kwatakihtāwak kōhtāwiy kikāwiy kistäs, äh-kōtawäyimiskik, " itik.

" hāh, namuya, nimusō ! namuya äwaku kā-pä-nātak, " itäw.

äkusi kāw utinamiyiwa ōm āspapiwin. äkusi mīna äh-mātātsimus-tākut, " kīhkīhk ta-nipāw, " äh-itäyimikut. māka namuya ta-kīh-nōhtähk-wasit, ä-nāh-nipāt ; wiya pikw awa kisäyiniw namuya äh-nipāt. äkusi kapäkīsihkwah ātsimōw. piyis mīna tipiskāyiw.

iyikuh mīna ä-nōhtähkwasit, āsay mīna. " niwīh-pimisinin, " itäw, äh-pimisihk, āsay mīna ōhi ; " kāh-kitus ! niwīh-nipān ! iyikuh māna kā-kuskuniyin, äkuyikuh kuskunihkān, " itäw, äh-kawisimut, wiy ōwa kis-äyiniw kapä-tipisk äh-ātsimut.

iyikuhk ä-wīh-wāpaniyik, äkuyikuh kuskunik mīn ōhi. piyisk wāpan-iyiw.

äkuyikuhk äkwah, " hāw, kika-kīwān äkwah, nōsisä ! mistahi kitim-ākisiwak kōhtāwiy kikāwiy kistäs, " itik ; " kisākōtsihin, nōsisä, " itik ; " hāw, äkwah wayawītān. "

äyak ōma kā-māyātahk aspapiwin äkwah pīsākanāpiy äw-utinamiyit, äh-wayawītsik, kā-wāpamāt ōhi misatimwah näwu ä-māh-miyusiyit, " äyak-unik ōki, nōsisä ! " äy-itikut.

" kitäm kā-pä-nātak, " itäw.

äkusi, " äha' ! "

äkwah sākahikanihk äh-ituhtätsik, äkutah uhtsi, " nitääm, pä-kapāā ! "

kätahtawä kā-wāpahtahk nipiy mistah äh-tsimatäyik, tāpiskōts äh-uhtäyik, piyis kā-wāpamāt äkutah äy-uhtsi-päkupāyit misatimwah, äh-pä-kapāyit, äh-mihkwawäyit. pōtih nāpästimwah.

" hāw, äyōkw āna, nōsisä ! utin ! "

" hā, nimusō, utin ! "

tāpwä utinäw awa kisäyiniw.

" hāw, äkwah, nōsisä, uyahpis ! "

" namuya ! uyahpitamawin ! "

tāpwä uyahpitäw awa kisäyiniw.

" hā, äyakw ana, nōsisä ! "

" tähtahin ! "

tähtahik. kāwih wīh-pahkupäyiwa.

" yahōh, nitäm [1] *äh-miyak anah nōsisim ! kapā, ä-wīh-kīwähtayisk ! " itwäyiwa.*

tāpwä kāwi kapāw.

" ā, nōsisä, wāhyaw k-ōhtuhtäyin. päyakwāw pikuh kika-nipān. itah nipāyani, äkusi kik-ātimikwak misatimwak. nsākihāw awa kā-miyitān. nätä takusiniyihi kīkiwāhk, mīnisāpuy asamihkan. äkwah awa kitäm päyakutās mihkwäkin tāpiskāhkan. äkwah tahtuh ihtasitwāwi misatimwak kahkiyaw ka-tāpiskahāwak mihkwäkinus. äkus äsi-kiskinōhamātān, nōsisä. mihtsät miyāhkasikanah kika-ntutamān, ta-miyāhkasamawatsik misatimwak. äkwah äyakuni miyāhkasikanah ka-papā-saskamōhāwak. ka-wītsōhkamākwak kiwāhkumākanak, ta-saskamōhātsik. äkusih äkutah uhtsih äkwah ta-mītsisōwak, maskusiyah ta-mītsitsik. namuy āni nihtā-mītsisōwak kā-wīh-kīwähtahatsik, " itik ; " äkutah uhtsi kik-ōkimāwin. niyōtinituyäku, tähtapiyani awa kitäm, nama käkway ka-pikwāskākun, " itik ; " kiwayäsihin ätsik āni, kāh-pä-utihtat niwīkimākan ! " itik ; " hāh, äkusi, nōsisä ! kīwäh ! "

äkusi pä-kīwäw aw uskinīkiw. kapä-kīsik äh-pimipayit, namwāts wāpamäw ōhkuma ; namuy äkutah ayāyiw wīkiyiwa. kinwäsk uma kā-käh-pimuhtät pīhtsāyiw itäh k-ōhtuhtät. iyikuhk itäh äh-tipiskāyik, äh-nōhtähkwasit, nīhtakusiw, " nika-nipān, " äh-itäyihtahk. ay-apiw, ä-mitsimāpäkināt ōh ōtäma, " kä-nakasit, wayäsimitsi nimusōm ! " äh-itäyihtahk.

kītahtawä kāh-pähtahk, " nōsisää, pakitin kitäm ! kawisimuh ! äwakwähkāk kitämak ! " kā-matwä-itwäyit.

äkusi pakitinäw, äh-kawisimut. sämāk nipāw. äh-mäkwā-nipāt, kītahtawä kā-pä-pitihkwäyik, ōhi misatimwah äh-pāpayiyit. takupayiyiwah, äkutah äh-wāskāpayiyit, ōmis īsi. piyis pōyōyiwa äkutah. äkusi mīna nipāw. iyikuhk äh-päkupayit, āsay wāpaniyiw. pōt ōhi kih-pa-pimapiyiwa ōhi misatimwah. äkusi pasikōw, äh-utināt ōh utäma. äkusi äh-tähtapit, äh-ati-sipwähtät, äkuyikuhk pāh-pasikuyiwa, äh-pä-pimitisahukut, wiya sōskwāts äh-pa-pimipayit.

äy-utākusiniyik, äkuyikuhk kā-wāpamāt ayīsiyiniwah. äkutah isi tähtapiw. ōh ōskinīkiwah äs ōhi nisitawäyimik. miywäyihtamiyiwa.

" ' māskōts misi-wanātisiw ! ' kikīh-itäyimikawin. mistahi kwatakihtāwak kōhtāwiy kistäs, " itik.

" hāw, kīwä ! ōhpimä ta-mānukäwak nōhtāwiy. iyikuhk wāpahtamāni uhpimä mīkiwāhp, äkuyikuhk nk-ätuhtān, " itäw ; " nāntaw ta-kakwäuhtinam mīnisah nōhtāwiy äkwah miyāhkasikanah. kīspin namuya mihtsät ayāw, kahkiyaw k-ähtahtikih mīkiwāhpah ta-ntutamāw miyāhkasikanah. mīna ta-kakwätsihkämōw mihwäkinus nāntaw tit-āyāwiht, ta-nitutamāt, " itäw ōhtäwiya ; " hāw, äkusi ntawi-wīhtamaw nōhtäwiy, " itäw.

äkusi kīwäpahtäw aw uskinīkiw, äh-ituhtät ōhi kisäyiniwa.

" kisäyiniw ! kika-miywäyihtän ka-wīh-ätsimustātān. päyāhtik nituhtawin, " itäw ; " kayās kā-wanihat kikusis, anuhts niwāpamāw. ōmisi kitik : ' patōtä ta-mānukäw. kīsi-mānukätsi, māskōts ihtakunwa mīnisah ;

---

[1] Perhaps *nitäm* : "my horse," is vocative; the inflexion of *miyäw* : "he gives (it, him, them) to the other" does not show the gender, number, person, etc., of the thing given.

äkutōwah t-ōsihtāwak', " itäw ; " ' äkwah mihkwäkinus ta-kāh-kakwät-sihkämōw, ta-ntutamāt. äkwah kīspin miyāhkasikanah tsikawāsis ayātsi, mīn äkutōwahk ta-papā-ntutamāw kiyām. mihtsät ta-kakwäh-ayāw,' kitik. ' iyikuhk wāpahtamāni mīkiwāhp, nik-ätuhtān, ' itwäw kikusis, " itāw ; " āh, äkusi ! "

ā, miywäyihtam awa kisäyiniw.

" nōtukäsiw, ntaw-ātsimustaw kikusisinaw, usīma äh-takuhtäyit ! kut-akah uskinīkiwah ta-wīsāmäw, ōma kīkinaw ta-ntawi-mānukätsik uhpimä. apisīs kitayānānaw mihkwäkin. nka-papā-ntutamān, mīna miyāhkasikanah. kī-wīhtamawatsi kikusisinaw, mīnisah sāpupatāhkan, " itāw.

äkus ä-at-sipwähtät awa kisäyiniw, äh-papā-ntutamāt äkwah.

äkwah awa ä-ntawi-wīhtamawāt ukusisah, " nkusis, takusin kisīm, äh-wāpamiht, ' uhpimäh ta-mānukäwak, ' äh-itwät äsah, uskinīkiwak kutakak ta-wīsāmatsik. "

miywäyihtam aw uskinīkiw, mīn ōk īskwäwak, wītimuwāwa ä-pmātisiyit. äkusi ntawi-mānukäwak ōhpimä. iyikuhk äh-kīsukätsik, äh-kīh-nahastā-sutsik, äkuyikuhk äkwah awa kisäyiniw pātāw ōhi ka-papā-ntutamāt. mitun äh-kīsukätsik, äkuyikuhk nāh ōskinīkiw päy-ituhtäw. nakatäw utäma. äkwah äh-pīhtukät, äh-miyāhkasikäwiht, miywäyihtamwak ōk āyīsiyiniwak äh-takusiniyit uskinīkiwa. pōtih tahtu käkway kā-ntawäyihtahk astäyiwa, äkwah kisäyiniwa äh-ntumāt, ōhō mīnsāpuy ta-mītsiyit, mīna ta-pīhtwāyit, äh-kiskinōhamawāt ōhtāwiya ōma mīnisāpuy umusōma äh-nīminamawāyit, mīn äh-taskunikäyit, māka tahtw itah k-āpitsik äh-mītsitsik ōhi mīnisāpuyah. namuya ntumäw ōhi kā-kīh-tahkamikut ustäsah ; namuya päy-ituhtäyiwa, äh-astāhāt, äh-kustikut. äkus äh-kīsi-mītsitsik mīnisah, äkuyikuhk äkwah wayawīw, äh-nātāt utäma. äkwah äh-pä-kīwähtahāt, kahkiyaw äh-päy-askōkut misatimwah, mistahi miywäyihtamwak ayīsiyiniwak, nama wīhkāts äkutōwahk äh-kīh-wāpamātsik ōhi misatimwah. mistahi māmaskātäwak äsinākusiyit ; ayis äkwäyāk wāpamäwak.

äkutah äh-takuhtahāt, äkwah ōhi miyāhkasikanah ä-saskahahk, tāpiskōts äh-tisamānihkät,[1] *äh-miyāhkasamawāt misatimwah, taht ōhi uskinīkiwa äkut äh-ayāyit, " wītsōhkamawik ; ōhi miyāhkasikanah saskamuhihkuk misatimwak, " äh-itāt.*

tāpwä wītsōhkamāk. iyikuhk äh-tipiskāyik, kīsi-atuskätäwak. äkwa mīna äh-wāpaniyik, äkwah mihkwäkinus ōma äh-tāpiskahātsik kahkiyaw ōhi misatimwah, utäma ōhi nāpästimwah päyakutās iyikuhk äh-tāpiskahāt. äkus äh-isi-pakitināt, nma wīhkāts wāhyaw papā-mītsisōyiwa ; ayisk äkwah mītsiwak maskusiyah misatimwak. ä-kīh-näwu-tipiskāyik, äkwah ntumäw ayīsiyiniwah, kahkiyaw ōhih mīkiwāhpah k-āhtahtiniyikih pāh-päyak nāpäwah. ōhi pikuh kā-kīh-tahkamikut ustäsah namuya nitumäw. ispīh kahkiyaw ä-takuhtäyit, pāh-päyak äh-ati-miyāt misatimwah, piyis kahkiyaw. ustäsah usīmimāwa nīsu miyäw. äkwah ōhtāwiya nīsu mīna. päyak iskunäw äh-māyātisiyit, " äyakuni aw ōstäsimāw nka-miyāw, " äy-itäyihtahk, wiya pik ōhi nāpästimwah äh-ayāwāt. äkusi äkuyikuhk.

äkwah pīhtäyisk äkwah ntayi-mānukäwān ōma mīkiwāhp, äkwah äh-miyikut ōhtāwiyah tit-ōkimāwit, ta-tipäyimāt kahkiyaw ayīsiyiniwa. äh-wāpaniyik, äkwah kā-ntumāt ustäsah wīwiyiwah kikih, ōhi kā-kīh-tah-kamikut.

---

[1] *tisamānihkäw :* "he makes smudge (thick smoke) to drive off insects."

äkwah äh-pīhtukäyit, " ā, tawāw ! " itäw ; " ā, kuntah ä-tsīsimitān ! " itäw ustäsah.

ä-wīh-atamiskākut [1] *ōhi wītimwa, namuya tāpwähtawäw.*

ōmis ītäw ustäsah : " ä-wīh-kakwätsimitān, " itäw.

" äha' ! kakwätsimin, nisīm, " itik.

" tānähki, ' nikitimākäyimik, ' ä-kīh-itäyimitān, anima ka-kīh-tōtawiyin, käkāts kā-nipahiyin ? käkway uhtsi ? " itäw.

ntsawāts nōhtä-wayawīw aw īskwäw.

" ya, äkā wiyah ! " itäw awa uwīkimākana ; " kāya wayawī ! pitah takīsātsimōw nisīm, " itäw.

äh-kīsi-kakwätsimikut, " hā, nsīm, tāpwä kikīh-kitimākäyimitin ; mīn āwa kītim kikīh-kitimākäyimik. nikīh-miywäyihtän äy-isi-pamihisk kītim. ' naspāts k-ätäyihtaman ; äh-päyakwapiyān, äh-pīhtukät kisīm, kā-kakwätsimit äh-wīh-nōtsīhkawit, ' ntik. äkwah nikisiwāsin, ' tāpwä kakäpātisiw ! ' äh-itäyimitān, mistah äh-kitimākäyimitāhk, " itik.

" wah, namuya, nistäsä ! nikiskäyihtän iyikuhk ä-kīh-kitimākäyimiyäk. tāpwä äy-ituhtäyān, kīkiwāhk äh-pīhtukäyān, päyakwapiw kiwīkimākan. kāwih ä-wīh-wayawiyān, ' pita mītsisu, ' ntik. ' usām kipäyakun, ' nititāw. ' nā, namuya nāntaw ä-päyakwapiyān, iyikuhk äh-kitimākäyimitāhk. ' tāpwä ninahapin, äkwah äh-asamit. äh-kīsi-mītsisuyān, ä-wīh-pasikōyān, ' pita ka-sīkahutin, ' nitik. ' usām kipäyakwapin, ' nititāw. ä-wih-ati-wayawiyān, nikipiskāk iskwāhtämihk. ' nītim, nōtsīhkawin, ' ntik ; ' tāpwähtawiyini, iyikuh kā-kitimākäyimitān, ayiwākäs ka-miyu-pamihitn. ' ' nā, mwäsih nka-kīh-tōtān ! usām nkitimākäyimik nistäs, ' ntitāw. ' itāp namuya ta-kiskäyihtam, ' ntik. äkus īs äy-īkatäkāpawit, äkusi nipä-wayawīn. nnäpäwisin, tāpiskōts nikāwiy äh-itäyimakik kahkiyaw nītimwak, iyikuhk äh-kitimākäyimitsik, " itäw ; " äyakō uhtsi kinwäsk äkā k-ōh-kīh-pīhtukäyān kīkiwāhk, ä-kīh-näpäwihit awa k-āpit. hāh, äkusi äwaku kā-wīh-kiskäyihtamān, ' tānähki k-ō-käh-tōtawit ? ' äh-itäyimitān. hāw, awa ōtah kā-sakāhpisut kīwähtah, äh-miyitān, " itäw.

" hay hay ! " itwäw aw ōstäsimāw.

māka kisiwāsiw.

" niyā, kīwätān ! " itäw uwīkimākana.

äh-ati-wayawītsik, nät ä-takuhtätsik wīkiwāhk, ä-kīh-sakāhpitāt awa misatimwah, äkwah itäw uwīkimākana, " sākäwätān uma k-äspatinäk, " itäw.

äkutah ä-kīh-nahapitsik, " mistah ätsik ōma äh-kakäpātisiyin ! kiy ätsik ōma kitäyihtamōwin ! nikitimākäyimāh nisīm ! käkāts kā-käh-nipahtwāsuyān ! " itäw, mōhkumān äh-utinahk, äh-tah-tahkamāt, äh-nipahāt uwīkimākana.

äkusi kīwäw.

äkwah awa aw ōskinīkiw ōhi wītimwah, kā-kīh-ntutamawāt pahkäkinus uskinīkiskwäwa, äyukunih äkwah miyik ustäsah uwīkimākaniyiwa. äkunih äkwah wīwiw wītimwa.

äkutah uhtsi aspin k-āskiwīk äkwäyāk misatimwak äkutah k-ōh-ōhpikitsik.

äkusi äkwah äy-iskwāk ātayōhkäwin, ātsimuwin. [2]

[1] In ordinary use this word implies shaking hands; I do not know whether this is always the case.

[2] After using the right word, informant corrects himself, substituting the wrong one.

Once upon a time, in a place where there were many people, a certain chief had three children, sons. Two of them had wives. As for the youngest son, this youth was handsome. He, then, had no wife, but both of his elder brothers, as well as his sisters-in-law loved him very much; he was cared for like an own child, so beloved was he, as he went in turn to the three tipis.

Then at one time—his eldest brother's wife was especially fond of him—when he had become quite a young man, as once he entered his eldest brother's dwelling, there was that woman alone in the tent.

When, accordingly, he made to go out, "Wait!" his sister-in-law said to him; "First eat a bit," she told him.

So she gave him something to eat. When he had eaten, she wanted to comb his hair, but he arose to leave the tent.

"Oh, but I meant to comb your hair, you know!" his sister-in-law said to him.

"No, for you are alone in the tent," he told her.

At that the woman rose to her feet and stood in the doorway, blocking the passage for her brother-in-law.

She said to him, "Brother-in-law, fond as I have been of you from the beginning, what I want to tell you is, ...

With that the young man went out of the tent.

Then the woman thought, "If, likely enough, he tells his brother about this, my husband will be very angry," she thought; "I had better tell my husband," she thought; "Before he tells his brother, I had better tell him myself," she thought.

When her husband came into the tent, she told him thus: "My husband, it was not in this way that I meant it, when from the first I showed affection to your young brother. . . . . she told him; "I was greatly surprised when he spoke in this way to me; that is why I am telling you of it. And so now I shall no longer be able to feel any fondness for your young brother," she told him.

At once that man was distressed.

"It was not in this way that I meant it, when I would say to you, 'Try to be fond of my young brother'," he told her.

Now the young man was embarrassed by what his sister-in-law had said to him. He did not feel like going there any more.

"It really seems that my young brother did intend something like that, seeing that he does not come to my tent any more," thought that eldest brother.

He was very angry at what his wife had told him. Then at one time, when the young man, after a long interval, did go there, as he was about to step into the tent, his eldest brother saw him. He seized a knife, thinking, "I shall kill my young brother." As the latter was coming in, and he made to stab him, the young man threw himself back. He managed to run the knife into him a little ways. He stabbed him in the abdomen, not deeply. The youth fled out of the tent; his sister-in-law who had slandered him kept crying out the while. Other women came out of their tipis and ran at the man who was pursuing his young brother. The man was seized and held. So he gave up his intent. He was taken home. When he went into his tipi, other men came in to admonish him.

"Why has he done thus to his young brother, when he is known to be fond of him?"

He told his story: . . . . is why I have done this to him," he told them.

Then the young man was brought into his father's dwelling and given medical treatment. It turned out that he stayed a long time, suffering pain, and nursed by the younger of his elder brothers, and by his sisters-in-law. This brother had two wives. They were very much distressed at what had been done to the youth, their brother-in-law, for they loved him like an own child. "Likely enough he will die," was the general thought concerning that young man. In spite of the curative treatment given him, for a long time, in the outcome, he was ill. At last the man took his young brother to his own tent, to nurse him, thinking, "It is too much of a strain for my father and mother to nurse my young brother; over here we can nurse him undisturbed." Accordingly, they nursed his young brother. The man who had stabbed his brother never came to see him, nor did his wife. Now that it was too late, the woman who had slandered her brother-in-law was sorry and wanted to see him. But whenever she said to her husband, "Let me go there," he would beat her, for he was jealous, and even for that had done thus to his brother.

At last the young man was on the way to recovery.

"Surely, when I get well, my brother will go even so far as to kill me. If I get well, I shall go away from here. What matter if somewhere or other I go to my destruction?" thought the youth as he grew better.

But when he became well, those sisters-in-law of his and his brother never slept, but took turns in attending to him and not sleeping of nights. Once, when the younger of his sisters-in-law was watching, toward dawn, he perceived that she was sleepy.

He said to her, "Sister-in-law!"

"What is it?"

"Please give me a small piece of leather and a sinew and an awl."

"What do you want to do?" she asked him.

"It is my moccasin which is torn that I want to mend," he told her.

"Take it off and give it to me; let me sew it. You are never to do your own sewing, even when you are well; do you suppose you will be allowed to do your work now that you are barely alive?" she asked him; "In any case, this is a little thing," she told him.

But the young woman was very sleepy. At last she gave her brother-in-law what he asked of her. Then the young man cut from it, cut the leather to shape. As soon as he saw that his sister-in-law was asleep, he took all of those things; he took his quiver.

Thus he went out of the tent and away, thinking, "I may as well go to my destruction, it matters not where. In any case my brother will always despise me."

So he set out, with no destination.

When that man woke up, he did not see his young brother.

He roused his wives, asking them, "Where is my brother?"

"The last I know was that he said he was going to mend his moccasins; and though I kept asking him to give them to me, he would not do it, until at last I gave him the things he wanted to use. Then, when I lay down, I must have fallen asleep and not noticed his going out," the one told him.

The man knew that his young brother had gone away. He went and told his father, that his brother might be looked for, for his father was a chief, and had power over the camp. So the old man went out of his tent and announced that they had lost his son, and ordered a general search for him.

By this time the youth was far off. Where there was heavy timber, he went into the woods. Well into the woods he sat down. At last he lay down, thinking, "May I not be found!"

Those people searched everywhere. He was sought here and there in the woods, but not found. At last night came.

When it was entirely dark, the youth set out. He did not know in what direction he was going. When daylight was again near, again he lay down, in a wooded ravine.

Now, those people searched also in the woods; but by this time the youth was far away. The searchers all turned back before they had come upon him.

The young man slept all day. In the evening he awoke. Presently he heard someone weeping. When he made to see the one who was weeping, he recognized his brother, standing motionless on a hill. So he kept hiding from him. His brother was weeping for him, because he had lost him. At last, as darkness was coming on, his brother departed to go home; when he heard him no more, he, too, set out, in the dark. All of that night again he walked. Toward daybreak he lay down, wherever he happened to be, thinking, "Now I am surely far off; now surely no one will see me." When he awoke, it was already bright day. "I may as well walk by daylight now," he thought. So he started off. He had not eaten from the time he set out. He walked all day, and when darkness was falling, again lay down where he happened to be. By this time he was hungry. The next morning he went on. He did not know, however, where he was going. He had never gone about seeing the world. He was very hungry now. Now he never walked at night, but only in daytime. In time he must have gone very far, walking every day, as he did.

Presently he felt himself growing feeble; indeed, he was almost prostrate with hunger. For he never ate, purposely refraining from killing anything he might eat.

"Oh, it really looks as if I should simply starve to death. It would be better if some creature should kill me. But if nothing kills me, and if I, by any chance, kill something, and if, besides, I find something that I can use, then I shall go home, if from any place I get something," he thought; "If I see anything I can eat, I suppose I had better try to kill it," he thought.

But he did not see anything. Then in time he could no longer walk with any speed, so weak was he from hunger; he hobbled along leaning on a stick, feeble from starvation.

Presently, after two nights, at last he saw a partridge, and thought, "I shall try to kill it, that I may eat." So he shot an arrow at it; he killed it. He took it and plucked off the feathers. Near by was a rise in the land; he saw that there was a wood beyond.

"I shall try to camp there for the night," he thought and set out.

When he got to the top of the hill, he saw a little lodge standing there.

"Truly, I am glad that I shall see some people," he thought.

He did not consider that they might destroy him; "Now I am surely destined to live; otherwise I should have died of hunger," he thought.

He went there. When he reached the place, he saw nothing outside the lodge, but someone spoke for him to hear, "Come in, grandchild! Come right in!" said an old woman, for him to hear.

When he entered, why, there she was, all alone.

"My grandchild, my grandchild," she said to him; "Heavens, it is a dangerous place whither he is bound!" she told him; "Sit down over there," she told him.

Then he gave her that partridge.

"Grandmother, take this to eat," he told her.

"Truly, my grandchild is giving me a treat!" she said to him; "And so my grandchild has been going hungry! I shall cook something for him," she said to him.

After hanging up a tiny little kettle, she put into the water two tiny bits of meat and two little berries; "Here am I, starving, and my grandmother puts so little food into her kettle!" he thought.

At once she said to him, "Grandchild, it is an evil place to which you are going. Never does anyone return, when people go there. In vain do I always try to dissuade the young men," she said; "Grandson, you had better go back home in the morning. It is an evil place to which you are going," she told him.

"Oh, grandmother, I am too far along by now. As it is, I shall die of hunger, to no purpose; if I reach that place and something or other destroys me, it will be as well. If to no purpose I starve to death on the way, then too I shall not reach home," he told her.

"Very well, my grandchild, stay here four nights, and I shall at any rate teach you something as to the way you shall do," she told him.

"Yes!"

Then she gave him food; he ate. He was not able to eat up those things which she gave him to eat. When he could not eat them all, he handed them to his grandmother.

"Goodness me! Truly my grandson is a poor eater!" she said to him.

Then she instructed him about the place to which he was going, telling him about it, and finally teaching him songs.

Presently she said to him, "Grandson, you must be tired! You had better sleep now," she told him.

And so he went to bed.

When he awoke, "Grandson, get up now! Eat! I have finished cooking," she said.

Then he arose. Then she brought her tiny kettle and set it before him, and he ate.

After a while he had enough, and, "Truly, little at a time does my grandchild eat!" she told him.

"When I have as much as this, I am always filled," he told her.

Then he stayed there all day, for several days. In the evening, when they had eaten, she would teach him songs, and when she thought he had enough of it, she would say to him, "Go to bed!"

When the fourth night had come, "Now then, my grandson, the time has come for you to go," she told him.

83186—18½

By this time he felt in good health again, when for four nights his grandmother had fed him; he was quite stout by this time; he no longer was feeble from starvation.

His grandmother told him as follows: "My grandson, even though I have taught young men in this same way, they did not follow my instructions, and, therefore, went, one after another, to their ruin. If you heed my words, you will fare well; but if he dissuades you to whom you will come, he will destroy you," she told him; "At any rate, carry this on your person," she told him, giving him the skin of a beaver-owl; "This thing, my grandson, you will keep for four nights. If he does not destroy you, when you are sleepy, 'Grandfather, let me lie down a while!' you will say to him. If he says 'Yes,' you will place this thing on your chest. 'Now then, if my grandfather speaks to you, answer him! I shall sleep. When daylight is near, then wake me!' you will say to this thing. And this," she told him, "You will spread under you as you lie," his grandmother told him, as she gave him her breech-clout; "Only by doing thus will you be able to overcome that old man. And when you are near there, as you go along you will pick up a stick, a stick that is not large. When you have slept twice on the way, you will see water. Not at all will you be able to see where that body of water has its end," she told him; "And so, after the day is past noon, then you will have come near that lake. It will be level land. You will see a very small rise in the land. To it you will go; there you will seat yourself. When you have seated yourself, there close to the lake you will see a tall man come into view. He will be dressed like a woman. You will not see his feet. When he comes to where you are, 'Ha, grandson, go back home! The one you have come to fetch you may take home with you,' he will say to you. At that a handsome white horse will come forth into view. 'There, this one I give to you. Go home!' he will say to you. Do you not heed his words. Say this to him: 'It is not this one I desire,' you will say to him. Then, 'Oh, yes, that is true, grandson!' he will say to you. He will take you back with him to the place from which he came. 'Go bring the saddle, that you may ride home,' he will say to you, when you reach his dwelling; 'Go, grandson, and take it! Go right in! It is a beaded saddle,' he will tell you. If you take it, persuaded by his speech, that horse will indeed come there. 'Take him; saddle him,' he will say to you. When you have saddled him, 'Mount!' he will tell you; 'Go home!' he will tell you. If he persuades you, and you mount, try as you may to depart, that horse will take you off straight to the lake. You will not be able to manage him. In the end he will go under the water. You must wait for a different horse to come up from the water; that one will destroy you," she told him; "Do not heed his words," she told him; "Four nights you will stay there. If you heed this which I tell you, you will overcome him, if you stay there four nights. But when you are sitting on that little mound, and he comes walking to where you are, if then you do not heed this which I have told you, he will talk you into acting against your will. 'Go ahead, walk right in!' he will tell you. 'Do you enter first!' you will say to him. If you persuade him, as he is about to go in, just as he enters the dwelling, with that little stick you will lift up his long skirt. You will see his feet. You will see that his feet are like a horse's. 'Heavens! What do my grandfather's feet look like!' you will say to him. 'What do they look like, grandson? Do you mean to say that you see them?' he will ask you. 'Yes! Your feet look like horses' hoofs,' you will answer him. My grandchild, be sure, by all means, to try to see his feet. If you see them, then indeed you will overcome him. But if you do not see them, if you do not do as I now am teaching you, he will overcome you," she told him; "But if you see his feet, then indeed you will overcome him. Then, if you succeed in staying there four nights, then every day he will give you one horse. 'Go home!' he will tell you. You will not obey him. It is really only if you defeat him that he will give you those horses. When the fourth night of your stay has passed, 'Now, grandfather, it is your own horse, the stallion, that I have come to fetch,' you will say to him. 'Very well,' he will answer you. By the door there will be lying an ugly saddle; and the rawhide bridle, strung together of small ends, will be ugly. For these you will ask him. 'It is those other saddles that are good, and those bridles,' he will say to you. Do not heed his words. He will defeat you with this one thing, even though you go unharmed through the four nights," she told him; "If you persuade him this time too, 'Very well then, grandson; now for my own horse which you have come to fetch!' he will say to you. Then he will go out of the lodge. He will take that very same ugly saddle and bridle. Then you will follow him. He will stand beside the lake. 'My horse, come to land!' he will call. At once the water will rise up high; it will look as if it were boiling. At last a stallion with a bay coat will come out of the water. It will come to the land. It will drag its tail on the ground. And its mane, here, too, will almost reach the ground. When it comes to land, 'There, grandson, take him!' he will say to you. Do not obey him. 'Take him for me!' you will say to him. When he has taken it, 'Saddle him for me!' you will say to him. When he has saddled it, then, 'Here you are, grandson!' he will say to you. Do not heed his speech. 'Put me on his back!' do you then say to him. If you do this, you will live; you will defeat him. But if you take the horse before he has set you on its back, that horse will destroy you; it will eat you," she told him; "But if he puts you on its back, then indeed you will come home. Having stayed there four nights, you will win forty horses from that old man. But though again and again I have taken pity on young men and instructed them even in this wise, yet they have not obeyed me. That is why any number of young men have not returned from there, but have been destroyed by him," she told him; "Very sad is your father, and your mother, and your elder brother, and those your sisters-in-law who are fond of you," she told him.

Then he set out, after she had given him the things she wished to give him. When he set out, "Twice you will sleep on the way," she had told him; and so, when twice he had slept, then he saw a lake. Not at all could he see to where the water had its end. At last he came there, close to that lake. At last, when the day was past noon, he saw a small knoll. There he sat down. Look as he might, he saw nothing. At last a person came into sight from the lake, and walked toward him. "Just like a woman," he thought of him, for his skirt was long.

Then, "Go home," this person said to him, "My grandson!" he said to him.

"Oh, no! The fact is I have come to visit you!" he answered him.

"Ha, grandson, the one you have come to fetch you shall take home with you!" the other told him, walking toward him; and at the same time a white horse came forth into view.

"It is not this one I have come to fetch. It is your own horse I have come to fetch!"

"Dear me, but this is my own horse that I prize very highly, which I am giving you!"

"Not this one!" he answered him.

"Oh, indeed? Well, then go to the place here from which I have come! Go on!" the other told him.

"No, grandfather! Do you walk ahead!" he told him.

The other tried to talk him down. At last, as he argued back, the other gave in to him and set out, saying to him, "Well, grandson, walk right ahead here!" "If I walk before him, he will see my feet," the other thought concerning him; that was why he said this to him.

So, when they went on and came to the other side of the knoll, there was a large tipi.

When they reached it, "There, grandson, go in! Over on this side you will see a beaded saddle, and an excellent rawhide thong bridle, that you may take to use on this my horse which I shall give you, when you go home."

"Oh, no! I do not mean to go home! It is another horse of yours which I have come to fetch!" he told him.

Then the other urged him by speech; "Do you go in first!" he told him. He, in turn, urged the other. In the end, again he persuaded the other. As he was entering, he lifted his skirt with the stick; he saw that he had horses' feet.

As he entered, "What kind of feet has my grandfather?" he said to him.

"Grandson, do you mean to say that you see my feet?" the other asked him.

"Yes."

"What do they look like?"

"You have feet just like a horse!"

"You don't say! So you really have seen my feet!" the other said to him.

Then night came on.

Then, as he stayed there, when it had grown fairly dark, "Grandson, let us not sleep, but tell stories," the other said to him.

"Very well! First let me go outside a moment," he said to his grandfather.

Accordingly, he went outside. Then he fastened on his grandmother's breech-clout down below here, and that skin of a beaver-owl he slipped between his garments on his chest. Then he entered the lodge. So then he sat there.

Then, "Now tell a tale!" the other said to him.

Then he told stories. He told of his journey to that place; he did not tell about the old woman. He told the story up to the point where he saw the other. At last he finished his tale.

At that, "My turn now!" said the old man, and began to narrate.

All night long he told tales, the youth saying, "Yes!" from time to time.

At last he grew sleepy.

"Grandfather, let me lie down! Let me listen to you that way!" he asked him.

"Very well!"—for if he slept, the old man would kill him.

So now he lay down.

"Now then," he said to that thing which he had between his garments here; this he said to it: "I am sleepy! I want to sleep! Speak to this old man whenever he speaks to you! When dawn is at hand, then wake me!" he told it.

"Yes!"

So now he went to sleep. And as the old man went on with his stories, whenever he said to him, "Grandson!" that beaver-owl skin would answer, "Yes, I hear!" and to his, "You are following my story, are you?" the other would answer, "Yes!"

But as for the youth, he had a good sleep. When it perceived that dawn was near, it waked the youth, like this, pecking at him with its beak. So he awoke; he rose to his feet.

Then daylight came. All this time he and his grandfather had been sitting up.

When it was almost noon, he gave him another saddle.

"Now, grandson, my horse that you have come to fetch is standing outside here, a black horse," he told him.

"Oh, it is not this one I have come to fetch!" he told him.

"Indeed?"

Then, when the other had put back the saddle, again he told him stories, intending that he should not sleep. At last darkness came again, while the other told tales without cease.

Again, when he felt sleepy, "Let me lie down," he asked him.

Again he lay down, and again placed that thing here.

"Always speak to him! I want to sleep! When dawn is near, you will wake me!" he told it.

So then, when he slept, whenever the other said to him, "My grandson!" that thing which was watching through the night would say to him, "Yes, I hear!"

When daylight was near, again it woke him. Then he arose.

When it was full day, the other again gave him a saddle.

"Now, grandson, here it is! Go home! Now I shall give you a roan horse. Go home! Your kinsfolk are suffering much with longing for you," he told him.

"No!" he said to the other.

At that the other took back the saddle. Then he again told him stories, intending that he should not sleep. All day he told him stories. At last darkness came, and still the other was telling him tales. At last it was deep night.

When again he felt sleepy, again he lay down, saying, "Always answer him!" to that skin of the little Round-Eye; "Talk always to him! I want to sleep! At the time when you always wake me, then you will wake me!" he said to it.

Then he lay down. That old man did not know that he was telling his tales to that skin of a beaver-owl, but thought, "It is that youth who always speaks to me; truly, he is a long time going to sleep," he thought of that youth, thinking, "For three nights he has not slept," as he kept on with his tales.

Again, when dawn was near, it waked him. So he arose, and truly, the old man was telling tales.

As day came on, and at last reached its height, again he took a saddle.

"Now, here it is, grandson! Go home! This horse of mine is a sorrel. This must be the one you have come to fetch. Go home now! Your father, your mother, your elder brother, are suffering much with vain longing for you," he told him.

"Oh, no, grandfather! It is not this one I have come to fetch," he told him.

At that the other took back the saddle. Thereupon again he began to tell him tales, thinking, "Whether he likes it or not, he shall sleep." But he could not possibly grow sleepy, since he slept all the time; it was only the old man who got no sleep. So all day long he told stories. At last again darkness fell.

When he again grew sleepy, again, "I want to lie down," he said to that thing; "Talk to him! I want to sleep! At the time when you always wake me, then do you wake me," he said to it, as he lay down, and the old man told tales all night.

When dawn was near, it waked him again. At last it was day.

Then at last, "Now then, you shall go home now, my grandson! Very pitiable are your father, your mother, your elder brother," he told him; "You have overcome me, my grandson," he told him; "Come, now let us go outside!"

When the other now took up that ugly saddle and rawhide bridle-thong, as they went out of the tent, there he saw those four horses, handsome, each one, and, "Here they are, my grandson!" the other told him.

"It is your own horse I have come to fetch," he told him.

Then, "Very well!"

Then they went to the lake, and from there, "My horse, come to land!"

Suddenly he saw the water rise up high, just as if it were boiling, and at last he saw a horse come from that water, and come to shore, a bay horse. It was a stallion.

"There, this is the one, my grandson! Take him!"

"Oh, grandfather, take him!"

Really, the old man took it.

"There, now, my grandson, saddle him!"

"No! Saddle him for me!"

Really the old man saddled it.

"There, there you have him, my grandson!"

"Set me on his back!"

The other set him on its back. It made as if to go back into the water.

"Ho there, I am giving my horse to my grandson! Come to land; he means to take you home with him!" said he.

Really, it came back to dry land.

"Now then, my grandson, you have come from afar. Only once will you sleep on the way. There where you sleep, horses now will overtake you. I prize very highly this one I have given you. When you arrive off yonder in your people's home, then make me an offering of stewed berries. And place round the neck of this your horse a garment's length of red cloth. And as many as are those horses, around the necks of all you will bind a piece of red cloth. These are my instructions to you, my grandson. You will ask for many strands of incense grass, that you may burn incense to the horses. You will have them go about with the strands of incense grass in their mouths. Your kinsmen will help you put the grass into the horses' mouths. And in that wise, from that time on they will eat; they will eat grass. For indeed they do not eat, whom you are about to take home with you," he told him; "In consequence of this you will be a chief among your people. When you are at war, if you are mounted on this your steed, nothing will wound you," he told him; "And so it seems, in fact, that you have deceived me, in that on your way here you came to the abode of my wife!" he told him; "Well, that is all, my grandson! Go home!"

Accordingly, that youth came home. Riding all day, not at all did he see his grandmother; her dwelling was no longer there. As he had walked a long time, far away was the place from which he had come. When it grew dark, at the place which he had reached, being sleepy, he dismounted, thinking, "I shall sleep." He sat there, holding that horse of his by the bridle, thinking, "He would run away from me, if my grandfather perchance should be deceiving me!"

Presently he heard, "Grandson, let go your horse! Lie down! Here come your horses!" he heard him call.

Accordingly, he let it go and lay down. He went right to sleep. While he slept, presently there came the thudding of those horses approaching at a run. They came there and ran about in a circle, like this. At last they remained still there. He was yet asleep. When he awoke, it was daybreak. There were those horses resting about the place. He rose to his feet and took his own horse. Then, as he mounted and started forth, then they all rose to their feet and followed him, as he rode straight on.

Towards evening at last he saw a human being. He rode in that direction. The youth, for such he turned out to be, recognized him, and rejoiced.

" 'Doubtless he has gone to destruction!' has been the thought concerning you. Your father and your brother are very unhappy," the other told him.

"Well now, go home! Let my father and his household set up a tent off to one side. As soon as I see a tent off to one side, I shall go there," he told the other; "From anywhere at all let my father try to get berries and incense grass. If he has not much, let him ask in all of the tipis, as many as they are, for incense grass. And let him inquire if any of his people have pieces of red cloth, that he may ask to have them," he said, as a message to his father; "There, go tell this to my father," he told the other.

Accordingly, that young man ran home and went to that old man.

"Old man! You will rejoice at what I shall tell you. Listen carefully to me," he told him; "Your son whom long ago you lost I have seen but now. This is his message to you: 'Off alone let him set up a tent. When he has completed the tent, perhaps there are some berries; these let them prepare,' " he told him; " 'And let him inquire everywhere for pieces of red cloth, that he may ask to have it. And if he have but little incense grass, this too let him go about demanding. Let him try to get much of it,' is his message to you. 'When I see the tent, I shall go there,' says your son," he was told. "Well, that is all!"

Oh, the old man was glad.

"Wife, go tell our son that his younger brother has arrived! Let him invite the other young men to come set up this tent of ours off to one side of the camp. We have a little red cloth. I shall go about asking for some, and for incense grass. When you have told our son, then put the berries into water," he told her.

With that the old man set out to go about asking for the things.

Then she went off and told her son. "My son, your younger brother has arrived and has been seen. 'Let them set up a tent off to one side,' it seems he has said; so you are to invite the other young men."

The young man was glad, and so were those women glad that their brother-in-law was alive. So they went and put up the tipi off to one side. By the time they had finished setting up the tent and arranging the interior, the old man came with the things he had been requisitioning. When they had the tent all in good shape, then that youth came from yonder place. He left his horses behind. Then, when he came into the tent, and the incense was being burned for him, those people rejoiced that the young man had arrived. And there were all the things he wanted; so now he called the old men to eat the stewed berries and to smoke, and he instructed his father to raise aloft those stewed berries to his grandfather, and to hold the stem of his pipe in that direction, but that all those who sat there were to eat those stewed berries. He did not summon that elder brother of his who had stabbed him; and he did not come, for he stood in awe of him and feared him. Then, when they had done eating the berries, then he went out of the tent, and fetched his horses. Then, when he came bringing them, and all the horses followed at his heels, those people greatly rejoiced, for never had they seen anything like those horses. They wondered greatly at their appearance; for this was their first sight of them.

When he had brought them there, he lit those strands of incense grass, just as if he were making a cloud of smoke, as an incense offering to the horses; and to as many youths as were there, "Help me; put these incense strands into the horses' mouths," he said.

Accordingly, they helped him. By the time it was growing dark, they had done working at them. Then, the next morning, they tied pieces of red cloth round the necks of all the horses, and he tied a garment's length round the neck of his own steed. When then he let them go loose, they never went far off in their grazing; for now the horses ate grass. When the fourth night had passed, he summoned the people, one man from each and every tent. Only that brother of his who had stabbed him he did not invite. When all had come there, he gave each one a horse, until he had gone the round. To the younger of his two elder brothers he gave two. And to his father, also, two. He kept out one poor one, thinking, "This I shall give to that brother of mine," and for himself he kept only that stallion. So much for this.

Then the people went and set up that tent for him in the centre of the camp, and his father gave him the chieftancy, that he might rule over all the people. In the morning then he summoned his elder brother, the one who had stabbed him, together with his wife.

As they entered, "Oh, come in!" he said to them; "Oh, I am merely putting you to needless trouble!" he said to his elder brother.

When his sister-in-law would greet him, he paid no attention to her.

He said to his brother, "The fact is that I want to ask you something," he told him.

"Very well, ask me, brother," the other answered him.

"Why, when I thought of you, 'He loves me,' did you do that to me, when you nearly killed me? What was the reason?" he asked him.

That woman saw nothing to do but go out of the tent.

"Ho, do not!" said that man to his wife; "Do not go out! First let my brother finish what he has to say," he told her.

When the other had finished asking him, "Now, brother, I really did love you; and your sister-in-law here also loved you. I was glad that your sister-in-law took such good care of you. 'You were badly mistaken; when I was alone in the tent your young brother came in . . . . she told me. Then I was angry, and 'Truly, his character is bad!' I thought of you, seeing how much we had loved you!" he told him.

"Dear me, no, brother! I know how much you loved me. It is true that when I came and entered your tipi your wife was sitting alone. When I wanted to go out again, 'First eat,' she told me. 'No, you are alone in the tent,' I said to her. 'Oh, it does not matter that I am alone, seeing how fond we are of you.' So I sat down and she gave me food. When I had eaten, and was rising to my feet, 'First let me comb your hair,' she said to me. 'No, you are alone in the tent,' I said to her. When I tried to go on out, she blocked me in the doorway. . . . . she said to me; 'If you do as I ask, much as I have loved you, I shall take even better care of you.' 'Why, how could I do such a thing? My brother is so good to me,' I said to her. 'He does not need to know of it,' she answered me. Then, when she stepped aside, I came out. I was embarrassed, for I looked upon all my sisters-in-law even as upon my mother, when they were so good to me," he told him; "It was for this reason that for a long time I did not come into your tent, because she who sits here had put me to shame. Well, this is what I wanted to know, for, 'Why has he done this to me?' was my thought concerning you. Now then, take home with you the animal that is tethered here; I give him to you," he told him.

"Thanks, thanks!" said the elder brother.

But he was angry.

"Come, let us go home!" he said to his wife.

When they had gone out, as they came to their tent yonder, after tying up the horse, he said to his wife, "Let us go over that hill there."

When they had sat down there, "And so it appears that you are of a most evil nature! It appears that you were the one who had that desire! Remember, I loved my little brother! And here I came near killing what was dear to me!" he said to her, and taking a knife, stabbed her repeatedly, and killed her.

Then he went home.

Then that youth was given his sister-in-law, the young woman whom he had asked for a piece of leather; his elder brother, her husband, gave her to him. So he had this sister-in-law of his to wife.

In this way, then, horses came to be, for the first time since the beginning of the world.

This, now, is the end of the sacred story, of the story.

(29) Rabbit

Mrs. Maggie Achenam

kā-wīhkaskusahk.

kätahtawä äsah wāpus kāh-kimutiw pakānisah. äkwah kisiwāhäw ōhih ka-kimutamawāt.

" tānisi kä-tōtawāyahk ? " itwäwak.

" ka-wanīhikamawānaw. "

pikiwah äs āhäwak. äkwah wāpus äh-ispahtāt, mitsimuskiwäw.

äkwah ōki ayīsiyiniwak, " tānisih kä-tōtawāyahk ! "

" mōnahipānihk ahpōh ukāminakasīskāhk ka-pīhtsiwäpinānaw ? "

" äkwah äsah k-kakwätsimānaw tānitah k-äsiwäpināyahk. tānimah kustahkih ōtah k-äsiwäpinānaw. "

äkwah nātäwak wāpuswah ; äkwah kakwätsimäwak.

" tānitah käy-isiwäpinitāhk, mōnahipānihk ahpōh ukāminakasīskāhk ? "

äkwah wāpus, " nikustän ukāminakasīskāhk. "

" äkutah k-äsiwäpinānaw, " itwäwak.

utihtinäwak wāpuswah ; ukāminakasīskāhk isiwäpinäwak. äkwah miywähihtam.

" nimätsawäwinisihk ! "

ati-pimipayiw.

" kitatamihināwāw äsiwäpiniyäk ! " itwäw wāpus.

äkuyikuhk päyak ātayōhkäwin äh-kīsihtāyān.

Once upon a time rabbit used to steal nuts. He angered the people from whom he stole them.

"What shall we do to him?" they asked.

"Let us set a snare for him."

They set some gum for him. Then when Rabbit ran there, he got stuck in the gum.

Then those people, "What shall we do with him?"

"Shall we throw him into a well or into the brambles?"

"Let us ask him where we are to throw him. Whichever he fears, there we shall throw him."

Then they fetched Rabbit and questioned him.

"Where shall we throw you, into a well or into the brambles?"

Then Rabbit, "I am afraid of the brambles."

"There we shall throw him," they said.

They took hold of Rabbit; they threw him into the brambles. He was glad of that.

"Into my own playground!"

He ran along.

"Very kind of you to throw me here!" said Rabbit.

And so I have finished one sacred story.

(30) Partridge and Quail

Adam Sakewew

sākäwäw.

kītahtawäh ä-misāk ōtänaw ayīsiyiniwak äh-wīkitsik, päyak ukimāw utānisa miyusiyiwa. pitsiwak kahkiyaw. päyak piku mīkiwāhp tsimatäw, äh-nakatiht päyak kisäyiniw, äkwah uwīkimākanah, nōtukäsiwah. äkwah nīsu iskwäsisah ayāwäwak. matukahpihk wīkiwak ōki kā-nakatihtsik. äh-wāpaniyik, papāmuhtäwak ōki iskwäsisak, äh-utinahkik uskanah, äh-pakāhtātsik. ä-mōsahkinahkik matukāhpihk, äh-mītsimāpōhkätsik, äkusi pikuh äy-isi-mītsisutsik.

äkwah kītahtawäh nāpäsisak, äy-ispatināyik, nātakām uhtsi matāwisiw nāpäsis päyak ; äkwah päyak itäy äh-pahkisimuhk isi kutak mina äyaku nāpäsis, tsatsäkahkwānah[1] *äh-takunahkik, ispatināhk äy-ituhtätsik. äh-āmatsiwä-tsikahkwät kutak mina, kā-pimakutäyik tsikahkwān. wāpahtam awa nistam kāh-ātsimak. mīna kīhtwām tsikāhkwäw, kutak mīna kā-pim-akutäyik. awa nistam k-ātsimak nāpäsis āmatsiwäw, utsikahkwān ä-nātahk.*

" iyahōh ! itah ätsik āwa äy-ayāt ! ' wīh-nitawi-wīwiw, ' kitikawih ! " ōma k-ätāt awa pahkisimuhk k-ōhtuhtät.

" hāā ! namuya ! kiy ätuk ōma ä-wīh-wīwiyan ! " itäw awa nātakām k-ōhtuhtät.

äkwah, " kintawi-wīwih ! " itäw.

äkwah nīhtatsiwäwak, matukāhpihk äh-ituhtätsik. päyak namuya wāpiskisiw. nātakām k-ōhtuhtät wāpiskisiw ; kiyāmäwisiw ; namuya mwāsih pīkiskwäw äyaku. äkwah awa kutak kīskwäw, äh-usāmitunät, äh-pīkiskwäskit.

" hāw, äkutah anih tsimatwātutān ! " itwäw awa k-ōsāmitunät.

ma-mätawäwak äkutah.

kītahtawä ōk āwāsisak iskwäsisak kā-pähtawātsik nāpäsisah äh-tät-wäwitamiyit.

" häy, nōhtāh, kähtsinā ä-kī-wäpinihtsik ōtah awāsisak nīsu kā-tsimat-wātutsik. kähtsināh ä-kīh-wäpinihtsik äwakunik mīna, kiyānaw mīna kā-wäpinikawiyahk ! "

" aha' , ntawāsimisitik. äkutäh anih akāmiskutäw nahastāsuk. wītsi-mätawämihkuk päh-päyak. äkusi namuya ka-pīkiskātänāwāw, wītsi-mätawämāyäkwāwi. ntawi-ntumihkuk, " itāwak ōk īskwäsisak.

mtun äh-utākusiniyik, ituhtäwak ōk īskwäsisak. kā-pīkiskwäskitsik äkutōwahk awa aw ōmisimāw. aw ōsīmimāw namuya mwāsi pīkiskwäw. näki mina nāpäsisak aw ōstsäsimās kāw-usāmitōnäsit.

äkusi äw-utihtātsik, " nīkināhk kiwī-päy-ituhtānāwāw ta-wītsi-ma-mätawämitāhk ! "

" wāpam nāha ka-wīh-wīwiyan ! " itwäw awa kaw-usāmitsōnisit ; " yah, kipä-wīwi ! ntawi-nahāhkapi ! " itäw usīma.

---

[1] The word *tsikahkwān :* "lance," (plural *-ah,* or reduplicated *tsatsäkahkwānah)* is used also of small darts with which boys played a game: one threw his dart so that it stuck upright in the ground, and the opponent tried to throw his so as to split the other. The same word in animate gender (plural *-ak*) is used of the girls' and women's gambling toy which consists (seen on Star Blanket Reserve) of four slabs of wood shaped like a knife-blade with surfaces slightly convex, and measuring perhaps 8 by 3 inches. On one side of two slabs are bear-tracks; on one side of the other two, weasel-tracks. The four slabs are grasped in one hand and tossed; the throw counts according to the combination of bear-tracks, weasel-tracks, and blanks that turn up.

" kiy ōma kā-wīh-wīwiyan, namuya niya, " itäw awa kā-kiyāmäwisit.

" äha' ! kitikuwāw awa ! " itäw awa k-ōsāmitōnisit.

äkus īsi kīwäpahtāwak ōk īskwäsisak. äkutah ay-ayāwak. nāh-nipāwak äkutah, pāh-päyak äh-wīhpämātsik ōh īskwäsisah.

kītahtawä awa, iskwāhtämihk äh-tsimatwātutsik, " hāw, pihäwukas ! " wīhäw usīma ; " awiyak ātahutsih, kita-nātsipahāw. kä-wāpahk, ōma kayāsi-pīhtukahān äkutah ta-pīhtukäpayiwak mustuswak. usām nōhtähkatāw kimanātsimākan, mītsimāpuy piku äh-mītsitsik, " itäw.

" äha' , " itik.

tsimatwātōwak. awa pihäwukas kīsiyawāw. pikuntah sākuwäw awa kā-kīskwät.

" nikīsiyawāw ! äkwah wiyah kä-nātsipahāt ! " itäw.

äkusi ä-kawisimutsik uwīkimākanah, " äkā wiya kita-paspāpiwak kōhtāwiy kikāwiy, käkway pähtahkwāwi ; niwī-nātsipahān. wīhtamawāhkanik mäyakwām. kīspin äkā paspāpitwāwi, pōni-pähtākwahki iyikuhk, ta-wayawīwak kōhtāwiy kikāwiy ; k-ätuhtäwak pīhtukahānihk, " itäw uwīkimākana.

äkusi käkāts äh-wāpaniyik, sipwähtäw aw āwāsis kā-kiyāmäwisit. äkwah wāhyaw äh-ayāt, wāpaniyiw, äh-nātsipahāt. äkwah mustusu-mäya utinam misahkamik, ä-nāh-nawayōstāt.

äkwah ōmis ītwäw : " ähyääāy ! "

äh-itwät, kā-pasikōyit mustuswah misahkamik.

" ähääā [1] häy häy häy ! " äkus ītwäw.

äkus āti-sipwäpayiyiwa. kīwähtahäw misahkamik.

kītahtawä ä-kīksäpāyāyik, nawats käkāts äh-āpihtā-kīsikāyik, wāwāstahikāniwiw.

k-ätwäyit ayīsiyiniwah pähtawäw, " mistiminihkuk atimwak, äkā kit-ōyōyōtsik ! " itwäw awa kā-matwä-täpwät, ispih ä-matwäh-askatāhk.

äkuyikuhk pähtawäwak ayīsiyiniwah misahkamik, kunitah atimwah k-ōyōyōyit ōtah matukahpihk, äkwah ä-sākōwäwiht, ä-pīhtukäpayiyit mustuswah.

" häy, nōhtāh, ' äkāy ōhtsi paspāpit ! ' äkusi kīh-itwäw kinahāhkisīm ! " itwäw awa iskwäsis.

äkwah awa kutak nāpäsis k-ōsāmitunit, " nā ! mātsikōttak ta-paspāpināniwiw ! äsi-mihtsätitsik ayīsiyiniwak ta-wāpamāwak ! " itwäw awa nāpäsis.

äkwah awa iskwäw, mwähtsi wāh-paspāpiyitsi unāpäma, wāh-wāpamāyitsi ōhi kā-tātwäwitamiyit, mitsiminäw unāpäma awa nōtukäsiw. ōki wiya iskwäsisak wāpamäwak ayīsiyiniwa mīn ātimwa matukahpihk äh-papāmipahtāyit. äkusi päyak ä-iskuhiht mustus, pikunta sākōwäwak ayīsiyiniwak. pähtawäwak ōki kähtä-ayak.

" mahtih ! miyāmay ōma ayīsiyiniwak ! " itäyihtam awa aw iskwäw.

iskwāhtämihk uhtsi paspāpiw : kuntah pīhtukahānihk pikunta kā-pikihtäyik, mustusu-yähyäwin äh-pikihtawätāmuyit mustuswah, ispimihk äh-itakutäyik, kuntah k-ōhpwähāyit nanātuhk pisiskiwah tahtuh kā-pipunihäwiyit, pīhtukahānihk uhtsi, kiyikaw mahīhkanah, nanātuhk mahīhkanah, matukahpihk äh-uths-īkatäpahtāyit. kīwäw awa nāpäsis. ayis nama käkway ihtakuniyiw. mahyakusiw, ōmanātsimākanah äh-mahyakōhikut.

---

[1] This and similar calls are made with lip-rounding at the end.

" ääh ! pihyäwukas äh-näpäwisit, äh-askōtawiskāt äh-āta-nātsipahāt ! " itäw ; " mahti mina mätawätān. awiyak kīsiyāhtsih, kita-nātsipahāw, " itwäw.

ā, tāpwä tsimatwātōwak. kīsiyawāw awa k-ōsāmitōnisit. mituni kīksäpā sipwähtäw. kutak äkwah ōma paskwāw, itah mustusu-mäyah kā-kīh-ōhtinahk awa kutak nāpäsis, äkutah uhtinam mustusu-mäyah, äh-nahnawayōstāt. äwaku mina päyakwaniyiw äh-tōtahk. " ähyääāw ! " äh-itwät, pōtäh mustuswah pasikōyīwa misahkamik.

äkwah awa iskwäsis, " nōhtā, näkā, päyakwā piku kā-kitahamākuyäk kinahāhkisīm äkā ta-paspāpiyäk. pähtākwahki pīhtukahānihk, mitsimin, nōhtā, nikāwiy. äwakw āna äsah ka-kīh-mahyakuhāt unahāhkisīma. mitunih pōni-pähtākwahkih, äkuyikuhk takusihkih ōyā kinahāhkisīm, kikanātänāwāw wiyāsah. äkāya nuhtaw kakwä-wāpahtamuk. iyikuhk takusihki kinahāhkisīmiwāw, äkuyikuhk kik-ätuhtänāwāw pīhtukahānihk, " itäw ōhtāwiya min ōkāwiya.

kītahtawä wā-wāstahikāniwiw.

" uskinīkītik, ntaw-āskatāk ! " k-ätwäyit ayīsiyiniwa, pikunita kā-pähtākwaniyik matukahpihk, tāpiskōts mīkiwāhpah äh-ayāyikih, ispih ä-pīhtukäpayiyit mustuswah, kahkiyaw ä-nipahimiht.

iyāt-āwa-pīhtukätsi awa nāpäsis, " nā, mātsikōttak ta-wāpamāwak ayīsiyiniwak ä-mihtsätitsik ! " iyāt-ītwätsi, nam āwiya paspāpiyiwa umanātsimākana.

wiyawāw wiya wāpamäwak ayīsiyiniwah.

äkwah ōtäh pīhtukahānihk äh-matwä-wīhimiht ōhtāwīwāwa, " awa kiya umustusu-mäy, kiya kinahāhkisīm päsiwäw mustuswah ! äwakō uhtsi äh-wiyinut k-ōh-miyitān ! " äh-itiht, ay-apiw ; namuya wīh-paspāpiw.

äkwah ōhi matukāhpihk ayīsiyiniwak äh-wāh-wīhimiht, " awa kiya, umustusu-mäy ! " wiyās kit-ōtinahk, mituni kahkiyaw ayīsiyiniwah äh-wīhimiht, äkwah matukahpihk äh-tatwäwitamiyit awāsisah, pähtawäwak ōki kähtä-ayak. ōki wiya utawāsimisah wayawītimihk ay-ayāyiwa, asitsi unahāhkisīmiwāwa. kītahtawä kā-matwä-takuhtäyit unahāhkisīmiwāwa.

" hāw, äkwah wiyāsah kit-āsah kit-āwātāwak kōhtāwiy kikāwiy, mīna ta-mītsiyäk kitaw-utinahkik. kahkiyaw mutakuhpihk tāsipitsikanah k-äyākih, äkutah kit-āt-ākutāwak wiyāsah, mīn ōtah kitāsipitsikaniwāhk tān āna äh-wiyinuyit, äyakunih kit-ōtinäwak, wiyāsah kitaw-utinahkik, ta-mītsitsik ! " itwäw awa nāpäsis k-ōsāmitsōnisit ; " äkusi tōtahkwāwi, äkā paspāpitwāwi, tahk äkusi kit-äsi-miyupayiw. māka wiya paspāpitwāwi, namuya ta-miyupayiw. kiyām awa piyäwukas nātsipahātsi, päyakwan kit-äspayiw, äkā paspāpitwāwi kōhtāwiy kikāwiy mīna. nīswāw kī-nātsipahātsi pihäwukas, äkuyikuhk ätukä ta-kīh-nīpinisinānīwiw. wiyās mistahi kik-āyānāwāw. namuya tāpwä awāsis awa pihyäwukas. niya mina, äh-kitimākäyimitāhk, äh-nōhtähkatäyäk, k-ōh-päy-ituhtäyāhk kīkiwāhk, " itäw ; " wīhtamōwāhkan kōhtāwiy kikāwiy : mina wāpahkih ta-nātsipahāw pihäwukas. äkutah uhtsi nānitaw näwu-tipiskāk mīna ta-nātsipahāw. piyisk mistahi kik-āyānāwāw mītsiwin, " itäw uwīkimākanah.

äkusi äkwah papāh-ma-mätawäwak ōk āwāsisak. kītahtawä utinamwak misāskwatwa pāh-päyak. pīhtukatāwak wīkiwāhk, äkwah äh-astawātahkik. miywāsiniyiwa. waniskānikanihk apasōhk äkutah tahkupitamwak.

ōmis ītwäw awa k-ōsāmitsōnisit : " nītim, äkāya wīhkāts utinamuk ōhi ; usām sākihtāw nīpisisah awa pihäwukas, " itäw.

pähtamwak ōki kähtä-ayak.

" *ā, äyakunik k-ōh-pimātisiyahk, äh-tōtamākuyāhk mītsiwin, nitawāsimisitik ! äkāya wīhkāts sāminamuk ahpōh ninahāhkisīmak wīpisisiwāwa, wiy ä-sākihtātsik !* " *itwäw awa kisäyiniw.*

äkwah wiyāpaniyik, nātsipahāw aw āwāsis päyak kā-kiyāmäwisit. päyakwaniyiw äh-tōtahkik. pīhtukäpayiyiwa mustuswa. päyakwaniyiw äh-tatwäwitamiyit ayīsiyiniwa awāsisah mīna, äkāy ä-wīh-paspāpitsik. kahkiyaw kwayātsi-wiyanihtsikāsuyiwa ōhi mustuswah, sōskwāts kā-kapäkīsik äh-āwatātsik wiyāsah ōki kähtä-ayak.

äkusi matukāhpihk äh-nakatamuht ōhi täsipitsikanah mitunih ä-sākaskinahtātsik iyikuhk, pōyōwak ōk āwāsisak.

äkwah ōmis ītwäw awa k-ōsāmitsōnisit nāpäsis : " *nītim, asaminān. nīmāhinān. māskōts kītahtawä namuya nka-takuhtānān, äkutah ta-mītsiyāhk,* " *itwäw awa nāpäsis k-ōsāmitsōnisit.*

tāpwä miyāwak kahkäwakwah mīnah wiyinwah mīnah utakisiya ä-sakāpihkātamuht, t-äsi-nayōhtahkik. äkus äh-tōtāhtsik, äkwah wayawīwak kīksäpā.

" *hāw, pihäwukas, nōhtähkatäwak ōki ōtah awah k-ōh-pitsit ukimāw. maht äkutä ituhtätān. kuhkuminaw ntaw-āsamātān,* " *itäw.*

" *äha'* , " *itwäw awa nāpäsis.*

uhpīwak, nayäwāts äh-pimakutsihkik. mitunih äw-utākusiniyik, utihtamwak mīkiwāhpah äh-mihtsäniyikih.

äkwāh ōki iskwäsisak pīkiskātäwak unāpämiwāwa, äkāy äh-pähtawātsik itah kita-tātwäwätamiyit.

äkwah näkih itah äh-sakāyik äkutah pakitsīwak.

" *hāw, pihäwukas, mituni kinäsōwäyimitin kiyah. niya mahtih nkantawāpamāwak ōk āwāsisak,* " *itäw uwītsäwākanah.*

uhpīw, äh-pihäwit. mītusihk twähōw.

" *äy ! āstamitik ! awa pihäw !* " *itwäwak awāsisak.*

pimwäwak. iyāta-pimuhtsi awa pihäw, uhpihāw. kisiwāk twähōw. äkus ōk āwāsisak nōsōskawäwak mihtsät. kītahtawä wāhyaw äh-ituhtahāt, sōskwāts uhpahōw. itäh kā-kīh-nakatāt uwītsäwākanah, äkutah twähōw. kāw āwāsisiwiw. äkwah mitihtäwak ōh āwāsisah. käkā-tipiskāyiw. äyikuhk äh-pä-kiwätsik ōki awāsisak, nāh-nakiskawäwak. kwahkunikwak, äh-kipiskawātsik. nāway ayāwak ; ayis kunt ītä si-kwahkunikwak. äh-āta[1] *wāh-pasikōtwāwi, kutakah äh-kwāhkunikutsik, piyisk nāway ayāwak. äh-ati-tipiskāyik, wāpahtamwak nōtukäsiwah wīkisiyiw, wīstäpahkwawikamik.*

" *äwak ōma, pihäwukas, kōhkuminaw wīkih. pīhtukätān. äkutah nipāhkāhk. namuya ta-kih-kīwäyahk anuhts,* " *itwäwak.*

" *äha'* , " *itwäw awa kā-kiyāmäwisit.*

äkwah äh-pīhtukätsik, " *hä, nōhkō ! ōtah nka-tsimatwātunān kitiskwāhtämihk !* "

" *äha'* , *nōsisimisitik !* " *itikwak.*

äkwah äōkutah ma-mätawäwak, äh-tsimatwātutsik. piyisk äh-tipiskāyik puyōwak.

äkwah näki iskwäsisak, äkā ä-kīh-nipātsik, kitāpahtamwak ōh ātsusisah nīsu. waskawīmakaniyiwa. kitāpahtamwak ōk īskwäsisak.

äkwah näki nāpäsisak, " *häy, nōsisimitik, äkwah ninōhtähkwasin. ntawi-nipāk äkwah. kīwäk. ninōhtähkwasin.* "

---

[1] Probably read *iyāta-* ; in either case we have a verb-form which is not finished, but is re-commenced in the *wāh-* of the next word.

äkwah awa k-ōsāmitsōnisit ōmis ītäw : " nōhkō, namuya nānitaw nikakīh-nipānān, " äh-itwät.

ōki āsay nipāwak nätäh näma kähtä-ayak. äkwah ōki iskwäsisak k-ōtinahkik uh ātsusisah, äh-waskawimakaniyikih, kītahtawä kā-pähtahkik äh-pīkiskwäyit, ōh ātsusisah äh-pīkiskwämakahkih. awa wäwīpisisit tānisi äh-itwät, äkutah pīkiskwäw wīpisisihk.

" nimisä, na matsikōttak āstam ! nituhtawātānik nītim äkwah kītim tānisi ätwätsik ! "

äkusi ōhi äh-itwämakahki atsusisah, itwäyiwa. äkwah nituhtawāwak, wāhyaw äh-ayātsik.

äkwah awa nōtukäsiw k-ätāt usisima, " nōhkō, namuya nānitaw wīhkats niwīkihkämunān, täpiyāhk äy-ayāsō-wīkihkämuyāhk. tānähk ōma, nōhku, äkā k-uh-mītsisuyin ? " itäw ōhkuma.

" häy, nōsisi, namuya uma mamiywä awiyak äh-mītsisut, äh-nōhtähkatähk ōma. āta kikiskäyihtänāwāw. nka-kitimākäyimāwak nōsisimak. nōsisimitik, äwakw āna nipākähkäk, " utanāskāniyiwa äh-isiwäpināyit, tanpākätsik.

" hā, nōhkō, aw āwa wiya pihäwukas äh-pä-ntaw-asamisk ! " ōhi itäwak, äh-miyātsik kāhkäwakwa mīna wiyinwa.

" äkusi, nōsisimitik ! ōtah awah ukimāw utānisah, ' awiyak ntaminahtātsi ōma ntōtänaw, äwakuh nk-ōnahāhkisīmin, ' äh-itwät, päyak āta āskaw wāh-wīhkāts nipahäw ukwāskwäpayihōsah ; māka namuya kihtäpahutōwak ayīsiyiniwak. usām apisīs, äh-mihtsätihk, " itwäw awa nōtukäsiw ; " nōsisä, niwih-kawisimun. itāp äkutah nka-mītsisun, " itwäw awa nōtukäsiw.

nipāwak äkwah näki iskwäsisak. atsusisah tahkunamwak. äh-itwämakaniyikih, ntuhtawäwak unāpämiwāwa.

" häy, pihäwukas, maht äkwah ntawi-nōtiskwäwä ! aw ukimāw utānisah ntawih-nōtiskwäwās ! "

" hā, māka mīn ätsik āni wā-mikuskātisiyan ! " itäw awa ustäsah.

" hā, wiy ä-sākwäyimuyin, kiyām itsi niya ! "

" häy, nimisä, wī-matwä-nōtiskwäwäw äkwah kināpäm ! " itwäyiwa utānisah awa.

hā, ntuhtamwak, ä-päkupayitsik.

äkwah awa ituhtäw awa nāpäsis. äkwah awa kutak kā-kiyāmäwisit namwāts äkwah waskawimakaniyiw wīpisis ; ayis nipāw ; awa pikuh k-ōsāmitsōnisit ka-waskawīmakaniyik wīpisis. äkwah ntawi-nōtiskwäwäw.

äh-pīhtukät, " mahtih wasaskutänah ! " itwäw awa ukimāw awa utānisah.

pōt ōhi awāsisah äh-kitāpamikut, wīst äh-kitāpamät, kā-wīh-pāhpiyit.

" āstawinah ! " itwäw aw ōskinīkiskwäw.

āstawinamwān ōm īskutäw. äkusi kawisimōw. nīsōhkwāmiwak, kutakah iskwäwah äh-utināt. ātsimustawäw äh-mīsihtātsik.

" ōhih k-ähtahtikih mīkiwāhpah kahkiyaw umatukāhpiwāhk täsipitsikanah sā-sākaskinäwah. kīhtwām nka-päy-ituhtān. äkuspi kōhtäwiy kika-wīhtamuwāw, kīh-pīhtukäyāni ; äkuspi ka-kiskäyihtänāwāw. kita-wīhtam kōhtäwiy. minah ōtäh äh-pīhtukäyān, kik-ātsimustawāw. äkuspi wāpahki nka-kīwānān ; nipä-wītsäwāw nisīm. hā, äkusi. niwīh-kīwān. kākāts wāpan. "

" äha' , " itik.

äkusi wayawīw. pīhtukäw ōhkumah wīkiyihk. kawisimōw. mayaw kā-kawisimut, näma wīpisis kāmwātastäyiw. nipāwak. wiyāpaniyik, kīksäpā kīwäwak. äw-utākusiniyik takusinwak wīkiwāhk.

" tāntäh ōma ä-kīh-ayāyäk ? " itikwak wīwiwāwa.

" hā, iyikuhk äh-kitāyāhk kā-kīh-nīmāhiyäk, äkuyikuhk k-ōh-päkīwäyāhk. usām apisīs kā-kīh-nīmāhiyāhk, " itäwak.

äkus äh-wāpaniyik, nātsipahāw awa usīmimāw. äkusi mihtsät päsiwäw mustuswah. kīhtwām äh-wāpaniyik, āsay mīna nitutamāw kita-nīmātsik ; äkwah itah äh-miywāsik mītsiwin miyāwak mistahi. äkusi kīksäpā wayawīwak. mayaw äh-ākawäwätsik, uhpīwak. päyakwan ; äw-utākusiniyik, takusinwak. äkusi pīhtukäwak ōhkumiwāwa wīkiyihk. äkwah sämāk miyikwak ōhkumiwāwa ta-nipākätsik. mayaw ä-tipiskāyik miyäwak ōhkumiwāwa.

" äh-miywāsikih, nōhkō, ōhi kanawäyihtah. wāpahki kīksäpā ntumimāhkan aw ōkimāw utānisah : itāp ta-päy-ituhtäw, " itäw ōhkumah.

nätä wīkiwāhk ntuhtawāw, wīpisisihk uhtsi.

" äkw anih wāh-uwīskwiyin, nimisä ! " itimāwa utānisa.

äkus äh-tipiskāyik, ntawi-nōtiskwäwäw. tāpwä käkāts ä-wāpaniyik, pä-kīwäw. āsay waniskāyiwa usīma.

" mistahi kimisi-wanātahkamikisin ! " itik usīma.

" kiy ōma kā-misi-wanātahkamikisiyin ! " itäw.

ntuhtawāwak wīpisisiwāhk uhtsi, ntawāts āskaw äh-pāhpitsik ōk īskwäsisak.

äkw ä-kīsikāk, " hā, nōhkō, ntawi-ntum awa uskinīkiskwäw ! miyāhkan ōhi ; ta-kīwähtatäw. māskōts ta-ki-pimātisiwak ayīsiyiniwak, utihtahkwāwi umatukahpiwāwa, " itäw ōhkuma.

äkwah ntawi-ntumäw.

" nōsisä, atsiyaw kiwīh-päy-ituhtān nīkihk. ä-uhtsi-ntumitān, usām npapāsimik nōsisim. itāp wiya kik-ātsimustāk. "

" äha' , " itäw.

ituhtäw. äh-pīhtukät, awin ōhi, kīh-apiyiwa kā-nōtiskwäwātikut. nahapīstawäw.

" hāw, ōh ōhi k-ōh-ntumitān. äkusi māka päyakwāw kīh-kapäsihk, äkutah nk-ōh-sipwähtānān, " itäw ; " hā, äkwah kā-kī-wīhtamātān kōhtāwiy kita-wīhtam, ōma kāy-itwäyān. mistahi mīsihtāw kā-kīh-nakatiht umanātsimākanah awa, " itäw usīma ; " äkusi. "

hāy, äkusi kīwäw aw uskinīkiskwäw. ōhtāwiya ntumäw wīkihk uhtsi.

" nōhtā, ōtah pä-pīhtukäw awāsis. äkusi itah äh-nipāyān äkutah nipāw. mīsihtāw kītsi-kisäyiniw kā-kīh-nakatiht. ' tahtuh k-āhtahtikih matukāhpah, äku-tahtuh ihtahtinwah täsipitsikana, wiyāsah äh-akutākih, ' itwäw kinahāhkisīm ; ' äkusi kit-äsi-wīhtam, ' äh-isit k-ōh-isi-wīhtamān. "

" äha' , ntānis. mastaw kiya kitayān, ' nāpäw ' ä-pakusīhtāyin. kakwämiyu-pimātisi. kitimākäyim ana kīskwa, " itäw utānisah.

ā, wīhtam : " kika-pitsinānaw anuhts. matwä-mīsihtāw nītsi-kisäyiniw ; matwä-mīsihtāw. sōskwāts itah kā-kīw-ōh-pitsiyäk, äkutah ka-kapäsināwāw," itwäw ä-wīhtamawāt utayisiyinīma.

tāpwä pitsiwak kahkiyaw. itäh äh-kapäsitsik, āsay mīna ntawi-nōtiskwäwäw awa. kīksäpā kīwäw. hāh, takusinwak wīkiwāhk.

hā, mayaw äh-pīhtukät, " nītim, kāhkwäyim kiwīkimākan ! äyakunih ukimāwa utānisiyiwa, äyakunih äh-wīwit, " itäw usīma.

" nā, nītim, kiy ōma kā-wīwiyin. kinituhtātin ōma tahkih," itik wītimwa.

" ahāw, ntawāsimisitik, kwayātsi-pānahamuk itah kita-wīkit kimisiwāw, kutak mīna kōhtāwiyiwāw ; nīswayak kika-pānahānāwāw," itäw.

tāpwä pāpitsiwak. sōskwāts kapäsimustawāwak. äkuyikuhk ati-kāhkīsupwäyāyiw.

äkusi äkwah, " hāw, nisīm, nātsipahāhkan. aswäyim māka : päyak kipakwātik. äkwah päyak niya nipakwātik ; māka nika-misawihāw niya," itäw ; " äkāya wīhkāts sāpu-pimuhtäh, piyäsiwatwāwi mustuswak," itäw usīma ; " kiya nīkān nātsipahāhkan," itäw.

" äha'," itik.

kīksäpā sipwähtäw. päyakwaniyiw äh-tōtahk, äh-mawatsihtāt mustusumäya ; päyakwaniyiw äy-isi-täpwātāt. pasikōyiwa. kawipayihōw. pänīkānuhtawäw. mākuhōk ä-sakiskamiyit ōhi mustuswah wataniyah, paspaskiw[1] *k-ätāyahk äh-äkutōwiwit awa kā-kiyāmäwisit. hāw, ä-wāstahamāmiht ōhi mustuswah, nama kī-säkupayihōw ; käsinātakutsin ; sāpu-pimuhtäw. ä-wih-āta-pakitsīt, nama kīh-pakitsīw. iyāyaw ä-nīpisīhkupāyik, iyāyaw äkutä ispihāw. kītahtawä käkway ispimihk k-ōh-pätuwäkutäyik. nama kīh-itāpiw ; pimi-tāwikipayihik. nama kīh-naskwänik. päyakwanuhk wāskāhakutsiniyiwa.*

äkwah awa k-ōsāmitsōnisit, " ähähäy, nisīm misi-wanātsihōw ! mahti nka-ntawāpumāw !" itwäw.

wayawīw ; utsahtsāpiyah utinäw ; äkwah ōhih nīsu atsusisah utinam. pōt ōhi sakāhk kīh-pimisiniyiwa usīma. äy-utihtāt, äkutah kisiwāk akusiyiwa pipunasiwa.

" häy !" itäw ; " häy ! päyakwan ōma kāy-isinākusiyin, äkusi kikäsinākusin. usām ayīsiyiniwak wītsäwatwāwi, tahk āyiwāk kika-tōtän. ntsawāts äkusi pikuh kik-äsi-mītsisun, ōma kā-tōtaman !" itäw.

nama kih-kwäskimōw ; nama kīh-ayisiyiniwiw. äwakuni " kipakwātik" kāy-itiht awa kā-nipahiht paspaskiw. äkwah usīma. ispāhkäw wīpisis ; kutak mīna ä-ispāhkät, pasikōyiwa usīma ; pimātsihäw.

iyāyaw pīhtukahānihk ituhtäw ; pōtih ayisiyiniwah wāpamäw, ähakusiyit pīhtukahānihk. utihtimanāhtanah kikiskawäyiwa. nīhtsipayihōw aw k-ōsāmitsōnisit, äh-ntunahk mōhkumānitusāpisk.

" yaōō ! ä-kanawäyihtamān anima, mästatäw, nimōhkumānitusāpisk !"

kitāpamäw ; mihkōwiyiw um ōtsihtsiy. ōmisi tōtam.

" kiy ätukä, mästatäw !"

äh-itāt, kuntah apsi-kāhkākīsa kā-muskōwäpahwāt uskisikuyihk.

" ōtah ntawats kiya-pakusihāwak ayīsiyiniwak ! namuya ka-kīhkwäskimun ! kāsiyāpih ; kika-wāpin anima !" itäw.

nama kīh-kwäskimōw.

" sakāhk kik-ōhtāpanihun !" itäw.

äh-itiht awa, uhpihäw ; kunt ītä ispihäw. nama kīh-ayisiyiniwiw kāwih.

---

[1] I here translate *pihyäw* : "partridge," and *paspaskiw* : "quail," arbitrarily, for I could not identify the birds; interpreters say "partridge" for both. The brother here called *paspaskiw* was above named *pihäwukas*.

"ntsawāts kä-wāpahk nīsihkahk; nātsipahāhkahk," itwäw awa k-ōsāmitsōnisit, "äkutah kit-ōyasōwātāyahkuk ōki ayīsiyiniwak," itäw usīma; "usām namuya kwayask wiy-ispayiw, ayīsiyiniwak ta-nihtawikiwak ōtah askīhk,—ta-sīkawistamōwāyahkuk ōm āskiy," itäw usīma.

"äha'," itik.

äkwah nīsiwak, äh-wāpaniyik, äh-nātsipahātsik. hā, nätä mustuswah usīhäwak; kīwähtahäwak mistahi mihtsät, tsikawāsis äkwah ä-pīhtukä-payiyit. awa pihäw mästakayitāsah kikitāsäw; awa paspaskiw mästakay-itāsah kikitāsäw. äkwah muhyāpitasäkōwak. mistahi miyusiwak. nīsukā-pawiwak, ä-mästsihātsik ōhi mustuswah. ātiht ayīsiyiniwak äh-mäkwā-wiyinihtākäwiht, pä-ntaw-asamāwak mīnsāpuy.

"hāw, ayīsiyinītik, ntsawāts kiyawāw nanātuhk kik-ätōwiwināwāw. tahtuh pisiskiw k-ähtasit, nanātuhk kik-äsi-pimātsihunāwāw. kahkiyaw ayīsiyiniw kika-sākōtsihikuwāw, uhpikitsih ōtä nīkān. äkwah niyah ōtäh tawāyihk nik-āyān, kā-nistitsik atsahkusak. kākikä nika-pimātisin. äkwah awa nisīm, ōtäh ta-nīsiwak atsahkusak, kākikä ta-pimātisit nisīm. usām wiyasiwäw kōhtāwiyinaw ta-sīkawiyahk, askīhk kit-ōhpikihitut ayīsiyiniw."

äkuyikuhk äskwāk ātayōhkäwin.

Once upon a time in a big town where people dwelt, a certain chief had a beautiful daughter. All moved camp. Only one tipi was left standing, where an old man was abandoned, together with the old woman, his wife. And they had two girls. On the deserted camp-site they dwelt who had been abandoned. In the morning those girls walked about, taking up bones, which they boiled. Picking up things from the deserted camp and making soup of them was the only way they got anything to eat.

Then at one time some boys, from over a hill, from the north, a boy came into sight, and another one, also a boy, from the west, and they carried throwing-sticks in their hands, and walked to a rise in the land. When one of them, the second one, threw a throwing-stick up the hill, and it sped through the air, the one of whom first I spoke, saw it. Again he threw a dart, and it, too, flew through the air. The boy of whom I spoke first went up the hill to fetch his dart.

"Yoho! So here he is! To be sure, 'He is going off to take a wife,' was said of you!" said he who had come from the west.

"Oh no! I daresay it is you, really, who mean to take a wife!" said he who came from the north.

But, "You were going off to take a wife!" he told him.

Then they descended the hill and went to the deserted camp-site. One was not white. He who had come from the north was white; he was bashful; this one did not speak much. But the other one was silly and talked too much and was a babbler.

"Now then, right here let us play throwing-stick!" said the talkative one.

They continued to play there.

Presently those children, those girls, heard the noise which the lads were making there.

"Oh, father, surely those two children who are playing with throwing-sticks have been abandoned here. Surely they have been abandoned, just as we have!"

"Yes, children. So put the lodge in order at the other side of the fire. Go play with them, each of you with one. That will keep you from being lonesome, if you play with them. Go invite them," those girls were told.

Late in the afternoon those girls went there. Of those who are talkative, such was the elder girl. The younger was not given to much speech. Of those boys, too, it was the elder who was a prattler.

So, when they came to where the others were, "You are to come to our house and play with us!"

"Look at the girl you are going to marry!" said the prattler; "Yah, do not forget you came here to take a wife! Go stay with your wife's people!" he said to his younger brother.

"But it is you are planning to take a wife, not I," the bashful one answered him.

"Yes! Now he has told you!" the prattler said to them.

Then the girls ran back home. They all stayed there. * * * * *

Then at one time, as they played with throwing-sticks by the door, "Now then, Partridge-Claw!" said the one, calling his junior by name; "Whichever is beaten will drive in the buffalo. Tomorrow let us make the buffalo run into this old buffalo-pound here. Our father-in-law is suffering too much from hunger, what with their eating nothing but soup," he said to him.

"Very well," the other answered him.

They pitched their throwing-sticks. Partridge-Claw was beaten. The babbler gaily whooped.

"I have beaten him! Now he will be the one to drive in buffalo!" he said of the other.

Then, when they went to bed, he said to his wife, "Let not your father and your mother peek out from the lodge, when they hear anything; I am going to drive in buffalo. Be sure to tell them. If they do not peek out, then, when the noise ceases, your father and mother are to come out of the lodge; they will go to the pound," he told his wife.

Accordingly, just before dawn, the bashful boy went away. When he had gone far, day broke, and he drove buffalo. He took a great amount of buffalo-dung, and laid it in little heaps in a row.

Then he said, "Hey hey heyey!"

When he gave this cry, great numbers of buffalo rose from the ground.

"Heyeyeyey hey hey hey!" he cried.

Thereupon they ran off. He brought a great herd with him.

Presently, as morning passed and it was nearing noon, the waving of signals began.

He heard people calling, "Hold the dogs, lest they bark!"—so cried the one who called out directions while the herd was awaited.

Then they heard a great crowd of men, and dogs baying everywhere in that deserted camp, and loud whooping as though of their fellow-campers, as the buffalo ran into the enclosure.

"Now, father, 'Let him at no time peek out!' said your son-in-law!" thus spoke that girl.

And that other boy, the talkative one, "Nonsense! Let them look out at a sight worth seeing! Let them see how many people there are!" said that boy.

But that woman, whenever her husband wanted to peep and see the people who were making all the noise, then just in time the old woman would hold back her husband. But the girls could see the people and the dogs running hither and thither about the deserted camp. Then, when only one buffalo was left, the people whooped everywhere. The old people heard them.

"I do wonder! Surely these must be people!" thought she, the woman.

She peeped out through the door: from all over the buffalo-pound smoke was rising into the air, the steaming breath of buffalo rising into the atmosphere, and at the same time all kinds of animals, as many as stay through the winter, came forth from the pound, all kind of wolves, every kind of wolf, and ran offside and away from the deserted camp. The boy came home. There was simply nothing left. His spell had been broken; his parent-in-law had spoiled his luck.

"Yaha, Partridge-Claw is coming empty-handed and ashamed, for all his buffalo driving!" he said to him; "Let us play again. Whichever is beaten, let him fetch buffalo," he said.

Accordingly, they played throwing-stick. The prattler was beaten. Very early in the morning he set out. Then on that other stretch of prairie, there where the other boy had taken buffalo-dung, from there he now took buffalo-dung, laying it in a row. This one did the same as the other had done. "Heyeyey!" he cried, and there, a great herd of buffalo rose to their feet.

Then that girl, "Father, mother, once and for all time your son-in-law has forbidden you to peer out. When the noise begins at the corral, do you, father, hold back my mother. Plainly it was she who spoiled things for her son-in-law. When the sound has entirely died away, then, after your son-in-law who has now gone away returns, then you will fetch the meat. Do not try to see things before that time. Only when your son-in-law arrives here are you to go to the pound," she told her father and her mother.

Presently the signals were waved.

"Young men! Go lie in wait!" cried the people, and all over the abandoned camp-site the noise began, just as if the tents were yet there, and then the buffalo came running into the corral and were all killed.

Even though he, that boy, said, "Nonsense, it is worth seeing, the crowd of people!" yet neither of his parents-in-law peeked out.

But they themselves could see the people.

Then, right there from the buffalo-pound they heard their father being called by name, "It is you, Buffalo-Dung, whose son-in-law is bringing the buffalo! That is why I am giving you the fattest one!" he was told, but he stayed right where he was; he would not peer out.

Then when the people who had lived in that now deserted camp were called, now one, now another, by name, "This one is for you, Buffalo-Dung!" (meaning that he was to take the meat), when all the people, to the last one, were called by name, and when even the children were noising about in the abandoned camp, that old couple heard them all. But his children were outside, with the old people's son-in-law. Presently they heard their son-in-law arrive.

"There now, now let your father and mother go fetch the meats, and let them take some for you to eat. On all the drying-frames that are on the camp-site let them hang the meats, and for this drying-frame of yours let them take the fattest one, to provide meat for them to eat!" said the boy who was a prattler; "If they do this way and do not peep, things will always go as well as this. But if they peep, things will not go well. Even if Partridge-Claw here drives buffalo, things will go just as well, if only your father and your mother do not try to look. By the time Partridge-Claw has had two turns at driving in buffalo, there will be enough, I guess, for a stay over the summer. You will have a big supply of meat. This Partridge-Claw is not really a child. And I, too; because we felt sorry for you when you were starving, is why we came to your dwelling," he told her; "Tell your father and mother: tomorrow again Partridge-Claw is to drive buffalo. Some four days after that he is to drive them again. In the end you will have a big supply of food," he told his wife.

Then those children went about playing. Then at one time each of them took a stick of saskatoon willow. They brought them into the lodge and put feathers on them, to make arrows. They were pretty. They tied them to the master-pole by which the tent is raised.

Thus spoke the prattler: "Sister-in-law, do you and the others never take these; Partridge-Claw is very particular about my arrows," he told her.

The old folks heard this.

"Now, it is to them we owe our lives, since they have provided food for us, children! Never so much as touch my sons-in-laws' arrows, since they are particular about them!" said the old man.

Then, the next morning, the child who was bashful went buffalo driving. They always did it in the same way. The buffalo ran into the pound. Even as before, the people and the children made their din, and they did not peer out. All the buffalo were skinned and cut up for them beforehand, so that without delay the old couple could set about fetching in meat day after day.

Then, when the drying scaffolds that had been left on the abandoned site were all full, the children ceased.

Then the boy who was a prattler spoke: "Sister-in-law, give us food. Give us provisions for the way. Perhaps some time we shall not get home; let us have food to eat off there," said the boy who was a prattler.

Accordingly, they were given pieces of dried meat and of fat meat and tripe, nicely wrapped into a bundle for them to carry on their backs. When this had been done for them, then early in the morning they went out of the tipi.

"Now, Partridge-Claw, that chief who moved away from this camp and his people are starving. Let us go there. Let us go give our grandmother food," he said to the other.

"Very well," said that boy.

They rose from the ground, flying through the air. Late in the afternoon they reached the place where there were many tents.

Meanwhile those girls felt lonely for their husbands, when they did not hear them at their noisy play.

But those others alighted in a grove of trees.

"Now, Partridge-Claw, I have no confidence in your powers. Let me be the one to go see those children," he said to his comrade.

He flew up in the form of a partridge. He settled on a poplar tree.

"Hey! Come here! See this partridge!" cried the children.

They shot arrows at it. Although the partridge was shot at, it flew up. Close by it settled again. So the children chased it hard. Presently, when he had drawn them off a long ways, suddenly he flew up. There where he had left his comrade, he came down. He turned back into a child. Then they followed those children's tracks. It was almost night. When those children were coming home, they began meeting them one after another. The children pushed them over and blocked their way. They were in the rear; for at every point the others pushed them over. Whenever they tried to get on their feet, others pushed them over, until they were in the rear. When night came on, they saw an old woman's little tent, a tipi of old bits of leather.

"This is our grandmother's dwelling, Partridge-Claw. Let us go in. Let us sleep here. We cannot get home today," they said.

"Very well," said the bashful one.

Then, as they entered, "Hey, grandmother! Let us play with our throwing-sticks here by your doorway!"

"Yes, my grandchildren!" she said to them.

Then they continued to play there with their throwing-sticks. At last, when it was dark, they ceased.

Meanwhile those girls yonder, who had not gone to sleep, looked at those two arrows. The things were moving. The girls watched them.

And the boys off there, "Hey, my grandchildren, now I am sleepy. Go and sleep now. Go home. I am sleepy."

Then the prattler said to her, "Grandmother, there will not be any place for us to sleep."

Off back yonder that old couple was already asleep. And as those girls picked up the arrows which were moving, suddenly they heard someone speak, as if those arrows were speaking. Whatever the owner of the arrow said, he spoke in the arrow there.

"Big sister, this is great, come here! Let us listen to my brother-in-law and to your brother-in-law and hear what they say!"

So now, whatever those arrows said, the others were saying. And they listened to them, though they were far away.

And when that old woman had thus spoken to her grandchildren, "Grandmother, we never stay anywhere with people, but pay at most a little visit here and there. How is it, grandmother, that you do not eat?" he asked his grandmother.

"Alas, grandchild mine, no one at all eats here, for here is a famine. But surely you know this. I shall befriend my grandchildren. My grandsons, use this to sleep on," and she tossed them her sleeping-mat, for them to sleep on.

"Well, grandmother, but this Partridge-Claw here has come to give you food!" they said to her, and gave her pieces of dried and of fat meat.

"Thank you, my grandsons. Now, the chief here, concerning his daughter, 'If anyone kills game for my town here, him I shall take for my son-in-law,' he has said, but, though from time to time one or another kills a deer, yet the people do not get enough to go round. It is too little, what with the great number of them," said the old woman; "Now, grandson, I want to lie down. Now I shall be able to eat," said the old woman.

The girls off yonder had gone to sleep. They held the arrows in their hands. When the things spoke, they listened to their husbands.

"Hey, Partridge-Claw, do you now go courting! Go court this chief's daughter!"

"Ha, so it seems you are again making trouble!" he said to his elder brother.

"Hoho, if you do not care to, it may as well be I!"

"Oh, big sister, it says your husband is going courting!" said that man's daughter.

They listened to it, waking up.

Then that boy went there. Then the arrow of the other boy, the one who was bashful, did not move at all, for he slept; only the prattler's arrow bobbed up and down. Then he went courting.

When he entered the lodge, "Make the fire bright!" said the chief's daughter.

Then, when she beheld the child looking at her, and in turn gazed at him, he smiled at her.

"Put out the fire!" said the young woman.

The fire was put out for her. * * * * * * * * * * * * * He told her of how they had acquired a supply of meat.

"Of as many tents as are in their camp-site, all the drying-scaffolds are filled. I shall come back here. When I do so, you will tell your father, when I shall have come into the tent; then you will all know about it. Your father will announce it. When I come in here again, then you will tell him about it. Now tomorrow we shall go back; for my brother has come here with me. Well, that is all. I am going back. It is almost daylight."

"Very well," she answered him.

Thereupon he went out of the tipi. He entered his grandmother's lodge. He lay down. As soon as he had lain down, his arrow off yonder lay at rest. They slept. When day broke, early in the morning they went back home. Towards evening they arrived at their dwelling.

"Where have you been?" their wives asked them.

"Well, far enough to use up the provisions you gave me, and then we came home. You gave us too little food for the way," they told them.

So when the next day came, the younger one drove buffalo. He brought many buffalo. On the next day after that he again asked for provisions; and they were given much of the very best food. Then early they went out of the tent. As soon as they were behind a rise in the land, they flew up. It was as before; in the evening they arrived. They went into their grandmother's lodge. This time at once their grandmother gave them bedding. As soon as night had fallen they gave it to their grandmother.

"Keep these good victuals, grandmother. Early tomorrow morning call the chief's daughter: she is to come here," he told his grandmother.

Off yonder where they dwelt he was heard through his arrow.

"So now you are to have a fellow-wife, big sister!" the man's daughter was told.

. . . .

"You surely do carry on in a dreadful way!" his younger brother said to him.

"It is you, rather, who go on in a dreadful way!" he answered him.

They were heard through their arrows, and those girls from time to time could not help laughing.

Then, when daylight had come, "Now, grandmother, go call that young woman! Give her these; she may take them home with her. Perhaps the people will be able to live, if they reach their old camp," he told his grandmother.

Then she was called for and invited.

"My grandchild, you are to come to my tent for a bit. My grandchild has been bothering me to invite you. The rest he will tell you."

"Very well," she said to her.

She went there. When she entered, who was that sitting there, but the one who had courted her! She sat down by his side.

"Well, these things are why I have called you here. Now, if once they camp on the way, that will be from where we others will depart," he told her; "Now then, now let your father announce what I have told you, the things I said. A great supply of meat has this one's father-in-law," he said, referring to his younger brother; "So there."

Accordingly, the young woman went home. She called her father from her tent.

"Father, a child has come in here. * * * * * * * * * * * * Your fellow-old-man who was abandoned has a store of meat. 'As many as are the deserted camps, so many are the scaffolds where hang the meats,' says your son-in-law; 'Accordingly, so let him announce it,' he said to me, and that is why I am saying it now."

"Yes, daughter. And so at last you have that which you begged for, saying, 'a man.' Try to live uprightly. Be sympathetic toward your fellow-wife," he told his daughter.

Then he announced it: "We shall move camp today. It is heard that my old friend has a supply of food; it is heard that he has a supply. Without delay you are to camp there whence you have moved camp," he said, instructing his people.

Accordingly, they all moved camp. There where they camped for the night, again that one went courting. . . . . They arrived at their dwelling.

Then, as soon as he entered, "Sister-in-law, be jealous of your husband! That chief's daughter, her he has taken to wife," he said of his younger brother.

"Nonsense, brother-in-law, it is you, rather, who have taken her to wife. I have been listening to you all the time," his sister-in-law told him.

"Now then, children, make ready by clearing the snow from the place where your elder sister is to stay and your other father; in two places you will clear the snow," he told them.

So they moved camp to that place. Without delay they joined them where they camped. By this time the warm weather was coming on.

Then, "Now, brother, drive in some buffalo. But watch for him: there is one who hates you. And there is one who hates me; but, as for me, I shall defeat him," he told him; "Never walk through the herd when you bring buffalo," he told his younger brother; "Do you first fetch buffalo," he told him.

"Yes," the other answered him.

Early in the morning he set out. He did as before, collecting buffalo-dung; as before, he whooped at them. They rose from the ground. He threw himself down. He came walking at their head. The buffalo pressed him close, stepping on his bird-tail, for the creature which we call the quail, that was the form the bashful one had taken. Then, when things were waved to drive on the buffalo, he found no place to go; he hung helpless in the air; he went past the herd. Although he wanted to come to earth, he was not able to. Hastily to a clump of willows, hastily he flew up and thither. All at once something came bearing down with noise through the air. He had not time to look that way; it came and struck him. But it failed to snatch him. In one place that other creature circled round in the air.

Then the prattler cried "Dear me, my brother is being destroyed! I must go look after him!"

He went out of the tent; he took his bow; and he took those two arrows. There in the grove he saw his brother lying. When he reached him, close by a winter-hawk was hanging in the air.

"Hey!" he called to it; "Hey! Exactly as now you appear, even so shall be your bodily form. . . . . you would always transgress. You will have to get your food always in the way of this which now you have done!" he said to it.

It could not change its form; it could not turn back into human shape. It was the one of whom the quail who was slain had been told, "He hates you." Now for his brother. He shot an arrow into the air; when he had shot the second one as well, his brother rose to his feet; he had restored him to life.

At once he hurried to the buffalo-pound; he saw a man sitting up on the hurdles of the enclosure. He wore a bracelet on his arm. The prattler descended to earth and began to look for a flint arrow-head.

"Oho! I prized it, Glutton, my flint arrow-head!"

He looked at him; his hand was bloody. He did like this.

"It must be you, Glutton!"

As he said so to him, it was a magpie that he struck full in the face.

"Here needs you will beg from human men! You will not be able to change your form! Wipe your face; you will have sight!" he said to it.

It could not change its form.

"In the woods you will get your sustenance!" he told it.

When it was told thus, it flew up; it flew somewhere aloft. It was unable to take on human form again.

"Let us needs both go tomorrow; let us drive buffalo," said the prattler, "Then let us plan for these people," he said to his younger brother; "For it will not go well—mortal men are to be born here on earth, and we must clear this earth for them," he told his brother.

"Yes," the latter answered him.

Then both went, the next morning, to drive buffalo. So off yonder they made buffalo; and they brought back with them a vast number, but only a few went into the corral. The Partridge wore breeches of hair, and the Quail wore breeches of hair. And they wore their clothes with the fur turned in. They looked most handsome. They stood together, the two as they slew all the buffalo. While some of the people cleaned the game, others came to give them berry-water to drink.

"Now then, people, you will have to turn into various forms. As many as are the beasts, as such you will find your sustenance. Every mortal man will overcome you, when off in the future he grows forth into life. But as for me, there in middle space I shall be, where are three stars. Forever I shall live. And as for this my younger brother, there shall be twain stars, and forever shall my brother live. For our Father has planned that we shall make way for mortal man to grow forth here on this earth."

This is as far as this sacred story goes.

(31) Hell-Diver

Mrs. Maggie Achenam

kā-wīhkaskusahk.

äkwah kutak.

sihkihp nōhtäh-ayīsiyiniwiw. kätahtawä usīhtāw utāsah uskihtäpakwah[1] *uhtsih. äkwah uhtsahtsāpiyah usīhäw, atsusisah mīnah. äkwah ituhtäw nähiyānāhk ōt ōma. ayīsiyiniwah wāpamäw ; ituhtäw.*

" tans ōmah äh-itiskāyan ? "

namuya nisituhtam äh-āta-kitōtikut.

" ahpuh ätukä upwāsīmuw awah, " itwäwak.

äkw ä-kitōtiht pwāsīmuwan, namuya nisituhtam.

" sätsāh, " itwäw.

" sihkihp äs āni ! " itāw.

tapasīw kuntah k-āti-naputukanäkutsihk.

äkwah kätahtawä mitātaht ihtasiwak ayīsiyiniwak, nāpäwak, äh-māh-mātsītsik, päyak pikw īskwäw kahkiyaw ōhih ustäsah äh-pamihāt. kätahtawä mānah äh-nikuhtät tahtu-kīsikāw, tahtu-kīsikāw mātsiyiwa ustäsah. kätahtawä iskwäwah päw-utihtik mäkwāts äh-mātahikät. äkusi wīsāmik tasipwähtätsik. namuya tāpwähtawäw. maskamik käkway ; sipwähtatāyiwah. äkwah pimitisahwäw ; wāhyaw äh-ihtātsik, miyik. äkwah sipwähtäwak ; wītsäwäw. äkwah sīpiy utihtamwak.

" äh-ntaw-unāpämiyahk, " itik, " mīkis-iyiniw. "

äkutah ayāwak sīpīhk. kitahtawä pätsitsimäyiwah ayīsiyiniwah äh-apisīsisiyit. äkwah pä-kapatäwäpahamiyiwa utōsiyiw. äyōkunik nīsu pōsiwak iskwäwak. päyak nakatahwäw ; äkwah äyōkō māh-mātōw. äkwah ōki pimitsimäwak.

" minahō, " itäwak.

mustuswah wāpamäwak. äkwah kapatäwäpaham utōsi äwakō sihkihp. minahōw.

" pita nka-mītsin wīsi ! "

" ā, namuya ! nama käkway ! nk-āpatsihtān mā-manitsōhkāhki. "

äkwah awa päyak iskwäw, " sihkihp awah, " itwäw.

kutak awah, " namuya ! mikis-iyiniw. "

äkwah kāwih pōsiwak ōsihk. äkwah kätahtawä kapatäwäpaham.

" ōtah apik, " itäw uwīkimākanah.

äkwah apiwak.

" äkwah kitsāhkus kā-pä-ntōmikuwāw, " itäw.

[1] Probably wrong; the translation is a guess.

ākwah sipwāhtāw. kātahtawā kā-pātsāstamuhtāt: nīsu uskinīkiskwāwak.

" āstam, nitsāhkus!"

wāpisk-atsimu-māyisah tāpihtāpisōwak. ākwah ituhtāwak. takuhtāwak nātā.

ākwah naha kutak kā-nakatahut takusin ākuta; kutakah nāpāwah miskamāsōw. ākwah āh-tipiskāk nīmihitōwak.

ākwah, " kāya paspāpik kā-wīh-nīmihituhk," itāw wīwah awah sihkihp.

ākwah āhtsi pikō paspāpiwak āyōkunik iskwāwak. pōt ōmah sihkihpah nāh-napwākiskāmawah, unāpāmiwāwah sihkihpah. ākwah iskwāw awa pakwātāw sihkihpah t-ōnāpāmit. sipwāhtāwak; kutakah ntaw-unāpāmiwak. utināwak mistikwah āh-yōskisiyit, manitsōsah āh-mihtsātiyit; kawisimunahāwak unipāwiniwāhk. ākwah ākusi sipwāhtāwak.

ākwah sihkihp āh-pōyōwihk kīwāw. kawisimututawāw pāyak uwīkimākanah.

" nitsāh-tsīstinik.—tānā k-ōh-tsāh-tsīstiniyan? kiyām, āh-kīh-mā-manitsōhkāhk.—mahti kutak."

kutakah mīnah tsāh-tsīstinik.

" kahkiyaw ākwah kitsīstināwāw, pikuh āh-kīh-nīmihituhk," itāw.

kākway itah: " kayās ōmah nitaw-ōnāpāmiwak; āh-tah-tahkwamiskik anikih manitsōsak; mistikwak aniki kā-kawisimututawatsik."

ākwah mātōw sihkihp. ntunawāw ākwah. miskawāw kutakah nāpāwah āh-wīkimāyit. kīskikwāswāw nāpāwah; nipahāw. kātahtawā iskwāwak pākupayiwak; nāpāwah ōhi nipahimāwah. sipwāhtāwak.

Now another story.

Hell-Diver wanted to be a man. Once upon a time he made some breeches for himself out of cedar bark. Also he made himself a bow and arrows. Then he went to this Cree country here. He saw people; he went there.

"What are you after here?"

He did not understand when they spoke to him.

"Maybe he is a Stony Sioux," they said.

But when they spoke Sioux to him, he did not understand.

"Shay chah," he said.

"Why, it's the diver-duck!" they said of him.

He fled, waddling off in no particular direction.

Now, once there were ten people, men, who spent their time hunting, and one woman took care of all these men, who were her elder brothers. Then, at one time—while she gathered firewood every day, her brothers went on their daily hunt. Then, at one time, some women came to where she was tanning. These women asked her to go away with them. She did not listen to them. The others took something away from her; they went off with it. Then she pursued them; when they had gone a long ways, the others gave it back to her. Then they went from there; she accompanied the others. Then they came to a river.

"It's a husband we're going after," the others told her, "the Bead-Man."

There by the river they stayed. Presently a little man came in a canoe. He beached his canoe where they were. Those two women got into the canoe. The other one was left behind as they paddled off; she wept and wept. And the others paddled along.

"Kill some game," they told him.

They saw some buffaloes. Then that hell-diver beached his canoe. He killed one.

"First let me eat the belly-fat!"

"Oh dear, no! I should say not! I am going to use it when religious rites are performed."

Then that one woman said, "He is the diver-duck."

The other, "No! The Bead-Man."

Then they got into the canoe again. In due time he beached it.

"Stay here," he told his wives.

So they stayed.

"Your sister-in-law will come call you," he told them.

Then he went. In due time someone came: two young women.

"Come, sister-in-law!"

. . . . Then they went there. They arrived over there.

Then that other woman who had been left by the canoers arrived there; she found another man for herself. Then, when night came they danced.

Then, "Don't peep in where the dance is going on," that hell-diver told his wives.

But those women peeped in just the same. There was the hell-diver being trampled on, their husband, the hell-diver. Then that one woman hated having the hell-diver as her husband. They went away; they went to take another husband. They took a crumbly old log that had many bugs on it; they placed it like someone lying down in their bed. Then they went away.

When the dance was over, the hell-diver came home.

. . . .

The other one, also, kept pinching him.

"Now both of you pinch me, even though there has been a dance," he said to them.

Something there spoke: "Long ago by this time they have gone to find a husband; it's bugs are biting you there; . . . .

Then the hell-diver wept. Then he looked for them. He found them staying with another man. He cut the other man's throat; he killed him. Suddenly the women woke up; that man had been killed. They went away from there.

(32) Hell-Diver

Coming-Day

kā-kīsikāw-pīhtukāw.

kītahtawā päyak kisäyiniw, äkwah päyak nōtukäsiw, äkwah nīs ōskinīkiskwäwak utawāsimisiwāwa awa kisäyiniw. kītahtawä āhkusiw awa kisäyiniw ; piyis nipiw. äkwah awa piku nōtukäsiw, äkwah utānisah nīsu, nistuwak. äkutah ay-ayāwak. piyisk kinwäs ayāwak. kītahtawä mina āhkusiw awa nōtukäsiw ; piyisk kinwäs āhkusiw. äkwah wīh-nipiw.

ōmis ītwäw : " nitawāsimisitik, sipwähtähkäk ; kakwä-miskawāhkäk awiyak. kīspin miskawāyäku nāpäw, unāpämihkäk ," itäw ; " māskōts äkutah uhtsih äkā wih-nipahāhkatusōyäk. "

" äha' , " itwäwak ōk ōskinīkiskwäwak.

äkusi kiyipah namuya pimātisiw awa nōtukäsiw.

äkwah uskinīkiskwäwak ōmis ītwäwak : " ōmisi kkīh-itikunaw kikāwiyinaw : ' sipwähtähkäk, nipiyāni, ' kīh-itwäw kikāwiyinaw, " itwäw aw ōmisimāw.

" tāpwä wāpahki ka-sipwähtānānaw, " itwäwak.

tāpwä äh-wāpaniyik, sipwähtäwak. kahkiyaw nakatamwak utsayānisiwāwa. piyisk nīswāw äh-nipātsik, sīpiy utihtamwak. mīnisah mihtsätiniyiwa. kwah nōhtähkatäwak. äkutah mīnisah mawisōwak, äwakuni äh-mītsitsik.

ōmis ītwäw aw ōmisimāw : " hāw, nisīmis, äkā wiya sipwähtätān. äwakunih kā-māh-mītsiyahk mīnisah nakatamahku, ka-nōhtähkatānānaw, " itäw usīmisah.

tāpwä äkutah ayāwak. niyōhtäyāpākwätwāwi, ituhtäwak nipīhk, sīpīhk äh-minihkwätsik. piyisk kinwäsk äkutah ayāwak.

kītahtawä kinwäsk äkut äh-ayātsik, äh-ntawi-minihkwätsik sīpīhk, kuntah mätawäwak äkutah, asinīsah äh-pāh-pakastawäwäpinātsik, kuntah äh-mätawätsik. kītahtawä kā-wāpamātsik awiya natimihk äh-pämāhāpwäwäyit, ōsihk äh-pimiskāyit.

" nimisä, awīna nāha ? " itwäw aw usīmimāw.

äh-itāpit aw ōmisimāw, " hä, nisīm, miyāmay nāpäw ! " itwäw aw ōmisimāw ; " nisīmis, ' nāpäw wāpamāyäku, wīkimāhkäk, māskōts äkā wīh-nipahāhkatusuyäku, ' kikīh-itikunaw kikāwiyinaw, " itäw ōsīma.

piyisk kisiwāk äh-pä-ihtäyit, kā-nisitawäyimātsik nāpäwa.

ōmis ītwäw aw umisimāw : " āstam ! pä-nātahunān ; ahpōh ka-wīkimitinān, " itäw aw ōmisimāw.

tāpiskōts äkā äh-pähtahk awa sihkihp äs āwa. äkutä iskwäwah k-āyāyit isi sihkōw, kā-wāpamātsik mīkisah äh-sihkōyit.

" nyā, nisīmis, äkw äs āwa mikisiyiniw ! " itäwak.

kītahtawä, " mīkisiyiniw ! " itäw.

ōmis ītwäw sihkihp, tāpiskōts äkwäyāk äh-pähtahk, " māh ! tānis ätwäyäk ? "

" āstam, mīkisiyiniw ! päh-nātahunān. ahpōh kā-wīkimitinān, äh-itwäyāhk. "

" äha' , tsäskwah ! " itwäw awa sihkihp.

äkutä isi kapāw. miyusiyiwa ōh ōskinīkiskwäwa. äkwah pōsihäw, pisisik ä-sihkut, mīkisah māna nipīhk äh-pahkisiniyit. äkusi kīwähtahäw. kītahtawä kā-wāpamātsik mustuswah.

" nāh, ka-minahōh ōma ! äh-nōhtähkatäyāhk ōma ! " itwäyiwa.

" äha' , äha' , nīwitik ! nika-minahun ; ka-mītsisunāwāw. "

äkwah äh-kapāt, " hāw, nīwitik, kanawäyihtamuk ōma kitōsinaw," itäw.

tāpwä ati-sipwähtäw, ä-wīh-minahut. äh-kitāpamātsik ōk ōskinīkiskwäwak, tāpwä pāskiswäyiwa ; päyak nipahäyiwa. miywäyihtamuk.

" äkwah kä-mītsisuyahk ! knōhtähkatāhtānaw, nisīmis ! " itwäw awa umisimāw.

tāpwä äh-pä-sākäwät awa sihkihp, " nīwitik, kika-mītsisunāwāw ; niminahun, " itäw.

äkusi sakahpitamuk ōm ōsi, äh-āmatsiwätsik. wāpamäwak mustuswah itah äh-pimisiniyit.

äh-takuhtätsik, " haw, nīwitik, kakwäyāhuk mihtah äh-utinamäk. nik-äspīhtsi-wiyanihtākān, ta-kutawäyäk, ta-nāh-nawatsiyäk. kinōhtähkatāhtāwāw ! " itäw.

tāpwä kiyipīwak äh-kutawätsik.

" nipapāsäyihtän, nīwitik. ōtäh ōmah äh-wīkihk, mistah ä-wih-miyawātikwahk, ä-wih-nīmihituhk, nipähikawinātukä, äkā mayaw ä-ntawitakusiniyān, " itäw.

äkwah ōki uskinīkiskwäwak k-ōtinahkik mihtah, " nā, nisīmis, kähtsināh awa äh-kīhtsäyihtākusit kināpäminaw ! " itäw.

" nāh ! " itwäw awa usīmimāw ; " nimisä, niya wiya äh-itäyimak, tāpiskōts äh-mōhtsōwit ! usām ma-mōhtsitunāmōw. "

" nāh, pasinaw tsī ntawäyimāw itä ä-wīh-nīmihitōwiht ? äwakw āwa miyāmay mikisiyiniw. "

" namuya, " itwäw usīmimāw ; " niwāpamāw ana kīmōts māna äh-utināt mīkisisah, äh-saskamut. äkutah māna, ' nikitāpamikwak, ' ätäyihtahkih, kā-sihkut, mīkisah māna kā-sihkwātät. namuy ān äwakō, " itäw, " mikisiyiniw, " itwäw aw ōsīmimāw.

äkusi äkwah äkwah ä-kutawätsik, käkats kīsi-wiyanihäw awa sihkihp. äh-kīsi-kutawätsik, ituhtäwak.

äkwah, " ahaw, nīwitik, itah äh-miywāsik wiyās utinamuk, ta-nawatsiyäk, " itäw.

tāpwä skwäwak ōki utinamwak wiyās. äkuyikuhk kā-pakutsänāt awa, wāpahtam awa usīmimāw wiyin.

" nä, wīsi niya nik-āyān, t-aspahtsikäyān ! " itwäw.

" yōhō ! " itwäw awa sihkihp, " käkway māka kiy-ōtakuhpiyān ōma kā-wīh-māh-mantsōkāhk ? " itwäw.

umisimāw awa, " niya wiya wīkwah nka-manaspahtsikanān ! " itwäw.

" yaw, käkway māka kiy-ōwīkuhkäyān ? " itwäw.

ntsawāts utastutiniyiw wīsi.

" yōhō, käkway māka kiy-ōtastutiniyān ōma ka-wīh-mā-mantsōkāhk ? " itwäw awa sihkihp.

äkuh ōki uskinīkiskwäwak ōmisih itwäw aw usīmimāw : " nimisä, kähtsin āwa äh-mōhtsōwit ! " itwäw.

" nāh ! äh-ukimāwit awa, k-ōh-ntumiht itä nānitaw ä-wih-isistāwiht. "

" a, päyakuh-kihtsäyimäw awa ! äh-mōhtsōwit niya wiya nitäyimāw ! "

" äkāy äkus īsi ! kika-pähtāk, " itäw usīma.

äkuyikuhk kīsitäpuwak.

" pä-mītsisw äkwa ! " āt äh-itikut, tāpiskōts äkā äh-pähtawāt.

" nā, kiy ōma k-ātitān, mīkisiyiniw ! "

" hā ! äkuyikuhk ! " itäw sihkihp.

" pä-mītsisu äkwah ! "

tāpwä ntawih-mītsisōw.

" ääh, nīwitik, kakwäyahuk äh-mītsisuyäk. mistah ätuk ōma nōtamihtāsun, ōm ītä k-ōh-ntumikawiyān, ka-wīh-nīmihituhk."

tāpwä kiyipa kīsi-mītsisōwak. ä-kīsi-mītsisutsik, äkwah pōsihtāwak wiyāsah, ä-sipwähtätsik. kītahtawä äh-atiy-utākusiniyik, äkutah uma māna, " ōma kā-näyāk kā-nīmihituhk, " k-ätwät ; māka nam āwiya wāpamäwak.

" ähä hehe ! " itwäw awa sihkihp ; " wāhyaw ätsik āni ätukä kāmāwatsihituh māna. ka-mwäsiskamāhtānaw ! " itäw ; " āta wiya uhtsita piku ta-pähikawiyān, kīspin äkā itah äyāyāni, namuya mōtsikihtāwak, " itäw.

tsīkih äh-ihtātsik, kā-pä-sākäwäyit ayīsiyiniwah.

" īh päyak kā-pä-sākäwät ! " itwäyiwa.

" nā, äkutah ätuk ōma kāy-itahk kināpäminaw ! äkwah kä-miywäyihtamahk, wāpamāyahkwäwi ayīsiyiniwak, " itäw usīma aw īskwäw.

ōmis ītwäyiwa : " hähwah, takusin sihkihp ! " kā-matwäh-twäwiht.

pōtih mihtsät pä-sākäwäyiwa iskwäwa.

" nääh, sihkihp pätahiskwäwäw ! " itäw.

" yah, nīwitik, nähā anih k-ätätsik, ' sihkihp, ' k-ätwätsik, " itäw.

" sihkīīhp, pä-kapā ! "

āhtsi pikuh pimitsimäw.

kītahtawä kā-pähtahkik ōk iskwäwak, " kinäpämāwāw [1] *sihkihp ! ' mīkisiyiniw, ' itihk ! "*

" mīkisiyinīw pätahiskwäwäw !—pä-kapā ! "

" hah, niyā k-ätikawiyān, nīwitik ! " itäw, äh-kapāt.

" mistahi kikaskäyihtamihtāsun, äkā mayaw äh-takusiniyin. äkus āni äkwah kī-nīmihituhk, " itimāwa unāpämiwāwa.

kītahtawä kā-pä-takuhtäyit nīsu uskinīkiskwäwah, usīma sihkihp, " hääy ! " k-ätwäyit ; " kitsāhkusinawak äh-päsīhtsik ! " äh-itwäyit.

äh-itāpitsik, awīn ōhi, kīh-tsāh-tsīpikutsäsiyiwa, äh-tāpihtsäpisōyit atimu-mäya äh-pāstäyik. äkusi wītsōhkamawāwak, uwiyāsimiwāwa äh-tahkuhtatsiwähtatāwiht uwiyāsimiwāwa.

" äkusi an äkwa kä-mānukähk itah kā-wīh-nīmihituhk, " k-ätwäwiht, äkusi wiyawāw mīna mānukäwak ōk ōskinīkiskwäwak, sihkihp awa wīwa. ä-kīsi-mānukäwiht wīkiwāw, äkwah äh-mītsisutsik, āsay kā-pä-ntumiht.

" sihkihp, äkwah kintumikawin, " itäw.

tāpiskōts äkā äh-pähtahk. äkusi kīwäyiwa kā-pä-ntumikut. piyisk kōtawi-pähāw.

" yō, tānsi ätat, äkā mayaw kā-pä-tuhtät sihkihp ? "

" ' kīpah äkwah kintumikawin, ' ntitāw. "

" yahahā, kinäpämāwāw ätukä ! ' mīkisiyiniw, kinitumik kītsi-mīkisiyiniw, ' ntaw-ītihk. "

" aha' . "

" mīkisiyiniw ! "

" wäh ! "

" ' kīpah äkwah ta-pä-tuhtāw, ' kitik kītsi-mīkisiyiniw. "

" aha' , " itwäw awa sihkihp.

" haw, nīwitik, pätāk ä-misāk wiyākan. mistah āni māna nitasamikawin itah äh-miywāsik kīsitäw. "

[1] Thus the record here and below; the usual form is *näpäwimäw* : "he shames him by speech."

äkwah wawäyīw.

" hah, umihtsim, pätāh wīsih ! "

miyäw. äyakw akwanahōw. wiyin äkwah pakwahtähōw.

" pätah anima wīyinuh[1] *! "*

itisinamawäw, äkwah äwakunih äh-pah-pīmuyit āyītaw. äkwah mīna utastutiniw, wīsi ä-pustastutinät.

äkusi äkwah ä-wih-ati-wayawīt, " ahāw, nīwitik, äkāya pä-ntawāpahkäk mäyākwām. misawāts nka-pätān ta-mītsiyäk pätunawān, " itäw wīwa ; " äkā wiya wiya pä-ntawāpahkäk. misawāts nka-kiskäyihtän, päy-ituhtäyäku, " itäw.

äkus āspin äh-ituhtät. mihtātamwak ōk īskwäwak, ä-kih-nōhtäh-kitāpahkätsik.

ōmis ītwäw aw ōsīmimāw : " nimisä, nama tsiw ōyā äh-pīwäyihtākusit ? äh-mōhtsōwit miyāmay ! "

" nāh ! " itwäw aw ōmisimāw ; " pasināw tsī mistahi ntawäyihtākusiw, ōma nāntaw k-äsistāwiht ? äh-ukimāwit ätukw ōyā ! " itwäw aw ōmisimāw.

" namuya ! " itwäw aw usīmimāw ; " ukimāwit ana, namuya tahakwanahōw wīsih. "

" nāh, tahki pikw āwa äh-pīwäyimāt ! " itäw usīma.

" tsikämō nama nipīwäyimāw, ä-ma-mōhtsōwit ! " itäw.

kītahtawä kā-pähtahk äh-matwä-sākōwäwiht, ä-nīmihitōwiht.

" nimisä, nka-ntawāpahkān ! "

" äkā wiya ! " itäw usīma ; " ka-kisiwāhānaw. äh-manitōwit ätukw āna k-ōh-kihtsäyihtākusit. "

" pasinaw tsī kihtsäyihtākusit, wiyinwa akwanahōw ? " itäw.

" tahki pikw āwa äh-pīwäyimāt ! "

" nah, kiya māka piku kā-kihtsäyimat wiyā mōhtsōyiniwit ! kiyām nka-ntawāpahkān, nimisä. "

" aha'. atsiya pikō. mātsikōtitān kä-tōtākuyahk, wāpamiskih ! "

" itāp namuya nka-kakwä-wāpamik. "

tāpwä ntawāpahkäw. äh-paspāpit, kā-wāpamāt ōhih unāpämiwāwa äh-tah-tahkiskāmiht, " sihkihp ayōtōtsikāniwiw ! " äh-itwäwiht, ustikwānisiyiw piku ä-sākamōyik, asiskiy misiwä äh-ayāyik, ōma wiyin k-ākwanahuyit mitunä ä-mästiskamuht. wāwīs äkwah pīwäyimäw.

kā-wāpamāt awa sihkihp uwīkimākana ä-paspāpiyit, kā-pasikusipahtāt awa sihkihp, nōtukäsiwa äkutah äh-apiyit, äōkunih äh-tah-tahkiskawāt awa sihkihp, " sihkihp āyōtōtsikāniwiw ! " äh-itwät, " nāāh, kitimahäw sihkihp nōtukäsiwah ! " äh-itwäwiht.

kīwäpahtäw aw uskinīkiskwäw.

ōmis ītwäw : " nimisä, mistah äs ōyā äh-pīwiyiniwit kināpäminaw kā-kihtsäyimat ! kiyām sipwähtätān ! niya wiya nipakwātäw, äh-mōhtsōwit, " itäw.

" nā, äh-manitōwit ätukw āna ! ka-nipahikunaw ana ! "

" pasinaw tsī tah-tahkiskawāw manitōwit anah ? namuya äksi tahtōtawāw. äh-mōhtsōwit anah, k-ōh-mätawākähk, " itäw.

" tānsi māka tä-tōtamahk ? "

" mistikwak nīsu nk-ōtināwak, " itwäw aw ōsīmimāw.

" äha', " itäw.

---

[1] If correctly recorded, for *wiyinwah :* (plural) "pieces of fat meat," but the particle *anima :* "that" is singular number.

tāpwä nätäw ōhi mistikwah, äh-iskusitsik, iyikuhk äh-iskusihāt ōhi mistikwah. itah äh-pimisihk aw uskinīkiskwäw, äkutah ahäw ōhi mistikwah.

" hāw, hāmōwak ōtah ka-mihtsätiwak !—pāskinikuyäkuh ōyā sihkihp, māmawōhkawāhkäk, ka-nōtināyäk ! äkusi !—äkwah kiya ! " itäw umisah.

äkutah mīna ahäw mistikwah, äh-akwanahāt.

" hāw, ōtah ta-mihtsätiwak mantōsak ! " itäw.

äkus äh-isi-akwanahāt, " wīh-kawisimutsih ōtah, tahkwamahkäk, mantsōsitik ! " itäw.

" ha, nyā, nimisä ! tapasītān ! " itäw.

tapasīwak.

äkwah iyikuhk käkäts äh-wāpaniyik, pōyōwān, äkwah äh-kīwät sihkihp. tāpwä pätäw ōm ītah äh-miywāsiniyik wīhkōhtōwin.

" ōm ītah, nīwitik, pätunawān ! "

namuya kitutik.

" wätstakäts ōki kā-pōsāhkwāmitsik ! " itwäw.

äkusi nahastäw, äkwah äh-nahapit, äh-kätayōwinisät, ä-wih-kawisimut. ōh ōmisimāwa kawisimututawäw. mayaw äh-kīsi-akwanahut, sämāk tahkwamik mantōsah.

" yā, äkā wiyah, umihtsim ! kiyām ōma kih-mā-mantsōkāniwiw, " itäw, äh-kisiwāsit, " äh-nīmihitōwiht, äh-wītsihiwäwak ! " äh-itäyihtahk, uwīkimākanah.

tahkih äh-tahkwamikut mantsōsah, piyis wanskäw.

" wätstakāh kā-kāhkwäyihtaskit ! " itäw ; " maht ōsīmim ! " itwäw, äkutäh mīna äh-kawisimut.

āsay mīna āmōwah tah-tahkwamik.

" äkā wiya, usīmim ! niwīh-nipān ; ninästusin, äyikuhk äh-nīmihituyān ! " ta-kih-nästusit, äh-kih-tah-tahkiskāht mitunih !

" namuy ätsik anih ta-kīh-nahi-wītsihiwäyān itah äh-nīmihituhk, iyikuhk kā-kāhkwäyihtaskiyäk ! " itwäw.

ntsawäts ōtah kunt ītah kawisimōw. äyikuhk äh-ākwā-kīsikāyik, äkuyikuhk päkupayiw. äh-ōhpiskwäyit, käyāpits nipāyiwa uwīkimākana.

" waniskāh, umihtsim ! ākwā-kīsikāw ! " itwäw.

namuya waniskāyiwa.

"kiya käkuts, usīmimāw ! "

äkā h-waniskāyit, wiya waniskāw. ōh ōsīmimāwa äh-pāskiwäpināt, kahkiyaw āmōwah uhpiyāyiwa, äh-māmäwōhkākut, pikw ītah äh-tahkwamikut, piyis misiwä uhkwākanihk, mīna usitihk uhi mantsōsah äh-tāh-tahkwamikut. piyisk wayawīyāmōw, apisīs äh-tōhkāpit, āmōwah äh-tōtākut.

ōmisi itäw, mistah äh-pähtākusit wīkihk : " nama tsi wiyah äh-nipahāt uwīkimākanah ? " itäw ; " mahtih ! " äh-itwäwiht.

wiyah nipīhk ituhtäw sīpīhk, äh-kīh-utinahk mihkuh. äkusi pōsiw, äh-ati-nikamut.

" nama tsi wiya äh-nipahāt uwīkimākanah, ä-wīh-nipahisut ? " itäw.-mōhkumān äh-utinahk, " äy, wīh-tahkamisōw ! " itäw.

tāpwä tahkahtam ōma mihkuh, kuntah ä-sīkipayiyik mihkuh, " nipahisōw ! " äh-itiht.

äkusi kwatapīw, äkutä sīpā äh-pimih-mitsimīt ōsihk.

" ä, nipahisōw sihkihp ! kwatapīw ! "

äkus ä-sipwäyāhukut.

" tāpwä kīsinātsihäw uwīkimākanah ! kakwä-utinihk ! " itwäwān, ōsihk äh-nātahuht.

utōsih ōma utinamwān ; namuya äkutah ayāw, äh-kōkīt.

" tāpw äs āni äh-nipahisut ! " itāw.

wāhyaw äkutä kapāw, kutak ä-sākahikanisiwiyik äkutäh äh-ituhtät. kītahtawä äkutä kā-matwä-nikamut, " äs āni ä-kakwä-tsīsihikuyahk sihkihp ! ōtäh matwä-nikamōw ! ntsawāts pahkupäk ; miskawāyäku, nipahāhkäk kā-kīsinātsihāt wīwah ! " äh-itiht.

äkwah misiwä äh-ntunāht nipīhk, piyisk käkway miskuskahkwāwih, kītahtawä äh-tah-tahkiskahkik, kītahtawä tāpiskōts äh-matwäwäyik äh-itihtahkik, " ukāwiyah äs ōhi äh-pāskatayäskāmiht ; äkusi kinipahānaw ! " äh-itwäyit ōh ayīsiyiniwah.

pōnihik.

ha, äkuyikuhk äskwāk ātayōhkäwin.

Once upon a time there was an old man, and an old woman, and two young women, the children of that old man and his wife. Then at one time the old man fell sick; at last he died. Then there were only three of them, the old woman and her two daughters. They stayed in the same place. They dwelt there, in the end, for a long time. Then, in time, the old woman, too, fell ill; in the end, she was sick a long while. Then she was about to die.

She spoke thus: "My children, go away from here; try to find some people. If you find a man, marry him," she told them; "Perhaps in this way you will not starve to death."

"Yes," said the young women.

Thereupon soon the old woman lived no more.

Then the young women spoke thus: "Our mother said this to us: 'Go away from here when I die,' said our mother," spoke the elder sister.

"And so tomorrow we shall go," they said.

Accordingly, on the morrow they set out. They left behind all their possessions. At last, when they had slept twice on the way, they came to a river. There were many berries. And they were hungry. There they gathered berries and ate them.

Thus spoke the elder sister: "Now, sister, let us not go away from here. If we leave these berries which we are eating, we shall starve," she said to her younger sister.

Accordingly, they stayed there. Whenever they were thirsty, they went to the water and drank from the stream. In the end they stayed there a long time.

Then at one time, when they had been there for quite a while, as they went to the river to drink, they played about there, casting pebbles into the water, to amuse themselves. Presently they saw someone coming downstream, paddling a canoe.

"Sister, who is that?" cried the younger one.

When the elder sister looked over there, "Why, sister, surely, a man!" said the elder sister; "Little sister, 'If you see a man, marry him, and perhaps you will not starve to death,' our mother said to us," she told her younger sister.

At last, when he had come near, they knew him for a man.

The elder sister called, "Come here! Come fetch us in your canoe; if you like, we will marry you," she called to him.

Exactly as if he did not hear it that Hell-Diver acted, for he it must have been. He spat in the direction of the women, and they saw that he spat wampum-beads.

"Goodness, little sister, this must be the Wampum-Man!" said one to the other.

Presently, "Wampum-Man!" she called to him.

Thus spoke Hell-Diver, as though only now he heard, "Why! What is that you say?"

"Come here, Wampum-Man! Come fetch us in your canoe. If you like, we will marry you, is what we said."

"Yes, just a moment!" said Hell-Diver.

He landed there. Those young women were handsome. So he took them on board, spitting all the time, and each time wampum-beads fell into the water. So he started to take them home. Presently they saw some buffalo.

"Goodness, you ought to take this chance to kill something! The fact is, we are hungry!" they said.

"Yes, yes, my wives! I shall kill some; you shall eat."

Then, when he went ashore, "Now, wives, do you keep watch over our boat here," he told them.

So he went off to kill game. As those young women observed him, he shot at the animals; he killed one. They were glad.

"So now we shall eat! We surely were hungry, little sister!" said the elder.

And so, when that Hell-Diver came back down the bank, "Wives, you shall eat; I have killed some game," he told them.

Accordingly, they tied fast the canoe and climbed up the bank. They saw the buffalo lying there.

When they got there, "Now then, wives, work as fast as you can, gathering faggots. In the meantime I shall skin it and cut it up, so that you can make the fire and do the roasting. You said you were hungry!" he told them.

So they were quick about making the fire.

"I am in a hurry, wives. Over yonder in the camp there is going to be a big celebration and a dance, so they must be waiting for me, seeing that I am not getting back in time," he told them.

Then, as the young women were picking up sticks, "Goodness, little sister, surely our husband is an important man!" she said to her.

"Pshaw!" answered the younger one; "Sister, as for me, he seems to me just as if he were crazy! He talks too silly."

"Why, do you suppose he would be in demand, then, for a dance? Certainly, he is the Wampum-Man."

"No," said the younger one; "I saw the creature taking beads, on the sly, and sticking them into his mouth. Then, whenever he thinks we are looking at him, he spits, and that is the way he always spits out beads. He is no Wampum-Man, not he," said the younger sister.

So then, when they made the fire, Hell-Diver had almost finished preparing the carcass. When they had built the fire, they went to where he was.

Then, "Now, wives, take the best parts of the meat to roast," he told them.

Accordingly, the women took the meat. When he had opened the belly, there the younger sister saw some fat.

"Ooh, me, let me have the belly-fat, to eat with my meat!" she cried.

"Hoho!" cried Hell-Diver, "And what am I then to have for my blanket-robe at the Spirit Dance?" he said.

The elder sister cried, "And I, I shall take the kidney-fat to eat as a titbit with my meat!"

"Oho, and what I am I to do for kidney-fat? he cried.

His headgear, for want of better, was belly-fat.

"Hoho, and what would I have for my head-dress at the Spirit Dance?" cried Hell-Diver.

Then of those young women, the younger said, "Sister, certainly he is crazy!"

"Nonsense! Because he is a chieftain is why he is called wherever there is to be a ceremony of any kind."

"Hee, this person is alone in looking up to him! As for me, I think he is crazy!"

"Don't. He will hear you," she told her younger sister.

By this time they had finished their cooking.

Although they called to him, "Come eat!" it was just as if he had not heard.

"Dear me, it is you I am calling, Wampum-Man!"

"Hah! At last!" Hell-Diver answered her.

"Come and eat now!"

So he went to eat.

"Now wives, eat in a hurry. I am delaying pretty badly with all this, seeing that I am being called over there for the dance."

And so they quickly finished their meal. When they had done eating, they put their meat on board the canoe, and went on. Presently, as it was going towards evening, every little ways he would say, "Just at that next point is the dance;" but they saw no one.

"Well, well, well!" said Hell-Diver; "It surely does seem that they have taken a far-off place for the council. We might miss the whole thing!" he told them; "Only, of course, they will be sure to wait for me, seeing that if I am not there, they never have any sport," he told them.

When they had got near, someone came into view.

"Over there is someone coming into view!" cried one.

"Dear me, I suppose this is the place our husband meant! Now we shall be glad, when we see some people," the woman said to her younger sister.

They heard that person cry, "Yoho, Hell-Diver has come!"

Then a great many women came into view.

"Goodness me, Hell-Diver is bringing women in his canoe!" was said of him.

"Yes, wives, it is that person over yonder they mean, when they say 'Hell-Diver,'" he told them.

"Hell-Diver, come, land!"

He kept right on paddling.

Presently those wives heard, "You are embarrassing Hell-Diver by the way you address him! Call him 'Wampum-Man!' "

"Wampum-Man is bringing women in his canoe!—Come to shore!"

"Ha, it is to me they are talking, wives!" he told them, and went to the bank.

"You deprived yourself of much pleasure, coming late. The dancing has gone on without you," their husband was told.

Presently there came two young women, Hell-Diver's sisters, and, "Hey!" they said; "Sisters-in-law have been brought to us!"

When they looked there, why, they were sharp-nosed little things, * * * * * * So then they were aided in the task of carrying their meat up the high bank of the stream.

"They are putting up the tipis by the dancing-place," the people said; so those young women, too, Hell-Diver's wives, set up their tent. When their tent was set up, and they were eating, already he was summoned.

"Hell-Diver, you are being called," he was told.

It was just as if he had not heard. Soon the one who had come to call him went back. At last they grew impatient waiting for him.

"Hoho, what did you say to Hell-Diver, that he is so long about coming?"

" 'You are summoned to come at once,' I said to him."

"Aha, no doubt you embarrassed him with your speech! 'Wampum-Man, your fellow-Wampum-Man summons you,' go say to him."

"Very well."

"Wampum-Man!"

"What is it?"

" 'He is to come right away,' your fellow-Wampum-Man says to you."

"Very well," said Hell-Diver.

"Now then, wives, bring a big dish. You see, I am always given a big share of the best hot food."

Then he put on his finery.

"Here, Aînée, bring the belly-fat!"

She gave it to him. This then he wrapped round himself as a robe. And a piece of fatty meat he used for a belt.

"Bring that fat!"

She handed it to him, and this he twisted round him at both sides. Then he put on his head-dress; belly-fat he wore as his head-dress.

So then, as he was about to go out of the lodge, "Now, my wives, be sure not to come and look on. Have no fear, I shall bring you some of the ceremonial food to eat," he told his wives; "Be sure, however, not to come and look on. I shall know it without fail, if you come there," he told them.

So off he went. Those women were disappointed, for they were eager to look on.

Then the younger one said: "Sister, cannot it be that that person who has just gone is held in contempt? It surely seems that he is crazy!"

"Nonsense!" said the elder sister; "In that case, could it be that he is so greatly in demand at whatever ceremony his people are having? No doubt that man is a chief!" said the elder sister.

"No!" said the younger; "A man who is a chief will not put on a blanket-robe of belly-fat."

"Yah, this girl is always belittling him!" she said of her sister.

"And I suppose I should not think little of him, when he is entirely daft!" she answered her.

Presently she heard the whooping, as the people danced.

"Sister, I am going to look on!"

"Do not!" she said to her younger sister; "We shall get him angry. I have no doubt that he has supernatural power, the way he is esteemed."

"Is it likely that one who is held in esteem would wear pieces of fat for his blanket-robe?" she asked her.

"She is always belittling him, this girl, and no one else!"

"Bosh, it is only you who hold him in esteem, that crazy-man! Please let me go look on, big sister."

"Very well. Just for a short while. You will see what he does to us, if he sees you!"

"Well, I shall try not to let him see me."

Accordingly, she went and looked on. When she peeped in through the door, why, there she saw her husband being kicked about, while the people cried, "They are having a lot of fun with Hell-Diver!" and there was only his little head sticking out, for he was all covered with dirt, and the fat he wore as a blanket was all trodden to bits. She despised him more than ever.

When Hell-Diver saw his wife peeping in, up he jumped to his feet, and an old woman who sat there, her he kicked and kicked, crying, "They are having a lot of fun with Hell-Diver!" whereupon, "Heavens, Hell-Diver is abusing an old woman!" the people said of him.

That young wife ran home.

She said, "Sister, that husband of ours must be indeed of small account, he whom you admire so! Come, let us be off! As for me, I hate the crazy fool," she said to the other.

"Goodness, I am sure he has manitou power! He will kill us!"

"Is it likely he would be kicked about, if he had manitou power? He would not be treated that way. Because he is crazy, they use him as a butt," she told the other.

"But how can we do it?"

"I shall take two tree-trunks," said the younger sister.

"Yes," she answered.

Accordingly, she went and got those trees and chopped them to the length of those women. In the place where she was to lie, the young woman laid the one tree-trunk.

"Now then, there are to be many bees here!—When he uncovers you, that Hell-Diver, assail him in full number, and fight him! There!—Now, you!" she said to her elder sister.

Over there, too, she placed a tree-trunk, and pulled the coverlets over it.

"Now then, here shall be many bugs!" she said to it.

Then, when she thus covered them, "When he lies down here, bite him, bugs!" she told them.

"Now, come, sister! Let us flee!" she said to her.

They fled.

Then, when it was almost daybreak, the dancing stopped, and Hell-Diver went home. He really did bring some of the good food from the feast.

"Here, wives, is the ceremonial meal!"

They said nothing to him.

"A nine days' wonder, what sound sleepers they are!" he said.

* *

So he needs lay down somewhere or other. It was broad daylight, when he awoke. When he raised his head, his wives were still sleeping.

"Get up, Aînée! It is broad day!" he said.

She did not get up.

"You, at least, Cadette!"

When she did not get up, he got up himself. When he threw back the younger one's covers, all the bees flew up, and the whole swarm went for him and stung him here and there, until his face was all covered, and meanwhile those bugs kept biting his feet. At last he ran out of the tipi, with his eyes barely a little open, what with the way the bees had treated him.

When people heard the noise he was making in his tipi, they said, "Is he not perhaps killing his wives? Let us go see!" they said of him.

As for him, he went to the water, to the river, taking with him some blood. Then he embarked, singing the while.

"Is he not perhaps, having killed his wives, about to kill himself?" was said of him.

When he drew his knife, "Hey, he is going to stab himself!" they said of him.

And really, he stabbed the vessel full of blood, and, when the blood spurted all over, "He is killing himself!" they said of him.

Then he tipped his canoe and got under it, holding to it as it drifted along.

"Hey, Hell-Diver has killed himself! His canoe has tipped!"

Then, as he was carried away by the current, "Truly he is bringing grief on his wives! Try to get hold of him!" was said of him, and they went to fetch him in a canoe.

They got hold of his canoe; he was not in it, for he had dived.

"It seems that he has really killed himself!" they said of him.

Far from there he went to shore, having reached a little lake.

Presently they heard him singing in yonder place. "So he is trying to fool us, is Hell-Diver! Over there he is singing! You will have to get into the water; if you find him, kill him; he is bringing grief upon his wives!" was said of him.

Then, when they sought him everywhere in the water, at last, when they felt something underfoot, and gave it a few kicks, then they heard something go off like a gun. "They have stepped on his mother's belly and it has burst with a bang; so now we have killed him!" said those people.

They left him alone.

Well, that is the end of the sacred story.

(33) The Foolish Maiden

Mrs. Maggie Achenam

kā-wīhkaskusahk.

kutak iskwäw sipwähtäw. sīpīhk ituhtäw, kā-wāpamāt nāpäwah äh-pätsitsimäyit.

" pōsih, " itik.

pōsiw. pōt ōhih äh-kitāpamāt, āyītaw kīh-uhkwākaniyiwa. äkwah mātōw.

" ' nika-pimātisin, ' äh-itäyihtaman tsī ? " itik ; " ä-wīh-mōwitān, " itik.

äkwah mātōw.

" kiyām apih ! uhtsitaw misawāts kiwīh-mōwitin. "

takusinwak ministikuhk. äkwah kapāw.

" nōhkō, " itwäw äkwah awa wīhtikōw, " pä-nās ; pakāsimāhkan awa kā-päsiwak. "

pä-nātäw nōtsukäsiw. päsiwäw wīkihk. äkwah kitāpamäw aw ōskinīkiskwäw.

" namuya kipa-pakisāpamin, " itwäw nōtsukäsiw ; " misawāts ä-wīh-pakāsimitān, " itäw.

äkwah aw ōskinīkiskwäw, " äh-nistawäyimitān, " itäw ; " ' nōhkum, ' äh-itäyihtamān. "

" nōsisimis ätsik āwah ! ntām-kitimahäw. nipahin, nōsisäh. pakastawäyāpäkastāhkan ntakisiy. äkutäh uhtsi ta-pä-mātahtam wīhtikōw. äkwah ka-kīskisän nispitun ; ' nikuhtä, nōhkōh ! ' kik-ätwān ; ' mistikuh katsīkahikān ! ' itāp anih nika-nikuhtān. äkwah kiyah ka-tapasīn. kakwäsōhki-tapasī. "

tāpwä äkwah tapasīw. äkwah ōhkumah nikuhtäyiwah. kätahtawä takusin wīhtikōw.

" nōhkōhō, pä-kīwä ! niwīh-mītsisun, " itwäw.

" tsäskwah ! ninikuhtān, " itwäw.

" äkusi kīpah ! "

" īspīhtsi-mītsisōh. wīpats nika-kīwān, " itwäw nōtukäsiw, uspitun piku äh-nikuhtämakaniyik.

mītsisōw äkwah wīhtukōw. mōwäw ōhkumah äkwah. ihkäyihtam äkā mi-mayaw äh-takuhtäyit ōhkumah. äkwah ntunikäw. äkwah äh-utihtahk, pōt ōmah ōhkumah uspituniyiw kā-pahkihtiniyik.

" tāntä äh-kiy-itāmuyan, kā-kīsinatsihiyin, nōhkum äh-nipahat ? nipapaminawatikuh ! kiwīh-pimitisahutin, " itäw.

äkwah nawaswäw wīhtikōw awa. äkwah tapasīw uskinīkiskwäw. kätahtawä kisiwāk pätwäwitamiyiwah. äkwah mākwäyimōw.

" nka-nipahik äkwah," itäyihtam.

utihtäw ayīsiyiniwah äh-uwaskāhikaniyit.

" tawinah ! niwīh-nipahik wīhtikōw, " itäw.

namuya tāpwähtāk.

" kīpah, nistäsä ! kitimākihtawin ! niwih-nipahik wīhtikōw, " itäw.

piyis yōhtänamiyiwah. pīhtukäw äkwah. āsay takupahtäyiwah.

" yōhtänamawin ! niwīkimākan nipäh-nawaswātäw, " itwäw.

namuya tāpwähtamawäw.

" kīpah yōhtänah ! niwīkimākan niwīh-wāpamäw. "

äkwah iskwäw, " kā wiyah, kā yōhtänah ! wīhtikōw anah, namuya niwīkimākan."

äkwah nāpäw, " yōhtänah ! niwīkimākan nipä-nātäw."

" namuya ! " itwäw.

kitahtawä nāpäw yōhtänam. āpihtaw iskuh äh-pīhtukäyit nāpäwah, kipiwäpinam ; nipahäw. äkwah iskwäw wayawīw. mihtah mihtsät utinam. äkwah pōnam. nāpäwah äkutah isiwäpinäw ; mästihkaswäw.

äkwah ustäsah, " kāyā käkway ōtinah ! "

kahkiyaw käkway pimastäw ; uyākanisah ämihkwānisak sīsīpaskihkusak paskwahamātsōwinisah äh-miywāsikih, ä-sīkwāhkasut awah wīhtikōw. utinam uyākanis ; sīhtihkōhkanāhtam. ati-kutawipayiyiw.

" nistäsä, nistäsä ! " itwäw.

pä-wayawiyiwah ustäsah ; utinamiyiwa.

" kāya kīhtwām käkway utinah ! "

pāh-pāstahamiyiwah kahkiyaw. äkusi äkwah pīhtukäw. äkwah usīhtāyiwa nāpäwah ayōwinisah. äkwah pustayōwinisäw äōkunih nāpäwāyōwinisah. äkwah sipwähtäw.

kätahtawä äh-pimuhtät kā-wāpahtahk sāpuhtawān äkut äh-akusiyit ayīsiyiniwah. pä-nīhtakusiyiwah äh-ākwāskākut.

"mätawätān, " itik.

" namuya, " itäw; " nikīwān, " itäw.

piyis sākōtsimik.

" kiya nīkān, " itäw ; " mätawäy, " itäw.

äkwah mätawäwak. skwäw awah sākōtsihäw. kīwähtahik nāpäwah ōhō ; sāpuhtawānihk tuhtahik. äkwah misakamik wāpamäw pisisik iskwäwah äh-kaskihtsikwanäskikāsōwit.

äkwah kakwätsimäw, " tānsi äh-tōtākuyäk ! "

" kīhtsäkusīw anah mistikuhk ; pä-kwāskwäkutsin ; nihtsikwaninähk pahkisin ; nikaskatiskākunān mānah. "

" äkwah namuy äkusi niya nka-tōtāk ! "

pä-pīhtukäw. nāpäw kīhtsäkusīw.

" ap äkutah ! " itäw iskwäwah.

äkwah iskwäw aw āpiw. äkwah kwāskwäkutsin awa. pīwāpisk itisinam iskwäw awa. kisisimäw ; nipahäw. äkus īsi äkwah pasikōw. miywäyihtamwak ōki iskwäwak, usām äh-kitimahihtsik.

" päyakwanuhk sipwähtäk tānt äh-uhtsiyäk ! "

namuya kiskäyihtamwak tāntä k-äsi-sipwähtätsik. piyis äkwah iskwäw ātiht sipwähtahäw wīkiwāhk isi. äkwah takusinwak nätä. mitātaht iskwäwah wītsäwäw. äkwah miywäyihtamiyiwah ustäsah äh-takusihk. mitātasiyiwah ustäsah. äkwah mīnah mitātaht kā-päsiwāt. miyupayiyiwah ustäsah. äkwah äkutah ayāwak. wīwiyiwah ustäsah.

kätahtawä kā-sipwähtät mīnah kīhtwām. wāwāskäsiwah kwāsihik. [1] *äkwah pakwātamiyiwah äh-kwāsihikut, kutakah mīnah pisiskiwah. äkwah wiya miywäyihtam iskwäw. unāpämiw wāwāskäsiwah. äkwah äh-watsistwanihkäyit äkutah nakatik. äh-kitōwit äkwah wāwāskäsiwah, äh-ppāmpahtāyit, sīpā pämpahtāyitsi iskwäwah äh-pimi-kīhkāmikut. ayis nama nāntaw kiy-isi-kīhtäkusiyiwah ta-pakamahukut. kätahtawä kā-pä-kitōwit kisiwāk äyakunih unāpämah. ōt ōmah misiwä uy-utsikisiyiwa äy-ispinatimiht, äkwah mitunih ä-wih-nipahāhkatusōwit.*

---

[1] From here on the story is obscure.

äkwah wīhtamāk : " kistäsak wīh-nipahāhkatusōwak, " itik ; " äkwah nka-ntaw-āsamāwak niyaw. kāwih itāp nk-āpisisinin, " itik.

" äha' ! "

äkwah ituhtäw ustäsah.

" kā wiya māka ta-pīkwahtamwak niskanah. uski-pahkäkinuhk ta-wäwäkastāwak ; nikutis ta-ntaw-āstāwak. näwu-tipiskāki kāwih nika-takupahtān. "

äkusi äkwah nipahäw. ustäsah ä-kīh-näwu-tipiskāyik takusiniyiwah.

" äkwah kīstawāw awītä ! " itäw ustäsah.

mātōw iskwäw ; mihtātäw unāpämah.

äkusi wiy äyōkō.

Another woman set out. She came to a river, and there she saw a man approaching in a canoe.

"Get in," he said to her.

She stepped aboard. There, when she looked at him, he had a face at either side of his head. Then she wept.

"Is it 'Do let me live!' you are thinking?" he asked her; "My intention is to eat you," he told her.

She wept.

"Sit still! It is no use; I mean to eat you."

They reached an island. He disembarked.

"Grandmother," cried that Windigo, "Come fetch her; prepare to boil this person I am bringing."

A little old woman came and fetched her. She brought her over yonder to her lodge. The young woman gazed at her.

"You don't stop staring at me," said the little old woman; "What matter, since I am bound to boil you?" she said to her.

Then the young woman answered her: "It is because I recognize you, because 'My grandmother,' is what I am saying to myself."

"And so it is my grandchild! I had almost been her undoing! Kill me, my grandchild. Then set the whole string of my entrails into water. That is what the Windigo will eat first. Also you will cut off my arm; 'Chop wood, grandmother!' you will say; 'You are to split wood!' Then I shall really split wood. And as for you, you will be running away. Run with all your might!"

Then she ran away. Her grandmother chopped firewood. Soon the Windigo arrived.

"Grandmother, come home! I want to eat!" he cried.

"Wait a bit! I am gathering wood," she said.

"Be quick, now!"

"Do you eat meanwhile. I shall be back soon," said the old woman, while her arm all by itself cut wood.

The Windigo began to eat. He ate his grandmother. He was impatient because his grandmother was not coming promptly. Then he began to search. When he came there, behold, there his grandmother's arm fell to the ground.

"Whither can you flee, you who have bereft me by killing my grandmother! She cooked for me. I will chase you," he called to her.

Then that Windigo started in pursuit. The young woman fled. Soon he came close with noise. She was in great distress.

"Now he will kill me," she thought.

She came to a man who had a house.

"Open! A Windigo is trying to kill me," she called to him.

He paid no heed to her.

"Quickly, big brother! Take pity on me! A Windigo is trying to kill me," she called to him.

At last he opened the door. She went in. The other had already got there on the run.

"Open the door for me! I come in pursuit of my wife," he cried.

His words went unheeded.

"Quick, open! I want to see my wife."

Then the woman, "Don't! Do not open! He is a Windigo, not my husband."

And the man, "Open! I have come to fetch my wife."

"No!" she cried.

Then at one time the man opened the door. When the other man had got half-way in, he flung it shut; he killed him. Then the woman went out. She took a great amount of firewood. Then she made a fire. She threw that man into it; she burned him up.

Then her big brother, "Do not take anything!"

All kinds of things were lying around; bowls, spoons, kettles, forks, all kinds of good things which had fallen out when the Windigo was burned. She picked up a bowl; she could not let go of it. It began to sink into the earth.

"Brother, brother!" she cried.

Out came her brother; he took the thing.

"Do not take anything more!"

He smashed all the things. Then she went inside. The man made some garments. Then she put on those man's clothes. Then she went away.

Presently, as she walked along, she saw a buffalo-lane and a man sitting up aloft on it. He came down and headed her off.

"Let us try our strength," he said to her.

"No," she answered him; "I am on my way home," she said to him.

But at last he talked her into it.

"You first," he said to her; "Show your power," he said to her.

Then they contended. The woman was defeated. That man took her home with him; he took her to the buffalo-lane. There she saw a great crowd of none but women whose knees had been broken.

Then she asked them, "What has he been doing to you?"

"This person climbs trees; he comes leaping down; he falls on our knees; as he lands he always breaks our bones."

"Now, he shall not treat *me* this way!"

She came inside. The man climbed up.

"Sit there!" he told the woman.

Then the woman sat there. He leaped into the air. The woman held out an iron bar. She impaled him and killed him. Then she rose to her feet. Those woman rejoiced, for they had been miserably dealt with.

"Go, all of you, to whatever place you came from!"

They did not know from where they had come. At last that woman took some of them away with her towards her home. They arrived at yonder place. She had ten women with her. Her brothers were glad when she arrived. Ten was the number of her brothers. And likewise ten were they whom she brought. Now her brothers fared well. They stayed there. Her brothers now had wives.

After a time she set out again. A stag took her away with him. He did not like it when in turn other animals took her away. But the woman herself liked it. The stag was her husband. Then he made a nest for her and left her there. Then when the stag bellowed as he ran about, whenever he ran by below there, the woman taunted him as he went by. For he had no way of climbing up there to beat her. Then at one time, hither came that husband of hers and bellowed. He was all covered with scars here on his body where he had been attacked, and he was lean to the point of starvation.

Then he told her: "Your brothers are starving to death. Now I shall go feed my body to them. Afterwards I shall come back to life," he told her.

"Very well!"

Then she went to her brothers.

"But they are not to crack my bones as they eat. They are to wrap them in a fresh hide; they are to put them away somewhere. When four nights have passed, I shall come running back."

So then she slew him. When four nights had passed, her brothers arrived.

"So it is you who have come!" she said to her brothers.

She wept; she grieved for her husband.

So much of this.

(34) The Foolish Maidens and One-Leg

Coming-Day

kā-kīsikāw-pīhtukāw.

mīkiwahpis äh-ayātsik, äh-nīsitsik, pisisik äh-papāmuhtätsik, äh-ntunahkik ka-mītsitsik, nama wīhkāts ayīsiyiniwa wāpamäwak. nōhtä-wāpamäwak ayīsiyinwa.

" māskōts nāpäw wāpamāyahkih, ka-wīkimānaw, ka-mītsiyahk ta-nipahtāt, " itwäw aw ōmisimāw ; " äkā wiya pakwātāhkan. kiyām pikw īsi māyātisitsi nāpäw ka-wīkimānaw, " itwäw aw ōmisimāw.

" äha' , " usīma.

äkwah äkutah ay-ayāwak päyakwanaw.

kītahtawä, äh-tipiskāyik, äh-wīh-nipātsik, äh-kitāpamāt aw ōmisimāw atsāhkusah, päyak kīhkānākusiyiwa ; päyak apisīsisiyiwa ; namuya kīhk-ānākusiw.

ōmisih itwäw aw ōmisimāw : " hä äy, nisīmis, tānik ōki unāpämiyahk, tāniki näki atsāhkusak ! nāha kā-kīhkānākusit äwakō niy ōnāpämiyān, äkwa kiya ana k-āpisīsisit, " itäw.

" äha' , " itik.

äkus äh-itäyihtahk : " äh-miyusit awa kā-kīhkānākusit, " äh-itäyih-tahk.

äkus īsi nipāwak. kīksäpā äh-päkupayit aw ōmisimāw, kā-kiskäyimāt nāpäwa ä-pimisiniyit. äh-māmīskunāt, " nāpäw ! " itäyihtam.

waniskāw, äh-kutawät.

" nisīmis, waniskāh ! " itäw.

wāpamäw mīna äkutä äh-nipāyit nāpäwa. awa äh-waniskāt usīmimāw, miywäyihtam nāpäwa äh-pimisiniyit. aw ōmisimāw itwahamawäw usīmisah uwīkimākana ōhi, tahkih ä-wīh-pāhpit, äh-miywäyihtahk nāpäwa äh-ayāwāt. äkus äh-kīsitäput, mīnisah pikuh äh-mītsitsik. äkusi waniskāw aw ōsīmimāw uwīkimākana : pōtih miyusiw uskinīkiw. āh, miywäyihtam awa aw īskwäw. mwästas ka-waniskāyit aw ōmisimāw uwīkimākana, pōt ōhi mituni kisäyiniwa, ä-wāpistikwānäyit. pakwātam ä-kisäyiniwiyit. äkusi äkutah ay-ayāwak. kapä-kīsik ay-apiyiwa. äyikuhk ä-tipiskāyik, aspin wāh-wayawiyiwa. äyikuhk käkāts äh-wāpaniyik, kā-takuhtäyit. äkusi äh-kawisimuyit. kīksäpā māna kāh-mītsisutwāwi, äh-papāmuhtätsik usīma, mīnisah äh-ntunahkik, mīna mistaskusīmina, äkutōwah piku äh-mītsitsik, nama wīhkāts mātsiyiwa ōwīkimākaniwāwa. kītahtawä kinwäsk äh-ayātsik, kītahtawä namuya nisitawinam askiy aw ōmisimāw. tāpiskōts äkā wīhkāts äh-wāpahtahk askiy itäyihtam. kaskäyihtam, pīhtaw äh-pakwātahk kisäyiniwa äh-unāpämit. piyisk pisisik papāmuhtäw. äkwah kaskäyihtam nam āwiya äkutah kā-kīh-ayātsik ; äyukō uhtsi k-ōh-kaskäyihtahk. kītahtawä māka mīna äh-papāmyhtätsik, mistaskusīmina äh-papāh-mōnahahkik, kā-wāpahtahk wistäpahkwayikamik.

" nisīmis, äkwah kiyōkätān ! " itäw.

tāpwä äh-ituhtätsik, äh-takuhtätsik, awan ōhi, nōtukäsiwa.

" nōsisimak, nōsisimak ! " itwäyiwa.

pīhtukäwak. asamäwak mistaskusīmina.

" häy, tāpwä mistahi kitatamihināwāw, nōsisimitik ! kayās nōh-akāwātān, äh-pähtamān ä-kih-päsīkawiyäk, ' mistaskusīminah äh-utinahkik tahkih, ' äh-itikawiyäk. "

" nōhkō, ä-kīh-tsī-päsīkawiyāhk ? " itäw.

" äha' ! " itäw ; " nōsisä, ' ntaskīnāhk äh-ayāyāhk, ' äh-itäyihtaman tsiw ōma ? "

" äha'. "

" namuya, nōsisä ! ispimihk ōma äh-ayāyäk, ōtä nīhtsāyihk ä-kiyuhtuhtahikawiyäk, " itik ; " nōsisä, ' ayīsiyiniwak tsī[1] *k-ōnāpämiyāhk, ' äh-itäyihtamäk ? "*

" äha'. "

" namuy āniki. k-āyisiyinīwiyin, ' atsāhkusak, ' k-ätwäyin, äkutōwāhk anah. nama tsī, ' anah kā-kīhkāyāsōwät äwaku unāpämiyān, ' kikīh-itwān ? äwakōw ana kōnāpämin kisäyiniw. äkwah, ' ana äkā kā-taspāsōwät äyakuni unāpämiyin, ' kikīh-itäw kisīm ; äyakō uhtsi anih ōskinīkiwa kā-wītsäwāt, " itäw.

" hääy, nōhkō, kah-kīh-tsī-pihkuhinān ta-kīwäyāhk ? nipīkiskātänān nitaskīnān, " itäw.

" hāha', nōsisä ; ayisk kikākäpātisin, äh-kīh-nōhtäh-unāpämiyin atsāhkus, " itik ; " haw, nōsisä, ntunah mistaskusīmin. mustusu-mäy itah äh-astäk, äkutah sākikihkih mistaskusīmin, äwakō kik-ōhpinän. äkutah

[1] The interrogative particle comes near the beginning of the sentence, usually after the first word; here it is inserted in a quotation of which it does not form a part. Compare its insertion in the verbal complex immediately below.

anima ä-pakunäyāk ōm askiy," itik ; " miskamäku, ka-pä-wīhtamawinäwāw."

" äha'."

wayawīwak, äh-ntunahkik. kiyipa miskamwak. äkusi ntawi-wīhtamawäwak ōhkumiwāwa.

" nimiskänān," itäw.

äkusi utinamiyiwa usäkipatwānäyāpīsiyiw.

" hāw, ōmah mistikuhk tahkupitamuhkäk. äwak ōma kik-ōh-pihkuhunäwāw. watsistwan usīhtāk, äkutah kit-āpiyäk. kīsihtāyäku, wīh-nīhtakusiyäku, kiya ka-wäwäkistikwānān. namuya ka-nanātawāpin, iskuh kitaskiyiwāw utihtamani. awa pikuh kisīmis äywaku kit-ätāpiw. äkwah nätä takusiniyäku, ' nōhkō, äwakwä kisäkipatwānäyāpiy !' kik-ätwān, nōsisä," itäw ; " haw, niyāk !"

wayawīwak, äh-ituhtätsik ōm ītah kā-pakwanäyāk askiy, äkwah äyusīhtätsik watsistwan. ä-kīsihtātsik, äkwah mistikuhk tahkupitamwak uma pīsākanāpīs, äkwah äh-pōsitsik watsistwanihk, äkwah ä-nīhtakusītsik, ähpakitāpīhkänisutsik. wäwäkistikwānäw awa umisimāw, äh-nīhtakutsihkik.

kītahtawä, " nisīmis, tānähki ? namäskwa tsīh kitaskiyinaw kiwāpahtän ?"

" äha' ! nama tsäskwah !" itäw.

kītahtawä kā-wāpahtahk.

äkwah aw ōskinīkiskwäw, " nisīmis, namā tsäskwa kiwāpahtän ?"

" äkwa ani niwāpahtän."

" hāy hāy ! äkwah ä-wīh-takusiniyahk kitaskiyinaw, nisīmis ! mahtih nik-ätāpin !"

" äkā wiya ! kikīh-itikunaw kōhkuminaw, ' iyikuhk kitaskiyiwāw takuhtäyäku, kik-ätāpin,' ä-kīh-itisk," itäw umisah.

tahkih äh-yāsipayitsik, tahkih kakwätsimäw usīma taskiyiwāw.

" käkäts äkwah ! mitun äkwah kīhkānākusiwak mistikwak," itäw.

" nisīmis, mahti nik-ätāpin !" itäw.

äh-,[1] *" äkā wiyah ! kisiwāk äkwah !" äh-itikut usīmisah, āhtsi pikuh wīh-kakwä-itāpiw. ātah ä-wäwäkistikwānänikut usīma, kītahtawä pāskipayikōw, äh-itāpit. paskipayiyiw ōma k-ō-sakāhpisutsik. nīhtsipayiwak äkwah. äh-kinusiyit mistikwah, äkutah akutāskutsiniyiw ōma watsistwan.*

" tāpwä kikakäpātisin, nimisä, ä-kīh-itikuyahk kōhkuminaw äkā kātāpwähtaman !" itäw ōmisah.

hāh, miywäyihtamwak utaskiyiwāw äh-wāpahtahkik. māka namuya kīh-pihkuhōwak ; äkutä ay-akusīwak. kītahtawä kā-wāpamātsik äh-pāpahtāyit mahīhkanah.

" häy, nisīmis, nka-wayäsimāw mahīhkan ; ka-pihkuhikunaw," itäw.

" äha'."

ā, kisiwāk äh-pimuhtäyit, ōmis ītäw : " mahīhkan !" äh-kitāpamikut, " pihkuhinān ! äh-mitsimuhuyāhk, nīhtininān. ahpōh itsih ka-wīkimitinān."

" yahōh ! namuya nnihtā-kīhtsäkusīn. mīna kik-ōtamihināwāw ; ma wīhkāts päyakwanuhk ntayān, pisisik äh-papāmätsihuyān," itwäyiwa.

" säsäy ! misawā tsī tapwä ka-kīh-wīkimitanān, äh-māyātisiyan, ähkinwāpäkihkwäyan, äkwah äh-kāsakäyan, käkway näpahtāyanih äh-päyakōhkaman !" itäw, äh-kīhkāmāt.

---

[1] Start toward including quotation in verbal complex.

äkusih ay-ayāwak äkutah. kītahtawä kā-wāpamātsik mīnah kutakah äh-pāpahtāyit. pōtih äyukunih pisiwah.

" *hä äy, nisīmis, äyakuw äkwah ka-wayäsimānaw ! nihtāwāhtawiwak äkutōwahk.—häh !* " *ōtah äh-pimuhtäyit,* " *hä ä äy, pisiw !* "

" *tānähkih !* "

" *pihkuhinān ! ahpōh itsi ka-wīkimitinān, äkā äh-käh-nihtinisuyāhk !* "

" *yahō ! namuya nnihtā-kīhtsäkusīn. īh wāpahtah nitsihtsiyah : nama käkway naskasiyak,* " *itwäyiwa.*

" *ä ä äy, misawā tsī tāpwä ka-kīh-wīkimitāhk, äh-māyātisiyan, äh-pitikuhkwäyin, äkwah äh-māmāhkisitäyin, äkw ä-nā-napakāskituyäyin ?* "

ay-ātawäyimäw. äkusi nakatikuk. ā, kaskäyihtamwak, ä-nōhtä-nihtakusītsik. piyisk kinwäsk äkutah ayāwak. kītahtawä kā-wāpamātsik mīna äh-pāpahtāyit.

" *nisīmis, äywakw äkwah nika-wayäsimäw. wīh-wawīwinawisiw*[1] *äwaku,* " *itäw.*

" *aha'.* "

kisiwāk ä-pimipayiyit ōtah, " *hä äy !* " *itāpiyiwa.*

" *kīhkwahākäs, kinihtā-kīhtsäkusīn. pihkuhinān. äh-kustamāhk äkā äh-kīh-pihkuhisuyāhk. ahpōh itsi, pihkuhiyāhkuh, ka-wīkimitinān,* " *itäw.*

" *yahō, kiwīh-wayäsiminäwāw !* " *itwäyiwa.*

" *namuya ! tāpwä ka-wīkimitinān,* " *itäw.*

" *aha' !* "

haw, pä-kihtsäkusiyiwa.

äy-utihtikutsik, " *niya nīkān !* " *itwäw aw ōmisimäw.*

" *namuya ! awa pitah kisīm.* "

" *äha'.* "

äkwah nayōmäw äkwah.

" *hāw, äkā wiyah mustsih sāmiskaw nitakuhp. mituni nikihtsäyimäw nitakuhp,* " *itäw ōh ōskinīkiskwäwa.*

mituni wäwäkīw aw ōskinīkiskwäw, äh-nīhtsatsiwähtahikut. piyis pihkuhäw. pitah ōmis īsi tah-tihtipīw awa kīhkwahākäs, ōhō utakuhpah äh-kāsīsimāt, ōh iskwäwa ä-sāmiskawāyit.

āsay äkusi itäyihtam nah ōmisimäw : " *nihtinitsih, nika-yīpātsihimāwa utakuhpah, kā-kistäyimut !* " *itäyimäw.*

äkwah päy-āmatsiwäyiwa mīna.

äy-utihtikut, " *hāw, mitunih wäwäkapih. nitakuhp nikihtsäyimäw,* " *itwäyiwa.*

äkwah nayōmik.

äkwah äh-nihtsatsiwäyāhtawiyit, päyāhtik äh-pimuhtäyit, " *kisiskāhtä, kīhkwahākis ! nikaskäyihtän, äh-nōhtä-sāmiskamān ntaskiy,* " *itwäw aw īskwäw.*

---

[1] Obscure; perhaps a nonce-formation. If really derived from *wīwah :* "his wife" (*nīwah :* "my wife," etc.), perhaps read *wīh-uwīwinawisiw ;* for the general rule in Central Algonquian is that secondary derivatives of dependent nouns are made from the form with third person possessor; those in *nī-, kī-, wī-* prefix *u-*, e.g. *wīstāwah :* "his brother-in-law": *uwīstāwiw :* "he has (as) a brother-in-law"; and those in *nō-, kō-, ō-* prefix *uw-*, e.g. *ōhtāwiya :* "his father": *uwōhtāwiyiw :* "he has (as) a father." But the Sweet Grass dialect seems to confuse this initial accretion with reduplication, e.g. *uyōhtāwiyiw :* "he has (as) a father," cf. below.

āhtsi pikuh päyāhtik äh-pimuhtäyit, waniskāpayihōw aw īskwäw, äh-kāhkapä-tähtapit, ōhi kīhkwahākäsah ä-sikitāt. kwätipipayihuyiwa, äh-nīhtsipayihuyit.

" tāpwä kikakwāhyakihāw nitakuhp ! nikatawatäyimāh nitakuhp ! " itwäyiwa.

äkwah aw īskwäw kā-nīhtsipayit, uhtsikwanihk kaskatäsin.

äh-ati-sipwähtäyit kīhkwahākäsah, aw ōmis ītwäw uskinīkiskwäw : " hä äy, kīhkwahākäs, iyikuhk kā-wīsakisimiyin, ntawāts anim ītah kā-sikitak kitakuhp kākikä äkutah ta-masinasōw, isku tit-āskīwik ! " itäw ; " mīna tsäskwa ayīsiyiniwak kā-wīh-uhpikitsik, nama wīhkāts kika-mōwikwak ; ka-wīhtsäkisin, ä-sikititān. ' kīhkwahākäs, ' k-äsiyihkātikwak. "

äkusi sipwähtäyiwa.

" hā, nisīmis, itah mihtah äh-mihtsäkih ituhtahin, " itäw.

ā, tāpwä utakuhpihk äkwah utāpātik usīma, itah mihtah äh-mihtsäniyikih, äkutah ä-takuhtayikut. äkwah usīhtāw wīkiwāw nīpiyah uhtsi uma wīkiwāw, äkwah aw ōskinīkiskwäw pisisik äh-nikuhtät, äh-pōnamawāt umisa, ä-wīsakäyihtamiyit ōm ōskātiyiw, äkā mwāsi äh-nipāyit, äh-wāh-wāpaniyik äh-pōnahk. piyisk kinwäs wīsakäyihtam ; namuya kīh-īniyiw. kītahtawä usīma äh-nikuhtäyit, utinam mōhkumān, äh-kīskisahk ōm ōskāt itah kā-nātwāhtiniyik. äkwah mistahi sākamuyiw ōma uskan. äkwah äwakō tsīkaham mōhkumān uhtsi, äh-atsiwikahahk. äh-kīwät aw ōskinīkiskwäw, kā-pähtahk äh-matwä-tsīkahikäyit umisah. tsīk äh-ihtät, pōnihtāyiwa, äh-akwanahamiyit, äh-kātāyit. namuya wāpahtam äh-tōtamiyit umisah.

ōmis äh-itäyihtak aw ōmisimāw : " nisīmis nika-wīwin, " äh-itäyihtahk, " ōmōw uhtsi niskāt, " äh-itäyihtahk.

äh, kītahtawä äh-nāh-nikuhtäyit māna aw ōskinīkiskwäw, kītahtawä mōyäyimäw umisah, kākikä äh-kitāpamikut, tahkih ä-wīh-pähpihikut. kītahtawä äh-nikuhtät, äkutah pitsikīskisīsah kā-tah-twähuyit.

" ay, iskwäw, ä-wih-wīhtamātān ! āsay äkwah kīsihtāw kimis uskāt äh-kīnikikahahk, äh-wīh-wīkimisk. kika-nipahik. tapasī ! " itik.

säkimik.

" tāntäh māk ōma k-ätuhtäyān ? "

" ōtä isi, nātakām, " itäw.

" aha'. "

äkwah kätikuskawäw wanakwaya.

" häw, nanakwātik, nikuhtäk ! nimis mätwä-täpwātikuyäku, ' tsäskwa ! ' itihk ; ' mäkwāts ninikuhtān, ' itihk. ' kiyipa ! ' itikuyäku, ' tsäkwah ! kīsāts mihtsät ä-wīh-nātwāhamān, sōskwāts t-āwatāyān, ' itāhkäk. "

äkusi nikuhtäwak äkwah ōki anakwayak. tapasīw äkwah aw īskwäw.

kītahtawä, " nisīmis ! " ka-matwä-itwäyit ; " pōni-nikuhtä ! "

äkwah, " tsäskwah ! " itwäyiwa.

" kiyipa ! " ka-matwä-itwäyit, kītahtawä, " nīwa ! " k-ätwäyit ; " pä-kīwä ! nikaskäyihtän, nīwa, äkā mayaw äh-pä-kīwäyan, " twäyiwa.

ā, tapasīw wiya.

piyisk ihkäyihtam awa, " pä-kīwä, nīwah ! " k-ätwät äyak ōmisimāw.

" tsäskwah ! "

" yahā ! "

kītahtawä, " ka-kisiwāhin, nīwa ! pä-kīwä ! "

" tsäskwa ! pit āni niwīh-nikuhtān. "

piyisk pasikōw aw īskwäw, äkwah ä-nitawāpamät usīma.

" wäsā nama kipa-pähtän ! äkwah kiwīh-ntawi-pakamahutn, nīwa ! sām nama mayaw kipä-kīwān ! "

äkwah päyak pikw uskāt äh-āpatsihtāt, itäh kā-nikuhtäyit usīma äh-ituhtät, tsīki äh-ihtāt, pōni-nikuhtäyiwa, kutak ä-sakāyik äkutä kāw ä-matwäkahikäyit, ä-matwä-nikuhtäyit.

" āhtsi pikw āwa kāh-nikuhtät, äh-āta-tā-täpwātak ! kikisiwāhin ani ! utihtitāni, kika-pakamahutin, nīwa ! " itäw usīma.

äkwah äh-ituhtät, kītahtawä kā-wāpamāt anakwayah äh-nikuhtäyit. äkwah pahkisinwak ōki anakwayak.

" hā hah, tāpwä nikisiwāhik nīwa, kā-tapasīt ! ntsawāts itah atimitāni, ka-nipahitin, nīwa ! " itäw, äkwah äh-ntunawāt.

kītahtawä kā-mātāhāt, äkwah äh-mitihtāt.

" namuya misawāts ta-pīhtsāw itäh tsit-ätāmuyin ! " itäw usīma.

ah-pa-pimāmut aw īskwäw, äkwah kisiwāk äh-päy-ihtāyit umisah, " hä äy ! tāntäh ōyā nimusōm ! " itwäw.

itah äh-at-ispahtāt, kā-pä-matāwisiyit wākayōsah.

" hä äy, nimusō, kakwä-pimātsihin ! nimis niwīh-nipahik. "

" hä hä hä ä ha ha, nōsisä, nīstah ni, nikustāw kimis ! manitōwiw kimis. äyiwähk māka ōtah kwayask itāmuh. "

hā, äkusi tapasīw aw īskwäw. hah, kiyipa ka-pä-sākäwāt aw īskwäw.

" näy, iskōh äwakunih äh-mamisīt nīwa ! " itwäw, äh-utihtāt ; " wākayōs, tāniwā nīwa ? "

" tāniwātukä ! " itäw.

" nama tsī kikātāw nīwa ? kiyipah wīhtamawin ! "

" namuya nikiskäyimāw. "

" kiyipah ! māskōts kikātwawin. käka ka-nipahitin. "

āta wīh-kisiwāsiw wākayōs ; māka namuya nāntaw kīh-tōtam. äyak ōmō uhtsi kā-kīskāyik uskāt, äyak ōhtsi tah-tahkiskawäw ōhi wākayāsah ; nipahäw. āhtsi pikw äkutah ntunikäw. āsay mīna mātāhäw usīma ; kwah mina mitsihtsipayīstawäw, kītahtawä mīn äkwah kisiwāk äh-atiy-askōwāt.

" häy, tāntäh ōyā nimusōm ? " itäw, pōt äwakuni misi-pisiwa.

mīn iyikuhk awa äyāta-takuhtät, " hä äy ! iskōh äwakuni āta äh-mamisīt nīwa ! " itäw, ä-näsōwisit, äh-takuhtät ; " misi-pisiw, tāniwā nīwa ? "

" tāniwātukä ? "

" kähtsināh kikātuwin ! kiyipa wīhtamawin tāntah äh-kātat niwa ! käka ka-nipahitin ! "

" namuya nikiskäyimāw. "

" kiyipa ! kititin uma ! wīhtamawin nīwa ! "

pisinä ä-wīh-kitutāt, āsay kā-tahkiskawāt ; nipahäw. tāpiskōts ayisk äh-pāskiswāt, äy-isi-sōhkäpayiyik uma uskāt aw ōmisimāw. äkwah ä-kīh-nipahāt, äkwah mina nitunam itah äh-pimuhtäyit usīma. tāpwä mīna mātāhäw. äkwah mina mitihtäw. kītahtawä mīn äkwah kisiwāk äkwah iskōwäw.

kītahtawäh ōmis ītwäw : " hä äy ! tāniwähk nimusō ? " itwäw.

pōtih, ä-sākäwäpahtāt, kā-wāpamāt misi-kināpikwa.

" hāw, nōsisä, äyiwähk ōtah pimāmuh ! āta wiy āni nikustāw kimis ; manitōwiw, " itik.

" hä ä äy, nimusō, kakwä-nipah ! ä-wīh-nipahit anah nimis ! " itäw.

äkus äh-tapasīt. kītahtawä äh-sākäwäpahtāt.

" häy ! iskōh äwakuni äh-mamisīt nīwa ! "

itah ōhi k-āyāyit, äkutah nakīw.

" misi-kinäpik, tāniwā nīwa ! "

" hā, namuya nikiskäyimāw. "

" wīhtamawin ! äh-kātwawiyin, ka-tah-tahkiskātin ! ka-nipahitin ! "

aha, pisinä äh-waskawiyit, tahkiskawäw ; piyis nipahäw. äkusi mīna äh-ntunawāt usīma. kītahtawä kā-wāpahtahk itah äsah ä-kīh-pimāmuyit. äkwah mīn äyakuni mitihtäw. äkwah nama käkway ta-mamisīt aw uskinīkiskwäw. kītahtawä äh-pa-pimipahtāt, kā-wāpahtahk sākahikan äh-āhkwatiniyik, kā-wāpamāt ayīsiyiniwah äkutah tāwakām. äyakunih äkwah mōskīstawäw. äh-utihtāt, awīn ōhi, päyakukātäyiwa, äh-misikitiyit asiniya äh-nayōmāyit, äh-tsīkahwāyit miskwamiya, äh-äskäyit.

" häy, nimusō, kakwä-pimātsihin, ä-wīh-nipahit nimis ! pimātsihiyini, ahpōh itsi kika-wīkimitin, " itäw.

namwāts kitāpamik ahpōh ; namuya kitutik.

" hä äy, ahpōh itsi kik-ōyōhtāwīmitin,[1] pimātsihiyini ! "

namwāts ahpōh wīh-ka-kitāpamik. äkwah kaskäyihtam, kisiwāk äkwah äh-päy-ayāyit umisah.

" häy, kiyipah kakwä-pimātsihin, ä-wih-nipahit manitōw ! "

äkuyikuhk kā-kitāpamikut.

" namuy āna manitōw. kimis ana, " itik.

" äha' ; māk ä-wīh-nipahit ! kakwä-pimātsihin. ahpōh itsi kik-ōstäsimitin, " itäw.

" aha' ! "

äkwah miywäyihtam awa päyakukāt.

" ōtah, " itäw, " ōtah pimipahtāh ! "

tāpwä äkutah ati-pimuhtäw tastawayakap.[2]

" äyakw āni anima mäskanās ati-pimuhtä. mäskanāhk kapāyani, kawāpahtän wāskahikanis. äkutah takuhtäyani, äkutah pīhtukähkan, nisīm, " itäw äkwah.

ā, miywäyihtam aw uskinīkiskwäw. tāpwä ati-sipwäpahtāw äkwah. ayis äkwah pätisāpamäw umisah. tāpwä äh-ati-kapāt um ä-sakāyik, äh-matāwisit, kā-wāpahtahk wāskahikanis mituni ä-miywāsiniyik. äkutah pīhtukäw.

äkwah awa utihtäw wītsi-päyakukātah.

" päyakukāt, tāniwā nīwa ? " itäw.

tāpiskōts äkā nānitaw äh-itāt, āhtsi pikuh äh-äskäyit.

" kiy uma k-ätitān, päyakukāt ! kanik ōt āw an [3] äkā wīh-kitāpamit ! tāniwā nīwa? kititin ōma ! käka ka-nipahitin, äkā kā-wä-kā-kitusiyin ! " itäw.

āhtsi pikuh ta-tsīkahikäyiwa, nanātuhk äh-itāt, " nka-kakwä-wīhtamāk, " äh-itäyihtah.

kītahtawä, " yahō, k-ätwäwitahk awa ! namuy āna kīwa ; kisīm ana ! namuya ōma kiya nāpäw ; kiy ōm īskwäw, ' nīwa, ' k-ätwäyin ! "

" namuya ! " itwäw aw īskwäw ; " kiyipah kiyām wīhtamawin : tāniwā nīwa ? tāntah kah-at-ītuhtät ? "

" ōtah, " itäw.

" tāntah ? "

" ōtah, " itäw.

---

[1] See preceding note.

[2] The only meaning I could obtain, "between the legs" does not fit One-Leg. If it is correct, the narrator has gone astray.

[3] Expression unfamiliar to me, or error of notation; the word division is a guess.

" tāntah māka, päyakukāt ? kiyipah wīhtamawin ! "

ōtah tastawayakap äh-wīh-ati-sīpāsit, ōhi kā-nayōmāyit asiniyah pakitsiwäpinäyiwa. mituni kīskiskōhik āpihtōsiyaw ; nipahik äwakuni.

āhtsi pikw āwa tsa-tsīkahikäw. kītahtawä äkuyikuhk kiskisiw äkwah ōh iskwäwa ; kīwäw. äkwah äh-takuhtät uwāskahikanisihk, awīn ōhi, kīh-apiyiwa usīma. äkwah nama käkway titā-mītsiyit. hāw, mihtsät wāpamäw pīhtatwānah äh-akutsiniyit aw īskwäw. ay-apiw awa päyakukāt.

" yahō, äkā käkway nisīm ntasamāh, k-ätapiyān ! " itwäyiwa, äy-utinamiyit kitsōhtsikanis, äh-miyāhkasamiyit, äkwah ä-yōhtänamiyit. ä-kituhtāt, kiyipa mustuswah kā-pāpayiyit. äyakuni pāh-pimwäw. iyikuhk äh-mästinahk päyak ōma upīhtatwāna, äkuyikuhk pōyōw. tapasiyiwa kahkiyaw mustuswah.

" hā, nisīm, nīpisisah kahkiyaw ntaw-ōtinah, " itäw.

äkusi wayawīw aw ōskinīkiskwäw, äh-utinahk atsusisah.

äkwah, " hā, nisīm, kahkiyaw utäyaniya pikuh utinah, " itäw usīma, tāpwä aw īskwäw ä-kīh-utinahk mōhkumān, äh-ntawi-manisahk utäyaniyah piku, kahkiyaw äh-utinahk, äkwah ä-pīhtukät, äkwah utäyaniyah äh-kīsisahk, äh-paminawasut.

äkwah aw ōskinīkiskwäw äh-wayawīt, ä-wīh-pōnahk, ōhi mihtsät kā-nipahāyit ustäsah namwāts käkway pimisiniyiwa. māmaskātam, mihtsät ä-kīh-nipahātsik mustuswah. äkusi äkwah ä-kīh-mītsisutsik, äkwah awa nāpäw utinam manitōwäkin, käkway äh-ati-miyāt ōh ōsīma.

" haw, nsīm, usīhtāh kitayōwinisah, " itäw ; " niya pisisik nitatuskān miskwamīhk, tahkih äh-äskäyān. äkāya wīhkāts,—kītahtawä awiyak ōtah ta-takusin, nisīm,—kāya wīhkāts tawinamaw awiyak, piyäyakuyini, " itäw.

tāpwä ka kāh-kaskikwātisōw aw ōskinīkiskwäw, äkwah äh-miyuhut, äh-nānapātsihut. äkwah miyusiw. täkuhtätsi awa päyakukāt, miywäyihtam äh-kwayātsih-paminawasuyit usīma. äkutah uhtsi mistahi kitimākäyimäw ōh ōsīma. nama wīhkāts wayawītimihk käkway nātamiyiwa, āt äh-päyakukātät.

iyikuhk kätātwāwi utäyiniya, " hāw, nisīm, nānapātsihuh ; wawäsī, " äh-itāt, kīsi-wawäsiyitsi, äh-miyāhkasahk ukitsōhtsikanis, " hāw, ispimihk akusī ōtah waskahikanisihk, " itäw ; " kituhtāh, " itäw ; " pāpayitwāwi mustuswak, iyikuhk kahkiyaw sipwäpayitwāwi, tapasītwāwi, ka-nīhtakusīn, " itäw usīma.

äkusi miyāhkasam ukitsuhtsikanis. ā, kihtsäkusīw aw uskinīkiskwäw. äkwah wiya päyakukāt äh-kīsi-yōhtänahk, kituhtāyiwa, kā-pāpahtāyit mustuswah, äh-waskāpayiyit wīkiwāw ōma. äkwah awa päyakukāt äh-nōtsihāt iyikuhk, äkuyikuhk ä-tapasiyit, äkuyikuhk nīhtakusīw aw uskinīkiskwäw.

ä-kīh-akutāt kitsuhtsikanis, " nhāw, nsīmis, nīpisisah ntaw-ōtinah, " itäw.

wayawīw, ä-ntaw-ōtinahk atsusisah.

äh-kīh-pīhtukatāt, " pisisik utäyaniya utina, nisīm ; wiyās wiya namuya. tahtwāw mänahuyāni, täyaniyah piku kit-ōmītsiwiniyin, äy-isi-takahkäyimitān, nisīm, " itäw ; " ä-kīh-kitimākisiyin, ' mahtih nka-kitimākäyimäw nisīm ! ' k-ätäyihtamān, " itäw.

äkusi ntaw-ōtinam pisisik utäyaniyah. äkwah äkutah ayāwak.

" nisīm, äkāya wīhkāts wayawī. iyāt-äwiyak-wāpamatsi, täkuhtätsi, namuya ka-wayawīn. mihtsätiwak ayīsiyiniwak äkā katawa äh-itātsitsik, " itäw.

" äha' . "

tāpwä kā-kapä-kīsik päyakōw aw īskwäw, wiya awa päyakukāt pisisik äh-ntaw-äskät miskwamīhk. äkwah wāh-tipiskāki, äh-kīwät awa päyakukāt, miywäyihtam kākikä äh-kwayātsi-paminawasuyit usīma. mistahi kitimākäyimäw, pikuh ä-kakwätsimāt ta-mästinahkik utäyiniyiw, iyikuhk miyästinamiyihki, äkuyikuhk, " nānapātsihuh, " äh-itāt usīma.

kiyīsi-nānapātsihuyit, " haw, äkwah mīna kīhtsäkusī, nisīm, ta-kituhtāyin. "

tāpwä kätuhtāyitsi, mustuswah pāpayiwa, ä-waskāpayit wīkiwāhk, äh-nōtsihāt päyakukāt. äyikuhk miyästinahk wīpisisah, äkuyikuhk äh-pōyut, äkus äh-tapasiyit. äkusi nihtakusīw aw īskwäw, äh-utinahk atsusisah, äkusi utäyaniya pisisik äh-utinahk. äkusi māna ōhi kā-nipahāt äh-āpisisiniyit, ä-sipwähtäyit.

äkusi ay-ayāwak, wiy āwa tahtu-kīsikāw miskwamīhk äh-atuskät awa päyakukāt. kītahtawä kiskäyihtam päyakukāt ä-wīh-takusiniyit awiya.

ōmis ītäw usīma : " nisīmis, wīh-takuhtäw wīsahkätsāhk.[1] *äkā wiya tawinamawāhkan. namuya kwayask äh-itäyihtahk. usām mistahi misiwä pähtākaniwiw äh-kitimākäyimitān, ' ta-kakwä-misi-wanātisiwak, ' äh-itäyimikawiyah, " itäw usīma.*

äkusi, ā, kā-kapä-kīsik äh-nakatāt usīma, kītahtawä äh-mästinahk kākāts utäyiniya, päyakwäw pikuh ta-mītsisutsik iyikuhk äy-iskunahk, kītahtawä ka-takuhtäyit : nāpäw. namuya nisitawäyimäw äwakuni wīsahkätsāhkwa.

" yāh, tawinamawin, nisīm ! " itik.

namuya wīh-ka-kitutäw, nanātuhk äh-āt-ītikut.

kītahtawäh ōmis ītik : " nisīm, ' ntaw-ispīhtsih-nōtsih mustuswak. kisīminaw ta-nitumäw. kākāts äkwah ta-kīwäyāhk ; usām nama kākway ta-mītsiyāhk kīksäpā, ' äh-itwät kistäsinaw,[2] *" itäw.*

äkusi tāpwähtam aw uskinīkiskwäw.

" niwih-wayäsimāw äkwah nisīm, " itäyihtam, " awa päyakukāt. "

tāpwä tawinamawäw wīsahkätsāhkwa. pīhtukäw.

" hāhā, nisīm, kakwäyāhuh äh-nanāpātsihuyin. kākah ka-tsatsiwihik kistäs, äkā kākway äh-kīsisaman, " itäw.

" tāpwä ! " itäyihtam aw ōskinīkiskwäw, usām äh-kitimākäyimikut ustäsah. ōm äh- , " äkusi kitik, " äh-itiht, k-ōh-tāpwähtawät. tāpwä äh-kīsi-kīhtsäkusīt wāskahikanihk aw īskwäw, kituhtāw, kā-pāpayit mustuswah.

ispih äh-kiskäyihtahk awa wīsahkätsāhk kisiwāk äh-ayāyit, " haw, ōhih atsusisah kahkiyaw ta-wīh-yōskihtakāwa ! " itwäw wīsahkätsāhk.

tāpwä, äkutōwahk. iyātah-pimwātsih mustuswah, pīkuhtiniyiwa ; namuya kīh-nipahäw. piyisk pīkiskwäyiwa mustuswa.

" maskamātān wīsahkätsāhk usīma ! " itik.

piyis mästinam atsusisah. äkuyikuhk pä-kīwäw päyakukāt. äkwah äh-āta-pä-kisiskāhtät, ä-sākäwät, āsay kā-kīpiwäpiskamiyit wāskahikan, äh-

---

[1] The whole motif, beginning where One-Leg befriends the young woman, occurs in a Menomini story, in which, however, the mischief-maker is not the Culture Hero, but the rabbit, and "prairie-weeds were his arrows." Three facts seem relevant, though I do not know in what relation they stand: (1) the story is not a typical Culture Hero tale, but one of the few in which he appears as a secondary character; (2) in general the Culture Hero plays a more important part in Menomini thought and story than in Cree; (3) his name in Menomini is *me'napus* : "Big-Rabbit," which may be an adaptation of Ojibwa *nānabuc* (Cree, eastern, *nänapus*), or of some earlier Menomini form.

[2] "Our elder brother," part of the deception, since everyone is Wisahketchahk's younger brother or sister, cf. immediately below, where he says *nisīm* : "my younger brother."

nīhtsipayit aw īskwäw. māka päyak awa mustus äh-wāpiskisit, māna äwaku māna äh-pä-nīkānuhtät, äkusi äyakuni nama wīhkäts wīh-nipahäw päyakukät; äwakw āwa kā-wāpiskisit mustus iskwäwa ōhi wäpahwäw, upakwahtäh-uniyiw äh-tāpisi-kwāskwahamwāt utäskanah uhtsi. äkus äh-tapasīt. kahki-yaw mustuswak tapasīwak. kwāsihimāwa usīma, aspin äh-ati-mātōyit.

äkwah awa wīsahkätsāhk mātōhkāsōw, tāpiskōts äh-mawīhkātät ōh ōskinīkiskwäwa, äkutä äy-isi-sipwäpahtät, " äkā nika-kisiwāhā päyakukāt ! " äh-itäyihtahk, tāpiskōts äh-pimitisahwāt ōh iskwäwa, māka äh-tapasīt, ōhi päyakukātah äh-tapasīhāt.

äkwah päyakukāt äkutah ayāw. mistahi mihtātäw usīma. äyikuhk äh-pōni-pīkiskātät usīma, äkuyikuhk usīhtäw wāskahikan, äh-ispāyik, äh-misāyik. äkuyikuhk äh-kīsihtāt, äkwah atsusisah usīhtäw ; piyis mihtsät sākaskinäyiwa upīhtatwāna.

äkuyikuhk äkwah, " mahtih nisīm nka-pimitisahwāw, " äkwah itäyih-tam, äkwah äh-sipwähtät, äh-mitihtät mustuswa.

āta kayās äh-kīh-pimuhtäyit, māka miyu-mitihtäw. kītahtawä, wāhyaw äkw äh-ayāt, kītahtawä kā-wāpahtahk sākahikan äh-misikamāyik. pōt ōma kīh-ministikōwiyiw, äkutah kā-mihtsätiyit mustuswah. ä-kitāpamāt, kā-wāpamāt ōhi äh-wāpiskisiyit mustuswa. kāsōw. piyisk utihtam sākahikan, sisunä sākahikanihk äh-pimisihk.

" hāw, ōma kā-wīh-pōtātamān t-āti-miskwamīwiw ! " itwäw.

ōma nipiy pōtātam : āpihtaw isku miskwamīwiyiw. kīhtwām pōtātam : äkwah āsuwakāmä-miskwamīwiyiw.

kīpipayihōw, " nka-wīh-āpakusīsiwin ! " äh-itwät.

äkusi sipwäpayiw, miskwamīhk äh-pimipayit. pihkuhōw. äkusi äkwah pasikōw. äkwah itah mānah ä-nāh-ntawi-minihkwäyit pisiskiwa, äkutä kāsōw, sakāhk äh-pa-pimisihk, " māskōts pä-kwāpikätsih nisīm, " äh-itäyihtahk, äkwah ä-wīh-kakwä-wāpamāt usīma. kītahtawä kā-wāpamāt ōhih kā-wāpiskisiyit mustuswa, itah äh-itiskwäpiyit, äkutah äh-apiyit usīma, mituni äh-kanawäyimimiht usīma. äkwah kustäw ta-kih-ituhtät, " tāns ätukä nka-kīh-isi-kisiwāk-usāpamak ? " äh-itäyihtahk.

äkutah äh-pa-pimisihk, kītahtawä kā-pä-takusiniyit sihkusa.

ōmis ītäw : " āstam ! " itäw.

takuhtäyiwa.

" tānähki ? "

" hāw, ōki tsī māna mustuswak kisiwāk kōy-ōtihtāwak ? "

" äha'. "

" hāw, wītsihin. äkāya wīhtamaw awiyak ōtah äh-ayāyān. kaskih-tāyani, nisīm ta-wīhtamawat itah ta-päy-ituhtät, " itäw.

" hä hä hä ha ha ! " itwäyiwa ; " āyiman ! mistahi kanawäyimāw kisīm. äkusi kwatakäyimōw kisīm, " itik ; " äyiwäh mahtih ! māk āni pakwātam tsīki awiya t-ätuhtäyit, " itik.

äkusi sipwähtäyiwa, kuntah tatāstawāyiyihk mustusunāhk äh-papā-mipayit awa sihkus, äh-wīh-kakwä-utihtät ōh īskwäwa. piyis tsīk äh-ayāt, āsay wāpamik ōhi wāpiski-mustusah. äkusi äh-at-ituhtäyit, tapasīw. äkwah tuhtäw ōhi päyakukātah.

ōmisih itäw : " āyiman. nama nikiw-utihtäw kisīm. nīstah nikustāw wāpiski-mustus, " itwäyiwa ; " mayaw äh-wāpamit, āsay nipä-nātik, " itik ; " āyiman ani ! " itik.

äkus īkatähtäyiwa. äkwah ay-ayāw äkutah. kītahtawā äkutah kā-pä-twähuyit tsāhkayōwa.

" āstam ! " itäw.

päy-ituhtäyiwa.

" ōmah kā-papā-māna-wīsāhkawatsik pisiskiwak, mituni tsī kinakay-āskawāwak ? "

" ääha' ! ahpōh māna wāwikaniwāhk tiwähōwak, āskaw ustikwāniwāhk mina, " itäw.

" māka awa wāpiski-mustus, askaw tsī mīn äyakō kisiwāk kusāpamāw ? "

" äha' ! āskaw ustikwānihk utäskanihk nitwähōwān. namuya māna pakwātam, " itik.

" hāw, kitimākäyimin ! wītsihin ! nisīm ana kīmōts kakwä-wīhtamaw ōtah äh-ayāyān. nāntaw isi ta-kakwä-kwāpikäw, " itäw.

äkusi, " äha' ; nka-wīhtamawāw, " itäw.

hā, äkusi aspin äw-ōhpihōyit, kuntah mäkwā mustusunāhk papāh-ta-twähōw awa tsahtsahkayōw. piyisk wāpamäw äh-apiyit ōhi wāpiski-mustus-wah, äkutah mina ōh ōskinīkiskwäwa äh-apiyit. äkutah tsīki ntawi-twähōw, kuntah ä-papāh-tsatsahkatahikäsit. piyisk wāwikaniyihk twähōw ōhi wāpiski-mustuswah. kītahtawā utäskaniyihk äkwah twähōw. ka-kitāpamäw awa aw uskinīkiskwäw, äh-wawiyatäyimāt, " tāpwä namuya kustam käk-way ! " äh-itäyimāt, äh-kāh-kitsōyit. kītahtawā k-ōhpipayihuyit, ustik-wānihk äh-twähuyit aw uskinīkiskwäw. namuya pisiskäyimäw, äh-wawiy-atäyimāt. kītahtawā utihtimanihk twähuyiwa.

ōmis ītik : " äkāya ka-säkimitin, äh-kitutsitān, " itik, uhtawakāhk äh-itiskwäyiyit ; " kistäs takusin, ' ntawi-wīhtamaw, ' äy-isit. ōtah kwāpik-äskanāhk pimisin ; ' ta-kakwä-pä-kwāpikäw ! ' kitik. "

" tāpwä tsī ? äh-tāpwäyan tsī ? " itäw.

" äha' . "

āh, äkusi uhpihāyiw. äkwah ōhpihāt awah, äkuyikuhk päkupayiw awa mustus.

ōmis ītäw aw īskwäw : " hāw, nka-ntawi-minihkwān. ninōhtäyāpāk-wān, " itäw.

" ō, namuya ! kutak awiyak ta-nātam, ta-minihkwäyin, " itäw.

" namuya ! uhtsitaw ä-nōhtä-ntawi-minihkwäyān. usām ninästusin, päyakwanuhk tahkih äh-apiyān, " itäw ; " piyis niskātah niwīh-wīsakäyih-tän. nika-sisāwuhtān, " itäw.

" āha' . kiyipa kakwä-takuhtä ; äkāya mīn āwiyak wītsäw, " itäw, äh-pakwātahk kutakah nāpäwah ta-kitōtikuyit ōh īskwäwah awa mustus.

" äha' , " itwäw aw īskwäw, äh-ati-pasikōt, äh-sipwähtät.

tāpwä äh-utihtahk sākahikan, " āstam, nisīm ! " k-ätikut ustäsah.

äh-utihtāt, " namuya tsiy āwiyak kisiwāk ayāw ? " itik.

" äha' . "

" ā, nisīm, äh-pä-nātitān ōma, " itäw, äh-utsämāt aw īskwäw ustäsah.

äkusi mīna pōtātam ōma sākahikan : āpihtaw iskuh miskwamīwiyiw. mīna äh-pōtātahk, äkwah akāmihk iskuh.

" hāw, nisīm, kawipayihuh, " itäw ; " nka-wīh-āpukusīsiwinān. "

äkwah miskwamīhk pimipayiwak. kākāts äh-kīsi-pihkuhutsik, äkuyi-kuhk ati-tihkisuyiwa ōhi miskwamiyah. piyisk āta wiyah pihkuhōwak, äkwah äh-tapasītsik.

äkuyikuhk äkwah wāpamikuk, " hayāhāy ! päyakukāt usīma kwāsihäw ! nawaswātähk ! " ka-matwä-itwäyit mustuswah.

äkusi äkwah sōhkih pimipahtāwak usīma. kītahtawä wāhyaw äh-ayātsik, äkwah wīh-atimikwak, usām nawats ä-yīkitsikawit aw īskwäw.

" ā, nisīm, kitakuhp wäpinah ! " itäw.

wäpinam, äwakuh äy-utihtahkik ōki mustuswak, kuntah äh-kitutsik, ä-nōhkwātahkik. ā, äkuyikuhk wāhyaw ihtāwak. äyikuhk äh-mästātahahkik um ākuhp, äkuyikuhk mīna nawaswäwak ōki mustuswak.

mīna ä-wīh-atimikut, " hā, nisīm, äkwah kanakwayak wäpin ! "

wäpinäw wanakwayah, āsay mīna äyakunih kunt äh-kitutsik, ä-nōhk-wātātsik wanakwayah. iyikuhk mīna äh-kitamwātsik, äkuyikuhk mīna sipwäpayiwak.

äyikuh mīna ä-wīh-atimikutsik, " nisīm, äkwah mīna kimaskisinah wäpinah ! "

mīn äyakuni äh-wäpinahk, utamiyiwak mustuswak, ä-nōhkwātahkik. äyiwähk māna wāhyawäs itāmōwak. äkwah mīna äh-mästātahahkik ōhi maskisinah, äkwah mīna pimitisahwäwak mīna. äh-wīh-atimikutsik, mīna utāsah wäpinam. mīn äyakuni utamiwiyiwa. äkwah mīn äyakuni äh-kitāyit, āt äkwah kisiwāk ayāwak mīna.

mwähtsy äkwah mīna ä-wīh-atimikutsik, " ā, nisīm, äkwah kipakwah-tähun wäpinah ! " itäw.

min äyakō wäpinam. wāwīs äwakō kiyipah kitāyiwa. kiyipah äkwah wīh-atimikwak.

äkwah kisiwāk äkwah wīkiwāw äh-ayāyik, " hā, nisīm, äyiwähk mahtih äkwah kiskutākay wäpinah ! " itäw.

wäpinam aw ōskinīkiskwäw. äyuku mīna mayaw äh-utihtahkik ōki mustuswak, äyuku mīna utamiyiwak. äkuyikuhk äkwah mituni tsīk äkwah ayāwak wīkiwāhk. äyikuhk äh-kitātsik, äkuyikuhk mina sipwäpayiwak. äkuyikuhk äkwah utihtam wīkiwāw. kīhtsäkusīwäpinäw usīma ; äkwah wiya wīstah kīhtsäkusīpayihōw. āsay äkutah takupayiwah. käkāts käsiskāk, iyikuhk äh-askōkutsik. äkwah äh-utinahk wīpisisah, äkwah äh-nōtsihāt ōhi mustuswah, miyästinahki, kutakah äh-utināt upīhtatwāna, piyisk mitun īskwahäw mustuswah. nama mayaw kīh-nipahäw ōhi ka-wāpiskisiyit mustuswah. kītahtawä äkwah kā-pikwastahwāt, tāpiskōts äkwah mistahi ä-maskawisiyit.

ōmis ītik : " päyakukāt, kisākōtsihin. āpihtā-kīsikāhk päy-isi-kawiw-äpinin. nīkān ōtä ayīsiyiniwak kit-ōhpikiwak. ' āpihtā-kīsikāhk wāpiski-mustus äy-ōtaskät nikitimākäyimik, ' itwätsi, ta-tāpwäw, " itik.

" hā, wāpiski-mustus, isi-kawipayihuh ! " itäw.

tāpwä äkutä isi-kawipayihuyiwa.

" yahōh, pōnihihk päyakukāt ! kika-mästsihikunaw. piyisk sāsay kōkimāminawa sākōtsihäw ! " itwäyiwa ; " pōnihihk ! "

tāpwä nanānis āh-isi-sipwähtäyiwa. äkwah nīhtakusīwak usīma.

äkwah äh-pustayōwinisäyit usīma, " mituni nanāpātsihuh, nisīm ! " itäw.

tāpwä nanāpātsihōw.

mituni äh-kīsi-wawäsīt, "hāw, wayawītān, nisīm!" itäw. ä-kīh-waya wītsik, " ā, nisīm, namuy äs āni kinwäsk äh-kīh-miyu-wītsätān. usām tahkih nka-mukuskātsihikawin kiy ōhtsi. piyisk ka-misi-wanātsihik awiyak. usām kikitimākäyimitn. tsäskwah ayīsiyiniwak kā-wīh-ihtātsik itah askīhk, ōtah äh-āpihtawitākusik k-ōtaskīn. päh-päyak ayīsiyiniw kika-kitimākäyi-māw, ōki tsäskwah kā-wih-ōhpikitsik ayīsiyiniwak. äkwah niya pahkisimō-

tāhk nik-ōtaskīn. ayīsiyiniw kīhkīhk päyak, ' nikitimākäyimik äh-päy-akukātät ! ' itwätsi, ta-tāpwäw. ha, nsīm, päskis äkutäh ōhtsi ä-wih-kana-wäyimitān, " itäw ; " niyā, nisīm, sipwähtä ! " itäw, wīst ä-sipwähtät, nīsōyak äh-ntaw-ōtaskītsik.

äkuyikuhk äh-iskwāk ātayōhkäwin.

The two had a small tipi, and all the time they walked about, looking for things to eat, and never saw any people. They wished to see people.

"If by any chance we see a man, we shall marry him, that he may kill things for us to eat," said the elder sister; "Do not then reject him. Rather let us marry a man, no matter how ugly," said the elder sister.

"Yes," said the younger.

There they stayed on.

Then at one time, after dark, as they were about to sleep, when the elder sister looked at the stars, one looked bright, and another was small and did not shine brightly.

Thus spoke the elder sister: "Oh, little sister, would we might have them for husbands, yon stars! Would I might have as husband that one that shines so brightly, and you the smaller one," she said to the other.

"Yes," answered she.

What she thought was, "The one that shines brightly is handsome."

* * * * * * * * * *

She got up and built the fire.

"Little sister, get up!" she called to her.

* * * * * * The elder sister pointed out her husband to the younger, smiling all the while with gladness at having a husband. Then she cooked; they had only berries to eat. Then the younger sister's husband got up: he turned out to be a handsome young man. Oh, she was glad, that woman. Then, after a bit, when the elder one's husband got up, he turned out to be a very old man with white hair. She did not like his being old. So then they stayed there. The men sat there all day. Only at nightfall they left the house and went away. When daybreak was near, they came back. Then they went to bed. In the morning, when they had eaten, the elder sister and the younger would always go tramping about, looking for berries and for wild turnips, for these were all they had to eat; but never did their husbands hunt. Then at one time, when they had been there quite a while, the elder sister did not recognize the land. It seemed to her as if she had never seen the land where they were. She was sad, and she disliked having for husband, as it turned out, an old man. Then she kept wandering about. And she was sad because there were no other people there where they dwelt; this it was made her sad. Then at one time, when as usual they were wandering about, digging wild turnips here and there, they saw a lodge of old leather.

"Little sister, now let us visit!" she said to her.

When, accordingly, they went there, when they arrived, there was an old woman.

"My grandchildren, my grandchildren!" she said.

They went in. They gave her wild turnips to eat.

"Dear me, you really please me much, my grandchildren! For a long while I have been hankering for these, ever since I heard that you were brought here, you of whom they say, 'They are always getting wild turnips.' "

"Grandmother, is it true, that we have been brought here?" she asked her.

"Yes!" she told her; "Grandchild, do you really think, 'We are on our earth?' "

"Yes."

"By no means, my grandchild! It is up aloft that you are, and from yon place below that you were conveyed," she told her; "Grandchild, do you think, 'They are mortal men whom we have as husbands'?"

"Yes."

"Not they. When you of mortal race say, 'Stars,' of that kind is he. Did you not say, 'The one that shines bright let me have for my husband'? That old man you now have for your husband. And, 'That one that does not shine so clear may you have for your husband,' you said to your younger sister; that is why she has that youth for her mate," she told her.

"Alas, grandmother, can you help us to get back home? We are pining for our earth," she told her.

"Yes, my grandchild; but indeed you were foolish to want a star for your husband," she told her; "Well then, grandchild, look for a wild turnip. The wild turnip which grows out from where the buffalo dung lies, that one you will pull up. That is where this land is pierced," she told her: "When you find it, come and tell me."

"Yes."

They went out of the lodge and looked for it. They soon found it. So then they went and told their grandmother.

"We have found it," she told her.

Then she took the little thong with which her braid was tied.

"Now then, tie this to a tree. By means of this you will get away and reach your destination. Make a nest in which you will sit. When you have finished it, and are ready to descend, you yourself will wrap your head. You will not look about to see things until you reach your earth. Only your younger sister here will look. Then, when you arrive down there, 'Grandmother, here is the thong of your braid!' you will call, my grandchild," she told them; "Well then, be off!"

They went out of the lodge to the place where the land was pierced, and made the nest. When they had finished it, they tied it to a tree with that little rawhide thong, and got into the nest, and descended, letting themselves down on the string. The elder sister wrapped up her head as they swung down.

Presently, "Little sister, how is it? Do you not yet see our earth?"

"No! Not yet!" she told her.

Presently she saw it.

Then that young woman, "Little sister, do you not yet see it?"

"Yes, now I do."

"Splendid! Now we shall come back to our earth, little sister! Do let me look!"

"Don't! Our grandmother told us, 'Only when you have reached your earth will you look,' she told you," said she to her elder sister.

All the time they were going down she kept questioning her younger sister about their earth.

"We are almost there now! The trees appear plainly now," she told her.

"Little sister, do let me look!" she asked her.

"Do not! We are near now!" her younger sister told her, but still she longed to take a look. Although her younger sister held the covering round her head, suddenly she threw off the cover and looked. The string broke by which they were tied. Down they went. The nest caught on a tall tree and hung there.

"Really, you are foolish, big sister, not to heed what our grandmother told us!" she said to her elder sister.

Oh, they were glad to see their earth. But they could not get there; they hung there aloft. Presently they saw a wolf who was running that way.

"Oh, little sister, I shall fool the wolf; he will get us down," she said to the other.

"Yes."

When he came near, she said to him, "Wolf!" and when he looked at her, "Get us down. Take us down from where we are caught. We are even willing to marry you, if you like."

"Yoho! I am not a good climber. Also, you would be a bother to me; I never stay in one place, but travel about all the time," said he.

"Faugh! Do you suppose we would really marry you, ugly as you are, and long-faced, and a glutton, who, whenever you kill anything, eat it all by yourself?" she told him, reviling him.

And so there they stayed. Presently they saw another who came running that way. He turned out to be a lynx.

"Oh, little sister, let us fool this one! The like of him are good climbers. —Hey there!" as he walked by, "Hey, hey, lynx!"

"What is it?"

"Get us down from here! We will even marry you, if you like; we cannot get down!"

"Yoho! I am not a good climber. Look here at my paws: I haven't any nails," said he.

"Ho ho, do you suppose we would marry you in any case, you ugly fellow, with your crumpled-up snout and your big feet and your flat rump?"

She gave up the chances of him. So he left them. Oh, they were sad, because they wanted to get down to earth. Finally they had been there a long time. Presently they saw still another come running that way.

"Little sister, now I shall cheat this one. This one will be eager to take wives," she said to the other.

"Yes."

As he came running close by there, "Hey, hey!"

He looked up.

"Wolverine, you are a good climber. Get us down from here. We are frightened and do not know how to get down. We are even willing, if you rescue us, to marry you," she told him.

"Hoho, you mean to fool me!" said he.

"No! Really, we will marry you," she told him.

"Very well then!"

So he came climbing up.

When he had reached them, "Me first!" said the elder sister.

"No! Wait; first comes your sister."

"Very well."

Then he took her on his back.

"Now then, do not rub yourself directly against my robe. I think a great deal of my robe," he told the young woman.

The young woman wrapped herself very carefully in her clothes, and he climbed down with her. At last he had got her down. Then, before doing any more, the wolverine rolled himself over and over, like this, to wipe his robe clean where the woman had come into contact with it.

Then that elder sister thought, "When he takes me down, I will dirty up his robe, the conceited fellow!" she thought of him.

Then he came up again.

When he had reached her, "Now then, sit carefully wrapped in your clothes. I think very highly of my robe," he said.

Then he took her on his back.

And as he climbed down, because he went slowly and carefully, "Hurry up, wolverine! I am miserable with longing to set foot on my earth," said the woman.

* * * * * * * * * * He rolled over and flung himself down to the ground.

"It is horrible, what you are doing to my robe! Did I not tell you that I valued my handsome robe!" he cried.

As the woman fell, she broke her leg just above the knee.

As the wolverine started to go away, the young woman said to him "Oho, wolverine, since you have thus given me a painful fall, let your robe needs forever be marked there * * * as long as there be, an earth!" she said to him; "And later, when mortal men grow into life, never shall they eat you; * * * * * * * * * * 'Wolverine,' they will call you."

Then he went away.

"Oh, little sister, take me where there is plenty of firewood," she said to the other.

So then her sister dragged her on her blanket-robe, taking her to a place where there was plenty of firewood. Then she made a lodge for them out of leaves, and then all the time the young woman gathered firewood, to keep up a fire for her sister, who was suffering from her leg and sleeping hardly at all; every morning she built a fire. At last she had been sick a long time; her wound would not heal. Then at one time, while her younger sister was gathering firewood, she took a knife and cut off her leg there where it was broken. The bone stuck far out. She whittled it with the knife, shaping it off small. When the young woman was coming home, she heard the sound of her elder sister chopping away at something. When she got near, the other stopped her work and covered it with her robe, to hide it. She could not see what her elder sister had been doing.

But what the elder sister thought was this: " * * * * * * * * " she thought.

Then presently, as the young woman continued to gather faggots, presently she suspected her elder sister, because she always stared at her with an unceasing smile. Presently, as she was gathering wood, a tomtit came and alighted here and there.

"Oh, woman, I want to tell you this! * * * * * * * * * * She will kill you. Run away!" it told her.

She was frightened by these its words.

"But where can I go now?"

"Off here, toward the north," it told her.

"Yes."

Then she took off her sleeves.

"Now, my sleeves, gather faggots! When you hear my elder sister calling to you, tell her, 'Wait a bit!' Tell her, 'I am just getting wood.' If she says to you, 'Hurry!' then, 'Wait a bit! I want to split a lot of it first, so that I can bring it without delay,' do you tell her."

Accordingly, those sleeves then gathered wood. The woman fled.

Presently, "Little sister!" came the other's call; "Stop gathering firewood!"

Then, "Wait a bit!" said those things.

"Be quick!" she was heard to call, and presently, "My spouse!" she cried; "Come back home! I am getting sad, my spouse, because you are so long about coming home," she said.

Oh, but as for her, she fled.

Then at last elder sister grew tired of calling, "Come home, my spouse!"

"Wait a bit!"

"Yah!"

Presently, "You will anger me, my spouse! Come home!"

"Wait a bit! I first want to get some faggots."

At last the woman arose and looked for her sister.

"You actually pay no heed at all! Now I am going to club you, my spouse! You are taking too long about coming home!"

Then, using her one leg, she went to where her sister had been gathering wood, and when she got near, the other ceased chopping wood, and then, in another grove, again the other was noisily chopping and making a din at the gathering of firewood.

"She keeps right on getting wood, when I call and call to her! Now you have made me angry! When I reach you, I shall club you, my spouse!" she said to her sister.

But when she got there, presently she saw the sleeves that were gathering wood. Then those sleeves fell to the ground.

"Oho, truly my spouse has angered me by running away! Wherever I overtake you, I will kill you, my spouse!" she said to her, and began seeking her.

Presently she found her tracks and began to trail her.

"In any case there will be no distance great enough for you to flee!" she called to her sister.

Oh, she was swift, even though she had only one leg. Presently, as that woman fled, and her elder sister came nearer and nearer, "Alas! Where is that grandfather of mine who once was here!" she cried.

In the direction in which she was running, a bear appeared in the path.

"Alas, grandfather, try to save my life! My elder sister means to kill me."

"Dear me, dear me, dear me, my grandchild, I too am afraid of your sister! Of manitou nature is your sister. At any rate, flee straight ahead in this direction."

Accordingly, the woman fled. Oh, quickly that woman came into sight.

"Fie, my spouse has come down to depending on this creature!" she cried, when she came to him; "Bear, where is my spouse?"

"I do not know where she is!" he told her.

"Are you not hiding my spouse? Quick, tell me!"

"I do not know anything about her."

"Quick. No doubt you are hiding her from me. I am ready to kill you."

The bear was getting into a rage, but he could do nothing. With her cut-off leg she kicked the bear; she killed him. She kept up the search in that place. Again she found her sister's track; again she set out on her trail, and presently again she was close upon the other's heels.

"Alas, where is my grandfather who once was here!" she said to one, and he turned out to be a Great Lynx.

And when that person arrived there, "Ha, my spouse has come down to placing vain hope even in this creature!" she cried to him, weary, as she arrived; "Great Lynx, where is my spouse?"

"Why, where can she be?"

"Surely you are hiding her from me! Quick, tell me where you are hiding my wife. I am quite ready to kill you!"

"I know nothing about her."

"Quick, I tell you! Tell me about my spouse!"

Before he could speak to her, she had already kicked him; she killed him. For it was just as if she had shot him, so powerful was that elder sister's leg. And when she had killed him, then again she looked for where her sister had gone. Again she found her trail, and again she tracked her. And presently again she was following close upon her.

Presently she cried, "Alas, where is my grandfather?"

There, as she went running round a bend, she beheld a Great Serpent.

"Now, my grandchild, at any rate, flee along here! But truly I do fear your elder sister; she is of manitou nature," he told her.

"Alas, my grandfather, try to kill her! That elder sister of mine means to slay me!" she told him.

She fled. Presently she came running into sight.

"Ha, even in this creature my spouse places hope!"

Where the other was, she stopped in her course.

"Great Serpent, where is my spouse?"

"Ha, I know nothing about her."

"Tell me! You are hiding her from me, and I am going to kick you! I'll kill you!"

As soon as the other budged, she kicked him; in the end she killed him. Thereupon again she sought her sister. Presently she saw where she had passed in flight. Then again she followed her trail. Now there was nothing in which that young woman could place hope. Presently, as she ran on and on, she saw a frozen lake and a man at the centre of it. She ran toward him. When she reached him, why, he was one-legged, and was carrying a huge stone, and pounding the ice to make holes in it.

"Alas, grandfather mine, try to save me; my sister means to kill me! If you save my life, I am willing to marry you," she said to him.

He did not even look at her; he did not speak to her.

"Alas, alas, if you like, I will even take you as my father, if you save my life!"

He would not even glance at her. She was in distress, for her sister was now coming near.

"Alas, quickly try to save me, for a manitou means to kill me!"

Only then did he look at her.

"That is no manitou. That is your elder sister," he told her.

"Yes; but she means to kill me! Try to save my life. I am even willing to take you as my elder brother," she told him.

"Yes!"

Now that One-Leg was pleased.

"Here," he told her, "run along here!"

So she went along there, passing through between his legs.

"Keep walking along that little path there. When you reach the main trail on the shore, you will see a little wooden house. When you reach it, then do you enter it, my little sister," he told her now.

Oh, the young woman was glad. And so away she ran. For even now she saw her elder sister approaching. Really, when on her way she came to the shore where were those woods, and came upon the trail, she saw a little wooden house, a very good one. She entered it.

That other one came to her fellow one-leg.

"One-Leg, where is my spouse?"

As though she had said nothing at all to him, he kept on breaking the ice.

"It is to you I am saying this, One-Leg! Truly he does not even mean to look at me! Where is my spouse? It is you I am asking this! I am ready to kill you, since you do not care to talk to me!" she told him.

He kept on pounding away, while she spoke to him in all manner of ways, thinking, "I will make him tell me."

Presently, "Oho, the noise this person makes! She is not your spouse; she is your sister! You are not a man; you are a woman, who go saying, 'my wife'!"

"No!" cried that woman; "Quickly now tell me: where is my spouse? Where has she gone from here?"

"Right here," he said to her.

"Where?"

"Right here," he told her.

"But where, One-Leg? Quick, tell me!"

When she made to go under between his legs, he dropped the stone which he was carrying. It fell on her and cut her straight through at the middle; it killed her.

The man went right on pounding. Presently at last he remembered that woman; he went home. When he arrived at his little wooden house, there sat his little sister. But there was nothing for her to eat. She saw a great many quivers hanging there. One-Leg stayed there.

"Ho, here I am sitting like this, and have not given my little sister anything to eat!" he said, and took a little flute, and burned incense under it, and opened the door. When he played on the flute, quickly the buffalo came running. He shot them with arrows. When he had used up one of his quivers, he ceased. All the buffalo ran away.

"Now, little sister, go take up all my arrows," he told her.

So the young woman went out and took up the arrows.

Then, "Now, little sister, take all their tongues, but nothing more," he told his sister, and so the woman, taking a knife, went and cut only the tongues; she took them all and came in, and cooked the tongues, preparing a meal.

But when the young woman went out to get fuel, none at all lay there of the many beasts her brother had killed. She was amazed, for they had killed many buffalo. When, then, they had eaten, the man took some black stroud and gave it to his little sister.

"There, little sister, make clothes for yourself," he told her; "I am always working at the ice, making holes. Do you never—for at some time someone will come here, little sister—do you never open the door for anyone, when you are alone," he told her.

So then that young woman kept sewing for herself, and then dressed in good clothes and decked herself out. Then she was handsome. Whenever One-Leg came home, he was glad, because his sister had already done the cooking. Therefore, he became very fond of his sister. She never had to fetch anything out of doors, even though he was one-legged.

Whenever they had eaten up the tongues, "Now, little sister, deck yourself out; put on your finery," he would tell her; and, when she had put on her finery, and he had burned incense under his flute, "Now climb up on the roof of the house," he would tell her; "Sound the flute," he would tell her; "When the buffalo come, then only after all of them have gone away, after they have fled, only then you are to climb down," he told his little sister.

Then he held his flute in the incense smoke. The young woman climbed aloft. Then, when One-Leg had opened the door, she blew the flute, and the buffalo came running, circling round their dwelling. Then, when One-Leg made war on them, and after they had fled, then the young woman climbed down.

After hanging up the little flute, "Now, sister, go take up my arrows," he told her.

She went out and took up the arrows.

When she had brought them in, "Take nothing but tongues, little sister; but not the meat. Whenever I kill game, you shall have only the tongues for your food, so highly do I esteem you, little sister," he said to her; "When you were in piteous straits, 'Let me befriend my little sister!' was my thought," he told her.

Accordingly, she went and took only the tongues. So there they dwelt.

"Little sister, never go out of doors. Even though you see somebody, even though somebody comes here, you are not to go out of doors. There are many persons of evil ways of life," he told her.

"Yes."

So daily all day long the woman stayed alone, while One-Leg always went to chop holes out on the ice. And, just before nightfall, when One-Leg came home, he rejoiced that his sister always had the meal cooked and in readiness at his coming. He took loving care of her, asking her only whether they had used up the tongues, and when they were used up, telling her to put on her finery.

Then, always, when she had put on her finery, "Now, climb up again, little sister, to play on the flute."

Truly, whenever she sounded it, the buffalo came, and circled round their house, while One-Leg attacked them. Only when he had used up his arrows did he stop, and then they would run away. Then the young woman came down and took up the arrows, and took only the tongues. And then always the creatures which he had killed would come back to life and go away.

In this way they dwelt there, and as for One-Leg, he worked every day on the ice. Then at one time One-Leg knew that someone would come there.

Thus he spoke to his sister: "Little sister, Wisahketchahk will come here. Do not open the door to him. It is no good he has in mind. Too much it is heard everywhere that I take loving care of you: 'Let an attempt be made to have them go to destruction,' is the thought concerning us," he told his sister.

And so, as all day long each day he left his sister, presently, when she had almost used up the buffalo-tongues and had left only enough for one meal, then someone arrived: a man. She did not recognize him as Wisahketchahk.

"Ha, open the door for me, little sister!" he said to her.

She would not speak to him, though he said all kinds of things to her.

Then he said to her, "Little sister, 'Do you meanwhile go hunt buffalo. Our little sister will call them. It is almost time for us to go home; and there is nothing for us to eat in the morning,' so spoke our big brother," he told her.

Then the young woman gave credence.

"I shall fool my little brother now," he thought, "That One-Leg."

Accordingly, she opened the door for Wisahketchahk. He entered.

"Ho, little sister, hurry and deck yourself out. Soon your big brother will come upon you and find you laggard, with nothing ready cooked," he said to her.

"That is so!" thought the young woman, for her big brother was so kind to her. When she was told this, "He bids you so," it made her give credence to him. So, after climbing to the top of the little house, she blew on the flute, and the buffalo came running.

When Wisahketchahk knew that they were near, "Now let the shafts of all these arrows be soft!" said Wisahketchahk.

Truly, so they were. Although he shot arrows at the buffalo, they broke and fell as they struck; he could not kill the animals. At last the buffalo spoke.

"Let us rob Wisahketchahk of his little sister!" they said of him.

At last he had used up the arrows. By this time One-Leg was coming home. But, though he came walking fast, when he came within sight, they had already knocked over the wooden house, so that the woman fell to the ground. Now, one of those buffalo, which was white, the one which always walked at the head as they came, this one One-Leg never tried to kill; and now this same white buffalo tossed the woman on its horns, pulling her up by her belt which it had caught on its horns. In this wise it fled. All the buffalo fled. His little sister was carried off, weeping afar as she disappeared from sight.

Then that Wisahketchahk pretended to cry, just as if he were lamenting the young woman, and ran off yonder, thinking, "I had better not get One-Leg angry at me!" and acting as if he were going in pursuit of the woman, but really making off in flight, fleeing from One-Leg.

One-Leg stayed there. He mourned greatly for his little sister. When he had passed the extreme of desolation at her absence, he built a high and great wooden house. He finished it, and then made arrows; at last he had many quivers all full.

Then, "Let me go in pursuit of my little sister," he thought, and set out, following the trail of the buffalo.

Although it was a long time since they had passed, yet he trailed them with ease. Presently, when he had gone a long ways, he saw a large lake. And there was an island, and on it were many buffalo. When he looked at them, he saw the white buffalo. He hid. At last he came to the lake, and lay down by the shore of the lake.

"Now, let that upon which I blow continue to turn into ice!" he said.

He blew upon the water: half of the way across it turned into ice. He blew on it again: all the way to the other shore it was ice.

He flung himself on the ground, saying, "Let me turn into a mouse!"

Then he ran off, running over the ice. He reached the other side. There he rose upright again. Then there where always the beasts went to drink, there he hid, lying among the trees, thinking, "Perhaps my little sister will come here to fetch water," for he meant to try and see his little sister. Presently he saw the white buffalo and by its head, as it sat there, sat his little sister, his little sister, closely guarded. Then he feared to go where she was, and thought, "I wonder how I can manage to see her from close by!"

As he lay there, presently there came a weasel.

He said to it, "Come here!"

It came to where he was.

"What is it?"

"Do you go close up to these buffalo?"

"Yes."

"Then help me. Tell no one that I am here. If you can manage it, tell my little sister to come here," he told it.

"Dear me, dear me!" it said; "That is difficult! Your little sister is closely guarded. Unhappy is your sister," it told him; "But at any rate, I will try. But he does not like anyone to come near," it told him.

So it set out, that weasel, running about here, there, and everywhere, between and under, through the buffalo country, trying to reach that woman. At last, when it had got near, already it had been seen by the white buffalo. So, when the other came toward it, it fled. Then it went to One-Leg.

It said to him, "It is difficult. I could not reach your little sister. I too fear the white buffalo," it said; "As soon as it saw me, it came for me," it said to him; "It is a difficult thing!" it said to him.

With that it went off. He stayed on there. Presently a blackbird came and alighted there.

"Come here!" he said to it.

It came to him.

"When in your way you go about delighting the beasts, have you got them much used to your presence?"

"Yes! I even perch on their backs, and sometimes on their heads," it told him.

"But this white buffalo, do you sometimes see him too from close by?"

"Yes! Sometimes I settle on his head and on his horns. He does not mind," it told him.

"Then, take pity on me! Help me! Try secretly to tell my little sister there that I am here. Let her try to come somewhere to get water," he told it.

Then, "Yes, I will tell her," it said to him.

Then up it flew and away, and here and there in the buffalo land the blackbird would alight. At last it saw the white buffalo sitting, and there sat the young woman. It went and alighted near by, pecking about here and there with its little beak. At last it perched on the white buffalo's back. Then presently it perched on the buffalo's horn. The young woman kept looking at it, pleased at its drollery, and thinking of it, "Truly, it fears nothing!" while it twittered away. Presently it flew up and perched on the young woman's head. She paid no attention to it, merely thinking it pleasingly droll. Presently it perched on her shoulder.

Thus it spoke to her: "Let me not frighten you by my speaking to you," it said to her, holding its head close to her ear; "Your brother has come here, and 'Go tell her,' he has bidden me. He lies there by the path where water is fetched; 'Let her try to come for water!' he says to you."

"Is it true? Are you speaking true?" she asked it.

"Yes."

Then it flew up. When it flew up, the buffalo awoke.

To it the woman said, "Now I want to go and drink. I am thirsty," she said to it.

"Oh, no! Someone else will fetch your drink," it said to her.

"No! What I want is to go and drink. I am weary of always sitting in one place," she said to it; "In the end I shall have pains in my legs. Let me stretch my legs by walking a bit," she said to it.

"Very well. Try to come back soon; and do not go with anyone," it told her, for that buffalo hated any other man to talk to the woman.

"Yes," said she, and arose and went off.

Really, as she came to the lake, "Come here, my little sister!" her big brother said to her.

When she came where he was, "Is no one near?" he asked her.

"No."

"Now, little sister, it is that I have come to fetch you," he said to her, as she kissed her big brother.

So then again he breathed on the lake: halfway across it was ice. When he blew on it again, then all the way to the far shore.

"Now then, little sister, lie down on the ground," he told her; "We shall turn into mice."

Then they ran along over the ice. When they had got almost across, the ice began to melt. At last, however, they got to the shore and made off in flight.

But now they were seen by the others, and "Ho, ho, ho! One-Leg is taking his sister away! Go after him!" they heard the buffalo cry.

So then he and his sister ran fast. Presently, when they had gone a long ways, the others were near to overtaking them, for the woman was too slow on her feet.

"Oh, little sister, throw down your blanket-robe!" he said to her.

She threw it down, and to it the buffalo came, wildly bellowing and licking it. Meanwhile they got far ahead. Only when they had devoured the blanket did the buffalo resume the chase.

When again they were close to overtaking them, "Oh, little sister, now throw away your sleeves!"

She threw away her sleeves, and again those creatures made a wild noise, as they snouted at the sleeves. Again, only when they had eaten them up, did they start out.

When again they had almost overtaken them, "Little sister, now throw away your moccasins!"

When she had cast away these too, the buffalo delayed to lick them. Each time they did, after all, flee quite a ways. And when they had entirely devoured the moccasins, they chased them again. When they were again about to overtake them, she threw off her leggings. Over these too the creatures delayed. When they had eaten these too, they were already near.

Then, as the creatures were again about to overtake them, "Oh, little sister, now throw your belt!" he told her.

She threw it too. This they devoured all the more quickly. Very soon they were now close to overtaking them.

Then, when their dwelling was already near, "Oh, little sister, now do you throw your dress!" he told her.

The young woman cast it off. As soon as the buffalo came to it, over it, too, they delayed. But by this time they were very near to their house. Only when they had eaten up the dress, did they start out again. But by this time he had reached their house. He threw his little sister to the roof; then he too flung himself up. Already the creatures arrived on the run. They nearly got there at the same time with him, so closely were they upon their heels. Then he took his arrows and made fight upon those buffalo, and when he had used them up, he would take another quiver, until at last he killed a great many of those buffalo. He had not yet succeeded in killing the white buffalo. But presently he wounded it, but it seemed to be as strong as ever.

It said to him, "One-Leg, you have defeated me. Come throw me toward the place of noon. Off in the future mortal men will grow into life. When one says, 'The White Buffalo that dwells in the place of noon has taken pity on me,' he will speak true," it said to him.

"Very well, White Buffalo, throw yourself thither!" he said to it.

Truly, to that place it flung itself.

"Ha, leave One-Leg alone! He will exterminate us. He has now defeated our chieftain!" they cried; "Leave him alone!"

And so in every direction they went away from there. Then he and his sister descended.

Then when his sister had donned her clothes, "Put on your best finery, little sister!" he told her.

Truly she decked herself out.

When she had put on all her ornaments, "Come, let us go out of doors, little sister!" he said to her. And when they were outside, "Now little sister, it appears that I should not long be able to stay happily with you. Too much always would I be assailed and troubled for your sake. In the end someone would destroy you. I am too fond of you. After a time, when mortal men come into being here on earth, then there in the place of the afternoon sun you will dwell. One and another mortal you will pity and befriend, of the mortals who in time are to grow forth. And I shall dwell in the land of the sunset. If in the course of time some mortal man says, 'The One-Legged has taken pity on me,' he will speak the truth. My little sister, at the same time from there I shall guard you," he told her; "Go, little sister, depart!" he said to her, as he too departed, and they went to dwell in two places.

That is the end of the sacred story.

(35) The Spirit Stallion

Mrs. Maggie Achenam

kā-wīhkaskusahk.

päyak iskwäw ntawi-mōnahikäw mistaskusīminah. kätahtawä wāyahtsāhk äh-ayāt, kahkiyaw kīwäyiwah uwītsäwākanah. äkwah wanisin. namuya kiskäyihtam tāntäh t-ätuhtät. kätahtawä misatimwa äh-wāpiskisiyit kā-pāpahtāyit. tapasīw ; nawaswātik ; kunt itäh itisahōk. äkwah tān-tahtu tipiskäw, nāntaw mitātaht kīsikāw nōtsihtāyiwa. itäh äh-ituhtahikut ōhi misatimwa, päyakwanuhk äkwah ayāwak ; iskwäw awa misatimwa unāpämiw. kätahtawä kutak äh-nīpiniyik, utsawāsimisiw misatsimusisah. äkwah māna papāmuhtäw pikw ītä iskwäw ; misatsimusisah wītsäwäw. wiyāpamātsih ayīsiyiniwah, tapasīw ; mihkawikīw mituni, tāpiskōts misatim.

kätahtawä, " kīwä äkwah, " itik unāpämah ōhi misatimwah ; " mihtsät ntawāsimisak ka-kīwähtahāwak ; kistäsak k-ätuhtamawatsik, " itäw.

" äha' . "

äkw āni ä-wayawīt, äkwah ä-wīh-kīwät. äkwah täpwäw ; kitōw awa misatim ; ukistakäwih pätsimäw misatimwah, nipīhk äh-uhtsih-mōskiyit ; äyakunih kahkiyaw äh-kīwähtatamawāt ustäsah. äkwah äh-kīwäpayit iskwäw, misatsimusisah ati-wītsäwäw. äkwah nätä takusin. misahkamik pätastimwäw. äkwah ōhi utsawāsimisah ōhi misatsimusisah awāsisah mätawākäyiwah ; tāh-tähtapiyiwah ; tapasīw awa misatsimusis. pimitisahwäw iskwäw utsawāsimisah.

äyaku mīna päyak ātsimōwin ä-kīsihtāyahk, misatimwah ä-kīh-unāpämit iskwäw. māmaskāts ä-kīh-ihkihk kayās äyaku mīna ; ka-pāhpinānaw mwästas.

A certain woman went to dig wild turnips. Presently, when she was in a marshy hollow, all her companions went home. Then she got lost. She did not know where to go. Then at one time a white horse came running toward her. She fled; it pursued her; it drove her all around. Then for how many nights? perhaps for ten days it did not cease from the pursuit. There where that horse made her go, there they stayed together; . . . . Then that woman would walk about here and there; the foal went with her. Whenever she saw human beings, she fled; she was very fleet of foot, like a horse.

Then at one time, "Now do you go home," her mate, the horse, told her; "Many of my children you will take home with you; you will lead them to your brothers," he told her.

"Very well."

Now the time came when she went out of the lodge to go home. Then he whooped; a loud call he gave, that horse; with his call he brought a great troop of horses that came out of the water; all these she took home for her brothers. And when she went home, the foal went along with her. Then she arrived yonder. She brought a great troop of horses. Then her children played with the foal that was her child; they kept trying to ride it; the foal ran away. The woman ran in pursuit of her child.

This is another story we have finished, of how a woman had a horse for her mate. This too is of a strange happening of long ago; we shall laugh afterwards.

(36) Aladdin

Mrs. Maggie Achenam

kā-wīhkaskusahk.

kätahtawä äsah ōtänaw ä-misāk. äkwah päyak awa kitsimākisiwi-wämistsikōsīs [1] *ä-papāmuhtät mānah ōtänāhk, käkway ä-wīh-kakwä-miskahk ta-mītsit. kätahtawä äh-kīwät, äh-tipiskäyik, mäkwāts äh-ay-apit, kā-pīhtukäyit mōniyāsah, tāpiskōts ukimāw äh-sīhōwit.*

" nikusis, " itik, " äh-pä-nātitān ; äkwäyāk ä-kiskäyihtamān äh-pimātisiyin, " itik.

äkw ōh ukāwiyah wäpimikuyiwah ; " nītim, " itik ōhi mōniyāsah, " nikusisinaw ka-pakitinamawin tsī ä-wīh-ōhpikihak ? "

" äha' , " itwäw.

mistahi sōniyāwah miyik. äkusi sipwähtahäw nāpäsisah. wāhyaw ituhtäwak misi-watsiy ; äkutäh takusinwak watsīhk. äkwah asiniy ä-misikitiyit yōhtänäw. nāpäsis äwakō äkutah pīhtukäw. mituni wanitipiskā-yiw ; apisīs pikō wāsaskutsäsiyiw. äkus īsi kipahuk ; kipaham.

" kahni pätā näma, nāpäsis, näma wāsaskutänikan ! "

äkwah utinam nāpäsis. äkwah ituhtäw iskwāhtämihk.

" pätāy ! muystas ka-pä-wayawīn ; nīkān miyin wāsaskutänikan ! " itäw nāpäsisah.

" namuya, " itwäw nāpäsis ; " usām ka-kipahun. "

äkusi, " kīpah pätāy ! "

---

[1] This word here, and *mōniyāw :* "Englishman," below, probably are intended merely as "white man."

piyis kisiwāsiw mōniyās awa. kipahwäw wātihk nāpäsisah. äkwah māh-mātōw nāpäsis. papāmitātsimōw pikw ītäh wātihkānihk. nama käkway wāpahtam. kätahtawä yāyīhtitäw utsihtsīs, kā-pustsipayiyit āhtsanisah.

" käkway, kā-tipäyimiyan ? " itik ōh āhtsanisah.[1]

" äh-nōhtä-wayawiyān. "

" umis ītwä : ' nikutwāsik iskwāhtäm, pāskihtäpayih ! ' itwä, nāpäsis, " itik.

äkwah nāpäsis, " nikutwāsik iskwāhtäm, pāskihtäpayih ! "

äkusi yōhtäpayiyiw. wayawīw nāpäsis. wāsaskutänikan päyak ayāw. äkw āhtsanisah tahkih äyakunih pīkiskwātikōw.[2] *äkwah sipwähtäw, äh-kīwät. äkwah äh-takusihk wīkiwāhk, ātsimustawäw ukāwiyah.*

" äkwah pätā kīkway[3]*; nika-kāsīhän niwāsiskutänikan, " itäw.*

äkwah miyik ; kāsīham.

" käkway nitawäyihtaman, kā-tipäyimiyan ? " itik mistāpäwah päyak. säkihik, wāsiskutänikanihk äy-uhtsi-wayawiyit.

" niwaskāhikan t-ōsīhtāyan äh-miywāsik mistahi, " itäw.

" aha' , " itik.

äkwah äh-nipātsik, āsay kīsihtāyiwa, mistah ä-miywāsiniyik. sākihtam wāsiskutänikan.

" pikō käkway nätawäyihtamani, ka-kāsīhän uma wāsaskutänikan, äkwah ahtsānis. pikw ītä nk-āyān ; itwäyanih äkutäh nik-āyān. nama käkway ka-pwātawihtān, " itik nāpäsis awa.

kätahtawä äh-ay-apitsik, awa matsi-mōniyās pihkwah utinam ; mistsikuwatsisihk asiwatäw. kiskäyihtam, äkut äh-masinahikähk pihkuhk, nāpäsisah äh-pimātisiyit, äh-ayāyit animah kā-mantōwaniyik wāsaskutänikan. äkwah wāsaskutänikanah māwatsihtäw äh-miywāsiniyikih ; äkwah äyakunih sipwähtatäw, itah täkusihkih, äh-māyātahkih wāsaskutänikanah ä-wīh-atāwät, mīskuts äh-miywāsiniyik äh-mäkit. piyis utihtäw nāpäsisah. päyakwapiw nōtukäsiw.

kakwätsimäw, " namuya tsī käkway kitayān wāsaskutänikan äh-māyātahk ? mīskuts äh-miywāsik ka-miyitin. "

äkwah, " päyak astäw ōtah ; ka-miyitin, " itäw nōtukäw.

äkwah nitunam ; miskam ; miyäw. mīskuts miyik äh-miywāsiniyik.

" äyukō kā-nitawäyihtamān, " itäw awa matsi-kimutisk.

äkwah nāpäsis awa namuya āpiw ; kīh-nakatam uwāsaskutänikan kā-manitōwaniyik. äkwah takusin. kakwätsimäw ukāwiyah, " tāniwä animah niwāsiskutänikan ? "

" nikusis, " itik, " äh-miywāsik mīskuts kkīh-miyikawinānaw, äh-atāmikawiyahk äwakōw kiwāsaskutänikan, " itäw.

kisiwāsiw nāpäsis.

" kikīsinātsihin. äwakōw wātihkānihk kā-kīh-kwästäwäpinit, kā-wayäsimisk, " itäw ukāwiyah.

äkwah sipwähtäw nāpäsis. kätahtawä äh-pa-pmuhtät, äh-tipiskāyik, npāw.

---

[1] In part the genies which are attached to the ring and the lamp are distinct from these objects, but in part the informant, more in accord with Cree views, does not distinguish them.

[2] Verb-form with inanimate actor, although *ahtsānis :* "ring," is of animate gender; in fact, even an inanimate noun in such a connexion would ordinarily be used in animate gender.

[3] Meaning "a rag"—temporary word-avoidance.

äh-päkupayit, äh-waskawīt, " kīkway, kā-tipäyimiyan, äh-ntawäyihtaman ? " itik uhtsahtsanisah äh-yāyisimāt.

" tāntä k-āyāt kā-kimutamawit niwāsskutänikan, äkutäh nik-āyān, " itäw.

" äha' , " itik.

äh-nipāt, kīhtwām äh-päkupayit, kisiwāk waskāhikan ayāyiw.

äkwah, " tānisiy äkwah kä-tōtamān ? " täyihtam.

äkwah wāpamäw ä-sipwähtäyit. äkwah ituhtäw.

" äyikus nik-äkutōwiwin ! "

kwäskämōw ; äyikusiwiw ; äkwah ispatsāw wāskahikanihk äh-tāskipayiyit mistikwah, äkutah kāsōw. äkwah wāpamäw uskinīkiskwäwah äkutah äh-ayāyit. kapä-tipisk äkutah ayāw, äh-pähāt ta-nipāyit. piyis nipāw awa kimutisk. äkwah utsāhtsanisah kāsīhwäw.

" kīkway äh-ntawäyihtaman, kā-tipäyimiyan ? " itik.

" awah kā-kīh-kimutamawit wāsaskutänikan ākamihk kihtsikamīhk kantawih-pakitināw. niwāsaskutänikan ka-nakatän, " itäw.

" äha' , " itik.

äkwah wiyah utinam wāsaskutänikan kā-manitōwaniyik.

" nīkināhk nik-āyān ! " itwäw nāpäsis.

äkutäh awah äkwah mīnah kākikä pimiwitāw uswāsaskutänikan ; nama wīhkāts nakatam.

kätahtawä mīnah kā-papāmuhtät awa kimutisk, äh-papā-atāwākät äsōniyāwiyikih sakāpīhkānisah. pīhtukäw äkutah nāpäsisah uwāskāhikaniyihk. nōtukäsiw päyakwapiw.

" māskōts ōma ayāyiki, wāwīs mistahi tah-ukimāwiw kikusis, " itik ; " tāwāyīhk ōtah kik-ākutān ; äkwah k-āsiwatān[1] *asinīwi-mitäh ; k-āsiwatān. äkutah mistahi ta-miyunākwan kiwāskahikaniwāw. "*

atāmäw nōtukäsiw. äkusi sipwähtäw awa kimutisk. äkwah awah takusin nāpäsis.

äkwah nōtukäw, " nikusis, " itäw, " ntatāwān umah k-ākutäk äkutah, t-āsiwatāyan asinīwi-mitäh. "

äkwah nāpäsis miywäyihtam. äkwah äh-tipiskāyik kāsīham wāsaskutänikan.

" käkway äh-ntawäyihtaman ? " itik uwāsaskutänikan.[2]

" uma k-ākutäk äōk utah k-āsiwatäk asiniwi-mitäh, " itik.

kisiwāsiw sämāk.

" käkāts kinipahitin ; ntäh animah, " itik awa nāpäsis ; " ä-wīhkakwä-nipahisk an, " ītik.[3]

äkusi namuya tāpwähtawäw.

kītahtawä kā-takusiniyit maskihkīw-iyiniwah. " äh-miyusit maskihkīwiyiniw, " itäw. āhkusiw a nāpäsis.

" äyōkw ānah, " itik, " ä-wīh-kakwä-nipahisk ; ka-pä-nitawāpamik ; nipahāhkan, " itik.

äkwah pä-ntawāpamik. nipäwinihk ä-pimisihk mōhkuman tahkunam.

---

[1] *asiwatāw* : "he puts it inside" (as into a box or bag), but we are not told into what. Immediately below the word is used in a common specialized meaning, "he puts it into his bag, bosom-fold, pocket"; farther on, similarly, the corresponding verb with animate object, *asiwahäw*, specialized: "bring (animal) under shelter."

[2] Either the nouns should be made animate obviative (ending *-ah*), or the preceding verb given inanimate actor (*itikōw*).

[3] For *anih itik* ; the sandhi is often carried from a quotation over to the verbs of saying, *itäw* (transitive), *itwäw* (intransitive).

" *kitāhkusin ?" itik.*

" *äha'," itäw.*

äkwah ōtah äh-pä-nawakiyit, tahkamäw ; nipahäw.

" *ā, tānähki ? maskihkīw-iyiniw kinipahāw !" itik ukāwiyah.*

" *ā, namuya maskihkīw-iyiniw !" itäw ; " kimutisk anah," itäw ; " ä-wīh-nipahit, äwakō k-ōh-nipahak."*

äkwah nitunikäwak ; pikw ītah utsasiwatsikaniyihk mōhkumān miskamwak, mīn īsawäsk äh-pimiwitāyit, mīnah pistsipōwin, ä-kī-wīh-pistsipuhikut awa nāpäsis.

äkwah ay-ayāw. kätahtawä nīpātipisk kā-takusiniyit mitātaht nāpäwah, sōsōwatimwah äh-nā-nayahtsikäyit. päyak pīhtukäyiwa.

" *nama wiya tsī nika-kīh-kapäsinān ?" itik.*

" *kapäsik ; kitämiwāwak asiwahihkuk," itäw.*

" *namuya ; äkus īsi ta-nīpawiwak."*

äkusi sakahpitäwak utämiwāwah. äkwah äkutah uskinīkiskwäw paminawasōw ; asamäw. äkwah äh-kīsi-mītsisōwiht, kāsīhiyākanäw. äkwah ä-ntawi-wäpinahk kāsīhiyākanāpuy, ituhtäw ōhi sōsōwatimwah, kā-pähtahk, " āsay tsī ?" äh-itikut, kīmōts ä-pīkiskwäyit.

" *namuya," itäw ; " kākāts," itäw.*

ōhi sōsōwatimwah kā-nayōmātsik kimutiskah mahkahkuhk. pīhtukäw äkwah uskinīkiskwäw. äkwah kisākamisam nipiy ; mistahi mitunih sīsīpaskihkuhk sīkinam. äkwah wayawīhtitāw. äkwah yōhtänam mahkahk.

" *āsay tsī ?" itik.*

" *äha'," itäw.*

pīhtsi-sīkinam nipiy mahkahkuhk ; nipahäw ōhi kimutiskah. nipahīhkāswäw kahkiyaw. äkwah pīhtukäw ; āmatsiwäw äkwah, utōkimāmah äh-ntawāpamāt. päyak ōhi äkutah apiyiwah käyāpits.

" *ntōkimām," itäw, " kayās mānah ä-nihtā-nōtinikäyān," itäw, " kayās tānsi ä-kīh-tōtamān ka-kitāpaminäwäw. nka-wawäsīn, tāpiskōts ä-wih-nōtinikäyān ; äkusi nik-āsihun."*

" *tāpwäh !" itäw awa utōskinīkiskwämah.*

äkwah nīhtatsiwäw uskinīkiskwäw ; nta-wawäyīw. äkwah pä-āmatsiwäw. isawisk tahkunam äkwah mōhkumān.

" *kayās äkusi ä-kīh-isīhuyāhk, kā-nōtinikäyāhk," itäw.*

äkwah äkutah pāh-pimuhtäw, pikw īsi äh-tōtahk. kätahtawä nāpäwah ōhi kīskwäwäpahwäw.

" *tāpwä namuya kwayask kitōtän, äh-kiyōkät ukimāw äh-nipahat !" itik utōkimāmah.*

" *kīspin äkāh kīh-nipahak, āpihtā-tipiskāk āsay kah-nipahik ; ä-wīh-nipahisk, k-ōh-päy-iytuhtät," itik ; " mātsikōtitān ntunikä. pikw ītah uskutākāhk umaskimutisihk utasikānihk, pikw ītah ka-miskän mōhkumānah," itik.*

tāpwäh ntunikäw ; uskutākayihk utasikaniyihk mihtsät mōhkumānah miskam.

" *äkwah tāpw äs ānih kipimātsihin !" itik utōkimāmah.*

äkwah wayawīhtahäwak ; ntawi-pakastawähwäwak kahkiyaw mitātaht kimutiskah.

äkusi wiy äwōkō päyak ātayōhkäwin nikīsihtān.

Once upon a time there was a large town. And a certain poor little French boy there was, who used to walk about the town, trying to find something to eat. Then at one time, as he came home after dark, while he was there in his house, in came an Englishman who was dressed like a lord.

"My son," said this man to him; "I have come to fetch you; I have only just found out that you are alive," he told him.

Then he urged the boy's mother: "Sister-in-law," that Englishman said to her, "will you give me our boy to bring up?"

"Yes," she answered.

He gave her much money. So he took the boy away with him. Far off they came to a great mountain; they arrived there at the mountain. Then he removed a large rock from an opening. The boy went in there. It was very dark; there was only a faint light. Then the other closed the door on him.

"Just you bring that thing over there, boy, that lamp!"

The boy took it. He went to the door.

"Hand me it! Afterwards you will come out; first give me the lamp!" he said to the boy.

"No," said the boy; "You will lock me in."

Then, "Hurry up and hand it to me!"

At last that Englishman got angry. He locked the boy in the cave. He could not see anything. Presently he rubbed his hand and found that a ring had slipped on his finger.

"What is it, you who are my master?" the ring asked him.

"I want to go out."

"Speak thus: 'Six door, go open!' Say that, boy," it told him.

Then the boy, "Six door, go open!"

Thereupon it opened. The boy went out. He had a lamp. And that ring always talked to him. Then he went from there, homeward. When he reached home, he told his mother the tale.

"Now give me something to wipe off my lamp," he told her.

She gave him something; he wiped it.

"What do you desire, you who are my master?" a giant asked him.

He frightened him, coming out of the lamp.

"That you build me a very fine house," he told him.

"Very well," said the other to him.

Then while they slept he had already finished it, and very beautiful it was. The boy took good care of the lamp.

"Whenever you desire no matter what, you will rub this lamp and ring. No matter where I am, when you bid it, I shall be there. You will fail of nothing," he said to the boy.

Then at one time, as they dwelt there, that evil Englishman took some ashes; he put them into a little wooden box. From the pattern of the ashes there he saw that the boy was alive and that he had that magic lamp. Then he collected beautiful lamps; he went off with them, to buy worthless lamps wherever he came, giving good lamps in return. At last he came to the boy. The old woman was alone at home.

He asked her, "Haven't you perhaps some worthless old lamp? I will give you a good one for it."

Then, "There is one here; I will give it to you," said the old woman to him.

She sought it; she found it; she gave it to him. In return he gave her a good one.

"This is what I want," said the evil thief to her.

Now the boy was not at home; he had left his magic lamp. Then he arrived. He asked his mother, "Where is that lamp of mine?"

"My son," she told him, "we have been given a good one in trade for that lamp of yours."

The boy was angry.

"You have done badly by me. This person was the one who threw me into the cave, this person who has cheated you," he told his mother.

Then the boy went away. Presently, as he walked along and night fell, he went to sleep.

When he awoke, as he stirred, "What is it you desire, you who are my master?" he was asked by his ring, which he had rubbed.

"Wherever he is who stole my lamp from me, there let me be," he told it.

"Very well," it said to him.

When he went to sleep and again woke up, there was a house close by.

Then, "What shall I do now?" he thought.

Then he saw the other depart. Thereupon he went there.

"Let me be an ant!"

He changed his form; he became an ant; then in a crack of a timber in the roof of the house he hid. He saw a young woman who was there. He stayed all night, waiting for the other to sleep. At last the thief went to sleep. Then he rubbed his ring.

"What is it you desire, you who are my master? it asked him.

"This person who stole my lamp from me you will go place across the sea. My lamp you will leave behind," he told it.

"Very well," it answered him.

Then he took the magic lamp.

"Let me be in our own house!" said the boy.

There he then always carried his lamp with him; he never left it.

Presently, there was that thief going about again, selling golden chains. He entered the boy's house. The old woman was alone in the house.

"Perhaps if this thing is here, your son will become an even greater man," he told her; "Here in the centre of the house do you hang it up; and inside it do you put a stone heart; put it inside. Thus will your house be very beautiful."

The old woman bought it. Then the thief went away. Then the boy arrived.

Then the old woman said to him, "My son, I have bought the stone heart that hangs there so that you may carry it about with you."

Then the boy liked it. When night came, he rubbed the lamp.

"What do you want?" his lamp asked him.

"The stone heart that is inside the thing which hangs there," he answered.

At once he grew angry.

"I could easily kill you; that is my heart," it said to the boy; "It was certainly that he wanted to kill you," it told him.

So he did not do what the other had told him.

Presently there arrived a physician. "An excellent physician," was said of him. The boy was ill.

"That is the one," the other told him, "who means to kill you; he will come to see you; then do you kill him," he was told by the other.

Soon he came to see him. He held a knife as he lay in his bed.

"Are you sick?" the other asked him.

"Yes," he told him.

Then, when the other leaned over, he stabbed him and killed him.

"Dear me, what are you doing? You have killed the physician!" his mother said to him.

"Oh, he was no physician!" he told her; "He was a thief," he told her; "Because he meant to kill me is why I killed him."

Then they searched; in his various pockets they found a knife and a sword which he carried with him, and poison with which he had meant to poison the boy.

Then he dwelt there. Then, at one time, in the darkness of night there arrived ten men who had donkeys as their beasts of burden. One of them entered the house.

"May we camp here for the night?" he asked him.

"Yes, do; and bring your beasts inside," he told him.

"No; they can stand where they are."

Accordingly, they tied up their beasts. Then the young woman prepared a meal; she gave them food. When her guests had eaten, she washed the dishes. When she went to pour out the dishwater, she went to where the donkeys were, and there she heard someone say to her in a whisper, "Is it time?"

"No," she answered; "Soon."

Those donkeys were carrying none other than robbers in boxes. Then the young woman entered the house. She heated some water; she poured a great amount of it into a kettle with a spout. Then she took it out of the house. Then she opened a box.

"Is it time?" the man asked her.

"Yes," she told him.

She poured the water into the box; she killed that robber. She scalded them all to death. Then she went into the house; she went upstairs to see her master. One of the others was still there.

"My lord," she said to her master, "in former time I used to fight, and you shall now see how I did, in former time. I shall deck myself as for the fight; that is the way I shall dress."

"Do indeed!" he told his young handmaid.

Then the young woman went downstairs; she went and dressed. Then she came upstairs. She held a sword and a knife.

"In former time this was the way we dressed when we fought," she told them.

Then she walked about there, acting in various ways. Suddenly she knocked that man out of his senses.

"Truly you are not doing right, to kill this lord who is our guest!" her master said to her.

"If I had not killed him, by midnight he would have killed you; in order to kill you was why he came here," she told him; "Just go and look. Everywhere in his coat, in his pockets, in his stockings, everywhere you will find knives," she told him.

"Now really you have saved my life!" her master said to her.

Then they took the man's body out of the house; they went and threw all ten of the robbers into the water.

And so I have finished this one sacred story.